The Long Lost Journal of Confederate General James Johnson Pettigrew

The Long Lost Journal of Confederate General James Johnson Pettigrew

Daniel F Bauer

Writers Club Press

San Jose New York Lincoln Shanghai

The Long Lost Journal of Confederate General
James Johnson Pettigrew

Writers Club Press
an imprint of iUniverse.com, Inc.

For information address:
iUniverse.com, Inc.
5220 S 16th, Ste. 200
Lincoln, NE 68512
www.iuniverse.com

ISBN: 0-595-12416-X

Printed in the United States of America

TO LINDSAY AND KIRBY:
MY PEARLS OF GREAT PRICE, LOVE DAD

Acknowledgements

My deepest thanks to those who helped prepare the manuscript: Elaine Engelke,Donna Wilde,and Jeanne Barry.

Special thanks to Lin Rosenstiel whose computer knowledge is unsurpassed!

To Bill Lanz and Diana Vance,many thanks for reading this manuscript and making many thoughtful comments.

I must single out for special thanks,Terri Erickson,whose support of this book has meant much to me.

To circuit court Judge James Beer:thanks for all those bike rides! Do you think we are ready for the Colorado mountains Judge?

All my love to my absolutely beautiful granddaughters,the twins, Mia and Paige and Cloey, two years and nine months old respectively. Do you think our telephone conversations will improve ladies?

To Josh Overcash of Fort Collins,Colorado,father of Mia, Paige and Choley...Thanks!

Advice and moral support were generously provided over the years by, Vicki Powell, Highland, California; Bob Cooper, Davis, California; Gene Vincent, Kingston, Jamaica; Addy Grini, Ed VanRavenstein, Jim Monro, Dr. Lee Knuteson, and Bill Wartenweiler, all of Monroe, Wisconsin.

To Don Sorn, Principal Extraordinaire,thanks and God Bless!

To Roy Thomas Ph. D...Thanks Doctor, it was a great 18 years! Someday we will collaborate on that book.

Finally, all my love and appreciation to Galina,my beautiful and talented Russian wife.

Introduction

Daniel Bauer
2211-16th Street
Monroe, WI 53566

Introduction

It was October 31, 1860, and a thirty-two-year-old Charleston lawyer, James Johnson Pettigrew, began keeping a journal to record the dramatic events swirling about him. He started his journal five months before the Civil War began and kept it faithfully during his rise from fledgling militia officer to brigade command in the Army of Northern Virginia, until his untimely death from a Yankee bullet during the retreat from Gettysburg.

All this time, overworked as he was, burdened with the heavy responsibilities of command and once gravely wounded, Pettigrew faithfully maintained his journal. The method he followed is indicated in a letter to his friend, James Louis Petigru, in July of 1861, in which he says: "This journalizing is hard work and I write whenever I can. I might easily have found incidents enough to double it, but some events occur when I have but little time to make the notes from which the journal is drawn off." That is, he made notes steadily when busy in the field, and then when he could find a few hours wrote his record in detail. In quieter times, he wrote every day; often he mentions sitting up late to finish, and several entries mention hastily dropping his pen before his command starts another movement.

A man of extraordinary intelligence, Pettigrew possessed an intense intellectual curiosity about contemporary events. The information in his journal comes from situations that he himself witnessed, through wide reading of newspapers, and through letters from far-flung friends and relatives in and out of the Confederate army. The result is an intelligent young man's penetrating and partisan insight into the Civil War South.

Although time has dimmed his stature as a historical figure, Pettigrew was deemed one of the more promising of the 425 officers who obtained the rank of General in the Confederate army. Matthew Fontaine Maury, the famed oceanographer and Confederate naval scientist, considered Pettigrew, "the most promising young man of the South." He felt in 1863 that, despite his youth, Pettigrew was the man in the Confederacy best qualified to be commander in chief of the Southern armies. "He was the coming man who should yet guide us to victory," wrote a North Carolinian. His untimely death coming after the catastrophe at Gettysburg added to the gloom then gathering around the Southern cause. "What is life," asked Governor Vance, the great wartime governor of North Carolina, "that so much labor and culture should be bestowed upon a man of so much genius and capacity and be shot down at such an early age."

Although many in the South believed he was to be the good genius of the cause there is little in Pettigrew's record to justify this assertion. With little or no formal military training, he rose to the rank of brigadier general and proved to be a competent brigade commander, but certainly no more so than a dozen others.

He first became interested in military affairs when in 1856 he was invited to join the Washington Light Infantry, a Charleston militia company. Later that year, Governor R.F.W. Allston appointed Pettigrew the senior of his ten aides-de-camp with the rank of lieutenant colonel of the militia. That he was a man of physical and moral courage is beyond doubt. When a plague of yellow fever ravaged Charleston in 1853, Pettigrew refused to look after his own safety but remained in the city to care for the sick and dying. Later as a member of the South Carolina legislature, he led a gallant fight against the reopening of the African slave trade, a highly unpopular position that ultimately cost him his seat in the legislature.

As the Civil War loomed on the horizon, Pettigrew was active in training and parading the militia before the admiring gaze of the citizens of the city. Although he was not one of the fire-eaters, he was appointed a colonel by Governor Pickens after the secession of South Carolina. During the Fort Sumter crisis, he was sent by Governor Pickens to demand the return of Major Anderson to Fort Moultre on Sullivan's Island. After the bombardment, he was eventually elected Colonel of the 22nd North Carolina.

He soon rose to brigade command and was severely wounded at Seven Pines and left for dead on the battlefield. He was captured by the Federals and, after a period of captivity, was exchanged in August of 1862.

The high point of his military career occurred as he led a division of Confederate troops in the heroic but costly charge ordered by General Lee on the third day at Gettysburg. A few weeks after the bloody repulse, he was killed at Falling Waters in a brief battle with Union cavalry. He died two weeks after his 35th birthday.

Tragically, Pettigrew's reputation seemed to have died with him, for with the close of the Civil War, he quickly disappeared into obscurity. His law partner, James Louis Petigru, who had possession of the journal, died in September, 1863; several years later his sister Adele donated the journal to Pettigrew's wartime aide, Louis Young.

The Pettigrew journal remained in the Young family for decades, unknown to and unused by Civil War historians. I managed to rescue the long-lost journal from obscurity after a series of strange coincidences.

Like many historians, I knew little, if anything, about General Pettigrew. During a 1994 trip to North Carolina's Outer Banks, I managed a side trip to the Gettysburg battlefield. Accompanied by my daughter Lindsay and son Kirby, we parked our van near the Lee monument on Seminary Ridge. We walked the length of Pickett's charge and stopped at the stone wall where Confederate Brigadier General Lewis Armistead died. After we finished the walk, I looked back from the stone wall and remarked to the children; "Pickett's men were very brave to have made that charge against such heavy fire."

A national park ranger standing nearby overheard my remark and said to me, "It's misleading to speak of it as Pickett's charge for Pickett only commanded one of the divisions in the assault, the other was commanded by the North Carolinian General Pettigrew."

"Pettigrew?" I stammered, "I never heard of him."

"Nevertheless," replied the guide, "in the charge, Pickett commanded only about one-third of the men engaged, at most a few hundred more than General Pettigrew."

After staying overnight in Gettysburg, we resumed our journey east the next morning. Our itinerary called for us to reach Morehead City and from there drive around the Outer Banks to Nags Head. Once at Nags Head, we planned to thoroughly explore Kitty Hawk, the origin of the Wright brothers' first flight. There was only one thing wrong with my plan; it is impossible to drive around the Outer Banks from Morehead City. I had misread my map and failed to note the fact that only by car ferry could we reach Highway 12 to Cape Hatteras and Nags Head.

We quickly revised our plan and drove north to New Bern, then to Washington and points north hoping to reach Nags Head that evening. Once at Plymouth, North Carolina, Lindsay noted that if we followed State Highway 64 it would take us to Nags Head. We turned east from Plymouth and followed the narrow two-lane highway through the

North Carolina countryside. As we passed through the tiny village of Creswell, I noticed a historical marker mentioning the burial place of Confederate General Pettigrew. Intrigued, I turned the car around and headed down the narrow country road to Phelps Lake and Pettigrew State Park. Once at the park, it took us 15 minutes to find the marker indicating that the Pettigrew family burial ground was a walk of one mile down a forest trail. Leaving the car, the children and I walked seemingly forever until we came to a rusty fence which bounded the gravesite of the Pettigrews. A simple cross marked the grave of the General.

Just as we were about to leave, a young man came down the trail to the gravesite. During the course of the ensuing conversation, I learned his name was William Young, the great-grandson of Lewis Young. He was a Richmond attorney and was also heading for the Outer Banks and on the spur of the moment had decided to pay a visit to the gravesite of his great-grandfather's commanding officer. As we talked I asked Mr. Young, out of curiosity, if he knew of the existence of any journals or diary that had belonged to his great-grandfather. The youthful attorney replied he knew of none but would inquire and be on the lookout for any.

Several months later, I received a phone call from Mr. Young explaining he had unexpectedly discovered a cache of his great-grandfather's correspondence in the cellar trunk of his deceased aunt whose effects he was pursuing. This dusty repository held over fifty letters of Captain Young's but, more importantly, the journals of General Pettigrew.

Mr. Young generously made the journals available to me knowing that as a historian I might be able to use them in my research on the Civil War. My reaction on reading the journals was that they provide many refreshing and poignant insights into "the real war," which Walt Whitman prophesied "will never get in the books." With this in mind, I undertook transcription and editing of General Pettigrew's papers for publication.

The journal that James Johnson Pettigrew kept from October 31, 1860, until just before his death on July 17, 1863, is in five notebooks approximately eight by twelve inches each in hard mottled covers with black leatherette binding and corners. The whole record fills over 2,000 pages. Although the ink is faded in places, the text is quite legible throughout. The volumes contain a few very rough diagrams of engagements and there are several drawings of the routes Pettigrew's brigade marched to battle or encampment.

While editing the journals I have made no attempt to definitively chronicle Pettigrew's life or assess his military career. My primary purpose is merely to have the General tell his own dramatic personal story.

There is not, to my knowledge, a statue or monument to the memory of General James Johnson Pettigrew. It is my hope that his journal, now just published after the lapse of over 100 years, may well become an even more enduring monument.

> Dan Bauer
> Professor of History
> South Central Wisconsin College
> Monroe, Wisconsin

THE LONG-LOST JOURNAL OF
CONFEDERATE GENERAL JAMES JOHNSON PETTIGREW

OCTOBER 31, 1860—WEDNESDAY
CHARLESTON, SOUTH CAROLINA

I take pen in hand on this warm but rainy October night to begin to record, in this journal, the future days and events of my life. As I write these words, I am a 32-year-old lawyer in the Charleston office of my relative and senior partner, James Petigru.

Although a native of North Carolina, I have lived in Charleston since 1849 and have come to hold a deep affection for the city of Calhoun and chivalry. The city has a population of 29,000 whites and 37,000 Negro slaves and is the largest American seaport south of Baltimore. It is a town of impressive beauty and grace, essentially English in tone and manner, reflecting the prestige and influence of the rice planters and landed aristocracy. Charleston is located on a peninsula bounded by the Ashley and Cooper Rivers with the Battery Square, the beautiful city park, at their junction.

Directly across the harbor, on the opposite side of the city is Sullivan's Island, on the point of which, and about seven miles from the city, is Fort Moultrie; in the center of the harbor stands Fort Sumter, with its massive walls and frowning port holes, looking down with defiance upon all craft that sail by. About three miles from the city on James Island rises Fort Johnson; and a mile or so from the mainland is Castle Pinckney. Thus in a military point of view, Charleston would seem almost, or quite invulnerable to the combined fleets of the world.

The city is regularly built and extends about two miles in length, and nearly one and a half in breadth. The streets are sandy and unpaved, except a few; but are frequently ornamented by trees peculiar to this southern latitude, such as the Magnolia. Many of the houses are of brick, some of which are in a style of superior elegance; others are of wood, neatly painted and embowered in the summer season amid a profusion of foliage and flowers. The dwellings are often furnished with piazzas extending to the roof, and ornamented with vines and creepers, while the gardens attached to them are adorned with the orange, peach and other choice trees, and a variety of shrubbery.

It is getting near the tenth hour of the evening, and as I look out the window of my house on 59 Tradd Street, I can see flashes of lightning in the distance. The clouds are low and dark, ominous, if you will, much like the times I live in. Here in my room I sit at my desk while the candle sends flickering light dancing off the white wall opposite me. The room is quiet except for the occasional boom of distant thunder. It is a good time for quiet reflection.

The atmosphere in Charleston has rippled and swelled with excitement all through this momentous fall. It would seem there is no business doing in Charleston but secession and its contingents, the sale of arms (principally revolvers, which are in universal demand). Those citizens not engaged in active military preparations spend their time entirely in talking, reading and discussing the news, the centers of intelligence and rumor being, of course, the newspaper offices and the great hotels. Of the latter, the Mills House is the most aristocratic, but the Charleston appears to be the headquarters of gossip; people throng there every evening to hear and retail it, while little Irish boys walk through the lobby shouting out, "Latest news! New edition!"

Both hotels are crowded with guests, many strangers being in tow; I need not say southerners, principally from Georgia and Alabama. I have heard of scarcely any Northerners at present, except those dispatched hither as agents by the manufacturers and patentees of revolvers, rifles, etc., in the North, the merits of whose respective weapons are duly paragraphed in the newspapers.

One of these northern salesmen, by-the-by, got into an argument the other day that almost led to violence. A Tennessean standing at the hotel bar said to the salesman, "If it were not for those wretched Republicans and horrid abolitionists, we might have peace!"

The Northerner replied, "The Republicans who want to elect Lincoln are not abolitionists, certainly not in your sense of that word. They only want to stop the extension of slavery."

"Ah, I tell you," the Tennessean rejoined, "it is all the same thing! Why stop the extension of slavery? It shows that they are against us. It is all very plain."

The salesman said, "Surely, it is wise to keep slavery outside the Free States and the territories."

At this the Tennessean showed intense feeling and shaking his fist toward the Northerner said excitedly, "If Mr. Lincoln has such sentiments as you express, there'll be blood, sir, blood. Now do you want it to come to that!"

"I am a Union man," was his emphatic response.

"What kind of a Union man are you?"

"I am this kind of a Union man," and he threw open his coat, which showed a huge revolver, strapped to his waist.

Calmer heads prevailed and a fight was narrowly avoided, as the South Carolinians present separated the two, while the gentleman who narrated the incident to me was extremely indignant that the honor of the South should have been risked by an unprovoked insult at the expense of a stranger.

The presidential election of 1860 looms on the horizon and all of the South holds its breath in the hope that a Black Republican will not be elected president.

If the Republican candidate Lincoln is elected, it will greatly strain the Union, and South Carolina will probably secede. I know each man of this state will do his duty and reply if South Carolina calls; and each woman will be ready to sacrifice her own heart on the altar of the South. We know our state is in the right and our cause, a just one.

Keeping this journal should also be good for my self-discipline. Recording my thoughts daily will require and add to my inner strength, which does not come by accident, but is made possible by hard work and effort. This will help me to despise indulgent softness and give me, hopefully, mastery over circumstance, because I have become the master of myself.

NOVEMBER 1, 1860—THURSDAY
CHARLESTON, SOUTH CAROLINA

Enormous excitement in Charleston as a slave ship, with hundreds of slaves on board, named the Echo, arrived in the harbor yesterday at about nine in the morning in charge of Lieutenant J.M. Duncan, of the U.S. Navy.

The slaver was captured by the U.S. Steamer Mohawk after an exciting chase off the coast of Cuba. It seems the captain of the Echo determined to slip out of Havana and make for the Georgia coast. The Mohawk learned of the departure and sailed off in pursuit. Captain Hamilton of the Mohawk soon observed several ships on the horizon. He identified the Echo by her white colors and the spread of her canvas. The Mohawk slowly gained on the slaver but a tornado sprang up and the two vessels were parted. When the sky was clear again, there was no sign of the Echo.

Hamilton assumed that her captain had sought refuge in a nearby channel, perhaps hoping that those dangerous waters would deter pursuit. As the Mohawk neared the shoals, he again caught sight of the slaver. It was trapped, but the Mohawk could not get close since she had a deep draft. Hamilton steered as near as he could and fired a shot at extreme range, and luckily scored a hit. The captain of the Echo hove to, and allowed a boat crew from the Mohawk to board.

Hamilton in person accompanied the boat, and putting revolver to the head of the slaver's captain, said he would shoot him if he did not surrender his ship. The revolver to his head had a way of persuading the slaver's captain and he surrendered his vessel. Hamilton then brought the Echo to Charleston.

Learning that the slaves were to be landed early yesterday afternoon, I determined to walk to the wharves on East Bay and watch the African's come ashore. I made a stop at the Charleston Hotel for some liquid refreshment and was surprised to find it full of numerous strangers, mainly of an unpolished type, dressed like rough planters and showing some of the qualities of hard drinking overseers or traders. The hotel corridors and barrooms were filled with dense tobacco smoke, and there was much serious talk, generously interspersed with profanity. The talk was, of course, almost entirely about the "niggrahs" or "niggers" on the slaver. What prices they might bring, if put up for sale, and if the reopening of the foreign slave-trade was possible, and if so, what effect this would have on the value of "home-raised niggers."

"Yes, sah," said one of the planters. "If it is right to buy slaves in Virginia and carry them to New Orleans, why is it not right to buy them in Africa and carry them to Charleston?"

"Neighbor," replied his companion, "I couldn't agree with you more. The politicians who vote to reopen the slave trade in Congress will be men whose names will be honored hereafter for the unflinching manner in which they stood up for the principle of truth, and the vital interests of the south."

After my sojourn at the hotel I walked to the harbor and secured a vantage point among a large crowd of spectators. Long lines of shipping, a mass of spars, smoke stacks and ensigns, stretched along the waterfront. I could see the Echo anchored about a quarter mile off shore. I thought the brig about 210 tons, with a length of 110 feet, and a beam of 26.

I walked to the periphery of a circle of onlookers who were discussing the presence of the slaver in Charleston harbor. One old salt, whose head looked like a ragged mop, reported that the Echo had been specially fitted for the slave trade with a double deck, and that the space between the two decks was designated "tween decks." This area was reserved for the slaves and was three feet, ten inches high.

After the buzz of comment that went around, another said he had been told that in storms the sailors had to put on the hatches, and seal tight the openings into the slave deck; here the slaves had to lie pressed together like herrings in a barrel, which soon caused an intolerable heat and stench. It was asserted by some naval offers he knew who were stationed on the coast to stop the slave traffic, that when the weather was just right, they could detect the odor of a slave ship further away than they could see her on a clear night. The odor was often unmistakable at a distance of five miles down wind.

After a short pause, another of the group hitched up his trousers, and rolled an immense "plug" over to the other cheek as if to preserve a proper balance and said, "This is the first slaver captured by an American man-of-war sent to a United States port. I have heard the ship left Africa with 470 slaves, of which number 140 have died. Even so the owners of the vessel expected to clear $130,000 in the advent of a successful landing."

Hearing this, a man, who from his appearance appeared to be a merchant, whistled in astonishment and announced, "A fellow could get rich fast if he could buy the niggers on that there boat!"

The man standing next to him laughed and commented, "Colonel, are you nevah goin' to stop thinkin' about buyin' niggrahs?"

Later, as the slaves passed from a steamer to Adgers wharf, I drew close to the roadside to view them. Escorted by U.S. Marshals, they presented a sad and affecting sight, which was closely observed by all present. As the Africans approached, I could see some were unchained, but most were chained in three companies, over a hundred in each, the right hand of one to the left hand of the other opposite one, making about fifty to each side of a large ox-chain, to which every hand was fastened and necessarily compelled to hold up.

As they plodded silently along many of the poor wretches looked half starved, and reduced to walking skeletons, with some evidently in a dying condition. .A few cases indicated dropsies and there were instances of hernia. Some also exhibited traces of other diseases, but a goodly number were apparently in good health; of course they smelled abominably.

One of the unchained women had obviously given birth during her captivity for she carried a babe of four to five weeks old. The baby was crying and the mother's efforts to get the child to stop were useless. One of the U.S. Marshals, a man who I knew to be from Mississippi, took the child by one arm, as you would a cat by a leg, and walked to the side of the road and remarked to a lady standing there: "Madam, I will make you a present of this little nigger; it keeps up such a noise I can't bear it." "Thank you, sir," said the lady. The mother's frantic appeals were not only in vain but caused her to be chained with the gang as she had not previously been.

Some time after the slaves were marched away, sixteen seamen of the captured crew were brought up to the city in the steam tug aid. Handcuffed, they were then marched guarded through the public streets while followed by a rabble of curious Negroes, to the jail in a distant part of the city.

The sight of this strange looking procession upset many in the crowd. "I tell you, this will not do," commented a gentleman of high standing. "How are our 'neegroos' to know their place when they see sights such as this?"

"How right you are, sir," replied a portly physician, looking on in disgust. "It is not too much to say that such an exhibition should not have taken place. There are thousands of other Negroes in our population and to see white men manacled and marched to jail only because they have been engaged in the trade of slaves, a thing which is done daily in our streets, undermines our laws and the sacred institution of slavery."

It is rumored that the United States Government is authorized to make provision for the safekeeping of the slaves here in Charleston. And now the question comes, what shall be done with them? Hitherto we have sent them back to Africa in government ships, and it is to be supposed that such will be the course proposed on this occasion.

For my own part I should consider it a hard case if they should be sent away. They have done no act that merits the punishment of being returned to barbaric Africa. Do we not want them? They are wanted everywhere—our planters want them; our mechanics want them; our railroads want them; our wastelands are in want of them. There are men here who are ready to buy them; one man offers in cash $50,000 for one hundred of them, and in the ordinary condition of slaves they would have a brighter life here than they have ever had the room to hope for.

When these Negroes shall be taken from the port of Charleston it will be a wanton insult upon our institutions. The blood boils in the vein of many men of this city at such a prospect, but so far there has been no attempt, and I presume there will be no attempt, to interfere with the operation of the law.

NOVEMBER 2, 1860—FRIDAY
CHARLESTON, SOUTH CAROLINA

There is a singular class of scoundrels in the North called abolitionists. They should be jailed or put in asylums. The fear and loathing they have brought upon the land!

We in the South slumber upon a volcano. Every day's information, every paper you read contains the same news—the constant warfare against us from the abolitionists, north, east and west. They rail against us from the pulpit and the press, demanding that our four million slaves be instantly freed. These crazed zealots completely ignore the problem of social re-adjustment if the Negroes were hastily freed. What steps would the North take in assisting the South to release this ignorant, penniless, and perhaps violent horde? The answer is that no help is ever offered by the North.

This open warfare against the South carries distinct dangers. This continual inciting of the slaves to revolt or run away will only lead to scenes of violence and raping as Haiti has witnessed; the abolitionists sow, but the South will have to reap the whirlwind.

Some believe it is not slavery that is the curse of the South; it is Africa. They believe we have living in the South an alien, inferior race with whom amalgamation is degradation and who can never be citizens—whose natural tendency is not improvement, but barbarism.

I think the majority of the American people are deeply sympathetic with the South in our attempts to govern the Negro. The white race must have superiority of necessity, to keep the black population from slaughtering us in our beds. A recent article in the Charleston Courier shows only too well the dangers we face from the slaves about us.

It seems that on the morning of October 24 at about three o'clock, the house of Mr. Isaac Middlebrook, who resides six or seven miles north of Charleston, was forcibly entered while Mr. Middlebrook was away.

The front door was battered down with an axe. Mrs. Middlebrook and two of her children were the only occupants of the house. The loud noise awakened Mrs. Middlebrook and the children, who were confronted by a drunken Negro with the demand that they be quiet or they would be killed.

The beast sprang to the bedside of Mrs. Middlebrook, grabbed her by the throat, lifted her from the bed, carried her out across the yard and threw her over the fence, where he abused her in a most shameful and sexual manner until a couple of Negro women, being aroused by her cries, came to her relief.

The fiend, becoming frightened, beat a hasty retreat. The alarm was immediately given in the neighborhood and a posse formed. Mrs. Middlebrook was questioned as to the identity of the perpetrator of the deed and stated that she believed it to be the Negro man named George. He is the property of Mr. Abel Nelson and had been hired out to Mr. Middlebrook.

Dogs were procured, and the track was pursued to a neighboring residence, where the boy, George, had a wife. The dogs caught George in an open field near the house. Once the Negro is cornered, the dogs are usually called off, but in this case the Negro struggled and so the dogs were allowed to rip and bite into him for a period of time.

Finally, the dogs were called off and the frightened and bleeding Negro was taken before a justice of the peace and committed to the jail, there to await his trial at the November term of the Superior Court.

The next morning, a crowd of men from the county assembled and made known their intention to forcibly take the Negro, George, from the jail and execute him in defiance of law or opposition. The efficient sheriff, Major Hargett, together with many citizens, remonstrated, persuaded, and even begged the mob to reflect for a moment upon the course and consequences that might follow their unlawful act. The pleas were to no avail. Major Hargett even promised to guarantee safekeeping of the prisoner by confining him in any manner they might suggest, and the others proposed to guard the jail night and day, but all to no purpose.

The hateful passion and frenzy of the mob knew no bounds. They rushed the jail, and despite all remonstrations and pleas, used axes, hammers and crowbars to beat down the doors to the jail and seized the slave, carrying him off in triumph.

The members of the mob left in high glee with the prisoner, whom they felicitated themselves they had captured without resort to the formidable weapons they carried.

The crying Negro pleaded for his life, but the leader of the mob determined he should be burned alive. That night the slave was tied to a tree and given fifty lashes upon his naked back, with a heavy "cotton planter's whip."

The next day, a large multitude assembled to watch the final punishment of the slave. All the slaves in the region were compelled to attend. George, who was to be executed, was the husband of a young wife, and the father of two daughters, who were forced to be present. The victim was led out from the place of his confinement to an oak tree, near the courthouse, where he was surrounded by a vast crowd of beholders, clamoring for the consuming fire. The single garment he had on was taken off and fat and light wood piled around him.

All was silent as death as the wood was set afire. George said not a word till he felt that the flames had seized him. He then uttered an awful howl, attempting to sing and pray. He then hung his head and suffered in silence. After the flames had surrounded the rapist, burned the eyes out of his head and his face to a cinder, some in the crowd more compassionate than the rest proposed to end his misery by shooting him. But it was replied that he was already out of his pain.

"No! No!" cried the Negro. "I am not! I burn all over! Shoot me! Shoot me!"

"No!" exclaimed Mr. Middlebrook, who had arrived on the scene. "No. He shall not be shot. I would sooner slack the fire if that would increase his misery!"

I regret that the mob took the law into its own hands. Yet the fiendish deeds of this black fanatic curdled the blood of the white residents of the area and they felt justice was done by the flames.

NOVEMBER 3, 1860—SATURDAY
CHARLESTON, SOUTH CAROLINA

I am fortunate to own two servants who take care of my Tradd Street residence. The Negro, Nat, and his wife, Ruth, share the domestic duties required to keep the house and yard clean. Ruth is also an artful cook who serves up the meals in a most delicious and delightful fashion.

Lately, Ruth has not been feeling well, and I am worried over her lack of vitality. She is a most valuable piece of property, probably worth eight or nine hundred dollars, and I would be reluctant to lose her. She seems to be suffering from some sort of nervous debility or neuralgia.

Yesterday, for example, Ruth claimed to be extremely tired and aware of a dull pain in her side. I realize that Negro women are especially susceptible to disorders and irregularities, which cannot be detected by exterior symptoms, but Ruth has always been healthy and a hard worker. I doubt if she claimed sickness to avoid work.

After talking to Nat about her condition, I decided to give her body the opportunity to assert its own curative powers. To this end, I rode over to Van Schaak and Griersons, who are druggists located at 221 King Street, to purchase a highly effective medicine, Doctor J. H. McLhan's Strengthening Cordial and Blood Purifier, that has been much talked about.

According to my good friend and fellow member of the bar, Benjamin Rutledge, the elixir is reputed to be especially efficacious for those in a weakened condition.

Upon entering the store, I noticed an advertisement posted on the wall for McLhan's remedy. It read in part:

"Doctor Mc Lhan's Strengthening Cordial is the greatest remedy in the world and a most delicious and delightful cordial.

"It is strictly a scientific and vegetable compound procured by the distillation of roots, herbs and barks. Yellow root, blood root, black root, wild cherry bark and dandelion enter into its composition. The entire secret remedial principal of each ingredient is thoroughly extracted by a new method of distilling, producing a delicious, exhilarating spirit and the most infallible remedy for renovating the diseased system and restoring the sick, suffering and debilitated invalid to healthy strength."

I observed at the bottom of the advertisement that over a million bottles had been sold. I purchased four bottles at generous terms and hurried home to let Ruth partake of the remedy. The druggist informed me that two or three bottles were guaranteed to cure most cases of neuralgia, with the suggested dosage being one bottle a day.

Nat, appearing most grateful, took one of the bottles to Ruth and promised to give her the remainder of the cordial over the next two days. I only hope that Ruth will soon return to her former strength and vitality.

Later in the evening, Rutledge and a friend, the planter Worthington, paid me a visit. Rutledge, bounding into the parlor with his usual wide grin, announced in his booming voice, "Hello, Johnson. How do you do?"

Not waiting for my answer, he introduced me to Mr. Worthington, who was in Charleston to procure supplies and to possibly buy a Negro or two for his rice plantation.

After pleasantries were exchanged, we took chairs by the fire and partook of some Madeira that Nat had brought in. The conversation was lively and delightful. Rutledge, being a bit of a raconteur, was in top form, and Worthington seemed very knowledgeable and informed concerning the events of the day.

At length, the conversation turned to Worthington's methods of rice planting and the treatment and work habits of his Negroes.

Worthington, a handsome and well-built man, well tanned by the South Carolina sun, took a long puff on his cigar and gave his opinion on the work habits of his slaves.

"All men are indolent," he stated in a grave tone of voice, "and have a strong inclination to avoid work, but it is a great deal stronger in the African race than in the white race. In working my niggers, I always calculate that they will do no labor at all except to avoid punishment, and they will never do more than just enough to save themselves from being whipped, and no amount of whipping or punishment will prevent them from working carelessly and indifferently. It always seems on my plantation as if they purposely try to break all the tools and spoil all the cattle that they can, even when they know they'll be directly punished for it."

"Worthington," I replied, "that may be the way your Negroes go about things, but I have never had that problem with my two Negroes, Nat and Ruth. They work hard and effectively. I could barely get along without them."

Worthington also bemoaned the trouble he has been having of late occasioned by his slaves running away. It often occurs, he stated, even when no immediate motive can be guessed at, even when the slave has been well treated and well fed.

Rutledge then asked Worthington if he had read a recent work by the learned Doctor Samuel Cartwright of the Louisiana State University, *A Report on the Diseases and Physical Peculiarities of the Negro Race.*

Doctor Cartwright, claimed Rutledge, believes that the slaves are subject to a peculiar form of mental disease, termed by Cartwright as

Drapetomania, which, like a malady that cats are liable to, manifests itself by an irresponsible propensity to run away.

Rutledge also stated that Doctor Cartwright devoted several chapters of his book to indispositions that effect the slaves. One chapter, claimed Rutledge, was devoted to idleness and sloth among the Negroes. According to Doctor Cartwright, the Negro does not take exercise enough to expand his lungs and vitalize his blood, but doles out a miserable existence being indolent and having too little energy of mind to provide for himself. The consequence of this indolence is that the blood becomes so highly carbonized and deprived of oxygen that it not only becomes unfit to stimulate the brain to energy, but also unfit to stimulate the nerves of sensation distributed to the body.

"Maybe, Johnson," said Rutledge, "you should read Cartwright's book. You may find the answer to what is troubling your Negro woman, Ruth."

The discussion and our evening ended with the agreement the Negro race was indeed an interesting, but vexing, one. "Perhaps," said Worthington as he rose to leave, "the great Thomas Jefferson was right when he asserted that 'slavery is more pernicious to the white race than the black.'"

So ended an evening of good conversation and company. As I watched Rutledge and Worthington take their leave, I could only feel deep inside me that the problem of how to live with the Negro race would be one that would haunt and perhaps destroy the South.

NOVEMBER 5, 1860—MONDAY
CHARLESTON, SOUTH CAROLINA

Later this afternoon after the company drill I was walking up King Street when I chanced upon Jackson Jarves, who owned a large plantation up on the Cooper River. He is a man of broad, coarse features, contracted and darkened brow, thick shoulders, bloated face and coarse black beard and hair. From the capacious side pocket of his large blouse there protruded the handle of a huge whip, the thong of which at the thickest part could not be less than an inch and quarter in diameter. Certainly a single lash from such an instrument on the naked back of a man or woman would make the blood fly in all directions. As I approached, he stopped in the middle of my path and extended his hand in friendly greeting. "Good day, sir," was my response.

As we conversed, he began to utter oaths and imprecations upon the abolitionists of the North declaring, "This question between the North and South must be settled now and forever, in the Union or out of the Union. South Carolina will take nothing more or less than the full measure of her rights. This I assure you, sir, is the position of her people." For his own part, he was willing "to carry a twenty-eight pounder twenty miles on his back if necessary to fight the dammed Abolitionists. "The Negroes," he said, "were kindly treated here, and when they were sick in the rice swamp, they were so much cared for as to be sent to the upper country to restore them to health! Rice could not be grown without niggers, and therefore, to abolish slavery would be to abolish the growth of rice in South Carolina!"

"How right you are," I replied. "And there is one thing I cannot understand. Why is it that Northern white men exhibit more sympathy for the Negro and his welfare than they do for themselves and their own children, and their own race and color."

We then discussed the recent news of the fearful tragedy at Lawrence, Massachusetts, one of these wholesale murders, commonly known in the Northern newspapers as an accident or catastrophe. A huge factory, long notoriously insecure and ill-built, requiring to be patched and bandaged up with iron plates and braces to stand the introduction of its machinery, suddenly collapsed into a heap of ruins, without the smallest provocation. Some five or six hundred operatives went down with it—young girls and women mostly. An hour or two later, while people were working frantically to dig out some two hundred still under the ruins, many of them alive and still calling for help, some quite unhurt, fire caught in the great pile of debris, and amid the hideous screams of anguish, those trapped were roasted.

"Of course," remarked Jarves, "Nobody will be hanged. But some greedy Northern capitalist has murdered about two hundred people, many of them with hideous torture, in order to save money. Where was Harriet Beacher Stowe to record this inhumanity? What does it become the citizen of the north to prate about the horrors of slavery? What southern capitalist trifles with the lives of his operatives as do the philanthropes of the North?"

NOVEMBER 6, 1860—TUESDAY—ELECTION DAY
CHARLESTON, SOUTH CAROLINA

Although busy with legal matters, I took the time in the morning to walk the short distance to City Hall where I cast my vote for John Breckinridge of Kentucky as the next president of the United States.

Rumors were flying like wildfire about the city, and talk of the election was on everyone's lips. One rumor being given great credence was that the election of Lincoln would set the stage for the Black Republicans to free the Negroes and force the whites to intermarry with them.

There has been speculation on what the election of Lincoln will bring. I found the views of *The Mobile Evening News* interesting:

"If Lincoln is elected president, it will mean war! The North may raise plenty of men, men who prefer enlisting to starvation— scurvy fellows from the back slums of cities, whom Falstaff would not have marched through Coventry with; but these recruits will not make soldiers, best of all, the soldiers to meet the hot-blooded, thoroughbred, impetuous men of the South. Trencher soldiers, who enlisted to war on their rations, not on men, they will be. Fellows who do not know the breech of a musket from its muzzle, and had rather filch a handkerchief than fight an enemy in manly combat. White slaves, peddling wretches, small-change knaves and vagrants, the dregs and off-scourings of the populace. These are the levied forces that Lincoln will array as candidates for the honor of being slaughtered by gentlemen such as Mobile will send to battle. Let them come south, and we will put our Negroes to the dirty work of killing them. But they will not come south. Not a wretch of them will live on this side of the border longer than it will take to reach the ground, and drive them over.

Mobile will send forth to wage this war of independence, the noblest and bravest of her sons. It is expensive, extravagant, to put such material against the riffraff of mercenaries whom the abolition power will call out to war upon us. We could almost hope that a better class of men would fall into the Northern ranks, that our gentlemen might find foemen worthy of their steel, whom it would be more difficult to conquer, and whose conquering would be more honorable."

As I write this entry, it is late, and the election returns are still trickling in via the telegraph. I am tired and it has been a long and exciting day. What the morrow will bring, I know not. The talk in Charleston is on nothing but secession. If it is to be secession, God grant that South Carolina will not have to do it alone.

NOVEMBER 7, 1860—WEDNESDAY
CHARLESTON, SOUTH CAROLINA

It is as if all Charleston has gone mad—such is the effect of the election of Lincoln on the populace of the city! Indeed, an array of Turks descending on the city from the sky in balloons could have hardly produced a greater frenzy.

Business during the day was largely suspended as the crowds filled the streets to read the bulletin boards for the latest election news. A large group of citizens took ship to Sullivan's Island and walked around the U.S. Army's Fort Moultrie, sporting secession cockades and shouting "down with Lincoln!"

James Conner, a fellow lawyer, came into our office at about noon and said, "Come, Johnson, let us join the madness."

"Why not," I replied, "it is a historic moment."

Turning to Mr. Petigru, Conner asked, "Do you want to come along, sir?"

"I have no desire to be one of the many lemmings running aimlessly and witlessly about the streets, chirping 'secession,'" replied my partner. "I hope to live and die under the Constitution of the United States."

"That," replied Conner, "would mean that we would have to live with the Northern states under a Black Republican president. I, for one," he continued, "view secession as the inherent right of South Carolina, and at this moment, her duty. All I have in property in South Carolina, I am prepared to stake, along with my life, on the issue of secession."

"If it comes to civil war, Conner," Petigru said softly, "you and many others may be required to honor that pledge."

After leaving the office, Conner and I walked to the Charleston Hotel. A large crowd had gathered and the scene was a most lively one. A band was present and the crowd was in a festive mood to serenade our public men and listen to their opinions.

The end of the day found me back in my house on Tradd Street, tired but pleased that the election at last is over and that the people of South Carolina seem sure what course they must take.

NOVEMBER 8, 1860—THURSDAY
CHARLESTON, SOUTH CAROLINA

Today the following notice appeared in *The Charleston Courier*:

"At the election of the various companies comprising the First Regiment of Rifles, held on Wednesday the 7th instant, the following gentlemen were elected without opposition:

J. J. Pettigrew, Colonel
J. L. Branch, Lieutenant Colonel
Ellison Capers, Major"

The men of the First Regiment of Rifles have paid me a great honor by trusting me to lead the regiment. I shall try to be worthy of the command they have bestowed on me. I am especially pleased with the election of Ellison Capers as Major of the regiment. A graduate of the South Carolina Military Academy, he has been serving as a professor at his alma mater. He is a stalwart fellow, with a thorough knowledge of military matters.

I take my command at a time when the City of Charleston is ablaze with excitement, flags and banners waving from the housetops and the heavy tread of embryo soldiers echoing through the streets. In the corridors of the hotels and public places, plumed cavaliers with their jangling spurs and rattling sabres discuss with infantrymen the relative merits of drill, musketing, southern valor, and diverse techniques of fighting.

I am well aware that all over the South many men are studying the mysteries of military tactics. Many feel as I do, that it is time to become desirous to know, not how to cultivate, but how to defend our soil.

NOVEMBER 9, 1860—TUESDAY
CHARLESTON, SOUTH CAROLINA

Yesterday I joined Mr. Petigru, my law partner, for lunch. After the meal, as we prepared to light our cigars, I said to Mr. Petigru, "Many think that if war comes, it will be a practically bloodless exercise. 'Johnson, I'll drink all of the blood that is spilled in a war between

North and South,' one ardent secessionist boasted yesterday when I encountered him on Church Street."

Mr. Petigru then drew a letter from his desk drawer and slowly unfolded it with trembling hands. Looking intently at me he said, "Johnson, I hold in my hand a letter from a William Tecumseh Sherman. He served on the garrison at Fort Moultrie on Sullivan's Island many years ago. As I have a summer house on the island, I often ran into Sherman on my rambles, and we became good friends."

"Is he still in the Army?" I asked.

"No, Johnson," Petigru answered, "Sherman now lives in Louisiana and is the head of the Louisiana State Seminary of Learning and Military Academy. We have, though, kept up a steady correspondence these many years. This letter is a most remarkable one," Petigru continued, "as it gives Sherman's views on the course any war between the North and the South must take."

Holding the letter toward the gaslight so he could see the handwriting more clearly, Petigru began reading parts of Sherman's letter to me:

"The people of the South believe there can be peaceable secession. You don't know what you are doing. If you will have it, the North must fight you for its own preservation. If South Carolina precipitates war, other Southern states will surely follow through sympathy. This country will then be drenched in blood. God only knows how it will end. Perhaps the liberties of the whole country, of every section, of every man, will be destroyed, and yet upon knowing that within the Union, no man's liberty or property in all the South is endangered, then why should any Southern state leave the Union? Oh, it is all folly, madness, a crime against civilization.

"You Southerners speak so lightly of war—you don't know what you are talking about. War is a terrible thing!

Now, the Northern people not only outnumber the whites of the South, but they are mechanical people with manufacturers of every kind, while you are only agriculturists—a sparse population covering a large extent of territory—and in all history, no nation of mere agriculturists ever made successful war against a nation of mechanics. The North can make a steam engine, locomotive or railway car; hardly a yard of cloth or a pair of shoes you can make. You are rushing into war with one of the most powerful, ingeniously mechanical and determined people on earth—right at your door."

At this point, Petigru put the letter down and said, "Magnificent, magnificent words, Johnson. Sherman has, I believe, seen through the mists of time and discerned the future."

"I think he writes eloquently, but falsely," I replied. "We Southerners are a brave fighting people who can overcome long odds."

"Let me finish the letter by reading the last paragraph," intoned Petigru. "I feel it is the most accurate of all." Picking up the letter, Petigru began to read from where he had left off:

"Finally, Mr. Petigru, let me warn you the South is bound to fail. Only in your spirit and determination are you prepared for war. In all else, you are totally unprepared, with a bad cause to start with. For how can Almighty God support a people that fights for slavery?"

With tears in his eyes, Petigru finished reading Sherman's letter. He took out a tiny handkerchief, blew his nose, dabbed at his eyes, and composed himself. Looking at me, he then said, "If Sherman is right, it means the ruination of the South." It was an emotional moment, and there was little I cared to say. For, like the cross, which the apostle Paul preached as unto the Jews, a stumbling block, and unto the Greeks, foolishness, this issue of secession had divided us, unalterable, into the unbelieving and the believing.

Now, I observe that what I had intended to be a small written tribute to James Petigru has ended, as all things do these days, in a discussion of secession and war. Will even this journal become a battleground between the contending forces?

NOVEMBER 12, 1860—MONDAY
CHARLESTON, SOUTH CAROLINA

I felt it my duty as a Christian to visit Dr. Malcom Banks, the surgeon of the slave ship Echo. He is presently incarcerated, along with the captain and other members of the crew, in the city jail. I had made Bank's acquaintance while a student at the University of North Carolina. No one seeing him stride across the campus would have mistaken him for a philosopher. He was swarthy and tall and might have looked distinguished except for a strabismus, a persistent squint in one eye. He was a curious personality who loved intoxicating liquors and engaged in many a drunken brawl. Who would have ever guessed he would later temper his licentious ways and become a priest? He gravitated to medicine after being unfrocked by the Catholic Church for writing an unauthorized version of the Spanish Inquisition and getting married.

Jail officials were kind enough to let me meet with Dr.Banks in a vacant room adjacent to the sheriff's office. As the guard escorted the doctor in he approached me with an amiable smile and shook my hand warmly. Without doubt Dr. Banks is one of the most cynical men I have ever known, yet I had always found him affable and enjoyed his company at the University.

"Johnson, it's been a long time, you look well."

"Doctor, I hope you are doing well."

"The truth is being confined to this jail has made me a melancholy case, for am I not correct, Johnson, in assuming that I and the other members of the ship could be hung for engaging in the slave trade?"

"True, doctor. National law prohibits the overseas slave trade and the penalty for engaging in it is death. But you have as much chance of being hung in Charleston for engaging in the slave trade as you would for engaging in monogamy."

"I'm not so sure, Johnson. The Northern abolitionists are raising a tremendous outcry over the Echo, and the United States District Attorney has made a personal issue of the case. I tell you things are in a hell of a fix."

"Pray tell, doctor, how exactly did you get yourself into such a fix?"

"Having been a fool in many things I was impecunious and became more concerned about food and shelter than my principles. I thought I could cure my financial ills in a short time by serving aboard a slaver."

"I would assume, doctor, you could make several thousand dollars a voyage?"

Banks got upright upon hearing my question and a new interest warmed his voice. "You have been misinformed, Johnson. A surgeon's berth on board ship never filled my purse or kept me long on shore. I served five years in His Majesty's Navy, but quit the King's service when I realized the financial rewards were poor. I was sometime later offered a surgeon's berth for an African voyage on the Echo, commanded by Captain Townshend, and made two rounds in her. It is the story of the voyage from Africa, across the Atlantic I should relate to you."

The doctor was in an expansive mood and I had always desired to hear first hand of conditions aboard a slave ship. I went to a nearby chair and holding up my hand to signal for a brief pause, took a cigar from my pocket so as to better enjoy myself as I listened to his tale. Once settled and with several puffs under my belt, I bade the doctor to continue.

There was a moment of silence, as Dr. Banks turned the memories over in his mind. He then moved to a nearby chair and began his most interesting narrative:

"Those several months the Echo lay at anchor off the Guinea Coast taking on slaves seemed to me the most dangerous part of the voyage.

Not only was the crew exposed to African fevers and the chance of being taken by pirates, but also there was the constant threat of a slave mutiny.

"To guard against this, as soon as an assortment of naked slaves came aboard the men were shackled two by two, the right wrist and ankle of one to the left wrist and ankle of another. Then they were led to down between the decks. Mr. Mansfield, the first mate, was employed in storing the slaves and he made the most of the room and wedged them in. It seemed to me that each had not so much room as a man in his coffin, either in length or breadth. It was impossible for them to turn or shift with any degree of ease.

"We followed the usual practice of lodging the males apart from the females, by means of a strong partition at the main mast, the forepart being for the men, the other behind the mast for the women. We had over 500 slaves aboard and the deck in which they were stowed was five feet high, thus being more airy and convenient for such a considerable number of creatures and consequently more healthy for them."

As the doctor paused to pour himself a glass of water from a nearby pitcher, I did a quick mental calculation and determined the Echo crossed the Atlantic with almost 500 slaves packed into a deck space 25 by 100 feet. It was obvious to me that they were packed as tightly as herrings in a barrel.

"At the front of each compartment were placed three large buckets of a conical form, nearly two feet in diameter at the bottom and only one foot at the top and in depth about twenty-eight inches, to use whenever the slaves felt the need to relieve themselves. It often happens that those who are placed some distance from the buckets, in trying to get to them, tumble over their companions, in consequence of their being shackled. Having to relieve themselves, but unable to proceed and prevented by the mass of slaves lying in front of them, they desist from the effort; and as their bladders and bowels are full, they ease themselves as they lie. This urine and feces often covers their naked bodies and becomes a source of boils and disturbances and tends to render the condition of the poor wretches still more miserable."

"Good God!" I uttered, trying in my mind's eye to imagine the horror of such an existence.

"Leave God out of this, Johnson," replied Doctor Banks. "Between decks of a slave ship is more like hell than heaven."

"As a doctor were you powerless to do anything?" I asked.

"Captain Townshend liked the ship tightly packed. He was a Christian and loved his Savior but he was also a Yankee and knew the more slaves he landed the more money he would make."

"Please continue, doctor," I said. "I'm anxious to hear more."

"Once the entire ship's cargo was together, the air became absolutely pestilential. The closeness of the place, the heat of the climate, added to the number in the ship, which was so crowded that each had scarcely room to turn himself, almost suffocated us. This malevolent smell brought on a sickness among the slaves of which many died. The wretched situation was further aggravated by the galling of the chains, now become insupportable; and the filth of the tubs into which the children often fell, and were almost suffocated. The shrieks and cries of the women, and the groans of the dying are with me yet.

"During the voyage I was frequently a witness to the fatal effects of the exclusion of fresh air. One instance will serve to convey to you, Johnson, some idea of the slaves' terrible sufferings. We had sailed into a storm and this caused the captain to order the portholes to be shut and the grating to be covered. This caused the confined air to be rendered noxious by the effluvia exhaled from the slave's bodies which by being repeatedly breathed, soon caused fevers and fluxes to ensue. While they were in this situation. I went down among them till at length the place became so extremely hot as to be only bearable for a short time. But the excessive heat was not the only thing that rendered their situation intolerable. The deck was so covered with blood and mucus that had proceeded from them as a result of the flux that it resembled a slaughterhouse. I ordered numbers of the poor creatures to be carried upon deck where several died and the rest with great difficulty were restored. The whole thing was dreadful and nearly proved fatal to me also. The area between decks was too warm to admit the wearing of any clothing, but a shirt and I had to pull that off in short order; and even though I only continued among them for about a quarter of an hour, I was so overcome with heat, stench and foul air that I nearly fainted and it was only with assistance that I could get back on deck. The consequence was that I soon fell sick of the same disorder from which I did not recover for almost a week.

"Once away from the African coast and under a favorable breeze the slaves are brought up on deck for exercise, which is necessary for the preservation of their health. Often they were asked to dance. If they go about it reluctantly or do not move with agility, they are flogged with the cat o' nine tail. I recall one occasion when a slave tried to snatch the cat from the first mate's hand. He was soon subdued and tied to a mast. The cat was then applied to his naked back until he was literally covered with blood. No cries, no screams, not tears from his gory victim seemed to move the first mate's heart from its bloody purpose. The louder the slave screamed, the harder he whipped, and where the blood ran fastest, there he whipped the longest. I shall ever remember this horrible exhibition. I shall never forget it whilst I remember anything.

"Often we had Negroes who refused to take food, and I have seen coals of fire glowing hot, put on a shovel and placed near their lips as to scorch and burn them. And this has often been accompanied by threats of forcing them to shallow the coals if they persisted in refusing to eat.

"If we found a slave who was particularly recalcitrant about eating, Captain Townshend had a method that always cured them of the habit. He would have the slave bound so he couldn't stir, then bind his knee over a block of wood, then he'd take a pair of pincers and pull one of his toe nails out by the roots, and tell him that if he ever refused to eat again, he would pull out two of them, and if he refused to eat again he'd pull out four of them, and so on, doubling each time. He never had to do it more than twice—it always cured them.

"I do recall one female who was determined not to be sold into slavery and she attempted to cut her throat. I sewed up the wound, whereupon that night she tore out the sutures, using her fingernails since nothing else was at hand. We found her dead the next morning and threw her body overboard where it fell a sacrifice to the sharks."

Doctor Banks then paused, spit a wad of tobacco juice into an empty glass and said, "Should I go on?"

"No," I replied. "I have heard quite enough. What you have told me only reinforces my belief that the overseas trade and the barbarous practices that are employed to maintain it are wrong. I can only contrast it to the system of slavery that exists here in South Carolina that is characterized by peaceful, industrious and virtuous slaves and honorable planters motivated by self-interest, custom and moral training toward paternalism."

"For my part, Johnson," concluded the doctor, "I am now vehemently opposed to the overseas trade. Custom, example, and pecuniary interest blinded my eyes. I did it ignorantly and should have been overwhelmed with distress and terror if I had known or even suspected I was acting wrongly. I can only pray God doesn't judge me too harshly for my actions."

NOVEMBER 16, 1860–FRIDAY
CHARLESTON, SOUTH CAROLINA

Messrs. Cressy and Harby, young gentlemen, were lately clerks together at one of Charleston's largest clothing houses. While working, they had a political dispute which ended in epithets and a fight. Cressy, whose violent and dastardly epithet provoked the assault by Harby, got the worst of the fisticuffs and prevented things from getting still worse by proposing to settle the affair according to the code.

My friend, Benjamin Rutledge, served as a second for young Harby. Rutledge asked me along to witness the duel and provide support if he was unable to do his duty.

As the principal agent for Harby, Rutledge was responsible for agreeing to the weapons to be used and where the duel was to be fought (the beach at Cummings Point). The seconds further agreed that the Cressy-Harby duel was to be fought at a distance of thirty paces with single-shot pistols.

Friday morning, shortly after sunrise, the aggrieved parties arrived at the place appointed and the respective positions of the duelists were spaded out with mechanical exactness. A coin was tossed by Rutledge for position and the giving of firing signals. Next, the dueling pistols were produced—each second loading that of his principal. The dueling pistol is an expensive affair, made of the very finest material. The pistols have a long slim rifle barrel with hammer underneath, the stock finely chiseled and elaborately ornamented with silver or gold. The pistols are about ten inches in length and carry a small bullet of .22 caliber.

The seconds then took their positions at an equal distance from each other and midway between Cressy and Harby. Both the principals stood facing each other, looking bold, calm and defiant; an insult to be wiped out and honor to be sustained.

The principals were in formal dress. Cressy attired in ballroom clothing—lace ruffles at his coat lapels, silk stockings, and black patent pumps. Harby wore black pantaloons, a white vest, and a grey cloth swallow-tail coat.

A physician arrived in a high-wheeled carriage to serve Cressy and another surgeon came alone in a light gig to serve Harby. The physicians appeared very businesslike and soon had their sleeves rolled up, ready for action with their forceps and tourniquets.

With all made ready, Cressy and Harby were summoned by the seconds to move to their respective positions. Cressy, known as a crack shot despite his tender age, smirked as he walked toward a nearby rock and carefully placed his burning cigar on top of it. He then said to his second, in a voice loud enough for Harby to hear, that he would soon be back to claim it before it burned out. This confident assertion seemed to unnerve young Harby.

Cressy and Harby then turned, facing the ocean, hands down with pistols in the right. The seconds would then call out in calm, clear, deliberate tones: "Gentlemen, are you ready?" Then, "Ready, aim, fire!" and, "One, two, three, stop!" The shooting must take place between the words "fire" and "stop" or during the count of "one," "two," or "three." If either of the principals fires before or after this count, it is considered murder, and he is at once shot down by the second of his opponent. But Cressy and Harby were, if anything, men of honor, and there was little chance they would fire before or after the appointed time. Honor was what had brought them to the field, and a true South Carolinian would make a sacrifice, give or take life, to uphold his name unsullied or the honor of his family untarnished.

As the word "fire" was given, Cressy and Harby wheeled and two sharp pistol shots rang out, piercing the stillness of the morning. As the smoke slowly cleared, Cressy stood till erect, a smile on his face, commanding and motionless as a statue. Harby remained steady for a moment, a quizzical look on his face, then he sunk slowly to his knees and fell face first to the ground. The surgeon ran forward making a hasty examination. "Blood!" called out Rutledge. A nod of satisfaction was given and acknowledged by both seconds. Cressy retired on the arm of a friend, stopping to pick up the still burning cigar, while Harby, then bleeding profusely from a wound in the chest, was lifted up and carried to the Marine Hospital in Charleston, where at this moment he hovers between life and death.

Thus sadly ended this Code Duello, the Southern gentlemen's method of settling personal disputes.

As I watched them carry poor Harby away, I could only think at what a high price a Southerner's honor and reputation was upheld. Surely in these troubled times with a civil war looming on the horizon, this senseless dueling extracts a heavy price on the manhood of the South.

Consider the tale currently sweeping Charleston of an incident that took place in Savannah. It seems a skilled duelist arrived in the Georgia city recently by steamer. Rumor credited him with having formerly shot to death two adversaries in duels and reported him as being quick to anger. This rumor became fact when he took a quick dislike to a young Savannah lawyer, goaded him into a duel and killed him with one quick shot to the head. Six friends of the deceased vowed their revenge by signing an agreement to challenge the murderer to a duel one at a time until one of the six should be successful in laying him low. They drew lots for the first honor, but the stranger killed this man also with a shot to the head. The remaining five then decided to disband, the group reasoning that none of them stood a chance before this crack shot.

There are too many men in the South like the Savannah duelist. Would-be gentlemen, who think it a greater disgrace to bear an imaginary insult than to murder a fellow human being in cold blood. It is time to end this needless bloodshed and prepare to weather the storm clouds gathering about.

NOVEMBER 23, 1860—FRIDAY
NEAR FLORENCE, SOUTH CAROLINA

The train has just left Florence. I had a delightful visit with my cousin, William, and his large family. Now, it's back to Charleston and the affairs of the day. After a jerky, rattling start, the train pulled slowly out of the Florence station, gaining speed while clouds of pitch-pine smoke interspersed with live sparks pounded from the enormous smokestack of the engine. The train now heads almost straight south to Charleston.

The return trip from Columbia has been a most interesting one. The train was advertised to leave at 3:00 p.m. I boarded shortly before that and found the cars crowded with passengers. The engineer, punctually at the scheduled departure time, gave notice that he was at his post by a long, loud blast of the locomotive's whistle. Five minutes afterwards, the train gave an impatient jerk and I thought, "at last we are underway." Ten minutes later, still sitting in the same spot, we advanced three rods; ten minutes later returned to the original position; and continued backing and inching forward for half an hour. At precisely 3:45, the train gave a huge lunge and we fairly started for Charleston.

Just before we started, I noticed thirty or forty slaves—men and women—chained together in gangs and accompanied by their owner or overseer—being put upon one of the rear cars. They were probably being taken to a slave market in Charleston to be sold at auction to the highest bidder. The women were sad-looking creatures who seemed to realize to some extent their debased and degraded condition. The men were a robust lot—strong, muscular fellows who were to all appearances unconcerned and indifferent to their fate.

In my car, I noticed that a large number of passengers were members of the fair sex who kept their tongues a-wagging and a-wiggling. When not straining their vocal cords with conversation, they filled the car with verse after verse of the song "Dixie."

Also on board my car was a member of the United States army garrison at Charleston, dressed in full uniform, who was returning to duty after visiting friends in Columbia. Seated beside the unfortunate officer was a trio of unusually venomous spitfires who gave their tongues full license and showered the hapless shoulder strap relentlessly with insults and epithets, almost drowning out the noise of the train.

The young officer braced against the arm of the seat opposite was completely at the mercy of his tormentors. To his credit, he took his medicine like a man, enduring such degrading epithets as "you Lincoln hireling—you Black worshiper" while they added insult to injury by flaunting miniature palmetto flags in his face.

The relief he felt was obvious on his face when the train stopped at a small way-station and the maidens made ready to depart. As they passed by the young man, resplendent in his blue uniform, they flashed upon him withering glances of scorn. If he had dared to reply to their insults, I am sure they would have fell upon him as one and attempted to scratch his eyes out, so great seemed their hostility.

Not surprisingly, soon after the pestiferous ladies departed, a calm settled over the car. The young officer, his feathers undoubtedly ruffled a bit, leaned back to read a book while other passengers attempted to sleep or talk in hushed tones. I couldn't help glancing at the soldier and noticing that he looked quite dashing and soldierly in his uniform. He appeared innocent enough absorbed in his book, and I could only think, "has it come to this?" To think that the mere sight of an army uniform could excite a bevy of females to such fury. Do the North and the South really hate each other so? I may live in interesting times, but it is also obvious that I live in difficult and dangerous ones.

Through the South Carolina countryside, the train hastens, rocking and dancing onward at over twelve miles per hour. It's a rather long affair with an engine, six passenger cars, a flat car and five freight cars. The Negro slaves, it appears, occupy one of the rear freight cars.

The passenger cars are like shabby omnibuses, but larger, holding thirty or forty people. There are entrances at each end with an aisle down the middle. The seats are placed crosswise, each seat holding two passengers. In the center of each car, there is a stove fed with charcoal or anthracite coal. At night, the stove turns red hot, and if you sit close enough, you can see the hot air fluttering between yourself and any other object you may happen to look at.

Whenever the train makes a scheduled stop, the aisle of the passenger car quickly becomes a place of business, with hawkers boarding to sell newspapers, fruit, candy, nuts, tobacco and patent medicines before the train starts again. The conductor, or captain, as he is often called, told me that one hawker usually sold $400 worth a week at a twenty percent commission.

A merchant I sat next to on the journey from Florence to Charleston said that trains would be "the perfection of traveling if one could stop when one wanted, if one were not locked up with forty or fifty tobacco chewers, if the engine did not burn holes in one's clothes, if the smoke would not poison one, and if one were not in danger of being blown sky-high or knocked off the rails."

The speed of the train is good, however, and we are making excellent time, but the cars of the train are old and dirty with dilapidated and moth-eaten furniture. Nevertheless, the seats are comfortable and I am in danger of dozing off. Sir Francis Bacon wrote, "Reading maketh a full man, speaking a ready man, writing an exact man." And I might add, a tired man! I've been worrying over the words in this journal too long. It's time to put the journal away, lean back and get some needed sleep before we arrive in Charleston.

NOVEMBER 30, 1860—FRIDAY
CHARLESTON, SOUTH CAROLINA

Suddenly I found myself sitting upright in my bed, my heart racing and my head and face drenched with sweat. What a dream—or was it a nightmare? Did the events of yesterday really take place? Yes, most assuredly they did and it was a day to be forever seared into my memory. But let me go back to yesterday and the beginning.

The day began innocently enough. I awoke knowing I was scheduled to ride patrol this day. Accordingly, I dressed and readied my big black,

"Madrid," my favorite horse. I armed myself with two colt revolvers and reported to the guardhouse on Broad Street to await the arrival of the other members of the patrol.

The purpose of the patrols is to prevent plots or conspiracies among the slaves. No Negro is allowed to go beyond the bounds of his master's plantation without a written pass. Some Negroes have a habit of secretly visiting the Negroes of other plantations by night. To stop this, overseers, policemen, and militia officers have organized themselves and are patrolling the countryside. Negroes off the plantations are stopped and checked for passes. If they do not have one, they are arrested and punished.

Also, no Negroes are allowed on the streets of Charleston between drumbeat at night (retreat) and drumbeat in the morning (reveille). Any Negro found on the streets during this period is also subject to arrest, if he does not have a pass signed by his owner. The drum is beaten at the main door of the guardhouse on Broad Street by a Negro named Percy Brown. During the day, the Negroes are only restrained from going where they please by their master's orders or by the needs of their daily routine of service.

I arrived at the guardhouse at about 2 o'clock in the afternoon. Upon arrival I was informed by Police Chief John Harleston, who was a graduate of West Point and a colonel in the militia, that I would be riding patrol with one of his police officers James Allen.

Harleston told me that Allen was no one to trifle with, that he had a hatred of all Negroes having once been stabbed in the abdomen by a Negro named Jack while attempting to punish him.

"He enjoys his reputation of being a first-rate hand at breaking young Negroes," remarked Harleston.

Upon introduction to Allen, I could see why the Negroes feared him so—cold, distant, morose. With a face wearing all the marks of hatred and malicious sternness, Allen presented an appearance all together ferocious and sinister. He was completely dressed in black topped with a wide straw hat with a black band, and when he walked, his large spurs jingled at every step. Attached to his belt was a vicious looking rawhide whip. He looked like a most malevolent creature.

Harleton informed us that we should ride north of the city between the Ashley and Cooper Rivers. A young Negro woman had run away from her master and we were to be on the lookout for her as well as any Negroes off their plantations without passes.

As we rode north out of the city, Allen informed me that runaway Negroes were a serious problem. These runaways indicated a spirit of insubordination which caused grave apprehensions of a general insurrection among the slaves. If enough Negroes were allowed to roam free in the countryside and woods they could form bands of murderers and incite the slaves of the whole area to a general insurrection. There was no graver offense a Negro could commit than to runaway.

"It is treason," remarked Allen, "and open rebellion against the only government that has any authority at all over them; running away threatens the stability of all government, the security of all property, and the safety of the very lives of the citizens."

A short distance from Charleston we found a man with a pack of dogs waiting for us at a curve in the road. Allen introduced him as Maurice Jackson, a professional hunter of runaway slaves. He was evidently an intelligent man, in a gossiping humor. Recalling a recent sale of Negroes in Charleston led him to boast to Allen and I of his own attractive qualities as a slave owner. He owned, he said, a parcel of likely gals which he would sell any day for a great deal more'n they were worth to him. He had been on the point of doing it several times, but he couldn't because they was of his own raisin'; and every time they heard he was talking of it, they'd come and cry so they'd make him change his mind. He felt he was a kind of soft-hearted man, and said he could not part with them gal's more than he could with his own children. Then pointing to the pistol tucked into his belt he said he always carried shootin'-irons with him, but he never yet shot a nigger—never shot a nigger. Some folks was mighty quick to shoot a nigger, but nary one of his niggers ever got shot, and he didn't expect they ever would—long as they behaved themselves.

"I won't have a bit of trouble shooting a nigger!" bellowed Allen. "You ought to have seen me a day or two since, in the midst of a group of niggers, with a revolver in one hand, an a bowie-knife in the other, ready to take the damn life of the first nigger that disobeyed my orders."

We were going to use Jackson's pack of bloodhounds to try and run the fugitive Negro girl down. "Ought to be easy," said Jackson, "as I have taught dem hounds to regard slaves as dere natural enemy."

He then gave me an account of how he trained his dogs in this business:

"The way to train 'em is to take these yer pups any kind o' pups will do, foxhounds, bulldogs, most any; but take the pups and keep 'em shut up and don't let 'em never see a nigger till they get big enough to be larned. When the pups gets old enough to be set onto things, then make 'em run after a nigger; and when they catches him, give 'em meat. Tell the nigger to run as hard as he can, and get up in a tree, so as to larn the dogs to tree 'em; then take the shoe of a nigger, and larn 'em to find the nigger it belongs to; then a rag of clothes and so on. Allers be careful to tree the nigger, and teach the dog to wait and bark under the tree till you come up and give him his meat."

"With these trained 'Negro dogs', we will have that Negro girl in no time Colonel Pettigrew," remarked Allen.

As we stood by our horses waiting for Jackson to give the dogs the scent of one of the girl's dresses he had procured, he informed us of the great skill his dogs employ.

"Once a pack of well-trained hounds has found the trail of a Negro," said Jackson holding the girl's dress up for us to see, "it is utterly impossible to confuse 'em or throw dem off the track. The nigger can run through squads of other niggers at work or even exchange shoes with another nigger in hopes of confusing the dogs, but it all is to no avail. Once these dogs have dat scent, dey follow the nigger to Boston and back if need be."

We mounted our horses, watched Jackson give the pack of eager bloodhounds the scent, and followed them as they ran off, noses to the ground, barking loudly.

We soon entered the boundaries of a large plantation and followed the dogs from one side to another. Twice we crossed a thick gully, at the bottom of which was a thick covering of brushwood. As we were nearly through it a third time, the dogs flushed a young Negro girl almost in front of us. As Jackson quickly called off his barking dogs to prevent the girl from receiving a severe mauling, Allen called out, "Who are you there?"

"Lucille, sir."

"What are you skulking there for, come up here so we can see you."

The girl rose and, saying nothing, approached us slowly.

"Have you been there all day?" asked Allen, his face flushed with anger.

"No, sir."

"How did you get here?"

Again the young Negro girl, who I guessed to be about 16 years old, made no reply.

"Where have you been all day? Do you have a pass from your master?"

The answer was unintelligible.

After further questioning, she admitted to having run away. "O, that I were free!" she half moaned. "I decided to run away, feeling that God would help me. You never would have caught me if it weren't for those hounds."

Allen looked at the girl, his jaw set, his eyes full of hate. "That won't do, come here!" he demanded. The girl walked toward him, her eyes looking down at the ground.

"That won't do," repeated Allen. "Get down." She knelt on the ground as Allen got off of his horse taking the rawhide whip off of his belt. The whip, a savage-looking instrument, was brown and made of about three feet of ox hide. It was an inch thick at the butt end, and tapered to a point, which made it quite elastic and springy. The rawhide was notorious for lacerating the skin and leaving gruesome scars.

"Mr. Allen, what are your intentions?" I asked.

"Colonel Pettigrew," answered Allen, "I'll ask you not to interfere. This girl is a runaway, a few runaways might form a mob. A mob may quickly grow into an insurrection or general revolution, which could sweep the whole country. She must be taught a lesson—a lesson she will never forget!"

Standing next to the kneeling girl, Allen began to strike her across the shoulders with the whip. The blows were well laid on, at arm's length, but Allen gave no appearance of angry excitement. At every stroke, the girl winced and exclaimed, "Oh my God! Oh my God!" Neither groaning nor screaming.

At length, Allen stopped and said, "Now have you learned your lesson?" There was no reply. "You have not had enough yet!" yelled Allen. "Pull up your clothes and lie down on your back." The young Negro girl, a look of defiance on her face, drew closely her dress and undergarments under her shoulders, and lay down on the ground, her back marking the grass with red streaks of blood.

Standing next to the girl, Allen began to strike across her naked loins and thighs. The blows were well laid on, at arm's length and every stroke brought away a strip of skin which clung to the lash or fell quivering on the ground, while the blood followed after it. The poor creature withered and shrieked and in a voice which showed her dreadful agony, screamed to Allen," O, spare my life! Don't cut my soul out!" But still fell the horrid lash; still strip after strip peeled off from the skin; gash after gash was cut in her living flesh, until it became a livid and bloody mass of veins and quivering muscle.

I turned away sickened by the spectacle taking place. I could watch no longer and gave Madrid rein and spur and we galloped up a steep acclivity. By the time I reached the top, the screaming and whip strokes had ceased. I could still hear the cries, sobs and groans of the young girl. I once again gave the black the spur and rode out onto the road, away from the scene of horror.

Shortly, Jackson and his dogs came up the road. "Mr. Allen will take the girl back to her master," stated Jackson. "You must look at the position of Mr. Allen," continued Jackson, "This is the only method by which slaves can be kept in subjugation."

Allen soon drove up, the young girl sitting tied up in the back of his one-horse wagon, an anguished look upon her pretty face. His contempt for the young girl was all too obvious and he seemed utterly indifferent to her condition as she moaned in pain.

I looked intently at Allen and decided he was one of the most cold-blooded men I had ever met. He had a calm, cruel look, which rendered him a terror in his vocation.

As he drove away, Jackson asked, "You don't approve of Mr. Allen, do you Colonel Pettigrew?" "How can I, Mr. Jackson. The man deals in agony! Torture is his stock in trade! He is a walking scourge and manufacturers tears about the vicinity of Charleston."

I felt only a flush of shame. It was the first time I had ever seen a woman flogged. I said little or nothing as we rode back to Charleston, glad to be done with the patrol and determined to never go on another. Much more of this, I feared, would make an abolitionist out of me.

Now, as I sit alone in my room, I once again recall the crack of the whip and the Negro girl's cries of agony. I can only conclude that Allen had enjoyed his work, even relished it. The man is, in my opinion, in league with the devil. But these seem to be the devil's days and he will have his due. Just before being hung over a year ago, the abolitionist fanatic John Brown had written, "I am now quite certain that the crimes of this guilty land will never be purged away but with blood." This prediction, I am beginning to fear, may well prove to be true.

DECEMBER 13, 1860—THURSDAY
CHARLESTON, SOUTH CAROLINA

Exciting news over the telegraph wires today. Seven senators and twenty-three representatives from the South issued a manifesto urging secession and the organization of a Southern Confederacy.

Major Capers marched a portion of the regiment outside of the city this morning for drill and target practice. Most of the men are excellent shots, accustomed to the woods and hunting; many have seen their share of deer or rattlesnake. Many of the men claimed that when armed with a rifle they could bring down anything within a distance of four hundred yards. In fact, nine-tenths of the company seemed born to arms, and were never so happy as when shooting.

Capers erected a target five feet high and fifteen inches broad. The men were placed at a distance of 150 yards and told to load their rifles. The noise of the ramrods filled the air as the men loaded and awaited Major Capers' order to fire.

"Now," said Capers, jocosely, "fancy the board is President-elect Lincoln." At the command, "ready, let all aim carefully," the men raised their rifles and took aim. At the word "fire," a volley was admirably delivered. As the smoke cleared, Capers rode to the target to count the holes. "Ninety-five holes counted, Colonel," he yelled back. "Ninety-five out of the hundred who had shot."

I smiled and said to the men, "Save your powder bags. You'll do." It was marvelous shooting and we were short of cartridges and powder.

"I think Old Abe was well covered, Colonel," announced Capers. "It would be a rough time for him or any of his hirelings if they were to come to South Carolina."

After drill, as the men marched back to Charleston, many expressed their desire for active service. They were tired of drill, guard-mounting, parades, etc. All wished to go forth and fight the Yankees—not that the Northerners were deemed worthy of that honor, but there was a strong desire to get to close quarters with the foe and settle the question without delay. There was not one of my regiment who did not fancy himself a match for any half-dozen New Englanders.

Later in the afternoon as the men prepared to return to their homes and occupations, Private Dick Simpson asked me to look over a letter he was preparing to send to the editor of a Yankee newspaper. Simpson, a patriotic young man, left his home in Spartenburg to come to Charleston to join the regiment. "This was not a rash act," he said, "but my love of South Carolina and feeling of duty compelled me to do it."

After reading Simpson's letter I felt it expressed almost perfectly the feelings of the majority of my men and I have included it below:

"To the editor of the N.Y. Tribune
Charleston, South Carolina
December 11, 1860

Sir, as your paper is the leading organ of the Black Republican part of the North I have concluded to let you know something about the condition of South Carolina as regards Secession. You are aware that South Carolina with Florida and the other Cotton States will soon be out of the Union and what next, Maryland or Delaware will also go off and can the South be coerce...no...never. The South can take care of the North and France will take care of...Johnny Bull. You people of the North think that we poor people of the South will never fight against the Federal Union. You are mightily mistaken. I am a poor man and am reddy now to fight rather than see the South subququated to the North. It is rumored here that Buchanan has sent a vessel of war to South Carolina to coerce her. It will take two millions of men to subdue South Carolina. Volunteer companies is forming all over the South. I saw an old man today seventy years old who had enlisted to fight you. Northern men know nothing about the condition of the slave. He is well fed, has plenty of time to eat and sleep and is not worked hard. We poor men of the South has the whole management of the slave, being overseers for their masters and we ought to be a judge of their treatment and condition. The Negro is satisfied with his condition, or a large majority are and I can tell you that if a Civil War were to take place with the North and South, you need not count upon the Negro, for there is no fight in him for ten white men well armed will whip a thousand Negroes for of all things in the world, the Negro is the scarest creature. I could take an old gunn barrel and scar ten Negroes to death even if they knowed there were no lead in it. I can tell you that the Ladyes of the South are taught to shoot the rifle and pistole and they use them with deadly aim. They can take care of the Negroes and we men will take care of you Yankees. Take care that when the war commences it will not end in the whole subjugation of the North. Who fought at the great battle of 1812, who was it that whip the solders that took Napolism Bonoapole at Waterloo, was it not the South and raw militia at that. But you Northerners think you have Gen. Scott to lead you. Do not be too sure of that and even if he should be able to lost all human feeling as to side with the North you never could subdue us.

Now, as you are one of the leading men of the North, I warn you people of the danger night and day and generations to the latest day will rise up and call you Blessed. Say to you men Lincoln if he have one spark of chivalry in him or one moment of love for this Union, to Resign for he can never be inaugerated in Washington he will find a Brutus. He can not be inaugerated unless he has a million of men at his back. You Republicans was fell off in your own by talking what you untended to do when Lincoln was elected. No I write this in the kindest of feeling. Take warning, I expect to meet your countrymen on the battlefield in deadly combat. I intend to do my duty and if I die I will die face formust to my enemies, but I had rather live in Peace with my brethern of the North."

Dick Simpson

Yesterday, Nat and I, armed with axe and shovel, spent most of the afternoon digging up a tree stump behind the house. Tonight, I have blistered hands and, in addition, in the palm of my left hand, there is a deeper-seated bruise, which has become inflamed. It seems to fester and worries me a bit.

DECEMBER 17, 1860—MONDAY
CHARLESTON, SOUTH CAROLINA

This mad existence I have been leading as of late continues. Early this morning I received a telegram from the new Governor of South Carolina Francis Pickens, stating that he was appointing me the first of his military aides. He further informed me in the telegram that he no longer advocated waiting for Lincoln to take office before seceding. Well, it seems the Devil is unchained at last. South Carolina has been talking fire a long time, and now we must face it.

Early in the afternoon, I took my cousin, Elizabeth Allston, for a walk on the battery. It was a lovely afternoon, a bit brisk, but the battery was thronged with equipages and pedestrians as on a "music evening" in the summer.

The walk was delightful, but the very air seemed to be charged with electricity by the approaching storm of contest. All about the battery were young men wearing conspicuously on their breasts blue cockades or strips of plaited palmetto fastened to their buttonholes. This attested that they were "minute men," all ready for duty.

Elizabeth was the personification of spring, wearing a beautiful sea-green tarlatan with white japonicas in her hair. Her dress was so simple, yet so elegantly neat and fresh looking. She attracted much attention from the many gallants strolling the battery who all inquired who she was.

While looking out at the harbor, I observed Colonel Wilmot Gibbes DeSaussure, who commanded the First Regiment of Artillery, approaching us. Colonel DeSaussure was mounted on a superb steed—glossy and black as night. The dashing DeSaussure, in his suit of grey, mustache and goatee of formal cut, waxed to a point, with boots and spurs and floating plumes, was young Mars from his golden head to his horse's hoofs.

Elizabeth, seeing this picture of manhood, lowered her eyes as the colonel said, "Good day, Colonel Pettigrew. May I have the honor of being introduced to this young lady of beauty at your side?"

"Colonel DeSaussure," I announced as gallantly as I could, "may I have the pleasure of introducing to you Elizabeth Allston."

Bowing from the waist and taking off his plumed hat and sweeping it across his chest in a noble gesture, Colonel DeSaussure said in a soft voice, "My pleasure, Miss Allston." Then turning to me the gallant DeSaussure said, "You keep beautiful company, Colonel Pettigrew."

This brought a smile to Elizabeth's face and the mounted colonel, always chivalrous, smiled and said, "Careful, Miss Allston, don't turn towards Fort Sumter with such a smile, for it is sure to melt the very walls of the grim old fort."

Blushing, Elizabeth smiled and replied, "You are most gallant, Colonel. I have heard my father talk of you in a most complementary manner."

Colonel DeSaussure then remarked, "As much as I hate to, I must break up this idyll. My compliments to you, Colonel Pettigrew, and to your fair lady friend."

With that, the colonel gave a light spur to the black and galloped slowly away. Elizabeth, watching earnestly, said softly to me, "Oh, Johnson, how gallant he is and how brave he seems to be."

We then hurried towards Elizabeth's father's home, for she had to gather her luggage. She was scheduled to take the steamer to Georgetown later in the afternoon. Walking up the street, we encountered a sea of mud and without a word of warning, I picked the fair Elizabeth up in my arms and carried her the distance to her house, ending a charming afternoon.

DECEMBER 18, 1860—TUESDAY
CHARLESTON, SOUTH CAROLINA

Yesterday, the South Carolina Convention met in Columbia, the capital of the state. General D. F. Jamison was in the chair as they passed a resolution to adjourn to Charleston, in consequence of the prevalence of the small pox at Columbia, which was declared an epidemic.

This must be fate, for no place in America could be more appropriate for a secessionist convention than Charleston. With its long tradition of resistance to the federal government and fanatic support of slavery, it is the perfect site. "Secession is the fashion in Charleston," an English newspaper correspondent writes. "Young ladies sing for it. Old ladies pray for it. Young men are dying to fight for it. Old men are ready to demonstrate it."

Recently, in a conversation with Major Capers, I learned that he has been keeping a diary.

"It may be dull and uninteresting to others," Capers explained, "but it holds and inexpressible charm for me. It may even be poorly written," he continued, "but by leaving this unpretentious record, I seek to do what I wish my father had done for me."

He went on to explain that his diary was not extensive, but more a record of daily events, appointments, dates, places, etc. One of the problems he had been having in keeping the diary was finding the time to record the day's events.

I told Capers of my journal. I explained to him that I wished to keep an extensive, detailed record of the times I lived in. Finding time to write in the journal is also a problem with me. I usually set aside some time late at night, when the feverish pace of the day has subsided. Then in the quiet of my room, I can meditate on and record the events of the day and my reaction to them.

Although a lawyer, and perhaps a soldier by profession, I enjoy language and my journal is an attempt to make it work for me. But even if my language or grammar is technically flawed, I trust it will still convey my thoughts and experiences as I have lived them.

The inflammation of my hand and palm continues to increase very slowly. I fear it will not be ripe and discharged soon enough for me to partake fully in the convention activities.

DECEMBER 20, 1860—THURSDAY—VERY LATE
CHARLESTON, SOUTH CAROLINA

Oh that feeble pen were able to adequately describe the momentous and historic events of this day. Thursday is a day destined to become famous in the annals of history.

The morning began, bright and cloudless, warm for the season. The town was overflowing with enthusiasm as people were sure the Secession Convention would vote to dissolve the Union on this day. In addition to the convention delegates, the entire South Carolina government, headed by Governor Pickens, was on hand.

I had ordered the First Regiment of Rifles to assemble on the Citadel Green at 10 o'clock. On the way to the green from my house, I encountered a myriad of people in town for the convention. Planters, newspaper publishers, judges, lawyers, clergymen, bankers—many wearing the bright uniform of the militia—were walking in the street, talking in groups, looking at the bulletin boards or scanning the newspapers for the latest news. It was a veritable volcano of excitement.

Reaching the Citadel Green. I conferred with the officers of the regiment. Once the Ordinance of Secession was passed, we were to parade down Meeting Street to the battery in celebration of the event. Until we received a message from the convention, I informed the officers to let the men do as they pleased, but to not leave the green.

At about 1:20 p.m. we heard a loud report, from a cannon. "sounds like the 'Secession Gun,'" announced Capers. "It was scheduled to be fired when the ordinance is passed." Off in the distance, down Meeting Street, we could hear cheering, which was rapidly expanding into a loud roar. Soon, bells tolled, more cannon boomed, people were running everywhere in a frenzy of delight and excitement. The bells from historic old St. Michael's began to peal and never did the chimes sound so musical.

A messenger came riding rapidly up Meeting Street—a cloud of dust trailing behind his galloping horse—and waved a piece of paper in his hand. He gave the horse reign and shouted, "I have a message for Colonel Pettigrew."

"He's here!" shouted Lt. Colonel Branch.

Dismounting, the messenger approached and said, "I have a message for Colonel Pettigrew from His Excellency, the Governor of South Carolina."

Taking the paper, I saluted and hastily read the contents. "Gentlemen," I announced to the assembled officers, "the die is cast! The Union is dissolved. Assemble the men!"

The bugle blew assembly and rapidly the men began to form ranks. The regiment was soon arranged in full force, over a thousand men, rank upon rank, facing me, Lt. Colonel Branch, and Major Capers.

"Soldiers of the First Regiment of Rifles," I announced, "the Ordinance of Secession has been passed. South Carolina is no longer a member of the United States!" A mighty roar and shouts of approval went up from the ranks.

Soon the regiment is aligned by companies awaiting the order to begin the parade down Meeting Street. The Palmetto Band would lead followed by the Citadel Band, next the Regiment of Rifles, composed of the Moultrie Guards, Washington Light Infantry, German Riflemen,

Palmetto Riflemen, Carolina Light Infantry, and Meaghan Guards. Behind the regiment would follow the Zouvare Cadets under the command of Lieutenant Chichester, the Charleston Riflemen, Captain Johnson, and finally the Palmetto Guards, Captain Middleton.

The bugle sounds. The officers mount. I look back. Major Capers is mounting. How lightly he springs to the saddle. How easy he sits, straight and slender, chin advanced, eyes to the front, pictured against the blue South Carolina sky.

Again, the bugle calls. The horses know it and tense for action. The Palmetto flag sways aloft, the hand of its young bearer trembling with trust, determined to do his duty. The bands begin to play, the drums rumble. Up Meeting Street we march, into a vast arena, bright with color—flowers, flags and people lining the street. Windows and balconies are thronged with happy and cheering crowds—around the column, murmurs, roars and thunders of greeting. The roar of welcome moves forward with our column. As we march down the street, intervals between companies, the men hold their rifles at right-shoulder arms as they swing with the route step up the thoroughfare.

As the column nears St. Michael's Church, thundering waves of sound surround the marchers and mounted officers, as the crowds roar their welcome to their patriot soldiers. Flags, banners, flowers and costumes swirl everywhere in bright drenching sun-kissed air. Throngs of people press close to the marching soldiers, at times almost impeding the way. I look back at Lt. Colonel Branch. His saber flashing, he gives a smile and a salute, as a bugle call fills the air.

As we pass St. Michael's, I sit erect on my horse, Madrid—my sword upraised in my right hand as we receive the applause and cheers of the throng. Madrid shakes his head and his nostrils flare, his black color gleams in the sunlight and he looks every inch a magnificent war horse.

Suddenly, a young woman dressed in white moves quickly toward me, a braided garland of flowers in her hand. Madrid, startled by the young lady's appearance, veers high in the air. I struggle with my bridle arm to control the animal. Madrid's front hoofs come back down, close to the fair young lady, but not injuring her. I bow low, almost touching the cheek of the young lass—my sword point near her feet. The crowd claps and roars approval at my gesture. A smile crosses her red lips. The air smells sweet about her. Is it the lovely smell of the flowers or the lush fragrance of her perfume that floats to my face? Romantic always, I take the garland of flowers from her trembling hand and place them over the neck of Madrid—the fragrant blossoms colorful atop his muscular black neck.

All the way down Meeting Street, a tumult of sound and motion follow us. The bands begin to play the notes of the popular song, "Dixie" and the crowd takes up the chorus. Nearing the battery, I look backward and take in the magnificent spectacle: the broad street full of the ranks of marching men, the chattering of horses' hoofs, sabers and bayonets flashing in the sun. "What a day," I think to myself. "What a day, and what a time to be alive." The memory of this march will last a lifetime.

Later, after the parade, the officers of the regiment and I stand near the center of the battery, pleased with ourselves and the regiment. President Jamison, the presiding officer of the convention comes directly toward us with a smile on his face. Jamison, a gentleman scholar who lives graciously on a large plantation of 2,000 acres with over 70 slaves, extends his hand in greeting and fairly shouts, "Well done, gentlemen. The spirit and enthusiasm of the men convinced me that when their services are needed to defend our cherished rights, they will be ready with strong arms and brave hearts to drive back the ruthless mercenaries who would invade the sovereign soil of South Carolina."

We all smile as Jamison walks away after his little speech. "You know," says Capers, "the position of South Carolina seems so now firmly taken that, though her past heroes should rise from the dead to urge her retreat, she would not take one step backward."

In the evening, the formal signing of the Ordinance of Secession took place in Institute Hall. Forming a solemn procession at St. Andrews Hall, the delegates marched over to the larger Institute Hall, which could accommodate almost three thousand people.

I attended the ceremony with my officers: Lt. Colonel Branch, Major Capers, Adjutant Gaillard Barker, Lt. James Conner, and Lt. Charles Henry Simonton. We took a place in the gallery, which was crowded with ladies who waved their handkerchiefs to the delegates as they entered. On either side of the President's chair were two large palmetto trees. The hall was densely crowded. The Ordinance of Secession, having been returned engrossed and with the great Seal of South Carolina attached by the Attorney General, was presented and signed by every member of the convention—special favorites of the people being received with loud applause. After almost two hours, the President then announced, "The Ordinance of Secession has been signed and ratified. I proclaim the state of South Carolina an independent commonwealth."

At once the audience broke out into a storm of cheers. In the streets, popular demonstrations of joy had continued from the afternoon. As night came on, the street became wild with excitement as the news spread like wild fire. Bonfires, made of barrels of rosin, were lighted in the principal streets. Rockets flashed through the night sky and innumerable crackers were fired by the boys. Men and women snake danced through the streets. Church bells rang out with "Auld Lang Syne" and uniforms were everywhere.

South Carolina now stands before the world a free and regenerated people. The chains that have so long oppressed us have been thrown off and consigned to the dust.

What a glorious day! The question has been finally settled and surely the news will go forth. Now, will the sister states of the South join us in our holy cause?

It has been an exciting day and I went to bed exhausted, but did not sleep more than an hour and a half, because of the pain caused by my hand. In the morning I found a small spot ripe enough to cut open which I did. The discharge of thick pussulent matter, though small, relieved me considerably for a time. The swelling has extended to the end of my finger and the pain sometimes extends slightly above my elbow.

DECEMBER 23, 1860—SUNDAY
CHARLESTON, SOUTH CAROLINA

I awoke very early, but, oh, so tired. The frantic pace of the last few days has finally caught up with me, I think. I wanted to lie in bed, under my warm quilt, but duty called and with superhuman effort, I arose. What a shock to my system it was when my bare feet hit the cold floor. It almost drove me back to bed. The opening of my inflamed hand now discharges a good deal and the swelling and pain continue so great that I think there must be more sufferation in progress and another place to break. I have thus far been able to ignore the pain and carry on with my duties, but it becomes more difficult every day.

After a quick grooming, I partook of an apology of a breakfast—a biscuit and a glass of buttermilk—as there was little time to prepare anything better. After leaving the house, my servant, Nat, gave me a ride in the carriage to Bird Shipyard on the Ashley River. Once we arrived at the yard, I found Lt. Colonel Branch, Major Capers and Secretary of War Jamison waiting quietly.

After a quick series of "hellos" and "good mornings," we went aboard the coastal steamer Nina, lying in wait by the wharf. Armed with field glasses, maps, and charts, we quickly made ourselves comfortable on the small ship.

The Nina, which usually plied the waters between Charleston and Georgetown, has been pressed into service as one of the first ships of the fledgling South Carolina Navy. The ship is a 300-ton, 147-foot side-wheeler able to carry about 40 passengers. She has one wood-burning boiler driving two engines supplied from Northern machine shops. Her shallow draft and speed make her especially valuable for duty in the harbor. A V-shaped wall made of heavy timber has been built on the front of the ship's superstructure to protect the engines from gunfire. On the bow of the ship, engineers have installed a 12-pound howitzer. Painted white with the name "NINA" visible in large, black letters on the port side of the vessel, the steamer, under the command of Captain Lockwood, steamed slowly down the Ashley River—a flame of black and white smoke trailing behind her.

The purpose of our voyage was to inspect the federal fortifications which dominated the sea approaches to Charleston harbor and the city. These forts irritate almost every South Carolinian, although they probably take up a total of no more than fifteen acres of good Southern ground. During our reconnaissance, we would attempt to determine the strength and weaknesses of the forts. Once this was completed, we would submit a written report to Governor Pickens suggesting possible courses of action if war should be declared.

As we journeyed down the Ashley, it was as bright a day as the most fastidious lover of nature could ask. The frost of the night had covered the thick surge grass, which extends for miles along the banks with myriads of icicles whose tiny points glowed and sparkled in the sunlight. Charleston, stretching from the Ashley to the Cooper River lay gleaming in the morning light. The dense and lonely woods of James Island in the far distance, unlighted by a single ray of the morning sun, were in sharp contrast to the hectic bustle and crowded shipping of the wharfs.

Soon we passed the federal arsenal, proudly displaying the stars and stripes high above its walls. The building edged the marshes of the Ashley River and occupied a full city block. It was rumored there were over twenty thousand pieces of ordinance inside, ranging from cannon to pistols. Governor Pickens had already placed a twenty-man guard detail of the South Carolina militia around the arsenal to make sure federal troops would not have access to the weapons within.

As we neared the battery, we could see the tall spire of old St. Michael's catching the morning rays of the rising sun. Smoke from a hundred or more chimneys curled upward into the bright blue sky. High above, buzzards and seagulls wheeled lazily through the air. It was a fair sight and it reminded me of how much I loved Charleston and its way of life. "Worth living for, and dying for, if need be," I thought to myself. "And the time may be coming soon when a man may have to choose."

Approaching close to the black sides and mounted ordinance of Castle Pinckney broke my reverie. This federal fort, situated on marshy Shute's Folly Island, is less than three-quarters of a mile from Charleston. As we sailed by the half-moon-shaped fortress named for Charles Pinckney, South Carolina patriot and framer of the Constitution, we counted the following cannons placed upon the walls: four 42-pounders, fourteen 24-pounders, four eight-inch seacoast howitzers, one ten-inch mortar, and four light artillery pieces. These cannons so close to the city could inflict great damage on Charleston if manned and used properly.

After our inspection of Castle Pinckney, Captain Lockwood turned the Nina toward Sullivan's Island, located on the northeast side of the harbor. Situated on the island was Fort Moultrie, which was the main base of the federal garrison stationed in Charleston Harbor.

We anchored the Nina near the fort and studied it with our powerful field glasses. Although the fort commanded the northern entrance to the harbor, it was obvious that the post-Revolutionary War brick structure was not of great strength. The fort was terribly vulnerable to attack from the rear. A hundred yards east of the fort were two high sand hillocks which would offer perfect cover for riflemen and cannon. We could easily see that Moultrie, with its 1,500 feet of works, was much too much fort to be held for long by the meager garrison of 60 regular army soldiers.

We next inspected the most distant, but imposing of federal strongholds, Fort Sumter, four times bigger than Moultrie and some 3.3 miles from the city. From the Nina, Fort Sumter looked ominous and formidable.

The fort, which was begun in 1829, was designed to be among the greatest forts in America—a stronghold commanding Charleston Harbor that could garrison over 650 men and hold 146 or more guns of different caliber. Its pentagon-shaped brick masonry walls, surrounded completely by water, stand 50-feet high and vary in thickness from 12 feet at the granite base, to over 8 feet at the top. Looking at the grim old bastion through our field glasses, we could see that although the fort itself was virtually complete, only fifteen of the planned guns were mounted. No garrison was maintained in the fort and it stood tall and empty above the water.

As we sailed seaward away from the fort, I reminded Secretary of War Jamison that Captain George Cullum, an engineer who had spent several years at Fort Sumter, had informed me by letter that it was the sole place in the harbor suitable for United States troops to be stationed.

"It is a perfect fortress," replied Jamison. "It commands the harbor and Fort Moultrie. If it should ever be garrisoned, it could cut off all shipping to and from Charleston."

"If we are serious about this business of being a republic," replied Lt. Col. Branch, "we should at once seize Sumter while it is still un-garrisoned."

"That is a question for the Governor to decide," countered Jamison. "Let us go about this business calmly. Such an action could precipitate a war with the United States."

Captain Lockwood had headed the Nina a short distance out to sea after our inspection of the harbor. The bow cannon had never been fired and he wanted to fire a couple of practice rounds. We sailed to a spot a mile or so off the east side of Morris Island while crew members loaded the twelve-pounder with a charge of double canister. Then turning the ship toward the open sea, Lockwood gave the order to fire. With a loud roar, the cannon belched its charge into the sea. The spattering of so many balls in the water looked very destructive.

"Such a shot would wreak havoc with a ship full of soldiers," remarked Major Capers.

"But not with a Yankee Man of War," replied Captain Lockwood.

"But if we seize and control Fort Sumter," Capers added, "no Yankee Man of War can enter Charleston Harbor."

I could only think to myself as Capers and Lockwood bantered back and forth, that talk was plentiful and rhetoric eloquent these days, but South Carolina was ill prepared to face the future. This issue of the control of federal forts could easily lead to war. Just the other day, *The Charleston Mercury* had alerted its readers to the potential problems that the fortifications could cause. Editor Rhett had warned President Buchanan that if he sent additional troops to Charleston, "it will be bloody."

As the Nina docked at the wharf, it suddenly dawned on me that Christmas was only two days away. The rush of recent events had left me totally unprepared for the upcoming holiday. With this and a million other thoughts on my mind, I hurried back to my house on Tradd Street determined to get my holiday affairs in order.

DECEMBER 24, 1860—MONDAY—CHRISTMAS EVE
CHARLESTON, SOUTH CAROLINA

Late last night, the pain in my hand became so extreme that I had to send Nat for Dr. Clark. He made a careful examination and, with the help of his assistant, administered sulfuric ether to me and then cut open my hand. He inserted the knife three times making an incision about an inch in length and three-quarters deep extending from the middle of the palm nearly to the junction of the middle and fourth finger. The cut was almost down to the bone and still deeper, reaching the cavity (before discharging) on the back of the hand. I asked Doctor Clark to make me completely insensible, if possible, and this he was able to do. As I was told, I cried out upon the entrance of the knife, but if I felt pain, I was unconscious of it, for when I came to my senses, a few minutes after the cutting, I did not realize the operation was over and supposed the surgery had yet to be performed.

When the sponge saturated with ether was first held over my nose and mouth, the ether fumes almost choked me and I pushed the sponge away. But when Dr. Clark's assistant held it farther off, I was able to inhale the fumes more gradually and it was not very disagreeable. I was perfectly conscious of the gradual coming over me of the stupefying and merciful operation of the gas. Soon after, I knew nothing more until I came to, in my clear senses, and with but little feeling of pain, except the sense of soreness of the newly cut wound.

After the operation, Dr. Clark gave me the stimulus of a strong drink of toddy. The doctor then dressed the wound with emollient poultices. The pain gradually increased and became quite severe.

Before two, I finally fell asleep and awoke at about six in the morning much refreshed and, for the first time in days, perfectly free from pain.

Early in the afternoon I left the house to do some last minute Christmas shopping. As I walked up Tradd Street, the worry regarding my hand finally behind me, I couldn't help saying aloud, "Tis the season to be jolly!"

Weary and footsore after my shopping binge, I returned to my house on Tradd Street in the afternoon. Nat, to his eternal credit, had a cup of hot steaming coffee waiting for me. No sooner had I settled into my easy chair than there was a loud knock on the door. Nat stuck his head into the drawing room and said, "Look like some members of your regiment come to see you, Colonel."

Going wearily to the door, I found Captain Gillespie and several members of the regiment. Handing me a wrapped Christmas present, the laconic Gillespie made the following presentation:

> "Here we are, Colonel Pettigrew, and here it is. This is a bully Christmas present, and it comes from the bully boys. Take it and use it in a bully manner."

> I took the present and opened it slowly, handing Nat the wrapping paper as I did so. The present proved to be a beautiful pair of matched silver spurs.

Turning to Captain Gillespie and the men I said, "Captain, that was a bully speech and this is a bully Christmas present. Come, let's all take a bully holiday drink."

DECEMBER 28, 1860—FRIDAY
CASTLE PINCKNEY, CHARLESTON HARBOR

The unthinkable has happened! Major Anderson has transferred the garrison of the United States Army troops from Fort Moultrie to Fort Sumter. This gross breach of faith may prove to be the opening act of a civil war.

Governor Pickens and the people of Charleston were unaware of what had transpired until the guard boat Nina, making her rounds of the harbor, passed Fort Sumter early on Thursday, December 27, and saw the entire federal garrison lining the ramparts of the fort examining the new quarters. As the Nina steamed at full speed back to Charleston, dense smoke was seen rising from Fort Moultrie. Major Macbeth, believing that the fort had accidentally caught fire, immediately chartered a steamer and ordered two fire companies to go to the aid of Major Anderson and his garrison.

The steamer was about to get underway when a man rowed across the harbor from Sullivan's Island with the report that the guns of Fort Moultrie had been spiked. The gun carriages were burning and Major Anderson and the entire federal garrison established at Fort Sumter. This information was shortly confirmed when the guard boat Nina arrived back at the city.

The utmost excitement now prevailed. Messengers were dispatched all over the city to ring doorbells and alert the people. Naturally rumors began to circulate like wild fire. One rumor had it that Anderson had craftily concealed his escape by drinking with the secessionist authorities the night before and pretending to get stone drunk. Another rumor spread that the guns of Sumter were now trained on Charleston and that a bombardment would begin momentarily.

Crowds soon began to gather and inquire for the latest reports. The newspaper offices were besieged, the hotel halls thronged and the rooftops and church steeples occupied by townspeople with telescopes to satisfy their curiosity and verify the fact that federal troops were actually at Fort Sumter. Others went by boat to Sullivan's Island to view the abandoned Fort Moultrie.

About noon, as the excitement mounted, the streets literally swarmed with people. Additional flags were displayed from the stores and houses on the principal streets. The Custom House, and other buildings formerly in the possession of the United States, displayed the bunting of the infant Republic of South Carolina. Everyone looked upon the war as actually beginning.

Governor Pickens, to his credit, recovered quickly from this rude surprise. Major Capers and I were summoned to his office at City Hall and ordered to go to Fort Sumter, meet with Major Anderson, and demand, courteously, but peremptorily, that the major and his command return immediately to Fort Moultrie. I felt that at this point in time, any incident, however small, could be dangerous. My greatest fear was that some unauthorized group of citizens would act foolishly and attack Fort Sumter, thus setting off the spark that would unleash civil war.

Major Capers and I took seats in a small boat and were rowed to Fort Sumter. As we departed from the boat at the fort's narrow esplanade, I could see the stars and stripes waving in the breeze high above the ramparts. "What strange twists life takes," I mused to myself. "This flag I have been taught to honor and respect is now the flag of an enemy nation." Once inside the fort, I sent my card to Major Anderson asking for an interview. We were soon escorted into Major Anderson's office on the second floor of the officers' quarters.

Major Capers and I, dressed in full uniform of the South Carolina Militia, entered the room not knowing what to expect. I noticed several federal officers, including Captain Abner Doubleday and Assistant Surgeon Samuel Crawford standing near a rear wall.

Major Anderson was sitting at a chair next to a small table. "So this is the man all of Charleston and South Carolina are talking about," I thought. At first glance, it would have been easy to mistake him for a kindly white-haired grandfather, but I knew him to be a brave, capable soldier, who had been wounded three times at Moleno de Rey, in the Mexican War. I took him to be about 5 feet, 9 inches in height, with dark eyes, swarthy complexion and thinning steel-gray hair.

His greeting was reserved and formal, and when the major offered Capers and I seats, I declined and immediately opened the subject of my mission.

"Major Anderson," I began, "Can I communicate with you now, sir, before these officers, on the subject for which I am here?"

"Certainly, sir." Anderson replied. "These are all of my officers. I have no secrets from them, sir."

I then informed Major Anderson that Governor Pickens was much surprised that he had reinforced Sumter. Major Anderson promptly responded that there had been no reinforcement of the fort, that he had moved his command from Fort Moultrie to Fort Sumter as he had a perfect right to do so being in command of all of the forts in the harbor.

I then explained to the major that when Governor Pickens took office, he thought an understanding existed between the previous-Governor Gist and President Buchanan. According to this understanding, South Carolina would make no attempt against the federal property in the state, and in return, the Washington government would not alter the military status in the harbor. By moving to Fort Sumter, Anderson had most decidedly altered the military status in the harbor. I then informed Anderson that Governor Pickens had hoped for a peaceful solution, but this violation seemed to make it uncertain, if not impossible.

Major Anderson replied that he knew of no understanding between the Governor and the President. He had tried vainly to get information and positive orders from Washington. Meanwhile, his position at Fort Moultrie had been threatened every night by the troops of the state.

"How?" demanded Major Capers.

"By sending out steamers armed and carrying troops." replied Anderson. "These steamers passed the fort going north. I feared a landing on the island and the occupation of the sand hills just north of the fort. One hundred riflemen on that hill would command the fort and make it impossible for my men to serve their guns, as any military man can see."

"To prevent this," Anderson continued, "I removed to Fort Sumter on my own responsibility, my sole object being to prevent blood shed."

Major Capers replied that the steamer was sent out for patrol purposes and the idea of attacking Moultrie was never entertained by the little squad who patrolled the harbor.

Anderson replied that he was totally in the dark as to the intention of the state troops, but he had reason to believe they had reason to attack him from the north, and to prevent this, and blood shed, he transferred his command to Fort Sumter. "In the controversy between the North and South," Anderson continued, "my sympathies are entirely with the South. These, gentlemen," he indicated, pointing to his own officers, "know it perfectly well. But," Anderson added, "my sense of duty as commander on the harbor comes first with me."

"Make my compliments to the Governor," Anderson said, "and say to him that I decline to accede to his request. I cannot and will not go back."

"Then, sir," I replied, "my business is done."

With this said, Capers and I took our leave from Major Anderson and Fort Sumter. I knew as we rowed back toward the city that our mission was unfulfilled, but both Capers and I were convinced of Anderson's lack of aggressive intent. The city of Charleston need fear no sudden bombardment from the guns of Fort Sumter.

Upon return, we found Governor Pickens in an agitated state. "Anderson's escape to Fort Sumter was the worst thing that could have happened," he exclaimed. "Now the federal garrison is situated in a fort that perfectly commands Charleston Harbor."

"We should have seized Fort Sumter while it was unoccupied," Major Capers said, to no one in particular.

"Yes, isn't hindsight wonderful," the Governor said to Capers. "What was that the poet Robert Burns wrote about…'the best laid schemes o' mice and men going oft a stray.'"

Then, turning to me, the Governor said, "Colonel Pettigrew, report back to me, at this office, later this afternoon. I will have a new mission for you to accomplish."

Later that afternoon, Capers and I reported back to the governor, as requested. Facing us, he read slowly from a piece of paper the orders he now wished us to execute:

"Orders to Colonel Pettigrew: Colonel Pettigrew, sir, you are hereby ordered to assemble the Washington Light Infantry and the Meagher Guards at the Citadel. Arm them there and then take measures for occupying Castle Pinckney.

F. W. Pickens"

As Capers and I turned to leave, the Governor added, "Your task may be a dangerous one, as there are an unknown number of soldiers still in the post and the approaches to the fort may be mined."

With a little luck and hard work, Capers and I soon had the troops assembled on the Citadel Green. I gave last minute instructions to the 150 men, who were dressed in winter uniforms and carrying rifles, revolvers, knapsacks, and blankets.

We double-timed to the wharf and boarded the guard boat Nina. Finding a place near the bow of the steamer, I had a splendid view as the ship set out across the three-quarter mile Cooper River Channel toward the marshy island. Pinckney occupied the southwestern portion of the island.

As we steamed across the harbor, a thousand thoughts raced through my mind. If the garrison offered resistance, we would soon come under heavy fire. How would I react? Could I give these men the leadership they deserved? Suddenly, my long hours of training for just such a role as this seemed pitifully inadequate. I had never been under fire—if there was only some way I could know what it was like. It seemed incredible to me that this group of fine, trusting men could accept an inexperienced lawyer to lead them into battle simply because he happened to be wearing the rank of colonel on his uniform.

As we neared the fort, my pulse quickened. "This is it," I kept thinking. "This is it." I would soon know if I could justify the faith of the men I was leading. I looked over at Major Capers. He seemed calm and intent on the fort just ahead.

Raising my field glasses, I scanned the battlements. From the front of the Nina, the walls looked undefended. Was it so? Maybe a cannon double slotted with canister was ready to sweep the pier as we landed? Perhaps a sharp shooter has his eye on me and is calculating the correctness of his aim, thinking about whether or not he should take me in the head scientifically, or make a sure thing of it by aiming a little lower down.

We reached the Pinckney wharf. It was nearly 4 o'clock in the afternoon. A voice in my brain kept repeating, "This is it! This is it!" I half-stumbled off the boat and heard myself shouting, "Follow me!"

We deployed the men quickly and advanced with caution, rifles at the ready. I gave the command, "Charge!" and we dashed toward the main gate. Finding the gate closed, I detailed a portion of the men to watch the parapet, with orders to shoot to kill if they spotted resistance. Still expecting stiff opposition, I called for scaling ladders from the Nina. These were quickly placed against the walls and I lead the ascent. Once over the wall and stepping upon the parapet, I encountered Lt. Meade of the United States Army. Still burning with excitement, I demanded to know who was the commanding officer of the fort.

"I am the commander," replied Meade.

I then informed Meade the forces of South Carolina under my command were taking charge of the fort. I then began to read my orders from Governor Pickens to Lt. Meade, but he stopped me by asserting that he refused to acknowledge the authority of the Governor, adding that he could only offer a verbal protest because he had no means to resist.

Meade then refused to accept receipts from me for the public property and declined to give his parole since he did not consider himself a prisoner of war, as war had not been declared.

Following this exasperating, if not ridiculous, conversation, Meade and I descended into the parade ground of the fort. Meanwhile, the wall had been scaled by many of the troops, who had unbarred the gate and let the rest of the troops into the fort.

I then told Lt. Meade he was free to go to Fort Sumter and that Ordinance Sergeant Skillen and his family, who lived at the fort, would be treated with consideration. As Meade saluted and turned to go, the loud cheers from the men filled the air.

Then came a rather fitting end to the ludicrous little drama. A flag had to be borrowed from the Nina. No one had thought to bring one from Charleston; thus, a nautical flag with a white star against a red background, instead of the palmetto tree of South Carolina, was hoisted over Castle Pinckney.

As the men stood at attention on the parade ground, the flag was slowly raised over the fort. While this was being done, Ordinance Sergeant Skillen's pretty fifteen-year-old daughter, Kate, began to weep. Major Capers walked over to her and assured her that she would not be harmed.

"I am not crying because I am afraid," she responded.

"What is the matter then," Capers asked.

"I am crying because you have put that miserable rag up there," she said, pointing to the new flag at the top of the staff.

The bloodless assault over, Major Capers and I made a careful inspection of the fort. We found a large quantity of powder, over thirty cannon, and a month's supply of food. This captured material was seized and appropriated for use by the forces of South Carolina.

JANUARY 1, 1861—TUESDAY—NEW YEAR'S DAY
CASTLE PINCKNEY, CHARLESTON HARBOR

The New Year! How quickly time flies. It seems that it was only yesterday that we hailed "60."

The year begins with feelings of apprehension and enmity, and as it is written in the good book, none of us, "knowest not what a day may bring forth."

Much work has been done since the occupation of Castle Pinckney. Ten twenty-four pound cannon are now mounted on the ramparts, along with fifteen cannon, which are case mounted in the lower tier. An abundant supply of ammunition has been provided and tomorrow, we will begin to drill the men in the use of the guns.

Upon inspection of the fort, Capers and I found that defective construction has somewhat impaired the power of the lower batteries. The fort, however, has an effective tier of rampart guns, which are capable of good service. The fort is beyond the reach of the largest guns of Fort Sumter, and commands the entire line of wharfs and shipping along the Cooper River. In the hands of an enemy, this would be capable of doing vast injury to the city.

Today, I gave out passes to many of the men so they could go into Charleston to be with their families for the celebration of New Year's Day. Those who left the fort are scheduled to be back on duty tomorrow.

It has been a rainy day with a cold sea breeze adding to the discomfort. We have kept a large fire going in the fireplace all day. Still, the chill in the air is felt almost down to the bones.

Major Capers' wife is visiting the fort today. Shortly before dinner, she walked to the window of the quarters and looked intently outside. "Are you going to keep that poor soldier out in the rain all day?" said the good major's wife to her husband on seeing a sentinel on duty in the rain.

When it was understood who she meant, we explained to her that it was necessary to do so, but that he didn't have to walk his watch more than an hour at a time. He was relieved by others in turn. This rather lengthy explanation didn't seem to satisfy her, for she soon asked again, "Couldn't you let him come down from the rampart and stand under shelter?"

Capers suppressed a slight smile, and explained once again that for the safety of the fort and garrison, a vigilant watch must be maintained, no matter how inclement the weather.

A short silence followed this explanation, during which it was obvious she was devising in her tender heart some scheme for the sentinel's relief. Presently, she looked up, her face aglow and looking at Capers with anxious hope, she said, "Dear, couldn't you lend him your umbrella?"

Despite the rain and Mrs. Capers' anxious concern, we enjoyed a royal new year's dinner and a pleasant time. A fine fat chicken, biscuits, fried mush, coffee, and peaches and milk, were on the table. Mrs. Capers is now engaged in heating the second teapot of water for punch purposes. Her countenance has become quite rosy, doubtless from the effect of the fire. Capers and I are currently debating whether to storm the punch or attack it with a flanking maneuver.

JANUARY 4, 1861—FRIDAY
CASTLE PINCKNEY, CHARLESTON HARBOR

Shakespeare's King Henry V may have given, "all his fame for a pot of ale and safety, but last night at Castle Pinckney there was too much ale and little safety.

Somehow, someone smuggled strong drink into the fort and several of the men overdid it and became a little tight. Soon there were strong words exchanged over the virtue of a young Charleston lady. Southerners are quick to anger and to fight, and in the presence of alcohol all reason flew out the window. The words led to fisticuffs and then pistols were drawn. In the confusion and struggle that followed a member of the Meagher Guards accidentally shot a member of the Washington Light Infantry. Fortunately the wound was not serious, but the situation threatened to break out into full-scale civil war. With some difficulty, Capers, Lieutenant Randle and I managed to restore order. To make sure that the situation would remain peaceful, I slept between the two companies all night. Today, reason and order have returned and we are all members of the same army again.

The pace of events regarding the federal forts in Charleston harbor has accelerated. Governor Pickens feels it will only be a matter of time before an attempt will be made by the federal government to reinforce Major Anderson and his beleaguered garrison at Fort Sumter. Accordingly, the Governor ordered work started on a new battery on Morris Island at Cummings Point. The governor has also ordered a second battery to be built on Morris Island, beyond the range of the guns of Fort Sumter. The Citadel cadets will man this battery of four 24-pound field howitzers. Its location is such that it commands the main ship channel into Charleston Harbor. The governor has also stationed troops in Fort Johnson on James Island, thus pulling the noose even tighter around Sumter.

Just minutes ago I received orders to report to Morris Island on or before January 6. Most of the First Regiment of Rifles has already been transferred to the island. The order states that I will be in command of all troops, artillery, and fortifications on Morris Island. It should be a post of great responsibility and excitement as Morris island lies directly south of Fort Sumter and is the closest point to it among the fortifications our troops are in the process of building.

There is a rain storm tonight. The sky is dark. The wind rising. And every few minutes a vivid flash of lightning illuminates the harbor and the thunder booms with a rumbling, echoing noise. Meanwhile the rain comes down in torrents.

I have been reading until the late hour the charmed pages of Dicken's *Tale of Two Cities*. I must now stop writing, not for want of matter, for I have much on my mind, but for brevity of candle.

JANUARY 6, 1861—SUNDAY
MORRIS ISLAND—SOUTH CAROLINA

I took the guard boat General Clinch to Morris Island this morning. Soon after we left Castle Pinckney, the sky cleared and the sun made a grand appearance.

On reaching the landing at Cummings Point, I proceeded down the gang plank where I was met by soldiers with crossed bayonets demanding "passports." My identity was soon established and with apologies and much saluting, I was allowed to set foot on the island.

Once ashore, everything that met my eye reminded me of the war. Sentinels patrolled the beach; drums were beating; soldiers marching and counter-marching; great cannons were drawn along the beach—hundreds of men pulling them by long ropes or drawn by mule teams. Across the bay, on the other side of Fort Sumter, with the aid of my field glasses, I could see on Sullivan's Island men and soldiers building and digging out foundations for forts. Morris Island was lined from the lower point to the lighthouse with batteries of heavy guns.

Morris Island is about three miles in length and from 300 to 400 yards in width. It is an island of sand, chiefly of beach and in part of sand hills of irregular size and formation, being blown up by the winds. Some of the sand hills reach up to the height of twenty feet or more. The hills continually change their formation and size due to the action of the wind and tides. On the interior, stretching toward James Island to the southwest, is an extensive impossible morass interspersed by creeks. Cummings Point at the northwesterly end of the island is the closest point to Fort Sumter.

I have established my command post a short distance inland from the beach. It is delightfully located. A high sand hill in front cuts off the rough sea breezes. The rear of my wall tent rests near a bold salt creek which affords oysters and crabs in abundance. The tents of Lt. Colonel

Branch, Major Capers, and Captain Simonton are nearby. I estimate our mini-village is only 1,260 yards from the guns of Fort Sumter.

In the company of Lt. Colonel Branch, Major Capers, and Captain Stevens, who is in command of forty Citadel cadets, I went out early in the afternoon on a short inspection tour.

Our first stop was the Morris Island battery, manned by the Citadel cadets. The cadets are here because they are among the few troops who have had any experience firing cannon. Sharing quarters with the cadets in an abandoned small pox hospital are two militia units, the Zouave Cadets and the German Riflemen. They are to serve as infantry support for the guns should the Yankees get it in their heads to try an amphibious assault.

The battery, which the cadets man, is a crude affair. There are four 24-pound siege guns resting on plank platforms set level with the sand bottom. Sand is then shoveled in front of the guns and strengthened with sand bags forming a parapet over which the long black barrels of the cannon appear. The cadets in their neat and jaunty uniforms are ready for any emergency—their only complaint being the sand, which is everywhere since the ocean winds constantly blow the abundant grit into their frying pans, gravy, coffee, and any other exposed food.

It was obvious on first glance that there was little protection for the cadet gun crews. One broadside from a Yankee warship could sweep the whole affair into ruins. The cadets I talked to were also concerned that Fort Sumter was only three thousand yards away and could destroy them with several well-aimed salvos. Yet despite the danger, they are cheerful and determined to remain at their posts.

After inspecting the Morris Island Battery, talking to the Citadel cadets and Major Stevens, I feel certain they lack neither resolve nor courage. Stevens informed me, "the cadets have been carefully and regularly drilled from the start." My main fear is that although well drilled, the cadets have never actually fired the 24-pounders.

Both Stevens and I agree that aiming the muzzle of a cannon at a distant and moving target is a complex task. To ensure a hit, the gunner must first correctly estimate the distance; then, elevate the gun barrel to lob the shell the exact distance; and finally, determine the effect, if any, of crosswinds on the shot.

The 24-pound smoothbores at the Morris Island Battery are powerful weapons. At five degrees, with a six-pound charge, they can fire a shell close to two-thousand yards. If accurately aimed, they will do good service.

Stevens has agreed to engage in a live firing drill tomorrow night with the battery. The cadets are excited about using live ammunition for the first time. We will soon see if the Morris Island battery is capable of sending a warm welcome to any hostile ships who attempt to cross the bar.

Other defensive measures have also been taken to protect the city of Charleston during the present crisis. All lights in the harbor have been turned off and the buoys marking the way across the bar have been removed. The Charleston Lighthouse has been closed and its powerful costly Fresnel-lens lantern smashed. This will leave the beacon at Fort Sumter as the only light operating at night. Also, the Vigilant Rifles have been ordered to guard the Southern end of Morris Island. This move should guard against any attack from the rear.

Tonight I was informed by telegraph that Governor Pickens has received a warning that the Yankee ship, Star of the West, is on the way to reinforce Fort Sumter. To protect Charleston from invasion and to prevent reinforcements or supplies from reaching Fort Sumter, the Governor has called for increased vigilance. The steamers General Clinch and Columbia have been ordered to nightly patrol between the bar and Cummings Point from 7:00 p.m. until daylight to intercept any vessel attempting to land troops or reinforce Sumter.

My hand is much better and, in other respects, I feel well. It no longer causes me pain to move my fingers or my arm.

JANUARY 10, 1861—THURSDAY
MORRIS ISLAND—SOUTH CAROLINA

Yesterday morning, January 9th, Citadel Cadet, William Stewart Simkins, a first classman from Beaufort, South Carolina, was walking his guard post along the Morris Island beach in the early morning fog. Suddenly he noticed the steamer General Clinch proceeding up the channel firing flares. Close behind, just visible through the fog, Simkins sighted what appeared to be a large passenger liner. The dependable Simkins immediately yelled a report to the Sergeant of the Guard Samuel Smith, from Charleston.

Major Stevens was quickly alerted and a long roll was heard summoning the cadets to their stations in the battery. A cadet messenger from Major Stevens alerted me to the emergency and I rapidly dressed, emerging from my tent the same time Major Capers and Lt. Colonel Branch were springing to duty. We quickly ran to a small sand hill overlooking the battery as the Zouave Cadets and German Riflemen took up their positions in the rear as infantry support.

Peering through the early morning light, I could see a ship steaming up the main ship channel—a huge United States ensign on the stern. Looking intently through my field glasses, I told Major Stevens it was probably the Star of the West steaming full speed toward Fort Sumter. "She looks to be about a half mile off shore!" I yelled to the major, who was beginning to sight the four guns in the battery.

With the guns sighted, the cadets stood at their posts ready to fire. Overhead a red Palmetto flag flapped in the ocean breeze. As the ship approached, the sun was just peeking over the horizon, the beginning to what looked to be a beautiful morning.

Stevens, mounted on the parapet, hesitated as the ship moved into range, apparently unsure of what to do.

"If that ship reaches Fort Sumter with reinforcements and supplies," I yelled to Stevens, "all hell will break lose in South Carolina!"

"But Colonel," Stevens answered, "what will history say if we fire on the American flag?"

"I hope it will say we manned the guns, fired accurately and did our duty," I answered. "Now proceed with the business at hand, Major."

Stevens quickly turned toward gun number one and gave the order, "Commence firing." Cadet Captain Whilden passed it on. "Number one, fire!" Upon this command Cadet "Tuck" Haynsworth, a lad barely sixteen, yanked the lanyard sending the shot on its way.

The loud roar of the big 24-pounder reverberated out over the water—the shot passing harmlessly over the bow of the steamer, splashing into the ocean beyond.

Lowering his field glasses, Lt. Colonel Branch turned to me and said softly, "Colonel, we have just witnessed the first shot of the civil war."

"God help us," answered Major Capers.

As the steamer continued up the channel, number two gun fired. This second shot struck the oncoming steamer inflicting slight damage. As the cadets cheered, gun number three was fired, the shot falling astern of the ship.

Soon, the firing became general as batteries on both Morris Island and Fort Moultrie on Sullivan's Island joined in. As the Star continued toward Fort Sumter, most of the shots passed over the ship or did minor damage.

Only a half mile from Sumter, the ship suddenly turned and began to head back out to sea. Puzzled by this sudden turn of events, I watched it until it sailed out of sight.

Major Stevens, his face beaming with joy, came up out of the parapet and walked toward us shouting, "What cowards Anderson and his garrison are, their flag has just been fired upon under the very guns of their fort and no help is extended. I always knew the Yankees wouldn't fight!"

Stevens then turned toward his young cadets, their faces streaked with powder and sweat and proclaimed, "Hurrah for the Citadel!"

With this, the cadets and other troops who now lined the beach went wild with joy. Cheer after cheer filled the clean ocean air. There were smiles, handshakes and hugs. It was a scene I'll never forget.

Now as I meditate upon the historic action of this morning, I realize although we have forbid the attempt to reinforce Sumter, the fort is still in federal hands. The problem of what to do with Anderson and his garrison remains much as it has been, only now the situation is only more agitated.

JANUARY 12, 1861—SATURDAY
MORRIS ISLAND—SOUTH CAROLINA

Although it has been unusually quiet here of late, passions in Charleston and elsewhere have been inflamed by the Star of the West incident. The January 10th issue of *The Charleston Mercury* crows about our repulse of the Yankee ship.

> "Yesterday, the 9th of January, will be memorable in our history. Powder has been burnt…perhaps blood spilled. The expulsion of the…Star of the West from the Charleston Harbor yesterday morning was the opening ball of the revolution. We are proud that our harbor has been so honored…Entrenched upon her soil, she has spoken from the mouth of her cannon and not from the mouths of scurrilous demagogues, fanatics and scribblers…she has not hesitated to strike the first blow, full in the face of her insulter…We would not exchange or recall that blow for millions! It has wiped out a half century of scorn and outrage."

There will be stirring times ahead! A fourth state has departed from the Union. Alabama, yesterday, joined South Carolina, Mississippi and Florida in deciding to form a new nation.

Although peace now reigns over Charleston Harbor, we are growing stronger by the day. Members of the militia and hundreds of slaves are laboring day and night to strengthen the batteries on Morris Island and Fort Moultrie. New batteries are being built at Fort Johnson on James Island, and other points to extend the ring of fire around Sumter. Guns have been taken from Castle Pinckney and shipped to Sullivan's Island where they are being used in a newly constructed battery at the east end of Sullivan's Island.

On Morris Island there are secret, hidden, treacherous foes which undermine one's happiness. Everyday I face enemies who give no quarter, whose ruthless tastes blood alone can satisfy. Now I am not alluding to any diabolical Yankees, they are only mortal—but to the insect kingdom. What a taste they have for Confederate blood! Mosquito bars are useless. They form regiments, divisions and corps, and pierce every obstruction imagination can invent, once they scent Southern blood. Flies hum and march over one in line of battle—whole pounds of them at a time. Mosquitoes go on flanking expeditions and strike at every exposed position. Sand flies make the blood flow copiously. Fleas form in battalions, which attack from front, flank and rear simultaneously. Ticks get into one's hair. Ants creep into one's stockings. Assaulted from all sides, you turn and brush your face, you slap at your arm, leg and writhe in agony. Outgeneraled, and outnumbered, you cry for mercy! In vain. These critters are ruthless, they give no quarter. You rush madly about. You look for some relief. Until utterly exhausted, you sink into unrefreshing sleep. Then begins a wild scene of pillage. Countless thirsty bugs, longing for blood, bite, tear and gorge into your skin. So it goes, day after day, here on Morris Island, insect capital of the Confederacy.

JANUARY 28, 1861—MONDAY
MORRIS ISLAND—SOUTH CAROLINA

There was a sad case of disappointed love in the regiment last night. A sergeant of Captain Vincent's company was engaged to a girl of Georgetown. They were to be married upon his return from duty on the island, and until within a month have been corresponding on a regular basis. Suddenly and without explanation, she ceased to write. Why? He could not imagine. The good sergeant never, however, doubted that she would be faithful to him. His anxiety to hear from home increased until finally he learned from her brother, a soldier of Maxey Gregg's regiment, that she was married. Strong, healthy, religious, good-looking fellow that he was, this incredible news prostrated him completely, and made him crazy as a loon. He imagined that he was in hell, thought the regimental surgeon was the devil, and became so violent that it was necessary to bind him.

This morning, he is more calm, but still deranged. He thought the straws in his bunk were thorns, and would pluck at them with his fingers and cry in a loud voice, "My God, they are so sharp!" Captain Vincent came to visit and the guards said, "Sergeant, don't you know where you are?"

"Of course I do," he yelled. "I'm in hell—red, hot, burning hell!"

When they were binding him, a strange look came over his face and in a mocking voice he said, "That's right, heap on the coals. Put me in the hottest place." While the regimented surgeon was preparing a medication to quiet him—laudanum perhaps—he said, "Bring on your poison. I'll take it."

Many of us, of course, are outraged over this affair. The sergeant was on duty, living roughly, exposed to hardships and dangers. Then, this woman of little or no honor breaks his heart

FEBRUARY 10, 1861—SUNDAY
MORRIS ISLAND, SOUTH CAROLINA

It is a custom, sanctioned by ancient military usage, for a colonel to have a servant. Peter, my servant, is a colored gentleman of much accomplishments. He has been a barber on a Mississippi River steamboat and a daguerreotype artist. He knows much of the South and manipulates a fiddle with wonderful skill. He is enlivening the evening hours now with his violin.

Peter has peculiar notions about certain matters and they are not always complimentary to the white man. One night over the supper fire as Major Capers and I were relaxing with coffee and cigars, we entered into a discussion on religion.

Peter, overhearing, drew close and, gaining our attention, entered into the fray by saying, "It jus' appears to me dat Adam and Eve were black, an' de Lord, he scare them 'til they get white cuz they was sinners."

"Peter, you scoundrel," replied Capers, "how dare you slander the white man in that way?"

"'pears to me dat we haf ta tell the truth, sah. That's my mind. Men was 'riginally black, but de Lord, he scare Adam and Eve 'til they get white. Dats de reasonable supposition, sah. Do a man's hair git black when he scared, sah? No, sah. It gits white. Did you ever know a man ta git black when he's scared, sah? No, sah. He gits white."

Capers, rolling his eyes, looked at me and said, "That does seem to be a knockdown argument, Peter."

"Yes, sah," continued Peter. "I've argued with more than a hundred white men, sah, an' they can't never git aroun' dat pint. When you strip dis subject of prejudice, an' fetch to bring on it de light o' reason, sah, yer can 'rive at but one conclusion, sah, de Lord, he rode into de garden in chariot of fire, sah, robed with de lightnin', sah, thunder bolt in his hand, and he cried 'Adam' in de voice of an earthquake, sah, an' the effect on Adam and Eve was so powerful they done turned white. Yes, sah, they been a beautiful black color, but when dey heard the Lord, they done turned white. Dat's my mind, sah."

Somewhat surprised at this novel and unique interpretation of the Garden of Eden story, Capers and I decided not to attempt to point out the inconsistencies in this tale of our philosopher and servant. Were we like Shakespeare's Hamlet to say, "There are more things in heaven and earth, Peter, than are dreamt of in your philosophy"?

We decided to let Peter go on his merry way, unchallenged, confident that Adam and Eve were originally black and that Capers and I have joined the list of foolish white men who have been vanquished by the force and logic of his argument.

FEBRUARY 13, 1861—WEDNESDAY
MORRIS ISLAND, SOUTH CAROLINA

We have learned this morning that at the Alabama capital, Montgomery, on February 8, the convention of seceded states unanimously adopted the Provisional Constitution of the Confederate States. We have also received word that Jefferson Davis and Alexander Stevens have been unanimously elected president and vice-president.

This afternoon, I received a telegram from Governor Pickens informing me that he had received a wire from Montgomery informing him that the new Confederate government had "taken charge of the questions and difficulties existing between the states of the Confederacy and the government of the United States relating to the occupation of the forts, navy yards and other public establishments."

It appears the question of peace or war has been taken out of Governor Pickens' hands. That momentous and awesome power now rests in the hands of President Davis. I hope God gives him the wisdom and foresight to do what is best for the Confederacy.

Despite the change in power from Pickens to Davis, the governor has informed me that the First Regiment of Rifles is slated for the honor of leading the assault on Fort Sumter if the attack has to be made. "Once our cannon have breached the walls," the governor stated, "your magnificent regiment will be able to land and take the garrison by storm."

The devilish Yankees have prepared pits and mines at the Sumter landings and the consequence will be that we should lose a great deal of life in the assault. Nevertheless, the very flower of South Carolina fills the ranks of the regiment and the best blood of the South will be a small price to pay to ensure the liberty of South Carolina and the Confederacy.

I read in the *Daily Courier* that two immense mortars are being sent by rail from Richmond to help in the reduction of Fort Sumter. The aggregate weight of the two mortars is said to be 11,500 pounds and the strain they place upon the floor of the flat cars is exceedingly great. Major Stevens has won me over to his way of thinking. If we can gather enough cannon perhaps the sheer weight of the bombardment will overwhelm Sumter and the infantry assault will be unnecessary.

FEBRUARY 18, 1861—MONDAY
MORRIS ISLAND, SOUTH CAROLINA

This morning, I received a telegram from Governor Pickens relieving the Regiment of Rifles from duty on the island by the newly enlisted six-month volunteers of the Confederate States Army under Colonel Maxey Gregg. The regiment is to take leave in Charleston before being assigned to other duty. Capers and I are pleased with the order as we have been on continuous duty since December 27, 1860.

FEBRUARY 24, 1861—SUNDAY
CHARLESTON, SOUTH CAROLINA

I could grow accustomed to this soft and pampered life I have led the last several days. Last night, I thoroughly enjoyed sleeping on my large, soft feather bed Nat recently purchased for me. As I slept, dreams of civic and military glory danced through my head. I awoke from my trancelike state to find I was not the commanding general of the Confederate Armies, leading them triumphantly across the long bridge into Washington City, but still a mere colonel in the First Regiment of Rifles.

After enjoying the steaming cup of coffee Nat brought to me, I undressed and went into the small bathing room. This room, not much larger than a spacious closet, holds only a bathtub. The tub, about four feet long, of polished metal and shaped somewhat like a rowboat, had been filled with hot water carried upstairs from the kitchen by Nat.

After dressing, I came downstairs to the aroma of a hearty breakfast prepared by Ruth. The table was replete with beefsteak, eggs, fried pota-toes and coffee. For dessert, there was the luxury of fresh strawberries and milk. After the Spartan fare of Morris Island, it was a veritable feast.

After breakfast, I walked down Church Street toward the battery. I was amazed at how the atmosphere of Charleston has changed in the short time I have been in the military service. The streets are full of colonels, majors, corporals and privates. It is obvious South Carolina's volunteer army has swollen to prodigious size, filling Charleston and the islands in the harbor with young bloods bored with inactivity and spoiling for a go at Sumter. Many of them claim Governor Pickens is a fool and a coward for hesitating to assault Sumter. "Isn't it the states' own property?" they ask.

Soldiering has become a "Palmettoland" craze, with the patricians lead-ing the way and the "best names" like Rutledge, Lowndes and DeSaussure taking their places in the ranks as well as accepting commissions. One merchant I talked to on Church Street informed me that there is a single regiment now stationed at one of the forts whose destruction would put every distinguished family in the state in mourning.

Another company, I was told, had an aggregate wealth of more than a million dollars. Yet another company is commanded by an Episcopal clergyman and has ten divinity students in its ranks. Enlistment has taken all but about 150 of the students at South Carolina College in Columbia.

It also appears that many of these young aristocrats, even in the military, lead pampered lives. Klinck and Wickenburg, Charleston's best provisioner, reports orders of such delicacies as champagne, Madeira, pate de foie gras, French green peas and Spanish cigars being sent to men on duty at the various posts. Lately, I have learned that the men have grown bored even with the fine food and drink and are getting restive and out of hand. Two days ago during tomfoolery at Fort Moultrie, young Private Thaddeus Strawinski was killed by an accidental revolver wound.

To be fair to the men, their enthusiasm knows no bounds. The mind of the young Southerner has been fired by reading the stories of heroes and soldiers in the old Southern Reader, and by the thrilling romances of Francis Marion and his men. The men of the South are hero worshipers. The stories of Washington and Putnam of Valley Forge, of Trenton, of Bunker Hill and of Lexington never grow old.

True, the men are nervous, perhaps dabble in drink too much and are hard to discipline; however, they labor day and night incessantly, if ordered, and wait anxiously the orders from Montgomery to begin the assault on Fort Sumter.

MARCH 4, 1861—MONDAY
SECESSIONVILLE, JAMES ISLAND, SOUTH CAROLINA

Yesterday, I observed the Palmetto Light Artillery Battalion at drill. They are armed with light twelve-pound field howitzers. The drill took place on a large level field near the Stono River, an ideal place for the artillery men to practice the various movements used by artillery in battle.

The battalion arrived on the field in fair condition, accompanied by many men of the First Regiment of Rifles who had turned out to witness the fun. The battalion was commanded by a Captain who had served in the artillery in the U.S. Army before the present crisis forced him to offer his resignation. The captain spent considerable time in explanation of the various movements to the drivers. Then the drill began and several movements and maneuvers were ordered. The drivers of the artillery pieces were able to execute the movements after a fashion, but the drivers of the caissons would stand fast, or keep on moving, or turn in the wrong direction. They were thinking they were independent of the artillery pieces. At last, the captain lost his temper and in very forcible language told the drivers of the caissons that they must follow the artillery pieces at all times, even if they went to hell.

Now, thoroughly motivated, the caisson drivers were determined to show that they were no dull scholars and that they now fully understood the orders. The horses on the first artillery piece were quite high-spirited and became very unmanageable by the frequent starting and stopping. So, at the next movement ordered, they suddenly wheeled from the line and started in the direction of Secessionville on a run, in spite of all the drivers could do to stop them. As the runaway artillery piece flashed down the road in a cloud of dust, the drivers of the following caisson, with the orders of the captain fresh in their minds to follow their piece even if it went to hell, wheeled out of line and with whip and spur urged their horses into a run after the piece—in spite of the captain who shouted fanatically for them to halt. It now became very exciting. The artillery piece was fast disappearing down the road. The caisson was following—making a lively good time—and the captain, yelling and waving his arms, was a close third in the race. Some men of the regiment watched this amazing spectacle and were doubled up with laughter. Others watched the proceedings with much perplexity and doubt. For in their ignorance of artillery field drill, they were unsure whether it was a race, a runaway, or a part of the drill.

The captain finally succeeded in stopping the drivers of the caisson. He asked them what they meant by leaving the line. They, very innocently, reminded the good captain of his instructions to them a few moments before, that they were to follow the piece no matter where it went, and they supposed that they were only obeying orders.

A sergeant who had been sent after the runaway artillery piece now returned with it. The drill was soon resumed when another mishap took place, this time with the second piece. On the limber chest were seated three men. The captain gave the order to countermarch and in wheeling, the driver made a cramped, short turn, breaking the pole short off. The horses became entangled in their harnesses. The weight of the three men caused the limber chest to tilt rapidly forward and the men on the ends jumped off. The limber chest, suddenly relieved of its weight, tilted back and the man in the middle—having nothing to cling to—was thrown backwards. He somersaulted off the limber and landed astride of the trail with his blouse turned up over his head. More laughter and cheering erupted from the men watching. The now furious captain helped him up and asked him why "in God's name" he ever joined the artillery. The man, dusting himself off and regaining his dignity, said that he was not in favor of that way for cannoneers to dismount and would rather be a driver.

Thus ended the first field drill of the Palmetto Light Artillery Battalion. Judging from what I witnessed yesterday, it will not be the last.

MARCH 15, 1861—FRIDAY
SULLIVAN'S ISLAND, SOUTH CAROLINA

The regiment has been transferred to Sullivan's Island to guard the northeast entrance to Charleston Harbor. Sullivan's Island is about three miles long and at no point more than a quarter of a mile wide. It is separated from the mainland by a scarcely perceptible creek, oozing its way through a wilderness of weeds and slime. The vegetation is scant, or at least dwarfish. No trees of any magnitude are to be seen.

Near the western extremity, where Fort Moultrie stands, are a group of frame buildings, occupied during the summer by fugitives from Charleston's dust and fever. There is also a large summer hotel on the beach halfway up the island. A horse railway connects the steamboat wharf and the hotel. Most of the island, with the exception of this western point and a line of hard, white beach on the sea coast, is covered with a dense undergrowth of the sweet myrtle. The scrub often attains the height of fifteen or twenty feet and fills the air with its fragrance.

The camp of the regiment has been set up about three miles above the Moultrie House among the famous Truesdell's oyster beds. We enjoy camp life in all its purity. The lopped off tops of the myrtle, overspread with a blanket, furnish many of the men a bed at night. The marks of the rough limbs on the bodies of the men are proof conclusive that under ordinary circumstances, it would not be a bed of ease.

My duty on Sullivan's Island will be a busy one, as I am in charge of troops and batteries spread miles apart, and of boats guarding the creeks by which federal vessels might seek entry into the harbor. This morning, I was at the eastern end of the island making sure the officers and men understood their duties as picket guard and the procedure of examining the papers of all passing vessels.

While inspecting the pickets along the beach, I noticed several of the men armed not only with muskets, but with bowie knives attached to their belts. A most sanguinary-looking weapon, the blade is about 15 inches long and about 3 inches wide at the broadest part, and a third of an inch thick at the back. When I asked one of the pickets about the knife, he informed me that he felt they would be indispensable in battle should the Yankees attempt to storm the island. He then explained to me the diverse uses to which this weapon could be put, assuring me that he could without difficulty seize the gun of a Yankee soldier by the muzzle, and with a dexterous blow, sever the barrel in twain. Another way of using the weapon, he explained, would be to attack a cord to the handle of the bowie knife and with a skillful throw, drive the blade into the heart of an advancing Yankee, and, after he fell, to haul the knife back by the long string, and repeat the operation on another of the enemy.

I received a letter from James Louis Petigru today. He still clings to the hope that the federal government will compromise and that Anderson will be withdrawn from Sumter, ending any occasion for bloodshed. He regards Lincoln as a low schemer who is using Major Anderson as a scapegoat. He cannot believe that the North will really invade the South.

MARCH 31, 1861—SUNDAY
SULLIVAN'S ISLAND, SOUTH CAROLINA

On March 29th, I received the following letter from Captain Gary, an old friend, who is on duty at Fort Palmetto on Cole's Island:

"My Dear Johnson:

"It would afford me much pleasure if I could communicate with you as often as my inclination prompts, but there is such monotony in camp life that it would puzzle the mind of the most ingenuous intellect to interest you. Since you left, we have been very hard at work in strengthening our position and making daily improvements. We have four twenty-four pounders mounted, whose range sweep the waters of the Stono. In addition, we have muskets and rifles in fine order and ready for use—and hands that are ready to use them. Indeed, there is no craven here; untrammeled we walk, free as the winds that fan our native land! Our Southern flag is waving from the ramparts; aye in the sunlight of heaven it is brightly streaming and flashing in proud defiance.

Do you remember Lt. Macy? You will recall him to be a good, honest, warm-hearted fellow, with a foible or two which no wife could have any trouble in accommodating herself.

About a week ago his young wife and infant son came to visit him here at the Fort. They subsequently decided to attend a party at the house of a friend some miles distant on St. John's Island.

"Charles, my dear husband, don't drink too much at the party today; you will promise me, won't you?" she said, putting her hand on his arm and raising her eyes to his face with a pleading glance.

"No, Ellie, I will not; you may trust me." And he wrapped his infant son in a soft blanket and they left the fort for St. John's Island.

Upon arrival she again reminded her husband of his promise as they passed up the steps to the house.

Poor thing! She was the wife of a man who loved to look upon the wine when red.

But his strong love for his wife, and their babe whom they both idolized, kept him back and it was not often he joined in Bacchanalian revelry.

The party passed off pleasantly, the time of departing drew near, and Ellie descended from the upper chamber to join her husband.

A pang shot through her trusting heart as she met him, for he was intoxicated—he had broken his promise.

Silently they rode back toward the fort, save when the drunken Lieutenant broke into snatches of songs or unmeaning laughter. But the wife rode on, her infant son pressed closely to her grieved heart.

"Give me the baby, Ellie. I can't trust you with him," said he as they approached a dark and somewhat swollen stream.

After some hesitation, she resigned her first born, her darling son, closely wrapped in the great blanket, to his arms. Over the dark waters the noble steed safely bore them, and when they reached the bank, Ellie asked for the child.

With much care and tenderness he placed the bundle in her arms; when she clasped it to her bosom, no babe was there! It had slipped from the blanket and the drunken father knew it not.

A wild shriek aroused him and he turned just in time to see the little rosy face rise one moment above the dark waves and then sink forever.

I must end this desolate tale, Johnson, and plead with you to warm those family men under your command to forgo indulging in intoxicating drinks, lest they suffer a fate similar to that of the luckless Lt. Macy.

I hope to see you in Charleston, once Sumter is ours.

With affection–Charles Grey"

Poor Macy! I do remember him as a fine fellow and a good soldier. This tragedy will undoubtedly cast a pall of gloom over his marriage which no amount of love will be able to lift. I fear he will eventually seek out death on the battlefield to avoid living with such guilt.

After putting down Captain Gary's letter, I felt the need to leave my tent for a short walk, perhaps to reflect on the difficulty and uncertainty of life. As I walked, I was alarmed by the constant and heavy coughing of the men. There is a great deal of sickness among the troops—many cases of colds, rheumatism and fever—resulting from exposure. I fear disease will send more to the grave than the bullets of the enemy.

Off in the distance, from the vicinity of Fort Moultrie, a band is playing. My mind wanders and I think, where, and under what circumstances, have I heard other bands? The question carries my thoughts into Charleston and from there, into half the states of the Union. Into a multitude of places. Into an innumerable variety of scenes, faces, conversations, theaters, balls, speeches, songs. The chain is endless.

APRIL 1, 1861—MONDAY
SULLIVAN'S ISLAND, SOUTH CAROLINA

What this new month will bring, who knows? It is hard to settle down to anything. The air is red hot with rumors and one's heart is in one's mouth all of the time. Any minute cannon may open upon us, the Yankee fleet come in, etc., etc.

Late tonight, I passed through the officers' tents, which occupy an elevated spot slightly removed from the rest of the camp. It was after nine in the evening and Bulger Cokely had sounded the last call, after which all lights in the tents must be put out and the camp made quiet. I made my way down a low sand hill and stepped upon the wet, hard sand which marked the outline of the beach. The night was dark and quiet and not a sentinel was in sight.

I walked slowly down the beach, cigar clamped between my teeth. The waves broke loudly to shore—lapping at my feet. Off to my left, out in the harbor, stood the dark outline of Sumter—the symbol of peace or war.

In the distance I could see the dim lights of Charleston. Above me appeared the stars beyond counting, pinpoints in the endless sky. Listening to the roar of the ancient ocean, alone in the blackness of the night, my soul stood hushed before the infinite. I looked out in awe at the spread of space and sea before me and felt insignificant compared to the vast universe about me. As I resumed walking, I could only think how trivial these issues of states' rights, abolition and the ownership of Sumter must be in the destiny of the stars and the God that oversees them.

I looked back just as the moon appeared from behind a large, dark cloud. The silver beams of light illuminated the outline of my footprints in the sand. Smiling at the beauty of it all, I walked slowly along, reciting to myself the lines of a poem by Prentice, A Name in the Sand, that I had come to love so well:

"Alone I walked the ocean strand,
A pearly shell was in my hand;
"I stopped and wrote upon the sand,
My name, the year, the day;
As onward from the spot I passed,
One lingering look behind I cast;
A wave came rolling high and fast,
And washed my lines away;
And so, me thought, 'Twill quickly be,
With every mark on earth from me'
A wave of dark oblivion's sea
Will sweep across the place
Where I have trod the sandy shore
Of time, and been, to be no more of me,
Of my day, the name I bore;
To leave no track as trace.
And yet, with Him who counts the sands,
And holds the waters in his hands,
"I know a lasting record stands,
Inscribed against my name.

Of all this mortal part has wrought,
Of all this thinking soul has thought,
And from these fleeting moments caught,
For glory or for shame."

APRIL 9, 1861—TUESDAY
SULLIVAN'S ISLAND, SOUTH CAROLINA

Journalizing is a serious job just now. We are living a month of common life everyday.

Today's papers give the latest news...

The *Macon Daily Telegraph's* editor is in Charleston. He concludes that public opinion is becoming "wonderfully impatient" with the delay in the occupation of Fort Sumter by our forces.

The editor of the Charleston Courier predicts that the Yankees will give up Fort Sumter without a fight, also Fort Pickens in Florida. But as we have no naval force, the North will hold Key West and Tortuga for a time.

Even though, during the last few days, preparations for war have accelerated, here on Sullivan's Island, the men are slumbering lightly. There is no noise, no confusion, no commotion. I write by flickering candlelight, secure in the knowledge that the machinery of battle has all been pre-arranged and, save the slow footsteps of the guard, silence reigns, undisturbed. I'm sure that in Charleston, the gaslights are burning low in a thousand chambers and many a pillow is wet with the tears of women and children praying in the stillness of the night for the safety of their loved ones sleeping at the guns.

APRIL 11, 1861—THURSDAY
SULLIVAN'S ISLAND, SOUTH CAROLINA

It has been reported that the ship Harriet Lane has departed from New York carrying relief supplies for Fort Sumter.

Yesterday, I received an order from General Beauregard to detail a company of men to mount a heavy Dahlgren cannon at the western end of Sullivan's Island.

"I know it will be hard for you to do this on short notice," he wired, "but this is one of those moments when the word impossible must be ignored, for the fate of Anderson and Sumter depends upon the number of guns we have in place."

I have also received word that another gun, the latest word in ordinance, has arrived in Charleston. This cannon, a rifled Blakely gun, just in from Liverpool, England, is the gift of a Charlestonian in business in England, Charles K. Prioleau. The Blakely can throw a shell or 12-pound shot with the accuracy of a dueling pistol. The gun has been shipped to Cummings Point on Morris Island in the hope that it can pound holes in Sumter's gorge wall.

It is a day of high excitement, but the men are going about their duty as ordered. Though there may be some concern as to what events will bring, no knees are trembling and no faces are blanched with fear.

The different commands have been ordered to look out for a signal shell from the battery at Fort Johnson. This will commence the bombardment of Sumter. The last boat bringing troops and munitions of war left Morris Island at five o'clock. Many of us stood on the ramparts of Fort Moultrie looking through our field glasses towards the signal point.

Eight o'clock came, no shell. Nine o'clock came and passed and still no sign of commencing hostilities. We began to think there would be no attack. Many wondered why. Some said they knew it would be so. At this time, the troops at the batteries have been dismissed. The sentinels are placed at customary posts. The men have retired to their tents, disappointed and perplexed. Their blood is up and they are ready for war. The camp is noiseless. Everything is hushed in sleep. The sentinels alone are wakeful and alert, walking their posts with unweary eyes alternately turned to Fort Johnson and to the bar, looking for the expected federal fleet.

The guard boats are ever watchful with their friendly lights sailing on the outskirts of the harbor, alert for the first sign of Lincoln's men of war.

Who can sleep at such a time! Fully awake, I pace the tent, cigar in mouth, smoking and thinking furiously. Are the men ready? The batteries? Have I done all I need to? Have I left anything important undone? What will the morrow bring? A thousand thoughts race through my mind. God how I wish something would happen to break the tension!

APRIL 12, 1861—FRIDAY
SULLIVAN'S ISLAND, SOUTH CAROLINA

4:30 a.m.

Capers, Lt. Colonel Branch and I stood quietly on the rampart of Fort Moultrie looking through the darkness toward Fort Johnson. Suddenly, we heard a loud report and we could with our eyes easily detect and follow the burning fuse which marked the course of a shell as it mounted the starry sky.

Leaving a scarlet train behind it, the shell exploded over Sumter, briefly illuminating the brick fort in the darkness. With this, the circle of batteries surrounding Fort Sumter opened fire after the first signal shot. All the islands and posts surrounding the fort were illuminated with a line of twinkling lights. The exploding shells brilliantly lit the sky above it. The solid shot clattered as thick as hail upon the sides of the fort.

At this point, I turned toward Capers and Branch and said, "Gentlemen, we all have our duties to perform and I propose to be about mine. May God be with you."

The sound of the firing awoke all camps. The sentinels gave the alarm and fired their guns. Men emerged in hot haste from their tents and ran quickly to their respective posts. Surgeons with bandages and lint in hand, with laudanum and chloroform all hurried to the stations assigned them.

As I left the rampart, I looked again out toward Sumter, standing quiet as death. No light was seen. Not a sign of life appeared. Not even a sentinel could be distinguished—but high above the fort floated her proud banner, the Stars and Stripes, waving defiantly in the midst of shot and shell.

The ball had been opened and, from end to end, Sullivan's Island was alive with men—officers and aides hurrying to and fro. The mortars and batteries fired at regular intervals. The loud reports echoed out over the harbor. The question was asked on all sides, what is Anderson doing? Why doesn't Fort Sumter return the fire?

On the left of Fort Moultrie was a little cottage in which by direction of Colonel Ripley was located a calcium light operated by two young students from the South Carolina College. I walked over to talk to these two patriots, one of whom, I. M. Logan, had served under me in the Washington Light Infantry. The calcium light was used to cover the channel through which ships could enter. At times during night it would snap on briefly to be sure the Yankees weren't trying to sneak reinforcements into Sumter.

Soon I could make out objects on the low coast becoming well-defined amid the shadows of the early morning. About then, from the casement of Fort Sumter, a sheet of fire rang out and a murmur rang through the men, "Sumter has opened fire!"

Short, sharp reports with spurts of flame told of bursting shells in and around Sumter, while splashes of spray or clouds of crumpled brick marked the violent force of round shot on its face.

At dawn, light rain began to fall and I put on my India rubber coat, while peering intently toward Sumter and the main channel with my field glasses. I was joined shortly by Colonel Ripley who said, "Well, Colonel Pettigrew, we have certainly rung the breakfast bell for Major Anderson this morning."

9:00 a.m.

The floating battery at the western end of the island has been struck eleven times, but the balls failed to penetrate. The guns from Sumter were concentrating their fire on the floating battery and the Dahlgren battery of Captain J. R. Hamilton that we just put in place yesterday. No houses on the island were on fire and there were no casualties, thank God. A steamer reported to be the "Nashville" came into sight, but upon hearing the firing, put back to sea.

Fort Sumter, under heavy fire, was badly damaged on the parapet and among the buildings. Fort Moultrie and the floating battery now received most of the fire from Sumter. Colonel Ripley, his face covered with dirt and sweat, was in his short sleeves working the guns himself. He appeared happy with the results of the bombardment at this point.

10:00 a.m.

Firing was perfectly regular. The men were cool and calm. A ball from Sumter came shrieking in and buried itself in the sand. Another bounced on the beach and went whizzing up the island. The men looked intently for another ball from Sumter.

"There it comes. Look out!" was the cry. Down went the men. Not a head could be seen. The noise was deafening. The loud reports seemed to shake the very island. Our shells continued to fall and burst upon Sumter. The men watched with great interest every shot and marked its effect with cries of "That's a good one!" and "Hurrah for that shot" or "That's a poor shot, try again!"

1:00 p.m.

Sumter was still combating furiously with Fort Moultrie and the floating battery. News was passed about that the federal fleet had arrived and was off the bar. It numbers three steamships and one transport vessel. Most thought they would try to land reinforcements at night.

7:00 p.m.

The firing and shelling continued. Fort Sumter was still firing back. The night was black and stormy with a heavy rain. Complete with lightning and thunder. Even the elements joined the battle. All the batteries were manned. Everyone was at his post—tense and anxious. The Yankee fleet was expected at any moment. If they come in, it will be hot and hard work.

10:00 p.m.

Wet and miserable, I watched for any sign of the fleet. Anderson had been signaling them, but they made no attempt to come in, miserable cowards that they are.

10:30 p.m.

Tired with the fatigue of two days and nights of watching and work—and the heavy responsibility of command—I walked, drenched to the skin, into my tent. I needed some sleep, even though I could be aroused at any time. Again the sentinels, wrapped in cloaks, walked their lonely posts.

During the night, fires were kept brightly blazing in the harbor for the purpose of detecting the Yankee fleet should they attempt to relieve the garrison of Sumter. The yellow glare of the light wood flames illuminated the darkness for miles around. The rain fell in torrents and the wind howled weird-like and drearily among the sand hills of the island. I was so tired, I didn't even bother to undress. I just removed my boots and practically collapsed onto my cot. So ended the first day of civil war.

APRIL 13, 1861—SATURDAY
SULLIVAN'S ISLAND, SOUTH CAROLINA

Saturday morning. No alarms or emergencies during the night. The firing has continued all night, but less energetically than during the first day.

Daybreak came, clear and balmy. The storm clouds had disappeared and once again God's good sunlight brightened the scene. The air was laden with the perfume of April rain and blossoms. The flags of each combatant were still flying with stately defiance while thundering tones of heavy cannon fire again resounded across the harbor.

Even without my field glasses the effects of yesterday's bombardment on Fort Sumter could now be observed. The walls were thickly pitted. The edge of the parapet cut away and several of the guns dismounted. Many of the embrasures were so battered that the regularity of their outline could scarcely be distinguished.

The men are in fine spirits and some sit about me eating breakfast—their first meal in over 40 hours. One of the men remarked how quickly he has become accustomed to Sumter's shots. "I wonder what my friends would think," he asked, "if they could see me so casually taking my meal while amidst the cannon balls."

At about eight o'clock in the morn, Colonel Ripley ordered the Fort Moultrie guns to throw hot shot at Sumter. Shortly thereafter, a thick black smoke was observed issuing from the southern portion of Fort Sumter. Soon a steadily ascending column of smoke filled the air. At first, it was thin and pale, but minute by minute it grew darker and darker until, shooting out from the base of the black pillar, yellow and red tongues of flame were borne eastward by the high wind, wrapping the entire parapet in dense clouds of smoke.

I stood watching the inferno, trying to light a cigar, when a wild shout of triumph rang along the island. Thousands of men stood on the sand hills, embankments and traverses, cheering loudly. This cheer of victory heartily echoed across the water—Morris Island and Fort Johnson. The sight of the burning fort infused new confidence in our men which caused the bombardment to immediately become far more rapid and fierce. The shells flew so fast and thick that I could see them exploding in groups over the flaming fortress. Only a few seconds intervened between the booming fire of the heavy cannon.

The fire blazed wildly until the whole line of the barracks on the south side of Fort Sumter was swept away, leaving only some of the crumbled blackened and tottering chimneys towering over the ramparts. In the course of the forenoon, I heard several violent explosions, apparently doing serious damage to the fort and probably caused by the fire reaching the hand grenades or the powder magazine.

At nine o'clock, the flames appeared to be abating, but at ten, another column of heavy white smoke suddenly arose above the fort followed by a loud explosion. It was obvious that the fire had reached an ammunition magazine. Then, from the island, we could make out the living quarters falling in. The blackened chimneys toppled over and, gradually, the flames sank behind the parapet. Even through this inferno, there would come at intervals a shot from one of the Sumter's batteries, as if to say, "you have killed me, but I'm dying game."

The defenders of Sumter made such an impression by their display of courage under desperate circumstances that at every flash from the muzzles of their cannon, our soldiers would leap to the crests of the earthworks and send up cheer after cheer as a salute to the enemy's bravery.

Shortly before one o'clock, another tremendous cheer from the men upon our batteries called me to my point of observation just in time to see the flagstaff bearing the Stars and Stripes fall heavily inside the fort. Many of the men now claimed that the fort would surrender before nightfall.

For fifteen or twenty minutes I could not see an ensign waving over the fort, but at the end of that time, I observed a large United States flag now flying above the smoke on the north wall of the fort.

Then a loud report issued from Fort Sumter and a large ball struck short of the Moultrie House, spraying dirt and sand high into the air. It then bounded over the heads of a group of frightened and astonished spectators. Then, with a loud crash, it tore through the large wooden hotel, which at the time was flying a yellow hospital flag. Terrified by the noise, a large group of people rushed out in a furious haste, tumbling over one another as they ran down the front steps. The 42-pound ball was shortly thereafter found lying behind the Moultrie House, half buried in the sand. Needless to say, many of us thought the act of shooting at a hospital barbaric, but something you would expect from the Yankee mercenaries.

The firing continued until about two o'clock, when suddenly a white flag appeared and the Stars and Stripes were hauled down. The scene that followed was altogether indescribable.

The troops upon the hills cheered and cheered again. A horseman galloped at full speed along the beach, waving his cap and shouting, "Sumter is ours!"

Many caught the cry and the whole island rang with the glad shouts of thousands. Lt. Colonel Branch turned toward me with a smile upon his face and said, "What I won't give to see Governor Manning and his bucket of Juleps now."

With the cessation of firing, the appearance of the harbor changed dramatically. General Beauregard despatched steamers with firefighting equipment to the fort. Sailing vessels could be seen darting about everywhere, carrying gentlemen from Charleston to see their friends on the islands. Shortly after the surrender, the bells of the city began to ring and salutes were fired from the Cadets' battery, the School Ship, and the cutter Lady Davis.

Walking back toward my tent, Lt. Colonel Branch, Major Capers and I came upon Captain Hamilton, who commanded the Dahlgren gun located near the floating battery. Understandably excited, Hamilton shouted, "Gentlemen, we have won a great victory and old Beauregard deserves the glory!"

"Sic transit mundi," replied Capers.

"What pray tell does that mean?" asked Hamilton.

"When a new pope is consecrated, the choir intones: 'Swiftly passes the glory of this world'," answered Capers.

"It may pass," I countered, "but there's glory enough in this victory for all. Don't forget Colonel Ripley who commanded the Moultrie guns and made the decision to use hot shot on Fort Sumter."

"Enough of this," said Lt. Colonel Branch. "There will be time for acclaim later and I have in my tent some applejack with which to celebrate the remarkable beauty of the day and the glorious victory we have just won."

"Yes, like glory, applejack also passes swiftly," laughed Capers, as he began walking toward Branch's tent.

APRIL 15, 1861—MONDAY
SULLIVAN'S ISLAND, SOUTH CAROLINA

The white flag flies over Fort Sumter. The first battle of the civil war has ended—a clear-cut victory for the Confederacy.

Now, a few incidents of the times...

During the negotiations with Major Anderson and General Beauregard's aides regarding the surrender of the fort, the meeting moved to the surgeon's quarters. Roger Pryor of Virginia, an ex-member of the congress of the United States was one of the Confederate emissaries negotiating with Anderson. This very embodiment of Southern chivalry was one of the many who had strongly urged the attack on Sumter. Standing in the surgeon's quarters, Pryor was literally dressed to kill—bristling with bowie knives and revolvers, like a walking arsenal. He swaggered about the room, making great play with that long hair of his. Now and then he'd toss it aside with a grim look on his face.

Walking about the room, Pryor noticed upon the table what appeared to be a glass of brandy. Thinking he needed something bracing, Pryor drank it without ceremony. Surgeon Crawford of the Sumter garrison, who had witnessed the feat, approached Pryor and said, "Sir, what you have drunk is poison. It was iodide of potassium and you are a dead man."

Pryor instantly collapsed and pleaded to the doctor to save him. Surgeon Crawford dragged him to the parade ground and saved him by applying a stomach pump. Colonel Pryor, it is said, left Sumter, "a wiser, if not better, man."

Today's *Charleston Mercury* carried the following ode:

"Jefferson Davis replies to President Lincoln's proclamation as follows: 'Fort Sumter is ours and nobody is hurt. With mortar, Pzixhan and petard, we tender 'Old Abe' our Beau-regard."

President Lincoln today called for, by proclamation, 75,000 volunteers to suppress the rebellion. In Virginia, the publication of Lincoln's message has greatly increased the secession feeling. Business of all kinds is reported completely suspended. Merchants are engaged in discussing the probability of a prolonged sanguinary civil war. The impression is that the Virginia Convention will instantaneously pass the Ordinance of Secession or call a border state convention.

In a *New York Tribune* editorial, Horace Greeley writes, "Fort Sumter is lost, but freedom is saved. We have a civil war on our hands and there is no looking away from the fact."

Still another Northern editorial has "Jeff Davis and company swinging from the battlements at Washington at least by the 4th of July."

Finally, it would seem that fate and Major Anderson of Fort Sumter have conspired to impede the financial success of the Wilber

& Son furniture dealers at 175 Meeting Street. In the morning's news-paper, Wilber and Son announced the following:

> "The furniture sale, which was to have taken place on April 12, was postponed in consequence of the bombardment of the har-bor by the renegade who commanded Fort Sumter. Now that the fort is ours and fairly won, the sale will take place on April 16th instead."

APRIL 18, 1861—THURSDAY
CHARLESTON, SOUTH CAROLINA

Early yesterday morning, I received the following message:

"April 17, 1861—7 o'clock a.m.

Colonel Pettigrew: You will report as soon as possible to my headquarters in Charleston. You are to act as an escort to the English journalist William Howard Russell while he visits Charleston and the nearby islands. Lt. Colonel Branch will command the regiment in your absence.

The Catawba Steamer will be at the island wharf this morning at 10:00 a.m. for the purpose of transporting you to Charleston.

I remain your obedient servant,
G. T. Beauregard
Brigadier General, Commanding"

At one o'clock p.m. I arrived at General Beauregard's headquarters at the Charleston Hotel. The general received me in almost cordial man-ner and informed me that the visit of the English journalist was extremely important to the Confederacy. As special correspondent of the *London Times*, William Russell was uniquely situated to influence the attitudes of the British people toward the American crisis. If Russell and the *Times* looked upon the Confederacy with favor, it could help influence the English government to formally recognize the

Confederacy. This diplomatic recognition would open the way to loans and arms sales to the South.

General Beauregard and I then went to the Mills House to meet the English journalist. The Mills House was full of notables. Present were ex-Governor Manning, Colonel Chesnut, Colonel Lucas, Aide-de-camp to Governor Pickens and Major Whiting. Major Whiting and I were to act as Russell's guides while he was in Charleston.

General Beauregard, with his usual charm, introduced me to Mr. Russell, who shook my hand warmly. After the introduction, Beauregard turned to Russell and said, "You shall go everywhere and see everything. We rely on your discretion and knowledge of what is fair in dealing with what you see. Of course you don't expect to find regular soldiers in our camps or very scientific works."

Russell smiled and replied, "You can be sure I will not make improper use of what I see in your country."

Just as Russell finished talking, a deep bell began to toll.

"What is that?" asked Russell.

"It is time for the colored people to clear out of the streets and go home," I replied. "The guards will arrest any who are found out without passes in half an hour."

Above the sound of the bells, we could hear loud noises in the streets—drums beating, men cheering and marching, soldiers seemingly everywhere.

I took my leave of Russell and made arrangements to meet him and Major Whiting early in the morning at the quay.

This morning, after an early breakfast, I walked along Broad Street toward the wharf, anxious that I be on time for my meeting with Russell and Major Whiting. The day was sweltering and a stiff breeze puffed the dust of Charleston about me, coating my clothes, irritating my eyes. The streets were crowded with lanky lads, clanking spurs and Sabres with awkward squads of citizen soldiers marching to and fro, with drummers beating and bugle calls renting the air.

I walked past the market filled with laughing Negroes selling their fruits and vegetables from their stalls and little Irish newsboys shouting out, "Battle of Fort Sumter! New edition!" Secession flags waved out of the windows and it seemed a holiday with all the glitter and excitement.

Approaching the quay, where the steamer, Russell, and Whiting were waiting, the uncertainty of the times was manifested in the hurried conversations of various friends who stopped to chat for a few moments.

"Well, Colonel, the old Union is gone at last! Have you heard what Lincoln is going to do?"

"Will Beauregard be placed in command of the Southern armies?"

"What do you think?"

And so on.

I boarded the small tug steamer at 7:00 a.m. and greeted Russell and Major Whiting who were waiting patiently for me. Russell, a powerfully built man of about forty years, shook my hand and appeared glad to see me. A handsome man of seemingly endless energy, he had the most peculiar habit of rubbing his brown beard and moustache with his lemon-colored kid gloves when he talked. He was dressed in what he called his "Crimean War garb." It consisted of high black boots, white pants, a three-quarter-length frock coat and a small brown cap with a small bill. Over his shoulder, he carried a leather pouch filled, he said, with his notebooks and pencils.

With a loud toot of its whistle, the steamer cast away and headed out across the harbor. A strong breeze was blowing and we literally bounced over the waves. Russell and Major Whiting soon became engaged in conversation about the English novelist William Thackenay. Whiting discussed at length his favorite books *Vanity Fair* and *The Virginians*.

I settled back on a bench and watched the seagulls swirling and diving around the boat, their shrill cries renting the sea air. One snow-white gull hovered almost a few feet from me, begging almost for some candy or food.

The shore opposite Charleston is more than a mile distant and as we steamed along, we could see Fort Sumter rising up out of the water near the middle of the passage out to sea between James Island and Sullivan's Island.

Passing to the south of Fort Sumter, we approached Morris Island, our first stop. Nearing Cummings Point, we could perceive a few tents in the distance among the sand hills. The sandbag batteries and a grim black parapet with cannon peering through portholes as if from a ship's side lay before us. Around them were swarms of men. A crowd in uniform was gathered on the beach to greet us as we landed from the steamer—all eager for news and provisions.

The whole of the island was filled with excitement. Officers were galloping about and sounds of laughter and reveling came from the tents. These were pitched without order and were of all shapes, hues and sizes—many being covered with rude charcoal drawings outside and inscriptions such as "The Live Tigers", "Rattlesnake Hole", "Yankee Smashers", etc. The smell was very bad in places as there were no latrines, bones and bottles were strewn about. When Russell called my attention to the health hazards arising from such conditions, I had to say with a sigh, "I understand, but it is hard to do anything. Remember, they're all volunteers and will often do just as they please."

In every tent there was hospitality to be found. Officers at dinner were drinking huge cups of champagne or claret. Toasts were offered to all and everything. Many were feeling the effects of too much drink. When the news was spread about that Russell was an English journalist, he was practically mobbed by half-inebriated officers asking him what he thought of Charleston, Lincoln and the Yankees, and the battle of Fort Sumter. In a quiet moment, Russell took me aside and whispered, "I feel, Colonel

Pettigrew, like a man in the full possession of his senses coming in late to a wine party. Am I crazy or are they?"

After a long and tiresome walk in the dust, heat and blowing sand, it was time to return to the beach and our waiting steamer. Reaching the pier, I was almost blinded by a gust of blowing sand and I wished I was wearing dust spectacles like many of the men on the beach. The sand and wind of Morris Island, I will never forget!!

We took boat and pushed off for Fort Sumter, heading straight for the Confederate flag fluttering in the wind, high above the walls. On near approach, the marks of the shot against the walls were visible enough and the edges of the parapets were ragged and pockmarked.

As the boat touched the quay of the fort, a tall, powerful-looking man came through the shattered gateway, and with stumbling uneven steps, strode over the rubbish to a waiting small boat, into which he jumped and rowed off. Turning, he recognized Major Whiting and suddenly stood up and, with a leap and a scramble, tumbled in among us. I immediately recognized that we were in the presence of Louis T. Wigfall, Colonel of the Confederate Army, an aide to General Beauregard.

Wigfall was dressed in the blue frock coat of a civilian, round which he had tied a red silk sash. From his waist belt hung a long straight sword and tucked into his pants was a Navy Colt revolver. His tan, muscular neck was surrounded with a white silk handkerchief. Wild masses of uncombed black hair, tinged with grey, fell from a large stove-pipe hat. His unstrapped trousers were gathered up high on his legs displaying ample boots, garnished with shining spurs.

Wigfall extended his hand in greeting to Major Whiting and smiled through his scrubby dark beard and moustache. It was obvious that Colonel Wigfall had been drinking, for he was decidedly unsteady in his gait and rather thick in speech.

Wigfall had gained instant fame during the bombardment of Sumter. When the fort was in flames, Wigfall procured a small boat and put off from Morris Island and steered through the shot and the slashing waters right for the battered walls of the fort. While a Negro rowed, Wigfall held up a white handkerchief from the end of his sword. After landing on the quay, he clambered through an embrasure and presented himself before the surprised Federals with a proposal to surrender. Although unauthorized by General Beauregard, Wigfall presented terms of his own making, which led to the final surrender of the fort.

Even though he reeked of alcohol, Wigfall's head was quite clear and he wasted little time in telling Russell about his exploit. Major Whiting and I had desired to show Russell around the fort, but we had no chance as Wigfall was determined to lead the tour.

Later as we stood on the parade ground a-talking, Wigfall turned to Russell and said, "The bombardment of Fort Sumter was one of the greatest victories in the history of warfare."

Russell shook his head as if to disagree and expressed surprise that the nearly four thousand shells expended by the southern-shore batteries had failed to make a breach in Sumter's walls and that no casualties had taken place on either side during the bombardment.

Then in a clear voice, not without emotion, Russell explained to us his opinion of the conquest of Sumter.

"Governor Pickens," he began, "has claimed you have defeated the Yankee government and their twenty million people, and humbled the flag of the United States before the Palmetto and the Confederate. The battle of Fort Sumter you call it! Good God! It wasn't a battle at all! It was little more than an exchange of civilities between gentlemen—more like a bloodless dual with pistols fired into the air. Commanding officers thanked God that their enemies had been spared!

"You boast that you have driven the Yankees from Fort Sumter, but you have only played at war and, to paraphrase St. Paul, you have only seen it through a glass darkly, but soon you will see face to face.

"Now the flame is no longer smothered. The fanatics of the North and South have made a gulf so deep that no friendly foot can pass it. Hatred so fierce that reason cannot allay it. Bloody civil war will be the fatal consequence. Passion rules and men will war against each other with a vengeance."

APRIL 20, 1861—SATURDAY
CHARLESTON, SOUTH CAROLINA

I awoke this morning thinking, once again, that words cannot express the delight I feel at being able to sleep in my own bed, to have the opportunity of a daily bath, to be able to change my clothes, not to hear reveille at four in the morning, not to be disturbed in the evening by the inevitable taps, to sit down at a table covered with a white cloth, not to be met at every meal by the unvarying menu of flapjacks and bacon or bacon and soda biscuits, and to have the services of my loyal Negro servants Nat and Ruth. Yes, to feast and to live, if you will, in a land of milk and honey.

After dressing, I hurried to the Mills House on Meeting Street where I joined Russell and Colonel James Chesnut for breakfast. As we conversed over coffee and biscuits, I looked at Colonel Chesnut and thought, "some people seem to get all the good things in life." A graduate of Princeton. Intelligent, handsome, owner of hundreds of slaves, a successful politician and married to a charming and intelligent wife. Colonel Chesnut, in the words of the Psalmist, "had more than heart could wish."

I was brought out of my reverie by Russell asking me for a cigar. After lighting the borrowed cigar, Russell held up a page of the morning paper and pointed his stubby index finger to a notice under the "City Intelligence" column. Having gained our attention, he began to read out loud. I had to listen carefully because of his English accent as he read the newspaper notice below:

"We would beg to call particular attention to the gang of 76 valuable Negroes to be sold singularly and in families this day at the Old Exchange Building at the foot of Broad Street on East Bay. The sale will commence at 11 o'clock by Wilnur and Son, Auctioneers. No postponement on account of weather. For particulars, we refer to their advertisement under Auction Sales."

After some discussion, it was agreed that Colonel Chesnut and I would accompany Russell to the morning's slave auction. Russell seemed most pleased with this decision, clapping his hands together and remarking, "I think the editors of my paper will welcome a first-hand account of a slave auction."

Taking a drink of coffee and a long puff on his cigar, Russell then said, "Most in my country think slavery is an evil thing."

Looking intently at Russell through the haze of cigar smoke, I said, "Mr. Russell, there is probably not an intelligent mind among the citizens of the South who doubts either the moral or legal right of the institution of African slavery. It is all a hallucination to suppose that the south will ever get rid of slavery or that it will ever be desirable to do so. To be sure, slavery has some potential evils, but as a practical matter, I can envision no bearable alternative—economic or social."

"And you, Colonel Chesnut," asked Russell, "your opinion of the institution of African slavery?"

Colonel Chesnut took a drink of his coffee, thought for a short time, and replied, "Our slaves are the happiest people on the face of the earth, sir! They are better fed and better treated than any peasantry in the civilized world. I've traveled in England, France and other countries of Europe and seen for myself, sir. What do you think of women—white women—working in the fields and living on nothing better than thin soup and vegetables as they do in France all the year around? You're an Englishman, Mr. Russell, while in England I've seen men with seven or eight children to support, working like dogs, breaking stones on the high road in winter for eight shillings a week? Such a thing couldn't happen in South Carolina—in all the South—sir!

"Mr. Russell," continued Chesnut, "as an Englishman you are a born abolitionist, but you know nothing at all about the workings of our institution of slavery except what the damn Yankees please to write about us. Why, I can tell by looking at you that the very word slavery shocks you. When you write your column, call it servitude, vassalage, or anything else that will make it more endurable to your readers. One of the advantages, by the way, that secession is going to bring with it is that the world will be brought into direct contact with us and thus see us as we are and not through the eyes of the North."

With this, the conversation ended and we left the Mills House to walk to the old exchange Building. Walking east, the sidewalks were crowded with booths kept by old Negro mammas, the food they were selling was tasty and the drinks cooling. We stopped at one booth and each bought a sassafras beer for a quarter dollar.

We soon reached the marketplace of Charleston, a mixture of swirling sound and smells. Here one finds no lack of supplies to furnish a feast and the array of fruits and vegetables is tempting. The fruits, as well as poultry, which are manacled in pairs, are sold by Negro and Mulatto females, whose gay turbans of Madras, and manner of sitting beside their wares has a very Turkish appearance. Arrayed in the various booths were colorful oranges, clusters of bananas, weighing twenty pounds, cocoa nuts, figs, peaches, melons of vast dimensions, cones of lemons and pyramids of yams.

In the vicinity of the market are hundreds of large sable, bald-headed birds called Turkey Buzzards. One sat high on a ridge pole looking intently at a shin bone lying in a nearby gutter. The buzzards are protected by law and make themselves useful as scavengers. Nothing escapes them. They can scent food from far off and they keep the streets around the market clear of discarded or unwanted food.

Russell, of course, had never seen anything quite like it and inquired about the efficiency of the Turkey Buzzards. I told him that I had once killed an old alligator nine feet in length and had him flayed upon the spot. When the skin was taken off, there was not a buzzard in sight, yet before I left the place, there were seventy buzzards crowded around the remains of the alligator and in an hour there was, on the bank of the river, the cleanest skeleton of an alligator that you would see in riding fifty miles.

We reached the Old Exchange, or "Custom House," shortly before eleven o'clock. This is perhaps the most historic building in all the South. Here, Stede Bonnet and other pirates were imprisoned and from here, Isaac Hayne was led to execution. Also here, in 1791, George Washington was entertained by his grateful countrymen.

The post office was also located in the exchange and visitors as well as residents called daily for their mail. Today, being a sale day, many still holding their unopened mail, were gathered about, waiting for the sale to begin.

Grouped in front of and just North of the building, waiting in the balcony under the blue sky were the Negroes who were to be sold. Dressed in bright, clean clothes, wearing striped cotton caps, or turbans, and crowded on platforms, they were very conspicuous against the background of brick walls. Grouped about them were planters and traders and curious on-lookers, wearing long coats, high hats and beards of formal cut.

Those who came with intent to purchase were busy with a general examination of the waiting Negroes, by feeling their arms, making them jump and stamp their feet, and throw out their arms and legs, turning them about, looking into their mouths. In short, they did everything they could to assure themselves the Negroes were sound and healthy.

On one platform was a Negro wife clinging to her husband. Next to them stood a sister hanging on the neck of her brother, shedding silent tears. At the side of the platform, were three relatives praying to be sold to the same master—using signs to signify that they would be content with slavery—might they but toil together.

The auctioneer, Alonzo White, began the sale by appealing for bids on a buxom Negress standing by him on the auction block and holding, tightly in her arms, her infant. Near the outskirts of the crowd, two pickaninnies, evidently forgotten for the moment, were crawling about. White's slave porter, a "black snake" whip in hand, sat on a large black horse, watching the Negroes and waiting to drive to the jail all slaves not taken in charge by their purchasers. On the side of the building flew the Palmetto flag—the revered emblem of South Carolina. In the foreground was a howitzer, point down and half-embedded, like a hitching post.

"Well, gentlemen," said White, "here is a capital woman and her three children all in good health. What do you give for them? Give me an offer. (Nobody makes a bid.) I will put the whole lot at 850 dollars…850 dollars…850 dollars…850 dollars…850 dollars…She's a good-looking woman. Will no one advance beyond that? A very extraordinary bargain, gentlemen. Look, she holds a fine healthy baby. Hold it up." One of White's attendants went up the first step of the block and yanked the baby from the woman's breast and held it aloft with one hand so as to show that it was a veritable sucking baby. With this, the proud-looking young Negro woman began to cry and tears ran freely down her face. I heard a man in the crowd behind me ridicule the Negress for her display of emotion.

White began once again, "A woman, gentlemen, still young, and three children, all for 850 dollars. An advance, if you please, kind sirs!"

A voice bid *860*.

"Thank you, sir, *860*. Anyone bid more?"

Another voice bid *870*.

"Come, gentlemen, 870 will never do. How much, how much do I hear for this splendid property? Good nurse, good seamstress and good cook. Look gentlemen, look what a rich development," at the same time placing his hand upon her round, full, bare bosom. "Do I hear a thousand dollars? Eleven hundred?" Twelve hundred is bid by a planter in the front row. "Twelve hundred? Going once, twice. Gone at twelve hundred dollars."

A man, his wife, and two children came next to the stand. "Now, gentlemen," sang out White, "we offer you a fine likely stock here, an entire family. We offer you the whole lump at once. We don't want to separate them. Our friends of the Abolition school up North, say it is wicked to separate families on the block, and you know it is, gentlemen," he added sarcastically. "How much for the family? How much do I hear? Do I hear nothing? Why, gentlemen, this man is a robust hand, a hard worker, and will till from morning to night." A thousand is bid for the man alone; then twelve hundred, fourteen hundred; gone at fifteen hundred to Mr. Paine of Charleston. His wife and the boy, a lad of ten, went for twelve hundred dollars to a planter from Georgia. The young girl, of some eight years, went for eight hundred dollars to a man from Columbia. But the scene of their separation, how shall I describe it?

The mother, realizing she was to be separated from her youngest child, was extremely distraught. She wept and raved and cried out in anguish in tones of desperation and despair which nothing but the heart broken, crushed and wrung to the very core, can ever give utterance to.

"They have sold my babe, they have sold my babe," she exclaimed as she tried to break away to get hold of her youngest, to grasp her in her arms, to press her to her bosom again; but fruitless effort, it was all in vain. The child was borne in one direction, and the mother in another.

A young Negro male was next told to step up onto the block. He was then ordered to take off his clothes, which he quickly did without a word or look of remonstrance. About a dozen buyers crowded to the step where the Negro stood naked. They then examined him carefully from head to toe. His clear black skin, back and front, was viewed all over for sores from disease. There was no part of his body left unexamined. The Negro was told to open and shut his hands. He was asked if he can pick cotton. Every tooth in his head was carefully looked at. As the investigation came to an end, he was ordered to dress himself and, having done so, was requested to walk once again to the block.

"Now, gentlemen," said White, putting his hand on the shoulder of the husky young man, "here is a very fine young boy, 19 years of age, warranted sound—what do you say for him? I put him up at 800 dollars...800 dollars. Do I hear a bid?

860 dollars was bid.

"Nonsense!" yelled White. "Just look at him! See how tall and well built he is? You see he is a fine, tall, healthy boy. Look at his hands!"

Several potential buyers stepped forward and caused the boy to open and shut his hands. The flexibility of the fingers was well looked to, then the hands and also the mouth. Having given satisfaction, an advance was made to 880 dollars. Then to 900 dollars.

At this point, Russell turned to Colonel Chesnut and me and said, "Gentlemen, I think I have seen enough. Can we leave now?" We then walked rapidly away from the exchange building. The rhythmic cry of the auctioneer, as he tried to advance the bid, rang in our ears.

Some distance away from the slave market, Russell stopped abruptly and took off his gloves. He slapped them fiercely against his leg. As he turned to Colonel Chesnut and me, a storm seemed to come over his face. "I wish to be polite, gentlemen, for I like you both immensely and I have enjoyed my stay in Charleston where I have met many warm and courteous people, but what we witnessed today was barbarous. This selling of slaves is behind the spirit of the age, as much so as the heathen gladiatorial combats of pagan Rome under the reigns of Nero and Caligula, of bloody memory."

Chesnut started to speak, but Russell held up his hand interrupting him by exclaiming, "You have lived amongst this all your life and have grown thus familiar and comfortable with slavery, but you are like men looking into the sun, blinded as to what you see."

Chesnut, appearing to grow angry, replied, "Mr. Russell, when I attended Princeton, I studied history carefully. I have found from careful study that from the time of Greece and Rome, human bondage has produced the world's greatest civilizations. Slavery has proven the social foundation for man's greatest achievements. I know, Mr. Russell, that you are a strong believer in democracy and the equality of men, but the experience of the ages has shown clearly the fundamental principals of the American Revolution to be sadly misguided. Men are not really created equal and free, as Jefferson has asserted. Nature has produced individuals and races strikingly unequal in both intelligence, strength, character, and circumstances."

Stung, as Colonel Chesnut had obviously been by Russell's words, I continued the pro-slavery argument by adding, "Say what you will about our institution, Mr. Russell, fed, clothed and protected, the slave in the South is far better off than the Northern factory worker whose employer has no interest in his health or survival. Free in name, Northern workers toil for virtually nothing and have the liberty only to starve."

"I have listened carefully to you, gentlemen, because as I said before, I like and respect you, but I must tell you that there is a curse against your nation, and its name is *slavery*.

"I believe that the Almighty Creator of the universe governs this world which he has made. That the sufferings of nations are to be regarded as the punishment of national crimes and their decline and fall, as the execution of His sentence. Indeed, to deny this would be to directly contradict the express and repeated declarations of the Holy Scriptures. If you admit these truths, gentlemen, and if it also be true that cruelty and human bondage are crimes of the blackest dye, then have you not cause for serious apprehension? God forgive you, but slavery is a monstrous system—one which a God of justice and mercy cannot permit to stand."

APRIL 26, 1861—FRIDAY
CHARLESTON, SOUTH CAROLINA

Yesterday, the greater part of the gallant Second Regiment, Colonel J. B. Kershaw commanding, left on the eleven o'clock train of the Northeastern Railroad for Virginia and the seat of the war. The officers of the various companies were engaged throughout the day in providing all the necessary equipment for their men and getting ready for the long journey north.

In the meantime, a number of the ladies of Sumter District, in order to show their devotion, had been busily engaged in preparing a beautiful regimental flag to be presented to the noble volunteers who were leaving their homes and their families to assist in driving back the foe. A foe who is preparing to invade the sacred soil of the Southland.

A little after nine o'clock in the evening, the regiment was formed in front of their quarters at the American Hotel and marched to the Charleston Hotel where a large crowd was assembled including a large number of ladies.

After the regiment was drawn up in front of the pavement, Governor Manning appeared, accompanied to the portico by three fair daughters of Carolina who wished to present a flag to the regiment.

The flag was then given to Colonel Kershaw by Mrs. Elizabeth Garden on behalf of the ladies of Sumter District. The flag was then spread to the breeze amid the cheers of the regiment while the band struck up a patriotic tune.

The flag is of the finest white Parisian silk and doubled. It is of the usual regimental size, six feet long and four feet wide, with a blue silk background and a Palmetto tree worked with white fidas silk in the center. The trimming is of golden fringe with golden tassels. On one side is the inscription, "Second Regiment, South Carolina Volunteers, 1861," encircled by a wreath of honeysuckles with roses in full bloom.

After the presentation, the regiment turned and began the march to the train station. The most intense excitement prevailed in the city, as this was the first regiment from South Carolina that was leaving for the war. Large crowds of people filled the streets as to impede the march of the gallant Second. Every window had its anxious, interested faces. Roofs of buildings were crowded with excited men. Cheers from the crowds brought forth cheers from the men of the regiment. Ladies lined the streets, waving handkerchiefs and flags while the regimental band played one stirring tune after another. How bravely they marched by, their bayonets glittering in the moonlight, although the shadows obscured their faces so we could not distinguish them. Many were very small, seemingly young boys of seventeen or eighteen

It was about ten o'clock in the evening when the regiment reached the railroad station. The yard was brilliantly illuminated by gas lamps and pine torches. The regiment, marching in splendid order, reached the front of the station with the band cheerily playing "Dixie."

A few short speeches were made and responded to, and then the ranks were broken and the colorful uniforms intermingled with the bustle and confusion of getting the baggage stored away and the men on board the train.

Amid the hissing of the steam engine and the noise and excitement of the crowd, I managed to say a fond farewell to Captain W. H. Casson of the Governor's Guards. He had read law in Mr. Petigru's office and was a noble fellow and good friend. As he boarded the train he smiled and said, "Goodbye friend, thank you for all you have done for me. I hold you in the highest esteem, sir."

Then, Captain Casson laid a tender hand on my shoulder and remarked, "Goodbye Johnson. I shall in all probability see you soon in Virginia. I'll leave a few Yankees for you to battle with."

He then boarded the train loudly remarking that he would write. The rest of his words were then drowned out by the blast of the engine whistle. I waved and yelled, "God speed," but I couldn't be sure he heard me as he passed out of sight.

The gallant members of the Second were all very gay, but I was saddened by the thought that many leaving would never return.

The whistle blew again and the train, with a clatter and deep, powerful rattle, bore slowly away. I followed the moving cars for a short distance, waving and cheering, watching, with tear-dimmed eyes, the trail of the last fading smoke of the engine.

APRIL 30, 1861—TUESDAY
CHARLESTON, SOUTH CAROLINA

I spent almost the whole morning at the dentist. Last night I suffered from a bad toothache until morning mercifully dawned, when I went in search of relief. I went to King Street to the dentist's office. Here I found a dentist who felt confident he could draw any tooth. He put on the forceps and crushed in one side, then cuts the gum, tries again, while pleasantly assuring me he could do it, and crunch went the old tooth again. He then grew radiant, and told me how he extracted twelve teeth from one lady the day before, and is now confident he can extract my tooth. He then put the forceps on tightly and by a succession of wrenches broke the crown of the tooth. Smiling, he laid the pieces on a sheet of paper and said that he had achieved what he most ardently desired. He made another effort, and smashed the root, and with the face of a angel told me it was going well–that now he was sure he could do it. Here human endurance failed. I objected to any further torture and took chloroform and sank into a state of insensibility. I recovered minus the tooth, and left his office glad to be alive.

With the First Regiment of Rifles having been disbanded after our victory at Sumter, I have returned, temporarily, to work in Mr. Petigru's law office.

All is not law work, however, for with the approval of Governor Pickens and General Beauregard and the active aid of a few prominent citizens of Charleston, I have set out to organize what I hope will be an elite regiment for service in Virginia. All members of the regiment will be select volunteers who will be trained in European light infantry tactics. Governor Pickens has assured me he will equip the men with the best available rifles before joining the service of the Confederate States Army.

Arlington Heights, overlooking the western part of Washington, has been seized by the Virginians and they are busily fortifying it. On the night of April 20, the federal Gosport navy yard near Norfolk, Virginia was evacuated and partially burned by the garrison and several vessels scuttled. A Norfolk paper—received here this morning—gives the list of the principle property destroyed. Six war vessels, including the celebrated Pennsylvania, the Germantown, and the Merrimac—a magnificent steamer just built—were burnt to the water's edge.

MAY 9, 1861—THURSDAY
CHARLESTON, SOUTH CAROLINA

A Virginia newspaper reports that, according to reliable intelligence, President Lincoln has been beastly intoxicated for the past thirty-six consecutive hours and that eighty Border Ruffians from Kansas, under the command of Lane, occupied the East Room to guard his majesty's slumbers. It is broadly hinted in a Washington paper that this Kansas guard exerts a despotic control over the bewildered President and that all decrees are of its inspiration.

Old Abe has at last fulfilled his threats of blockading Charleston and the Southern coast by sending the warship Niagara here. The whole Yankee fleet does not consist of more than 24 vessels, although some are very fine ones. The Niagara is a splendid steam propeller, so contrived that she can withdraw the wheel from the water and thus use either steam or her sails at the captain's pleasure. The Niagara is probably the fastest ship in the U.S. Navy. It carries 12 guns, is manned by 600 men, and is fully supplied with provisions, implements and munitions of war.

Ruth preserved a large quantity of strawberries yesterday. Sugar will soon be scarce, but I am a lover of strawberries and cannot think of living without them. Mr. Petigru is worried the blockade will soon cut off all needed supplies and is laying up large quantities of salt, cotton bagging, rope, coffee, sugar and I know not what. I think I have household supplies sufficient to last for some months.

Let the Yankees try their blasted blockade! Who cares? Who will be the most hurt—the South? The North or England? Not the South, for here we make the necessities of life. But what will England do for cotton when her looms are idle? What will her starving population then do for bread? England cannot do without our cotton. Once we have a large supply and say to the English, "Come and get it," the Royal Navy will sweep the navies of Mr. Lincoln away like dust.

I received a letter from Mr. Russell, the English journalist today. He has just arrived in Montgomery from Savannah, Georgia. He reported that at one of the train stops, General Beauregard, attended by Governor Manning and others of his staff, got into the car and tried to elude observation.

Much to the general's displeasure, however, the conductors took great pleasure in announcing to the passengers that the hero of Sumter was aboard. The crowd then insisted upon a speech. The general told Russell he hated speech making and he had besides been bored to death at every station by similar demands. So, as the next best thing, the handsome Manning made a speech in the general's name in which he dwelt on Southern rights, Sumter, victory, and

Beauregard as the man of the hour. The eloquent Manning had hardly warmed up when, with a lurch, the train began slowly moving, carrying the astonished Manning away from the cheers of this audience in the midst of an unfinished sentence.

Russell sent his regards and told me he would write again if the opportunity offered. As engaging in print as he is in person, he wrote that I was a fine specimen of the Southerner and that, minus my broad-brimmed hat and military frock coat, would be a good representative of an English squire at home.

The Courier today carried the copy of a letter that was recently sent to President Lincoln.

"Georgetown, South Carolina
"Confederate States of America, April 1861

"His Excellency, Abraham Lincoln:

"Sir, I recently read your proclamation calling for 75,000 mercenaries to invade these states. With all proper respect, I offer you a wage of $50,000 that we meet you half-way and whip you and your Yankee hosts.

"Respectfully, Ernest Steffen

"P.S. If the bet is accepted, the money will be deposited in the Farmers Bank of South Carolina."

MAY 11, 1861—SATURDAY
CHARLESTON, SOUTH CAROLINA

True to his word, I received a letter today from Captain W. H. Casson. It read as follows:

"Second South Carolina Volunteers
"Camp near Richmond, Virginia

"Dear Colonel Pettigrew:

"The good people of Virginia can sleep soundly in their beds at night. The Second South Carolina has arrived at the seat of the war and the Confederacy will now be safe.

"After the train left Charleston, it need hardly be stated that there was too much excitement for the first half of the night to get much sleep. The men laughed, danced and sang as if possessed by hysteria. We were young boys on our first trip away from home having the time of our lives. The sardine boxes which we brought along to be eaten when rations had run short were opened before we reached the first stations and the various flasks, much sooner.

"In spite of all the heat and dust, the eternal swaying and rattle of the train, and the drawback of having no place or opportunity for comfortable sleep, most of the men were in excellent spirits. Indeed, our upward journey to Richmond was one all the way of wild excitement.

"As the train rumbled on, the older and more serious members began to settle down to pipe and tobacco, to staring out at the trees which seemed to rush homewards like an army of great phantoms, and to realize that there were sober, earnest, thoughtful faces among them. Where are we going? How many of us will return?

"The loud talkers—who had told story after story which the noise of the train prevented anyone, but themselves, from hearing—began after a time to show signs of exhaustion. As the long night wore on, there would sometimes be a brief lull, undisturbed by anything except the heavy breathing and snoring of the sleeping men. Then the train would stop at a station and one man would be heard complaining of the oppressive boots of his vis-a-vis neighbor against the pit of his stomach, while another would complain of the legs which projected over the top of his seat and made sleep impossible for him.

"As we passed across your home state of North Carolina, Colonel Pettigrew, I had gratifying evidences at almost every station of the unanimity and enthusiasm of the people for secession. I heard of many acts of rare and remarkable liberality of individuals, lately Unionists, in contributing money to the support of the cause, and devotion to it in other ways. Individuals of the county of Dublin, for example, had subscribed $50,000 and one hundred and fifty of the residents had volunteered for military service on one day. This county, I am told, is neither larger or richer than the average. It seems that North Carolina is now a true member of the Confederacy.

"I must now record an interesting incident that happened to the Second Regiment to illustrate to what foolish lengths men will go when excited.

"The train was rattling along at a good speed, something like fifteen or twenty miles an hour, consisting of a long string of cars loaded with soldiers—our baggage scattered promiscuously around in the cars, (trunks, valises, carpetbags, and boxes of all conceivable forms, holding the belongings of the regiment.) It was a glorious day and all were light of heart. Spirits once again flowed in liberal dimensions—congenial friends in a congenial cause. Just below Weldon, with long stretches of lowlands on one side and the Roanoke River on the other, curling streaks of grey smoke made an appearance from under one of the forward cars. At first, the merry, good humor and jesting of the soldiers along with the occasional round of a friendly bottle prevented the men from noticing this danger signal of fire; however, this increasing and continuing volume of smoke soon caused an alarm. Men, now alerted, ran to the doors on either side. They shouted and called, waved hats, hands and handkerchiefs, and at the same time pointed to the smoke below. As there was no communication between the cars, those in the cars to the front and rear had to be guided by the wild gesticulations of those in the car that was smoking. The engineer did not notice anything amiss and sat blissfully upon his high seat watching the fast receding rails as they flashed under and out of sight beneath the ponderous driving wheels of the engine.

"At last someone in the forward car, not accustomed to, but familiar with, the dangers of fire in a railroad car, made a desperate leap from the car. This was followed by another, now equally excited. Those men in the front cars, clutching to the sides of the doors and looking anxiously out the windows, craned their necks as far as possible outward, but could see nothing but leaping men. They, fearing a catastrophe of some kind and stricken with panic, leaped also, while those in the rear cars (as they saw along the sides of the railroad track men leaping, rolling and tumbling on the ground) took it for granted that a desperate calamity had occurred to a forward car. There was no time for questions. No time for meditation. Reason had fled the scene. Anxious to leave the train, the men's only concern was to watch for a soft place to make a desperate leap and, in many cases, there was little choice. Men leaped wildly from the speeding train—some with their heads up—others falling on their heads and backs—some rolling over in a mad scramble to clear themselves from the perceived danger.

"The engineer, not being aware of anything wrong with the train, glided serenely along, unconscious of the pandemonium taking place in his rear. But when all had about left the train, (I must confess that, stricken with panic, I, too, jumped to what I thought was safety) and the great driving wheels began to spin around like mad from the lightening of the load, the master of the throttle finally looked to the rear. He must have been amazed at the sight behind him. There lay stretched prone on the ground or limping on one foot or rolling over in the dirt— some bareheaded and coatless with boxes and trunks scattered about in profusion as if in some awful collision—upwards of one thousand men of the gallant Second South Carolina along the railroad track. Many of the men thinking, no doubt, that the train hopelessly lost, or was about to explode in a fiery blast, threw their baggage out before making the dangerous leap into the unknown. As last, the train was stopped and backed to the scene of desolation. It terminated, Colonel Pettigrew, like the bombardment of Fort Sumter—no one hurt and all this confusion and panic occasioned by a hotbox that could have been cooled in a very few minutes.

"When the truth was discovered, much swearing and good-humored jesting was now engaged in. There were also, as you can imagine, many who were embarrassed by their frenzy to leave the train. Such is the result when panic spreads unchecked by reason.

"The sound of taps now echoes across the night air meaning I must extinguish this flickering candle and end this letter. Give my love to all in Charleston and write if the opportunity offers.

"Affectionately yours,
"Captain W. H. Casson"

MAY 15, 1861—WEDNESDAY
CHARLESTON, SOUTH CAROLINA

Breakfast was a delight this morning. Colonel Wilmot DeSaussure and I were the guests of Colonel and Mrs. Wigfall. There was on the table a profusion of dishes—grilled fowl, eggs, ham, iced water, coffee, tea, varieties of homing, mush and African vegetable preparations. During the meal, we discussed the morning papers which were pursued eagerly with exclamations such as: "Do you hear what the Yankees are doing now—infernal villains!", "That Lincoln must be mad!", and the like.

As we ruminated over the news, the Negro waiter brought Colonel DeSaussure a mint julep—a concoction of brandy, sugar and peppermint beneath an island of ice. After taking a sip, Desaussure smiled and said, "Delicious. An obligatory panacea for all the evils of our hot Southern climate."

DeSaussure then turned to the intelligent-looking Negro who had just waited on him and asked if he knew how to read and write. "We must not do that, sir. Massa Wigfall has dun told me to work hard, not tell lies, not ta steal and be a good servant. Massa says that before God I am as white as he is."

After the Negro left, Wigfall lit a cigar and amid a great cloud of smoke said, "I'm not sure we can trust our Negro slaves in these perilous times. You must always be careful what you say around them."

Mrs. Wigfall, obviously concerned, agreed and added, "I'm sure I will not sleep soundly amid these complaints and rumors of growing insolence and insubordination among the Negroes."

Then, in a quiet and observant manner, Colonel DeSaussure told of an English friend who has been traveling through the Southern states for the last several months. This friend who recently arrived in Charleston reported that the greatest alarm and fear exists among the slave owners in consequence of certain evidences which they have discovered. These evidences suggest the slaves may have, in some locations, organized schemes for rebellion.

Wigfall agreed with this observation remarking that everyone who has lived in the South knows the manner in which intelligence is passed among the slaves. The hotel waiters, the barbers, and the private servants of gentlemen and families in cities are the first to learn what is going on. Constantly present with their masters, they hear all conversation and if it bears on their own interests, they treasure it up with a very retentive memory. There exists among the slaves a very general belief that an army from the North is soon to march down to the South and liberate all the slaves. Many think this liberation will be accelerated if they make a rising themselves and some such revolts have been made.

"There have been," agreed DeSaussure, "alarmingly frequent cases of slaves killing their owners."

"Was it not Spartacus," asked Mrs. Wigfall, "a slave in the Roman Empire, who headed a slave revolt for freedom. We will have to fight the Yankees in front, with one eye behind for a Negro Spartacus."

"Gentlemen," said Colonel Wigfall, "there is only one way to end these revolts and that is to deal out retribution to the perpetrators with dispatch."

"My English friend," said DeSaussure, "informs me that the revolts he has heard of have been put down with great severity. They are hushed up as much as possible. Some slaves have been burned at the stake. Others hung. Others sold to go further South and everyone says as little about the insurrection as possible."

"We live in the midst of a smoldering volcano, gentlemen," added Wigfall, "and I fear that sooner or later an eruption will take place."

Colonel DeSaussure, stroking his beard in a thoughtful manner, looked intently at Mrs. Wigfall and said, "I understand your fear, Mrs. Wigfall, but most of us are not afraid of our own Negroes. True, some are horrid brutes—savages, monsters—capable of foul deeds, but I would go down on my plantation tomorrow and stay there if there were no white person in twenty miles. My Molly, who practically raised me, and half a dozen others that I know, would keep me as safe as I should be in the Tower of London. Many among us are ready to slaughter the Negroes indiscriminately, and I believe the Negroes in this climate of fear to be in much more danger from the whites than the whites are from the Negroes."

At this, Mrs. Wigfall looked at me and said, "You have kept very quiet during this exchange, Colonel Pettigrew. Your thoughts, if you please?"

"I think, Mrs. Wigfall, that when confronted by menace, or what is perceived as menace, people will usually attempt to smash it. Rarely do they attempt to examine or understand it. I believe along with Colonel DeSaussure that the Negroes have more to fear from us, than we from them."

"You do not fear the Negroes then, Colonel Pettigrew," asked Mrs. Wigfall.

"No, Mrs. Wigfall," I replied, "but I do believe one thing, that regardless if we win or lose this war, it will mean the freedom of the slaves. James R. Gilmore, a wealthy merchant here in Charleston and a man of mildly emancipationist views, has talked to several intelligent Negroes who are perceived to be leaders of their people. One, who goes by the name of Sapo, told Mr. Gilmore that the South would lose the war, 'cause you see dey'll fight wid only one hand, when dey fight de Norf wid de right hand, dey'll hev to hold de nigga wid de leff.'"

As I finished my remarks, a hush settled over the table. I had mentioned the unthinkable. I believe my messmates would have been more willing to conjecture what lie on the far side of the moon than discuss the possibility of the South losing the war, or freedom for the slaves.

Colonel DeSaussure cleared his throat and broke the silence by signaling the young Negro waiter to bring him yet another mint julep. As the waiter approached with glass number two, DeSaussure looked at us and said, "This will be good for me. The air is very bad this morning, much dew." Then looking closely at the waiter, DeSaussure asked, "Where did you say you were born Sambo?"

MAY 30, 1861—THURSDAY
CHARLESTON, SOUTH CAROLINA

I received word today that the regiment I hoped to lead will not be accepted into the Confederate service. I am extremely disillusioned by the whole affair. My high hopes, like gallant, many-masted sailing ships, have navigated afar never to return. My dreams, like the early morning dew, have vanished into the thin air. I was confident that the War Department would hear my plea, but instead my expectations have been dashed.

The rifle regiment has been disbanded and the companies are being accepted into other regiments now forming. The Washington Light Infantry, for example, will become part of the Hampton Legion. Governor Pickens, bless his kind soul, has offered me the post of adjutant general, or, in effect, Chief of Staff of South Carolina. But I feel I must decline the offer as such a position would keep me in South Carolina carrying out administrative duties. It is my wish, dream, hope to go to Virginia and lead troops in combat.

Yesterday, I received the following note from Ellison Capers' wife, Charlotte:

"Dear Johnson,

"I am sorry to tell you that our little daughter, Mary, is suffering from scarlet fever. She was very restless all last night with fever, which continues very high today. Her reason appears to be unaffected, as she talks and remains quite sensible. Her neck and face are covered with a fiery red rash and she has a terrible sore throat. Ellison and I are greatly distressed and filled with fearful apprehension.

"Doctor James hopes that the attack may not prove very severe. Most of the cases, and there have been many in the city this season, have proven manageable—yielding to treatment. We hope for the best."

Little children are so frail and I can only pray that Mary will have the strength to overcome this illness.

Here I am brimming with abundant health and yet feeling sorry for myself because the regiment will not be accepted to the Confederate service. It seems a small thing now, when compared to the cruel fate that has come upon Mary.

JUNE 1, 1861—SATURDAY
CHARLESTON, SOUTH CAROLINA

Yesterday while having breakfast, James Louis Petigru asked me if Confederate losses during the bombardment of Fort Sumter had been suppressed to keep Southern morale high. I expressed surprise at the Judge's statement, explaining that Southern casualties had been put at five or six wounded, including Roger Pryor's stomach from drinking poison at the fort and an old horse killed on Sullivan's Island by Union guns.

"Do you have reason to suspect," I asked Mr. Petigru, "that the contest was not as bloodless as represented?"

Mr. Petigru then informed me of several rumors presently in circulation. One mentioned a list of Confederates killed and wounded which had been posted on a bulletin board in Charleston. It was soon torn down for fear it would discourage the troops.

Another concerned a rigger from Boston who had found employment as such during the winter at Charleston and Wilmington, North Carolina. He claimed he was on the battery at Charleston during the first day of the bombardment. The news that circulated that day among the crowd was that nobody had been hurt. Doubting this story, he determined to go down to the wharf at night and see if any killed or wounded were brought in by boat.

At about ten o'clock that evening, one of the two steamboats which plied between Charleston and the forts came in. Three or four long, covered vehicles with a tarpaulin curtain hanging down behind had been standing near the wharf for some time. One of them backed up on the wharf and there began to bring dead bodies on handbarrows from the steamer and put them into the covered vehicles where they laid them in long boxes. There were three of these boxes in each covered vehicle and they put two bodies in each box.

After the vehicles drove away, the rigger waited until two o'clock in the morning when another boat came in with yet another load. More bodies were loaded onto covered vehicles and carried away. He estimated the number of bodies carried away at nearly one hundred.

The next night, he also went down to the battery and saw more bodies brought ashore, about half as many as on the first night. Many of these he believed were killed at Fort Moultrie when a shot fired from Sumter entered an embrasure and killed thirty men. He learned that the dead were taken to Potter's Field near the Cooper River and buried there.

I couldn't help but laugh loudly at the story of the thirty killed at Fort Moultrie. I reminded Mr. Petigru that I had been at or near the fort during the entire battle and had neither seen or heard of any deaths caused by Yankee shells. I also informed the judge that I knew personally many officers and men who had served at the various forts and posts during the bombardment and they all assured me there had been no deaths in any of their commands.

"I fear we shall need no rumors of casualties," I said, "for we will soon have more than enough real ones."

Today I received another note from Charlotte Capers:

"Dear little Mary has improved. We hope and pray she is quite out of danger now."

These are long days and long nights for Ellison and Charlotte. I and Mr. Petigru have offered to help in any way we can. I pray often for little Mary and hope she will recover.

Several years ago, there was a scarlet fever epidemic in the Charleston Orphan House in which sixty children were afflicted, but only one died. Those are good odds and give me hope of Mary's return to health.

JUNE 2, 1861—SUNDAY
CHARLESTON, SOUTH CAROLINA

Virginia has been invaded! A short time ago about 5,000 Union troops took control of Alexandria. The few hundred Confederate soldiers who were there were able to retreat successfully to Manassas Junction.

Hampton, Virginia, has also been seized by the Yankees. As expected, they have struck the first blow by invading our soil and the consequences of this act will be upon their own heads. The mail from the North has been stopped and the telegraph wires cut beyond Richmond, but, as our own post office department went into operation yesterday, it will not incommode us.

The Congress has adjourned and the provisional seat of government is to be moved from Montgomery to Richmond. The Congress will again meet on the 20th of July.

This morning James Louis Petigru and I went for a cruise aboard a small steamer. We left the wharf very early in the morning. As we steamed out through the quiet harbor, I could not but contrast it with the excitement and danger it held during the bombardment of Fort Sumter.

As we passed Castle Pinckney, the shadows lay long and cool upon the water. The shipping, the docks, the wharves, so still and quiet, all impressed a Sabbath tranquility upon us, while the chimes of St. Michael's and other churches called their congregations to the early morning service–which is held in some of the Charleston churches in hot weather–came floating delicately over the water. The scene was one of beauty and worked to attune our hearts to thankfulness and peace.

As we steamed past Sumter, inspecting carefully the battered walls with our field glasses, a black object struck our eyes in the dim distance.

"What is that?" I inquired, while Mr. Petigru turned his glasses toward the ocean.

"That is the blockading squadron, Colonel Pettigrew," said a passenger. Looking long and intently toward the Yankee vessels with my field glasses, I cannot adequately describe the rage which came over me. Angered, I felt a powerful urge to take control over our steamer and head to seaward, there to seize, grapple and sink the enemy. There they lay, three vessels, insolently barring our way from the sea.

"Oh," I said to Mr. Petigru, "for a navy that could cope with them we would soon drive the hated Yankee flag from the entrance to Charleston."

"Don't worry, Johnson," replied Mr. Petigru, "they do not so effectually shut us out as they suppose, for blockade runners slip past them every dark night both to and from the West Indies."

"That may be," I answered, "but the sight of Yankee ships has robbed me of my Sabbath peace and quietness. I am thinking most unChristian thoughts toward them at present."

This afternoon, I was able to talk with Major Capers. He feels that his dear little Mary is better, although what the final result will be is known only to Him, in whose hands are the issues of life and death.

We are all praying for the best and Capers said the attending physician thinks the severity of the attack is well-nigh passed.

JUNE 5, 1861—WEDNESDAY
CHARLESTON, SOUTH CAROLINA

Last night, Little Mary had a more comfortable night than she has had for some time. Her fever has somewhat increased this morning, but we all hope and pray that a good God will preserve her precious life.

Charlotte Capers is doing reasonably well. Her tender attentions to Mary have been unceasing and, according to Dr. James, most valuable.

As I reflect on Mary's battle against scarlet fever, I am well aware that life can be brutal and short. I remember all to well the yellow fever epidemic that struck Charleston in 1858 and killed nearly eight hundred inhabitants of the city.

During that appalling epidemic, I saw more people die than I ever expect to again. I felt for a time as if I were living in a graveyard. The fever that year was of a new and deadly type, which was ultimately traced to a steamer from Havana. Some of the passengers eluded quarantine and spread the disease to Charleston and Sullivan's Island.

I stayed in the city that summer even though I was considered especially vulnerable to the disease since I had never had yellow fever. I had determined to help those in need and go about my usual business. I have always felt it would be better to die than be fearful as some people are. I trust in God and if He is for me, what can be against me?

That terrible summer, which now seems like a bad dream, Joseph Blythe Allston, my close friend came down with yellow fever and was pronounced by the physicians as certain to die. Determined to save my friend, I nursed him day and night and I think had some influence on saving his life. Many of my friends said I was crazy to stay with Allston and that I should be placed into the lunatic asylum.

Once the summer ended, the epidemic seemed to have passed, but it suddenly broke out again in November. During the second week of the month, I contracted the fever and became deathly ill. For five days, I hovered between life and death, vomiting endlessly and hallucinating. The attending physicians gave me large doses of calomel and castor oil. I received the tender nursing of Allston and Henry Deas Lesesne, another close friend. Mr. Petigru has told me many times he considered me lost, but somehow, the fifth-day crisis of the disease passed and, by the grace of God, I was spared.

Now, the skeptic will laugh and say, "by the grace of God, indeed" but as I ended my hallucinations, I reached for the Bible that had been placed by my bedside. As I picked it up, the pages fell open to the book of Psalms. I glanced at the page and my eyes fell, for some reason, on Psalm 116. Imagine my astonishment when I read the following words:

> "I love the Lord, because he hath heard my voice and my supplications. Because he hath inclined his ear unto me, therefore will I call upon him as long as I live. The sorrows of death compassed me, and the pains of hell got hold upon me; I found trouble and sorrow. Then called I upon the name of the Lord; O Lord, I beseech thee, deliver my soul. Gracious is the Lord, and righteous; yea O God is merciful. The Lord preserveth the simple: I was brought low and he helped me. Return unto thy rest, O my soul; for the Lord hath dealt bountifully with thee. For thou hast delivered my soul from death, mine eyes from tears, and my feet from falling. I will walk before the Lord in the land of the living. I believed, therefore have I spoken: I was greatly afflicted..."

JUNE 8, 1861—SATURDAY
CHARLESTON, SOUTH CAROLINA

This evening, I was to have attended a small party at Sara White's, but, due to a tremendous thunderstorm, decided to stay home and read. While lightning flashed through the darkened sky and loud cracks of thunder literally shook the house, I rested dry and comfortable in bed and read from Carlyle's *Heroes and Hero Worship*.

I must admit surprise that Charleston would be so gay with the dark clouds of war looming on the horizon. So many are away at the front, but it seems to be a reaction after the long depression of winter and absence of friends on duty on the islands. During the last month, I have been invited to a good many parties, almost all rather small dinner get-togethers.

Now that I am no longer on active duty, I must watch what I eat at these dinner parties, or I may soon be a large corpulent mass and have to roll to duty in Virginia.

Now, I must record something that pains me dearly. Today Dr. James informed me that he entertained little or no hope for the recovery of dear little Mary Capers. For many days now, she has had no sleep, tossing from side to side, throwing herself with violence against the sides of her little crib. High fever. Small running pulse. Great difficulty in swallowing—her throat greatly swollen. She is now apparently sinking under the protracted nervous derangement and fever. The doctor feels her kidneys may also be inflamed and not working well.

Dr. James reminded me of how vicious a killer scarlet fever can be when he told me of James Lindsay, a Georgetown merchant who had six of his eight children—between the ages of four and eleven—succumb to scarlet fever in eleven days.

JUNE 10, 1861—MONDAY
CHARLESTON, SOUTH CAROLINA

We have been kept ignorant here in Charleston with reference to the true movements of our army in Virginia. President Davis' presence in Richmond inspires great enthusiasm and confidence. He appears to be, in every way, the man of the hour. Equal to any emergency. He is at once soldier and statesman. Indeed, many here hope that if there is to be a battle in Northern Virginia, Davis will take command of the army and lead it into battle.

How I long to be in Virginia. I have no doubt there will soon be a fierce battle there. Many of my friends and comrades are on duty there, exposed to hardship and danger and here I sit, doing nothing of importance in Charleston.

I have still received no word from Governor Ellis of North Carolina regarding my offer to services to my home state. I know he suffers from a terminal illness and is also probably overwhelmed with applications. I must learn to be patient, but it is so hard in these frantic times.

Little Mary still lies extremely ill, with little or no change in her condition. If she was not a child of vigorous constitution, I should utterly despair of her recovery. Yesterday prayers were offered in both St. Michael's and St. Phillips' churches for her recovery.

JUNE 12, 1861—WEDNESDAY
CHARLESTON, SOUTH CAROLINA

Yesterday morning at about nine o'clock, the beautiful daughter of Ellison and Charlotte Capers passed away.

Sweet Mary, how we all loved her. She has been removed, we trust and believe, to be with God. She is not dead, but sleepeth. As least her pain and suffering has ended and nothing now remains of her short pilgrimage but treasured memories of her smiling face and gentle voice.

Ellison informed me that as Mary was breathing her last, just as the last breath was escaping from her disease-wracked little frame, he sat watching at her side. As he watched, looking intently into her eyes, one little tear drop, pure as crystal—the only one she had shed during the course of her frightful illness—fell from her eye. It was, Ellison believes, Mary's farewell to earth and to her sorrow-stricken father. It may have been purely accidental, but to Ellison, it was of the greatest significance.

Because she died of scarlet fever of the most virulent type, the physicians decided that Mary must be interred as soon as possible to limit the spread of the disease.

Accordingly, at seven o'clock in the evening, Mary Capers was laid to rest. The scene at the grave site was one of great solemnity. Charlotte Capers was desolate with grief and it appeared that her mind was wandering. She said many things that made little or no sense. Later that evening as we gathered at Ellison's house, Charlotte, overcome with grief and adversity, experienced a morbid conviction that Mary was not dead, just in a deep sleep and that she had been buried alive. It was only with the greatest difficulty that Charlotte was restrained from hurrying to the graveyard and attempting to exhume the body.

After this tragic scene, Ellison took me aside and said, "I know I must be dreaming, Johnson, because reality could never be this tragic. I know I am literally numb because my heart doesn't beat and my hands don't shake."

Now, as I sit alone in my own room, the remembrance of little Mary comes over me in overpowering vividness. She was so young, beautiful and gentle. She would have grown to be a lovely and talented woman. How sudden and awful was God's summons.

I pray God will ease the grief that Ellison and Charlotte feel. Their family troubles have come at a time when we have as much national anxiety as we can sustain.

JUNE 30, 1861—SUNDAY
CHARLESTON, SOUTH CAROLINA

I am remiss that I have been inconsistent in the practice of writing in this journal as of late. This year of all the years of my past life, I should have been most faithful in keeping this record for it is probable I shall never pass through so stirring a time again.

These are historic times and I am becoming increasingly restless here in Charleston as the sectional crisis increases in intensity. I imagine in peace times, I would have lived and died a quiet, happy-tempered fellow, but the peril that now faces the South forces me to act.

Frustrated at my attempts to command either a South or North Carolina Regiment, I have determined to go to Virginia as a private in the Hampton Legion. I have assurance I will be able to serve in the Washington Light Infantry commanded by my good friend James Connor. Connor has reluctantly accepted this arrangement, writing me, "plenty of men can make privates. Few are as capable as yourself of being in command."

This afternoon, Mr. Petigru and I walked about the battery. As we strolled along the greens of this beautiful old place, with the ocean air and the fine breeze, the idea of going to war seemed a turning point in my life. Perhaps I would journey north to Virginia and find military glory and fame, or maybe a Yankee bullet in the head. Mr. Petigru thought me a fool to join the Legion as a private and strongly urged against it. But his arguments were of no use. A man must march, when it is his plain duty, and all the more, if he has had in this world, more than his slice of cake.

I read in one of the Richmond papers this evening a strong editorial recommending that, once the South wins this civil war, moves should be made to legalize the renewal of the African slave trade. The renewal of the trade by law, or even against law, to bring slaves to this country was obviously impossible under the old union. Once the war is ended, all the Southern states will suffer greatly from the scarcity and high price of labor. They could obtain no supply from abroad because the only available and useful supply of Negroes was prohibited by law.

Nothing, claims the editorial, can exceed the horrors and the amount of suffering it inflicts unless it is its modern substitute, the transportation of so-called free men—like the hordes of destitute whites who immigrate from Europe to the North—but the sufferings of the slave trade were caused by its prohibition and the dangers of capture and severe punishment. To lessen this danger, the transportation of slaves was effected in small and swift sailing vessels in which the slaves were packed so closely that they could scarcely live through the speedy voyage; but, if the business was legal, it would be the interest of the owners to take care of the lives, the health and the comfort of their slaves. Also, the government could prescribe all humane and needful regulations for the slave ships, which could be as operative as for passengers in immigrant ships. Under such enlightened laws, there is no reason why the African slaves, even on the "Middle Passage," should not even be more comfortable than their lives were before under their barbarous and inhuman African masters and rulers.

JULY 7, 1861—SUNDAY
ON THE TRAIN TO RICHMOND, VIRGINIA

Behold me, installed in solemn state, seated uncomfortably on the seat of a railroad car watching the North Carolina countryside flash by.

The train is full of soldiers and the reception given to the volunteers, along the line of railway, whenever a town, a village, or even a log hut appears in sight, evidences the most profound warm feelings on the part of the spectators, who principally consist of women. The Secession Flag floats wherever I observe a human habitation—the sight of which frequently occasioned a shout from the soldiers aboard the train that literally fills the air and echo beyond the distant forests.

During the night, the water in the car tanks was exhausted, and as soon as it was known, the men suddenly became extremely thirsty and did some vehement swearing and complaining. While the train lay on a siding near Willmington, a poor fellow from one of the forward cars got out and, while standing on another track, was instantly killed by a passing fast train. This threw a damper over all.

This afternoon, while the train was in motion, we passed a small town and near the track, a very pretty and patriotic young girl appeared with a bouquet of flowers in her hands—of which to her evident regret, she had no opportunity of disposing. The rear of our long train was composed of platform cars laden with cannon and underneath whose rattling chains at night some of the men would crawl and sleep. Upon the last of these platform cars, a young sentinel was standing who thought it a pity that such a pretty bouquet should be left behind. As the train went slowly around the curve, the sentinel jumped off the train without accident, ran to the pretty young miss, and took the bouquet, and a kiss besides, from the fair lips of the astonished donor. Then, accompanied by the shouts and cheers of the many soldiers who witnessed this gallant act, he succeeded in regaining the train.

Now, in the front of the car, a couple of the boys are singing "The Girl I Left Behind Me." I left no girl behind, but many friends, a house and ten years of my life's work. It's a strange feeling to head into the unknown. I wonder if I will ever return to Charleston and if I do, will my life be the same?

JULY 10, 1861—WEDNESDAY
CAMP BEAUREGARD—OUTSIDE RICHMOND, VIRGINIA

Camp Beauregard is not my idea of paradise. Heat, cold, dust, rain, flies—each tent looking as if a swarm of bees had been hived in it—contribute to making us of the Washington Light Infantry the most wretched band of patriots upon whose heads ever descended a hot sun or drenching rain. It is a soldier's life with all its hardships, with none of its pleasures or excitements. Our only amusement is cleaning sabres, rifles, mounting guard, and sleeping under the shade of two stunted trees—the only chance for shade there is in camp.

I was able to go into Richmond on leave. The streets of the capital city are crowded with soldiers. I walked all over the city without counting more than ten young men who were not in uniform. Bar rooms and hotels are swimming in money. Plain drinks (whiskeys, for instance) which usually cost, perhaps twenty-five cents per gallon, sell for fifteen cents a glass and mint juleps and sherry cobblers, at twenty-five cents, so that a campaign of six months would be in what a private gets for pay worth exactly three hundred and sixty five drinks!

Last night we experienced one of the most severe thunderstorms conceivable, and sad havoc was made of our tent.

Private Brown shared my tent and as the wind howled and the thunder rolled, we sprang from our blankets and each seized a tent pole. Hanging on desperately, we tried to steady our frail canvas habitation as best we could. We were strong and brave, but soon proved no match for the elements. Just as Brown cried out, "It is glorious to die for one's country!" down went the tent upon the ground with the rain pattering on our backs. As we stood there, drenched and cold, Brown looked at me and said, "I can't swim and I want to live so bad, even in this mud and water."

"Yes," I answered, "it's so glorious to live, and the South needs us. Now what are we going to do about this tent?"

"Why, I'm going to stay right here," answered Brown, "just to be revenged upon the whole Southern Confederacy!"

So we did. We stayed right there, two glorious wet soldiers, trying to sleep upon wet blankets in the mud and the tent cloth flapping wildly over us.

At daylight, we discovered the whole camp in much the same condition and Captain Conner had fared no better. The wind had carried the good captain's loose articles, including his extra drawers and socks, to a neighboring fence corner.

Such are the trials of Private Pettigrew of the Washington Light Infantry. I now realize I have left civilization and comfort far behind.

JULY 11, 1861—THURSDAY
CAMP BEAUREGARD—NEAR RICHMOND, VIRGINIA

Today I received the following telegram from Governor John Ellis of North Carolina:

"Executive Mansion
"Raleigh, North Carolina
"July 11, 1861—8:00 a.m.
"Private James Johnson Pettigrew:
"Washington Light Infantry

"It is my pleasure to inform you that yesterday you were elected Colonel by a vote of the men of the Twenty-Second North Carolina Regiment, now organizing at Raleigh.

"Please inform me if you will accept the command, and if so, when you can report for duty.

"Governor John W. Ellis"

There is no way to describe the shout of joy that escaped from my lips upon the receipt of this telegraph. This summons came at a time when I had just about given up hope of ever commanding a regiment. I thought I was to be Private Pettigrew for the duration of the war.

I have now resolved to join the Twenty-Second as soon as possible, even though a battle is looming here in Northern Virginia.

I hurried to Captain Conner's tent to inform him of my good news. He expressed surprise and happiness for my sudden good fortune.

Having had nothing to eat since early morning and having stood in the ranks for several hours, my appetite was keen and I gladly accepted Captain Connor's invitation to "dine" with him. My host provided the meal by dipping a tin cup into a black camp kettle and procuring one iron spoon. He then invited me to a seat on a barrel beside him and we took turns at the soup with the spoon—each also having a piece of hardtack for his separate use. Alas and alack! My dinner so eagerly expected, was soon ended, for one or two spoonfuls of the greasy stuff that came out of the camp kettle completely turned my stomach. I then excused myself, telling Captain Connor I did not mind dying on the battlefield, but would prefer not to die at the camp kettle.

I must now pack and make arrangements for my journey to Raleigh. It will be a hurried metamorphosis from private to colonel, but it must be done.

JULY 18, 1861—THURSDAY
CAMP CAROLINA, RALEIGH, NORTH CAROLINA

I arrived here last night to take command of the Twenty-Second North Carolina.

The regiment is made up of ten volunteer companies numbering nearly 1,000 men raised in the western part of the state. The men of the regiment range in age from mid-teens to late twenties. Most are farmers or the sons of farmers. Others list themselves as laborers or mechanics. A few are clerks or professional men. They are a stout, athletic set and look as if they will fight well.

I am getting to know the officers of the regiment, having Lt. Colonel John Long, a graduate of West Point, as the second in command and Thomas Galloway, Jr., a graduate of the Virginia Military Institute, serving as Major. First Lieutenant Graham Davis serves as adjutant and fifteen-year-old Walter Clark as Second Lieutenant and drill master. Doctor James Hall serves as the surgeon of the regiment and James Litchfield as Quartermaster. We are still searching for a chaplain.

Early this afternoon, Lt. Colonel Long and I went to watch the Raleigh Howitzers at inspection. The battery is at this time short of cannoneers, so several new and rather raw recruits have been drilling with the regular gun crews.

A first class battery needs cool and intelligent cannoneers who are quick to understand their duties. They must also be able to perform the duties of two or more posts at the gun, in case of casualties in battle. A slow, awkward person has no place in a gun detachment of light artillery.

A battery of artillery is like a machine. No one works individually but all in unison and with the precision of clockwork. In drilling, the men are taught to work at "reduced numbers." Each man in position is known by a number when on drill or in battle. For example, Number One rams home the cartridge. Number Two inserts the cartridge. And so on. Each number has a certain part to perform during the loading and firing of the cannon.

The newcomers to the Raleigh Howitzers had been recruited and drilled, but they still had much to learn. The only occasion upon which they equaled their fellow battery members was when they drew their pay and rations. They were, however, kept with the battery in the hope that they would soon learn their duties and become integral parts of the battery.

As the inspection began, a smart-appearing artillery officer, dressed in a new and colorful uniform, started on the round of inspection examining critically every man, cannon, carriage, horse and other equipment. At times, the inspector would stop suddenly at one of the cannon and, placing his hand on some part, would ask one of the cannoneers, "What is this?" (Every part of the gun or carriage has a name, for instance, the gun has the bore, muzzle, face of muzzle, muzzle band, swell at muzzle, neck, chase, trunnions, vent, breach, etc. The men were supposed to know all the parts of the gun and carriage and answer promptly any questions asked.)

Lt. Colonel Long and I watched intently as the inspector passed slowly along. Suddenly he stopped and, placing his hand on the face of the cannon, said, "Number Two, what is this?" Number Two, a raw recruit, looking very worried as this was his first inspection, looked at the inspecting officer and then at the gun, but did not answer.

The inspector sharply repeated the question. Number Two, now realizing that he must answer, hesitated and in a low, frightened voice replied, "The end of the gun, sir." This answer staggered the inspector, who, giving a scornful glance at Number Two, walked quickly to the rear of the gun where stood Number Four, a quick-witted, fun-loving Irishman, who was a veteran cannoneer and could easily answer any question pertaining to his duty. The inspector placed his hand on the knob of the cascable, the extreme rear end of the gun, and said, "Number Four, what is this?"

The Irishman saw a chance for eternal fame in the battery and a smile came over his face. As quick as a flash, he answered, "The other end, sir!" This answer paralyzed the inspector, who, followed by the other officers, quickly left the gun as if in fear of it, as well as themselves, exploding.

The battery commander who had started to walk away with the inspector suddenly turned on his heels and returning, dismissed the men of the battery. The men, trying not to guffaw, ran quickly to the privacy of their quarters to give vent to their pent-up laughter.

Later in the day, Lt. Colonel Long and I were not surprised when we passed by the battery camp and noticed cannoneers Number Two and Number Four, walking back and forth in the front of their tent carrying a heavy log shaped like a cannon barrel. At one end of the log was a large white sign on which was written in large letters, "the end of the gun." At the other end of the log was another large sign on which was written in large letters, "the other end of the gun."

It seems queer and almost magical to be transported in such a brief time from the post of a private in the Washington Light Infantry to the command of a regiment of almost 1,000 men. My only regret is that I had to leave Virginia on the eve of what appears to be a great battle.

It appears that the Union and Confederate armies, each 60,000 strong at least, now sleep within five miles of each other. Their pickets, it is reported, are hourly having affrays along the whole line—which is now said to be upwards of eight miles in length. I feel strangely enough the same way now as I did before the bombardment of Fort Sumter began. Apprehensive and fearful, yet strangely excited about the prospect of battle. I pray that my friends and associates in the Confederate Army will be spared should the two armies chance to join in battle.

Today's *Raleigh Banner* has little doubt about the outcome of the impending battle. It says:

> "The army of the South is composed of the best material that ever made up an army, whilst that of Lincoln is gathered from the sewers of cities—the degraded, beastly offscourings of all quarters of the world serve for pay and will run away just as soon as they can when danger threatens them."

JULY 22, 1861—MONDAY
CAMP CAROLINA, RALEIGH, NORTH CAROLINA

Sunday, July 21, was a quiet day in Raleigh with the streets practically deserted and with no sign of the newspaper bulletin boards that had attracted great crowds during the last three days. At about six o'clock, we began to hear news that a great battle had taken place at Manassas that morning, but no details were received. Later in the evening, great crowds besieged the newspaper and telegraph offices, clamoring for news about the great battle, but the details were very slow in coming in. Thankfully, late at night, under a full moon, a telegraph dispatch from Richmond was read to the crowd in front of the Yarborough House Hotel on Fayetteville Street announcing that the Confederates had gained a "glorious, though a dearly bought, victory," and that the enemy was in full flight, closely pursued by General Beauregard's forces.

The news was of course received with a delirium of joy by the crowd, but I felt as many of my fellow soldiers felt that I could not rejoice until I heard how it had fared with my friends and comrades who were in the battle.

There was still a vast crowd around the Yarborough House this morning. Their enthusiasm was mingled with grief however, when an affianced young lady whose betrothed had been in the battle with the Fourth Alabama lost control of herself and, breaking away from her escort, raced shouting to the nearby telegraph office. There her frantic and loud appeals to the telegraph operator for information about the names of the killed and wounded brought tears to the eyes of the sympathetic spectators.

We were told that it was raining heavily in Richmond this morning and that weather interference with the functioning of the telegraph would cause reports from the battlefield to come in slowly. At noon it was learned that President Davis had officially communicated the news of the victory to the War Department. About an hour later, this dispatch, addressed to Adjutant General Samuel Cooper, was posted on the newspaper bulletin boards.

At about four o'clock, a telegraphic report transmitted by Pritchhard's Southern Press made it clear that President Davis had arrived on the battlefield in time to take a prominent part in the battle. Part of the dispatch read as follows:

"When the center of the Confederate line began to yield before the mighty federal host, this order was passed along the line: 'Stand firm! President Davis is on the field and in command!' This appeal made the wavering men stand firm and contest every inch of ground against the most fearful odds. The news that the man whose bravery had been tested on the bloody fields of Mexico War is in command inspired our gallant troops with a courage such as the world has never seen and the palm of victory was the reward."

Here at camp, we had to issue strict orders against the use of rifles and revolvers, as many of the men were yelling and firing their pieces into the air as a result of our great victory at Manassas. It would be a shame if someone was killed by some half-drunken fool firing rifle or pistol in celebration of a victory he had no part in.

JULY 26, 1861—MONDAY
CAMP CAROLINA, RALEIGH, NORTH CAROLINA

This day I received a letter in the mail, from Ellison Capers in Charleston. I shall enclose the specifics of the letter below:

"Charleston, South Carolina

July 22, 1861

"Dear Johnson,

"I have enclosed a small locket containing a small portion of little Mary's hair. I know you would want to have it.

"What I must tell you now saddens and angers me and has deeply compounded the grief Charlotte and I have felt over the loss of our beloved Mary.

"As you know little Mary was buried in her favorite dress made by her Aunt Sally. Several days ago Aunt Sally visited a washer woman for the purpose of employing her to do some work. While conversing, Aunt Sally's eyes were attracted by a child's dress which hung upon a clothes line. She was startled for the dress resembled the one in which Mary was shrouded.

Aunt Sally asked permission to examine it, and her request was complied with. What was her horror to find that it was the very dress which she had put together with her own hands, and which her little favorite loved to wear. There could be no mistake about it for Aunt Sally knew her own work, and the materials were of unique pattern. Aunt Sally asked the washer woman how she came by the dress. The answer was that one day she was washing at Doctor Hoge's house, and that the Doctor's wife made her a present of it for her little girl. Aunt Sally immediately left the house and stated her suspicions to me. The result was that little Mary's coffin was opened and to my horror found empty. The discovery created such a sensation that the police were appealed to, and other coffins, buried in the church graveyard by the same undertaker, were opened and found vacant. The bodies had been removed and sold to a surgeon for dissecting purposes. The thought of little Mary's body being cut up by some cold-hearted surgeon is more than I can bear.

"The funeral director who has enjoyed the confidence of his community for some years is little better than a vampire who has been fattening upon the bodies of the dead. Were I not a Christian I would have his head. As it is, he has been jailed and is awaiting trial. What punishment can there be in this world for such an evil man?

"As I am pressed for time, I will end now. I will write more soon. Charlotte sends her love.

"Respectfully,

"Ellison.

These are difficult times we live in, but it is still hard to believe that such sacrilegious transactions could be performed in this enlightened age.

My prayers go out to Ellison and Charlotte and may they find comfort in the Lord.

JULY 29, 1861—MONDAY
CAMP CAROLINA, RALEIGH, NORTH CAROLINA

It is clear after our great victory at Manassas that the Yankees make poor opponents for our men. But in retrospect how could anyone think that the retiring consumptive Yankees could stand up in battle against the Southerner who is well-versed in the skills of riding, shooting and personal combat.

The rosy enthusiasm of the Yankees has departed and there is now little talk of the magnificence of Yankee mechanics for making war. Even many of the Northern newspapers now speak of the invincibility of the Southern soldier and his terrible propensity for battle. A recent article in the *New York Herald* illustrates how awed the Northern soldiers are by the savage ferocity with which our men use their deadly weapons:

The Washington correspondent of the *Herald* writes:

"One of the New York Fire Zouaves who was wounded at the battle of Bull Run, a stalwart, hardy fellow of unquestionable intelligence, came home to New York yesterday. He, of course, has the privilege, like all others, of telling his own tale. From him I obtained a thrilling narrative of an encounter between his regiment and a regiment of Mississippians.

"After the battle had been raging for some hours, according to the account of this Zouvian hero, he saw an immense body of Mississippians, accompanied by some (believed to be) Baltimorians rush furiously from the Confederate line. They at once saw the conspicuous uniform of the Zouaves and made at them. The Mississippians after approaching near enough sent a tremendous rifle volley into the Zouave ranks. This done, they threw their guns aside and charged onward until each contending enemy met face to face and hand to hand in terrible combat. The Mississippians, having discarded their rifles after the first fire, fell back upon their bowie knives; These were of huge dimensions, eighteen to twenty inches long, heavy in proportion, and sharp or two-edged at the point. Attached to the handle was a lasso, some eight or ten feet in length, with one end securely wound around the wrist.

"My informant says when these terrible warriors approached to within reach of their lasso, not waiting to come within reach of bayonet range, they threw forward their bowie-knives at the Zouvaes after the fashion of experienced harpooners, striking at a whale. Frequently the knives plunged in, and penetrated through a solder's body, and were jerked out ready to strike again, whilst the first victim sank in death. On several occasions the bowie knife was transfixed in a Zouave and the Zouave"s bayonet in a Mississippian, both impaled and falling together. So skillfully was this deadly instrument handled by the Mississippian that he could project it to full lasso length, kill his victim, withdraw it, again, with a sudden impulse, and catch the handle unerringly.

"If by any mischance the bowie-knife missed its aim, broke the cord fastening it to the arm or fell to the earth, revolvers were next resorted to and used with similar dexterity. The hand-to-hand closing in with both pistol and bowie-knife, cutting, slashing and shooting almost in the same moment was awful beyond description. Blood gushed from hundreds of wounds, until amid death, pitiful groans and appalling sights, it staunched the very earth. My Zouave companion says himself and his comrades died hard, fighting, stood up manfully to the murderous conflict but never knew before what undaunted bravery and courage meant. He felt no further ambition to engage in such encounters. Having been shot through the wrist by a revolver, after escaping the fearful Mississippi weapons and disabled from further active participation in the struggle, he willingly retired to reap the glory convinced that to fight against Mississippians with bowie-knives and pistols, after receiving a volley of their sharp-cracking rifles, is no ordinary fun. 'The southerners,' the Zouave concluded, 'Common as they look, are not common men; such men as these won the battle of Bull Run and could rule the world if they choose to.'"

The feeling among us after reading the article in the Herald was one of profound contempt for an enemy who were defeated under so many disadvantages.

JULY 30, 1861—TUESDAY
CAMP CAROLINA, RALEIGH, NORTH CAROLINA

I was worried we were never going to receive the rifles we had been promised. The men were grumbling about not having any weapons and having to fight the Yankees with bowie knives and swords. Today, like manna from heaven, our arms arrived and we received 200 .69-caliber smooth bore muskets. The musket can be loaded with either a single round ball or with "buck and ball" (that is, three buckshot behind a regular-sized ball). It's a formidable weapon at close range.

We also received 900 .54-caliber Mississippi rifles. It's a very dependable and accurate weapon that is prized for its deadly long-range accuracy. This rifle was used most effectively by the Fourth Alabama Regiment at Manassas when they scattered a force of advancing New York Fire Zouaves with one volley. We also received 800 barrel wipers, 800 screw drivers, 800 cartridge boxes with belts over 1,000 cap pouches, 1,000 bayonets, and 30,000 rifle and musket cartridges. I believe the regiment will now be able to adequately defend itself if the need arises.

In addition, I took care of some personal needs today. I purchased a larger wall tent for the sum of $50.00. I also squandered my money on six sets of knives and forks and four sets of spoons for myself and my staff. Peter, my servant, is busy cleaning and rearranging the culinary weapons as I write.

AUGUST 3, 1861—SATURDAY
VIA RICHMOND, VIRGINIA, BY TRAIN

The welcome telegram arrived several days ago: "Break camp and proceed by train to Richmond. Detailed orders will follow shortly." This was wonderful news and great was our rejoicing to leave Camp Carolina and start for the war.

I had hoped that the regiment could stay long enough in camp in Raleigh to get some cohesion and practice in marching together, but I wasn't about to protest our orders to move north. My problem now was to take this mob of one thousand men to Richmond.

As the moment approached for departure, the busy note of preparation was heard throughout the camp. With knapsacks well filled with two days' rations, the regiment formed ranks in marching order and, with new rifles shouldered, stood at attention, encircled by relatives and friends who had come to see them off.

I stood in front of the regiment and made a few last-minute remarks as we waited for the word to board the train. I told the men that if any feared to meet the enemy, now was the time to say so, to retire; for none were desired in the 22nd who feared to fight for their country. The time of our trial would soon come and we must show that the sons of North Carolina would fight for what they believed to be right at all costs.

When I finished, no one stirred—not a sound could be heard in the whole assembly, save occasional sobs from the family and friends present. Then, suddenly, like the sudden eruption of a volcano, a mighty yell from the men rented the air. I could only smile and think to myself what a magnificent group of men this was and how honored I was to command them.

Then the band struck up "Dixieland" and our beautiful colors were unfurled to the wind and, amid cheers and tears from young and old, male and female, we marched resolutely through Raleigh to the train station.

The train was waiting, gathering steam, the eight-wheeled locomotive polished brightly. Behind the cowcatcher, a large Confederate flag had been placed to wave boldly as the train sped along.

Departing was difficult. There were tears as men clasped their children to their bosoms for the last time and bashful sweethearts and sisters wept copiously. It made my heart bleed to hear the men talk to the dear ones they would leave behind. I realized this cruel war had frustrated plans, nipped many a love in the bud, and shattered the little worlds of these great and good people.

By railroad it was the same. The telegraph signaled our approach and the stations were crowded with all sorts of people—tables with breakfasts, dinners or supers were spread for our accommodations. As we traveled along the polished rails, the people along the way seemed to vie in rendering our journey an unbroken ovation; many would approach close to the track and rent the air with shouts. Fair ladies would toss bouquets upon us by the hundreds.

At Rocky Mount, an artillery battalion joined us and the train lengthened to fifty cars, with two engines puffing along at the rate of twenty miles an hour. Some of the men were in passenger cars, but the greater number had to put up with baggage cars, having temporary seats and in want of sufficient ventilation. Muskets were freely used in knocking out the panels to admit air.

Near Weldon, North Carolina, the steam horn of the train sent forth tremendous blasts. "Cows on the line," said Lieutenant Clark, who was sitting near me and, on looking out, we saw three of the cows had been killed, the head of one taken clean off. The demise of the cows was directly attributable to the cowcatcher in front of the engine, an immense iron beak made of open bars projecting about four feet in front of the engine, a few inches above the rails. The pointed bars are expected to impale any animal straying along the track and keep it from falling in front of the engine and throwing the train off the rails. The extraordinarily loud noise of the steam horn, if it fails to scare the cows or other beasts off the track, is sure to give notice to some laborers who come to drive the cows off the track.

Weldon is a grand junction station, the rails branching north to Richmond, south to Charleston, east to Norfolk, west to Raleigh, Clarkesville, etc. Close to Weldon flows the majestic and rapid Roanoke River, over which the railroad runs on a wooden bridge a quarter of a mile long. The Yankees, realizing the importance of the bridge, have offered, it is said, $20,000 reward for its destruction. Thus the bridge is strictly guarded at each end and in the middle where it rests on an island.

The bridge tender, a Mr. Butler, was formerly a sea captain who used to salt his vessel to make it fireproof. As he did to his boat, he also salts this wooden bridge over the Roanoke River. His plan and practice is to place salt, rock salt, generally, along the timbers in the evening. The dew of the night will dissolve it and the timbers will become impregnated with salt. When sparks from a passing locomotive chance to fall on the bridge, the salt will ooze out in moisture and smother the fire. Several times, small fires have accidentally started on the bridge, but the salt has saved it.

We reached Petersburg at two o'clock in the afternoon and are now waiting on a siding as a southbound freight train flashes past. Once through Petersburg, it is only about another twenty miles to Richmond and the end of our journey by train.

AUGUST 5, 1861—MONDAY
RICHMOND, VIRGINIA

It was a joy to leave the train and begin our march into Richmond. The city, which contains a population of about 20,000, has spacious homes and full-foliaged trees. The streets are not paved, and but few of them are provided with sidewalks other than earth or gravel.

As we marched along Broad Street, we had to halt and take to the side of the road as a brigade of artillery of 36 guns passed us. Almost all the guns were drawn by six horses. Each battery, consisting of six guns, had its battle flag—a red St. Andrew's cross in a blue ground. One I saw borne on a branch fresh cut from wood. The Second Regiment of North Carolina Cavalry also rode past, about 800 strong. Colonel Baker, the regimental commander saluted as he rode by. He was mounted on a magnificent white horse and looked like one of the old Cavaliers, with his slouched hat and feather, blue eyes, jet-black hair, and splendid moustache.

We had been directed to bivouac on the capitol grounds. The capitol, a Grecian edifice, stands alone and is finely placed on open and elevated ground in the center of Richmond. It was built soon after the Revolutionary War.

When we reached the capitol, a staff officer rode up and informed me that I was to march the regiment to a nearby tobacco warehouse where we were to spend the night.

At eight o'clock this morning, the command fell in for breakfast and, with the regimental band playing, marched to the Exchange Hotel where we were served a hearty meal. This concluded when we were ordered to march to the location selected for our camp.

We arrived at Union Hill at about noon and found a literal bald spot—not a tree or shrub was to be found on it. There, tents were furnished us and by dark, our canvas city was pitched. The men went about making supper.

The tents we have been furnished with are called Sibley Tents. When erected, they form a large cone of canvas 18 feet in diameter and 12 feet tall, supported by a center pole. The tent has a circular opening at the top for ventilation and a cone-shaped stove for heat. The tent will comfortably hold a dozen men. The men sleep in wheel-spoke fashion with their feet at the center. On cold or rainy days, with the tent flaps closed, the atmosphere inside can become intolerable. Our regimental surgeon, Doctor James Hall, told me this morning when he first heard we would be issued the tents, that to enter a Sibley on a rainy morning and encounter the night's accumulation of nauseating exhalations from the bodies of twelve unwashed soldiers who differed widely in habits of personal hygiene, was an experience for which medical college had not prepared him.

In time, I hope the Sibleys will be replaced with smaller, simpler tents, but for now, the Sibleys will have to do. Thank God the nights are warm and the tent flaps can be kept open and some of the men can sleep outside if they choose.

Early this evening, I went down to see the Yankee prisoners captured at Manassas who are confined in the tobacco factory at the foot of Main Street. There are four very large buildings there, apparently crowded with prisoners on every floor. This lot of men is as miserable, filthy and degrading as I have ever seen. They were barefooted, ragged and hungry. Bread was being distributed to them as I arrived and they seized and devoured it like hungry wolves. The wounded prisoners are still being brought in in large numbers. Their name seems to be Legion.

The Yankees tell me they had orders to hang our men as fast as they took them prisoners. One shudders to think what would have happened if they had won the battle.

Most of the Yankee prisoners say they will never be caught in another fight, but, indeed, I do not trust them—though it may be they value their lives enough to never fight such determined troops as ours again.

Some of the wounded I talked to took the fire of the Eighth Georgia Regiment. They were incredulous after the battle to learn there were only 600 men in the Eighth Georgia. They told me such heavy fire never could have come from only six hundred men. If they all magnified our numbers in that way, it is not strange that they report us as having such a tremendous force in the field. There were many surgeons taken among the Yankee prisoners. They were put to take care of their own wounded and sick, but in many instances they utterly refused to do it.

As I left the tobacco factory, I chanced to meet Captain Todd who is one of the officers in charge of the Yankee prisoners. He is a character and has won some notoriety because he is President Lincoln's brother-in-law.

A native of Kentucky, Captain Todd is a tall, good-looking man, fond of a dashing uniform and is jovial and convivial with his acquaintances. He has the reputation of treating the Yankee prisoners now under his charge with arbitrary severity. As a general thing, the people of Richmond like and admire the captain, while the prisoners hate him. I cannot tell if he looks like Mrs. Lincoln because I have never had the pleasure of seeing the lady. Captain Todd's wish is to visit his sister in the White House while General Beauregard and General Johnson dictate peace terms to President Lincoln. Although he wouldn't mind seeing his sister again, he is emphatically "down" on Abraham.

AUGUST 7, 1861—WEDNESDAY
RICHMOND, VIRGINIA

Madame Rumor is visiting the camp again. It is said that the United States Navy is making preparations to take armed Negroes south in large numbers and put them ashore at points on the Southern coast to burn, plunder and kill. I very much doubt whether the Yankees will find many Negroes willing to engage in so hazardous an enterprise, but if the Yankees should, they are mistaken if they suppose the people of the South will dread them more than the whites—no Negroes can certainly exceed Yankees in barbarity.

If this rumor proves to be true, I hope our Southern coast is in a state of preparations, for no doubt landing or expeditions of Yankee troops will occur on some distant day. A few more weeks will close the hot season and then free from the danger of yellow fever or malaria, they will think to come on us with impunity. They will be the more anxious to do so because Virginia has blocked them so effectively from her coast.

My grey horse, Charleston, was missing this morning. Lieutenant Clark looked for him the greater part of the day and finally found him in the possession of Captain Isaacson of a Louisiana regiment. It happened this way:

Captain Isaacson told his men he would gladly pay any farmer or horse trader fifty dollars for a good horse. The officers of his regiment, seeking a little fun at Captain Isaacson's expense, took my horse out of pasture and delivered it to him saying that they had bought the horse from a nearby farmer. The captain, thinking he was making a great buy, gladly paid the men fifty dollars in return. The captain, proud as a peacock, then rode Charleston around to the various camps, showing all of his friends what a wonderful horse he had and bragging considerably over how gallant he looked mounted on his new purchase.

About dark, Lt. Clark got wind of the fraud and interviewed the luckless Isaacson, informing him that his dream horse was just a mirage. The air was quickly let out of Isaacson's balloon and the gullible captain reluctantly returned Charleston to Lt. Clark.

So, as the dejected captain sat by his tent, bemoaning his fate, the officers of his regiment arrived and began to ask Isaacson about the fine points of his horse and wondered if they could borrow him while others wanted to know when he would go riding again.

Isaacson, with the vision of this dream horse evaporated like the morning mist, enjoyed the joke as much as anyone. When they tried to return his fifty dollars, he suggested they use the money for a party instead. When last seen, Isaacson was drinking from a bottle of wine, thoroughly elevated, or drunk, if you prefer, and telling two young lieutenants that it was quite easy to acquire a good horse, but rather hard to keep one.

AUGUST 12, 1861—MONDAY
RICHMOND, VIRGINIA

I drilled the regiment in a large clover field just outside the picket line this morning. The men were in fine condition, well dressed and well equipped. I kept them on the jump for two hours. I doubt if any regiment in Richmond can execute a greater variety of movements than mine or go through them in better style. My voice is excellent. I can make myself heard distinctly by the whole regiment without becoming hoarse by hours of exertion.

I have spent long hours studying General Hardee's *Rifle and Light Infantry Tactics*. This pocket-sized two volume textbook is the basic training manual for our army. Hardee's *Tactics* was for a month or more a book of impenetrable mysteries. The words conveyed new ideas to my mind and the movements described, such as a regiment marching from line of battle into a column by the right flank, were utterly beyond my comprehension, but now the whole thing comes almost without study.

Just as I was ready to march the regiment back to camp, President Davis rode up on his splendid iron-grey, almost white, horse. The men broke ranks and rushed eagerly forward to be near him.

He raised his hat in greeting and called to me, "Are your men all well, Colonel Pettigrew?"

"Only three on the sick list," I replied, "but some are indisposed today in consequence of getting wet in the drenching rain of last night."

"Do you men have India rubber overcoats and good tents?" he asked.

"We have good tents, Mr. President, but some of the men lack rubber overcoats for use when on guard duty."

"In that case, Colonel, you must present a requisition to the Department for rubber overcoats. Our men must not be unnecessarily exposed. You can call on it for anything you need for the regiment. I hope you will not leave Richmond until the comfort of your men is secured as far as it can be."

Then, after a brief exchange of pleasantries, and a salute from the regiment—which was acknowledged by President Davis with uncovered head and a graceful bow—he replaced his hat and rode away as the regimental band played "Ever of Thee I Fondly am Dreaming."

Oh how proud our hearts were as our gallant President rode away. There wasn't a man present who wouldn't have followed him to the gates of hell or Washington City if he would have commanded. He is a great man. There is nothing too trivial for his attention, and nothing escapes his notice that can promote someone's comfort. He seems to regard the people as his family, himself the patriarchal head.

The President's visit and manly bearing reminded me of a recent article in the *New Orleans Advocate* in which the editor wrote:

"President Davis is the very soul of courage, honor, chivalry; Lincoln is a cowardly sneak. In the midst of the present storm, Davis is calm, cool, generally cheerful, comprehensive in observation, rigidly keeping his own counsel. Lincoln is filled with abject fear, drunk half the time, occasionally foolishly facetious, whistling to keep his courage up!"

Now, on a more somber note, a young soldier of the regiment died Sunday at the house of Mrs. Brooks where he had been ill for over a week. He had the measles, then lung fever. He was beginning to recover we thought, when he was taken suddenly worse about midnight on Saturday. Mrs. Brooks and her daughters had given him their undivided attention all day, at night he was watched over by some of his comrades. He awoke suddenly that night, delirious, and said to his absent tentmate, "Calvin, I am going to die."

Mrs. Brooks, whose room adjoined his with an open door between the two, was awakened by it and was at his bedside in a moment.

He repeated, "I am going to die, but I am not afraid to die. Jesus is with me." They sent immediately for a physician who came and stayed with him until morning dawned, but he never rallied and gradually sunk, until evening, when he calmly breathed his last.

Throughout his illness, he had clung to Mrs. Brooks' kindly sympathies. He called her mother and if she left his presence for a brief half-hour, he would beg for her return. A short time before his demise, he said, "Comb my hair once more, Mother." I was so glad this young sufferer, so far from home, was able to receive the very best of care in a private house—instead of dying almost unnoticed in a crowded hospital.

The death of this young man has cast a pale over the regiment. He is the first one of us to cross that river from which no one returns. I rode to Mrs. Brooks' house as soon as I heard the bad news. I was shown into the bedroom where the young lad lay lifeless on the bed. He was a emaciated-looking, sandy-haired youth. A bespectacled Negro servant sat nearby with a brush to keep the flies off the boy's face.

After I returned to camp, I sent a small detail to a warehouse near the railroad station to secure a wooden coffin to bury the lad in.

AUGUST 14, 1861—WEDNESDAY
RICHMOND, VIRGINIA

We have had little sickness in this regiment and I believe that is because we have practiced good hygiene. The officers and I have kept the camp in good order by careful policing and looking carefully after the quartermaster and commissary departments.

In many of the regiments, ample and wholesome rations are served to the men, but the food in many instances to my personal knowledge so badly managed and cooked that it impairs the digestive organs and undermines the health.

The men, it seems, fry everything, usually using a greasy frying pan. When the soldiers do get vegetables, some of the more creative roast them on a stick or throw them in the fires' coals until they are done, but mostly the men fry them in pork fat along with everything else. They soak their hardtack in water until soft and fry it in fat, too, and often heap it with undone beans or burned rice, creating a sloppy, slimy mess.

The larger camp kettles used by many of the regiments are also not often cleaned properly. These big, black iron pots frequently double as laundry tubs when they are not being used for cooking. As a result, are often coated with a barely noticeable film of soap suds and dead lice, which the company cook often overlooks, or forgets to wash.

In addition, many of the men neglect to wash their dishes or simply mop them up with a piece of bread which they then pop into their mouths joking to their comrades that they are "eating the dishrag." Others pour hot coffee over their utensils and dry them with grass. The tin plates are black from use over the fires and I have often seen knives and forks jabbed carelessly into the ground a few times to remove food particles.

Many of the regimental camps are rife with garbage that is unburied and that attracts rats and insects. Few recruits bother to use the slit-trench latrines (and those who do usually forget to shovel dirt over their feces). Many just urinate just outside the tent and, after sundown, in the street. Garbage is everywhere, rats abound, and dead cats and dogs turn up in the strangest places.

The emanations of slaughtered cattle and kitchen offal, together with the stench from the seething latrines, produce a smell impossible to put into words—particularly on a hot summer day when the heat of the sun makes the stink increase.

I think my regiment is fortunate in that Dr. Hall understands the relationship between sickness and food, even if the individual soldier does not. He has been indefatiqueable in forcing the men to keep their campsites clean, wash their clothes, eat wholesome food, etc. Many of the men do not appreciate his efforts, but I do. Every man we do not lose to disease is another man we can take into battle.

AUGUST 20, 1861—TUESDAY
RICHMOND, VIRGINIA

I was pouring over the regimental sick list, when an orderly came into my tent, saluted and said, "There's a correspondent from the *Charleston Courier* here to see you, Colonel."

"Send him in, Corporal."

"Yes, sir, Colonel," replied the orderly, a strange smile coming over his face.

Presently, the tent flap opened and in stepped a tall, sharp-featured, black-eyed lady of about thirty years. She was an attractive vixen, but what made me take a second look was that she was wearing bloomers with a Rebel soldier's belt around her waist and a small, gold palmetto tree pin beneath her beautiful chin.

Puzzled about the reason for her sudden and mysterious appearance, I stood and bowed gracefully (I thought) and said, "I must have misunderstood the orderly. I thought he said there was a correspondent from the *Charleston Courier* here to see me?"

"I am that correspondent, Colonel."

"But you are a woman!"

"It is estimated that about half the population are, Colonel."

"And you are wearing bloomers," I stammered.

"If you had to wear a voluminous skirt and bear the weight of many flannel and taffeta petticoats, you'd wear bloomers too, Colonel Pettigrew."

"And what would you think if I did wear bloomers, Madam."

"I'd think that you would have to endure what I endure. That no matter how modestly you go about your business, base rowdies congregated around street corners, hotel steps and beer saloons will look at you, make coarse and smart remarks, and stare and laugh. Yet I consider bloomers more sensible for the work I am engaged in than the traipsing skirts and multiple petticoats most women wear."

"Very well then, Madam, let's talk about the work you are engaged in."

"Thank you, Colonel. I am presently the Virginia correspondent for the *Courier*. I arrived in Richmond yesterday to begin my duties. You may, Colonel, perhaps think a woman is not competent to grasp the issues now presented to our people. I dispute this. I think a woman proves many times a more attractive correspondent than a man. Her perceptions are keener. She picks up items of interest almost intuitively and can often times glean stories or facts from a mass where a man would detect nothing. Here in Virginia, I plan to remain in as close proximity to the camp and battlefield as is consistent with my dignity as a woman, seeking shelter in farmhouse or village as the case may be. Should there be wounded to nurse, my mission will be among them."

"But why have you come to see me, Madam?"

"I pray you to remember, Colonel, that the *Courier* is a daily newspaper, or meant to be, and not a historical record of past events. Newspaper stories to be of any value should be prompt, fresh, and full of facts. I realize how difficult it will be under the censorship to write, but there must be facts enough of general interest for me to write a daily column. Many in Charleston remember you fondly and appreciate the services you rendered during the Fort Sumter crisis. Many are disappointed you do not command a South Carolina regiment or brigade. They wish to know about you. What you are doing. Etc."

"You wish to interview me then and write a story from it?"

"Yes, Colonel. If you will give your permission. Incidentally, were you at the Bull Run battle?"

"No, I left for North Carolina to take command of this regiment shortly before the battle."

"Then you would not know if it is true or rumored that the Louisiana Zouaves had cut off the heads of wounded Union soldiers and kicked them around as footballs?"

"I would doubt the veracity of that rumor. It sounds like something another correspondent would make up."

"I thought so," she replied.

As she turned to go, I stepped to her side and said, "There are many officers in this army, Madam, who think special force of character and intellect are dangerous things in a woman. They have created a stereotypical female who they think too delicate for any physical effort beyond a languid game of croquet and too refined to discuss—let alone engage in—politics or other issues of the day. You will have large odds to overcome if you are to be successful in your mission. I can only wish you well."

Looking intently at me, she said, "You have never married, have you, Colonel."

"No," I answered, blushing somewhat under her steady gaze. "I have concluded that a bachelor's life is not so bad after all. You know the old song, 'No Wife to Scold or Children to Bawl.' Happy is the man that can go to bed with his boots on if he chooses, get up when he pleases, take his toddy when he wishes, eat when it suits him, smoke his pipe if he feels so, and lean back and put his foot on the table if he desires. Now this is liberty in the broad sense."

"That's unfortunate, Colonel, your good looks are only exceeded by your gallantry. You would make some woman a good husband. I hope you soon receive your promotion to Brigadier General. God bless you. I shall call again."

AUGUST 30, 1861—FRIDAY
RICHMOND, VIRGINIA

I thought I would forego my usual after-dinner cigar tonight in favor of a cup of hot tea and a smoke on my new pipe. I filled the bowl with some newly purchased fragrant "Killokaleeka" tobacco. This is the mildest and finest-flavored tobacco of Virginia and is sold in solid lumps of about two pounds.

Several nights ago, while perusing one of the Richmond papers, I came upon the following advertisement:

THE RICHMOND THEATRE
PRESENTS
THE CELEBRATED ETHIOPIAN SERENADERS
AS
THE ETHIOPIANS OF THE SOUTHERN STATES.

PART I

AIR   JOHNY BOWKER...By the Band

SONG   N TUCKER, a Virginia refrain in which is Full Chorus described the ups and downs of Negro life...by the Minstrels

SONG   OLD TAR RIVER, or the incidents of attending a coon hunt...Full Chorus

A NEGRO LECTURE ON LOCOMOTIVES, in which he describes his visit to the wild animals, his scrap with his sweetheart, and shows the white folk how the niggers raise steam...by Billy White

PART II

SONG   DE COLORED FANCY BALL, Napoleon Sinclair Brown, Dandy Broadway and other aristocratic niggers preen and dance on their way to De Colored Fancy Ball...Full Chorus

SONG   LUCY LONG, a very fashionable song which has never failed to be received with unbounded applause...Full Chorus

SONG   UNCLE GABRIEL, or a chapter on the trials of life...Full Chorus

PART III
THE SURPRISE PARTY....
Billy White, Dan Fiels, George Abingdon and Ralph Connor
PLANTATION JIG...
W. Norton WHO STRUCK BILLY PATTERSON?....
Introducing the whole troupe in their festival dance
Doors open at half-past six, to commence at seven o'clock
ADMISSION—Twenty-Five Cents

Thinking it would be interesting and enjoyable to attend the performance at the Richmond Theatre, Doctor Hall and I rode into Richmond late in the afternoon. As we entered the city, we had to wait at the first intersection as two horsecars with all seats full, standees clinging to overhead straps, and others holding to the steps outside rolled past.

We rode up a thoroughfare passing four immense wagons drawn by six mules each, the teamster riding on the back of the near-wheeler. The wagons were loaded with tobacco, flour and a great variety of raw country produce.

Near the post office, we came upon a comfortably dressed white man leading three Negroes by a rope, the first a young man, the second a girl of perhaps twenty, and the last a middle-aged man. The arms of all three were secured before them with handcuffs, and a heavy rope by which they were led passed from one to another, being made fast at each pair of handcuffs. They were thinly clad, the girl especially so, having only an old red ragged handkerchief twisted around her neck over a common calico dress and another handkerchief twisted around her head. They were dripping with sweat as they were being pulled along at a brisk pace.

Doctor Hall and I stopped to let them pass, the young girl looking very sad and the middle-aged man quite doleful. "Came in a canal boat," shouted the white overseer as he trotted by, "sent here to be sold. The young lady's a likely gal, she'll bring a high price." Struck by the looks of resignation on the faces of the slaves, I wondered out loud, "I wonder what they think, or do they think at all of their condition?"

After they passed, Doctor Hall turned toward me and said, "What does it matter what they think! It's a hallucination to suppose that we are ever going to get rid of slavery or that it will ever be desirable to do so. It is a thing that we cannot do without. It is righteous, profitable and permanent. Southern men should act as if the gates of Heaven were inscribed with a covenant, in letters of fire, that the Negro is here, and here forever—is our property, and ours forever—is never to be emancipated—is to be kept hard at work and in rigid subjection all his days."

"They are interesting creatures," I replied, "and with all their faults have many beautiful traits. I can't help being attracted to them, and if we can treat them well and not use ropes and handcuffs and other means of terror, I am sure they would come to love us."

Riding on, we arrived at the Richmond Theatre at about seven o'clock. Through the courtesy of the manager (a friend of Doctor Hall's) we, in company with several members of the press, were shown through a private entrance to the box, thus saving ourselves the necessity of elbowing through the crowd.

We had purchased tickets for the more expensive box seats as they offered a bit of privacy and decorum. Sitting below us, in front of the stage, was the pit where the working classes sat. Looking down, we could see a diverse section of humanity, with men spitting tobacco juice on the floor, cracking peanuts and drinking what looked suspiciously like liquor. They milled about like a herd of buffaloes, stomping their feet, laughing and hollering back and forth to each other.

At exactly a quarter past seven, a full head of gas was turned on, brilliantly illuminating the interior of the theater. Across the way, seated in the boxes, I could make out a bevy of handsome and bright faces. Behind us, a captain of the cavalry walked by with his immense circular-saw spurs jingling like so many sleigh bells. With him, walking arm-in-arm, was a lovely young lady with that beautiful rose tinge upon her cheeks and lips which nature alone gives. They made a gallant-looking couple.

At half-past seven, the curtain went up to a burst of applause from the audience. Now, imagine the scene before Doctor Hall and me as the applause subsides and the Negro extravaganza featuring entertainment by white performers who blacken their faces with burnt cork is about to begin.

One the stage sit four black-faced performers with a middleman or interlocutor in the center and two endmen, known respectively as "Tambo" and "Bones" because one plays the tambourine and the other the bone castanets.

The minstrel performers wear exaggeratedly sharp-cut, wildly colored tailcoats with great burlesque shirt collars framing the blacked-up faces set off by the smeary red travesty of the Negro's everted lips.

The program was steered by the interlocutor who, dressed like a yokel's idea of an elegant Southern gentleman, served as the master of ceremonies. Dialogue seemed to be the principle concern of a character named Mr. Bones seated at one end of the chairs across the stage and of another named Mr. Tambourine at the other.

The interlocutor's "Good evening, Mr. Bones," had the whole audience on the edges of their seats, for they knew this simple greeting was to be the start of an evening of fun and laughter.

Soon the interlocutor gave way to the irrepressible endmen and to the delight of the audience, Mr. Bones and Mr. Tambourine were engaged in a lively crossfire.

"How is you tonight, Mr. Bones?'

"Jus' fine. How's you feelin' Mr. Tambourine? Ho's yo' symptoms seem to segashuate dis ebenin'?"

"Well, Mr. Bones, to tell da truth, I feel jus' like a stovepipe."

"How's dat, Mr. Tambourine?"

"A little sooty!"

At this delicious answer by the grinning Mr. Tambourine, the audience howled. Doctor Hall, who had been pulling on a bit of Brooks Haily's peach brandy, nearly fell out of his seat with laughter.

Doctor hall and I delighted in the jokes, songs and dances of the minstrels, but to me the finale was the high point of the performance. As the curtain rose for the closing scene, we witnessed the entire troupe on stage in darky costumes. Then there were a number of individual songs and dances, which concluded with a rousing rendition of "Dixie." Oh how the rafters of the old Brooks Theatre must have rattled as the audience rose to its feet amid cheers and thunderous applause and joined in singing "Dixie." I found the sound deafening and Doctor Hall became so excited he began to pound me on the back in exuberance as he sang at the top of his lungs.

There was not a dry eye in the theatre as the curtain rang down on what I felt was a memorable and highly entertaining evening. Doctor Hall was hoarse from singing while bemoaning the fact that his bottle of peach brandy was empty. As we left the theatre, the good doctor shuffled along, now and then attempting a darky dance step while singing a slightly inebriated version of "Dixie."

SEPTEMBER 6, 1861—FRIDAY
NEAR DUMFRIES, VIRGINIA

For some time, it had become evident that the regiment would soon be moved to an area along the Potomac River. On September 2, I received orders to move to Evansport on the Potomac and there assist engineer officers in constructing batteries.

Although I am not overjoyed with this move, because it takes us away from Manassas and the field of active operations, there are excellent strategic reasons for the move. Union forces have been moving lately in a threatening manner in the direction of the Occoquan River, some twenty-five miles below Washington. There is also reason to suspect that a Yankee force might land in the vicinity of Dumfries and thus flank our position at Manassas. To intercept such a movement, it is necessary for us to take up positions somewhere in the vicinity of Dumfries, near the Occoquan River.

In addition to the 22nd North Carolina, I now have under my command an artillery company, five unattached infantry companies, and two troops of cavalry. The artillery company is a splendid one made up of young Marylanders devoted to the cause, who yearn to avenge the Yankee occupation of their state.

Despite the surveillance of the federal pickets who line the shores of the Potomac River and the care taken by the Federalists to prevent communications with us, numbers of adventurous young men escape from thralldom every week, bringing frequently arms and equipment. I imagine there are not less than from three thousand to thirty-five hundred men from Maryland now in the Confederate service. It is by no means improbable that to them will be assigned the honor of leading our Southern troops onto their soil. Nothing would be more *apropos*, and nothing more conductive to our success, in the event of a movement to the opposite shore, than to give them front place in the picture.

Speaking of the constant influx of Marylanders, I am reminded of a Baltimorean, Mr. John Hill, now an officer in Hampton's Legion who, a few weeks ago, swam his horse across the Potomac at a point where it was two miles in width without the slightest injury to either man or beast. Subsequently on the strength of his previous experience, he swam another horse across in the same manner, a distance of a mile and a half. The next day, he rode him sixty miles. As hard to believe as these statements are, I have introduced them to show the extent to which men have gone to reach Virginia and join our noble cause despite the numerous difficulties they must overcome.

SEPTEMBER 7, 1861—SATURDAY
NEAR DUMFRIES, VIRGINIA

We have established our camp near Dumfries, an old Virginia river port which was founded in the early eighteenth century. The main road, or telegraph road, between Washington and Richmond passes through the center of the town, giving an atmosphere of importance to the vicinity. There are some elegant buildings, a tavern or two, but only about twenty residences remain to mark the site of a flourishing city of 10,000 inhabitants two generations ago. Whatever the glory of Dumfries may have once been, it is now largely faded.

The Evansport batteries we are presently constructing lie about three and a half miles below Dumfries. We are doing almost all of the work at night to conceal our activities from the Yankees. Once the batteries are finished, they should effectively block the Potomac River and prevent passage of federal ships upstream to Washington.

This is important work we are doing, and I have issued orders appointing a provost marshal and provost guards to maintain order in Dumfries and the immediate vicinity. The provost marshal has orders to imprison all officers and privates he finds in his premises without a written pass. I have also made special provisions regarding the sale of spirituous liquor. Lastly, the articles of war dealing with conduct of troops are to be published at each regimental dress parade and strictly enforced.

Yesterday was a fine day, clear and rather cool with gentle winds. I rode almost all day from 9:00 a.m. until sundown visiting all the various detachments of my command, and finished up by following the river pickets for miles. My command has been picketing the river bank for several miles, from the mouth of the Occoquan to Evansport. About 200 men are put on each afternoon carrying 24 hours' rations and returning the following evening after being relieved.

It is a hard duty, as the poor men are not allowed fires and the weather has been rather inclement. Still, they go out with wonderful cheerfulness. There is a strange excitement at the prospect in shooting Federals across the river. We have had, however, very little picket firing and do not encourage it. The Yankees appear on the opposite bank, but so long as they remain quiet, we do not trouble them.

We have also established a signal system and every night, lights can be seen gleaming all along the shore from Fort Washington to below Evansport. If a United States steamer leaves the navy yard on a cruise down the river, these lights are displayed in a particular manner as soon as she passes Fort Washington and the signal thus made is taken up and repeated all along the line and answered by corresponding signals from our side (the Virginia side) of the river. If the steamer stops, fires a gun, or turns back, this movement is indicated by signal lights of a different color. This signal is repeated in the same manner. Because of this efficient signaling system and the placement of our batteries, we have been successful in blockading the Potomac River and preventing the landing of any federal expedition having Richmond in view.

A few days ago, the butchers belonging to the regiment, while hunting cattle through the woods, found the skeleton of a man sitting upright against a tree. They said he had on very fine clothing, splendid boots, a handsome revolver, and a valuable watch. He was a Yankee who was probably a scout or spy and was wounded by a picket and then strayed away to hide. He then died alone in anguish. It will probably be many a year before all are found who have died under similar circumstances.

Lately I have been receiving letters about as often as it rains in the Sahara. I have no doubt, Madrid, my horse in Charleston, would write if he could, but others more literate seem to have run out of ink. Therefore, imagine my delightful surprise this morning when I received letters from Ellison Capers and my father, Ebenezer.

The envelopes were adorned with the new five cent postage stamp which has been adopted by the Confederate states. The stamp features an engraving of the head of President Davis with the words, "Confederate States of America, Five Cents." The new stamp is something we have needed and all have wondered at the tardiness of the issue, but with so many problems of grave import to attend to, it is not strange that the government has been delayed in the issue of the stamp.

SEPTEMBER 14, 1861—SATURDAY
NEAR DUMFRIES, VIRGINIA

The news from North Carolina startled me as much as any important event since the fall of Fort Sumter. There was a vague undefinable feeling of uneasiness at the words heading the bulletin, "North Carolina invaded—Fort Hatteras Captured."

I assume the Battle of Fort Hatteras will be duly magnified by the Northern newspapers. I fancy I see the big heading to the news in the *New York Herald*, "Brilliant Victory", "Bombardment of Fort Hatteras", "Surrender of the Fort After a Terrific Combat", and, perhaps, "Onto Raleigh."

My father, Ebenezer, in his latest letter, which I received several days ago, wrote in an almost hysterical tone that he was worried that General Butler has taken possession of Fort Hatteras with the design of making it the nucleus for an invasion of North and South Carolina, as soon as troops and war material can be collected.

I suspect the Yankee attack on North Carolina is just a diversion. By harassing the seacoast with sudden attacks, short incursion into the interior, the burning of villages and stealing of Negroes, a large portion of southern troops will be forced to remain home instead of aiding the Confederate government in its designs upon Washington. If Butler can successfully alarm us for a month and draw off a few regiments from Virginia, his object will have been accomplished. He will withdraw upon the approach of Confederate troops and suddenly pounce down upon another part of the coast—probably South Carolina. We must not fall for his diversions. The war, I feel, will be won or lost here in Virginia.

SEPTEMBER 15, 1861—SUNDAY
NEAR DUMFRIES, VIRGINIA

It has been a short walk of about a half an hour, with my notebook and pencils, from the canvas village of the 22nd North Carolina to the forest banks of the Potomac River and here I have seated myself down under the shade of a wild persimmon to write part of this journal entry.

It is a sunny and warm day, with birds singing and the wind rustling gently through the trees above me. Behind me rises an abrupt ascent, whose bushy surface would be impenetrable but for the many paths which lead from shore to summit. Immediately in front, stretching away on either side until lost in the circuitous winding of the river, is a broad white beach which echoes to the music of the rippling water.

Across the river, the distance to the Maryland shore is three-and-a-half miles. Transports loaded with provisions are floating upwards toward Washington City. I count no less than thirty, looking some of them like white-winged swans so far away are they on the edge of the horizon. As I look through my field glasses, I can see ships of the Federal fleet. Across the river are five ugly-looking steamers, black and defiant, squatted low upon the water in the shadow of the opposite woods.

What the purpose of these gunboats is I cannot guess. They may attempt to land forces of a few thousand to secure a position on the Virginia side of the river. If they try this mad scheme, it will be bloody work. Therefore, we must watch and be always vigilant.

Having seen enough, I headed slowly back toward camp. I walk out of the thick woods and gaze upon the tents of the regiment. Before me lies a broad field where Providence has created three hills as if He intended them to correspond with the three departments I command—infantry, cavalry and artillery.

In the rear of each hill is a row of trees. That behind the cavalry being a pine thicket, which makes a very respectable natural barn for the stabling of their horses. In front of the pines stand the horses, tethered together, dripping, steaming, chewing their hay. Some of the men are cleaning sabres, wicked-looking things, some brushing boots, some laying off, reading, writing—some cooking, some sleeping. On long, temporary cross sticks back of the tents are cavalry accoutrements—blankets and overcoats hung out to air. Near a pyramid of stacked muskets stands a group of horses continually stamping and whisking their tails to keep off the flies. The smell of the horses and their droppings is a strong one, and I move to a more favorable location;

Walking away from the cavalry outpost, I approach the small strip of woods containing the camp kitchen, where the men find almost everything necessary for their culinary purposes. In front of the camp runs a broad, clear stream which serves at once as a magnificent bathing tub, a watering trough for horses and a reservoir for fish.

Not too far from the stream on a small knoll are located the tents of most of the regimental officers. As I walk towards my tent, I pass that of Major Galloway.

The major is a highly efficient officer who graduated from the Virginia Military Institute. After graduation, he became an instructor in ancient and modern languages at the Albemarle Female Institute in Charlottesville, Virginia. In 1859, he went west to Little Rock, Arkansas, to take control of St. Johns College, an institution under the special care of the Masonic order. Although a good deal under the average size, the major has a commanding presence. He is a fine-looking man with a wealth of rich auburn hair, almost verging into red. Over his lips he wears a thin moustache. He is fond of sports and exercises and is an excellent horseman. He is widely read, especially in languages, mathematics and metaphysics. Just before the war started, he was preparing for publication a grammar of the Latin language. Although Major

Galloway does not have many intimate friends, he is loved by those who know him well.

I walk up and glance into the major's empty tent. The floor is of straw, the bed a cot, the washstand is the body of a tree with a board nailed across the top, the dining table is a camp chest; there is one chair. A camp table with a pair of folding legs is in one corner and just now upholds a field glass, one or two military works, a writing case and a flask. The latter is an indispensable "article of war," and go where you may, you will find them as plentiful as prayer books on the family table at home. From end to end of the tent is a strong line, which acts in the capacity of a wardrobe, sustaining everything from a clean shirt to a soiled napkin. A peg or two on the posts supports sword and pistols, dress coat and pants, while the trunk that stands in the corner contains the remainder of Galloway's clothes. I smile when I see Galloway's pet, which is a Yankee chicken named McClellan, that morning, noon and night is as much an occupant of the tent as the master himself. When the major is present, ten chances to one that she is either on his table or roosting on his shoulder. McClellan is a rather lazy chicken that neither lays nor crows, the height of her ambition is to do her setting on the headboard of the major's bed, whether she retires with as much regularity and punctuality as he does himself.

Lately, McClellan has developed illusions of grandeur. She has come to believe that she is the imperial monarch of Galloway's tent. She put Doctor Hall to flight one day with several well-aimed pecks on his shins. This unprovoked attack so incensed the doctor that he thought of riding to Dumfries and purchasing a Confederate chicken to do battle with the supercilious, feathered Yankee pecking machine.

Lieutenant Clark suggested instead a nocturnal raid on Galloway's tent with a clandestine snatch of McClellan and an untimely death for the unrepentant Yankee in a large boiling pot. "That will end this irrepressible conflict to the joy of all," smiled Clark, licking his lips in anticipation.

"No, I command this regiment," I answered, "and as much as I abhor civil strife, we will leave the belligerent Yankee alone. We must remember that God favors those who wait. Major Galloway has said that the fowl's bones are not to be picked this side of Washington City. Then, in the just triumph of our noble cause, McClellan, like her Yankee counterparts, will have to pay for her crimes."

Moving from the major's tent, I came across Doctor Hall sitting on a box of cayenne pepper, making a medicinal preparation. Doctor Hall graduated from Princeton college in New Jersey and then attended the Medical School in Philadelphia where he received his medical degree in 1844. In 1856, he was tendered the appointment of surgeon on board the clipper ship, Ocean Foam, destined to ply the waters between the East Indies and New York. After twenty-four months at sea, he went to work for the Manassas Gap Railroad until the beginning of the war. The doctor is a man of striking and splendid physique, fine athletic proportions and great muscular strength. Yet, he is devoted to music and flowers. No warbling bird can raise its morning song or evening carol near his tent that he does not pause to drink in the melody; I have often seen him stoop to study the lowest flower that has lifted its dewy head in his pathway. The doctor has a sunny heart, which makes him the delight of our evening campfire circle.

The doctor is laboring over a long board, six inches from the ground and covered with everything in the range of healing art from "syrup simplex" to strychnine. His tools are a broken graduating glass, a spatula with no handle, a corkscrew, a table fork, and a few bits of brown wrapping paper. A dozen men are standing around him with prescriptions, each waiting to be served in turn. As bottles are a scarcity in camp, the doctor makes them bring their own.

Doctor Hall sits quietly and passes out his medicines to the waiting men. One has a prescription for a couple of ounces of turpentine, with a little sugar; another needs colchicine for his rheumatism; another belladonna for a stimulating action to his central nervous system; and others just a small glass of whiskey for whatever ails them.

The sick in camp receive all of the attention that the good office of Doctor Hall can supply. It is often pitiful to see the poor, helpless fellows—gentlemen who have been accustomed to every delicacy—stretched out on their cots, feeding perhaps out of a tin cup and pewter spoon, yet making the best of circumstances without murmur.

Luckily, most men of the regiment find the rough and open life of campaigning an exhilarating experience. The exposure to the open air and constant exercise has actually improved the health of many of the men. Hopefully that trend will continue even as the weather turns colder.

Finding Doctor Hall busy with his medicines and patients, I walk toward my tent, passing quickly by the tent of Lieutenant Colonel Long. The lieutenant colonel is one of the more corpulent officers of the regiment. He is haughty, humorless and always immaculately uniformed. He takes great pride in his appearance and does not walk through camp, but struts. "He is so proud," remarked Doctor Hall, "that he would make a peacock look humble."

When I assumed command of the regiment in Raleigh, Long was already a very unpopular officer. If he had remained much longer in command, the regiment would have been lost beyond redemption. The men were at a point where almost anything would have caused a mutiny. Long tried to implant into the men a few of his military school notions, but did not know how or would not alleviate the severity of his discipline by a kind word or act. In a democratic army, legitimate discipline must be carefully distinguished form arbitrary actions or brutal punishment. The more I see of Lieutenant Colonel Long, the more I am disgusted with the idea that to know how to drill men or to know right face from left entitles a man to a high position or command.

Nearing my tent, I receive the salute of the sentinel, Private Neal. As I return the salute and enter my tent, I laugh to myself, for Private Neal was not always so efficient. Just last week when General Samuel Gibbs French visited the camp and my headquarters, Neal failed to salute him. Later, after General French had left, I upbraided the private and asked why he had failed to salute. Neal, a tall youth from western North Carolina, coolly replied, "Why, Colonel Pettigrew, that general was never introduced to me."

Of all people in the world, however, who deserve sympathy, give me the sentinel, especially when he has the night watch. Solitary, with no companion but the stars, no solace but his thoughts, armed with only a musket, shivering in the cold, even under his blanket, imagine the condition of such a man. How slowly the hours drag themselves, how tedious the constant pacing through the dark, how frightening the night when alone and every shadow looks ominous, every sound is magnified. What a fund of patience and courage the soldier must have to endure all this and then sit down to a dish of fat bacon and corn bread for breakfast. But such is the experience of thousands these days.

SEPTEMBER 20, 1861—FRIDAY
NEAR DUMFRIES, VIRGINIA

Captain Andrew Worth of Company One narrowly escaped death during the thunderstorm yesterday afternoon. He was standing by the pole at the entrance of his tent, supporting it against a heavy gust of wind while his servant was standing at the opposite end doing the same thing. The bolt struck the head of the pole in the hands of Captain Worth, passed down across his breast leaving a bright red streak and entering the body of the Negro, killing him instantly. Another servant in the tent was also stunned, but has since recovered.

Sitting in my tent this evening, I was rather surprised when Lt. Clark handed me a letter from Lt. Colonel Long. It was late and I was tired, but feeling the letter might be important, I opened it and found that he had written a long letter about drills, parades, etc. It seems the Lt. Colonel feels the regiment should spend more time learning the manual of arms and parade ground drill. "A well-drilled regiment is an efficient one," he writes. I am now sure he is an ass and he begins to greatly annoy me.

Often after supper, many of us sit around the campfire smoking our pipes or cigars, telling stories, tales, etc. It is usually a pleasant time unless the pompous Lt. Colonel Long joins the group. Then it is hardly necessary to remark that he does most of the talking.

Last night, Dr. Hall and Major Galloway entered into a conspiracy against the talkative Long. They proposed for one night to do all the talking themselves and not allow Long to edge in even a word. After supper, Dr. Hall was to commence with stories of his duty on the Clipper ship and without allowing himself to be interrupted, continue until he had given a complete narrative of his sea-going adventures. Then Major Galloway was to strike in talking about the Virginia Military Institute and the Albemale Female Institute and finish up the night. Lt. Colonel Long was not to be permitted to open his mouth except to yawn.

After supper, they adjourned to the campfire and took their respective places, lighting their cigars and anxious to spring their clever plan. Before Dr. Hall was fairly seated on his camp stool, he began to earnestly discuss the exulting life of a ship's doctor. He dwelt eloquently on the most interesting details of medicine and thrills of the sea. Galloway was not only an attentive listener, but seemed wonderfully interested. Dr. Hall proceeded with his tale, telling of the wonders of the Pacific and the East Indies until, unfortunately for the scheme, he made a reference about receiving a letter from his mother. Just then, Long, gesticulating eagerly, and with his forefinger levied at the speaker, cried, "Just a word, just a word right there. Let me tell you about my mother." So persistent was Long that Dr. Hall was required to yield. Thus Lt. Colonel Long got in his word and held the floor the rest of the evening, discussing not only his mother, but also his father, aunt, uncle, nephew, niece, and all other relatives back to the dawn of time and Adam and Eve.

At midnight, when Dr. Hall and Galloway left, he was still talking, this time to the unfortunate Lt. Clark who had happened to wander by.

Dr. Hall and Galloway could only shake their heads and bemoan their fate as they prepared for bed. They had been hoisted by their own petard.

SEPTEMBER 23, 1861—MONDAY
CAMP NEAR DUMFRIES, VIRGINIA

The latest antics of the overbearing Lt. Col. Long border on the ludicrous.

This Sunday past, the Lieutenant Colonel, Dr. Hall and several of the company officers decided to ride South of Evansport to visit the establishment of a man named O'Niel, who sells whiskey and other products which contain heavy doses of brandy and rum.

Arriving at their destination, the party found a canvas-covered log store built on two levels of ground with plank stairs running to the higher level where the bar room was located. Once inside, Lt. Col. Long began the fun by proposing a toast to "the 22nd North Carolina, the best-drilled regiment in the Confederacy." The next toast was proposed by Lt. Evans Turner, "To Lt. Colonel Long whose dedication to the principles of West Point have made the 22nd a great regiment!" No one, it seems, drank with more gusto to this toast than Lt. Col. Long. So it went, the party having a high time and consuming whiskey in rivers.

Dr. Hall had begged off drinking after the first toast, when he found he couldn't in good conscience and loyalty to me drink to the second. He then sat back to observe the merriment taking place around him. He was not long in perceiving that the lieutenant colonel was drinking heavily and keeping it up at a rapid pace. He soon became stupid in speech and staggering in gait. This was the first time Lt. Col. Long had shown signs of intoxication in Hall's presence, and the doctor was greatly alarmed by his condition which was fast becoming worse.

Dr. Hall's attention was soon distracted by conversation with a fellow officer and he lost sight of Lt. Col. Long amid the general hum of conversation and laughter. Sometime later, curious to see how Long was doing, Dr. Hall pushed in among a crowd of officers, of all ranks, and found himself standing in front of a table covered with bottled whiskey and baskets of champagne.

Sitting in a chair holding a glass of whiskey, the obviously inebriated Lt. Colonel offered Dr. Hall a drink. The doctor, who had concluded his drinking for the evening, declined the treat.

"What!" said Long, "why so, why so?"

"Because," the doctor replied, "I have found that when I haven't much to do, if I accept a drink the desire for the repetition keeps growing upon me. I try to limit my indulgence to only special occasions."

"That's it, is it?" Long said. "Do you know what I do when I feel that desire?"

"No," said Hall. "I can't conceive what you do."

"Ah," said Long, holding up his whiskey glass close to his mouth. "I always take a little more."

And with that he drained the glass to the bottom, smiled and began to pour another drink.

Dr. Hall after much argument finally managed to convince Long it was time to leave and that it would be some time after dark before they could return to camp. Long was not pleased with Dr. Hall's interruption of the festivities.

Over the protests of Lt. Turner and the other junior officers who were enjoying the bounty of O'Niel's bar, Dr. Hall managed to lead Lt. Col. Long outside to the waiting horses.

Lt. Col. Long had taken on this trip, for his own use, a horse belonging to Colonel Bellard of the Maryland Artillery Battalion. This spirited animal was called "Kangaroo" from his habit of rearing on his hind feet and making a plunging quick start whenever mounted.

Dr. Hall succeeded, with much effort, in assisting the unsteady Long atop Kangaroo. On this occasion, Long gave him the spur the moment he was in the saddle and Kangaroo flashed away at full speed before Dr. Hall was ready to follow. The road back to camp was crooked and tortuous, following the firmest ground along the river and was bridged over in several places.

Each bridge had several sentinels stationed at it, but the inebriated Long paid little or no attention to bridges or sentries. He rode at full speed, swaying in the saddle, through the bridges, past astonished sentinels, literally tearing through everything in his way. The night air was full of dirt, dust, ashes and embers from campfires, and shouts and curses from those he rode down in his mad race.

Through the mercy of Providence, horse and rider escaped impalement from bayonets and equally fortunate, were not fired upon by the bridge guards. Dr. Hall rode after him as fast as he could go, but his horse was no match for the speedy Kangaroo.

A short distance from camp, Dr. Hall finally caught up with Long who by this time was riding at a slow walk. The doctor seized Kangaroo's bridle rein and managed to steady the weaving lieutenant colonel in the saddle.

The pair reached camp about midnight and found Major Galloway and the officers of the guard waiting at the entrance to the headquarters area. Helping Lt. Col. Long off Kangaroo, they approached the major and waiting guards. Long shrugged his shoulders, pulled down his vest, shook himself together as one just rising from a nap. Seeing Galloway and the guard, he bid them good night in a natural tone and manner. He then started to his tent as steadily as he ever walked in his life. Dr. Hall's surprise could only turn to astonishment as he watched the metamorphosis taking place before his eyes.

Of course, the talk of the camp today is the drinking bout of Lt. Col. Long and his wild ride in returning to camp. The lieutenant colonel has not yet said a word to anyone about the incident, but looks rather pale and nauseated.

Now, as complaints from bridge sentinels and officers of the guard pour in regarding Lt. Col. Long's "big bender," I know that I must call him into my tent for censure. This will only widen the gap between us. I know he feels our roles should be reversed and that a graduate of West Point and veteran of the Mexican War should not have to take orders from an upstart former colonel of a South Carolina militia regiment. Yet I am the elected Colonel of the 22nd North Carolina Regiment and must do my duty as I see it, regardless of the enmity I occur from Long. Public drunkenness in the officer corps is highly dangerous to morale and order and Long must take the consequences of his actions. There is a rumor afloat that several of his supporters in the regiment are trying to get him to the colonelcy of a new regiment that is forming in North Carolina. I can only hope this is true, because I feel that his departure will not hurt the morale or be a loss to this regiment.

SEPTEMBER 26, 1861—THURSDAY
CAMP NEAR DUMFRIES, VIRGINIA

Yesterday morning, Major Stephen D. Lee was ordered to unmask his battery at Firestone Point by gradually cutting away a small copse of wood which stood between it and the river. At about ten o'clock, a small Federal gunboat discovered the battery's position and ran close to the Virginia shore to reconnoiter. After firing several shots, to which Lee's battery did not reply, the gunboat made off up the river.

Major Lee reasoned the gunboat would soon be back—probably with reinforcements. Accordingly, he sent me a message asking for infantry support should the gunboats return and attempt to land infantry to attack his position.

Within half an hour of receiving the message, I had started on the way with the regiment, each man carrying only his rifle, cartridges, a loaf of hard bread, a blanket and a canteen. We marched the three miles to the battery in record time, the last mile or so on the double-quick. Soon the regiment was posted behind adequate cover, protecting the flanks of Lee's battery.

Major Lee, having one battery already in place, had sent an orderly for his reserve battery. Looking anxiously up river through his field glass, Lee wondered out loud if Captain Hart and the reserve battery would arrive before the expected Federal gunboats. Soon, however, the reserve came into sight, the drivers slinging their strong whips, the teams at a brisk trot, with gun carriages rumbling, harnesses rattling, and the iron hooves of the horses striking sparks on the flinty road.

As they moved closer, I counted six guns, three rifles and three Napoleons. What a sight to gladden a soldier's eye! In front rode Captain Hart on his black stallion, "Beauregard"—a pace behind rode the adjutant and the chief bugler.

I knew from experience that Hart's battery is an excellent one. Some time ago, when we were in camp near Richmond, I had observed the battery drawn up on a farm adjoining the camp, unlimbered for action, the cannoneers standing about the guns. At a command from Hart, they sprang at their guns, each man with a special part to perform. The handspikes, sponge buckets and other implements were stripped off with utmost dispatch; the trail was raised in the air, the gun at once tipped and poised on its muzzle, freed from the carriage, and dropped with a thud on the ground. The wheels were next removed and laid beside the axle and, when the crew stepped back, the battery was lying in pieces on the ground. At the next command, the crew sprang back to work: the wheels instantly slipped to their places; with a strong team effort, four men quickly lifted the gun with handspikes until it was again poised on the muzzle; meanwhile, the carriage had been pushed up with elevated trail and the heavy piece fell back promptly with its trunnions in their appointed sockets. Next, the implements were restored to their respective places and the battery was ready for action. On the day I observed this drill, the guns were taken apart and put together again and the motion of loading and firing gone through with in less than a minute. On one other occasion, I was told it was accomplished in forty-nine seconds!

At about two o'clock, seven vessels were sighted coming down the river—black, formidable-looking affairs with their decks cleared for action. As soon as it became clear that the Federals meant business, Lee's guns were loaded and made ready for action.

Soon all eyes were on the leading gunboat as she silently steamed toward us. Suddenly, a belt of fire gleamed from her side and a heavy shot came streaking through the air, exploding with a loud roar some distance in our rear.

Then two more of the vessels opened fire, the white smoke from their guns rolling and heaving in vast columns along the shuddering waters. Two more rapid broadsides were quickly fired, the deafening explosions echoing up and down the river. One young cannoneer, frightened out of his wits by an exploding shell, turned and ran toward the rear. Captain Hart tried to stop the fellow, but he fled past and vanished from the scene of the action like a scared rabbit.

Lee, calm amid this hurricane of shells and explosions, gave the order to return the fire as his voice rang out, "Fire by battery! Fire!" The two Blakey 3.4-inch rifles, which fired ten-pound shells, were soon in action along with the "Long Tom" captured at Manassas. Their first shots fell twenty rods short and skipped over the tops of the two leading gunboats.

The men at the guns worked like demons, loading and firing the pieces with incredible rapidity. The leading gunboat was the main target, a slow steamer clear against the horizon while much of Lee's battery was hidden in earth and bushes. The next three shots ricocheted across the water, aimed at the gunboat's water line, but they fell short.

As I stood behind an embankment with Lieutenant Clark, watching the action through my field glasses, several of their shot and shell went over my head about nine or ten feet from the ground I would estimate. Some burst short of us and one well-aimed shot burst behind us, fragments of the shell flying about our position. Luckily, no one was hit.

One well-aimed shell from Lee hit the second Federal gunboat, cutting away the main stays and scattering bits of iron chain down on the deck. A thin wisp of smoke struggled upward from the steamer, indicating she had been severely hit.

The gunboats continued to fire, salvo after salvo. When Lee and Hart returned the fire, the men of the regiment cheered and yelled loudly. Several more shells, sounding like slow-moving freight trains, flew overhead bursting harmlessly.

As I stood watching, I could only think how the balls do hiss and the shells sigh aloud; a perfectly distinct, fascinating, locust-like song, growing louder and faster as they come nearer, plunging, hissing and bursting through the air. Lieutenant Clark was perfectly cool, standing erect, taking notes of the time and effect of the shots both ways.

After a time, I began to grow anxious and began to envy the men at the guns who, in the intense excitement of battle, had lost sight of danger. Feeling the mental strain of doing nothing under heavy fire and driven by my duty to see how my men were faring, I left the cover of the parapet and began to walk behind the support lines of my men, who were lying on the ground. As the shot and shell came near, hissing and exploding, a cry rose from the ranks that I should lie down also, but I continued to walk up and down the line and replied to their entreaties, "No, you men have stood guard on picket and at camp. It is my time to stand guard now. I will not lie down!"

Finally, through the smoke, I could see the enemy flotilla begin to steam off after about two hours of firing. As they retreated, they took one of their badly damaged gunboats in tow. Another of the gunboats was beached and sunk during the night within view of our position, but beyond the range of our fire.

The battle ended, the officers and men cared for the few wounded and repaired as far as possible the damage done. Soon the moon came peacefully up over the dark night sky, fires were lit, coffee and bread were taken from the haversacks and, by the light of burning fence rails, the much-needed food was enjoyed. At taps, the fires were put out and soon no sound broke the stillness save the tread of the sentinels or the stamp of the artillery horses as they stood munching their corn or wheat.

This morning, I marched the regiment back to camp. It had been a good baptism of fire. The engagement had been a hot one and reflected great credit upon all engaged. All who witnessed the action said that guns were never better handled than those of Lee's. Every shot was well aimed.

After our return to camp, and just as I was about to enter my tent, Major Galloway approached me and said, "Did you know you captured a regiment at Firestone Point?"

"I did no such thing," I replied.

"Yes. When you so resolutely walked the lines amid that storm of shot and shell yesterday, you captured the 22nd North Carolina. You have not a man who would not now die for you."

SEPTEMBER 28, 1861—SATURDAY
CAMP NEAR DUMFRIES, VIRGINIA

Sometime ago, I received the following letter:

"Fayetteville, North Carolina

September 5, 1861

"Dear Colonel Pettigrew,

"As it is the praise-worthy custom of our Christian country to afford their soldiers during military service the means and consultations of religion, I thereby offer myself as a volunteer to the service of the Confederacy, and my God in the capacity of Chaplain to the 22nd North Carolina. Should you accept my offer, I will depart from here for the front within a week.

"This present civil war is, in many of its aspects, a religious one. It is a battle for truth and righteousness—for liberty and freedom against Black Republican despotism. Of the cause for which they fight, our soldiers should be constantly reminded. Ministers of the gospel are the most likely persons for this service. Those who fight for and believe in religious principles are mighty in the day of battle. David, an unknown shepherd, sang and wrote psalms and defeated the giant Goliath. The Roundheads of Cromwell prayed and sang psalms and were invincible. The beloved Washington prayed and believed and led the colonies to victory.

"My proposed service is, by God's good grace, to make of those under your command better men and, hence, better soldiers, to comfort the sick and wounded, and to console the dying. Yet if danger comes near and you should require me to wield the sword or handle the rifle, I would have no hesitancy, having been early trained in the use of weapons by a brave old father, who commanded a volunteer company in our glorious war of the revolution."

"Alfred Keys

"Pastor, St. James Church, Fayetteville, North Carolina"

Yesterday, I am happy to report, Chaplain Keys began his services with the regiment. His first duty has been to distribute testaments and hymn books among the men. Last night, from many tents, the evening hymn ascended to heaven and the sacred songs were sung with an emotion hitherto unknown for they reminded the men of home and dear friends and brought back afresh the most solemn and impressive scenes in their lives.

The picket war, as I call the occasional shots exchanged between the two opposing lines of sentinels, continues. It is not a game, but deadly earnest business, with men who are deliberately engaged after the fashion of Indian warriors in the task of taking each other's lives. All is silent, and you are surrounded by beautiful scenery, the river flowing majestically toward the sea before you, when suddenly a white puff of smoke suddenly flashes out from the edge of some green thicket, and you listen fearfully to the cold, ominous whiz of the flying balls and the occasional sullen "whack" or loud thud, into a tree near where you stand.

The firing is necessarily desultory, each picket lying in wait until he finds a chance to take a shot. Resort is made to various stratagems to draw the enemy's fire, and reveal their position, but strange to say, the execution done is of the most trifling character. Frequently many days will pass without a man on our side receiving a scratch and then, one day, one or two will be killed. I believe, however, that the number *four* will cover all the casualties that have thus far occurred to our men.

OCTOBER 5, 1861—SATURDAY
NEAR DUMFRIES, VIRGINIA

Yesterday morning, Chaplain Keys and I rode to a nearby hospital where we found the patients clean and comfortable, many of them suffering from rheumatism. As Pastor Keys passed along the beds, he had a cheerful and pleasant word to speak to all. How kindly he was received by the men! Some tried to get up that they might speak or catch his hand. His influence is wonderful. The lady nurses speak in the highest terms of him.

We had almost ended our visit when the chaplain was summoned to the cot of a gravely ill soldier who had been admitted several days before with a severe case of diarrhea. The patient was very weak, having ten to twelve stools daily and having not eaten in several days. The doctor's treatment called for a prescription of ipecacuanha and opium, alternated with grains of chlorate and potassa. He was also receiving beef-tea, wine-whey, and brandy.

Chaplain Keys had visited the young man the day before with confident hopes of a speedy recovery—hopes which were shared by the doctor and the young man himself—but a sudden change had taken place and the surgeon had called Keys to tell him that the youth could live but an hour or two at most and to beg the chaplain to make the fearful announcement to him.

I watched from a respectful distance as Chaplain Keys knelt at the side of the cot of the dying lad and, overpowered by his emotions and concern for the youth, was utterly unable to deliver his message. The dying young soldier, however, quickly read the terrible truth in the altered looks of Chaplain Keys, his faltering voice and ambiguous words. The soldier, up until that moment, had not entertained a doubt of his recovery. He was expecting to soon be well and receive a leave to journey back to North Carolina and see his mother, and with her kind nursing make a complete recovery. He was, therefore, entirely unprepared for the announcement and, at first it was overwhelming.

"I am to die then…and how soon?"

As the youth had before expressed hope in Christ, Chaplain Keys replied, "You have made your peace with God; let death come as soon as it will. He will carry you over the river."

"Yes, but this is so awfully sudden, awfully sudden! I am scared, Chaplain! I am terribly frightened for this world seems a fine place and

I don't especially want to leave it." With this his lips quivered, tears began to well up in his young blue eyes and he half moaned, "And I shall not see my mother."

"Christ is better than a mother," murmured Chaplain Keys, wiping a tear away from his cheek.

"Yes," the word came softly, almost in a whisper. The lad's eyes were closed, his lips pressed tightly together as he struggled with his emotions. But as the minutes passed, his countenance grew calmer, his lips steadier; and when he opened his eyes again, he looked at peace with himself and the world he was about to leave.

"I thank you for your kindness," he said tenderly while taking the hand of Chaplain Keys. "The bitterness is over now and I feel willing to die—not my will but Thy will be done. Tell my mother," he paused, gave a soft low sob and full of anguish continued, "tell her how I loved her and longed to see her, but if God will permit me, I will be near her. Tell her to comfort all who loved me and say I thought of them all. Tell my beloved father that I am glad he gave his consent for me to be a soldier and many fathers will mourn for their sons before this cruel war is over. Tell my younger brother by word or letter that I love him dearly and will miss him so. Tell him I find Christ will not desert the departing soul and that to live is Christ and to die is gain. And now, Chaplain, will you pray with me?"

Once again, Keys knelt beside the cot and, restraining his tears, recited with the young soldier the 23rd Psalm. When they finished, Keys pressed upon the youth's forehead a fervent kiss.

Smiling, the youth slowly raised his hand and wiped a tear from the chaplain's cheek. "Thank you, Chaplain," he said. "Thank you."

"The Lord God be with you," was Keys' firm response.

"Amen," trembled the fading soldier.

We left the room as the surgeon moved closer to do all that he could to alleviate the lad's suffering. Another hour passed. Keys paced uneasily, quietly about the room. There were sounds outside, then footsteps on the stairs. Keys opened the door and encountered the surgeon who whispered one little word, "Gone."

OCTOBER 6, 1861—SUNDAY
NEAR DUMFRIES, VIRGINIA

This morning, we buried the young soldier who died yesterday. I will never forget the scene as the regimental band, with slow rolling muffled drums and measured step, preceded the simple pine box. The squad, with reversed arms and solemn visages, slowly winded their way through a light drizzle to the open grave on the quiet hillside. In the distance, we could hear the low sound of looming thunder. The sad strain of the dead march sent a chill through every heart. He has been one of the first of our regiment to die. It is hard to get used to such things. After the body was lowered into the shallow grave and three volleys were fired over it, the band struck up a lively march and the poor fellow was left on the lonesome hillside, soon to be forgotten by all, except his grieving mother, father and brother who would weep bitter tears over the loved one who would return no more and whose forgotten grave they would never see.

As I write these words by candlelight, it is a splendid moonlit night. Off in the distance I can hear the braying of a lonely mule and the hoot of a nocturnal owl. Lately, I have considerable work to attend to, so much so that I have had an additional clerk, Corporal Sam Harper, from Caldwell county, detailed to my staff. I must approve all the issues from the quartermasters and commissaries, all charges for court's martial, all applications for furloughs and leaves and all reports; in short, everything for over 1,000 men has to pass under my supervision, besides the daily detail of guards, officers of the day, etc. I must also find time, often morning duties, to visit the various commands to examine the condition of the camps, hospitals, kitchens, etc. Each morning, my field officer of the day, whose duty it is to visit and supervise each camp night and day, makes one a long written report. All of his complaints and suggestions I generally attend to in person as the most effectual way of correcting error and improving matters generally to accomplish all this, I am usually up at sunrise and to bed whenever the work is done and I finally collapse, exhausted, into my cot.

OCTOBER 18, 1861—FRIDAY
NEAR DUMFRIES, VIRGINIA

While there is an overabundance of good men in the regiment, there are some who enlisted who are weak in character and have proven false to the colors. Private Jack Yates of Company A has proven to be such a man. Yesterday morning, Yates was drummed out of camp for desertion. Yates' case is a curious one because he did not desert to the Yankees, neither did he leave the regiment and return home, but he left his command and in partnership with the sutlier O'Niel went on a huckstering tour, peddling goods and whiskey from O'Niel through the different camps, while receiving a percentage of the profit. Of course, while being absent from the ranks on his profit-making scheme, he was marked on the rolls as a deserter. He had been peddling for some time when he was arrested and returned to the regiment. Yates, of course, had many elaborate excuses for his absence, but was nevertheless found guilty by a court martial. His sentence was that he should have the buttons cut off his uniform, half his head shaved, be branded on the hip, and then drummed out of camp.

I went to visit Yates in the guardhouse and sat down beside him. He was a rough-looking, shady character. As we talked, I learned his father and mother had thought him incorrigible and had disowned him. He had made ends meet by working as a hired farmhand before he enlisted. Yates said his father had considered him the black sheep of the family...Yates had tried to return to his father's good graces, but his father had not treated him as the prodigal son and refused to allow him to return home.

I sent for a bowl of mutton broth. I sat at his side while he ate and said, "I know that you have had a hard time, been neglected, and often imposed upon. I think had you given soldiering a chance, you would have found a home here and come to enjoy it. Now, however, you have left me no choice but to have you drummed out of camp. I do this for the good of the regiment, not for any personal dislike for you."

Yates finished his soup, put the bowl down, and, wiping some of the broth off his chin with his hand, said, "I deserve my punishment, Colonel, and will take it like a man. Even a villain can have an occasional spark of pride."

Lieutenant Neal was the officer of the guard on the day Yates' sentence was to be carried out. The prisoner was in the guardhouse. When he knew what was coming and began to realize the enormity of his offense, he determined that the guard should not cut off his buttons— a mark of deep degradation. So Yates pulled all the buttons off his blouse, thus expecting to baffle the officers in charge of his punishment. Lieutenant Nesbitt, equally determined, had every button sewed on again and then deliberately cut them all off, thus carrying out that part of the sentence. The next punishment was shaving half the head. Yates kicked and fought most vigorously against this, but the guard overpowered him and he was forced to submit. The razor opened several bloody cuts on his shaved head.

The next punishment was brutal, but deserved, as Yates was marched down to the regimental blacksmith shop. The letter "D" was branded on his right hip. Yates was plucky, however, and he never winced, even though I could distinctly smell the pungent odor of burning flesh. A lid of a cracker box was then hung on his back with the word "DESERTER" painted on it in large red letters. Eight men from Company A then formed behind him with bayonets fixed. Members of the regimental band were placed in front of him and struck up the "Rogues March." The procession marched toward the edge of camp, accompanied by several hundred spectators. As soon as Yates was marched out of camp, he received a parting salute from the members of the regiment in the form of a volley of old shoes, tin pans, and other miscellaneous matter. Yates was then turned loose to go where he saw fit. He was a disgrace to the Confederacy and to North Carolina. When he wandered off, Yates remained plucky to the end as he stopped, turned, and gave a long salute toward Lt. Neal and the guard.

OCTOBER 26, 1861—SATURDAY
NEAR DUMFRIES, VIRGINIA

It is a miserable day, with cold rain and high winds that send a chill almost to my bones.

Last week, I sent my Negro body servant, Peter, back to Charleston because of illness. He was a loyal, hard-working servant, responsible for doing the cooking, mending clothes and care and grooming of the horses.

Imagine then my astonishment when, tonight, Captain Gibson came to my tent conducting a peculiar looking and most singular specimen of the Negro race. As he took off his drenched slouch hat, I could see he was not over four-and-a-half-feet tall, hump-backed, crooked-legged and about forty years old.

Captain Gibson explained tome his name was Elias and he had been the faithful servant of Lieutenant Eliza DeKalb, who was recently killed in a cavalry skirmish at Pohick church. I learned that Elias is quite intelligent, very respectful and had been perfectly devoted to his late master.

After our introduction, Elias gave me the particulars of Lt. DeKalb's sad death. After being wounded, he was taken to a house in Fredericksburg where the young daughters of Mrs. Lee nursed and tended him as kindly as if they were his mother and sisters. The young ladies would not allow a servant to make his nourishment, but cooked all with their own hands. After an amputation, fair hopes were entertained of a recovery by his friends, though he himself would often tell

Elias that he knew he was going to die, but he was prepared and willing. He would laugh and chat gaily with the ladies, enjoying their society very much, but when alone with his favorite servant, who never left him, he would speak of his approaching end.

At last, secondary hemorrhaging took place and, though a physician was immediately sent for, one could not be procured for some time. When he came, it was too late. He could not rally from this fearful exhaustion and died the next day in Elias' arms as quietly as an infant going to sleep. So gently that Elias could not believe it for a little while.

Five minutes by the watch before he died, he feebly traced a letter to Captain Gibson asking him to please look after Elias and find a good master for him. When the captain heard of Peter's return to Charleston, he determined to bring Elias to me, thinking I would find him most loyal and useful.

I told Elias that working as my servant could bring danger for he might, at times, get caught up in the tide of battle. He smiled and, shaking the rain off his hat, told me that he had no fear of danger because one thing was certain and that was the fact that we all had to die at sometime. There was no way to get away from death when it came. The Lord above had permitted him to live some forty years and had given him food, drink and clothing all that time. He believed that God was good and nothing could harm him, not even death. If he didn't believe that, he would be the biggest sinner in the world.

I was uncertain if this deformed Negro would have the strength and skill to perform the many duties I required of Peter. Captain Gibson assured me, however, that Elias was a willing worker who through persistence was able to perform most tasks.

Taking the captain at his word, I decided to have Elias remain with me to serve as my body servant. Captain Gibson departed, pleased that he had paid his debt to the late Lt. DeKalb. Elias, pleased with his new situation, cheerfully told me he could now take off his "traveling shoes" and have a place to call home.

NOVEMBER 2, 1861—SUNDAY
NEAR DUMFRIES, VIRGINIA

Interesting was a scene upon which I chanced tonight. Strolling in the cool moonlight, I was attracted by a brilliant light beneath the trees, and cautiously approached it. A circle of ten or fifteen camp darkies sat around a roaring fire, while one old uncle, Jupiter by name, was narrating an interminable tale, to the insatiable delight of his audience. Noticed by only a few, I stood in the background and listened. At this point in the narrative, Uncle Jupiter and his wife were out of money and wondered what to do so he thought and then said to his wife, 'I am going to Massa and ax for money to bury you!'

"Then he gone on down the road. When he came to the big house, the Massa been sitting on the porch cooling his foots.

"'Massa,' he say, 'I in trouble.'

"'What the trouble, Jupiter?'

"I lose Mom Lizzie last night!'

"'What?'

"'Please, Massa, you always ben kind to me. Loan me twenty dollars to put Mom Lizzie away right.'

"'That enough, Uncle?'

"'Twenty dollars enough, Massa.'

The money was delivered and Jupiter thoroughly dramatized every word as he told how he walked happily home to show the Massa's money to mom Lizzie.

"'Lizzie, old gal, I got the money. Now you seen the Massa coming, you better been dead. I tell Massa you dead!'

"Next morning mom Lizzie goin' down the road and she meet up with her white missus. Mom Lizzie pass de time of day, but when she think how she got to be dead, she look sad. So Missus say, 'Mom Lizzie, I am troubled. You say you good as common but you look like you seen a ghost.'

"And Mom Lizzie say, 'Well Missus, now you ax, got troubles sure 'nough. Don't feel none too good. Miss Jupiter too much!'
"'Where Uncle Jupiter?'
"'He dead!'
"'Dead? Jupiter dead?'
"'Yes, Missus, and I sure could use twenty dollar to put him away right!'
"'Twenty dollar?'
"'Yes, Missus. Twenty dollar send Jupiter to Hebben in style.'
Then Jupiter narrated how Lizzie came home and informed him of what she told the master's wife. The gifted storyteller then had Mom Lizzie say, 'Told my Missus you been dead so here! I got my money too!' (*Immense applause from the darkies and one appreciating auditor says chuckling, "Now you gots forty dollar of Massa's money!" which brings down the house.*)
"Ain't that pitiful! Ain't that pitiful! And dat night the Massa and Missus meet, Massa say, 'So Mom Lizzie dead?'
"And missus say, 'No! Uncle Jupiter the one dead. I know cause I loan Mom Lizzie money to put poor Jupiter away right.'
"'You must be wrong, say Massa. 'I loan Jupiter twenty dollars to bury Mom Lizzie.'
"Dey look at each other and smell a rat and dey say, 'We best ride over to de cabin and find out who is dead!'

"So Massa and Missus get in de buggy and gone on. Well the two old colored folks been finishing up the best supper in years. Yes, sir, de in de land o' milk and honey. De just sitting on de porch—just setting dere slapping mosquitoes. Den dey hear hoofs comin' and dey know it's Massa's horse and Jupiter say, 'Sho as Moses a meek man, that de Massa!'
"And Lizzie say, 'And I hear de Missus!'

"And they ain't got but one thing to do. Both Lizzie and Jupiter fall dead—stretch out! Lay same as two old fat possum! Soon Massa and Missus hit dey step and see their two favorite slaves stretch out! So de Massa say, 'Missus, I would give ten dollar to know which one dead first.'

"And Jupiter jump up and say, 'Me dead fuss!'

"And Mom Lizzie jump and say, 'Me dead fuss!'

"Den both lay down and stretch out again—after all dey dead! Massa smile and place ten dollar on Jupiter and ten dollar on Lizzie. Then Massa and Missus ride away. So both dead first!"

The loud laughter and dancing eyes which greeted the end of this story was something to behold. As I walked away I could only think the darkies are the most good-natured, careless, light-hearted and happily constructed human beings I have ever seen.

NOVEMBER 19, 1861—TUESDAY
NEAR DUMFRIES, VIRGINIA

The notes of war continue to sound in our ears. Daily and hourly cannonading is heard at intervals all along the river. The blockade of the river is considered effectual. It is felt that McClellan is hesitating about meeting his great foe—our noble Beauregard. McClellan will never meet him this autumn at Manassas. He may possibly venture as far as the neighborhood of Fairfax with his grand army for another trial of arms—partly for the purpose of rendering himself still more celebrated in the eyes of his countrymen and to endeavor, if possible, to retrieve the fallen fortune of his predecessor. I wish McClellan would advance at once, if such is his intention, and decide to give battle.

The cold weather is fast making its appearance in this region. The rains have been very heavy and with the cold, makes camp life very arduous. It is especially trying during the silent hours of night while performing guard duty. The sentry walks his lonely ground with no companion but the screech owl.

The monotony in camp is very great, but I am fortunate to be associated with a genial group of officers. Dr. Hall, Major Galloway and Chaplain Keys and I mess together. We have even hired a cook. Each member of the mess contributes in proportion so that we manage to live very well, although prices are high in this country. The demand is so great for butter, eggs, and chickens. Butter is worth fifty cents per pound, geese $2.50 per pair, turkeys the same, and so on. The teamsters bringing in supplies to our camp often act as hucksters by bringing in a lot of delicacies to sell on their own account for enormous profit.

It has been noticed that many of the men in camp have been indulging in drinking. Accordingly, I gave orders to the camp guards to search every man coming into camp. If any liquor was found on him, it should be destroyed. This stopped the smuggling, but only for a short time. It soon became evident that considerable amount of John Barleycorn were still being smuggled into camp. It was a mystery how it was done, but at last it was discovered.

There were, for some reason, many watermelons available in Dumfries and most of the boys who went to the village would bring back a watermelon which, of course, was not considered contraband. These were not seized or searched. Now this is where the diabolical drinkers resorted to great cunning. One would purchase a large melon, cut a square hole in it, and then with a spoon, scrape out all the soft inside. After filling it up with whiskey, they would insert the plug and with his melon under his arm, march proudly into camp. One day a member of Company B came to grief. Just as he nonchalantly passed the guard at the gate, he lost hold of his melon and it fell to the ground, bursting into many pieces. Along with the burst, over a quart of whisky ran onto the ground. This ended the carrying in of liquor by the professed lovers of watermelon.

Through the good work of Major Galloway, it was then determined that two rogue settlers were selling the liquor to the men. They were ignoring the order that no liquor should be sold to soldiers and that anyone selling it would be severely dealt with. Galloway had them arrested and placed in our guardhouse for safekeeping. The regiment's court martial was convened and the settlers tried. They were each found guilty and sentenced to receive 15 lashes on their bare backs and to be sent adrift on the Potomac in an open boat without oars. The sentence was confirmed by the government in Richmond and the punishment soon carried out.

Two young pine saplings were selected close to the guardhouse. The shirts of the protesting prisoners were torn off after a brief struggle. They were then tied to the trees. Two guards had been detailed to execute the flogging. One had a coach whip and the other had a long wagon whip.

Lieutenant Dickson, being officer of the guard, gave the order to begin. At the first cut, the ridges were raised and the men writhed and yelled for mercy. Soon Lt. Dickson ordered the guards to lay it on harder (under the penalty of receiving a dose themselves if they didn't comply) and the two prisoners fairly howled. Each whip stroke struck home with a loud "crack" and the blood flew freely from their backs. One sutler, hung from his bonds barely conscious, moaning and crying. The other yelled with every stroke, pleading he would never sell liquor again and to please let him go.

When they had received the 15 lashes, their backs looked like raw, bloody beef. After the sentence had been carried out, they were cut loose and, after tenderly putting on their shirts, they were led from the camp muttering threats of vengeance on those they considered responsible for such vile and unfair punishment.

NOVEMBER 28, 1861—THURSDAY
NEAR DUMFRIES, VIRGINIA

I am writing this journal entry in my tent almost suffocated by the smoke that insists on coming out of the wrong end of the stove.

Solomon, the great king of Israel, was right when he said, "a smoky chimney and a scolding wife are evils." I know all about the first, but nothing of wives, and don't care to.

Last night, I was not feeling well and took to my bed. I told Elias to wake me when Dr. Hall arrived. Later in the evening, when he attempted to wake me, I was in one of my sleepy moods and he couldn't shake me awake. I awoke much later, tired and sick to find Dr. Hall sitting over me. I was quite feverish and the doctor administered quinine to bring down the fever. After this, Dr. Hall told me that he had never seen such a miserable Negro in his life and that Elias was frightened nearly to death when he couldn't wake me. "He is most attached and faithful to you, Colonel," remarked Dr. Hall.

I can only say thank God for the ever faithful Elias and the thousands of loyal slaves like him. Their faith and loyalty toward their masters is often touching.

It was while engaged in such thoughts that I came across an article in the *Delaware Enquirer* entitled, "What Will Become of Sambo." According to this Yankee newspaper, the enemy is putting into practice a new policy in Virginia and Maryland. They are proceeding upon the hypothesis that the slave owners of Virginia will either be slaughtered or driven from the soil and that their lands will be confiscated. The newspaper then proclaims the following as the policy to be pursued with regard to the slaves:

"We should take the slaves from the Rebels, even if we have to sell them to the persons who will become the owners of the soil confiscated. If the army does not pursue this course, if the slaves are not taken care of by the victorious army, they will have no one to take care of them. We think there should be enough slaves captured to pay the expenses of the war and every effort should be made to turn everything available to account. Virginia has enough slaves within her borders to pay the whole expense of the war and every one of them should be captured and placed in safe keeping until they can be turned into money to defray the expenses of the war. At all events every nigger in the Confederate states should change hands for the benefit of the Union."

Such is to be the fate of Elias and thousands like him in the event the bloody program of these northern robbers and plunderers is carried out. The Negro is to have the privilege of changing masters after the war is over. Northern invaders started into this war with the promise of freedom to the Negro, under the hope that he would rise up and fight their battles for them. Finding themselves deluded in this hope, they have eagerly come to the conclusion that Sambo should be captured, put in chains, and, after the war is over, sold to the new owners of the soil, the proceeds of the sale to be applied to defraying the expenses of the war! Such a proposition of wholesale robbery is without parallel, even in the most barbarous ages, and I venture the prediction that these northern philanthropists and psalm-singing hypocrites will yet fall victims to the barbarities and spoilation which they have allotted to the people of the South. I have great faith that in the providence of God, a day of retribution for such wickedness must inevitably come.

DECEMBER 6, 1861—FRIDAY
NEAR DUMFRIES, VIRGINIA

Lt. Col. Long went to Richmond on leave last week and came back to camp with a most remarkable purchase. Long, believing that someday soon the regiment must be ordered into battle, had purchased a steel plated vest to ward off bullets. He took it into the woods one day to try it out. Propping the vest against a tree, he took careful aim with a rifle and watched in dismay as the ball went clean through the vest. One morning several days later, Long found a new steel vest propped up against his tent. The vest was an exact replica of his old one except that a bulls eye had been painted over the area which would cover the heart. Furious, Long is trying to discover the perpetrators of this little joke.

Yesterday, Mrs. Long reached camp to stay for a while with the lieutenant colonel. I have not and do not intend to call on her even at the risk of seeming rude. Her husband and I, like east and west, seem to be far from each other at the moment.

You have heard of big, bigger and biggest. If Lt. Col. Long is big, Mrs. Long is biggest. I overheard Lt. Clark ask one of the captains how she got here? "Perhaps by horse," replied the captain.

"No." answered Lt. Clark. "It is a mystery to me. There is no horse that can carry that big of a load and I'm not aware of any elephants that are presently in the service of the Confederacy."

On a much more somber note, a poor woman arrived in camp today from Alamance County to see her soldier husband. She had come to visit him in the hospital, but, poor creature, she was stunned to learn that he had died of pneumonia and had been buried four or five days prior. She had spent her last cent to get here. Once arriving in Dumfries, she walked four miles through rain and mud to the camp.

Upon learning of her husband's death, she was completely distraught. Finding his grave, she threw herself upon the ground and sobbing, tore at the earth in a vain attempt to uncover the body. We finally managed to calm her and sent her back to Dumfries in the ambulance. I gave her $20 for her return journey to North Carolina. I knew of no better way to spend the money. I'm afraid I am a poor comforter and her case was such a hard one.

DECEMBER 29, 1861—SUNDAY
NEAR DUMFRIES, VIRGINIA

The Occoquan is a sluggish stream that flows into the Potomac about three miles from Mt. Vernon. The Richmond Road from Alexandria crosses it about six miles from its mouth. At its crossing, the old dilapidated village of Occoquan is located. About five or six miles above the Occoquan, and running parallel with it, is a stream called the Accotink, which also flows into the Potomac. The Yankee picket lines are on the Accotink, while our pickets guard the Occoquan. Between the two streams is a tract of country which might be called debatable ground and is overrun by the scouts of both armies. Parties from either side collect forage and pick up every-thing of portable nature that can be used in camp. The people living on this disputed territory are in a sad predicament—being robbed by both sides. Not a chicken, sheep, hog, or anything edible is left them. They save things only if they can securely hide them from the keen-eyed foragers. Sometimes, commands of the opposing sides will meet and there will be a skirmish. Just such an affair occurred several days ago near Pohick Church.

On Friday, 27th instant, I accompanied Captain Hayes and fifty cav-alrymen to join Major Butler and one hundred cavalry of the Hampton Legion. We had ordered two days' rations for men and horses to be issued to the joint command.

Our plan was to ride out and sweep the country between the Occoquan and Accotink rivers in an attempt to pick up straggling scouting parties of the enemy. There was enough show of danger to make the reconnaissance exciting and a good chance to successfully attack and capture some of the enemy. Expeditions such as this can also teach lessons for the bivouac, if not the battle, bring to light what faults there might be in the disposition of equipment, practice men and offi-cers in their duties and suggest to them the labors of a campaign.

Major Butler, who was to lead our little foray, is twenty-six years of age and handsome as a Greek god. He sat his horse like a typical South Carolina cavalier. Descended from a distinguished family of heroes, soldiers, and statesmen, Butler attended the South Carolina College and later studied law under his uncle, Judge Butler, one of the leading lawyers in South Carolina. Brave as a lion, he never orders a soldier to go where he will not go himself. He loves his men and they love him.

At two o'clock in obedience to the successive calls of the bugles, the command assembled and were formed. With one impulse, the men lifted themselves into their saddles. About thirty of the men, in addition to their ordinary arms, were provided with Enfield rifles. These rifles are extremely accurate and the ladder back sight allows the trooper to advance the slider for ranges of 100, 200, and 400 yards. It is an ideal weapon for skirmishing in rough terrain.

Major Butler fearlessly mounted his magnificent bay, "Don," who was seventeen and a half-hand high. As he did so, I overheard one of the troopers say, "that big horse is full of mettle, but Major Butler can ride anything." Watching the major on his charger, I thought of the words of Job regarding the horse, "Hast thou given the horse strength; hast thou clothed his neck with thunder; can'st thou make him afraid as a grasshopper? The glory of his nostrils is terrible. He passeth in the valley and rejoiceth in his strength. He smelleth the battle afar off, the thunder and the captains and the shouting."

Major Butler took the lead, ordered the ranks dressed and, with fluttering guidons, the column moved off, receiving a farewell cheer from those who had gathered to watch our departure.

We took the well-known road toward Pohick Church, riding in files to the right and left, winding among the trees, or breaking through fences into adjacent fields. Soon, a dozen miles were traveled. Meanwhile, the sun declined into a bank of black and sullen clouds until, at last, simultaneously with the beginning of a light drizzle, the command bivouacked close to Pohick Church.

The area around Pohick Church is some of the most historic in Virginia. The church itself stands to the left of the Richmond Road and twelve miles west of Alexandria, being situated high on a green hill above Pohick Creek. The church was constructed by some of the distinguished families who formerly lived in this neighborhood, such as the Lees, the Masons, Washingtons and Fairfaxes. The walls of the church have suffered with the advent of war. They are blackened with hundreds of names—testimony to the many soldiers who have passed this way. The seats have been cut to pieces and borne away as memorials of the church of George Washington. Some of the old square pews remain and the pew of Washington has been untouched.

In the same neighborhood, about three miles from Mt. Vernon, on the heights overlooking the Potomac River, are found the shattered walls of the house of Lord Fairfax. This once great house is now a heap of rubbish and large trees are growing out of the ruins. One can still trace the outline of the garden walls.

The weathered tombstone of one of the Lady Fairfaxes now lies broken in the forest overlooking the Potomac. On the stone, she is described as "very beautiful and too pure for the world."

Lower down on the Potomac, but still near the area of Pohick Church is the famous Funston Farm. This was formerly the Mason estate. For nearly a century, it was the home of that famous family. Here George Mason, who was one of the distinguished founders of our government, lived and died. He was a signer of the Declaration of Independence and a member of Congress for many years.

His son, George Mason, was also a lawyer, and a man of varied accomplishments. Unfortunately, he was also of dissolute manners and the basest passions. He had traveled extensively over Europe, mingled with the best society and had conversed with the greatest men of his times.

At the age of thirty, already dissolute, he met a very charming young lady of the name of Powell. Her beauty, vivacity and charm induced Mr. Mason to propose marriage, even though his heart was dead to love. After some hesitation, she accepted his proposal, not that she loved him, but because her family were in moderate circumstances and her marriage would improve her position.

Mason was a brutal husband. His aim from the first was to subject his wife to all those moral and social indignities which would degrade her and bring her down to his own level—by exposures, the most revolting and vicious, to make her the pity and scorn of her slaves. For twenty years, this beautiful woman bore the inhumane treatment of this beast. Humiliated and shamed, she exiled herself from society, only finding enjoyment in the company of her child and some peace in the days and weeks absence of the man she now loathed to call her husband.

Mason, while in his prime, became ill and began to sink rapidly. Around his bed in his last hours stood many relatives and friends of the family, and the long-suffering wife. When Mr. Mason crossed the river of death, she closed Mr. Mason's eyes and said aloud to all that this was the first act that she had performed for her husband in twenty years with pleasure.

Mason was then buried in the family graveyard, while Mrs. Mason had a tombstone erected which completed her revenge. Under the letters which recorded his name, age, year and day of death, she had placed the following lines: "Brandy, brandy, bane of life. Source of evil, cause of strife. If men could half thy vices tell, they would wish thee safe in hell."

Mrs. Mason lived on the estate some years after the unlamented death of her husband, leaving after her son died in his youth. The widow now, if still alive, resides with relatives in another part of Virginia.

While the men were preparing camp for the night, a Negro called Humphrey, who lived in the area, alluded casually to a party of Yankee cavalry which had bivouacked in the neighborhood of his home. As we questioned the slave, we learned that the Yankees were spending the night at the house of a Dr. Goulding.

It appeared from talking to Humphrey that the enemy were isolated from any adjacent post from which they could expect prompt reinforcement. They had not posted sentinels and were not particularly vigilant or apprehensive of attack. Once we determined to attack the enemy at the doctor's house, Humphrey promptly volunteered to guide our party to the enemy's location.

Major Butler and I quickly selected twenty men to accompany us on the raid. Captain Hayes was ordered to stay in camp with the remainder of the men, but to be on the alert should we need support or reinforcements.

The rain began to increase at night, making the air raw and cold. It was a night of Egyptian darkness. The obscurity was so great that only a practiced eye could distinguish the most prominent object.

As the camp grew quiet and the hour late, Major Butler led the column silently toward the enemy. Through the dripping woods and tangled brush we rode, at each moment shaking from the leaves a shower of suspended rain drops. The night was cold and dark and we rode silently along over the oozy surface of the fields and lanes. The only sound was the occasional neighing of a horse or the muffled cough of one of the troopers. I fixed my eyes on the back of Major Butler and Humphrey riding ahead of me, my breath sending out a cloud of white vapor barely visible in the cold night air.

Our course was along plantation roads and devious by-paths. Through woods strewn here and there with rotting trunks of fallen trees. Until at last we came upon a country lane, across which it was necessary for us to proceed.

Finally, we halted on the edge of a large field and Humphrey, with intense excitement pointed forward and whispered to Major Butler, "Dar 'tis!" Off in the distance, through the thick, wet night air, we could faintly discern the outline of a large house. A few yards apart from the main building there was a small office and Humphrey told us that this is where the Yankees were quartered for the night. As the men waited silently behind us, we questioned the Negro as to the ground between us and the building, and the arrangement of its interior. Humphrey excited by the prospect of battle, gave confused answers to our questions and as a result, we determined to ignore his remarks and make plans for the attack on our own instincts.

I ordered Sergeant Davis and another trooper to the rear of the building. Major Butler and two other men would rush the front. The rest of the command under my direction would surround the building at a distance and, hopefully, capture any Yankees who might successfully escape.

Once Sergeant Davis was in place, Major Butler and the two troopers drew their revolvers and rushed the building. Jumping upon the front porch, Butler drew his sword and cocked his Navy Dragoon. Reaching the front door, Butler flung it open and found himself face to face with five Yankees sitting at a table playing cards, while two others were resting on a nearby bed. "Surrender, or you're dead men!" shouted Butler.

One of the Yankees at the table began to stand, his hand upon a weapon. There was a loud explosion and wheeling half around, the Yankee exclaimed, "You've shot me, sir!" as he fell to the ground.

Butler and the two privates leveled their guns at the remaining Yankees while Sergeant Davis alarmed at the sound of the shot, rushed to the rear window and, seeing one of the Yankees on the bed reach for a musket, discharged his carbine. The ball struck the Yankee in the back and he threw his hands into the air as he fell forward mortally wounded. There was no more firing, the surprise had been complete, and the remaining five of the enemy surrendered.

When I arrived at the building, the young Yankee soldier who had been shot by Butler was writhing in mortal agony, while the other lay dead in a large pool of blood by the bed. There was little that could be done for the wounded soldier, and shortly, there was a small rattle in his throat and his eyes closed forever.

Leaving the building, we dashed to our horses with the prisoners, their arms, and their horses, and started upon our return. Moving more rapidly then when we advanced, we retraced our steps in safety. Late in the evening, we made our return to camp, tired and weary, but infused with a spirit of satisfaction over our bold adventure.

Early the next morning, the day broke cool and clear. The order was given to saddle up and we soon found ourselves on a road north of Pohick. Along the way, we fell in with Major Connor, who had been out by another route with part of the infantry. The major could not resist the temptation. He left his men, who were in good position, and accompanied us. When about a mile from the church, the enemy made their appearance at the top of a hill, which is approached by a deep, straight road, a half mile long, with a fence on either side. Major Butler always spoiling for a fight, moved steadily forward with some ten rifles. The enemy formed a line of battle and began firing on the advance. As the deadly balls whistled overhead, Butler and his small group found themselves suddenly in a novel and perilous position.

Major Butler halted the advance and ordered it to fire while he dismounted and endeavored to open the fence for the purpose of leading the column around to the rear of the Yankees. It is difficult to say which the enemy indulged in most all this time—loud shouting or vulgar cursing—but both fell harmless on the steadily advancing men. The stakes of the fence were secured at the top and it could not be broken without much delay. Disappointed in this, the major remounted and, drawing his sword, led his small command in a charge.

At that moment, his horse fell and threw the major head over heels, senseless to the ground. Seeing this, I ordered the men into formation and gave the orders, "Gallop! Charge!" With, the whole command plunged forward to the attack. The thunder of the horses hooves shook the hills.

When the Yankees saw this yelling host charging at them, they began a cowardly flight at top speed. The men, showing their high spirit, aimed their pistols and commenced shooting at the retreating enemy.

As soon as the top of the hill was gained, I dispatched Major Connor with ten men to examine the wood on our left. In the meantime, I moved the column forward slowly—alert for an ambuscade. After we moved about a quarter of a mile, we encountered the enemy, drawn up in double rank about 300 yards in front of us. Major Connor and I studied the terrain with our field glasses and determined the enemy could not be charged without passing a point where a fire from an ambuscade would have been most destructive. I then ordered the men with the Enfield rifles to the front.

At the same time, the enemy unslung their rifles and carbines. Firing was commenced by us and was promptly returned by them. We could see the puffs of smoke rise from their rifles as the Yankees shot at us. Once or twice a momentary slackening of our own volleys allowed us to hear the whistle of bullets.

Soon our marksmen proved too much for them and they retreated as fast as their horses could carry them. It was evident from their confusion that they had experienced some casualties. We have since learned through persons in the vicinity that two were killed and three wounded. We also learned that an ambuscade of three hundred infantry, with two pieces of cannon, awaited our approach at the points we avoided. Corporal Griffin, of the Edgefield Huzzars, received a painful but not a dangerous wound.

Later, back at camp, I was sitting on a chair, cleaning the mud off the rowels of my spurs when Major Connor approached, saluted and said, "My compliments, Colonel Pettigrew."

"How so, Major?"

"When we encountered the Yankees today drawn up in double ranks, many a fool who now commands, yearning for glory, would have impetuously ordered a charge and ridden right into an ambush, with double charges of canister from Yankee cannon. You sir, study the terrain, think of all the possibilities, judge the strength and position of the enemy and keep the welfare of your men constantly in mind. There is many a man in this command who is alive today because of the judgement and wisdom you used."

"I have learned, Major Connor, that in war, it is good to play the fox as well as the lion."

With this, the major smiled and slapped me on the back in the gesture of an old friend. He then smiled and said, "You have come a long way, Colonel, since we read law together in old Judge Petigru's office in Charleston. I think you just might make a soldier yet."

To that I could only laugh and say, "Amen."

DECEMBER 31, 1861—TUESDAY
NEAR DUMFRIES, VIRGINIA

The last night of a climatic year...no one will grieve its passing, but all wonder what 1862 will bring.

I wanted to make the last day of the year as joyous as our surroundings would permit. In a festive mood, I invited many of the regimental officers and Major Connor, Major Butler and Colonel Wade Hampton of the Legion to join me in celebration with a genuine Southern eggnog. I had Elias and Major Galloway's servant, Jim, scour the countryside far and wide for eggs which were exceedingly scarce. The boys did their duty well and returned with a basket full of splendid-looking eggs. We had on hand a reasonable supply of sugar. Elias and Jim, looking like two black alchemists, superintended the concoction of this favorite beverage, adding just enough peach brandy to make a right-tasty and powerful drink.

After a very palatable supper, all present were eager to sample the delicious potion and stood anxiously waiting with camp cups in hand. Jim started toward the table with a full and foaming bowl. He held it out before him with almost painful care. He had taken but a few steps when he struck his toe against the uneven floor of the rude quarters and stumbled. The scattered fragments of crockery and the aroma of the wasted nectar cast a deep pall over the expectant and thirsty group.

As we all stood there looking agape, with thoughts of how we could best strangle or draw and quarter Jim running through many minds, Major Butler with a broad grin on his handsome face, stepped to the front of the group and told us not to despair.

"You remember, gentlemen, that when Major Connor, Colonel Hampton and I rode into camp and up to your headquarters that several of you commented on the pair of new boots tied together at the top and flung over my saddle in the fashion of hostlers.

"I believed that, for some reason, you had brought the boots to present them to Colonel Pettigrew," answered Major Galloway.

"A logical deduction, Major," said Butler, "but things are not always as they seem. Never let it be said, gentlemen, that Major Butler came to a party unprepared. Major Galloway, please ask your servant to bring in those boots that hang on my horse."

In came the boots, which were remarkably heavy. "Now," said Butler, "have you any glasses? If so, have them filled with snow." I had glasses and snow aplenty outside our quarters. Elias and Jim quickly filled the glasses with snow. Then, to our surprise, the laughing Butler pulled out of each boot a bottle of champagne. It was a delightful surprise! Pop went the corks and amid much laughter and conviviality, the sparkling fluid was poured into the
snow-filled glasses. It was delicious and we all agreed it was the best champagne we have ever tasted.

JANUARY 24, 1862—FRIDAY
NEAR DUMFRIES, VIRGINIA

This has been a day of great activity for me. The long lost paymaster finally came this morning and in addition to the excitement and bustle of the men finally receiving their pay for the first time in five months, the paymaster, himself, got very drunk, taking all day to pay three companies when he should have paid the entire regiment before night. I stood it for as long as I could in camp and then, leaving Major Galloway in command, and seeing everything in good order, I mounted Charleston and rode over to a little Methodist church near the river, there to pray for strength and patience as I had a strong urge to strangle the paymaster to death.

Riding back to camp, I came very near to being killed. Approaching a small stream, my horse broke through some concealed ice in crossing a very bad hole at a rapid gait and we both rolled over and over in the mud. I am surprised I survived the fall, for Charleston fell with great force and, doubling his head completely under him, turned a complete somersault. Maybe my prayers at the little church helped, for I was thrown forward hard, but escaped with only a slight sprain of my wrist.

But such sad-looking objects as my horse and I could not be imagined. I was completely covered with black mud from head to foot, and Charleston, my big horse, was worse, for he was considerably cut and bruised.

After recovering from the fall, I was struck with the behavior of animals when terrified. As I brushed the mud off Charleston, he was no longer the high-spirited beast of the morning, but was entirely subdued and trembled and shook and seemed scarcely able to stand. Then, as I regained my composure and looked at my wrist, he showed no disposition to wander or leave me, but stood with his nose close to me. It was scarcely necessary to hold his bridle, he was so quiet and compassionate.

Tonight, as it is very cold and I feel damp and chilled after my fall, I have arranged matters with a view to keep as warm as possible. I have had a very large wood fire built right in front of my quarters, and the sentry on guard will keep it going all night unless the wind changes. In which case, his orders are to "stop putting on wood" as it will certainly smoke me out. I intend to go to bed in my overcoat and hope that I shall keep warm.

FEBRUARY 2, 1862—SUNDAY
NEAR DUMFRIES, VIRGINIA

Yesterday morning I was sitting in my quarters reading a copy of the day's Richmond Examiner when I heard loud voices. Summoned outside, I saluted the corporal of the guard and was informed that Lieutenant Odell of Company M had sent a prisoner with whom he could do nothing.

Standing in front of the guard was Private Stiles of "M" who has long been regarded as one of the best soldiers in the company. In recent days, young Stiles has become utterly indifferent to and negligent of duty, and dirty and bedraggled in person and clothing. Stiles has thrown away his pants, preferring as a substitute his blouse, into the sleeves of which he had thrust his legs. The body of his garment was indifferently secured around his waist by a broad belt of yellow cloth. In an act of amazing genius, he had pinned pieces of red flannel to his shirt and on each shoulder as marks of imaginary rank. As he stood before me, his countenance was rigid, as if cut from marble, and his strange appearance drew roars of laughter from those of the regiment who had turned out to look at him and ascertain what manner of reception he would receive from me.

"Ah! Stiles, is that you?" I asked. "What dress is that, and your rank is a most unusual one—how do I address you?"

"This is a uniform of my own, Colonel!"

"Your own, is it? Do you outrank me, sir? I am not sure that I have ever encountered a uniform with two pieces of red flannel for rank. For all I know, you may have transferred to the Turkish army and now have the rank of sultan."

"No, you still outrank me, Colonel. I just prefer to wear my own uniform."

"Good enough! Corporal of the guard, please enter upon the guard book that Private Stiles is not to change his uniform in any particular, except by express orders from these headquarters."

"But Colonel Pettigrew, I am sick!"

"Sick are you? Well, orderly, give Doctor Hall my compliments, and ask him to report here at once!"

Doctor Hall soon arrived and thoroughly examined Private Stiles. He could detect no evidence of sickness, but after consultation with me administered a powerful cathartic, which is a strong laxative, good for purging the bowels. Stiles swallowed the medicine, but with a wry face, and the poor fellow has kept busy in more ways than one ever since.

Private Stiles reports he is much better this morning. Indeed, he says he feels quite well and really sees no need for more medicine. Now that he is healthy, he is at work under guard, picking up the thousand and one little pieces of paper lying about camp. The wind is blowing raw and cold, and Stiles' unique uniform has uncovered a most substantial part of his body, including that part of the anatomy used to sit on. He is very contrite and has sent forward a request to be allowed to exchange his own for a Confederate uniform, but we are not issuing new uniforms just now.

Like Private Stiles, the esteemed Lieutenant Colonel Long is also having his share of troubles these days. But, like the book of Genesis, let me start at the beginning.

The lieutenant colonel, in some mysterious manner, became the proud possessor of a good fat goose, which he directed his Negro cook,

Fred, to prepare for dinner. Young Lieutenant Clark, his eyes wide in wondrous amazement, described the goose as looking absolutely succulent while the cook prepared to place it in a large kettle suspended over a blazing fire. Long invited a few of his favorite officers to partake of his hospitality and made great preparations to entertain them in lavish style. Word of the impending feast became known about the camp and some of the more devious boys, perhaps with the knowledge of Doctor Hall and Major Galloway, undertook to disarrange and disrupt the repast, at least so far as the goose was concerned. Plotting long into the night, they came up with a brilliant scheme to kidnap the goose. Their plans had to be well laid, for the cook was very alert and suspicious, keeping close to the fire over which hung the camp kettle with the goose inside and a cover on.

The key to the success of the plot was to get the Negro cook, Fred, away from the fire for a few moments. Quite a number of the boys gathered around the fire, inhaling the fragrant odors and trying to distract Fred's attention, but to no avail, for he was on to their scheme and guarded the kettle with a diligence that was exemplary. Fred underestimated his adversaries, however, and one bright and ingenious lad put the well-laid plan into action. He slipped around quietly from one to another of the boys around the fire and whispered to each one and then walked slowly away, passing in front of Lieutenant Colonel Long's tent. Once out of sight of the vigilant cook, he approached the sentinel who was standing guard in front of the lieutenant colonel's tent and held a short, whispered consultation with him, then went merrily on his way. Soon after, the guard, when he reached the end of his beat nearest the cook's fire, stepped out a little farther so he could see Fred and, in a low voice, not loud enough for Long to hear but sufficiently loud for the cook to hear, said, "Fred, Lieutenant Colonel Long wishes to see you."

Fred, a trusting soul used to obeying orders, was completely taken off guard and at once turned around and started to walk to the front of the lieutenant colonel's tent. He had barely turned the corner when it suddenly flashed upon his mind that skullduggery was taking place and that it was only a ruse to get him away from the fire. He turned and with his eyes wide with fright, retraced his steps in hot haste. He reached the fire and removed the lid, only to discover that the goose was gone.

Fred ran quickly to Lieutenant Colonel Long's tent and told him the awful news. Long rushed from the tent and began a frantic search for the missing goose. He ran madly up and down the company streets, sniffing with nostrils distended, trying like a bloodhound hot on the trail to catch a whiff of the pleasant aroma of cooked goose.

It was no use, the goose had disappeared and has not been heard from. It vanished as surely, swiftly and effectually as though it had evaporated into thin air. Nobody knows who took it and no one seems to know what has become of it. Lieutenant Clark, wise beyond his years, said to Doctor Hall that it was a fowl conspiracy if he ever saw one.

FEBRUARY 8, 1862—SATURDAY
NEAR DUMFRIES, VIRGINIA

For the past several weeks, the officers and non-commissioned officers have been diligently studying Lt. Col. William J. Hardee's *Rife and Infantry Tactics*. This manual of over 500 pages has been adopted to replace Scott's *Infantry Tactics*. Hardee's manual is almost exclusively concerned with drill and offers step-by-step instruction in the words of command and necessary evolutions to change from one formation to another.

The regimental officers have benefited greatly from this study of military tactics and it must be confessed that almost all of them were as ignorant of things military and as awkward in the drill as the privates. To give the devil his due, often Lt. Colonel Long, who graduated from West Point and knows Hardee's *Tactics* backwards and forwards, was seen taking his sword, or a stick, from some young captain or lieutenant while drilling a company, showing him how to go through the various maneuvers.

This morning, the entire command had its first lesson in regimental tactics. Following an idea put forth by Lt. Colonel Long, the movements were directed by bugle call, the officer ready if necessary to supplement the call by verbal order. The color guard, strengthened by details from each company, formed the reserve. It was a mild day, the sun shined forth brightly and when the regiment deployed in line and extended, covering nearly a mile of ground, the sun flashed off the thousand bayonets, creating a dazzling reflection almost blinding in brilliance.

At my order, the chief bugler sounded "the forward." The advance was then stopped by the bugle call to "lie down." While lying, the men receive the order to "commence firing," and, as they use nothing but caps, there is no damage done. The order to "rise up" is soon sounded and, in fear of an imaginary enemy, the call comes to "rally by fours," then "by sections." The call is then sounded to go forward. The system works wonderfully. The bugle almost talks to the men. Up and down steep inclines, across ravines and morasses, through almost impenetrable thickets, the men moved in obedience to the imperative note of the bugle. Sweating, puffing, and a little tired with the constant call to go forward, the men welcomed the new notes sounding "the retreat." The call to disperse liberally interpreted sounds like "spread out a little." That to rally, hurry up, hurry up, hurry up, boys. Associating familiar phrases like the above with the calls, they become strongly impressed upon the memory of the men. The regiment drilled in this manner for some two-and-a-half hours, and, for a first-time performance, the drill was a great success.

Afterwards, I came across Lt. Colonel Long, his hair was spongy and covered with sweat. He was breathing like a horse after the exertions of the drill. I gave him a sharp salute and said, "My compliments, Colonel. The bugle calls were a great success. Well done!" A slight smile turned up the corners of his lips, breaking if only for an instant, the icy exterior he showed to the world.

"Thank you, Colonel Pettigrew. I have waited a long time for that compliment. I thought the regiment was magnificent today!"

"I agree," I replied. "I value a day of good drill higher than a week of oratory; however, we must not forget that battle is the swiftest of all schools of military instruction, and until we pass our examinations during that severe test, we must continue to drill and prepare."

As the other officers slowly rode up to join us, they were all smiling and laughing, elated and proud of the way the troops had performed.

"Colonel Pettigrew," shouted Major Galloway, "the regimental maneuvers and the extraordinary precision and unison with which the many motions in the manual of arms were made was so machine like, as if to indicate that all the muskets were controlled by one lever."

"The 22nd North Carolina is without a doubt the best regiment in the Confederacy," added Captain Evans Turner.

"The 22nd is the best regiment in the world!" shouted Lt. Clark.

"I feel sorry for any Yankee regiment that we would meet on a fair field," said Major Galloway.

"Yes," said the irrepressible Lt. Clark, "their goose would be cooked in short order."

At the mention of the word goose, Lt. Colonel Long stiffened, like he had been suddenly stabbed. His black eyes glared at Lt. Clark from his ruddy face while many of the officers put their hands to their face or turned away to suppress smiles.

Ignoring the young lieutenant's unfortunate use of words, I ordered the officers to begin the march back to camp. It had been a long day and the men were tired and hungry.

Riding back to camp, the sunlight turned deep gold. It was beautiful, much like my mood. Feeling a great inward glow of satisfaction over the day's drill, I rode down the road until it turned and passed by a church with old grey walls and a small house with a thatch roof. After that, I paid little attention to my surroundings. All I could think of was the pride I felt in the men and officers of the regiment. There just isn't any way to record how good I felt. I was honored and proud to command these men, these officers. It was a glorious feeling and I wished it could last forever.

FEBRUARY 10, 1862—MONDAY
NEAR DUMFRIES, VIRGINIA

The weather has been tempestuous as of late, snowing, sleeting, freezing and altogether of the most unpleasant character. The high winds and low temperature make the camp a dreary place.

To multiply the depth of a "blue Monday," I had to witness an execution by hanging today. The culprit was named Dennis Lanaghan, who murdered in a most brutal manner a man by the name of Adam Patterson. Lanaghan was a member of a roving band of guerrillas made up of mostly deserters. He entered, with others of his motley gang, the house of Patterson, who lived near Dumfries and was known to have money hidden in the house. The guerrillas demanded the money, but Patterson would not comply and he was seized, his ears cut off, his tongue taken out, and then stabbed.

Lanaghan was captured by one of our cavalry patrols, his compatriots escaping into the woods. He was tried by a military court and condemned to death.

At twelve o'clock yesterday, a crowd commenced congregating at the Dumfries courthouse, eyeing with curiosity a large uncovered army ambulance hitched to six splendid horses. The ambulance was to convey the prisoner and his coffin to the gallows.

At one o'clock, the Sixth North Carolina Regiment, commanded by Colonel Dorsey Pender and the Hampton Legion cavalry commanded by Major Butler arrived upon the ground and formed in line. The ambulance and military then moved to the jail, a rough wooden coffin was placed in the ambulance and the prisoner escorted from the jail. Lanaghan had been intoxicated at the time of the murder, but even when sober was a very bad man. Leaving the jail, he had a pale and haggard look, unshaven, glancing about nervously. His step was firm and he got into the wagon with but little assistance. He was accompanied by Chaplain Keys. The procession then moved off toward the gallows erected a short distance from the town upon the Alexandria Pike. The eager crowd followed to the place of execution, swearing, laughing and yelling, many carrying bottles of whiskey or wine.

The day, as I have mentioned, was half-sleety, half-snowy with a cold wind. The ceremonies were kept short. General Order Number 123 from headquarters was read. The prisoner then knelt and was baptized by Chaplain Keys. After the baptism, a Catholic priest made a most fervent and eloquent prayer. Lanaghan was on his knees, with his eyes lifted to heaven, and seemingly praying with all the fervor of one who will soon be facing his Creator. After the Catholic priest had finished praying, the prisoner was told he had five minutes to live and could make any remarks he wished. Lanaghan arose with steady limbs and, turning to the crowd, said, "Gentlemen and friends, I am not guilty of the murder of Adam Patterson. I did not kill him. I hope you will all live to one day find out who was the true murderer. I believe Jesus is waiting to receive my eternal soul. I repeat, I am not guilty of Patterson's murder. I was there, but too intoxicated to kill him."

After this short speech, he stepped forward on the scaffold to have the fatal rope placed around his neck. As the rope was being adjusted, he said out loud, "For God's sake, don't choke me before I am hung." Then when the black cap was drawn over his eyes, which would see the world no more, he yelled, "Lord, have mercy on my soul!"

The words were scarcely uttered when the hangman pulled the cord and let fall the drop. Lanaghan fell about two feet and literally died without a struggle. There was but a small imperceptible drawing up of his legs and a twitch or two of his feet, but little other evidence of movement.

Slightly before Lanaghan's hanging, Sarah Ann Patterson, the youngest daughter of the murdered man, had made her appearance near the gallows. She asked Captain Goodwin and Major Wert of the Sixth North Carolina the privilege of adjusting the rope around his neck, but they would not grant her wish. She is a young woman of about seventeen years, attractive and intelligent-looking. She stood there watching intently for a long time while Lanaghan hung dangling between heaven and earth. She seemed to take great satisfaction that the murderer of her father had now paid the penalty with his life. I asked her what she thought of the gruesome affair, and she curtly replied, "He will never murder another man, I think. I hope, Colonel, that he rots in Hell!"

After the body had remained about fifteen minutes swinging in the air and the surgeon of the Sixth North Carolina pronounced Lanaghan dead, it was cut down and placed in the wooden coffin. The crowd slowly broke up and moved away, their moods somber like the weather.

FEBRUARY 11, 1862—TUESDAY
NEAR DUMFRIES, VIRGINIA

Major Galloway, Doctor Hall, Chaplain Keys and Colonel Dorsey Pender of the 6th North Carolina have been stretching their legs before my fireplace all afternoon. Pender, a handsome man of medium height with an olive complexion and thick dark beard, is a 1854 graduate of West Point. He has served with the artillery in Florida and the Dragoons in New Mexico. Shortly before the war, he served in California, Oregon and Washington, engaging in several bloody skirmishes with the Indians. At Spokane Plains in 1858, He was suddenly attacked by an Indian chief, the leader of a large war party. To his dismay, Pender discovered that his sword had become entangled in the scabbard and could not be drawn out. Out of desperation, he grabbed the Indian's arm with one hand, and his neck with the other. He then pulled the savage close and galloped back toward the ranks of this men. Once there, he lifted the Indian from his horse and hurled him among his soldiers, who quickly stabbed the chief to death.

As we drank coffee and smoked our cigars, enjoying Pender's interesting tales of the Indians and the West, an orderly came into my quarters and handed me a copy of the following telegram:

> "Intelligence has reached Norfolk that the enemy captured Roanoke Island Saturday afternoon at four o'clock.

> "The enemy landed a force of fifteen thousand against less than three thousand Confederates.

> "All of our troops are prisoners in the hands of the enemy, excepting twenty-five who made their escape. Many of our officers are wounded and among them, O. Jennings Wise, it is feared mortally. Captain Cox of Charlottesville is reported killed. Particulars received are very meager, but that the island has been captured is certain. General Wise was not captured."

This terrible news threw a dark shadow over our little gathering. We soon learned that the Yankee force (under General Burnside) that had captured Roanoke Island, landed and somehow got through a swamp which our engineers had pronounced impossible. With this tactic, they flanked our men and forced surrender.

"Why," asked Major Galloway, "did not our men have a leader worthy of them? Roanoke Island is called the back door to Norfolk. Why did they not find that out before putting it in the hands of our enemies!"

"Not only that," added Dr. Hall, "Albermarle Sound and its tributaries are now open to inroads and incursions of all kinds. It opens up a large extent of the state to the enemy. Wherever their gunboats can go, they will be masters."

"Yes. Many who live in that part of the state, including many of your family, Colonel Pettigrew, will have to flee inland," said Galloway.

This despondent talk continued for some time when Chaplain Keys stood up and said in a loud voice, "Gentlemen, you tire me with your talk of disaster. I say this may be the best thing that could happen to us. Maybe this defeat will infuse many with a will to volunteer and also give our people a determination not to be conquered. We should count our blessings! Even when things seem to go wrong, we should thank God and take courage."

"I see few blessings to count, Reverend," replied Dr. Hall. "I think instead I'll go to my tent, bend my elbow and count my drinks."

"I agree with the good doctor," added Galloway. "Confederate affairs are certainly in a blue way. Roanoke Island, captured. Fort Henry on the Tennessee River open to the Yankees and the Mississippi River in danger of being under their control. We have evacuated Romney in Western Virginia and it seems new Yankee armies and fleets are swarming and threatening everywhere. I believe that God has abandoned us and our cause."

"I think as a people and as a nation, we tend to take the manifold blessings of God for granted," replied Chaplain Keys. "As for me, doctor, instead of feeling blue and turning to strong drink, I count my blessings."

"I agree," said Colonel Pender, taking a long puff on his cigar. "We as a people and nation must count our blessings or the gloom cast overall by these defeats will erode our will to win. We face a deadly determined foe, and the prospect of a long and bloody war."

My quarters are now quiet. All have left and I sit here alone puffing madly on my cigar. Chaplain Keys' may be happy, but I am dismal without and within. I find the Roanoke affair perfectly incomprehensible. Since the beginning of the war, the newspapers have been filled with extravagant laudations of Southern valor. The annals of Greece and Rome offer no parallel, they write. Whole Yankee regiments are defeated by companies of our troops and we yield only to death. Yet at Roanoke, our men surrender with no blood on their bayonets.

The troops who surrendered on Roanoke Island may have had reason to do so, but I have no pity for any soldier in this war who surrenders.

FEBRUARY 20, 1862—THURSDAY
NEAR DUMFRIES, VIRGINIA

This afternoon I looked at my desk and found it piled high with paperwork that needed to be completed. There is, alas, no escape from the daily reports that are made to me by the captains, adjutants and orderlies. I must review and sign them before forwarding them to brigade headquarters. These daily reports descend to the most minute details: the number of sick in quarters, the sick in the hospital, the number in the company present for duty, the number detailed for special service, and the whereabouts of those absent from camp—whether on passes or furlough, the rations drawn, etc., etc. These reports must in all things conform to strict military rule, which, like the law of the Medes and Persians, changeth not. There must be no mistakes in this cascade of paper. Nothing to be corrected or left to be understood.

Not only is Dr. Hall a fine surgeon, but also has the eye of a hawk, the nose of a bloodhound, and the ears of an elephant. Nothing escapes him. Somehow he learned that I acquired four bottles of Madeira and Champagne from Richmond.

Accompanied by Major Galloway, the doctor appeared suddenly at my quarters looking like a little lost boy. I was suspicious of this nocturnal call and could tell they were up to no good, but I let them enter my quarters.

"Good evening. Good evening, Colonel," said Dr. Hall.

"Good evening, gentlemen. Take a seat. What can I do for you this evening?"

"Nothing special, Colonel. It's a friendly call. It's pretty cold weather, Colonel."

"Yes!"

"It's dry, too. Very dry, wouldn't you say, Colonel?"

"Yes."

With this, Dr. Hall pulled out a harmonica from his coat pocket and said, "The men sing a great deal, Colonel."

"Yes," I replied, "sometimes they do."

"Major Galloway and I sing a song or two ourselves, Colonel, and we have been practicing. Perhaps you would like to hear us now."

"Isn't it a bit late to be warbling a tune," I asked innocently.

"No. It's a short tune," said Major Galloway.

With this, Dr. Hall put the harmonica to his mouth and with a sound anything but musical, the two of them began singing in a slow time at the start, but increasing time gradually, until the last line, which was rattled off a double-quick. Thus was sung:

> "Between you and us, we really think,
> "Between you and us, we really think,
> "Between you and us, we really think,
> "It's just about time to take a little drink."

Just as they finished the last line, they stood, stomped their feet in perfect harmony and took from behind their backs each a small tin cup and simultaneously extended their arms toward me, a smile on their expectant faces. It was rather entertaining and I decided that such a show should be rewarded. I produced a bottle of my Madeira and filled the two tin cups. The two minstrels drank heartily and soon drained the cups dry. Much to my surprise the harmonica was again produced and suddenly, they were singing again:

> "Between you and us, we really think,
> "Between you and us, we really think,
> "Between you and us, we really think,
> "It's just about time to take a little drink."

I poured another round and, as they sat drinking and conversing, I asked for the harmonica, blew a strange sound and sang:
"My Madeira is just about gone,
"My Madeira is just about gone,
"Now you must depart,
"Even though it will break my heart."
The hint was taken and they drained their cups. I put my nearly empty bottle of Madeira tenderly away. With a quick salute, the two songsters left my quarters. As they left, Major Galloway remarked as he stepped outside, "You're a good host, Colonel!"

With that, Dr. Hall smiled, blew a little sound on his harmonica and said, "Amen!"

FEBRUARY 27, 1862—THURSDAY
NEAR DUMFRIES, VIRGINIA

What a glorious scene lies before me! The night sky filled with stars. The rising moon. The rapid river. The thousand tents and log quarters dotting the hillsides and valley. The boys in groups about their camp-fires. In short, just enough of heaven and earth visible to put one in a contented, reflective mood.

I am sitting on a log in front of my quarters enjoying my usual after-supper cigar. It is one of life's little joys. I have just finished re-reading a long letter I am going to sent to Judge Petigru in far away Charleston.

I am including the letter below as it gives, I think, a good picture of our life here in winter quarters.

"Dear Judge Petigru:

"Wouldn't it be wonderful if you could by some miracle peep in on me some evening as I sit by my stove, trying to amuse myself until it is time to retire. I have been reading a great deal lately, usually late at night when the day's work has been done and the camp is quiet. Among the works of literature that have occupied me as of late are

Macablay's essay on Madame D'Arblay and his novel *Evelina*. Also, Carlyle's *Heroes and Hero Worship*.

"Often my fellow officers pay me a visit and we sit around the stove in happy discussion and laughter. We amuse ourselves with the many-tongued rumors which float about on the popular breeze that England or France has recognized the Confederacy, or that the Confederates have gained a new victory.

"At times, the discussions grow quite educational and among the subjects discussed are: Vattel and Philmore on International Law; Humboldt's Works and Travels; The African explorations of Harth, the great German traveler who went from the Atlantic to the Red Sea in a line a few degrees above the equator; the influence of climate on the human features; and the beauty of European as compared to Southern women.

"Chaplain Keys will often take center stage and propose his usual question for discussion: 'People have always professed religion, but to profess religion and to have religion are two very different things. If one considers the history of the world for thousands of years that we know of, and especially the centuries of so-called Christianity, and sees how people have behaved, then he will know how much religion they have had. The history of mankind has been a history of war's aggression, hatreds and injustices. Why?'

"This question usually sparks a lively debate. Lately, however, whenever the Chaplain attempts to interject this into our discussions, he is shouted down, for we have found that no matter how long we debate this question, we are further from the answer when we end, than we were when we began.

"Sometimes we get Dr. Hall to tell of his travels in Europe and on the high seas. He served as a ship's doctor for some years and is a natural-born raconteur. His stories are so entertaining and interesting that it is delightful to listen to him.

"One of Dr. Hall's favorite stories concerns the man who died of fright. I have heard this story several times and always find it interesting.

"It seems that one evening about dark, sometime after supper, Dr. Hall was sitting in front of his office enjoying the evening newspaper and an after-supper smoke. He soon observed an ambulance drive up filled with several sick men. It was a daily occurrence to have sick men arrive at his office from a nearby camp and the arrival of this ambulance load was no unusual occurrence. As soon as it stopped, Dr. Hall got in to find out the condition of the men and to determine how to best treat them. Once in the ambulance, he smelled small pox and said to the driver, 'You've got small pox here.'

"The driver seemed very surprised and said, 'No, I reckon not.'

"Dr. Hall said he was certain of it and directed the driver to take the men to a nearby hospital. Dr. Hall looked closely at the driver and noticed that he was a robust, heavily built man, a picture of perfect health. The driver started to drive his team as directed and seemed to be drawing the reins together to back the horses, but he suddenly fell backwards off the wagon seat, landing at Dr. Hall's feet, as he was standing in the ambulance. Dr. Hall guessed that the driver had lost his balance and had fallen back and would right himself, but he did not move. Dr. Hall bent down and examined him and found that he was, to all appearances, dead. Whether or not the driver had died from fright, Dr. Hall could not determine. The next day, however, the doctor had the driver's body taken from the dead house and carried to a nearby examining room where, with the assistance of two other doctors, they made a careful post mortem. They could find nothing abnormal in his brain or other organs. Dr. Hall has speculated that the mere mention of the dreaded words *small pox* caused the driver to die from fright.

"I could recount numerous other stories of Dr. Hall and the campfire, but I will wait until we meet again on that happy day when I return to Charleston.

"Of course, all our entertainment does not take place around the stove or in the comfort of our tents. Just the other day, we had the good fortune to witness an exhibition by a group of soldiers from the Louisiana Zouaves. They created a sensation among the men of my regiment when they appeared on the drill field dressed in their Algerian Zouave uniforms of brilliant red Turkish trousers, red kepis, blue jackets and vest, and white garters. These Zouaves are a tough, dare-devil, hardy-looking set of fellows with a dashing rakish air. It is said that on the way to Virginia from Louisiana, one of the Zouaves fell under the cars and was killed at just about the same time that a young officer had to shoot one of the Zouaves for insubordination. When they detrained at Richmond, they headed straight for the nearest saloons. A correspondent of the *Charleston Courier* described them as stampeding into the saloons like famished cattle into a river, snatching up everything in sight and drinking it down, yelling and threatening if it did not come fast enough and not bothering to pay. After leaving the bars, they were quartered temporarily in a five-story warehouse close to the train depot. Coming downstairs like ordinary people did not suit these Zouaves. As one would hang by his hands from a windowsill, a second would slide down his back and hold onto his heels. While a third would turn four or five somersaults, go out the window, and roll down this novel bridge into the window of the story below.

"The Zouaves marched to the drill field with a cat-like elasticity of step. Their officer gave the orders in French. They then proceeded to give a demonstration of their superior skill in handling their rifled muskets. They drew a vast crowd around them and their movements were watched with evident delight and much interest. They handled their muskets with extraordinary skill, the sharp bayonets glistening in the sun as they demonstrated to what beauty and perfection the manual of arms can be brought to through intelligence and drill. The bayonet exercises were a complete triumph, as every movement elicited shouts of approval and applause. Their movements were remarkable as they threw their rifles with fixed bayonets high into the air, or made them revolve with great speed. Now the point up. Now the butt of the gun up. As the rifles descended, they would catch them near the point of the bayonet and revolve the rifles around their heads with great velocity, passing the gun under their arm, over the shoulder, then around the neck and under the other arm. Etc. Etc.

"After the exhibition, the men of the regiment were so thrilled by the performance that they took up a collection for the Zouaves which amounted to over one hundred dollars. After pocketing the money, the Zouaves marched toward the camp of the Sixth North Carolina where I am sure their performance was likewise hailed with delight.

"I have not heard from Ellison Capers lately, but trust he is doing well. I see Major Connor of the Hampton Legion from time to time as they are camped not too far from us.

"The disaster at Fort Donelson is much to be deplored. Yet our men fought well until they were overpowered. I am sure you know that my Uncle Peyton's son Dabney Harrison was killed gallantly leading his company. He was a Presbyterian minister, but felt the call to defend his state from the invader and, doffing his ministerial office, raised a company in his own congregation and was elected its captain. My uncle has borne this loss like a noble Roman—or rather like the Christian which he is. The story of this loss is like that of many another in the South.

"I have gone on far too long. Give my love to all who remember me in Charleston.

"God bless,

"Johnson"

MARCH 12, 1862–WEDNESDAY
CAMP BARTOW—FREDERICKSBURG, VIRGINIA

On Friday, the seventh of March, we received orders to pack and be prepared to fall back to a new defensive line on the Rappahhannock River. We were surprised by the order and hardly knew what to make of it. Earnest hope was expressed by the officers and men that we might yet be ordered to remain and defend the gun positions and breastworks upon which we had spent so much time and labor.

Saturday morning, we began packing and soon every knapsack was filled to bursting. What we couldn't carry with us, we destroyed. The commissary and Sutler's stores were thrown open for the soldiers to help themselves. What a feast it was for the troops. There seemed everything at hand to tempt the men to eat, drink or wear. The soldiers, who suddenly found themselves in a veritable land of plenty, were soon loaded down, hating to leave anything of value behind to the Yankees. Such an assemblage of heavy-weighted men was never seen before. They looked for all the world like a band of bloodthirsty pirates who, having sacked a coastal city, were returning laden with booty. Many of the men had immense knapsacks bulging out ready to burst. Others carried carpetbags, old valises and even kettles filled with every imaginable article that could be of use.

As our tramp proceeded, the men began to grow weary under their heavy loads. As mile after mile was traversed and heavier grew the burden, the road began to be littered with disregarded clothes, cooking utensils and provisions. Despite the terrible condition of the roads, we reached Austin's Run just before dark. This camp will long be remembered as a place of great quiet and beauty. The run flowed between two hillsides facing each other which were each occupied by two regiments. The night was dark and cold, but there were plenty of trees and brush at hand for firewood.

Countless fires soon sprang up and the men cooked dinner, weak coffee, hard bread and fat bacon. As they sat around the fire cooking their bacon with the aid of a stick or ramrod, the dark shadow of the surrounding forest was illuminated by the crackling flames, while the dusky forms of the soldiers moving to and fro lent a wild grandeur to the nighttime scene.

We left our nighttime bivouac early the next morning and marched through the rain, which soon rendered the roads in horrible condition. Traveling through the mud and slush amid the deep ruts cut by the wagon trains, a number of heavy guns became bogged down and the horses were no longer able to pull them. My men, weary and not accustomed to marching long distances, felt it was an indisposition to have to halt and attempt to move the heavy guns. But many were tugging and pulling with good grace, while others stood around giving unneeded advice when I rode up from the rear. I could see that only an extraordinary effort could save the guns. I dismounted from my horse and waded into the deep mud, calling upon the men to help save the artillery. Good men that they were, those watching raised a shout and crowded around the wheels. Thanks to their efforts, not a gun or caisson was lost. I mounted my horse, thanked the men and rode slowly away, the muddiest colonel in the Confederate Army.

The next day, it once again began to rain and a continual down pour fell as we marched along. Blankets were taken from the knapsacks to cover the men as they marched, but they soon filled with water and had to be thrown aside. Both sides of the road were strewn with blankets, shawls, overcoats, and clothing of every description. The men found it impossible to bear up under such loads. The mud-filled road made marching very disagreeable to soldiers unaccustomed to it. Soon the men were strung out for miles and all organizations were lost sight of, but at night, they collected together in groups joined the wagon trains and bivouacked for the night.

On one occasion, I found one of my youngest soldiers—a mere lad of 15 years—lying on the roadside, weeping bitterly. I dismounted and asked him what was the matter. He explained that his feet were so sore that he could not walk any further. He feared he would be captured by the enemy. His feet were swollen, sore and bleeding. I said to him, "You shall not be captured," and ordered him to mount my horse and ride forward until he could get into an ambulance or wagon. Then he would tell the quartermaster to send my horse back to me as soon as possible. He thanked me, wiped his eyes, got into my saddle, and rode a few rods to where the company of which he was a member had halted to rest. He stopped the horse in front of his comrades who were sitting, resting on the roadside, and, straightening himself up, he lifted his old slouch hat with all the dignity of a commander-in-chief and called out in his youthful voice, "Attention men! I'm about to bid you farewell and I want to tell you before I go that I am very sorry for you. I was once a private myself!"

Having given his little oration, he galloped away, bowing and waving his hat to his comrades in acknowledgment of the cheers which greeted him.

We have, at last, come to our place of rest, about six miles from the city of Fredericksburg on the south bank of the Rappahannock. We crossed the river late last night on a railroad bridge which has been laid with planks to accommodate the passage of our wagon trains.

This afternoon, Melvin Russell, orderly-sergeant of Company K, died of congestion of the lungs several hours after the arrival of the regiment. He was an educated man and had formerly been a school teacher. He was the only man we lost during our tiring march. The notes of Surgeon Hall give a glimpse of Russell's illness and death.

"March 9—Orderly-sergeant Melvin Russell, Company K, age 23. Complains of lassitude—dispirited—some headache—pains in the lungs—has taken some remedies of his own.

"March 10—Feels relieved—rested well. Was placed in an ambulance during the march—complains of fatigue—Diet of tea and soft bread.

"March 11—Endured the day's march quite well. At night, was removed without knowledge of surgeon to quarters of the company bivouac. Was called to visit him at eleven o'clock. Found him cold and uncomfortably situated. Complained of chills and fever. Administered stimulant of brandy.

"March 12—Slept well during the night and expresses himself as feeling better—complained last evening of inability to use lower extremities. Thinks he was numb, but not paralyzed. Twelve o'clock—appears quite elated at our arrival in camp and end of march. Remains in ambulance hospital. Half-past-three o'clock—found patient out of ambulance—cold and suffering from severe chill. Removed directly to hospital tent. Stimulants administered—congestion of spinal column and general congestion. Died at six o'clock, conscious to ten minutes before death."

I am now living in a tent on the edge of a large pine forest. We are getting on very well here. I am in excellent condition. This kind of life which kills men of delicate health such as Sergeant Russell, for some reason, agrees with me most wonderfully.

The line of the army now extends from Staunton to Gordonsville. I hope there will be no more falling back.

MARCH 14, 1862—FRIDAY
CAMP BARLOW, FREDERICKSBURG, VIRGINIA

Shortly after dark last evening, we buried Melvin Russell. Many of his comrades had been his schoolmates and all felt his death deeply. He was tenderly wrapped in his blanket and prepared for burial. The men of Company B followed the wagon carrying the body in a silent and sorrowful procession. The remains were carried back for a mile to a little churchyard that was located near our camp. The body was then laid on the ground while the men stood sorrowfully around. Pine torches lit up the dark woods and gave light to the men who, with pick and shovel, were digging the lonely grave.

Once the grave was prepared, the men gathered around and Chaplain Keys said a prayer. Then the chaplain opened his Bible and read the words from John 11:25, which have echoed down the centuries and offered comfort to so many.

"I am the resurrection and the life; he that believeth in me, though he were dead, yet shall he live: And whosoever liveth and believeth in me shall never die."

When the chaplain finished, the men stood silently around the grave, their heads bowed in sorrow and prayer, the crackling flames from the pine torches sent dark shadows of the men flickering off the nearby trees. In the distance, the lonely cry of an owl carried across the still night air.

Then, Russell's body was lowered into the grave, the blanket marked C. S. A., his only shroud. The tears of his comrades sanctified the soil where they laid him and though buried far from his home in North Carolina, hands as gentle and loving as those of his family laid him to his last rest.

Upon our arrival back at camp, I observed candles flickering in many of the tents where men were writing letters home, while in the distance, I could see several groups of men sitting by the smoldering embers of the camp fire in quiet thought, gazing at the distant dark outline of the Blue Ridge Mountains, or listening to the wash of the Rappahannock's waters.

Several of us gathered around a cheerfully crackling campfire and our faces ruddy with the fire's warm glow talked later than usual of young Russell and the uncertainty of life.

As we continued our conversation, Major Galloway poked at the fire with a ramrod and remarked, "You know, this has been a most trying night and young Russell lies dead and buried. I feel that before this war is over many of us will die a soldier's death and follow him to the grave."

"Maybe Russell is the lucky one," added Colonel Pender.

"How so?" asked Chaplain Keys.

"Because he was at least laid to rest with loving hands, by those who know him, and his grave marked with a wooden cross. However, we are poor, naked wretches that will soon have to face the pitiless storm of battle. Perhaps we will die an agonizing death and then be buried in a mass grave by the enemy or those who don't know us. There we will molder, be abandoned and forgotten by all those we hold dear."

"That well may be," remarked Chaplain Keys, "but I firmly believe that men do not end with this life and maybe what we are and what we do here will have an influence on the hereafter. Who knows?"

MARCH 17, 1862—MONDAY
CAMP BARLOW—FREDERICKSBURG, VIRGINIA

We are delightfully situated here about the right distance from town. Nice camp. Comfortable quarters. Lots of troops. The only drawback is that the 11th Mississippi Regiment is camped too near us for quiet. General Whiting who commands the troops in the Fredericksburg area has three brigades consisting of twelve regiments and Hampton's Legion. General French's brigade is also located near us, accompanied by four light batteries.

Major Galloway and I rode into Fredericksburg yesterday morning to meet with General Whiting on regimental business. We are in need of overcoats, socks, drawers, canteens, axes and blankets. The meeting was a productive one as General Whiting ordered his quartermaster to issue the needed supplies as soon as possible.

Galloway and I reached Fredericksburg in good time to walk around the scenic little town. Located in the beautiful valley of the Rappahannock, the city lies halfway between Washington City and Richmond. It is a regularly planned and well-built town with straight and wide streets, substantial brick houses and an appearance of rising prosperity.

General Whiting has established his headquarters at the Planters Hotel. Outside the main entrance of the hotel, at the corner of Charles and William streets, stands the slave market auction block where Negroes are sold or hired out for a fixed term to the highest bidder. The proprietor of the hotel informed us that President-elect Lincoln had stayed briefly in the hotel after the 1860 election. Entering the hotel through the front entrance, you emerge into a spacious lobby. On the far wall hangs a large lithographic view of Fredericksburg that was produced in 1856 by the E. Sachse Company of Baltimore. The print presents a view of the city that one might see if he were high in a balloon on the north side of the river looking south. The print is surprisingly accurate and many houses, churches and buildings can easily be identified. A train, smoke trailing from its stack, heads north over the bridge, while large and small ships sail up and down the river. Galloway and I spent some time studying the print and were easily able to identify such familiar landmarks as Mayre's Heights, the Washington Woolen Mills, the Fallmouth Bridge and Rapids, and Scott's Island.

The shades of night were falling fast when we mounted and left Fredericksburg for our camp. Snow had fallen and the paths through the woods were obliterated. We had only traveled a short distance from town when we halted at a crossroads unsure of which direction to take. After some confusion over which road to take, Major Galloway, who was supposed to be a good woodsman, took the lead. He claimed to know the exact route to take back to our camp. He was mounted on a large grey-colored steed and directed me to "follow the grey," which I did, in Indian file. After proceeding a mile or so down a dark and narrow path, Galloway halted and confessed himself at fault. He had evidently gone astray. Just then, a light was seen shining dimly through the thick, dark woods. We rode towards it "following the grey." It was the campfire of the Eighth Georgia Regiment.

Galloway asked the sentinel for directions and, satisfied he now knew the way back to camp, cried, "follow the grey," and away we went. After riding for some time, we saw a light again and a lone sentinel. "What camp is this?" said Galloway.

The answer came, "The Eighth Georgia."

"I'll be damned," said a puzzled Galloway. "Which way to the camp of the 22nd North Carolina?"

"I told you before," replied the sentinel, and he again gave the directions.

Away we went, Galloway saying very confidentially, "All right now, just follow the grey."

We rode for more than an hour through the thick woods, the branches sometimes scraping our faces. For all I knew, we could have been in the wilds of China when we approached what seemed to be another campfire. Galloway, not quite his old confident self, again asked hesitantly, "What camp is this?"

In answer to the question, came back the same reply, "The Eighth Georgia."

I rode near to Galloway, thinking perhaps I should find my own way home, when an officer appeared and said, "Gentlemen, you are evidently lost. You have already stopped at this fire three or four times. I am the adjutant of this regiment, and the colonel sends his compliments and invites you to dismount and come into his tent and warm up."

The "Great Pathfinder" and I did not wait for a second invitation, but discounted at once and Colonel "Dignity Smith" gave us a warm welcome and hot punch, after having a laugh at our mishaps. It was in the small hours of the night when we again started for camp with a guide furnished by Colonel Smith.

Galloway, now in disgrace as a woodsman and pathfinder, was banished with his grey to the rear.

MARCH 20, 1862—THURSDAY
CAMP BARLOW—FREDERICKSBURG, VIRGINIA

The night is grand. The moon, a crescent, now rests for a moment on the highest peak of the distant Blue Ridge and, by its light, suggests rather than reveals the outline of hill and valley.

The boys of the regiment are wide awake and merry. The fair weather has put new spirit in them all, and possibly the presence of the paymaster has contributed somewhat to the good feeling which prevails.

The campfire is blazing away, and Major Galloway, Doctor Hall and I have just fired up fresh cigars. We are busy making small talk when Chaplain Keys suddenly steps through a cloud of campfire smoke, unfolds a portable chair near the blaze, and settles down in front of the flickering light.

Lighting his cigar, Keys takes a deep puff and then drops a bombshell into our pleasant conversation by exclaiming, "Have you heard, gentlemen, that throughout the North, Negro regiments are being raised, drilled and equipped as soldiers? General Hunter of the Union Army in South Carolina has a regiment of them he styles the First South Carolina Volunteers. Amo writes me that he has seen two men who were taken prisoner at Port Royal, guarded by Negroes in the U.S. uniform."

"Our only chance it seems to me," replied Doctor Hall, "is to get ahead of the Yankees by freeing our Negroes and putting them in our army. Wade Hampton's Negroes offered to fight for him if he would arm them. He pretended to believe them and felt he could trust those he would select. He proposed to give so many acres of land and freedom to each one he enlisted."

Major Galloway then entered the fray by saying, "The proposition to make soldiers of our slaves is a most pernicious idea. You cannot make soldiers of slaves, nor slaves of soldiers. The day you make soldiers of them is the beginning of the end of our revolution. If slaves will make soldiers, our whole theory of slavery is wrong."

"You know," I added, "the Negro by long habit and training has acquired a great horror of firearms, and this war will be ended before any body of Negroes can be organized, armed and drilled so as to be efficient."

"I think the Yankees will have a great deal of trouble raising a large number of Negroes to serve in their army," stated Keys. "That there exists a moral hate on the part of the slave population towards their owners, which may be made available for the organization of Negro troops to operate in the field, is one of the most absurd of all the crotchets that fill the noodles of those Yankee fanatics."

"It is a miserable policy for the Yankees to muster runaway Negroes into their army," I stated. "If twenty million free men of the North are not able to suppress a rebellion of six millions of white men, let this acknowledgment at once be made. The plan to raise Negro troops will not scare the South."

"This may well be," said Doctor Hall, "but I am dismayed at the presence of black soldiers in South Carolina. Men lately released from slavery, men who are but a degree removed from savagery…such men sometimes do terrible things when suddenly entrusted with power. While we fight the Yankees here in Virginia, they may burn, rape and pillage all of unprotected South Carolina."

"Gentlemen," shouted Keys, clamoring to be heard, "I think we make too much of this Yankee plan. What kind of soldiers can these ex-slaves make? The Negro has a long stride yet to make before he reaches the degree of intelligence of even the most ignorant class of whites. The minds of the Negroes have not yet embraced the most elementary ideas and truths of our civilization, and despite the great progress and improvement they have made in two or three generations from a state of besotted barbarism under the admirably devised educational system of the mild domestic servitude in which they have been held, it will require many years and generations of progress and development before they have attained the capacity to think and act as free men and soldiers."

I agree wholeheartedly," added Major Galloway. "How infinitely absurd is the idea that the African slave, whose parents two centuries ago were roaming savages, perhaps cannibals in the most benighted region of the earth, can be brought to comprehend the duties of citizens and soldiers under our political system and to assume a position on a level with the white offspring of two thousand years of freedom and civilization."

"I agree, I agree!" I fairly shouted. "Slavery has supplied the very best probation through which the Negro may be gradually conducted to a full knowledge and comprehension of all his social and political duties. Slavery has certainly advanced him with no inconsiderable progress in the domestic arts and in social ideas. If the Yankees will free the slaves and attempt to arm them, they will add enormously to the bitterness that now prevails between the belligerents of the North and the South."

"If the North continues to arm the slaves," shouted Major Galloway, "then I think we should caution those white officers who lead them that if captured they shall be deemed as having incited servile insurrection and be hanged or shot. Likewise, captured black soldiers should be shot or hanged or sold into slavery. That will put an end to this nonsense!"

"And if the Yankees retaliate in kind?" I asked.

"Then we must continue our policy regardless of the consequences," replied Galloway. "It is fatal to wage war without the will to win it!"

As we paused to consider the chilling consequences of Major Galloway's proposal, the sound of "Tatoo" drifted through the camp and our little group broke up. Keys, Hall and Galloway scurried back to their tents while I remained by the dying embers wondering if, when the first shot was fired on Fort Sumter, any of us thought the war would come to this.

MARCH 24, 1862—MONDAY
CAMP BARLOW—FREDERICKSBURG, VIRGINIA

As I sat by my desk trying to put into words my feelings on being promoted to brigadier general, the string band of the 22nd struck up at the door of my tent. Going out, I was surprised to find all the commissioned officers of the regiment standing in line. Adjutant Clark nudged me and said they expected a speech. I asked if beer would not suit them better. He thought not. I am not much at speech making but I knocked the ashes off the end of my cigar and began.

"Gentlemen: I am informed all the officers of the regiment are here. I am certainly very glad to see you. The newspapers inform us that I have been very highly honored. If the report of my promotion to brigadier general is true, then I am indebted to your gallantry and that of the brave men of the 22nd for the honor. You gave me your loyalty and your trust and if now I have obtained a higher command, it is because I have had the good fortune to command good soldiers. The step upward in rank will simply increase my debt of gratitude to you.

"Shortly before your arrival, I was pondering over what this promotion would mean to me. Although greatly honored, I am not so impressed with myself or my new rank to forget from whence I came and those who have aided me. Further helping me to keep my promotion in perspective is a tale I heard some time ago.

"It seems that during the desperate battle at Manassas, there was a colonel who very largely distinguished himself and, as a result, had most of the top of his head shot off. He was carried tenderly to the rear and the surgeon, in charge of the field hospital, seeing that it was a severe case, applied a unique medical treatment. He scooped out the colonel's brains and proceeded to wash them in an old army bucket nearby. While this was taking place, a message came from the commanding general saying that the wounded colonel had been promoted to a brigadier generalship for gallantry on the field. It requested him to report to the front immediately. With the top of his head in the hands of the surgeon and his brains in the bucket, the colonel mounted his horse and prepared to obey the general's order. Thereupon the surgeon said to him, 'Wait, you are preparing to ride off without your brains!'

"'What of it?' said the late colonel as he cast a glance of pity toward the men with whole heads around him. 'What need do I have of brains? I am a brigadier general now!'

After the laughter subsided, the officers responded cordially by assuring my that they rejoiced over my promotion and were pleased I would command the brigade to which the 22nd was attached.

Then the band played sundry airs while the officers imbibed rather copiously of some applejack to celebrate my promotion and protect against the night air, which, by the way, is always dangerous when applejack is convenient. Thus ended a momentous and wonderful evening.

APRIL 1, 1862—TUESDAY
CAMP BARLOW—FREDERICKSBURG, VIRGINIA

The brigade which I have taken command of consists of the 22nd North Carolina, the 35th Georgia, the 47th Virginia, an Arkansas battalion and a small four-gun battery manned by young artillerymen from Baltimore. The brigade numbers over three thousand stalwart, well-fed men, splendidly uniformed and accoutered.

To serve as my adjutant, I have summoned from Charleston my old friend Louis Gourdin Young, a veteran of the First Regiment of Rifles and the bombardment of Fort Sumter. I am very much attached to Young personally and can endorse him as a true and honest man, willing to do all in his power for the service. I have enlisted several other aids who are all persons with whom I had previous acquaintance. They have been appointed by me for what I believe is their merit as men and soldiers. Thus far, they have given entire satisfaction.

After my promotion, I moved my headquarters to be in close proximity to all my command. Nevertheless, the move was not without incident.

Elias came to the conclusion that my mess kit might just as well be carried by a mule as by Elias and, in fact, that the mule might carry Elias too. He took one of the brigade mules for this purpose. He had only his belt and some old scraps of rope for a tackling, but he thought this would serve well enough. He ingeniously contrived a pad out of his own and my blankets and endeavored to balance his load and tie it securely to the sides of the mule, which were all festooned with pots, pans, gridirons, camp kettles and tin dippers. This gave the animal the appearance of a "hawkers" donkey. After all this varied assortment of wares had been precariously piled on the beast, Elias kindly allowed a knapsack or two to be strapped on behind and then mounted, guiding the mule with a rope halter.

He had not proceeded far down the road before some of the knots began to slip, for Elias was not a sailor, nor a very skillful disposer of weights. The best laid plans often go astray and soon one of the knapsack straps got loose and insinuated itself on the inside of the mules hind leg. It tickled him and he did what mules do best, kick. This displaced a camp kettle, which slipped under his belly. He buck jumped and unseated Elias rather ungraciously. Then the entire load shifted, most of it swinging under the mule's belly. Now the show began as the mule curveted and pranced, reared and kicked, and cleared the road right and left for more than a mile. The men scattered on every side for the mule was in earnest and was, like the Lord, no respecter of persons, kicking just as viciously at the officers as at the men.

This tale, alas and alack, has an unhappy ending, for newly appointed Brigadier General James Johnson Pettigrew had no dinner that day save what he got through the kindness of others, for his coffee, hard bread and bacon, tin plates and cups, flour, butter and precious eggs—all the materials of many a savory feast—lay in the dust.

APRIL 6, 1862—SUNDAY
CAMP BARLOW—FREDERICKSBURG, VIRGINIA

I have begun to enjoy brigade command immensely. I feel I have come to understand all the peculiarities of volunteer soldiers and when they operate to the disadvantage of good discipline, I seek to correct them, not as would most others, by punishment, but by some ingenious device hopefully salutary in its effects. One of the traits of the volunteers of my command, the outgrowth of their free Southern life and their habits of study and self-reliance is a keen desire to know the object and reason of every order given them. If not told the object of the order, to guess at it, and then execute the order with sole reference to what they suppose to be its intent. This propensity, needless to say, annoys me exceedingly. To effectively break up this habit and to substitute for it the obedience of the regular soldier is my desire. I am ever alert for some good opportunity to teach this lesson to all my officers.

Yesterday, just such an opportunity presented itself. A Yankee side-wheel steamer has been converted into a gunboat for service on the Rappahannock. She is admirably adapted for such purpose, being armed with a heavy battery consisting of two nine-inch Dahlgrens.

These Dahlgrens are pivoted, one forward, the other aft. The gunboat also holds two thirty-pound Parrott rifles and three howitzers. Because of the large number of guns she carries, we are constantly obliged to be on the alert and keep a bright and sharp lookout. The gunboat usually patrols the river at night, in order to prevent supplies and dispatches from reaching us.

The moon was full last night and I could easily see the steamer gliding up river, hugging the far shore. I ordered one of the guns of the Baltimore Artillery Battery to fire at the steamer with 14 degrees of elevation. Lt. Channing in charge of the battery, thought 16 degrees would be better and, giving the gun that range, made a superb shot, sending a ball directly through the smoke stack of the side-wheeler.

"Now you have the range, Lieutenant. Fire away," was my sole remark as I turned and left the battery. The Yankee ship turned and made a hasty retreat and was soon out of range. Lt. Channing, who thought himself highly complimented by me, related the incident to his brother officers with great gusto, not hesitating to assert that his knowledge of artillery was superior to that of the commanding general.

At midnight, I sent for Captain Barnes who commanded the battery. I began innocently enough by stating, "I was wakeful tonight and thought you might be willing to relieve me of my uneasiness by giving me a little of your company."

As Captain Barnes relaxed, I continued by saying, "The officers and men of your battery are all good, but they are volunteers. They are better than regulars in one respect—they are zealous, but they are very bad in one important respect—they think of the object of an order and execute it zealously in the direction of the object they imagined is intended. Now, let's consider Lieutenant Channing of your command, a fine officer, very zealous and intelligent. He has a first-rate notion about artillery. He makes excellent shots. I told him to fire at the Yankee steamer today and to give the gun 14 degrees elevation, but he gave it 16 degrees and made as good a long shot as I ever saw. He hit the boat, but his zeal carried him away. He didn't obey my order. He thought I wanted him to hit the steamer. I wanted instead to hit her right near the water line, to force her to stop, and then I could have easily blown her out of the water. Lieutenant Channing thus spoiled my whole plan. Now, go back to your quarters, call the lieutenant in, and tell him what I have just told you. Make him understand it. Battle is the swiftest of all schools of military instruction and maybe now that the Yankee boat has escaped, hopefully Lt. Channing will be more receptive to obeying an order as it is given. That is all the punishment I think he will need."

Lieutenant Channing was duly summoned and received his reprimand. He now has little to say of his skill as an artillerist and has had to endure the jests of his fellow officers. But through his example, I trust the whole command has learned a lesson in the implicit obedience of orders.

APRIL 10, 1862—THURSDAY
CAMP BARLOW—FREDERICKSBURG, VIRGINIA

News has just arrived of the glorious victory in Tennessee, saddened, however, by the fall of General Albert Sidney Johnson. In ten hours of hard fighting, we have taken 6,000 prisoners and 100 guns, artillery and, of course, many small arms.

Truly we have cause for the proudest exultation and for most profound thanks to the Almighty who has in mercy sent us such a great victory. New Orleans is, for the present at least, safe from any approach of the enemy down the Mississippi valley. Island Number Ten will not now be outflanked. Memphis will remain in undisturbed security. And, if the flying legions of the Lincolnites are closely pressed, Nashville may be retaken and Tennessee delivered from the vile presence of the insulting Yankees.

The news reports are as yet incomplete, but Beauregard and Polk lead the pursuit. It is rumored the large Yankee reinforcements lead by General Buell are nearby, but I trust that these reserve columns will not stay the tide of victory. I do not think they can with the horrors of defeat in a hostile country resting on the Yankee army. While ours is jubilant with enthusiasm and draws courage and inspiration which is based on issues that are sacred in honor, pure in principle, true in religion, and valuable in life.

Our troops must have fought with a bravery and desperation worthy of the cause to which they have pledged their lives and sacred honors. Just think of it, eighteen field batteries captured! The naked fact gives an idea of the magnitude of the victory and the peril and daring involved in their capture.

I never knew General Johnson, but he died a glorious death on the field of battle. It appears that he fell while leading a successful charge which turned the enemy's right and gained a brilliant victory. During this action, a minie ball cut the artery of his leg, but he rode on until, from loss of blood, he fell exhausted and died without pain in a few moments. Although the brave soldiers of his army will not again catch the inspiration of his presence on the field of peril, he will live long in the grateful remembrance of his countrymen.

Now if we can whip the Yankees at Yorktown where we are bound to have a fight—if it has not already commenced—they will have their plans considerably disarranged again. General McClellan is there with nearly all of his army. We have an insignificant part to play here, along the Rappahannock, for we have scarcely no one in our front.

When the battle does come off at Yorktown, it will be a fearful one, for the stake is enormous, being nothing less than the fate of Virginia. Having taken months to prepare, having assembled such a force as the world has not seen since Napoleon advanced into Russia, McClellan feels that to him, defeat would be ruin, while our leaders and soldiers feel that not only their fate but the fate of the South is staked upon the issue. The contest cannot long be deferred. The news of a terrible battle may come at any moment. I trust the people of the South are prepared not only to call upon God to defend the night, but, under God, to defend it themselves with brave hearts and strong arms.

I presume that with so much at stake, President Davis, himself, will be on the field as he has intimated. He will bravely share the fate of his soldiers in life or death, in victory or defeat.

APRIL 14, 1862—MONDAY
ASHLAND, VIRGINIA

Here we are at Ashland on the railroad, a mere fifteen miles from Richmond. The trip down here was a difficult one. We left our camp near Fredericksburg on Friday morning at 9:00 a.m. We had a hectic time the day previous. As usual, in moving large bodies of troops, there were a thousand things to be attended to at the last moment. We were up at daylight Friday and got ready to move at eight. At about half past, we began our journey and the weather, which up to that time had been spring like, changed to winter's cold.

We bivouacked Friday night and it rained all that night. The same on Saturday, and that night it rained, hailed and sleeted and snowed all in one night. Our blankets were in wagons and they were fifteen miles behind us. We have not seen our blankets during the trip and they have not come up yet, being water bound by high rivers. We built big fires and I stripped the horse covers from off my horse and laid down on that. When I was too cold and wet to sleep, I got up and tried to get warm by the fire. I had one of my raging headaches and was soaked to the bone. I could only think what a miserable existence this was.

The wet and the cold were terrible and, to compound our misery, we had nothing to eat but hard biscuit and fat bacon, just one steak of lean and five inches of fat, but it tastes wonderful when put on a stick and toasted on the coals. From Friday morning to Monday afternoon, that was all our diet. All our provisions are in the wagons.

Strange to say, the men of the brigade stood the trip admirably. Very few sick and all in good spirits. By some miracle, I did not even catch cold, even though my clothes and overcoat were soaked. But the recruits caught it. Sixteen new men from Savannah joined the 35th Georgia a few days before we moved down here and three of them have died from the trip. It shows how much hardier the men are who have been in camp all winter.

We marched through Bowling Green and camped for a couple of hours a mile from it. Very soon, large numbers of ladies in carriages came around to see us, bringing food and drink for the tired and thirsty men. A prayer for our success was offered by the Reverend Mr. Barnwell. I replied with a little speech thanking the people of Bowling Green for all they had done.

Later that night, the brigade prepared to board the cars at Milford. I arranged all the details about transportation, baggage, guards, etc., and turned over the command to Colonel Lewis of the 47th Virginia. I went up to the Railroad Hotel to lie down, leaving orders to be called when the brigade was ready to be moved. After a brief rest, the call came and I went down and found everything in horrible confusion. There were 20 men from the 35th Georgia who had sneaked into town and left their arms and knapsacks without anybody to take care of them. I certainly thought they would be left, but they came back on time.

We were, from twelve that night until three the next day, going to Ashland. All of us were stowed away in freight cars. Once here, the good ladies turned out with baskets of provisions and fed us well. The ladies of Ashland must have known of our hunger and came like angels of mercy to feed us.

One has no idea of how good a thing water is. I never before appreciated the blessings of good water and plenty of it. It was always the first thing the men of the brigade called for as the cars stopped. Last night, as we stopped on a switch to let another train pass, near the switch was a large farmhouse. An old lady—a motherly-looking soul—and her two daughters came out. The men began shouting lustily, "Water! Water!"

The men had been without water for some time. The good lady and her pretty daughters were mighty distressed and they turned out all their Negroes and piggins and buckets and sent them down the line of cars. The mother said, "It hurt me so to hear the poor fellows hollering for water." We gave her a rousing cheer as the cars glided off.

It is hard to tell how long we will remain here. Probably only long enough to gather in our baggage and our wagons and we will then, I think, be ordered town to some point between the James and York rivers. The whole army is being concentrated. Up to this time, it has not been fully understood by the authorities which route McClellan would take to reach Richmond, whether by way of Fredericksburg or Yorktown, but now scouts have reported large transports, laden with soldiers, being shipped down the Potomac to the mouth of the James and York rivers. This leaves little doubt that the peninsula will be the base of operations.

APRIL 19, 1862—SATURDAY
RICHMOND, VIRGINIA

The brigade arrived at Richmond safe and without adventure on the sixteenth. Soon after, we marched down through the streets and pitched our tents in an open field near the Richmond and York River Railroad Depot. We are now waiting orders to board the cars for West Point.

I had occasion to walk around Richmond this morning and the town is all bustle and excitement. The sidewalks are crowded to excess—currents of humanity moving up and down from early morning to dewy eve. Carriages, rail cars, baggage wagons, public hacks and all sorts of vehicles obstruct the crossings so that it requires more real genius to cross upon one of them gracefully and with safety than to ascertain the plans of the Yankee General McClellan.

Not less than ten thousand men, every man of whom would prefer death in glory to a life of dishonor passed through this place in the last 24 hours. Most of these soldiers were Georgians and a sturdier, more cheerful set I never saw. Thousands of people lined the streets along their line of march. When they stopped to rest, the lower part of Main Street for many squares was perfectly lined with soldiers sitting on the curb stones as comfortably as if they were in rocking chairs, smoking, talking, laughing and hurrahing at every stray dog that came along, just as though they were not going to perhaps the deadliest of all the battle of wars.

If was amusing to see many of them eating fat bacon as if it were cheese. General Toombs was in command. He rode a large, grey horse and wore a big, high-crown, brown slouch hat and a long red worsted comfort around his neck.

As I returned to the railroad depot, I watched long trains pass by, loaded with soldiers. The men in the open cars were most picturesquely huddled—some in group—some singing—under any shelter they could find—the corner of a tent—the body of a baggage wagon—wheels and men thrown together at random—on their way to war.

I haven't seen General Joe Johnson during my sojourn in Richmond, but, according to the camp gossip and the daily papers, he is in firm control of events. Between him and President Davis, there is a perfect and harmonious understanding.

APRIL 24, 1862—THURSDAY
YORKTOWN, VIRGINIA

The brigade assembled early Tuesday morning at the Richmond and York River Railroad Depot. After roll call, the men broke ranks and laid down. We had orders to be ready at nine o'clock, but it was a good two hours later before we loaded aboard the train. We rode on platform cars from Richmond to West Point.

After traveling 38 miles, we reached West Point, which is simply a tongue, or spit of land, dividing the Mattapony from the Pamunkey rivers at their junction. The village consists of a few houses built upon the shallow. Some wharves, half demolished, mark the terminus of the York and Richmond railroad. A paltry water battery is the sole defense.

At three o'clock, the brigade began embarking on waiting ships, which were to carry us the last part of the journey to Yorktown. After watching the bulk of the brigade sail away, I boarded the steamer Sarah Washington with a portion of the 35th Georgia.

The men gathered in little knots on the deck, here and there, a party playing "penny ante." Others slept or dozed, but the majority smoked and discussed the upcoming campaign. The general opinion among us was that at last we were on our way to fight the real battle of the war and, hopefully, secure nationhood for the Confederacy.

I gathered near the bow of the ship with Dr. Hall, Chaplain Keys and Colonel Mayo of the 35th Georgia. It was a warm night and occasionally we could see a dim light or the flicker of a far away camp fire near the shore of the York River. A million stars filled the sky above and in front of us, the ship cut a foamy path through the murky waters.

Colonel Mayo took a deep puff of his cigar, causing the tobacco to burn brightly in the darkness and light his face in an eerie glow. Outlined against the bow of the ship, his face illuminated by the burning cigar, the colonel dug deep into his pocket and offered us each a cigar from a trio he held in his hand. Once the cigars were lit, we passed the time pleasantly in telling stories. Among the stories told was one about a gentleman who had an unfortunate impediment in his speech and who resorted to many expedients to hide or amend it. The story was a good one and elicited many expressions of sympathy, especially from Chaplain Keys, whose good heart always went out to anyone who struggled with life.

Dr. Hall, after listening to the story, said that it reminded him of a mate of a ship who had an impediment of speech which forced him to say all he had to say by singing it.

The story, according to Dr. Hall, was that a ship was approaching the coast of South Carolina in foggy weather and the captain, being a very careful man and desiring to make doubly sure of his location, ordered his mate to throw the lead. The mate was the unfortunate soul who had the speech impediment. As he hauled up the lead after his first sounding, he sang out (to the air of the hymn "There Will Be No More Sorrow There"), "There is plenty of water down here-r-r-ah!" At the next throw of the lead, he warbled, "Full fifty fathoms down here-r-r-ah!"

A short time later, he shouted at the top of his lungs, finding the water rapidly shoaling, "I would have the captain keep the ship clear of here-r-r-ah!" By then, the danger became so apparent to the mate that he forgot his impediment in speech and shouted excitedly, in a clear voice, "For heaven's sake, Captain. Put her about at once!"

The shock occasioned by a full realization of the danger of the ship was such it cured him of the speech impediment.

We listened with unusual interest and attention to the good doctor's recital, which was made realistic by the way in which he acted the part of throwing the lead by the mate. It was a good story to end our gathering and we all departed our separate ways to get some much needed sleep.

Early the next morning, we reached Yorktown and the steamer came to a stop and anchored. The captain of the Sarah Washington, explaining that the water was too shallow to permit him to approach the landing pier, said that the troops could not land until the scows, which were being towed by another steamer, came up.

After a short wait, the scows came up and began unloading the troops. Dr. Hall was one of the last to reach the landing and the doctor, who cannot swim, in attempting to get on the wharf, slipped and fell into the water. There was excitement aboard as Chaplain Keys and I looked for a line or rope to throw the doctor. When the doctor struck the water, he went down, but he soon reappeared, splashing and frantically waving his arms, and shouted, "Gurgle, gurgle. *Blub. Blub.* Save me! Save me!" At the most, there wasn't over six or seven feet of water and with all the men around, there was little real danger.

The second time Dr. Hall came to the surface, he flung his arms around one of the wharf piles and, in this position, uttered another vehement appeal to be saved. Just as he cried out, Colonel Mayo, in a spirit of mischief, leaned out over the wharf and shouted, "Dr. Hall!"

The doctor's only response was a very loud "Save me! Save me!"

Mayo again called to the imperiled doctor, who finally said, "Yes, yes. What is it?"

Then Colonel Mayo, with a smile on his face, sang in a loud voice to the tune employed by the mate, "Is there plenty of water down there-r-r-ah?"

Dr. Hall failed to appreciate Colonel Mayo's humor and used many loud words, not to be found in the Lord's Prayer, and threatened that, when he reached terra firma, he would end the military career of Colonel Mayo.

The doctor was soon rescued from the deep. When his anger had subsided, he walked over to Mayo and shook his hand. They had a good laugh together with the jolly old doctor enjoying the little joke about as well as any of us.

We marched through Yorktown, if a few old tumbled-down houses and a row of wooden wharves could be called a town, and went into camp a mile or so from the historic old city. During the day, many of the brigade visited Yorktown, through curiosity, and watched the federal fleet anchored off the old Point Comfort.

APRIL 25, 1862—FRIDAY
YORKTOWN, VIRGINIA

Today, we were shelled by Yankee gunboats lying about four miles away on the York River. These infernal monsters threw 120-pound shells toward our position at irregular intervals. The whirring, screaming approach of the shell preceded it, as if a box car were hurling through the air. When it hit, there was a resounding explosion. They seemed to rock the earth around us.

This morning, Lieutenants J. B. Updike and Robert Bruce, and myself, were quietly seated on a parapet, watching with interest the puffs of smoke from the great guns, when we suddenly became aware that one of these great shells was screeching toward us! We fell to the ground and spread out to evade the storm of shell pieces, debris, and dirt which did us no harm. But we soon discovered the shell had gone down through a quartermaster sergeant's tent and through his dinner table, which was a store box. The explosion made a hole you could have buried a large horse in. The quartermaster sergeant had been eating his dinner, but had just gone into his cook tent after a drink of water. On his return, he viewed, with astonishment, the hole that was now located where his dinner table had been.

Lt. Bruce said, "Sergeant, I would advise you, in the future, to sit your table in the other corner of the tent."

Later, during the evening ramble from our camp, Chaplain Keys and I came up on an old church. Although not large, the church was a fine structure, having been built in the form of a Greek cross. As we approached the edifice, Keys fell to his knees and said a short, silent prayer.

Rising, he turned to me and said, "Like the prophet Daniel, I try to pray at least three times a day. It's strange, General, but I can almost feel the presence of God near this church. I thought it a most opportune time and place to give thanks for His many blessings."

"You're a good man, Chaplain, and I know your prayers come from the heart, so I'm sure God listens. I often feel guilty when I pray. It seems that I am often merely begging selfishly for the things I desire. What good can come of such a prayer?"

"If you pray enough, General," replied Keys, "it will cease being a duty and become a privilege. The privilege of prayer is one of my most cherished possessions. I know God hears and answers me when I pour my heart out before Him. The Lord's answers I never venture to criticize. I can only ask, it is the Lord's decision to answer according to His will. If it was my will that was always done, I would not dare to pray at all. In the quiet of camp, in the strife of life's daily troubles, or even in the face of death, the privilege of praying to God is inestimable. I value it so much because it calls for nothing that the way-faring man, though a fool, cannot give—that is, the heart felt expression of his simplest desire. If I should be terribly wounded in some great battle and could neither see nor speak, I could still pray so that God could hear. When I finally pass through death's door, I expect to pass through it in conversation with the great shepherd."

About the church were the graves of many forefathers of Yorktown, reposing under the shadow of a cluster of old trees. Near a corner of the churchyard, we discovered overgrown with underbrush, a bluish marble tombstone, in a good state of preservation. On one side was engraved a fleet of sailing vessels. On the other side, a cross, surmounted by a crown underneath which was inscribed a long memorial. The beginning and ending of which ran thus:

> "Here lies the body of Sir William Cole. Master of the Rolls to King Charles of the county of Warwick, who departed this life ye 4th of March, 1690, in the 56th year of his age * * *Of him may this be loudly sounded—'He was unspotted on ye Bench, unstained at ye bar.'"

I could only look at the weathered stone and think that this is what comes to human fame and greatness. Such will be the fate of us all. We will soon pass away and be forgotten! We may not even have a friend to remain behind and remove the underbrush from our tombstone, should one be erected over where our dust reposes.

Keys and I walked slowly away from the church. Above, in the trees, a bird warbled a melodious tune and the late afternoon sunlight turned a deep gold. The late Sir William Cole, "unspotted on ye bench, unstained at ye bar," was long dead and buried and it was no good thinking about him anymore. I was here and I was alive.

We went down a muddy road until it turned and then across a large field. There was another church with old grey walls and a few houses with thatched roofs. Along side the houses were some little children chasing a pair of ducks toward a muddy pond. It was good to be there, just to be alive. Good just to be walking in the late afternoon sunlight back toward camp.

APRIL 27, 1862—SUNDAY
LEE'S MILL, VIRGINIA

Yesterday morning, the brigade marched to a position in reserve near Lee's Mill. By six o'clock, the men were in line and on the road. The morning was indescribably beautiful. The vapors that rose from the broad expanse of the York River were tinged with a thousand gorgeous hues as they rolled away, dispersed by the morning sun. The tall yellow pines, which lined the road, were crowned with rich golden coronals of light.

The men were in good spirits and the road, at the start, was perfectly level and dry as we began our march. We marched through a portion of the peninsula that was absolutely delightful. Large, rich groves of stately oaks just sending forth their foliage were beautifully interspersed with the holly, with its bright red berries and rich evergreen leaves. Peach orchards in full bloom added to the splendor of the scene and, when at times I could see the line of troops over a mile in length, their muskets glittering in the bright sunlight, my enthusiasm for my command and our cause was unbounded.

Each regiment in my brigade had several baggage wagons assigned. To each baggage wagon were attached four or six mules driven, usually, by a colored man, with only one rein or line. That line was attached to the bit of the near leading mule and the driver rode in a saddle upon the rear-wheel mule.

To each train of baggage wagons, a guard was assigned. While the guard urged the drivers, the drivers urged the mules. The drivers were usually expert and understood well the stubborn, wayward natures of the long-eared creatures over whose destinies they presided. On the way to Lee's Mill, our baggage train became blocked as the leading wagon had become stuck in a large mud hole in the road. This wagon was heavily loaded. To facilitate movement, its contents were unloaded by the guard. Even then, the wagon would not move and the whole column ground to a halt.

Hurrying to the front, I found the wagon badly mired, but not enough to justify the stopping of the whole brigade. Several guards and wagon drivers stood along side the blocked wagon. Apparently, they were trying to figure out what to do. The lazy colored driver of the mired wagon was half-dozing in the saddle.

"Get that team out of the mud!" I yelled loudly, bringing the sleeping Sambo to his senses.

He hastily flourished his long whip and, cracking it over the ear of the lead mule, shouted his mule lingo at the team. In response, the mules pulled frantically, but not together.

"Can't you make your mules pull together?" I shouted.

"Dem mules pull right smart!" said the driver.

"Well, maybe you can make them pull a little smarter," I replied. I then cocked my Colt Dragoon, fired a shot into the air, and commanded, "Now get that team out of the mud."

The Negro rolled his eyes wildly and snapped to action. He first patted his saddle mule, then spoke to each one. He then, once again flourishing his long whip, flung it over the head of the mules with a loud crack and shouted, "Go 'long dar! What I feed yo' fo!" and praise the Lord, the mule team left the slough in a very expeditious manner.

As we reached Lee's Mill, it was early evening and commenced to rain. After I had assigned the various regiments to their places, Elias and I hastily began to improvise a small tent for shelter. Nearby, I watched a teamster drive near a large pine and unhitch his mules, tying them to the front part of the wagon.

Once inside the tent, which opened at both ends, I crept forward and lay down with my head close up to the rear end. Lying there quietly, I listened to the rain pattering on the canvas covering and such a delightful sense of comfort stole over me as I have very seldom experienced. I was soon sleeping profoundly. Sometime during the night, one of the mules broke loose from the nearby baggage wagon and thrust his head in under the cover of the tent. His mouth could not have been more than six inches from my face when he began to bray in a most un-confederate manner.

How I got out of that tent is beyond me, but I do know that I was at least twenty feet beyond it when I awoke running. I thought I was making good time, when I noticed Elias hobble past me, eyes wide with fear. Rank has its privileges and I overtook Elias and raced toward the end of the camp. I soon noticed that the camp was still and quiet and Elias and I appeared to be the only frightened beings in it. I stopped and gazed around and, just then, another mule in another part of the camp began a song. The truth struck me. Elias and I sneaked quietly back and crept into the tent.

I was almost asleep again when a young mule awoke from his evening nap and expressed his disgust for the military life by an earthly bray. This was taken up and re-echoed by several of his fellow beings until it sounded like all the asses in Christendom were in our camp.

APRIL 29, 1862—TUESDAY
NEAR LEE'S MILL, VIRGINIA

Today for the first time the brigade was brought face to face with the enemy. We now man a portion of the defensive lines of Yorktown and the Warwick River. This line of defense designed and located by General Magruder extends from Yorktown (on the York River) southwesterly to Mulberry Point on the James River—a distance of almost nine miles.

At proper intervals along the Warwick River, we have thrown up dams to back the water over the swampland to keep the Federals from crossing it. Dam number one, for example, is located about two miles from Yorktown. The river here is usually only 12 to 15 feet in width, but by the use of dams, its width is increased to 75 or 100 feet. Opposite Dam number one is a redoubt occupied by two 12-pound Napoleon guns, double charged with canister. All along the line for a space of 50 or 75 yards, the timber has been cut down clear through the swamps.

These fine works are a monument to Negro labor, for they were the hewers and the diggers. Every slave owner in Eastern Virginia was ordered to send one half of his male servants between the ages of sixteen and fifty to work on the fortifications. In some cases, particularly bright Negroes have been put to military service and used as sharpshooters.

The works are occupied by lines of battle relieving each other every 24 hours and, just after night, as no movement of troops can be accomplished during the day due to a heavy fire from the Yankees.

The brigade we relieved told us of the many nights they would sit in the lines near a dam with water up to their knees and sleep under the inspiring music of the frogs. We have learned that there is music in the hollering of the frogs, for it is a well-known fact that the frogs will not holler when the water is disturbed, and in that fact, lies the music. As long as they keep up their music, we know that the Yankees will not be crossing the swamp.

So admirably designed are the fortifications that General Magruder says that with thirty-five thousand men to man the fortifications, that all h_ _l can't take them. We are reported to have a force of sixty thousand here at present.

McClellan, it is said, is on the peninsula with one hundred and fifty thousand men. It is reported that the Yankees are making railroads to transport siege guns near our lines to shell us out of our fortifications. The great battle will probably soon begin.

Bad news from New Orleans. Two Yankee steamers have succeeded in passing the forts and are on their way to the city. There is considerable uncertainty as to the safety of the city. We have some iron boats above them, however, which they will have to pass. One is the gunboat Louisiana and I know it will give a good account of itself.

Just as I finished writing the above words, Colonel James Orr, commanding the First South Carolina Regiment called. I knew him in Charleston during what now seems another lifetime and his presence brought recollections of other days when we were younger, thought more of sweethearts than of war, and when the word *battery* meant a delightful promenade at the tip of Charleston, not six brass cannon double-shotted with canister enough to blow men into a hundred pieces.

The colonel is a very industrious talker, chewer, spitter and drinker. He took part in the battle of Manassas and has been under some tremendous hot firing I tell you! Well, if he don't know what heavy firing is and the d_ _ _ _dest, hottest work, too, then there is no use for men to talk! The truth is, his command stood its ground at Manassas and never retreated an inch.

No, sir, no d_ _ n Yankee regiment that ever marched was a match for his. Bullets came thicker 'n hail, but his men stood up. He was in the thick of it with 'em. Damned hot, you better believe. Well, if he must say it himself, he knew what hard fighting was.

This blather went on for quite some time until I gently took the colonel by the arm and escorted him toward the door, claiming it was late and I must get some sleep. He left my tent still talking, muttering something about the firing being hotter 'n hell, and yes, Colonel Orr knows what hot firing is, sir!

MAY 8, 1862—THURSDAY
NEW KENT COURT HOUSE, VIRGINIA

We evacuated Yorktown and the line extending across the Peninsula last Saturday night. During our retreat, we have had a very trying time through anxious and laborious days and sleepless nights, such as I fancy would make old age come prematurely.

It was, of course, well understood by all of us that McClellen, having complete control of the navigable rivers by virtue of his overwhelming naval power, could at any time turn either of our flanks and land a heavy force between us and Richmond, and that, therefore, our Yorktown line could not be a permanent one. We were not surprised then at receiving orders about the 2nd of May to withdraw and march toward Richmond.

After nightfall on May 3, we opened a tremendous bombardment with our heavy guns. The atmosphere was in a condition eminently favorable for conveying and prolonging the sound. And, as one great gun followed another, it rolled like mighty thunder over by and field and forest, and echo mingled with echo. The shells were not directed at any one spot but seemed rather to be aimed at random, driving the Yankees to ground everywhere. The burning fuses traced the brilliant red arcs across the dark sky. It was a magnificent pyrotechnical display.

Masked by the heavy artillery fire, the troops moved out of the trenches which we left intact with only the heavy naval guns still in place. Our men made "dummies" and put them on the embrasures besides stuffing old clothes to represent sentinels. It was a well-managed retreat and without a noise and in perfect order, we sallied forth towards Williamsburgh.

The army retreated along two roads, one from Yorkstown that angles westward and then turns northwest up the center of the Peninsula, and one that crosses the Warwick at Lee's Mill and then runs parallel to the Yorktown Road and a mile or so from the James River. The two roads converge eleven miles beyond Yorktown and two miles short of Williamsburgh.

Whitling's division, of which my brigade is a part, served as a rear guard on the march. Through the night we trudged, often wading through long ponds and pools of water up to our knees. About midnight, we came to a large opening surrounded by a rail fence. Here I ordered the men to build fires from the rails nearby. This was done and soon the heavens were lit up by this great stretch of roaring fires. Many of the men spread their blankets and lay down for a good sleep while others sat around the comforting, warm, cracking blaze wondering what next. Scarcely had we all become quiet when orders came to "fall in." Back over the sloppy, muddy and deep-rutted road we marched.

At one point, shortly after dawn, an artillery piece became so deeply mired in the mud that I had to call a company of men from the 22nd North Carolina to assist the gunners. Watching carefully was a monocled Englishman who was a member of General Stuart's cavalry. He was a lord of some sort and had come over to witness the war in the colonies. As the men struggled to free the gun, he noticed Yankee cavalry coming into sight on the road behind us. Turning to one of my aides, he asked why we were bothering with "that damned thing."

"We can't afford to leave it," the aide replied.

"Pardon me again," said the Englishman, ever so politely, "if I ask how much it is worth."

The aide said he would guess the gun to be worth about a thousand dollars. The Englishman glanced again at the approaching Yankees, who were now close enough to let loose a few shots at our party. "Well then, let's move on," he said to my aide. "I'll give you my check of a thousand dollars for the gun at once."

We managed to move on, the gun in tow, the English lord riding rapidly ahead of us and the Yankees. I formed a regiment in a line of battle to cover the retreat and traded long-distance shots with the enemy for a time, the rattling, bang, bang proceeding in fine style. A heavy fire from behind is hard to bear—in advancing, you hardly think of the bullets, but they seem relentless when you are retreating from them. Then there is also the fear of being left if wounded and we all thought that could be equivalent to having our throats cut in cold blood for the amusement of General McClellen and friends, although there has been no proof of any barbarity on the part of the Yankees at this time and it is pleasant to think that such accounts have been exaggerated.

As we neared Williamsburgh, Stuart's cavalry took over the rear guard duties and I ordered the regiment from line into column and began the march through town. As the sound of musketry echoed through Williamsburgh, a young woman rushed up to Captain Hanks of the 2nd Arkansas battalion and pleaded with him to turn his men back and repel the Yankee invaders. "You must defend this cradle of liberty just as your forefathers had defended it against the Redcoats!" she cried. "If you won't lead your men, let me be the captain and lead them!"

We had passed on through the town when the continual roar of cannon and musketry told a battle in earnest going on in the rear and our troops hotly engaged. My brigade and that of Kershaw were ordered back at the double-quick. As we passed back through the town, the citizens were greatly excited, the piazzas and balconies being filled with ladies and old men who urged our troops on with all the power and eloquence at their command. Captain Hanks, riding at the head of his company, once again came upon the young beauty who had pleaded so earnestly before. This radiant Joan of Arc, as Captain Hanks described her, inspired by the return of our troops, was preparing to lead the men into battle until the captain looked down from his horse and cautioned her, "Oh no, sis, don't go—you might tear your dress!"

The woods had been felled for some distance in front of the earthworks and forts, and as we neared the former, we could see the enemy's skirmishers pouring out of the woods in the clearing. The 2nd and 8th South Carolina regiments of Kershaw's brigade were ordered to occupy the forts and breastworks beyond Fort Magruder and they had a perfect race to reach them before the Yankees did. The battle began to rage in all fierceness when suddenly the Yankees withdrew, but not before losing 44 men and one gun. As one of the lieutenants of the 8th South Carolina told me, "The balls whistled and shells burst over us, but God was with us and we pushed on them and they withdrew."

A very heavy rainstorm fell on us during the night of the 4th—this had to be endured as best we could. On the following day, the 5th, the storm continued with even greater violence, until the wagons of the army, containing commissary stores and ammunition, sank so deeply in the mud that for miles the whole army train remained motionless, and it became impossible to move our supplies.

During this fearfully stormy night, I somehow lost my India rubber cloak. I was wet and would have suffered and slept little but for borrowing a dragoon overcoat from my guard. This kept me warm and dry and I slept most soundly and got a little to eat and drink.

By noon of the 5th, it was still bleak and gray with a cold, hard downpour. It soon became apparent to General Johnson that his supply lines and artillery would be a long time moving any distance on the single muddy road leading out of Williamsburgh toward Richmond. While the rest of the army was set in motion, Longstreet's division was to act as the rear guard to block pursuit. As the peninsula is only seven miles wide here, it was Longstreet's good fortune that he had an excellent place to make a defensive fight.

At about two o'clock in the afternoon, the ball opened with heavy cannonading about two miles east of Williamsburgh. The battle was soon joined and continued until evening. In this battle, the Federals were repulsed with a heavy loss, amounting in killed, wounded and prisoners to about 5,000. Our loss was also severe and amounted to about 2,500. The courage and endurance of our troops was fearfully tried in this engagement, but they stood the test like true Southerners and patriots, battling for freedom.

Several incidents that came under my notice are illustrative of events that happened along our whole line. At one point in the battle, the 19th Mississippi formed ranks (seven hundred strong) and charged a portion of the Yankee line. They rushed across an open field, clambered over a fence, and delivered a volley at ten paces, which drove a Yankee brigade several hundred yards before them into a woods, capturing many prisoners. The gallant colonel of this regiment (Colonel Lomax) was shot during this time. His Negro servant recovered his body and carried it on his back several miles and conveyed it to Richmond to the bereaved wife, thus keeping the promise he had made to her—namely, never to let his master's body fall into the hands of the enemy.

After the charge, a ghastly scene was spread across the road nearby. Those men of the Mississippi regiment who had been killed in the charge were brought by their comrades and laid in rows with hands crossed upon the breast but eyes wide-staring. The rain continued to fall and the faces of the dead were bleached with more than death's pallor. Strangely, the Yankees must have been firing a bit high because almost every man struck in the charge was killed and most through the brain. Now, as they lay motionless in death, every eyeball was strained upward to the spot where the bullet had crashed through the skull and every forehead was stained with the ooze and trickle of blood. Men were passing slowly through the silent lines of dead, bending low, seeking in the distorted faces identification of their friends and comrades.

During a lull in the fighting, our cannons had been withdrawn and were parked in column parallel to the road in a common on the outskirts of Williamsburgh. The artillery men were lounging about resting and talking, awaiting orders, when a number of wounded Yankee prisoners were brought up in an ambulance and laid temporarily on the grass while a field hospital was being established nearby. Among them was a suffering Yankee shot through the bowels, who was rolling on the wet and blood-stained ground in excruciating agony, beseeching the nearby artillery men to put him out of his misery. There did not appear to be anything that could be done for him, at least not until the surgeons arrived, so I was in the act of turning my horse and riding away from the painful spectacle when a couple of Louisiana Tigers, the most rakish and devilish-looking beings I ever saw, appeared on the scene.

These men belonged to Rob Wheat's command. He had raised a battalion of the hardest set of men in New Orleans. The soldiers called them "wharf rats" and "cut-throats" and "gutter snipes." They knew no subordination and defied law and military discipline. While in camp near Yorktown, several had been shot at the stake for mutiny and insubordination. Afterwards, when the soldiers heard a volley fired, the word would go out, "Wheat is having another tiger shot."

The tigers were soon peering over the shoulders of the circle of onlookers watching the Yankee writhe in agony on the ground, his bloody hands clutching his stomach, his face contorted in pain.

As the Yankee once again screamed to be put out of his misery, one of the tigers pushed through the ring saying, "Put you out of your misery? Certainly, sir!" And before anyone had time to interfere, or even the faintest idea of his intention, brained the Yankee with the butt of his musket; the bloody club still in his hands, he looked around upon the other wounded men and added glibly, "any of you other Yankee gentlemen here'd like to be accommodated?"

I was shocked! It is impossible to express my feelings and I sat almost stupefied as the demon suddenly disappeared and a gasp of horror escaped the spectators. I am sorely disappointed that I didn't shoot the Louisiana savage down in his tracks and my inaction is something I will have to live with for eternity

Finally, there was another of those never-to-be-forgotten things that a soldier bears in his heart as the mementos of battle. Lying at the side of the Williamsburgh Road, with upturned face, as if gazing into the heavens, was a dead Confederate soldier, the lower half of his body buried in the mud. The storm has washed his face; it was strikingly beautiful, like that of a lovely woman; a smile of the sweetest peace lingered on the face of death. That calm, angel-like expression in such a scene struck every passing soldier with wonder. Hundreds stopped and looked; many said that he died dreaming of his mother or that his last moments were cheered by the presence of angels. I have heard many of our men speak of this as one of the most affecting incidents of the battle.

May 6th dawned clear and pleasant, and as the Yankee pickets edged forward, they found our lines deserted. The troops had quietly slipped through Williamsburgh and taken the road to Richmond. Our rear guard had beaten back the Federal pursuit and we were able to continue our retreat unmolested.

About noon, the men were allowed an hour's rest. This was also ration day and the commissary was missing. This being the case, the men were informed they could go across the road to several corn cribs and help themselves to some corn on the cob, to be eaten raw or roasted in the ashes as their different tastes might prompt. All were hungry enough to appreciate this liberality and such corn cracking as followed has seldom been heard outside a hog pen. While enjoying this feast, a half-grown hog sprang from hiding and ran across the road. At least fifty men threw their corncobs in the air and gave chase. The hog ran a good race but at last was bayoneted and brought back to the ranks. A roaring fire was soon going and the roast pig added to the menu.

Later that day, we ended our march and made camp. Shortly thereafter, Adjutant Young and I walked over to the camp of Hood's brigade. We found General Hood and several of his officers sitting around a blazing fire, having just finished supper. Hood is a giant of a man, blond-bearded and looking like a Viking warrior. His brigade—1st, 4th and 5th Texas, plus the 18th Georgia, which the Texans have adopted as the 3rd Texas—are perfectly willing to follow the gallant Hood wherever he may lead.

As we sat around the fire talking, General Hood picked up a Bible and opened it. The first sentence that his eye rested upon read, "I shall not die but live," (Psalm 118:17). Hood then proposed that each of us open and read in like manner. As I was near him, I opened and read. Then, Colonel Marshall, then Captain Ryan, next Doctor Ester, followed by Colonel Robert Smith of the 18th Georgia, and last, Adjutant Young.

A short time later, Colonel Smith and I went for a walk. We strolled leisurely across a field overgrown with wild flowers and forget-me-nots. When Colonel Smith noticed the profusion of the little blue flowers, he was deeply affected. He stood gazing upon the ground wrapped in thought and he spoke in a strangely poetic strain of the goodness of the Creator in covering the fields with such beauty and perfume. We lingered thereon that sweet spring evening and talked of the matter for some time.

As we walked back toward camp, Colonel Smith suddenly stopped and said, "General, if I fall in the next battle, as I now believe I shall, I wish you would have them bury me under this tree, where I indicate by these lines." He then proceeded to mark with the point of his sword the outlines of a grave. After drawing the lines, conversation was resumed, and no further attention was paid to the incident.

Early the next morning, we received news of a Federal force coming ashore at Eltham's Landing. This posed a threat to our wagon trains. If the Federals should attack at this juncture, it would mean a serious threat to our retreat. The Yankee force had to be neutralized, and Whitling's division was given the task. His orders were "to prevent the enemy from advancing upon Barhamsville until all the trains had passed."

Whitling gave orders to General Hood "to feel the enemy gently and fall back." With Hood in the advance, my brigade was to follow in reserve.

All was then hurry and bustle in camp. Some with gloomy countenances, some with buoyant spirits, went to work filling their canteens and haversacks. I was busily engaged in getting the brigade ready to march.

At about 6:00 a.m. on the 7th, we were ready to leave camp to take up the line of march toward Eltham's Landing. I rode over to the tent of Colonel Smith of the 18th Georgia and found him lying in bed, awake. I silently approached his bed. "Ha!" said he. "You are up already, General? Well, soon will be the time." He was quite feeble and feverish, suffering from an onset of fever that had come on during the night—no doubt brought on by the heavy rain and chill of the last few days.

"Colonel, you are very feverish—you are not trying to go out with your regiment this morning are you?"

"I must," he replied weakly.

I was quite anxious to have him go with us had he been able; but I know he was not able. Every man in his regiment had he been consulted would have said that he wanted Colonel Smith to be in command in case of a fight. I remonstrated against his going, but to no effect. He said, "I must go!"

Soon the order came for us to get into line and I left to form my brigade. When we were ready to march, Colonel Smith came out and was assisted to mount his horse. The orders then came to "Left face!" and then, "March!"

We started toward Eltham's Landing, but the road was muddy and we had to stop frequently so that the troops ahead of us might get out of our way. I was riding a short distance behind Colonel Smith and about the second time we stopped, the colonel beckoned me to him. When I was by his side, he said to me, "I am very sick; help me down."

His orderly and I took him under each arm and assisted him from his horse. When I had lead him back to a log, he sat down and very soon began to vomit. The orderly held his head some time as Colonel Smith was very weak and sick. After he finished vomiting, I entreated him to return to camp or go to some house, assuring him that he was not able to proceed further.

"No," he said, "I will go on."

I assisted him to and upon his horse and again we moved on.

Soon Colonel Smith was vomiting again, leaning over the side of his horse to do so. I rode to him and told him that he was doing great injustice to himself to go on, but he persisted and said that he was determined to go on. "My men need me," he said.

The column soon reached a thick woods and Hood ordered his brigade from column into line. At the crossing of the dotted crossroad leading into the woods, Hood sat on his fine horse directing the men into line. He is a cool man, this Hood, quite a wonder, a glorious soldier indeed.

To avoid the chance of his men shooting each other by accident in the thick woods, Hood had his men advance with unloaded guns. Upon reaching a small cabin on the brow of the hill overlooking the slope which led down to Eltham's Landing, Hood ran unexpectedly into Yankee pickets. The enemy was only fifteen feet away and a Yankee corporal drew a bead on Hood with his musket. Fortunately, Private John Deal of the 4th Texas beat the Yankee to the draw and shot him dead. Private Deal apparently felt that fighting a war with unloaded rifles was a lot of foolishness. He had disobeyed orders and carried his gun ready for use and had saved Hood's life.

Shortly after this incident, the affair assumed the appearances of a real battle. Leaving the battery of artillery at the cabin, the Texans pressed on through the woods, driving the Yankee pickets ahead of them.

It was at this time that Colonel Smith passed me and, as his regiment wheeled into line on Hood's left, Smith smiled and waved his sword toward me as he rode by. I called out wishing him good luck. Then having formed his line of battle, he spoke a cheering word or two to his men and then told them to follow him.

Returning to my brigade, I formed line of battle and ordered the few cavalrymen who accompanied me to guard the flanks. My brigade was to wait in reserve and support Hood's brigade when needed.

Hood's men soon collided with a solid line of Federal infantry and the firing became general. The lines of the Federals had been reinforced by more troops from the landing and a flanking movement against Hood's left was attempted. Seeing his 1st regiment in a difficult spot,

Hood gave the order to charge. The 1st Texas responded magnificently and Hood's left was saved. My brigade was then moved up in close support just in case the Yankees renewed the attack. In the meantime, Archer with the 5th Texas had joined in the attack on the right. Then the entire line surged forward, driving the enemy back toward the protection of the gunboats on the York River.

During the retreat, a company of Yankees, numbering over eighty men, took the wrong directions and, coming upon the 5th Texas where it was lying down in line of battle, were greeted by a volley which left not one standing.

General Whitling, who had been watching the battle from a hill in the rear, ordered up a battery of artillery to shell the enemy landing, but the range was too great and the battery was withdrawn. The Federals responded with a few salvos from the gunboats.

Once the Yankees withdrew to the protection of their gunboats, the battle was, for all purposes, over. General Hood had accomplished his mission. He had neutralized the Yankee threat to our rear while the wagon trains were retreating closer to Richmond.

Was Whitling and I rode up, Hood greeted us with a salute. "General Hood," inquired Whitling, "have you given an illustration of the Texas idea of feeling an enemy gently and falling back? What would your Texans have done, sir, if I had ordered them to charge and drive back the enemy?"

"General," Hood replied gravely, "I suppose they would have driven them into the river and tried to swim out and capture the gunboats."

Looking about, I asked General Hood if he had seen Colonel Smith. "The colonel is dead, General Pettigrew," replied Hood. "I did not see him after the battle began, but I have learned from others who saw him that he most bravely rushed forward until he fell, pierced by an enemy ball. Then, after he had fallen, to those who went to assist him, he cried aloud: 'Charge, men charge!' Although sick, he knew his men needed him and he knew that they would fight under him better than any other living man. Georgia has given one of its finest sons to the cause."

Dr. Ester, of the Texas brigade, Colonel Mayo and I rode to the east looking for the body of the gallant Smith. We found the colonel lying in the middle of a large field, his face toward the enemy. We carried the body to the roadside where Chaplain Davis of the Texas brigade was waiting. As we laid the body gently down, Chaplain Davis said a short prayer and remarked, "What a day or an hour may bring forth, the God omniscient only knows. Before another Sabbath shall have come and gone, the storm of war may again burst on us and we may also be torn and bleeding on the field."

Then a cart loaded with sacks passed on its way to a hill. The cart belonged to the Westwood, the family seat of Mrs. Catherine Brockenborough that lay a few miles away on the main road of the peninsula. The cart was speedily emptied and the sacks hidden in the brush. The body of Colonel Smith was tenderly laid in the improvised hearse and Dr. Ester, Chaplain Davis, Colonel Mayo and I walked by it to the large tree where the colonel had indicated he wished to be buried.

Old Aaron, one of Mrs. Brockenborough's slaves, was set to work digging a grave while the colonel was prepared for burial. A simple coffin was quickly fashioned at the plantation carpentry shop.

At sunset we gathered about the grave Old Aaron had dug and Chaplain Davis, standing at its head, sent Colonel Smith to his eternal rest with the solemn ritual of the Episcopal Church. As the gentle chaplain spoke the promise and said the words, "I am the resurrection and the life; he that believeth in me, though he were dead, yet shall he live," Mrs. Brockenborough and two pretty little children she had brought along strewed flowers over the cavalry overcoat that covered the rough bier.

The old oak tree marks the spot where Colonel Smith was laid to rest. It is a beautiful place and, after Old Aaron finished filling the gravesite, I picked several wild flowers and forget-me-nots and laid them tenderly over the grave. Then I gave one last lone salute to my fallen comrade and walked slowly away.

I am writing this in the woods where we are bivouacking for the night. For nearly a week now, I have not had my clothes off and for perhaps not more than two nights of the time have I had my boots and spurs off. I have usually arisen at three in the morning and not lain down until ten or eleven at night. My appetite is good and health excellent. I hear an owl hooting off in the distance, but other than that, all is quiet. With God's help, we will soon reach Richmond and end this long retreat.

MAY 20, 1862—TUESDAY
CAMP AT WILLIAMS HOUSE—NEAR RICHMOND, VIRGINIA

Our army is now behind the Chickahominy and directly in front of Richmond, some of our lines are just three miles from the city. We can retreat no further without giving up Richmond.

General Johnson has chosen his position well, I believe, because the Chickahominy poses a formidable barrier to any federal advance. The river rises some ten miles northwest of Richmond and makes its way in a generally east-by-southeast direction around and in front of the city—coming as close as three and a half miles at one point—before stretching away down the center of the peninsula to empty into the James, 36 miles away.

One of our scouts described the Chickahominy to me as "a narrow, sluggish stream flowing through swamp land, covered with a rank, tangled growth of trees, reeds, grasses and water plants. Vines climb and mosses festoon the trees. Its stagnant water is poisonous, water moccasins and malaria abound. Flies and mosquitoes swarm." In dry weather, the river does not seem unduly imposing, but in the rainy season, its bottom lands quickly flood and what has been a river becomes a broad lake as much as a mile across.

It is good we have the river in front of us for the Yankee General McClellan has proven an able strategist. In two months, he has just maneuvered us out of Norfolk and Yorktown, opened both the James and York rivers, compelled us, ourselves, to blow up the Merrimac, and established his own pickets within six miles of Richmond.

My headquarters tent has been struck in a beautiful little nook in the hills. There are pine trees and honeysuckle vines all about the area with a pleasant stream close by. The men have dammed this up to form a swimming place. This is a pleasant location for the brigade after our arduous retreat.

My tent is located near the 47th Virginia and there was a great deal of excitement in their camp this morning. They had filled a large cauldron with water the night previous for the purpose of making coffee early in the morning. Some time during the night, a couple of large rats got in the water and, being unable to get out, drowned. These creatures were not discovered until the coffee had been made, issued and drank. The effect of the discovery can be better imagined than described.

My old nemesis, Colonel Long, has been selected by General Whiting to lead the 22nd North Carolina. James Connor is moving to be Colonel of the Hampton Legion. I must admit my dislike for Long and am not happy to have him command one of the regiments in my brigade.

A relatively large man, Long is inclined to strut and bluster to make his presence felt. He can be friendly and gracious one moment, and impatient and insulting the next. An exaggerated preciseness of speech and manner, accompanied by a habit of delicately taking snuff, make him seem ridiculous to the enlisted men who call him "Old Granny." They tell and re-tell true or exaggerated tales of this egotism, the favorite being that he once demanded a private railroad car because he was too good to ride with common soldiers.

Long is in many ways a complete martinet. He is fussy about everything, especially detail.

I recall so well an incident that happened when I commanded the 22nd North Carolina and he was my lieutenant colonel, and second in command. Dr. Hall on one occasion sent up through channels a certificate recommending the discharge of a soldier afflicted with chronic rheumatism caused by his limbs having been broken in a railroad collision. The document received the approval of the company captain, major, etc. until it came to Lt. Colonel Long. He sent it back disapproved with the notation, "the Lt. Colonel is not informed that railroads ever collide."

For all his faults, he knows his trade thoroughly. He will, I feel, continue to keep the regiment on the rigorous routine of training that has transformed it from a raw mass into a disciplined unit.

MAY 24, 1862—SATURDAY
CAMP AT WILLIAMS HOUSE NEAR RICHMOND, VIRGINIA

There is a balloon encamped near us, in charge of Captain Langdon, Cheves of South Carolina and thirty men of the Tenth. Captain Cheves has collected virtually every yard of dress silk in Charleston and Savannah, stitched together an envelope, filled it with illuminating gas from the Richmond Gas Works, and dispatched it to the front, roped to a boxcar on the York River Railroad.

As this balloon is the only one attached to the Confederate Army, its ascension is regarded by the soldiers as an event of extraordinary interest and they had gathered around the clearing where the aerial contraption was located in considerable numbers. So many, in fact, came to gratify their curiosity that the crew, engaged in maneuvering the balloon to its take-off spot, found it difficult to perform their task for the pushing, staring crowd about them.

But, finally, their work was finished and the aeronaut, Major Edward Porter Alexander, stepped into the basket. Major Alexander, I have been informed, disliked heights and accepted the balloon assignment from General Johnson with profound skepticism. To his surprise, he has found ballooning at great heights agreeable. He suffers an occasional touch of giddiness when looking down, but a short pull from a flask of Old Hurricane brandy (my brand also) ends the sensation.

Soon the windlass began to turn and the balloon rose from the ground. It went up very smoothly until it reached a height of about two hundred feet when, with the suddenness of a pistol shot, it fairly darted straight up into the sky as if it had been discharged from some gigantic catapult. The rope had been cut and the balloon and its intrepid aeronaut were at the mercy of the winds.

The accident had happened in a strange manner. It seems that one of the soldiers, in his burning eagerness to watch every stage in the ascension of the balloon, had, without knowing it, stepped in the open center of the great coil of rope that was to be wound around the windlass as the balloon went up. So, soon as the ascent began, this rope started to run out so fast, and with such a disturbing noise, that the young soldier, in his surprise and confusion, permitted his feet to become entangled. Upon seeing himself drawn helplessly toward the windlass, he screamed at the top of his voice for assistance. A comrade standing near, thinking that his friend would certainly be caught in the windlass and killed, picked up a hatchet and, with a quick blow, severed the rope. The soldier was thus saved from death, but the balloon was now let loose upon the mercy of the wind.

The morning was clear and bright, without a cloud and as the balloon rose higher and higher in the heavens, the beams of the sun gilded her like gold. I could see plainly Major Alexander in the basket when his cry came down, "Oh! What shall I do! What shall I do!"

Soon, the balloon reached a height of over six hundred feet and was rapidly drifting toward the James River. The balloon being now entirely beyond Alexander's control, the prospect before him was not a cheerful one. Indeed, it seemed as if he would either come to the ground within Yankee lines or be dropped into the river. In one case, he would be drowned; in the other, imprisoned.

Suddenly, a shift in the wind blew the balloon lazily toward the Confederate lines and the watching host below gave a thankful cheer. Then another current of wind struck the sides of the great bag and gradually diverted its motion in the other direction. In a short time, Alexander was once again headed for Yankeedom. But once again, the balloon became the sport of an air current, antagonistic to the one propelling it. Under this new pressure, it slowly turned and floated back towards the Confederate entrenchments.

Major Alexander had been pulling on the valve rope and this caused the escape of the gas. The balloon began to descend. It was soon only a few hundred feet above the ground. But this fact created new danger. Traveling so low to the ground, the balloon was in great risk of being shot at by the Confederate batteries, as they would be ignorant of the balloon's identity. Alexander was now so near the surface of the ground that there would be little difficulty in hitting so enormous a target.

Hardly had the balloon arrived over the first Confederate encampment when it was greeted with a fusillade of musketry. Although Major Alexander frantically waved his signal flag, the soldiers below ran forward some distance as he receded, firing at the huge object overhead.

Slowly the balloon drifted away until it stood above the margin of the James River and, as it passed over the stream, it had sank so low that Major Alexander could distinctly hear the rope that was trailing beneath it splashing in the water.

Luckily, the balloon, under the influence of another current of air, drifted back to land. About three miles from the river, it fell upon the

Sibley tent of some officers who were seated at a table eating breakfast. Suddenly there was a crash—the tent staggered, the ropes broke, the inmates rushed out, and, in a second, the balloon and the tent lay fluttering together. Major Alexander, as one who had descended from another world, climbed out of the basket in the presence of the surprised and speechless officers and, without exchanging words or offering an explanation, left the astonished men to their own conclusions.

Major Alexander, greatly mortified by the morning's aerial experience, hurried back to his tent. When last seen, he was sitting on a camp stool taking a long, long pull from a flask filled with Old Hurricane brandy.

MAY 26, 1862—MONDAY
CAMP AT WILLIAMS HOUSE NEAR RICHMOND, VIRGINIA

It was a pleasant party that Colonel Mayo and myself met in Richmond last night. Many old friends we had not seen since the war commenced. The party consisted of a major of artillery and one of infantry, a lieutenant colonel of cavalry and ourselves.

We dined at a hotel near the center of Richmond and the meal was bountiful. Salads, meats, hot bread, ices and sauces were in abundance. For drinks, a preparation of gins, cordials, sugar and lemons, all deftly concocted, invitingly floated in a cask tub. The feast was thoroughly enjoyed and when properly disposed of, wit and humor, song and story triumphantly asserted their mastery. They reigned supreme until the beverage was exhausted.

Later that evening, a theatrical party was formed by Captain Alexander, the assistant provost marshal of the city, to see Ida Vernon's performance. We were with it. Among the ladies of the party was Mrs. Rose Greenhow, who had just been released from the old Capital Prison in Washington where the Federals had held her as a spy. She is a remarkably attractive woman and had just come across the lines. She is being much feted in Richmond.

Our party at the theatre occupied a private box, which had been provided by Captain Alexander. Ida Vernon was just performing the grand Finale Fabliau scene, with the red lights and slow music accompaniment representing the Virginia coat-of-arms, the Goddess of Liberty standing with her foot on the breast of a prostrate tyrant, with sword in one hand and the Confederate flag in the other, and proclaiming, "Sic semper Tyrannis," amidst thundering applause, when Captain Alexander brought to the door of our box an orderly bearing a small note from General Whiting to me. It read:

"General Pettigrew,

"Come at once, the division moves in the morning. Your brigade will lead the column."

"Yours,

"General W. H. C. Whiting"

Leaving the theatre, we hurried to our waiting horses, Colonel Mayo had quaffed deeply of the inebriating concoction in the cask tub that had sat so invitingly by our dinner table. Coming to the spot where his patient orderly had presumably, through all the weary time, watched his horse, his generosity for such a lengthy service overcame his dignity and, lurching forward to mount, he steadied himself and, addressing the soldier in maudlin tones, said, "By George, orderly, with all this hilarity going on tonight, do you know I'd like to take a drink with you." But then recovering himself, he continued, sternly, "It wouldn't do, sir. It wouldn't do, sir. By George, sir, you're an orderly, sir, and I am a colonel, sir. Recollect that, sir."

From the orderly's reply, it was quite evident that he had also had an opportunity to sample John Barleycorn. Promptly asserting himself, he quickly responded, "By George, Colonel Mayo, hadn't you better wait 'til you're asked?"

It was too much for the colonel in his then condition, even to administer a reproof to his orderly. I had overheard the conversation and during the ride back to camp, I couldn't resist pleasantly twitting Mayo about the incident.

Early this morning, orders were issued to send off surplus baggage, which always accumulates with amazing facility when the camp is near a city or town. Shortly before noon today, we departed and, marching most of the afternoon, we soon reached our new location and camped between the Mechanicsville Turnpike and Central Railroad. Where we will be ordered next is anybody's guess. All we can do now is wait. A bloody battle appears imminent.

JUNE 18, 1862—WEDNESDAY
UNITED STATES ARMY HOSPITAL—FORT MONROE, VIRGINIA

I lie here on the cot and close my eyes—it all seems like a dream—am I here—prostrated with wounds in the throat, arm and leg—far, far away from my brigade, my men, from home and loved ones? I look through the small window on the wall opposite me and see that the day is coming to a close, so that the light in the room is poor. However, that is of no concern to me because the wound in my throat throbs and my head trembles under the weight of great fatigue. A fly is buzzing through the still air and I occasionally have to swat it away.

There is another man in the same room I am in. It looked like he would die all day yesterday with pains in his side and all through his body. He has been shot through both lungs. It hurt him to even lie down and, while he was in great pain, he would pray and would say, "Lord, what have I done that I suffer so and the pains are sharper than any two-edged sword!" He prayed for mercy. I could not help shedding tears for him for he had a wife and one child in Georgia.

The other night, one of the nurses came to him and read him the second chapter of Mark, but he was suffering great pain. After reading from the book, the nurse told him to trust in the Lord and he replied by saying, "Don't do a damned bit of good to trust in the Lord!"

This evening, he is better, but never have I seen a man suffer as he did.

It is hard to write now, the frightful scenes I have witnessed. The last five days make my heart almost like a stone. It seems a lifetime since I was wounded at the Battle of Seven Pines and I am troubled that I have been reported killed in the Charleston papers. I am, however, much alive and, to tell the story of the events that led to my incarceration here, I must rely on my memory, for I had little or no time to record the events daily in my journal.

Early on Friday, the 30th of May, our camps presented nothing unusual and all was quiet and peaceful. The day was terribly hot, one of the hottest days of a very warm month. Not a breath of air stirred and the rays of the sun poured down in a blistering flood. About noon, it assumed a curious aspect, the sun was no longer there, and yet no clouds were to be seen. The light was white and ghastly. It was evident to all that nature was preparing for some terrible convulsion of the elements. The men lay around in their tents and under the trees in a listless manner and a fearful hush seemed to pervade all nature.

About three o'clock in the afternoon, the sky assumed a coppery color, which was frightful to behold. Flashes of lightning of the most vivid character followed each other so rapidly that the whole sky seemed to be aflame, while the thunder crashed and roared in a manner that caused a thrill of fright to strike the hearts of the bravest. The rain fell in perfect sheets and the wind blew a veritable hurricane. The storm partially ceased about six o'clock and the troops prepared their scanty supper. In a short time, the thunder, which was rumbling in the eastern part of the heavens, began to grow louder and it was soon apparent to all that the storm was returning.

All night long the fearful war of the elements continued overhead with the rain falling in torrents and lightning flashing almost continuously. The thunder sounded like hell's artillery. A bolt of lightning struck the camp of the 4th Alabama and killed four men.

The storm ceased about daybreak on the morning of the 31st and the sun rose bright and clear. The camp was soon astir and the troops were drying their clothing and laughing and joking as usual. The sluggish Chickahominy, in front of us was now a raging torrent, flooding the bottom lands.

Two federal corps, those of Keyes and Heintzelman, had recently crossed to the south of the Chickahominy while the remainder of the federal army was on the high ground north of the river. Early in the morning of the 31st, it was whispered that General Johnson intended attacking the Yankees south of the river. In answer to the inquiry, "In such weather?" it was answered that the bridges were washed away, rendering it impossible for McClellan to send over any of his troops in his right and center to the assistance of his left. That a large force would be thrown against his left, effectively crushing it before it could be reinforced.

I was informed of the intended advance at 6:00 a.m. and began issuing the necessary orders to put the brigade in motion. Soon arose a bugle note, then a fife and drum. Presently another. Soon the whole bivouac is jarred out of its tranquility by the merciless call of the bugle and the rattle of the drum.

Next the drums sound the assembly and the regiments fall into line. The marching order of the brigade and its movements are directed by the bugle. From the head of the column, staff officers gallop from place to place and indicate to the brigade and regimental commanders the order of march. Soon the regiments fall onto the road and the column is en route.

We marched from our camp on Meadow Bridge Road Saturday morning. Wading through mud and water, we reached the field near General Magruder's headquarters at about two o'clock. Whiting's, Hood's and my brigade were placed near the fork of the Nine-mile and New Bridge roads. Hatton's and Hampton's were in reserve near Mrs. Christian's farm. Here we waited, listening for the signal to begin the battle, which was to be the roar of firearms on our right.

It subsequently appears that General Longstreet had begun the attack at or near nine o'clock a.m., but, owing to some atmospheric phenomenon, the sound of battle was not heard until five hours after, when the enemy had been driven from his position and had fallen back near the York River Railroad.

At about four o'clock, heavy musketry was distinctly heard and General Johnson directed General Whiting to move the three brigades to Longstreet's assistance and the two brigades at Mrs. Christian's were ordered to move up, follow and support them.

I, at once, impressed upon my staff officers the idea of telling the troops the necessity of moving rapidly forward. It was unnecessary because the order to advance was never hailed by any troops with more welcome than by those of my brigade. The order was obeyed with spirit and alacrity and the troops, notwithstanding the mud and difficulties of the ground, moved forward in double-quick time, driving in the advance pickets of the enemy.

My brigade was in the advance and Whiting's followed in reserve. After marching half a mile, the brigade was put in the wood on the right of Nine-mile Road and ordered to sweep through them. It was here that I heard the whistling of the first bullet and was simple enough to look up a tree for it thinking it a flying bird.

Next, I noticed a bunch of pine leaves falling and looked again. While looking, another bullet passed just over my head. Riding on, I heard one strike and, glancing around, found one man on the ground, shot in the foot. A short distance further, I heard another and, looking sideways, discovered that a man was shot in the head, killed instantly. These shots were thrown a distance of a half-mile. Our men advancing soon drove the Yankees off.

In our advance, we reached the spot where generals Johnson and G. W. Smith were standing. Whiting stood with them. It was at this time that the Yankee battery stationed on the left of the road opened. This battery was assigned to us, together with Colonel Wade Hampton's and one other brigade that came up later. "The battery must be taken!" was the order from General Johnson.

Trying to quickly size up the situation amidst the din and confusion of battle, I ordered the 35th Georgia, Colonel Mayo commanding, into the woods to flank the battery and held the other regiments in reserve. The Georgians entered the woods in gallant style. I thought the 35th should be able to take the Yankees by surprise and capture the entire battery, but I found that the Yankees, although they cannot stand in the open field against even half their numbers of Southerners, can fight very well behind breastworks and in rifle pits.

Realizing the 35th Georgia was stalled in the woods by Yankee infantry, I ordered the 22nd North Carolina, the 47th Virginia and the 49th Georgia to attack the battery. The men formed in two lines of battle in front of me as I spurred my horse along the line shouting, "Forward for God and the Confederacy, men!"

I soon found that Lt. Col. Willingham, as gallant a soldier as ever rode through fire, was killed on the right and his horse with him. Major Nesmith, whose towering form I could see on the left, was riding abreast of the men, shouting in trumpet tones, "Forward men! Forward!" But a ball soon silenced his voice forever.

By this time, the fire from the Yankee lines had become terrific. The ground for 800 yards in front of the Federals was mostly open and slightly rolling. My brigade and that of Colonel Hampton attacked straight ahead in line-of-battle formation. One charge of Hampton's men advanced to within 20 to 40 yards of the enemy's line when the Yankees fired a tremendous volley, marked by a line of bright flame. Unable to stand such accurate fire, Hampton's men were forced to retreat, leaving their dead and wounded littering the ground.

The Yankee cannon also took a tremendous toll as we attempted to storm their lines. Their spherical case shot are terrible missiles. Each of them consists of a clotted mass of 76 musket balls, with a charge of powder in the center. The missile acts as a solid shot, ploughing its way through masses of men and, when exploding, hurls forward a shower of musket balls that mowed down our men in heaps. When we advanced to within 400 yards, they switched from case shot to canister and such destruction I have never witnessed. At each discharge, great gaps were made in our ranks. Indeed, whole companies seemed to go down before that murderous fire, but the men closed up and came on with an order and discipline that was awe inspiring.

The day was fast declining and Colonel Hampton and I decided to make one more attempt to overrun the enemy position. As our brigades lay in close rank, we marked the flash of exploding shells that kissed the brow of the small ravine in front of us, while the incessant firing of the massed batteries filled the air with constant roar and deafening crash.

The scene was solemn and grandly inspiring. All the men waited with great impatience for the order to charge—that order, when given, which will fire the heart of the soldier. At last Hampton gave the order. I repeated it and the men sprang forward raising the well-known "Rebel Yell," which for that moment drowned out the roar of the artillery. The men ran forward at their greatest speed toward the enemy lines. We assumed they had a much larger force than ours, but we cared not for numbers. We had never been dismayed by superior numbers, feeling that our courage would enable us to triumph.

I observed Colonel Long riding ahead of me yelling "22nd North Carolina, charge!" Danger seemed to be banished from every bosom. Victory and glory absorbed every other feeling. We rushed on and forward to within a short distance of the crown of the hill on which the enemy was massed. On it was concentrated the shell and canister of many cannon and the volleys of massed infantry. It was murderous and a useless waste of life to go further. Thick battle smoke covered the scene and the men fell back. By lying on the ground, they had a better view and resumed firing.

I rode along the line and came upon one young boy of the 47th Virginia who was sitting flat on the ground and discharging his musket in the air at an angle of forty-five degrees as fast as he could load.

"Why do you shoot in the air?" I yelled.

"To scare 'em," he replied.

Even in the midst of battle, it would seem, there is time for humor.

Our troops held their position close to the enemy's line until given the order to retreat. I rode back among the last and was not interfered with by the enemy in any manner.

I had not ridden far back when I came upon an old man, sitting up leaning against a tree. Across his lap lay a young lad whose fine features, pale face and light waving hair would readily be taken for those of a young girl. Stopping, I dismounted and addressed the old man, inquiring as to his command.

"Hampton Legion," he replied.

"Where are you wounded?"

To this he replied by unbuttoning his coat with his left hand and displayed an ugly wound in the right arm. I then asked the lad what regiment he belonged to and he answered, "Hampton Legion."

"Then you know each other?"

"Yes, he's my son," said the old man. "He fell badly wounded in the leg and when I went to help him, I was wounded myself. I have tied his leg up as well as I could in my crippled condition. We have both lost much blood and I am afraid we cannot stand it much longer."

Adjutant Young, who was with me, asked if he had received any attention yet.

"No," he answered. He then told us how he had dragged his son to the tree, taken off his own shirt, torn it into strips, tied up the wounds as well as he could and then sat down, taking the boy's head on his lap. They had remained there waiting to be taken to the rear.

I went to my saddle and removed my flask of Old Hurricane brandy and filled half a tin cup with brandy, then filled the remaining half with water from my canteen. I then raised the boy's head and gave him about half and the old man the remaining contents of the cup.

"General, you have saved our lives," replied the old man. "I don't know how to thank you."

By this time, Adjutant Young had redressed their wounds and left them far more comfortable. Remounting our horses, we prepared to ride away as the old man smiled and gave a feeble salute. Returning it, we rode off toward the rear, as Adjutant Young remarked, "With men such as these, how can we not conquer?"

On sudden impulse, I rode toward the right and into the woods where the 35th Georgia had fought so valiantly. The men were retreating slowly and I rode past them toward Lt. Colonel Gustavos Bull, who was at the edge of the woods attempting to get a better look at the enemy position.

I rode up to Bull and pulled out my field glasses and peered at the enemy position. I remember as I stood there, I looked upon the enemy with great admiration. They were enveloped in the smoke of their guns and had a shadowy appearance, yet I could easily discern their cross belts. I watched them go through the regular process of loading and firing. They seemed to be firing with as much steadiness and regularity as if on dress parade. It was a grand sight and I was impressed with their courage and discipline.

Bull and I decided we had seen enough and had ridden a short distance back into the woods when a sharpshooter's bullet crashed into my throat, grazing the windpipe, severing an artery and tearing bone and muscle in my right shoulder. Blood splattered from my face and I was literally knocked from my horse, falling heavily to the ground. I tried to breathe, but felt the strange sensation of my breath gushing through the wound making a loud sucking sound.

The blood flowed freely, soon soaking my jacket and shirt and running down my chest on to my drawers and grey trousers.

When Adjutant Young and Lt. Colonel Bull came to my aid, I delivered to them what was my first and what I then regarded as my last dying request, for I then thought the wound in my throat must soon prove mortal. It was in these words which I have, ever since, borne freshly in memory. "Tell my friends in Charleston that I did my duty."

These words expressed all that I felt at that moment. I well remember that supreme moment, how I was without fear and was perfectly willing to die—to die the death of a patriot—and how then came upon me the tender thought of home and of home friends. All my earthly aspirations concentrated into the one wish that my memory might be kindly linked to the recognition that I gave my life honorably and bravely in duty, to my country and to my God.

As Young dismounted, he cried out for water, while Bull quickly held his finger to the wound, applying pressure to stop the bleeding. I noted more men bending over me, but I could barely make out their forms as I stared up into the darkened sky. I felt my blood wetting the ground and, once again, became aware of the strange sucking sound as I gasped for air.

Then I heard the sounding thud of the minie ball, which had become such a familiar sound, when Lt. Colonel Bull was hit at my side. He staggered and fell beside me. Another shot crashed into my leg. It felt like I had been burned with a red-hot poker. At this fuselage of shots, Adjutant Young and those about me scattered for cover.

Dust and the sulfur smell of battle smoke tinged the darkening night air. I drifted in and out of consciousness. Presently four men, sent by Young, appeared carrying stretchers. I asked one of them how the battle was going.

"Against us," one of them replied.

"Our troops are retreating," added another.

I ordered them to rejoin their unit, saying that I was beyond help.

As our troops continued their retreat, an officer from the Hampton Legion stopped to check my condition and found me insensible, my eyes fixed and neck and chest covered with blood. He decided that I was dead and so reported my condition to General Whiting.

I next remember waking up in what seemed to be the dead of night. The moon, nearly at its full, threw over the dark forest and lonely fields a robe of silver and her rays filtered down through the pines in radiant shafts of light. It was an eerie scene. In my dazed condition, it was not difficult to imagine I was on the brink of entering another world and that spirits in white flitted amongst the pines ready to usher me over the threshold.

Soon my attention was directed to the movements of a Yankee soldier who came sneaking into the woods and commenced to rob the dead. From a dead officer lying about twenty feet away he took a large Navy revolver. The man detected me watching him and came over to me, pointing the Navy pistol directly in my face.

I cried out, "Don't shoot! I'm wounded!"

"Where's your sword?" said he.

It lay not far off and I pointed to it. Taking the sword in his left hand he again pointed the pistol, this time almost touching me. It seemed as if my time had come, and almost involuntarily, I made a weak movement toward when he stepped back and cocked the pistol saying, "Lay down!"

Just then, one of our batteries began sweeping the woods with terrific fire. One of the cannon in its discharge, fired a sponge-staff which came hurling over our heads with a sound that was positively horrible. The shells were raining all about and I feared I would be hit again.

Just then, a shell burst over our heads, instantly killing the Yankee and sending the revolver flying. He fell over my body just as another shell burst nearby, sending a shell fragment passing through his body, but its force was spent. So it happened that the Yankee unconsciously saved me from the fate that had befallen him.

I must have lost consciousness once again for when I awoke it was early morning and I could faintly hear a great owl hooting amongst the trees and a far away whip-poor-will, the only sounds to break the silence of the dawn.

JUNE 20, 1862—FRIDAY
UNITED STATES ARMY HOSPITAL—FORT MONROE, VIRGINIA

I once again take pen in hand to continue my account of the battle of Seven Pines.

When I regained consciousness on the morning of June 1st, I was lying flat on my back, dried blood covering my neck, chin and chest. I tenderly felt for the crucifix I wear around my neck and pulled it slowly in front of my face. Both the cross and chain were covered with blood. As I attempted to wipe the cross clean, I heard a voice announce.

"Here's one that's still alive."

There suddenly appeared a squad of Yankee soldiers from the Ambulance Corps detailed to look after the wounded. One of these, a sergeant of the 20th Massachusetts Infantry, assured me of my safety. The Yankees then gave me water and carefully laid me on a stretcher. Lt. Colonel Bull, who was lying a short distance away, was wounded grievously.

A bullet had struck the left side of his lower jaw and, as the surgeons say, "carried away the body of the interior maxilla to the angle." It tore off his lower lip, tore the chin so that it hung down, and knocked out all the lower teeth but two, while badly lacerating the tongue. He was in great pain and unable to speak. One of the Yankee corporals told me he doubted if Bull would live a day or two longer.

Both Lt. Colonel Bull and I were taken to a full hospital located at a Captain' Carter's house. As we approached the house, the shrieks and groans of the wounded with which the house and grounds were filled made it seem that the scene before us was located in the infernal regions. Entering the yard, we were laid upon the ground and a Dr. Seeley dressed my wounds. He looked carefully at the leg wound and was uncertain whether the leg should be amputated or not. In my own mind, I resolved to die before submitting to its loss. After tending to my wounds, the doctor crossed over to Lt. Col. Bull and laid a clothlike a mask over his face with holes for his eyes. With a sponge soaked with water, he went to work bathing the tongue to reduce the swelling.

The wounded men of this hospital were mostly New York and Pennsylvania troops of General Summer's corps. Near me, lying on the ground, was a dead federal officer who had just died. Under his hand was a pocket Bible. I gently lifted up the hand and removed the book so that, if possible, I might find his name. On the front leaf was written, "Captain Joel Chesten, 3rd Pennsylvania Reserves."

"Sir," said to me a soldier lying by the side of the dead man, "be so good as to leave the book, for the print is plainer than any in my testament and I can sometimes read a few words."

"I had no intention of taking it, my friend. I only wished to learn the name of the dead captain. I am glad you wish to have the book. I know its words and promises can give you the most precious solace in this hour."

"Yes, sir," he replied. "I know it to be true. The captain, while living, read the Bible aloud as long as he was able, and when he could no longer hold it up or see the words, then I read. We prayed together and, last night, as we lay wounded on the field, we encouraged each other by repeating hymns and passages of the blessed book. The captain was a good man and died in perfect peace. He entered into his final rest only a few hours before me."

"You expect to die?" I asked.

"Yes, they have told me my wound is fatal. I do not expect to ever rise from this cot, but if I die, I have no regrets or misgivings. I left my profession and entered the army as a private soldier because I felt that when my country needed me, I could not remain at home without disgrace. I know that we had no desire to trample upon the South or to inflict any injury upon her people, but were compelled, by the strongest sense of duty to God and man to defend our most precious Union. This cause never appeared to me more worthy the sacrifice of my life than now."

I wasn't surprised to hear this testimony from the lips of the soldier, speaking as he did with great difficulty, often panting for breath, his words were most sincere and listened to as the last utterances of one who was not afraid to give his life for the cause he was defending. I had never doubted the courage or mettle of our foe.

I found on inquiry that his name was John A. Prien, Sergeant 3rd Pennsylvania Reserves. He was evidently near death and, when I was carried off to surgery, I bade him farewell and watched him lying there very still, the open Bible of his friend lying on his bosom. I afterwards learned from the doctor he died the evening of that day.

Wounded men continued to arrive until every available spot in the yard was occupied. A large hole was dug in the yard about the size of a small cellar and, into this, the arms and legs were thrown as they were lopped off by the surgeons with a coolness that would be a terror to persons unaccustomed to the sights of military surgery after a battle.

The day was hot and sultry and the odor of chloroform used in the operations and the effluvia arising from the receptacle of mangled limbs was sickening in the extreme. Flies came down on us in clouds and tormented us with their bites. Where did they come from? They seem to scent a battle from afar and are always in at the death.

One young soldier wounded under the arm asked the surgeon to look at and dress his wound. He could not raise his arm. The doctor stepped away from the soldier and took hold of his hand, jerking it violently up. As he did, a handful of maggots fell out. I turned away from the sight, disgusted with the horrors of war.

Sleep in the yard was almost impossible as the groans, shrieks, sighs, prayers and oaths of the wretched sufferers, combined with my own severe pain, banished all thought of rest. One of the noble women who lived in Captain Carter's house walked among the wounded and distributed sandwiches and cups of coffee with cheering words of comfort and sympathy.

She came to where Lt. Colonel Bull was lying and handed him a cup of coffee. When he took off his mask to drink it, the woman took one look at Bull and burst into tears as she ran away.

There arose the voice of a young Yankee corporal crying in prolonged loud wails and screams. His voice soon became hoarse and husky. Then I heard his cry no more. I imagined he had fallen asleep. With great difficulty, I hollered to a wounded man lying near, "Where is the boy that was in such agony a short while ago?"

The wounded soldier raised himself on his elbow, pointed over a few others, and said, "That's him. He is now dead."

I sat up and looked over at him. He was a boy of about sixteen, smooth faced as a woman and handsome. He was dead. One of his feet was torn into an unrecognizable mass of flesh, bone and sinew. Gangrene was evidently the immediate cause of death. I could only wonder if early amputation would have saved the boy's life.

I laid in the yard of the house until early evening ruminating on my situation and that of Lt. Col. Bull. The pain from my wound was great, but it was nothing compared to the mental agony when I thought of being a prisoner and absent from the command of my brigade. The feeling of loneliness was the most bitter I ever experienced. I was also anxious to know our fate. Would we be sent to prison? Tried for our lives and hung, or sent away to some distant country? I had heard warnings to expect the most cruel treatment from the Yankees, but at this point, I had seen nothing that indicated anything but humane treatment.

Finally, occurred a most pathetic incident. A young soldier, a mere boy, was brought into the yard, carried on a stretcher while a soldier walked alongside and, with his hand, held pressure on a wound in the thigh, near the body. The surgeon quickly examined the wound and said to the boy, "Nothing can be done for you. You must die. If you have any word or message to send home, attend to it at once. You will die within a few moments after your comrade takes his hand from your wound and that must be soon."

The boy asked for paper and pen which were quickly furnished. He wrote a letter to his mother, stated his condition and that a fellow soldier was holding the wound while he wrote to her, saying that as soon as he finished the letter his comrade would let go and he would bleed to death in a few minutes. The letter was finished. He fell back to the ground, looked upward, as if in prayer, hesitated a moment, then said," Now you may let go." The soldier slowly withdrew his hand and in a few minutes, life left the young soldier.

Presently, I was taken to the area where surgery was performed. Most of the operating tables were placed in the open where the light was best, some of them partially protected against the rain by tarpaulins or blankets stretched upon poles. I was carried to a long table made of rough boards, near which lie an assortment of surgical instruments, conspicuous and handy.

Near the table stood the surgeon, Doctor Smith of the 105th Pennsylvania. His sleeves were rolled up to his elbows, his bare arms as well as linen apron, smeared with blood. Dr. Smith directed me to the operating table and, after carefully examining my wounds poured ice water into the wound in my neck which caused intense pain.

The sponge saturated with chloroform was then applied to my nostrils and a sweet feeling of repose gradually pervaded my tired body while the form of the doctor and view around me seemed to recede farther and farther in the distance, until all was salient and dark.

Recovering consciousness before the operation was completed and hearing the cutting and scraping at the shattered wounds in my neck and shoulder and not feeling any pain, I requested the surgeon to apply again the sponge of chloroform, which request was quickly complied with. I had to call a second time for the chloroform before the operation was finished.

On recovering consciousness, I found my arm and shoulder nicely bandaged and in a sling. There was also a bandage covering the wound in my neck. The surgeon informed me that the neck wound, despite considerable bleeding was not dangerous. He was worried about the wound in my shoulder and arm and said that it would inflame greatly. If gangrene would develop, amputation might be necessary. He had also applied sulphate of iron and bandaged my leg very tightly from the foot to the knee, thus checking a dangerous hemorrhage.

Just as I was to be taken from the table, Dr. Smith gave me two large doses of morphine. I asked Dr. Smith my condition and he said that once foreign bodies had been removed from the wound and repairs effected, the management of surgical cases was exceedingly simple, consisting in the majority of cases in the fulfillment of the following conditions: absolute rest, keeping down inflammation by cold fomentations, relieving the pain by opiates and supporting the natural healing process of the body by liquor and quinine to enable it to go through the necessary process of suppuration. He thought that if gangrene or secondary hemorrhaging didn't develop, I should recover quite well.

I must add a word here, in contradiction to the assertion often heard that Yankee surgeons were unsympathetic and brutal in their treatment of wounded Confederate soldiers, I wish to bear testimony to the fact that, in my experience while under their care and my observation of their conduct and treatment of Southerners, I always found them kind and courteous and ever manifesting a sincere solicitude for the welfare of their patients.

Several days later, Lt. Col. Bull and I were moved to a nearby house which seemed to be vacated. We were laid on the floor of the parlor and that morning, a captured Confederate surgeon, Dr. Wilson Taney came to see us. "I'm glad to see you're not going to die as I heard you were," he said bluntly after examining me. "Our old crowd is getting too small."

Even Dr. Taney winced when he observed for the first time the mangled condition of Bull's jaw and mouth. He did manage to secure a piece of charcoal and a slate for Bull so he could communicate in writing, for his tongue was still too swollen for him to speak.

Early on June 13th, we were informed we were to be moved to the railroad and then by train to the White House on the York River and thence by ship to Fort Monroe and prison. Bull was told he was still too weak to make the journey and many of his friends who were about to be marched off came to bid him good-by, but, using his slate, he declared in writing he would not be left behind, that he could and would make the journey. Both his comrades and the federal surgeons and nurses, who were kind and attentive, protested that this was out of the question that he would die on the train or before.

"Very good," wrote Bull, "I'll die then. I am going, and if you don't bring a litter and put me on it and carry me, then I will simply get up and walk 'til I drop."

Finally, the surgeons yielded, saying that, in his condition, it would be as fatal to confine him forcibly in bed as to lift him out and attempt to transport him. That either course was certain death. So, the litter was brought and he was placed upon it. His friends sadly took hold of the bearing poles and started feeling that the marching column of prisoners was really Bull's funeral procession.

The journey to the railroad would have been trying enough, even for a lightly wounded man, but for one in Bull's condition, it was simply fearful. Why he did not die, they could not see, yet he did seem to grow weaker and weaker until at last, as the column halted in a small village near the railroad, and his bearers put the litter gently down in the shade. His eyes were closed, his breathing labored and the majority of those about him thought he was gone. The whole population of the village was in the streets to see the Rebel prisoners go by. Some stared with gaping curiosity at the man lying on the stretcher with the mask over his face.

I was laid next to him and, along with Major Parker, kept sort of a guard, or watch, over him. Soon Bull opened his eyes and beckoned feebly for Parker to come close to him. Bull took up his slate and began to write weakly…"Parker!"

Parker said he confidently expected Bull to write some message for his family, or a tender farewell to his friends. He watched as Bull, who was supposed to be dying, wrote with extreme difficulty just these words:

"Parker! Did you ever see such an ungodly pair of ankles as that young woman standing over there on that porch has got?"

We knew then that Bull could not die and that such a man would survive the journey to Fort Monroe and years beyond.

Upon reaching the railroad, Bull and I were lifted onto a caboose. This car was equipped with a cookstove and most of the seats were taken out and good beds put up to lie on. These were arranged so that they could be turned back out of the way when not in use. Most of the other prisoners were either laid on flat cars or crowded 25 or more into boxcars.

We were loaded onto the train at a place called Sneed's Water Tank. The train was standing on the main track while the plump man, with a mule harnessed to a lever on the water tank slowly pumped the tender full of water. Once the tenders were full of water and wood, the engineer would fire the engine and we would be off.

While we were waiting to depart, I watched one of the Yankee officers scanning the road to the rear with his field glasses. Looking down the road, he spotted a moving column and shouted a warning. Officers seized their glasses and watched with concern.

"Cavalry," someone muttered. The remark caused consternation. Was this Confederate cavalry, raiding the federal rear?

Then some keen-eyed officer saw the sunlight flashing from bayonets and shouted that it was not cavalry, but infantry. There was the national flag and the flag of Union General McCall's division. As the long line of soldiers came into view, the band leading the column struck up the "Old John Brown" battle hymn. As the marching troops heard the chorus, first a score of voices joined the words to the music. Then a hundred. Then a thousand. Soon five thousand voices were singing the great battle song of the Army of the Potomac.

"Glory, glory, hallelujah. His soul is marching on."

It was a stirring sight even for us Confederates watching from the train. As this magnificent body of young men was marching past us, I could not but look upon them with envy, for their condition and equipment was so much better than that of the Confederate Army, which had been laboring and fighting in the peninsula for the last three months.

At one o'clock in the afternoon, with a clickity-clack, clickity-clack, the train lurched down the tracks. Imprisoned in the caboose, we sped down the iron rails further and further into Yankeedom. Little did I realize what loomed ahead of us.

At about this time, Southern Cavalry led by General Stuart swept into Tunstall's Station and overwhelmed the small contingent of federal infantry posted there. Even as the cavalry were seizing the village, some of their number cut the telegraph wires to prevent precise information about their strength and intentions from reaching McClellan's headquarters.

Then, the troopers heard a rumble on the railroad tracks and the whistle of what proved to be our approaching train. A lieutenant and two troopers quickly caused a tree to be cut down which was standing on the side of the road. It fell across the tracks. In addition to this, they placed across the tracks an oak-sill about a foot square and fourteen feet long. They barely had time to do this before our train thundered into view.

The engineer, seeing the obstructions on the track and a large force of cavalry there, suspected danger. Being a plucky fellow, he put on all steam and came rushing down. The engine, striking the obstructions, knocked them out of the way and passed through the station. General Stuart had dismounted a number of his men and posted them on the high banks overlooking a cut in the road, just below the station through which the train was about to pass.

They fired their carbines and pistols as we passed, riddling many of the cars and wounding and killing a number of men. Obviously they had no idea there were Confederate prisoners or wounded on board or they would never have opened fire.

One of Stuart's more aggressive scouts, Captain Will Farley, grabbed a shotgun and spurred his horse after the train passed through the cut. He rode alongside the engine and killed the engineer with a blast from both barrels. Most of those aboard the train survived the gauntlet of Southern fire, thanks to the bold engineer who did not. A fireman took over control of the engine and safely ran the train the last 5 miles into the depot at the White House.

After the train came to a stop, the wounded and dead were brought out of the cars and many officers and soldiers sprang out to tell the story. It was a scene of great excitement.

After the dead were gathered, there were ten or more lying side-by-side along the tracks. A light mist had fallen on their faces and the lights from the train glittered on their brows like gems. Sergeant Williams seated at a window of the caboose looked down on them and said, "General, the sweetest tears that heaven sheds are the light rain that falls on a dead soldier's face."

There were hundreds of Negroes about the place, most of whom were runaways and had left their masters when the Union army came along. When they learned that the Confederates were likely to arrive, they were scared through and through. They ran to the miserable shanties where they had taken up their abode, gathered up their little belongings into bundles, then, not knowing what to do or where to go, they filled the air with dismal groans. While some prayed loudly and fervently, others, too badly scared to pray, uttered wild and incoherent cries of despair. On all sides could be heard, "Lawd, save us po' sinners. Oh, de good lawd, look down an' help us."

Great confusion also occurred on the river as the signal was given for various vessels at anchor at the White House to sail down stream. The whole night was one of the greatest commotion and alarm. This was a part of the celebrated raid of General Stuart in which he, with 1,800 cavalry, swept entirely around the federal rear.

By early the next morning, it was obvious, even to the Yankees, that Stuart and his cavalry had moved on and that the danger of any attack had ended. At ten o'clock, Lt. Colonel Bull and I were taken with a large number of others to the wharf. Many of them were badly wounded, but all were in high spirits.

In the middle of the York River lay at anchor a big hospital steamboat which would carry the wounded to Fortress Monroe. A small stream tug conveyed the soldiers from the wharf to the hospital ship. Bull and I were placed at the front end of a procession of some eight hundred men, four in a column moving at a snail's pace in the direction of the wharf. The badly wounded, those who had to be carried on stretchers, were first taken across. It was a slow process to transport them to the tugboat and thence to the hospital boat. The tug was required to make many trips to convey so many men.

While on the tugboat, I had an opportunity to examine my wounded leg, which had now become quite swollen and was very painful. On removing the bandages, I discovered that they were as dry as powder. The water which I kept pouring on at short intervals in compliance with the instructions given me by Dr. Smith at the field hospital never penetrated beyond the outer layers of the bandages because the swelling of the leg had drawn them too tightly. My wound had not been dressed for several days and the area around it was quite black. I feared that mortification had already set in.

It was already dark when the last of the wounded were loaded into the hospital boat. Once aboard, our condition was changed as far as outward circumstances were concerned, from a state of misery to one of solid comfort. The boat was large and commodious. It was furnished with excellent beds and there was an abundance of good, substantial food. An attendant took Bull and I to a small room where our stretcher bearers placed us gently on a tier of bunks. The accumulated dust and dirt of the past week rendered my clothes somewhat untidy in appearance and I hesitated to get in between the white sheets. But the attendant said, "Get in, we'll attend to that and in a few minutes, we will bring you some supper."

I was helped into the bed, a real luxury to which I had been a stranger for the past several months. A bowl of excellent soup was then handed to each of the patients.

I had trouble sleeping because of the pain. About midnight, a surgeon appeared and gave me a dose of laudanum which had the effect of allaying the pain considerably. Seeing that Bull was very weak, he gave him a stimulant and placed his head on a pillow so he could rest.

The boat glided smoothly down the York. It did not jar our lacerated limbs and bodies and was, therefore, a great improvement on ambulance transportation across corduroy roads.

I slept well, but awoke about four o'clock in the morning to find an attendant and surgeon working feverishly over Bull. During the night, his bandages became drenched with blood from some small arteries under his tongue which had sloughed away. The surgeon stopped the bleeding by cramming a towel under his tongue. This weakened Bull a great deal and made him fearful of sleeping again.

When the sun arose in the morning, the boat was already tied to the wharf at Fortress Monroe. The severely wounded, who were to be hospitalized here, were taken off and speedily distributed among the various waiting ambulances. The lightly wounded were to be taken north and hospitalized at various cities.

Fort Monroe is the largest coastal fortress in America. It is an enormous hexagonal masonry work a third of a mile across that had been completed in 1845 on Old Point Comfort, the finger of land that marked the tip of the Virginia Peninsula. The fort's great guns commanded the channel from the Chesapeake Bay into Hampton Roads. The fort had been too strongly defended for the Confederate forces to capture at the start of the war and now it was a secret sally port from which McClellan's army had based its advance on Richmond.

Bull and I were placed in Ward A of the hospital and laid in cots about two feet apart. The first ceremony to which we were subjected to after our arrival was that of purification—that is, we were taken to the bathroom and scrubbed. Hospital apparel was then given us along with clean bedding. The condition of my wound in my leg was such that I feared amputation might be necessary.

Lt. Colonel Bull was also in a weakened condition. His wound was sloughing freely and his tongue greatly swelled, almost black in color. He was in a great deal of pain and for him to swallow was exquisite torture.

Such was our condition when we were brought to the hospital at Fortress Monroe. Ward A is full of wounded officers, including one from the 20th Massachusetts Regiment who occupies a cot on my left. Also in our ward is Major G. M. Hanvey of the 12th Georgia. He was shot through the lungs at the battle of Seven Pines, has an unpleasant cough and looks very delicate.

Thus ends my account of the battle of Seven Pines and its after-math. I have tried to give an accurate description of the battle, but that is almost impossible. For as the Duke of Wellington said when asked to describe the battle of Waterloo, "No man is more incapable of giving you the information than myself of that battle. I only saw what came within the limited range of my own vision. The remain-der I heard from others."

JUNE 26, 1862—THURSDAY
PRISON HOSPITAL—FORTRESS MONROE

Almost all the patients in my ward have been quite severely wounded so that most of them are confined to their beds continually. Having been accustomed to the bustle and excitement incident to camp life in the army, and for the last several months the tension of skirmishing and doing battle with the enemy at the front, the sudden transition from these scenes of strenuous activity to a state of helpless and utter inaction have a tendency to produce a feeling of loneliness and even homesickness. The scenes of suffering and distress ever present to me and the never ceasing groans of some of the wounded tend to make the situation still more gloomy and intolerable.

The various dispositions manifested by the wounded on Ward A are remarkable. There are those who, only slightly wounded, moan and lament continually to the great annoyance and disgust of the other patients. There are those whose wounds cause pain of the most excruciating degree, but not a groan or a word of complaint escapes their lips. They grit their teeth and bear their torture in silence. When I arrived here, within a few yards of me was a big Yankee lieutenant whose left arm was severely hurt and his right leg still more seriously. His leg lay in a tin trough. Both it and the arm were suspended by ropes fastened to the rafters above. A few days ago, we heard something drop into the tin trough in which the leg was suspended. On examination by one of the nurses, it was discovered that the bullet which had caused the wound had dropped out, having by its own weight, penetrated through the rotten flesh. Thus he lay, unable to change his position in the least, except his right arm. He suffered terribly until relief came—death. But he never complained. Never groaned. He just smoked his pipe in stoical silence.

On the other hand, many died that to all appearances should have survived. On my first day here, I noticed a great swarthy stalwart federal, a lieutenant of cavalry. He was minus one leg. We struck up a pleasant conversation and I was impressed with his dark, coarse face with its busy beard and his muscular neck and arms. He was said to be a man of great strength and bravery. He had suffered amputation of his wounded limb at Williamsburg, but, being remarkably strong and vigorous, had stood the surgery well. He was very good humored and patient in his affliction and, evidently deeming me a sympathizing friend, always received me with a beaming smile and cheerful greeting.

Then, the stalwart cavalryman began to sink under the heat and the loss of blood. I watched him carefully and could only look with pain on the huge frame, as it changed in a few hours. The pallor of death had overspread the once ruddy face while the vigorous form grew limp and tremulous. He lingered but a day or two and, one morning, I awoke to find a great wooden coffin at the foot of his bed. A moment or two later, two men appeared and, one bearing the head, the other the single foot, lifted the brawny fellow out of the bed and took him to the coffin. I closed my eyes to the scene, but the heavy fall of the body as the men dropped it into the coffin reached my ears and sent a shudder through my body.

Another illustration: A young robust Confederate was slightly hurt at one of his little fingers. The surgeons took it off, but the wound inflamed and the hand was amputated. Next it was found necessary to take the arm off near the shoulder. Then he died. It was said that the young man had been addicted to the use of strong drink for which reason the wound failed to heal.

However, praise the Lord, Lt. Colonel Bull, contrary to all expectations, continues to improve. His wound was sloughing freely when he was admitted to the hospital and it was very offensive to the sight, but the doctor has applied a solution of chlorinated soda for two days. As a result of this treatment, the slough has all disappeared and the wound is now granulating. The doctor also dressed the wound four times a day, cleaning it freely with cold water. It is believed the water will keep the wound "clean and sweet" plus prove very soothing. Swelling and discoloration of his tongue is abating slowly. However, the doctor has not attempted to remove any of the spicula on account of the tendency for the wound to hemorrhage while sloughing.

The night is gloomy enough and our spirits need rising. I draw closer to the candle and take out my little Bible. As I open it, my eyes fall on the 38th psalm. I read aloud from it for some time.

I put the little book down. There were tears in Lt. Col. Bull's eyes. He took up his slate and wrote in his painfully slow way, "Thank you, General. In all this affliction, the Lord is kind."

JUNE 29, 1862—SUNDAY
PRISON HOSPITAL—FORTRESS MONROE

The battle for Richmond has commenced. We have received sketchy details of the fight. McClellan is reported to be routed. And we have 12,000 prisoners. For the first time since Joe Johnson was wounded at Seven Pines, we may breathe freely.

Shiloh was a victory—if Albert Sidney Johnson had not been killed. Seven Pines—if Joe Johnson had not been wounded. I pray God will preserve R. E. Lee through this fight and he will lead us to victory.

A large, grey-headed, stern-looking old doctor called a "contract surgeon," as he is not commissioned, is in charge of Ward A today. He is, I find, very unpopular with the wounded officers. His name is Boyd. I saw him approaching my bed like a malevolent storm cloud, his steel gray eyes cold and unfeeling.

Dr. Boyd came to my bed, inquired carelessly about my wounds and asked if he could remove the bandage on my leg that he might see it. I allowed him to, telling him at the same time to be careful, as my doctor was fearful of any hemorrhage. Without uttering a word in reply, he removed the bandage, took hold of my leg and began to roughly press the flesh surrounding my wound. I winced and told him he was causing me great pain, but he continued to press the wounded leg until it began to bleed and jets of bright red arterial blood spurted from it. I saw he had unnecessarily and designedly produced hemorrhage and cursed him while taking the Lord's name in vain. I denounced him as an inhuman wretch, as he stood smiling grimly and sardonically over me, and ordered him to leave my presence. The malignant old renegade, a doctor of pain, not of mercy, did not even offer to check the rapid flow of blood, but instead walked unconcernedly away and out of the ward.

The nurse of the ward, a young lady from Baltimore, came to my rescue and wrapped strips of cloth very tightly around my wound. The blood saturated them through several thicknesses, but finally arrested the hemorrhage. The sheet had to be changed as it was soaked with blood. Bull had watched the whole affair and, tapping his slate to get my attention, he wrote, "The doctor is an ass and an incompetent one at that."

I tried to laugh, but the pain caused by Dr. Boyd's rough treatment of tearing loose the flesh which had begun to knit together was intense. As I reflected on the affair, I was sorry that I lost my temper and indulged in profanity, but Boyd's' cruel provocation makes it seem somewhat justifiable.

This Boyd would suit as a companion for the devil and ought to be on his medical staff. They could work together in the infliction of pain and suffering. I learned that Boyd is a Presbyterian elder and a very bitter abolitionist.

How can such a hard-hearted hypocrite be either religious or an abolitionist? I guess it's easy. As easy as setting John Brown to come down here and cut our throats in Christ's name.

JULY 8, 1862—TUESDAY
PRISON HOSPITAL—FORTRESS MONROE

Very early this morning, the hospital was alive with excitement when it was learned that President Lincoln had arrived at Fortress Monroe on the steamer Ariel accompanied by several officers, including General Halleck. As Ward A is now completely filled with wounded Confederate officers, I felt justified in believing the President would hardly choose to visit a group of unrepentant rebels intent on overthrowing his government. I would have been much happier had I learned that President Davis and about 70,000 of his armed admirers were about to pay the fort a visit.

Much to my astonishment at about nine o'clock in the morning, the long and lanky form of the Yankee President appeared in the ward accompanied by a group of doctors and staff officers. How the swords and spurs of the troopers did rattle and jingle as they followed the president down the center aisle. Not far from my cot I heard the ubiquitous Dr. Boyd say, "Mr. President, you really shouldn't be in here, they are only rebels."

The president stopped and gently laid his large hand on Boyd's shoulder and quietly answered, "You mean Confederates."

I then noticed one of the doctors pointing toward me. Shortly, the president slowly approached my bed, his stove-pipe hat in hand. As he came near, I looked on a man of about 180 pounds and extreme height. Part of him did not seem to fit. His head appeared too small for his height. His chest was narrow and thin in contrast to his long arms and legs, his huge hands and feet. His black hair appeared coarse and unruly.

He stopped at the bed next to mine. His grey eyes sparkled as he said, "Howdy" and shook hands with a surprised Lt. Col. Bull. I observed how rough and bony his hands were. These were the hands of a man who had known hard, physical toil in his youth. I also noticed he had a dark, leathery complexion with a mole on his right cheek, large ears, and a scrawny neck with a conspicuous Adam's apple. His neck was too thin to fill the collar of his white dress shirt, even when it was pulled tight with a black cravat.

After shaking hands with Bull, he turned to me and said softly, "General Pettigrew, if you have no objection, I would be pleased to shake your hand."

I extended my good arm and, as we shook hands, I thought to myself that he was much better looking than any of the pictures represent.

He then said, "I have heard of your bravery in the battle of Seven Pines, General, and the cause of your wounds. It is always a pleasure to shake the hand of a brave man. How were you able to keep so cool and utterly insensible to danger in such a storm of shell and bullets as rained about you during that day?"

I thought a minute and then replied, "Mr. President, my religious belief teaches me to feel as safe in battle as in bed. God has fixed the time for my death. I do not concern myself about that but am always ready, no matter when it may overtake me."

"You are an able officer, General, but for this war I am sure we would be friends and not enemies; however, I must inform you that the solemn obligations we owe to our country and posterity compel the prosecution of this war. I bear you no malice."

"And I bear you none, Mr. President."

"Now, General, are there any terms under which this war can be peacefully ended?"

"I think that this war could be ended if our Negroes were restored to us, or paid for, that all debts incurred during this war be paid by the United States, that half the territories are to be ours, that border states—Missouri, Kentucky and Maryland—be left free to choose the Confederacy or the old Union as the majority shall determine."

"Be assured, General, that if I should return North and be the advocate of peace on the basis you ask. I should not be ridden on a rail, nor hung to a lamp post, but rather consigned to a lunatic asylum."

"You asked my opinion, Mr. President," I replied.

"And I thank you for honestly giving it to me, General, for I now know the spirit of the men we have to deal with. But so that you understand the spirit of the North and what you contend with, let me tell you a story."

"A short time ago, a Northern general and his staff were riding along in the valley of Virginia and spied a plantation. They were thirsty and rode up to the gate and dismounted. One of the orderlies took the general's horse, while the rest of the party walked upon the porch where there was an old gentleman, probably sixty years of age, white-haired and very gentle in his manners, evidently a planter of the higher class. The general asked the planter if he would be kind enough to give him some water. He called a Negro boy. Soon he had a bucket of water with a dipper. The general then asked for a chair. The planter and the general then engaged in a conversation as the troops of the general's corps passed by the roadway closely by fours. Every regiment had its banner, regimental or national, sometimes furled and sometimes afloat. The old gentleman then said, 'General, what troops are those passing now?'

"As the color bearer came by, the general commanded, 'throw out your colors! That is the Seventy-third Ohio.'

"'The Seventy-third Ohio! Seventy-third Ohio! Seventy-third! What do you mean by Seventy-third?'

"'Well,' said the general, 'habitually a regiment when organized amounts to 1,000 men.'

"'Do you pretend to say that Ohio has sent 73,000 men into this cruel civil war?'

"'Well, my friend, I think that may be inferred.'

"'Well,' says he, '73,000 men from Ohio? You must have a million men.'

"Says the general, 'I think about that.'

"'What may that be?'

"The general called out to the color bearer, 'Throw out your colors and let us see!' It was the Twenty-sixth or Twenty-seventh, I have forgotten which—Wisconsin.

"'Wisconsin! Northwest Territory! Wisconsin! Is it spelled with an *O* or *W*?'

"'Why,' said the general, 'we spell it now with a *W*.'

"'The Twenty-seventh! That makes 27,000 men?'

"'Yes, I think there are a good many more men than that. Wisconsin has sent about 50,000 men into the war.'

"Then again came along another regiment from Minnesota.

"'Minnesota!' yelled the planter. 'My god! Where is Minnesota?'

"'Minnesota is away up on the sources of the Mississippi River. A beautiful state.'

"'A state?'

"'Yes.' has senators in Congress. Good ones, too. They're very fine men—very fine troops.'

"'How many have they sent?"

"'Well, I don't exactly know. Somewhere between 10,000 and 20,000 men probably. Don't make any difference—all we want.'

"'Well,' said the planter. 'Now we must have been a set of fools to throw down the gauge of battle to a country we don't know the geography of! When I went to school, that was the Northwest Territory and we looked upon that as way off and didn't know anything about it. Fact is, we don't know anything at all about it!'

"Said the general, 'My friend, think of it a moment. Down here in Virginia, one of the original states which formed this great union of this country, you have stood fast. You have stood fast while the North has been growing with a giant's growth. Nine-tenths of the country's manufacturing capacity, my friend, is situated in the North, which also has two-thirds of the railway mileage, to say nothing of nearly all of the facilities for building rails and locomotives. The North contains most of the nation's deposits of iron, coal, copper, and precious metals. The North controls the seas and has access to all the factories of Europe; it also produces a huge surplus of foodstuffs which Europe greatly needs and these will pay for enormous quantities of munitions.'

"'My God,' said the planter, 'it's awful. I didn't dream of that.'

"'Well,' said the general, 'I was once a banker and I have some knowledge of notes, endorsements, et cetera. Did you ever have anything to do with endorsements?'

"'Yes, I have had my share. I have a banker in Richmond and I give my note and he endorses it. I get the money somehow or another. I have to pay it in the end on the crops.'

"'Well,' said the general, 'now look here. In 1861, the Southern states had four million slaves as property, for which the states of Pennsylvania, New York, Ohio, Indiana, Illinois, and so forth were endorsers. We were one country. Your slaves were protected by the same law that protects land and other property. Now, you got mad at the North because they did not think exactly as you did about the tariff, or slavery in the territories and another thing. Like a set of fools, you first took your bond and drew your name through the endorsers. Now you will never get paid for those slaves at all. They are gone. They will be more than likely free men someday.'

"'Well,' said the planter, 'we of the South are the greatest set of fools that ever were in the world.'"

As the president finished his story, the doctors and staff officers surrounding him burst into laughter. I tried hard to suppress a smile and remarked, "Your reputation as a storyteller is well founded, Mr. President. There was even a moral, which every good story should have. A moral I disagree with, but, nevertheless, a moral."

The president smiled and, once again, extended his hand. I took it and wished him well. As he turned to leave, he gave a wave and said in a low voice, "God Bless and God Speed, General Pettigrew."

Mr. Lincoln and General Halleck then walked forward by the side of those who were wounded too severely to be able to arise and bade them to be of good cheer, assuring them that every possible care should be bestowed upon them to ameliorate their condition. It was a moving scene and there was not a dry eye in the ward, either among the Federals or Confederates. It appeared to me that Mr. Lincoln was just as kind, his hand shaking just as hearty, his interest just as real for the welfare of the men as if he had been among his own soldiers.

JULY 10, 1862—THURSDAY
PRISON HOSPITAL—FORTRESS MONROE

No newspapers arrived today and we are impatient for news. We all await word concerning McClellan. Will he retreat or entrench? Entrench, I say, and wait for reinforcements. Then he'll advance upon Richmond up the James River to Drury's Bluff, perhaps on the south side under cover of his gunboats.

After President Lincoln left Fortress Monroe, it was reported he went to Harrison's Landing to confer with McClellan. I'm sure they discussed the best way to attack Richmond. I doubt if they will withdraw the Union army from the peninsula and return it to Washington City or thereabouts.

I applied for crutches today, as I am tired of lying helpless in bed. A very rude and awkwardly made pair were brought. After tying a strip of cloth around my neck and extending it around my knee also, in order to hold up my wounded limb and thus prevent the painful rush of blood to my leg and foot, still very sore from the severed nerves and muscles, I attempted to walk a few steps. Every step jarred my wound and gave me pain, but I persisted in the effort for some time. After working up a good sweat, I was able to get about quite well.

Tired from my effort with the crutches, I ate a meager breakfast and laid down, discouraged and troubled at my failure to be sent off for exchange. I gave myself up to unpleasant thoughts of the unpromising and gloomy future as a prisoner before me. While thus ruminating, I noticed a matron of the hospital, a large, rough-faced woman, walking slowly up the center of the ward, glancing from right to left at the wounded men lying on their bunks. She stopped at the bunk of a wounded captain and said, "You are looking pale and I guess have been right badly hurt."

He replied that he suffered a good deal and needed more to eat than was furnished.

To which she said, "I guess you get all you are entitled to." Then she proposed to cheer the captain up by singing to him. To which he readily assented. To my surprise and amusement, she began the well-known, threadbare Yankee song, "Rally 'round the flag, boys, Rally 'round the Flag." Its inappropriateness didn't seem to strike her until at the close of the first stanza, someone hollered out that the damn song suited Union soldiers, not unrepentant "rebels" like those in the ward. She attempted to start another stanza, but was hooted down and left the ward in tears.

A short time later, she returned with Dr. Boyd and several guards. They gathered up several of the prisoners who had been rude and severe in their conversation to the matron and two others who had complained of the neglect and mistreatment by Boyd. They have been taken away to be punished by being locked up tonight in the "Dead House" where those who have died are placed while preparations are being made for their burial. The room is kept in utter darkness. The dead bodies lie uncoffined, frequently on the floor. I imagine that keeping forced company with the dead in such a manner will be anything but cheerful and arguable. Who but an unfeeling wretch like Boyd would think of such heartless punishment.

Lt. Col. Bull is continuing to improve. He now subsists largely on a diet of coffee and pea soup. He still is unable to talk, but continues to believe in his recovery. Yesterday, he wrote on his slate to me, "No matter what happens in my life, I have to be able to believe that this too, shall pass. If I keep persisting, I'll find a way."

As bad as Bull's wound is, it is nothing to that of a lieutenant of a Texas regiment who was brought to the ward several days ago. The lieutenant was wounded at the battle of Malvern Hill by a fragment of a shell. The missile entered the right side of the face, destroying both eyes, the nose and part of the forehead. After receiving this gruesome wound, he was left on the field until cared for by the Union surgeons. After a light dressing was placed over the shocking laceration and painkillers given, he was carried to a hospital transport steamer and then conveyed to Fortress Monroe.

On admission, he was placed at an isolated bed at the far end of the ward with a curtain drawn around it. Word soon spread of the wounded man without a face who was behind the curtain. I have heard that the wound is so extensive that the frontal sinuses are freely exposed; therefore leaving an opening direct to the cranial cavity. No one can long, or would desire to, survive such a wound. I pray that the Lord will soon take this suffering soldier home.

JULY 20, 1862—SUNDAY
WEST BUILDING HOSPITAL—BALTIMORE, MARYLAND

Last Friday, all of the Confederate officers who had been confined at Fortress Monroe for any length of time, were very suddenly and unexpectedly ordered to pack up. At four o'clock, we were put on a steamer bound for Baltimore and waved Fortress Monroe goodbye.

We arrived in Baltimore the next morning. After leaving the steamer, we were conveyed through the city in cars on a railway laid in the streets. As we traveled toward the center of town, we saw many Negroes swarming about the streets. We were told that many of these are free men. As we rounded a corner near the depot, a Negro was driving a cart across the line of railway and our conductor thought he'd been indolent in getting his cart on the tracks when he could clearly see us approaching.

"Give it to him! Give it to him!" the conductor roared to the engineer who immediately drove up very quickly so as to almost hit the cart. Fortunately, though, it was just beyond reach. This near miss made the conductor very angry and, turning to where I was sitting on the platform in front of the car, he remarked, "If I had been driving, I would have taken two wheels off that damn nigger's cart."

Rather surprised at his anger over so trifle an affair, I asked if the railway had the prior right of passing.

He replied, "Well, the city gives us the right of way through the streets. As to the right to pass first, I take it. I guess that is just about how the law stands. If we did not act so, we could not get along at all. However," he continued, "I see your sympathies lie with Sambo. I would have you know I like to spare the chaps and don't wish to wantonly harm them, but that fellow had no business to get on the track when he saw the car coming."

Our destination was the West Building Hospital, a building that consists of a center 346 feet in length with three transverse wings. The central building contains a lecture room, office parlors, et cetera. The wings with connecting buildings are distributed into sleeping and sitting rooms for the patients. The rooms open into a common corridor, wide, lofty and airy, where the patients lounge or walk. The sleeping rooms are not large. There are no iron bars on the windows. The sashes only open three or four inches and the frames are of iron. The panes of glass being small, the substitution of iron for wood in the structure of the window obviates the necessity while serving their purpose of iron bars and, at the same time, avoids the appearance of restraint. It is a welcome change from the austere environment of Fortress Monroe. The quiet, order and comfort prevailing throughout the hospital are admirable.

The surgeon in charge, Dr. George Vincent, tried to make believe, by his growling and unsmiling countenance, that he was an old bear, but he can't deceive me. He is simply an old gnarled Oak with rough bark, sound and all right at the heart.

Lt. Col. Bull and I have been reunited with the redoubtable Major Thomas Edgefield. The major is doing quite well and was extremely happy to see us. His wounds have almost healed and he is looking forward to being exchanged.

JULY 29, 1862—TUESDAY
WEST BUILDING HOSPITAL—BALTIMORE, MARYLAND

The last several weeks have been difficult ones for Lt. Col. Bull. As his grievous wound has healed ever so slowly, he began to face the issue of his facial deformity. Still wearing the masks over the lower part of his face and only able to mutter a few unintelligible sounds, the future stretched before him like a dark cloud. Doubt and discouragement were beginning to dig deeply into his gallant inner heart and his indomitable will was beginning to falter.

We had often talked of how life requires character and courage, but what courage wouldn't falter and what character wouldn't fail against so insidious an enemy as his wound. It was an obstacle that no amount of striving or struggle could prevail against. He began to feel his life didn't matter and could only blame blind, unfeeling fate for striking him down in so impartial a manner. I greatly admired his perseverance and his great and good disposition as he fought to conquer the corroding bitterness that deformity engenders in the mind and which, while preying on itself, sorrows one towards all the world.

Often at night, watching him struggle to eat his pea soup or drink his buttermilk, I could only stand silent and reflect upon the difficulties his sanguine soul must endure. It was a lonely battle and often I watched him wipe the tears off his slate as he attempted to write me a message.

It was with great pleasure that several days ago, the lieutenant colonel underwent an examination by Dr. Buck. There was hope that the good doctor might be able to alleviate Bull's condition with an operation. After the examination, Dr. Buck explained that now and then, by removing disorganized parts and paring and approximating the sound tissue by twisted sutures, favorable results could be obtained.

Yesterday, Lt. Col. Bull passed through the ordeal of a surgical operation. It was performed in the United States Army Hospital here in Baltimore by Dr. George Buck, one of the most skillful plastic surgeons in the country.

I remained with Bull through the whole operation and helped hold his hand during surgery. He was an hour and a half under the surgeon's knife and not under the influence of chloroform. During the time that intervened since the wound was received, the jagged flesh had been put together and a sort of chin formed, how we hoped that the operation would not be an extensive one, but in this we were disappointed. The flesh was all cut loose, then a gash cut through the cheeks on both sides to the angle of the jaw. Slits were then cut parallel with them in the same direction so as to get a loose strip of flesh an inch wide which was attached to the face at the angle of the jaw.

These strips were pulled and stretched so as to meet over an artificial underjaw and teeth, to form an upper lip. The tightening and stretching of these strips caused the upper lip to be pushed out of place and protrude, so a gore had to be cut out of each side and sewed up. Then the flesh which had been loosened from the chin was put back and trimmed so as to fit in with the new under lip.

Bull lay upon the operating table unbound while I held his left hand and watched great beads of sweat form upon his forehead and face as the doctor cut and stretched the tender skin. His self-possession was remarkable, obeying every direction of the doctor, turning his head as directed, until the agony and the loss of blood exhausted him and caused a shiver to run through his frame.

During the operation, he came near strangling from the blood in his mouth, and in a spasmodic effort to get his breath, blew out the false teeth. After this, he was able to spit out a mouthful of blood and regain his breath and composure.

Near the end, one of the nurses remarked that the operation was over. Then, Dr. Buck, looking at his work, said, "Colonel, I must finish up with two more stitches."

The colonel raised up one finger to plead for only one.

I cried, "Dr. Buck, don't touch him!" Then Bull bravely raised up two fingers and the two stitches were taken.

After the ordeal was over and stimulants administered, he rose and walked upstairs to a room to rest. Dr. Buck considers the operation a great success. He had invited a number of physicians to be present. One of whom told me that a man who could endure what Lt. Col. Bull had that day would tolerate burning at the stake.

AUGUST 14, 1862—THURSDAY
WEST BUILDING HOSPITAL—BALTIMORE, MARYLAND

Took a ramble around Baltimore this morning. Much of my time was spent, as all travelers' time must be, in asking questions and seeing all that the answers told me was necessary to see. Perhaps this can be done in no city with more facility than in Baltimore; you have nothing to do but walk up one straight street and down another till all the parallelograms have been treaded. In doing this, I saw many things worth looking at.

I enjoyed the stately column erected to the memory of George Washington, which bears a colossal statue of him at the top and another pillar of less dimensions recording the decisive battle of

Bunker Hill. Both of these are of brilliant white marble. There are also several marble fountains in different parts of the city which greatly add to its beauty.

I sat on a bench by one of the fountains that rushed its water high into the air. The water then flowed down into a marble cistern, which you descend by a flight of steps of delicate whiteness and return by another. These steps are never without groups of Negro girls, some carrying water on their heads with that graceful steadiness of step that requires no aid from the hand. Some walk gaily with their yet unfilled pitchers and many of them sang in the soft rich voice peculiar to their race.

As I enjoyed the colorful scene before me, many free Negroes walked by who were dressed in the latest style of fashion. Indeed, I noticed many more well-dressed and highly dressed colored people than white. Among this dark gentry the finest French clothes, embroidered waistcoats, patent-leather shoes, resplendent brooches silk hats and kid gloves were quite common. Nor was the fairer, or rather softer, sex at all left in the shade of this splendor. Many of the colored ladies were dressed not only expensively, but with good taste and effect after the latest Parisian mode. Some of them were very attractive in appearance and would have produced a decided sensation in any European drawing room. Their walk and carriage were more often stylish and graceful. Nearly a fourth part seemed to me to have lost all African peculiarity of feature and to have acquired, in the place of it, a good deal of that voluptuousness of manner which characterizes many of the women of the South of Europe.

I did notice that although many are undoubtedly free, they invariably gave the way to the white people they met. Once, when two Negro ladies were engaged in a conversation and looking at each other, I watched a Baltimore gentleman approach and lift his walking stick to push them aside. Later, I observed three rowdies, arm-in-arm, taking the whole of the sidewalk hustle a black man off it, giving him a blow as they passed that sent him staggering into the middle of the street. As he recovered himself, he began to call out to and threaten them. "Can't you find anything else to do than to be knockin' quiet people around! You jus' come back here. I'll teach you how to behave…knockin' people around! Don't care if I does hafta go to der watch house."

They passed on without looking back, only laughing jeeringly as he continued, "You come back here! I'll make you laugh. You is jus' three white nigger cowards. Dat's what you be!"

The day was warm and I sat on the bench and began to muse. Sitting there, I built a huge castle in the air. 'suppose I thought that I was the happy owner of say three or four million Yankee dollars, what would I do? Then came my mighty castle and as its broad portals, massive pillars, huge domes and shining minarets came slowly into view, I became entirely lost to all external influences. What a delightful journey I had with some agreeable companions to England, France, Germany, Italy, Spain, in fact all around the world. What a magnificent residence awaited me in Charleston when I returned. Et cetera. Et cetera.

I also thought of what I would do with my life after the war is over, if I live. I thought of practicing law in St. Louis, or perhaps California, but I suppose there is no use thinking much about such things until the war is over and peace comes to this divided land.

As my reverie ended, I walked a few blocks and hailed a horse car to take me back to the hospital. On the car, I found myself sitting immediately fronting a very pretty young lady. She had dark hair, dark eyes, fair complexion and regular, handsome features. I admired her in a discrete manner. I soon became aware that she kept her eyes almost continually on me—and I never looked towards her but once. She was gazing at me. I finally worked up the courage to attempt to make her acquaintance in some way. With this very laudable end in view, I drew from my pocket the morning edition of the *Baltimore Sun*.

"Would you like to look over the morning's paper, Miss?" I engaged in my most polite Southern manner.

"How do you sell 'em?" she asked.

I explained to the fair maiden that I was not a newsboy but a visitor to her fair city and added that I offered her the paper thinking she would like to read the news. She said she never read the news because it was never good news, always bad. As the ice was now broken, we continued the conversation for some time. I soon discovered that she was very illiterate. She wasn't able to read the newspaper even if she wanted to.

I noticed that she was constantly spitting some dark colored fluid from her mouth. I thought she had a toothache and had perhaps something in her mouth to cure it. I looked on the floor to find a great puddle at her feet. It resembled tobacco juice very much. By George! It was tobacco juice, for I saw her spit out the old chew and put in a fresh one. Then she gave me a slight smile and I took one look at her brown-stained teeth and felt slightly sick to my stomach.

As I watched her continue to chew and spit, I could only think of the ladies of Charleston. Those pure, chaste undefiled creatures of grace and charm. How lovely they seemed compared to the not-so-fair maiden who sat across from me.

After she left the car, a soldier sitting near me remarked, "She is mighty good looking, but hard as hell on tobacco and the floor of this horse car."

AUGUST 19, 1862—TUESDAY
WEST BUILDING HOSPITAL—BALTIMORE, MARYLAND

Last night, Dr. Warren and I secured a pass from Dr. Vincent to leave the hospital and visit friends of ours in the city. Dr. Warren is from Kentucky and, like all her sons, thinks there is no place more beautiful. The doctor, however, enlisted in the army from Mississippi.

He is naturally proud of his native state but is equally as much of his adopted one that has done so much for Southern rights and honor.

We decided to first visit the residence of a Mr. Keifer some distance away from the hospital. I no longer need crutches to get about, but my leg often pains me, even after walking short distances, and my right arm is still in a sling and very sore. Accordingly, we determined to ride to the Keifers and hailed a passing two horse carriage. It was driven by an aged Negro, very much bent, seemingly with infirmity; he moved very slowly and undecidedly, a tired expression upon his face. When we told him our destination and asked him to hurry, he did not look at us but muttered unintelligibly.

"Hurry, we said, hurry!"

"Think I can drive fast in this traffic?"

"We don't want to spend all day in this carriage. You must drive fast."

"Nebber let de old nigger have no rest—hundred gemmen think I can tak dem where dey wants to go in a minit; all get mad at an ole nigger; I ain't agoin to stan it—nelber get no rest—up all night—always takin someone somewhere—haint got nautin to eat nor drink dis blessed day—hundred gemmen—"

After his harangue the old-timer got busy with his whip and we hurried on for some distance until we pulled to a stop to take aboard an officer in the Yankee army with a red flannel shirt peeping from above the collar of his uniform. He looked as though he were in the habit of going to bed but very rarely and retiring to rest in his clothes. The Yankee proved o be Major James Van Donburg, a quartermaster for a militia regiment stationed on Federal Hill. As I sized him up, Major Van Donburg had reached middle life. He was of rounded figure and apparently a generous liver. He was perfectly affable, and his conversation was mainly made up of complaints about the "biz" of making out quarterly reports all in triplicate. He cheerfully asked why my arm was in a sling.

I said I had been wounded.

"Oh, you're in the army?" he asked.

"Yes," I replied.

"Where were you wounded?"

"Seven Pines," I answered.

"What command were you with?" he asked.

"Pettigrew's brigade, Whitings division, Army of Northern Virginia," I answered.

The rest of the trip passed in silence and when the carriage stopped, he saluted and said, "Give my compliments to General Lee or do you report directly to President Davis?" With this, he walked rapidly away, departing, I think, with the thought that he had just traveled with a raving madman.

We finally arrived at the residence of Mr. Keifer. While there, Miss Julian Gurnie, a high-spirited lass and a sister of Mrs. Keifer, appeared and made to us a very pretty speech in honor of the Confederacy. She also told us that the Yankee authorities continue to wage war upon the females of Baltimore.

It was with regret that we left this patriotic young lady and her family, but we bade them a goodnight and started for another portion of the city. On the way thither, we dropped into the store of a Mr. Armstrong and imbibed rather copiously of apple-jack to protect us against the night air. After fortifying ourselves, we proceeded to the residence of a Mr. Storey. His doors were thrown open and we entered his parlors. Here we had the honor to be introduced to Miss Storey, a pretty young lady, and the gallant Lieutenant O'Brian, a nephew of Reverend Hill.

Lt. O'Brian is an officer in Longstreet's corps. He accompanied Reverend Hill to Baltimore under a flag of truce and has been loitering on his way back until the present time. He was wearing the Confederate gray. When we entered the room, he was seated on the sofa with Miss Storey. How delightful it was to again see someone wearing the uniform of the Confederacy! Young O'Brian's astonishment on being introduced to a brigadier general of the Confederacy was amusing. Miss Storey enjoyed the lieutenant's surprise as much as I did.

After the introductions, I placed myself by the young lady and endeavored to at least divide her attention with my fellow Confederate. The apple-jack expanded most engagingly on the remarkable beauty of the evening, the pleasantness of the weather generally, and the delightfulness of Baltimore and life away from the dreary confines of the hospital.

There was a piano in the room and, finally, after having occupied her attention jointly with O'Brian for some time, I took the liberty to ask her to favor us with a song, but she pleaded an awful cold and asked to be excused. The apple-jack excused her. The Storeys are pleasant people and I trust that, full as we were, we did nothing to lessen their respect for us.

Our last call was at the residence of Mr. Weasner. The doors were thrown open and a cordial invitation given us to enter. A pitcher of good wine was set out and, soon after, Miss Weasner, a very beautiful young lady, appeared and played and sang many patriotic Confederate songs.

After her last song, she stood up at the piano and said, "General Pettigrew, Dr. Warren, I can't begin to tell you how it warms my heart to have two heroes of the Confederacy in my father's house. Playing and singing for you has been an honor."

She continued, "In this life of deepest shadow and occasional sunshine, there is but one thing for which I am altogether devoutly thankful, that I was born and bred in the South. To that land every drop of my blood, every fiber of my being, every pulsation of my heart is consecrated forever. These are dark days and Yankee rule hangs heavy over our fair city. Our enemies are vile, cruel creatures and I never see a Yankee soldier but when I roll my eyes, grit my teeth and almost shake my fist at him. Then I bite my lip and turn away in disgust. How vile are they? Well just the other day, I passed a group of Yankee soldiers on the street and, as I walked by a sergeant in the rear, I couldn't help but say out loud, 'Hurrah for Jeff Davis.' He turned to me, his face full of hate, and said, 'By God, Madam, your cunt is all that saves your life.'"

Dr. Warren was so touched by Miss Weasner's patriotic fervor and the injustice done to her that he made a bow so low that his nose almost touched the floor. Facing her, he gently kissed the back of her hand and said, "It is small wonder that the true men of the South fight as well and as hard as they do. As it is for women like you, fair maiden."

At this, her beautiful dimples all appeared as she smiled and replied, "God Bless you, my gallant doctor."

He bowed again and answered, "Your beauty, fair lady, has made it easy to laugh and enjoy this night."

She walked close to the doctor and I. Motioning us to her, she said, "The Confederate people of Baltimore are still alive and true to the cause. I must tell you that an organization exists with a Confederate general at its head ready to take the field at a moment's warning."

"General _____, whom President Davis has kept so long in this state to be ready to take command of the Maryland forces when they have the privilege of joining the South, is very restive and says he has been stalled long enough. If his services are not brought into action speedily, he will go abroad. He cannot stand this oppression any longer. The Yankees keep a close watch on him in common with hundreds of others among our first gentlemen, but they very little dream that they are watching a major general of the Confederate Army. Our men are indeed crest-fallen. How could they be otherwise when our hated and insolent Yankee foes are at all times in our streets threatening us with their bayonets. But we still hope and be assured, as the poet says, 'There's life in the Old Land yet.' We, the ladies of Baltimore, are ready to make forts of our homes and arm ourselves with hot water, stones, or any other effective appliances within our grasp to free our state from the foul invaders."

It was then time to leave and the good doctor was blushing, whether from the influence of the apple-jack or the radiant features of the paragon of beauty before us, I couldn't tell.

I took her hand as we turned to go and will forever have her features before me. She was a veritable daughter of the Gods, divinely fair and most divinely tall with jet black hair, pearl white teeth and wondrous expressive eyes. She was lithe and sensuous of motion and infinitely graceful.

When we finally bade this pleasant family and their young goddess goodnight, it was late and we, fortunately, had little trouble weaving our way back to the hospital.

AUGUST 20, 1862—WEDNESDAY
WEST BUILDING HOSPITAL—BALTIMORE, MARYLAND

I spent much of the day thinking of the enchanting Miss Weasner. Her beauty is only exceeded by her courage. I cringe when I think of the vulgar words of the Yankee sergeant falling upon such a pure and chaste creature. It is indeed extraordinary that the ladies of Baltimore are willing to fight the Yankees with sticks, stone, or any weapons at hand. With such courage, how can the South not conquer.

In a flight of fancy I envisioned myself seeking to marry Miss Weasner and thus live happily ever after. Lonely and far from home such thoughts brought a smile to this wrinkled old face. It would seem that my thoughts of matrimony are not uncommon these days as a recent article I clipped from the *Vicksburg Whit* demonstrates:

"Even in this army, and in the hearts of men who have wives and families at home that blind God, Cupid, will occasionally find his way. In their hearts there seems still to be a longing for the beautiful, the good, the pure that cannot be eradicated, and many a sweet and lovely damsel has a charm cast over her by these gay young soldiers so full of enthusiasm and zeal.

In Virginia, throughout the valley, and about Fredericksburg, we are told of soldiers who left devoted wives and prattling little "tow-heads" behind, and have since taken innocent Virginia maidens "for better or worse." A letter writer tells an instance of this sort which recently leaked out in General Lee's army, which bids fair to get a handsome officer in trouble, and bring sorrow and shame to the soul of an interesting girl who in him had gained her highest ideal. A "nice young Lieutenant" of a Louisiana regiment wrote a very long and endearing letter to his wife and children in Louisiana and at about the same time wrote a most affectionate loving letter to his newly married bride who was staying a few miles from camp, and accidentally, but unfortunately for him, he sent the wrong letter to each, so that his lovely bride received the letter intended for the wife and she the other. The finale of the affair has not culminated yet, but the Vesuvian outburst at the home of his new bride indicates very clearly that he has got into a predicament out of which he will find no small amount of trouble in extricating himself.

An instance of this kind is also said to have occurred recently near Vicksburg, but fortunately for the young lady, the "gay deceiver" was not permitted to call the guileless maiden "mine own." The officer saw and admired the sweet Mississippi girl, and shortly both conceived, formed and cultivated a tender passion for each other, and the truant husband, in a short time was the betrothed of the fair one whose reason had been beclouded by Cupid, until in him she saw the ideal hero in which feminine hearts at eighteen usually dream. Everything was arranged, for the wedding, and borne on the gentle current of anticipation the pair glided along smoothly, awaiting eagerly the great day.

While things were being selected for the make up of femininity on such occasion, over the glowing scene of joy and tranquillity came a cloud which overcast it all, and obscured its brightness forever. The recreant husband received a message from the capital of the state advising him of the arrival there of his wife and children, closing with an injunction to go after them. Here arose an irresistible conflict between the old lover and the newer passion, but after dire deliberation, the officer took the iron horse for Jackson and there met his wife and household goods, whom he has since concluded not to abandon, fearing they might suddenly "turn up again." When the news was broken to the fair one who had longed for the hour that would make her a wife, she was grieved and mortified, but there being no remedy, contented herself by exclaiming: "Oh, that dream, so sweet, so short enjoyed, should be thus sadly, cruelly destroyed."

After reading the newspaper article I recalled Miss Weasner's parting words to me last night, "Fain would I stand by your side and face the cannon ball, but this is denied me." I could never, I told myself, deceive one so lovely and pure. Nor should we deceive any of our ladies, for they are the soul of the war.

AUGUST 29, 1862—FRIDAY
WEST BUILDING HOSPITAL—BALTIMORE, MARYLAND

Southern prisoners in Baltimore have suddenly become a political issue. A part of the Northern press and public have become aroused at the notion that fiendish rebel officers are living at ease and receiving courtesies from the citizens of Baltimore. Flaming this sentiment are accounts from escaped or released Northern soldiers which detail the "suffering, privations, indignities and discomforts" they have undergone in Southern prisons.

The inevitable reaction of the people of the North is to demand that Southern prisoners be given similar treatment. A short time ago, a committee of the Ohio Senate, investigating conditions at Camp Chase, found that the prisoners were accorded the best of treatment. Negro slaves accompanied their masters to the prison and were confined with them as servants. As a result of this, many Northern newspapers are calling for the rebel prisoners in the North to be put on an allowance similar to the coarse cornbread, bad meat and cold water given to Northern prisoners in the South.

Dr. Vincent has warned me that I might soon be sent to Fort Delaware. It seems that the zealot Secretary of War Edwin Stanton has taken a personal interest in my case. It appears there will be no chivalry for me and my days here at the hospital are numbered.

Some time ago, I heard of the despondent condition of a fellow prisoner, Captain James Fletcher of the Third Virginia Cavalry. My fears concerning his condition were not unfounded as yesterday the captain attempted suicide.

He had requested to be taken to the bathroom and while there alone, it was ascertained that he had placed the muzzle of an old revolver in his mouth and pulled the trigger. The cap snapped, however, and before he could try it again, an attendant came upon him and forced the pistol out of his hand. Captain Fletcher then attempted to cut his throat with a large pocket knife, but this was also taken from him by the attendant. The revolver is one of Allen's old patents and is commonly called a "Pepper Box." It has four barrels, all of which were loaded. Captain Fletcher gave as the reason for the rash attempt that he was in miserable health and would never get well, which made him very despondent and he would rather die than live.

Dr. Vincent has said he will do all in his power to have Fletcher exchanged and sent to his home in the South.

Lt. Colonel Bull, on the other hand, has improved greatly. To the casual observer, no trace of the wound appears under the full beard he now wears, but a careful glance will show the marks of the "gores" cut in his upper lip. He has regained his speech, but speaks quite softly as of yet. He will also shortly be exchanged. His recovery has been nothing short of a miracle.

SEPTEMBER 1, 1862—MONDAY
FORT DELAWARE PRISON

Who am I? A prisoner of hope? No, of war. But now not of West Building Hospital in Baltimore, but of Fort Delaware. Here I expect to remain until exchanged or until freed by the end of the war. How came I here? I answer by the machinations of certain cowardly Northern officials who transferred me from Baltimore to this bastion of Yankee-doo-dledom.

My removal from Baltimore is considered an act of Yankee cruelty by my friends and family since I still do not have full use of my injured arm. Only in Baltimore can I secure the medical skill and the galvanic battery treatments that might restore the full use of the arm. My imprisonment here has dampened my spirits, but I will keep the faith and battle on.

The place of my imprisonment, Fort Delaware, is built on a small flat island of a few acres in the middle of a bay about thirty or forty miles below Philadelphia and opposite the town of Salem, New Jersey. The island, on which the fort is situated, is called Pea Patch Island and a doubtful story is that it was originally formed by the sinking of a vessel loaded with peas which germinated and caused an accumulation of mud and sand.

The fort itself is perhaps octagon in shape, at any rate many sided, and one section of the upper casements is used as rooms divided by thick partition walls of brick and opening at the back on connecting passages. Here I have my room, along with other Confederate officers of higher ranks. Life here is more comfortable and has some special privileges and advantages that the mass of prisoners don't enjoy.

Separated from the fort by some distance is the "pen," quarters for the many hundreds of prisoners. The part for the officers and the part for the enlisted men has a fence between that is twelve or fifteen feet high with a narrow platform on the top patrolled by sentinels. No communication between officers and men is allowed.

As I settled down in my new quarters, I soon became aware of the host of flies swarming about the room. These winged pests are a source of great annoyance. Not only are their bites painful, but I am required to be constantly on the watch to prevent their depositing eggs on my bandages and so produce maggots. The attendants here are furnished with codeine, turpentine and pulverized charcoal with which they make war on our persistent enemies, the flies.

We are fed twice a day, once at ten a.m. and six p.m. Our rations consist of two thin slices of bread and a pail of fresh meat which my roommate, Captain J. C. Brown, and I share. The meat is boiled fresh and when there is any salt, the attendants bring it around in cups and give each man a small pinch. The water in which the meat is boiled is called "soup" and is given to us during our last meal.

My roommate, Captain Brown, late of Stonewall Jackson's army of the valley, was captured at Winchester. The captain is a perpetual letter-writing machine, often sending three a day to various folks and friends in Dixie.

Captain Brown attempts to send some of the more interesting of his letters through the underground railroad, that is, through soldiers or laborers on the island. These letters, however, are often discovered by the Yankee authorities.

The following letter was addressed by Captain Brown to Samuel Arnold, Howard Street, Baltimore, and sent by the underground railroad:

"Fort Delaware, August 30, 1862

"Dear Sam—Thinking that you would like to hear from me, I avail myself of this opportunity of giving you the news, that is, such as I can get ahold of. It is most mill-dam hot here today and I am certain if it is any warmer in Baltimore you will have a good many drinks of whiskey. Old fellow, what do you think? I have opened a faro bank and, today, I am about four hundred ahead in Southern money, but you know that is a damn sight better than Abe's shinpasters—in fact, if McClellan makes another flank movement soon, the Confederate states' money will be worth (even in the North) dollar for dollar. Sam, please go to Sweeney's and see if my girl has been there. If she has not, tell her that I expect to get out of this place soon and write to her and smooth things over. As I cannot write at this time, please try and see her if you can and write me what she has to say. Please send me some chewing and smoking tobacco and two pipes and some anti-bilious pills. Also, if you can, get me a couple of cans (say peach cans) and fill them up with whiskey. Get a tinner to seal it and have it labeled "Peaches" or "Pickled Oysters." It will pass the lines by packing them all in a box. When you write your letter, be particular and don't say anything about the war. I remain your friend.

"J. C. Brown"

As luck would have it, this missive fell into the hands of the Yankee authorities and J. C. Brown was immediately sent for. As he sat in front of the Yankee commander, he shrunk under his keen gaze and was a picture of emphatic discomfort. "You have $400 in Southern money, sir. Give it to me."

"Why, Colonel?" replied Brown. "I think I can take care of my own money."

"That is not the point. I'll take it. You shall have a receipt and it will be returned when you leave."

The pocketbook was emptied, the receipt given, a lecture administered for sending surreptitious letters and J. C. Brown departed a poorer, but wiser, man, glad that matters were no worse.

SEPTEMBER 8, 1862—MONDAY
FORT DELAWARE PRISON

There have been many attempts at escape. Some time ago, it was not usual for the Yankees to call any roll, they thought that no man could evade the vigilance of the guards or, if he could do that, swim the stream. The confluence of the Brandywine nearly opposite, produced a counter current when the tide was coming in, which greatly added to the danger and labor of a swim. Sharks were invited to that neighborhood by the sinks, boxes, vessels, etc., and, doubtless, made food of several of our number.

On evening, I am told, the moon and tide being right, several men examined the privy and determined that a hole could be cut through. That night, no less than seventeen were said to have made their escape. None of them ever returned and though some perhaps were drowned, others undoubtedly returned to Dixie. This exodus was kept secret, but they soon found the hole and made the place so strong they thought no one could get through. In a few days, however, the new wooden bars were sawed through and three officers escaped, one of whom was rumored to have drowned. Then the Yanks put in large sills so near to each other that no one could get through. They also erected a platform behind the sink on which a guard was placed whilst another sentinel stood at the top of the sink revolving a large railroad reflector, which rendered it almost as light as day for one hundred yards around.

Not withstanding all this, one month after, when the tide was right, fully half a dozen Confederates got under the privy at a new hole and had nearly cut through the outer bar when a shot fired at a private who was attempting to escape, produced such vigilance that escape was impossible. All this labor was necessarily performed with every part of their bodies in absolute contact with the foul human waste contents of the privy. What will a prisoner not do for liberty?

About a week ago, some Yankee officers were walking through our quarters for curiosity. Taking advantage of this, an enterprising Confederate dressed up as a Yankee officer and walked boldly out by the sentinel, who supposed he had come in at the large gate near the sutlers. Once out, he began to reconnoiter the island. Finding that a steamboat had brought a large party down from Philadelphia on a picnic excursion, which would leave that evening, he returned to his quarters and forged papers in Commander Holcomb's name to go on the boat. He, unfortunately, returned too late to take the boat. He tried to hide that night, but was soon found and returned to the prison.

This attempted escape, of course, produced a great sensation. Commander Holcomb ordered him to tell where he got the Yankee uniform, but he refused. He then threatened to tie him up by the thumbs, but the officer told him the threat of death would not cause him to reveal the secret. Holcomb ordered the guards to tie him up, but they relented and put the brave Confederate in the dungeon. The next day, he was brought out, but refused to do so flatly that Commander Holcomb released him and said, "Sir, I honor you for your fidelity to your friends." This trick, of course, stopped the visits of all Yanks, except the officer of the day and certain well-known sergeants.

Finally, there occurred yesterday a comic-opera escape attempt. One of the handsomest men in prison, Captain Kiel of Florence, South Carolina, shaved off his magnificent beard, trimmed a head of luxuriant ambrosial locks and dressed in citizen's clothes, which had been smuggled in. He then secured a fake pass which allowed him to sell religious materials in the prison and started for the gate with a basket of biblical tracts on his arm, the remainder of numbers supposed to have been distributed to impenitent rebels. Had he left five minutes sooner or later, he would have been under the broad canopy of heaven, without the walls, but as luck would have it, Commander Holcomb happened to pass the gate as the guard ushered the pretended minister of God out.

"Good morning, my Christian friend."

"Good morning, Colonel Holcomb."

"Have you a pass?"

"Oh yes."

"Let me see your pass. I'm in hopes you will convert these rebs. Your name is…"

"Well, Colonel, it is in the pass."

"Well, sir, what is it?"

This war too much for the Confederate and his patience giving way, his rebellious spirit broke out. "Darn you, Colonel Holcomb! Can't you read?"

"Hello, guards, gobble this reb!" Which was done.

Moral? It is bad enough to forget your own name, but unpardonable in prison to forget an assumed one. Captain Kiel lost his whiskers and hair and, as a quid pro quo, received a night in the dungeon and a reprimand. It might have been worse.

SEPTEMBER 9, 1862—TUESDAY
FORT DELAWARE PRISON

Great cheering and rejoicing in the prison today as the details of our late great victory come in. The guards and Yankee officers say nothing nor do they attempt to stop the celebration as the news spreads throughout this dismal place.

We fought on three successive days, Thursday, Friday and Saturday, the 28th, 29th, and 30th of August. On Sunday night, the enemy acknowledged a loss of 17,000 and several entire batteries of cannon and yet that scoundrel and liar General Pope, although in full retreat, sent a dispatch to his government claiming a victory and at the same time, wrote to General Lee requesting a suspension of hostilities and leave for his ambulances to pass through our lines to attend his wounded. We have killed and taken many officers, several generals amongst them.

The battle was fought precisely on the battlefield on Manassas, where we routed the Yankees in 1861. We captured some batteries in precisely the same spots as those then taken. The bayonet charge of our men was reported to be splendid in the extreme. We have only the enemy's account of it, but they admit it to have been beyond praise. The Yankee General Kearney was killed in a most disgraceful and inglorious manner, so as to deprive him of all claims to a hero's laurel crown. He rode up to one of our regiments, the 49th Georgia, by mistake during the fight. Instantly, a hundred muskets were aimed at him when he called out, "I surrender! I surrender!" But no sooner were the guns lowered than lying down on his horse, he started off at full speed.

Before he was out of range, however, he fell pierced with innumerable bullets. So, another Yankee scoundrel meets his death! I suppose he will be defied and made a martyr of by his countrymen who do not understand the concept of honor and who will all declare that he was shot after having surrendered. What is strangest of all is that he belonged to the old army and has had the opportunity of knowing better by association with Southern gentlemen of honor.

The Northern army has fallen back to the lines about Washington and Alexandria. They have burnt the long bridge (according to rumor) over the Potomac and destroyed the Aqueduct. We hear that panic pervades Washington and that McClellan has been placed in command of his own, Pope's and Burnside's armies. Stonewall Jackson is said to have crossed the Potomac at Leesburg or Edwards Ferry, and three divisions of our army are said to be now menacing the Relay House. It now remains for Maryland to prove her devotion and loyalty to the Southern cause.

On Monday, General A. P. Hill succeeded in capturing a long train or wagons at Germantown. The Yankees deployed in line of battle to receive the shock of our troops, but before our gallant men came close enough to charge they broke and ran in inextricable confusion! The

Yankees are said to be completely demoralized and represent themselves as sick of fighting and desirous only to go home.

But we must not get overconfident! They are terribly afraid of Stonewall Jackson and their generals cannot comprehend his rapid movements and unexpected assaults. The boldness of his march around Pope's rear and its completeness of execution has immortalized old Stonewall. One of Jackson's men was captured and taken before Lincoln's Dutch General Sigel. As soon as the Confederate entered, his presence he demanded with great vehemence, "Vere is he? Vere is he?"

For some moments, the Confederate could not understand his broken Yankee (for their language is not English). At last, however, the prisoner took it in and asked, "Who? Who do you mean?"

"Why, Shackson! Vere is he? Vere is Shackson now?"

The papers hint that Jackson may swoop down upon the railroad between Baltimore and Washington and cut the arteries which connect Washington with the West and North. The road via Annapolis will be open, it is true, but that is not only round-a-bout but runs through a hostile (to the Yankees) country. Ah such news! Glorious news! New which I hope will lead us to peace.

Rumor in abundance this morning to the effect that many of us are to be exchanged. Commander Holcomb and his officers all say that we are to leave in a day or two by the order of General McClellan. I have now been a prisoner of the Yankees for 102 days; how I wish I were in Dixie.

The days pass so changeless and with so little variety that it is a chore to find events to record. I was quite sick last night with my bowels, but with the aid of opium, I feel better today.

During the night, Captain Brown's beer barrel near my bed became so full of gas that he had to get up to fix it. When he pulled the plug out, the gas, beer and all, flew in every direction with a terrible noise, wetting both of us. The noise and commotion brought lieutenants Spring and Newman into the room. They had a good laugh watching the foam cover Brown's repeated efforts to stop the hole. After a long time, quiet was restored and Captain Brown contented himself with the reflection that his beer was fully advertised, and so it seems, for it sells well today. It is made of molasses, water and a preparation of dandelion with yeast to work it. It tastes something like sarsaparilla and Brown makes all believe it is an old Virginia recipe.

SEPTEMBER 14, 1862—SUNDAY
RICHMOND, VIRGINIA

Parole or exchange has been the common topic and the Baltimore and Philadelphia papers kept us on the qui vive all the time by the rumors they published from day to day. Our hopes were raised by one issue, only to be dashed by the next. At last on the tenth of September, the severely wounded prisoners were actually sent away and we were given assurance that we would soon follow.

About eight o'clock in the morning of Thursday, September 11, a train of wagons of all shapes, sizes and colors drew up near the prison. The wagons were called "ambulances" because they were set on springs. After the welcome order to move out, Captain Brown and I left our room for the last time. Once outside the prison, a flat-nosed clerk took my name and wished me well. I was soon mounted on a seat beside a wagon driver as we started for a large waiting steamer at the wharf. I had with me a copy of the *Baltimore Sun* of September 10, 1862 and intended to preserve it as a souvenir of my imprisonment, but on the voyage south one of the ship attendants borrowed it and I never saw it again.

As we boarded the ocean steamer Daniel Webster, I could only think that our confinement was almost at an end and only the sea trip and the run up the James River lay before us. Soon, the steamer was cast adrift and I watched the walls of Fort Delaware recede slowly in the distance.

Away! Praised be a merciful God! Away from the prison walls which barred us from freedom. Away forever from the land of the Yankee.

For a while, I sat meditatively in the bow of the boat, full of strange thoughts and a sense of thankfulness. I had escaped death and now captivity and was about to return to my homeland, but there was still a war to be won and many hard battles undoubtedly loomed ahead. I hope that I could rejoin my command and play some part in the eventual victory.

The Daniel Webster was one of a series of transports supplied for the exchange of prisoners by the federal government. Her woodwork was shining and glossy. Her steel shone like mirrors. She was as cool as paradise. There was ice in abundance on board and savory lemonade lay conveniently around in great buckets. Among the female attendants on board, there was one very large, angular and sanguine, who had a large vessel of boiling coffee from which she drew quantities at intervals. When the Confederates thronged around eagerly, she rebuked the more forward and called up some emaciated, bashful fellows, giving them the preference. Every rebel who accepted coffee was obliged to take a religious tract and she gave them away with a grim satisfaction.

The fresh sea breeze was very refreshing and many sat up nearly all night talking of home. I spent some of the time writing in this journal and making lists of people in Baltimore I owed letters of thanks to. The next evening, we reached Fortress Monroe, where we expected that our baggage would be searched or confiscated, but, by some good fortune, it was allowed to pass and we reached Verina, ten miles below Richmond, without any trouble.

Our commissioner of exchange was expected to meet us, but he was at church in Richmond with some fair lady, or too happily engaged otherwise to hurry down to attend to the wants of a few hundred prisoners who were pining to be ashore again. So we remained many hours within ten paces of the shore before the necessary forms were complied with and we were allowed to land.

There was some talk of sending us to Camp Lee to remain there until we should be exchanged, but, as soon as I stepped ashore, I recognized an old friend, Major Charles Spaulding of Charleston. He embraced me as if I were his brother and joked about my return from the North saying, "What right have you to come back and eat the fatted calf and drink the old Madeira that the South gives to its living heroes?"

Major Spaulding took me in his carriage to Richmond, where we arrived at night. I was surprised that my joy at my deliverance was not so visible on my face that it would be noticed on the streets. I half expected that even strangers would congratulate me. I had finally reached Richmond and my days of captivity were over, but it seemed to me that I had been gone for an eternity.

SEPTEMBER 28, 1862—SUNDAY
RICHMOND, VIRGINIA

I was bitterly disappointed today to find that I was not to rejoin my old brigade, now somewhere in Maryland with Lee's army, but to command a new brigade in North Carolina. I resent being stuck with a new command in a backwater area, away from the glorious field of war. I prefer the risk of being killed by the Yankees in Virginia to the risk of dying of fever in the low country.

I have also learned I am to be granted a thirty-day leave of absence until my exchange is finalized. Being of no service to the army for a month I have determined to return to Charleston, that home of beauty, graciousness and boundless hospitality, until it is time to rejoin my new command.

A month in Charleston, where the temptation to do nothing but sail or stroll by the seashore, or lie under the trees, or recline by the windows and gaze on the water and white sails. Sounds like a serene existence that will be almost too good to be true. Anticipation of this leave and the desire to see old friends makes me impatient to get away from Richmond and the endless bureaucratic delays.

Richmond has been wild with rumors again. The reliable gentleman has multiplied himself and arrives at every train from all quarters of the country. Mr. Rumor left Washington only the day before yesterday. He was in Lexington, Kentucky at the close of last week. He is just twenty-four hours from Fortress Monroe. To this well-traveled gentleman, we owe the many startling reports that have relieved the dullness of the capital since Lee marched the army north.

The last rumor is this. Seventeen thousand men have risen in the city of Baltimore and taken possession of the strong fortifications on Federal Hill—the provost marshal has been killed—a considerable force of Maryland secessionists had blown up the fine stone viaduct over the Patapaco, at the Relay House, and were marching upon Annapolis junction—all Maryland is in a flame of insurrection accompanied by the resurrection of long-buried arms.

Another rumor that our invincible Stonewall Jackson had been sent by Lee to Harper's Ferry and has taken it, is TRUE. Nearly 12,000 men surrendered there on the 15th last after the loss of two or three hundred on their side and only three killed and a few wounded on ours. We captured 90 guns, 15,000 stand of arms, 18,000 fine horses, 200 wagons and stores of various kinds worth millions.

Next came news that Lee had concentrated his weary columns at Sharpsburg, near Shepherdstown, and on the 17th last, gave battle. We received the first news of this battle from a Northern paper, the *Philadelphia Inquirer*. This edition described the battle as a crushing Confederate defeat, having killed and taken 40,000 of our men, made Jackson prisoner and wounded Longstreet! The 21st was a day of gloom. The streets were full of newsboys crying extras. Today we learn the truth is we lost 5,000 men and the enemy, 20,000. At the next dawn, Lee opened fire again, but lo! The enemy had fled!

Another newspaper report contains accounts of the landing of Yankees at White House, York River and of reinforcements at Williamsburg and Suffolk. They might attempt to take Richmond, while Lee's army is away for they know we have no large body of troops here.

As if to confirm the above account, a full battalion of artillery passed through the city this morning early, at double quick, going eastward. What a glorious sight it was—enough to gladden a soldier's eyes. See the sixteen guns! What beauties—rifles and Napoleons taken from the enemy at Manassas and Seven Pines. Sixteen caissons, thirty-two carriages in all, nearly three hundred men and two hundred horses. In front rode the colonel on his black stallion, a pace behind rode the adjutant, then the chief bugler and the guidon bearer carrying the little scarlet banner with the blue cross. Just behind came the batteries, the captains riding in front of each.

Horrible! I have talked to men just returned from Manassas and the battlefield of the 30th August, where they assure me not less than 1,000 Yankee dead lay unburied—1,000 copses, black swollen and decomposed by a month of hot suns and beating showers were still refused a covering of earth.

My informants tell me that in one small clearing and along the excavations for an unfinished railroad, where some of the heaviest fighting occurred, where Schurz and Kearney and Stevens fought, lay ridges of mangled bodies where they fell. Among the blue-clad corpses were scores of wounded men, still uncared for, some of them dying. Some of the gentlemen who were on the field tell me that, for some time, they were so overcome by the unpleasant sights and smells that reached their senses that they could not set themselves about their benevolent labors.

OCTOBER 3, 1862—FRIDAY
ON THE TRAIN—SOUTH OF WILMINGTON, NORTH CAROLINA

I travel ever so slowly to Charleston, patience Pettigrew you will soon be there.

It is the sickly season and the yellow fever is raging in Wilmington. The mortality is very great, thirty or forty reported to be dying daily.

I reached Wilmington at half-past six and, disembarking from the train, I immediately noticed the dense black smoke canopy that hung overhead. People believe the epidemic can be smoked out so rosin fires are burning all over the city. The smoke seems a malevolent symbol of the suffering beneath it.

The *Wilmington Journal* reports that Thursday there were 29 interments—20 from yellow fever. Those who can flee Wilmington have done so, but many physicians and ministers have stayed behind, working around the clock to keep up with the many calls.

A boat to take passengers to the railroad was scheduled to start at half-past eight. When I looked at my time piece, I found it was already shortly after eight, but being pretty sure that she would not get off punctually and having a strong resistance to staying overnight in a city deviled by a yellow fever epidemic, I shouldered my baggage and ran for the wharves. At half-past eight, I was looking at Wilmington over the stern of another little wheel-barrow steamboat pushing back up the river.

Presently, we reached the wharf near which stood a locomotive and train. It was here that I took leave of Mr. Sennec and his family who were to run the blockade later this evening. Miss Sennec is much too pretty to risk a collision with a fragment of a shell, but here no one seems to think anything of the risk of passing through the Yankee fleet, as the blockade runners, though often fired at, are very seldom hit or captured.

I left the ferry via a long, narrow plank and, with a half dozen other white men, went on shore. Then followed as many Negroes who appeared to be a recent purchase of their owner, a rice planter from near Georgetown, South Carolina. Owing, probably to an unusually low tide, there was a steep ascent from the ferry to the wharf and I was amused to see the anxiety of the planter for the safe handling of his property and especially to hear him curse them for their carelessness, as if their lives were of much greater value to him than to themselves. One was a woman. All carried over their shoulders some little baggage—probably all their personal effects— and slung a blanket. One was leading a small puppy whose safe landing caused him nearly as much anxiety as his own did the planter.

"Gib me da puppy now," said the puppy's owner, standing half way up the plank.

"Damn the puppy," yelled the planter, "give me your black hand up here. Let go of that mongrel. D' ye hear! Let him take care of himself."

But the faithful darky hugged the puppy and brought him safely ashore.

After a short delay, the train started, hopefully leaving Wilmington and the yellow fever far behind. The single passenger car was a fine one (made at Wilmington, Delaware) and just sufficiently warmed, as to be comfortable.

Passing through long stretches of cypress swamps with occasional intervals of either pine barrens or water ponds, in almost two hours we came, in the midst of the woods, to a stop for water and fuel. The conductor told me the stop would last for about an hour and a half.

The Negroes who had been riding in the freight car were immediately let out on the stoppage of the train. As they stepped on the platform, the owner asked, "Are you all here?"

"Yes, massa, we is all heah!" answered one.

"Do dysef no harm, for we's all heah," added another in an undertone.

The Negroes immediately gathered some wood and made a fire for themselves. Then they opened their bundles and formed a circle around the fire. The oldest Negro of the party, armed with a banjo, and two young Negroes, one with a tambourine and the other with a drum, began to play and sing. The others began to clap their hands and pat their feet while their bodies swayed to the syncopated rhythm.

Now this was a lively and happy song. It was almost as if sitting there in the pine woods, the fire flickering off their black faces, casting long shadows on the surrounding trees, that they felt a need for excitement, a desire for something to sing.

Without warning, the tempo began to increase. The hand clapping became louder and faster. The black bodies began swaying and moving in rhythmic unison. Then, singing with his eyes closed, the old Negro marked the tempo by swinging his head and body. Warming to his work, it was easy to see that he was transported and utterly oblivious to his surroundings.

With wonderful harmony, he lead the group to the tune of this piece:
"As I walked down the new-cut road,

"I met the tap and then the toad;
"The toad commenced to whistle and sing,
"And the possum cut the pigeon wing."

"Along come an old man riding by,
"Old man, if you don't mind, your horse will die;
"If he dies, I'll tan his skin,
"And if he lives I'll ride him agin.
"Hi ho, for Charleston gals!
"Charleston gals are the gals for me.
"As I went a walking down the street,
"Up steps Charleston gals to take a walk with me.
"I kep' a walking and they kep' a talking.
"I danced with a gal with a hole in her stocking."

As the group sang the chorus, two or three began to dance. What wonderful dancing it was, surpassing anything ever exhibited by Carncross and Dixey or any "pale-faced" Ethiopian band of minstrels. The dancing was most a violent exercise, but so irregular I am not able to describe it. The whole group of darkies appeared to be exceedingly happy at this singing and dancing and seemed if they had forgot or were not sensible of their miserable condition. Fortunately, if they have nothing else, all God's children have a song.

I almost forgot to mention that the lone woman of the group, bare headed and very inadequately clothed as she was, stood back from the group alone, erect and statue-like, her head bowed, gazing at the fire. She took no part in the singing or dancing and had not given any assistance in making the fire.

This attractive mulatto woman was not dressed in the usual plantation apparel. I had noticed how engrossed the planter had seemed in her movements and the solicitous manner in which he treated her. It was all sadly suggestive and I felt shame at the situation this young, unwilling black woman found herself in. I didn't think any worse of her for being a thing I can't name, but my disgust boiled over at this so-called Christian man, the keeper of a black harem.

OCTOBER 6, 1862—MONDAY
59 TRADD STREET—CHARLESTON, SOUTH CAROLINA

And then there is Charleston! How I have often wondered if I would ever return alive. Now, in the fullness of time, the wandering pilgrim has returned to the celestial city. Ah! Home, how wonderful you are! Would that I were never compelled to leave you!

As I arrived in Charleston, the Eutaw regiment, which had been encamped on James Island, was marching up to the Northeastern depot upon the firm plank road. First came eight or ten instruments braying discordantly, then an enormous Confederate flag, followed by about six hundred men moving by fours—dressed in every variety of costume and armed with shiny Enfield rifles. The men were a fine, determined-looking lot. I saw among them a short stout boy of twelve who had taken part in the Secessionville battle.

As the men neared the cars, which were to take them north to Lee's army, they began to smartly change from column into line. It was here that they began to sing:

"An exile from home, splendor dazzles in vain, Oh give me my lowly thatched cottage again; the birds, singing gaily, that come at my call. Give me them, with the peace of mind dearer than all. Home, home, sweet home, there is no place like home; there is no place like home."

As my carriage took me away from the depot, their tender song ringing in my ears, I wondered how many of the gallant lads of the Eutaw regiment would ever return to their "home sweet home."

I found Louis Petigru where I suspected I would, reading in his study—he reads incessantly—a book on science is propped open on the mantel piece while he dresses, a book on law lies on his bedside table, the shelves of his study are stacked with volumes of philosophy and theology, the overflow is piled on the sofa, magazines litter the table and chairs and his sponge is used to support the reading of English novels in his bathtub.

As I entered, he looked up from his book a look of surprise on his face and loudly he exclaimed, "Have we not reason to be grateful to the divine mercy that you were spared? When I learned you were only wounded and not dead, I passed from the extreme of despondency to that of hope and now, that hope stands before me."

"The soldier has returned to those he loves," I replied.

Later, during our reunion, he asked, "Tell me, how did it feel to be shot and not know if you would live or die?"

I thought a bit and then answered, "When we began our attack at Seven Pines, I would have given all I was worth to have once more been safely in Charleston. But after the first shot was fired, I could not restrain myself. I thought only of my brigade and had no thought of any personal danger. The balls would whistle and hum over our heads and every now and then a shell would explode and cover us with mud and too often with blood. But it seemed to me as though something told me not to fear. I said one short prayer for myself. Then, I thought of nothing but pushing the Yankees out of the woods. As we made the attack, I cannot describe the exultation I felt that we would help win a victory for our beloved Southland.

"Then," I continued, "when I was wounded, I thought I was a gone coon. As I lay there on the field, drifting in and out of consciousness, I determined to live, but if I must die, to die like a soldier anyhow. I don't think I felt afraid, only proud that I had been shot doing my duty. I don't recall much pain. That came later. It's a hard sensation to describe, for one isn't shot everyday you know and all things considered, I hope I can avoid Yankee bullets in the future."

"I would have thought," he replied, "that you would have had enough of powder ball and reconciled yourself to a quiet life, at least until you regain your full strength."

"I regard our cause as sacred and my honor as a soldier and gentleman require that I return to my command."

"There is no hope for you," he said, obviously exasperated.

"I have given it much thought. It is something I must do. I believe with all my heart that South Carolina was right when she left the Union and I am optimistic we will win our independence."

"I don't share your optimism, Johnson."

"Please explain, dear friend."

He looked at me intently and then, in a deep, solemn tone, his voice trembling with emotion, he expounded on a theme that he had obviously thought deeply about.

"When South Carolina seceded and the church bells were ringing and everyone was running about madly rejoicing that she had left the Union, a dreadful feeling came over me, like I had never had in my life. I couldn't help feeling there was something terribly wrong. After much thought, I have come to the conclusion that this great conflict is being urged between two principles: one looking toward liberty and human advancement, the other madly drawing the world back to barbarism and the dark age. It is my strong conviction that the Union cause represents the will of God and that he has decreed that slavery is to be abolished by the war."

He continued, "Slavery will be abolished and the South will fail because the Almighty, in his infinite wisdom, will not allow the Confederacy to gain the final victory! How else can you account for the failure to capture Washington after Bull Run, or the death of Albert Sidney Johnson, from a mere scratch, just at the height of his victory at Shiloh and the calling back of Jackson, by Lee, when in the act of making his final attack on McClellan at Harrison's Bar. The issues of war often turn upon trifles too small for man to see or consider, but God has His grand design and uses all things for His own wise purpose."

Although I listened respectfully, I went away unconvinced that the Almighty had taken sides with the vile Yankees. But, had Judge Petigru claimed intervention by the devil on their behalf, I would have most whole-heartedly agreed.

OCTOBER 9, 1862—THURSDAY
59 TRADD STREET—CHARLESTON, SOUTH CAROLINA

The morning papers carried the announcement of Lincoln's Emancipation Proclamation, which announces freedom to all slaves after January 1, 1863. In my opinion, this is the crowning act of the series of black and diabolical transactions which have marked the entire course of this administration.

Lincoln's proclamation has been answered by our Congress with another, proclaiming that after the same date, all Yankee officers captured, whether commissioned or non-commissioned, shall be put to "hard labor," either in prison or otherwise. They shall be considered as inciters, aiders and abettors of servile insurrection. Many I talk to these days feel that it is certainly full time that the severest retaliatory measures be taken.

In the afternoon, I found myself at Van Schaacks and Garrisons apothecary where, by chance, I encountered several planters who had come from James Island to buy supplies. Dressed in white suits with broad straw hats, they were very talkative. I believe they had imbibed rather freely of the elixir sold by the druggist in the rear of the store. It was their opinion that Lincoln's proclamation was a direct bid to start an insurrection and a most infamous attempt to incite flight, murder and rapine on the part of the slave population.

Then, the oldest of the group told of the house where he had spent the previous night. The owner of the house made a white boy, fourteen or fifteen years old, get up and go out into the rain for wood when there was a strong nigger fellow lying on the floor doing nothing. "God! I had an appetite to give him a hundred lashes right there."

"Why, you wouldn't venture out into the rain yourself, would you, if you were not forced to?" inquired one, laughingly.

"I wouldn't have a nigger in my house that I was afraid to set work at anything I wanted him to do at any time," answered the older planter.

"But now," said another, "with this Yankee proclamation, if you don't treat you niggers well, they may run away and try to reach the Yankee lines at Hilton Head."

"Well," said another, "if I couldn't break a nigger of running away, I wouldn't have him anyhow."

"It's obvious to me," said another, "that the Yankees don't understand niggers like we do. Now Lincoln and the Abolitionists hope to abolish slavery, but there wouldn't be any use in that. Why, the thought of it is ridiculous unless you could find some way to get rid of the niggers. Why, they'd murder us in our beds—That's what they'd do. Why, over to Georgetown, there was a Negro woman that killed her mistress and her two little ones with an axe. The people just flocked together and hung her right up on the spot. They ought to have piled some wood around her and burned her to death, that would have been a good lesson to the rest."

I left the apothecary with a new toothbrush, shaving cream and the conviction that it does indeed appear impossible to conjecture where this all will end.

OCTOBER 10, 1862—FRIDAY
59 TRADD STREET—CHARLESTON, SOUTH CAROLINA

Today while eating breakfast at the Charleston Hotel, a Lieutenant Colonel Arthur Fremantle of the British Army introduced himself to me. He is here, as he put it, "to see something of this wonderful struggle." He openly confessed his initial sympathy for the North, which he attributed to his own dislike of slavery, but says that he is now openly sympathetic to the South. He admires the "gallantry and determination of Southerners and disapproves of the foolish bullying conduct of Northerners."

Fremantle is small and slight, a diminutive Ichabod Crane. He was dressed in wide corduroy pants and boots that reached mid-calf. Long side whiskers accentuated his already elongated face. Drooping eyes peered out from beneath a high-crowned hat set at a jaunty angle. With his head cocked slightly in the direction his hat pointed, the colonel seemed to list precariously to the right.

Despite his rather strange appearance, I enjoyed his good humor during our breakfast conversation. He convulsed me with the tale of his arrival at the Charleston Hotel. Shortly after receiving his room key, he was approaching the door to his room when he overheard a colonel conversing mysteriously with an attractive young quadroon. He could not help but hear the following dialogue.

"Colonel, you overwhelm me with you kindness."

"Do not thank me, young slave, and believe me when I say there is no sacrifice I would refuse to make to merit your affection and esteem."

"And you will buy me, Colonel?"

"I will buy you, pretty colored girl. And without any haggling over price either."

"And when I am yours, you will take me home with you, Colonel?"

"Everything is ready, dearest, do not doubt my word. In a few days, the two of us will travel to my home where you will be free and I your slave."

Fremantle said he was on the point of turning the hall corridor to confront the impudent seducer of the young, susceptible and credulous slave, but at the first noise he made, the colonel slipped off in one direction while the quadroon fled past him down the hall.

When I returned home late in the morning, Ruth was still at the washboard. Ever resourceful, she had enlisted one of the young servant girls from across the street to help her. As I stood near the back door, I could hear Ruth, a strong Baptist, stick up for her own faith against the servant girl, who belonged to the Episcopalian church her master attended.

"You kin read, now can't you, child?"

"Yes."

"Well, I s'pose you've dun read de Bible, haint you?"

"Yes."

"You've read about John de Baptis', haint you?"

"Yes."

"Well, child, you never read 'bout any John de Episcopalian, did you? You see, I has de Bible on my side den."

OCTOBER 12, 1862—SUNDAY
59 TRADD STREET—CHARLESTON, SOUTH CAROLINA

At the Charleston Hotel this afternoon, I found four newspaper correspondents. We fraternized immediately and they all pooh-pooed Lincoln's Emancipation Proclamation and the attempt to enlist Negro regiments to serve in the Yankee army.

One, a rather stout fellow, inclined to panting and perspiration, had just returned from the West. He wore glasses upon a most pugnacious nose. His large, round head was covered with short bristly, jetty hair.

"Since the passage of the bill in the Federal Congress allowing Negroes to enlist," said this person, "the greatest demoralization exists in Sherman's army. This is frequently manifesting itself in open mutiny."

"Has it infected just the officers or all men of the army?" asked one of the group.

"Both!" Officers and soldiers of Democratic faith daily allow their obstinate determination not to fight in the same ranks with Cuffy and Sambo, or to draw another sword in the abolition crusade to make a St. Domingo of the South."

At this point, he took off his glasses and wiped his face. The water was running down his cheeks like a miniature cataract and his great neck seemed to emit jets of perspiration.

"I know," he continued, "that an Indiana and an Illinois regiment are said to have recently stacked their arms and voted to return home. Most of the officers resigned and numbers of the soldiers marched through the streets of Memphis in mutinous demonstration, free to proclaim their intention. The colonel, lieutenant colonel, and major with five or six captains of a Kentucky regiment are also stated to have sent in their resignations and left for their homes. The Missouri troops, too, are kicking against the pricks and, unless bayonet rule can quell the growing disaffection, we may soon have a war of the races between two hostile components of the Federal Northwest Army. Reports of a little bloodletting have already reached us, but I think they are a little premature."

"The federal soldiers have been grossly deceived by their political leaders," said another of the company. "They did not enlist thinking that they joined the army for the sole purpose of liberating the Negro."

"I agree," said the perspiring one, "and I have also learned that the majority of the army at Memphis are greatly estranged from the federal cause by the Negro equality military bill passed by the reckless Congress at Washington and that a respectable minority for the same reason are ready at anytime to mutiny and desert. Many pickets around the city no longer support their cause. They talk of insurrection in the presence of refugees who pass the lines when driven from their homes and refuse often times to take from these persons pistols, bowie knives and other arms which they bring with them contrary to order.

"You have actually seen this?" I asked.

"Oh yes," he answered. "One day, at the edge of the city, I heard a refugee ask a sentinel to examine his trunk. 'No sire,' said the surly soldier, an Illinoisan, I believe. 'I don't care by God if you've got it full of arms. I don't intend to fight any longer for a government that allows a damn nigger to fight by my side.' Such is the present spirit and temper of the Northwest and its soldiers, who have achieved every victory for Yankee arms yet recorded in the calendar of this cruel war."

After further conversation, the stout one and two of the other correspondents left the hotel leaving me with the *Charleston Courier* correspondent, Flex Gregory de Fontaine. I had first met his likeable Frenchman when he came to Dumfries, Virginia, back in the days when my regiment was guarding the Evansport batteries on the Potomac River.

A likeable rogue, De Fontaine, although born in Boston, is of foreign parentage. Two of his uncles, after whom he is named, were Italian professors attached to the Austrian and French courts. His father, Louis Antoine de Fontaine, was a French nobleman who accompanied Charles X into exile. Leaving France behind, the elder de Fontaine came to America and married a Boston girl who was connected with the family of the Revolutionary War patriot, Ethan Allen.

Educated by private tutors, de Fontaine managed to learn phonography and this system of writing has helped him greatly in his career as a reporter. In time, he became a Congressional reporter in Washington City and was also charged with preparing the official reports of the famous trial of Harvard professor John Webster for the murder of Dr. Parkman in Boston in 1849 and that of Congressman, now Federal General Dan Sickles for the shooting of Barton Key in Washington in 1859. In March of 1861, de Fontaine moved to Charleston where he covered the stirring events of the start of the war for the *New York Herald*. He made the first report of the attack on Fort Sumter when he telegraphed an account back to New York.

By May, 1861, de Fontaine had decided his sympathies were with the South and he accompanied the First South Carolina Regiment to Virginia as a military correspondent with the rank of major. His credentials are impressive, as he has covered the first battle of Manassas, Balls Bluff, the Battle of Shiloh, the Seven Days Battles, the second battle of Manassas, and Sharpsburg. He has returned to Charleston from the front only because he suffered an accident when his horse was frightened suddenly and he was dragged 75 yards, severely lacerating him. But fortunately, he broke no bones. Somewhat battered and bruised, he was forced to leave Lee's army and return to Charleston.

"I would like to believe that fellow who just returned from the West," I said to de Fontaine, "but I believe that we must rely upon our own strength rather than upon any weakness of the enemy if we expect to win in this game of war."

"I wouldn't believe everything he says," answered de Fontaine. "I know he was attached to the provincial press and has been with the Army of the West until recently, but without any exception, he is the fussiest, most impertinent, most disagreeable man I know. He always makes a hero of himself in his reports and, if I remember rightly, their headings run after this fashion:

> "Tremendous Battle at Belmont! The Correspondent of the Blunder Hoists the Stars and Bars in Front of the Yankee Lines!!!" Or again, "Great Battle at Shiloh! Mr. Twaddle, Our Special Correspondent, Taken Prisoner!! He Escapes!! He is Fired Upon!! He Wriggles Through Four Swamps and Seven Hostile Camps!! He Is Again Captured! He Strangles the Sentry! He Drinks the Yankee Commander Grant Blind! Grant Gives him the Password! Our Correspondent Gains Our Lines and Is Feted by Beauregard!! His Welcome! Description of His Boots! Remarks" et cetera. Et cetera.

Laughing at de Fontaine's graphic description of the stout blowhard, I managed to order some apple whiskey and we returned to the front door a moment to catch the free air and continue our conversation. Just as we stepped outside the hotel, a little Negro boy came dashing up and said, "Do you know where I can gets a paper. Missus wants a paper. Wesley flinged hern over de fense in de yard and de puppy tored it up."

After the gallant de Fontaine secured the ebony messenger a paper and admonished him to keep it away from Wesley, he watched the lad run down Meeting Street. Apparently, this chance encounter once again led de Fontaine to muse over the role of the Negro in this war.

"You know," he said, "the belief even prevails among the Federals that Negro troops will be cowardly. I don't think you can make soldiers of slaves, for freedom is punishment to the slave and servitude, his normal condition. He loves, looks up to and depends on his owner as a good dog does his master. He will despise and reject emancipation just as a good dog would dislike being discharged from his duty of guardianship and kicked into the street to get his own living as best he could."

"Regardless," I said, "there are those in the North who will do all in their power to arm the Negro and send him into battle against us."

"Then, if captured, it will be a nice question whether they are to be realized as belligerents or outlaws and hung," replied de Fontaine. "If they take up arms against us, we must either shoot them or hang them. There can be no other course."

OCTOBER 19, 1862—SUNDAY
59 TRADD STREET—CHARLESTON, SOUTH CAROLINA

Fremantle and de Fontaine came to call on me at 9:00 a.m. They then accompanied me to General Ripley's office. At twelve o'clock, we took the general's boat to inspect Fort Sumter. Our party consisted of a congressman named Nutt, Captain Walters of Ripley's staff, Fremantle, de Fontaine, the general and myself. We reached Fort Sumter after a pull of about three-quarters of an hour.

Arriving at Fort Sumter, we met General Beauregard, as had been previously arranged. The general was with Colonel Rhett, the commander of the fort's garrison and his aide, Captain Mitchell. I had not seen Beauregard since the halcyon days of 1861. He would still be very youthful in appearance were it not for the color of his hair, which is now much grayer. Some people account for the sudden manner in which his hair turned gray by allusions to the cares and anxieties of command, but the real and less romantic reason is to be found in the rigidity of the Yankee blockade which interrupts the arrival of his hair coloring chemicals from England.

From the summit of Fort Sumter, a good general view is obtained of the harbor and of the fortifications commanding the approach to Charleston. General Beauregard pointed to Castle Pinckney, Fort

Ripley, Fort Moultrie and Fort Wagner, for Fremantle and gave the number of heavy guns at each location. It appears that both sides of the harbor for several miles bristle with forts mounting heavy guns.

We then looked to the east toward the open sea. Beauregard explained that the bar, beyond which we counted thirteen Yankee blockaders, is nine miles from the city. He said that if the Yankee blockaders and ironclads should try to enter the harbor, he would hose them with flat-headed bolts out of the smoothbore guns, which he thinks could travel accurately enough for 500 or 600 yards. He felt, however, that Fort Sumter could be destroyed if a vessel could be found impervious enough to lie pretty close in and batter it for five hours. But with the forts' heavy armament and plunging fire, this catastrophe was not deemed probable. General Beauregard then told us that, in his opinion, the proper manner to attack Charleston was to land on Morris Island, take Fort Wagner on Cummings Point, and then turn their guns on Sumter.

Later in the afternoon, we surprised General Beauregard with a small presentation party. Ripley, Fremantle, de Fontaine, Rhett and I gathered with the general in the middle of the fort on the parade ground. Facing the general, I then proceeded to read to him the following letter:

"Fort Sumter, October 19, 1862.

"General Beauregard—Sir, as a testimonial of our respect for you and admiration for the chivalrous instincts which, when the Southland was assailed by vile legions, induced you to spring unhesitatingly to its defense, we have the honor to present to you a beautiful field glass. Trusting that, by its assistance, you will be able to see through your enemies and better serve the admiring soldiers under your command. We have the honor to subscribe ourselves.

"Your most obedient servants,

"General James Johnson Pettigrew, Lt. Col. Arthur J. L. Fremantle,

Flex Gregory de Fontaine."

I then handed the general the box containing the gift. He thanked me and carefully opened it, taking out the necks and upper parts of two whiskey bottles fastened together by a piece of wood. He seemed greatly surprised at first sight, but soon joined the rest of the party in the merriment of the moment. He then lifted the field glass to his eyes and leveled it upon our small group remarking that we appeared to be thirsty. Fremantle then replied that we had anticipated the general would be able to see the situation clearly with the aid of this new field glass and had come prepared. With this, he held up a bottle of champagne and proposed a drink to celebrate the occasion and the high estimation with which the general was held by his friends.

After our return to Charleston, I spent a pleasant evening that concluded with a walk on the battery with Beauregard and Fremantle. De Fontaine had reluctantly left us to attend to business at the *Courier* office. The night was lovely! The tide was full. The waters of the bay rippled up against the stones with a pleasing gurgle. The shore of the opposite James Island was dimly seen in the distance, a clump of tall pines stood out a darker shade in the haze. The whole bay was light, silver like, with ships spotting it, their watch lights trembling like stars and reflecting below in the water. The sky was perfectly cloudless and the moon full and sharply defined. The soft night air was full of fragrance and the houses along the bay with their long piazzas were so tropical looking. All was still and calm. I had to wonder if it was real or was I dreaming. Could there be such peace in the midst of war?

We sauntered up and down discussing the current military situation, dwelling especially on the defense of Charleston. Beauregard was firm in his conviction that the Yankees would spare no effort to attempt to capture the city. He felt that with all the Yankee blathering about Richmond, the capture of Charleston was really the prize they coveted the most. Even though Richmond is the Confederate capital, its capture, except in name, would prove a barren victory. If the Federals could take Richmond, that event would probably be fore-seen by our government in time to remove from the capital every-thing of value. He said that Virginia and the South abound with nat-ural facilities for manufacturing purposes and the workshops already in existence in the interior would be increased to a great extent. The government archives could be transferred to another locality without any difficulty. In the language of President Davis, the war could be carried on in Virginia for twenty years. After the first inconveniences of the loss of Richmond, our national defense would proceed with fresh energy and we should still possess the only means of transport-ing supplies we have ever had—the railroads. For our rivers have been, and still are, of use only to the enemy.

Moreover, the frequent discomfiture which the Yankees have met in their "On to Richmond" and the increasing improbabilities of accomplishing that object are beginning to make the grapes sour in the estimation of those amiable foxes. But the Charleston grapes still hang in tempting clusters and the grudge they owe South Carolina is older and more venomous than that toward Virginia. The Yankee journalists never refer to Charleston without calling it the "adder's nest of treason," manifesting a burning desire to stamp out this nest of "vipers." South Carolina committed the unpardonable crime of lighting the flames of this unholy rebellion and of first crushing the flag of the United States to trail in the dust. Moreover, she is an old offender, having for thirty years been chafing in her chains and loathing with intense disgust her compulsory companionship with Yankee Doodledom. Also, her proud and pure character is a standing affront to the vile Yankees that can never be forgiven. How they would delight to humble South Carolina in the dust, to tread over her in the mud, to jump and hallo and whoop over her prostrate form.

Beauregard next mentioned that the condition of New Orleans would be an Elysium compared to that of Charleston if it should fall into Yankee hands, for he felt that there is no indignity its people would not be made to suffer. No atrocity the Yankees are not capable of perpetrating. It would be better that not one brick should be left standing upon another in Charleston, better that its whole population should be driven out houseless and homeless to the interior than to surrender to the Yankees and be governed probably by Butler the beast—who might be sent here as the most efficient agent to make Charleston drink to the dregs of the bitter cup the Yankees have prepared for her lips. But, thought Beauregard, we have no fears of any surrender. If Charleston should be destroyed, it will only be the loss of a few acres of Carolina soil leaving intact the strength and independence of the state. Beauregard was satisfied, however, that Charleston would drive back the invaders in ignominious confusion and come out of the conflict with all her banners flying.

The general's discourse and our stroll on the battery was a happy ending to an interesting day. As I walked home, I knew that with Beauregard at the head of Carolina's chivalry, there will be such an entertainment ready for the Yankees at Charleston that it will satisfy their appetite for invasion for generations to come.

OCTOBER 25, 1862—SATURDAY
59 TRADD STREET—CHARLESTON, SOUTH CAROLINA

I woke yesterday morning with a terrible headache. The doctor prescribed six onions, cut fine, eaten raw, with vinegar, pepper and salt. It was difficult, but I followed the prescription and they cured my head. Later I left my house and stepped out onto narrow Tradd Street to walk the fifty paces or so to Meeting Street and thence north a short distance to St. Michael's Church.

A few happy steps from my front door, I observed coming toward me Miss Laura Randolph, one of the young beauties of Charleston society. She looked very lovely, all silk and satin under an umbrella. She looked as though she were going to a dinner party. She came rustling toward me, her wide dress taking up much of the narrow street. I advanced trying to think of something clever to say, when I instantly remembered the horrid onions and felt like a culprit! I would have fled, but it was too late. What should I do? I had to remain and greet her. I bowed low in a mock-heroic gesture, but I dared not open my mouth lest my breath should betray the fatal secret! So I monosyllabled her and stood as far off as possible. At last she went off, her handsome eyes flashing like two stars.

I took a carriage ride this evening with Judge Petigru through the environs of the city. After getting beyond Magnolia Cemetery, there was nothing to remind us of war; all was peaceful loveliness. We talked of days past and almost forgot that our land was the scene of bitter strife. At one point, I almost fancied that we were taking one of our usual summer trips with the power to return when it terminates. Then, I was suddenly aroused from my sweet dream to find myself a Confederate general, surrounded by the desolation and horrors of a war which my Christian fancy had never conceived a possibility, in this Christian land and enlightened day.

A length, we turned the carriage around and headed back toward Charleston. Following a dirt road near the Cooper River, our attention was attracted to a burly-headed old Negro with a long beard, feet that were encased in stout cowhide boots, hickory-colored jean clothes and a huge white felt hat—the wide brim cocked up before and behind in military style, giving him a rakish and somewhat dignified appearance. He sat high on the driver's seat of a small Dutch wagon being pulled by two oxen. The bed of the wagon was filled to overflowing with ears of corn and topped off with vegetables and fresh-killed pigs and poultry "fixin's" of various kinds bound for the Charleston Market.

In his right hand, he held a tall whip, several inches thick and braided from hemp of some six feet in length. He looked out at us with a jaunty air as we pulled aside. He cheered on his sturdy team by singing in a melodious tone to the popular old Negro air of "Long Time Ago," an improvisatory song. Every stanza, in order to take fresh breath and give vent to the exuberance of his feelings, he wound up in a chorus of loud cracks of his whip.

"Den goin' down to Charleston, long time ago.
"Where all de w'gons chucky fill, stan'in a row.
Crack! Crack! Crack!
"Ob pig an' turkey, chicken big, long time ago.
"Who never more his foot he dig, in garden ob Sambo."
Crack! Crack! Crack!

After the last sharp crack of the whip, I took the opportunity of questioning our ebony serenader.

"So then, Sambo, you have planted a garden?"

"Yes, sartin, master give me small garden and one day a week to work it."

"And what, may I ask, do you raise there?"

With this he walked to the back of the wagon and handed out sundry vegetables, beginning with a huge carrot about as big as an Enfield musket.

"Pray, Sambo, how did you produce that?"

Thinking a bit before answering, he replied, "Master think his garden never grow nothin', poor dry soil. I knows better and I wheels in several barrel loads of manure. Then I work garden late. I work it 'arly."

Judge Petigru, intrigued with this skillful horticulturist, joined the conversation by asking, "Sambo, you are a genius to grow such carrots. A real scientific agriculturist. Did you ever read Davy or Tull?" (Noted English chemists and agricultural writers)

"Tull," he replied with a grin. "Who he be? Dog that tree de coon?"

"Not exactly," replied the judge, suppressing a laugh, "but do you produce other vegetables equally large?"

Stopping to think once again, he replied, "Pa'snip in the spring—him grew a might smart chance all winter."

"Very well, Sambo. Very well indeed, but now pray tell me how do you contrive to make such fat luscious-looking poultry there as I see in the wagon? I fancy that they did not grow in the same way that your carrots and parsnips have here."

"I reckon not ezakly," said he. "Raise them 'pecial, don't steal them like some niggers. And my mammy sure know how ter fix chicken. Lissen. Clean de chicken an' leave him whole. Put wet paper roun' him an' put him in de hot ashes in de fiahplace. Cover him wid coals. Oh, my laudy, laudy!" Then he burst into a loud laugh and commenced dancing all around the wagon.

We ended our conversation without waiting for the dancing Sambo to elaborate further his method of fattening fowls. The last we saw of him, he was again sitting atop his wagon, cracking his whip and singing out at the top of his voice:

"What now you ask de pound for coon? Long time ago.

"Ah, massa, cheap at Picayune, times be so low!"

OCTOBER 26, 1862—SUNDAY
59 TRADD STREET—CHARLESTON, SOUTH CAROLINA

My time in Charleston is nearly at an end. I leave soon to join my new command in North Carolina.

I have begun to hope that I may pass safely out of the valley of the shadow of death. I have escaped so far and the idea is taking root in my mind that I could possibly live through the remainder of the war. Still, there is active duty before me and the campaigns I have passed through remind me not to be sanguine. The North and South are now getting down to serious business and all hope of compromise appears to have departed. Both sides have mutually decided to fight it out to the bitter end. One flag or the other must be hauled down forever.

If I can only get through next summer, I think my chances will be of a hopeful nature. We shall, perhaps, be down below the belly of the bottle by that time and can make short work of the dregs.

Thank God for pine knots. Gas, candles and oil are all disappearing in the Confederacy. I sat by the fireplace tonight and read the day's newspaper with avidity from beginning to end—embracing Southern rumors, official statements, army telegrams, Yankee extravaganzas, and various et cetera.

The newspaper also has Bragg's report of the battle of Perryville. He beat the enemy from his positions, driving the Yankees back two miles before night set in. But finding overwhelming masses accumulating around him, he withdrew in good order. He is now in full retreat, leaving Kentucky and racing for Chatanooga, the point of interest now.

Reading Bragg's report reminded me of a recent talk I had with Colonel Harrison Scott, who commanded a brigade at Perryville. Wounded during the battle, Colonel Scott has been recuperating in Charleston and anxiously awaiting the surgeon's permission to rejoin his brigade.

I found Colonel Scott to be a fair type of the Southern planter—full of bluster and bravado, mixed with good sense and an ordinary amount of intelligence; terribly in earnest on the war; confident of the ultimate success or our cause and withal what might be called a very "good fellow." We conversed freely and unreservedly on our domestic troubles. "Do you think the Yankees can subjugate us?" he asked.

"Subjugation is not their word now," I replied. "It is extermination."

"Well," said he, with an oath, "extermination let it be then. The Yankees will have to exterminate us before we have peace; for we can never live under the same government again. I will tell you, I opposed secession with all my might—stumped the entire state against it until I would have been treated as an abolitionist if I had not been one of our own people. But now I find the fire eaters were right and I was wrong. I have gone into the war and expect to stay in it until I die or we are a free people. If the Yankees whip us and there is no hope, I will return to South Carolina, place my wife on a pack mule, and go to Mexico, for by God, I will never live under the old government again."

The colonel was not an admirer of General Bragg, saying that if he had fought an hour longer, he would have annihilated the enemy at Perryville. He had little Christian charity where Braxton Bragg was concerned. In his eyes, Bragg was "a poor, feeble-minded, irresolute man of violent passions." Scott claimed that in the old army there was a story that in Bragg's younger days, as a lieutenant commanding one of several companies at a post where he was also serving as quartermaster, he had submitted a requisition for supplies. Then, as quartermaster, had declined by endorsement to fill it. As company commander he resubmitted the requisition, giving additional reasons for his needs, but as quartermaster, he persisted in denial. Having reached the impasse, he referred the matter to the post commandant, who took one look at the correspondence and threw up his hands, "My God, Mr. Bragg. You have quarreled with every officer in the army and now you are quarreling with yourself!"

Colonel Scott and I parted in the most friendly manner. As I left, he said that if Beauregard was restored to command in the West, within thirty days, there would not be a Yankee in Tennessee or Kentucky.

OCTOBER 30, 1862—THURSDAY
NEAR GEORGETOWN, SOUTH CAROLINA

as as beautiful an evening as a traveler could ask, the 28th day of October, 1862, that I bide my good friend James Petigru one last good-bye and started in my sulky for Pawley's Island. I left Charleston in the evening, that the wearisome task of crossing the Cooper River might be over, and the earlier start upon my journey be made the following morning. Tarrying at the house of a fine old planter during the night, who amused me until nearly cock crowing with long stories of his service in the Mexican War, I arose after a very slight refreshment from sleep and was on my way toward Georgetown an hour before sunrise. It was a toilsome way though, as the road runs parallel with the seashore the whole distance of sixty miles, just far enough inland never to catch a glimpse of the water and leading over a narrow road through mile after mile of pine trees, where neither house, cultivated field, nor flowing streamlet occurred to divert my attention for the whole day. It was pleasant enough at first to feel one's self alone in the boundless forests of pine and imagine Francis Marion, the Swamp Fox, eluding British soldiers in and among a welter of labyrinth trails, as he had done here so often during the Revolutionary War. But by degrees, as the Carolina sun began to rise above the trees, the never-changing scenery about me grew dull and wearisome. I found myself looking forward in the hope of finding some place by the roadside where my horse might shake his thirst. No such place however appeared and onward we jogged over the apparently unending level of creaking sand, without one sign of human industry or human life. As matters began to grow serious and my weary stead to manifest symptoms of dissatisfaction which could not be mistaken, a kind Providence led me to a large dwelling house, which served as a way station for the Charleston stage.

Encamped in front of the house sat the stage, the driver, Tom McCarthy, engaged in watering the mules. Mule driving is an art of

itself and McCarthy is justly considered a professor at it. In appearance
he is a tall, handsome old man, much given to chewing tobacco and
blowing his nose with his fingers. When driving, he is always yelling,
generally imprecations of a serio-comic character. He rarely flogs his
mules, but when one of them rouses his indignation by extraordinary
laziness, he barks out, "Come here, mule, and let me give you hell!"

While the animal is receiving such discipline as comes up to his idea
of the infernal regions, McCarthy generally remarks, "I wish you was
Uncle Abe, I'd make you move, you God damn son of a ____!" His idea
of perfect happiness seems to be to have Messrs. Lincoln and Stanton in
the shafts. Another trick McCarthy uses to handle his mules is kicking
the footboard. Strangely enough this noise gratifies the mules quite as
much as licking them. McCarthy accounts for his inhumanity by saying,
"It's the worst practice in the world licking niggers or mules, because
the more you licks 'em, the more they wants it."

I was also introduced to another "character" who was riding the
stage. Captain Chubb told me he had been born in Boston and served
as Coxswain to the United States ship Java in 1827. He was afterwards
jailed at New York on suspicion of being engaged in the slave trade, but
he escaped. At the beginning of this war, he was captured by the
Yankees, when he was in command of the Confederate blockade runner
Royal Yacht, and taken to New York in chains where he was sentenced
to be hung as a pirate. But he was eventually exchanged. I have learned
that the slave trading escapade of which he was accused consisted in his
Buying slaves in Cuba and then coolly selling them once his ship made
port at Charleston.

Although evidently a remarkable and clever man, Chubb seems
extremely egotistical and vain. He is on his way to Charleston to assume
command of the blockade runner Arabia.

I ought not end this brief sketch of stagecoach notables without mentioning two volunteers who were on their way to Charleston to enlist. These two fresh, youthful-looking fellows were accompanied by their Negro body servants. They were also accompanied by a great number of bottles of champagne and brandy. They also had huge hampers containing roasted turkeys, chicken, hams and all sorts of good things. Each volunteer also had several trunks containing their necessary wardrobe. I could only laugh to myself and think how incomplete their military education was. Soon, they would be on campaign and dressed partially in rags. They would gnaw on ears of hard corn and would gladly exchange their extensive wardrobes for a square meal or a decent bed to sleep on.

Eventually, the stage left for Charleston and I resumed my journey north. I met few people along the road. Now and then, a man and a woman riding together on an antiquated horse, or a darky on a poor, doleful-looking mule. I met large wagons, canvas covered, drawn by four or six mules and driven by Negroes, taking rice and vegetables to Charleston. As night approached, I saw the campfires of these drivers— they, sitting on the ground, about the fire, cooking "hog and homily," cracking rude jokes, singing corn songs and laughing their loud "Yah! Yah!" as the whiskey bottle passed among them.

Just after dark, I stopped at the doorway of a very small and rudely-constructed hut and inquired if I could stay for the night. At first, I was refused, but, upon representing myself as an officer in the army of the Confederacy, I was welcomed in, as they had a boy with Stonewall Jackson.

The cabin contained but one room, with no windows. The chimney, built of mud and stones, was outside the house. The furniture of the house was scanty in the extreme, a roughly-constructed frame on which was laid a corn-shuck mattress, a pine table and a few shuck-bottomed chairs.

I had not been long in this place before preparations for the evening meal began. An iron vessel called a spider was brought and set over the fire. In this dish was roasted some coffee. Afterward, in the same dish, a corn cake was baked and still again, some rank old ham was fired and the corn cake laid in the ashes to have it piping hot. This constituted our supper which, being placed on the table, three of us sat down to partake of while Cynthia, the young daughter, held a blazing light-wood knot for us to see by.

After this repast, the man of the house, a kind-looking fellow with a ruddy complexion and bright, crimson proboscis, aptly nicknamed, "Old Barrels," poured a small nightcap. I took a seat by a flickering candle and pulled from my saddle bag a Charleston newspaper, seeking the latest war news.

Old Barrels, who sat near, said, "Appears you've read a good deal, hain't you?"

"Oh, yes. Why?"

"You look as though you liked to read. Well, it's a good thing. S'pose you take pleasure in reading, don't you?"

"That depends of course on what I have to read. I suppose everybody likes to read when they find anything interesting to them, don't they?"

"No. It's damn tiresome to some folks it appears to me. 'Less you've got the habit of it. However, I guess it's a good thing. You can pass away your time so."

As the hour became late, one by one, the family retired to the corner and all lay together on the corn shucks and were soon sleeping soundly. Taking my saddlebags for a pillow and wrapping my blanket around me, I laid down before the fast-dying embers looking forward to a peaceful slumber. Just as I was about to doze off, Old Barrels managed to roll over on his back and begin to snore. I tried to ignore this cannonade, but the nasal bombardment soon reached head-splitting proportions. Then, by the grace of God, Old Barrels gave an extra loud snort and rolled over on his stomach. Quiet descended over the cabin. With harmony restored, I was soon slumbering peacefully. Morning came and as I had to leave early, all were up at sunrise. I asked the hostess for a wash and the vessel which had served for roasting, baking and frying in the evening previous was now brought. I washed myself in the dish out of which twelve hours before I had eaten a hearty supper. I paid Old Barrels and his wife well and thanked them kindly for they had given me the best they had. Destitute as they were, they seemed contented and happy.

NOVEMBER 1, 1862—SATURDAY
PAWLEY'S ISLAND

After a long and tedious journey, I arrived at cousin Elizabeth Allston Pringle's house early Friday morning. Usually when visiting here, I stay at Chicora Wood, the plantation house located some seven miles inland. The Pringles are rice planters and the cultivation of rice necessitates keeping the fields flooded with river water until it becomes stagnant. As this happens, the atmosphere becomes polluted by a dreadful smell and no white person can remain on the plantation at this time without the danger of incurring Yellow Fever. To escape the dreaded disease, the planters remove their families from their plantation homes the last week in May and do not return until early in November, by which time the cold weather has come and the danger of Yellow Fever is gone. The formula is three white frosts make a black frost. That means that all the potato vines and other delicate plants have been killed so completely that the leaves are black.

The house on the island actually consists of two houses, each with two immense rooms downstairs with very high ceilings and many windows and doors. Two rooms occupy the above, equally large, but only half stories. The two houses are placed at right angles. The front one toward the beach, runs north and south. The other, toward the marsh, runs east and west. Both have wide piazzas around them which makes a large, cool and shady hall where they come together.

I mention the size of the houses because, with Colonel Pringle away serving with Lee's army, Elizabeth, like many women of the South these days, has a large household to manage and control. There are so many Negro servants I have almost lost count. There is Mary the cook, Milly the laundress, Caroline the house maid, Cinda the seamstress, Peter the butler, Andrew the second dining room man, Aleck the coachman, and Moses the gardener. And lest I not forget George, the scullion, and the boy in the yard besides! After breakfast, they line up and ask, "Miss Elizabeth, Wha' you want me of' today?" It is then that Elizabeth assigns the day's tasks, for the house and grounds are large and keeping the place perfectly clean requires constant work.

As we talked after my arrival, Elizabeth said to me, "Oh cousin, I do not see how I can live my whole life amid these slaves. To be always among people whom I do not understand and whom I must guide and teach and lead on like children! With Colonel Pringle gone, it frightens me so!"

I laid my hand gently on my cousin's hand and said, "Elizabeth, it is a life of self-repression and effort, but it is far from a degrading life. It is a very noble life if a woman does her full duty in it. It is the life of a missionary really. One must teach, train, uplift, encourage—always encourage, even in reproof. I grant you it is a life of effort, but, my dear, it is the life of many women of the South during this cruel war; the life of those who have the great responsibility of owning human beings. We are responsible before our Maker for not only their bodies, but their souls. Never must we for one moment forget that. To be the wife of a rice planter is no place for a pleasure-loving, indolent woman, but for an earnest, true-hearted woman, one who loves her husband and the noble cause for which he fights."

Later, Elizabeth and I journeyed by carriage to the grave site of her son, Edward Jenkins Pringle, who lost his life at Sharpsburg. The day was lovely, the sea sparkling in the brilliant sunlight, the air crisp with clearness and purity. We drove under a varied shade for a short time and saw lovely vistas of the ocean through openings in the woods. At last, after tearing and crackling along through a thick growth of timber and underwood, we emerged upon a truly magnificent panorama. We were on a small height and on either side were dark woods. In front, the Atlantic.

After enjoying this beauteous view for a short time, we took a short walk to a still secluded part of the woods. There, in the midst of a sunny clearing, surrounded by partly overshadowing trees, was a single grave, that of the only adored son of my cousin and her husband. In front of this simple grave was a semi-circular seat.

"Here often," said Elizabeth, "I come during the day and often spend part of the evening. It is a melancholy happiness to feel he is near—almost as it were with us."

Here we remained for some time. The birds were singing. The sea so calm that you could scarcely just then at that distance hear the everlasting resounding voice of the waves as they washed ashore. I could look through the opening in the woods up and up and the clear cloudless sky seemed to almost recede from my gaze, yet bluer and bluer, brighter and brighter. All was beauty and enchantment while in front of us lay the lonely dead on hallowed and consecrated ground.

"When I heard he was wounded," said Elizabeth, "I prayed God as I have never prayed Him before that He would not take my son away. Yet despite my prayers, Edward was taken from me."

"Elizabeth," I replied, "some years ago, when traveling in Spain, I was told a story by an old Jesuit priest that tells us of the love of God. It is the story of a gardener who, in his garden, had a most favorite flower which he loved much. One day, he came to the garden to find the flower gone. He was vexed and sad to see his lovely flower gone. In the midst of his sorrow, he met the master of the garden and hurled his complaints a him. 'Hush my child,' said the master, 'I plucked it for myself.'"

"Thank you, Johnson," said Elizabeth, smiling at me. "That will give me great comfort." After this, we stood in silence, there where nature was so wild and beautiful and nature's creator seemed so near.

That young Edward lies buried here in his native South Carolina and not some unknown grave in Maryland or Virginia is largely due to the admirable efforts of his body servant, Andrew. Like Elias, who was loyal to his first master, Lieutenant DeKalb, so Andrew was loyal to Edward to the point of death and beyond.

When the annals of humble folk who were brave are written, I hope they save a few pages for Andrew. I found him, broad of grin and bare of foot sitting in the doorway of his cabin. I have attempted to record his story to the best of my ability below.

Andrew began, "In de war with Edward, Gen'ral Pettigrew? Sho' was! Massa Pringle say ter me, 'Andrew, When my son goes, you go an' take care o' him. You hy'ar dat?' So Edward go to war an' I go wid him. We fight wid Gen'ral Lee."

The loyal slave continued, "Battles? Yes sah! In all o' dem 'til de dark day. I follow Massa Edward ever'whar he go. Stay wid de tents 'til we move again or de men fall back an' come of' us. I was sid him all de way—'til de Yankee bullet got him. Dats right. Tore up his side. Battle o' Sharpsburg. Same one whar Gen'ral Stark done got killed. Wors' battle o' de war. Took two de bes' men—young Massa Edward an' Gen'ral Stark! Dey say ter me, 'Andy, you Massa done wounded. De major say, better go see 'bout him!'"

Andrew found the brigade hospital. The surgeons let him in and he went to young Edward's cot and fell on his knees. Edward was weak and pale, but he took Andrew's hand and held it tightly. He smiled. Talked in a low voice about Chicora Wood and the folks at home. For twelve days, Andrew watched by his side. Then Edward died.

"All de po' soljers dyin', an' dey bury 'em in Virginny. Way off thar. I knowed Massa an' Missus be right powerful grieved to have him buried off up thar. 't wouldn' do. I mus' git him back home. How do it—dat's de question! Yes sah. How do it. I axe de hospital man an' he jus' laugh. Carry him back? Naw sah. One doctor say, 'Andrew, you crazy! We goin' put him in ground ter-morrow.'"

Andrew said he watched the preparations for burial and felt disheartened. He couldn't bear the thought of a lonely grave in a far off place for his master. Watching closely, he seized a favorable moment to cut off a piece of Edward's uniform and a little finger so he could easily identify him that night.

He continued, "I tole Major Davis what I gonna do. He say, 'You black devil, what you mean?' An' he terrible upset 'til I tell him I jus' got ter take my Massa back to South Car'lina. Couldn't bury Edward off like dat. Major Davis, he's a Charleston boy. He knows how 't is. He apologized for bein' mad. Sure looked sad. He say, 'Andrew, maybe you can do it.'"

"Dat night, I go to hospital an' talks low to de guard. 'How much money you got nigger?' de guard say. I say I got fiddy dollar. What young Massa give me when he die. Dicker back an' fo'th an' fine'ly de guard take de fiddy dollar. I lif' young Edward up off de ground onto my shoulder and with Major Davis' help, we carry him out, put him in de wood coffin-box we got waitin', an' de boys help load it onto de freight car that de train pick up befo' mawnin'."

At night, the freight train rumbled south. Andrew sat beside the coffin-box, calm and determined, while his childlike ignorance and strong faith in what he is doing blinded him to the fact that what he proposed to do was all but impossible. Andrew was over three hundred and fifty miles from Pawley's Island. Bodies couldn't be carried as freight and a slave couldn't take charge of one.

Andrew recalled it was daylight when they passed through Roanoke. At a nearby stop, a railroad bossman discovered the coffin-box with

Andrew guarding it and raised a ruckus. He swore he would arrest Andrew and send the coffin straight back. Seven men of authority gathered to discuss the matter and were trying to dissolve a violent disagreement about it with several rounds of drinks when the whistle tooted two times and the train suddenly rolled past the now inebriated authorities.

They came to South Carolina. Here Andrew found some friends who gave him the first food he had eaten on the trip. Furthermore, they arranged with the train men for the rest of the trip to Florence.

Andrew looked down in recollection as he said, "Nex' stop was Florence, down in good ole South Car'lina. Nobody gonna botha me down thar. When we get to Florence, it was afternoon o' de fo'th day. De ole town neva look so sweet! Get off train and get me a tumble cart an' put de coffin-box on. Afta two mo' days, got to de lane dat turn to de big house at Chicora Wood 'bout ten 'clock. All de lights out. De wasn't 'spectin' us attall. We git up to de gate an' I holla 'Hello!' Ole Massa hy'ar me an' he raise de window an' holla, 'Is dat you Andrew?' 'Yes sah, 'tis,' I say. 'Whar's Edward?' He say anxious-like.' 'He's out hy'ar,' I yell. 'I got him in ole coffin-box.'

Andrew paused in an effort to remember more. "De all come out an' start weepin' 'bout Edward bein' kilt at Sharpsburg, but dey right glad he's back an' not liyin' in some unknown grave in Ole Virginny. Servants come an' fetch de coffin-box. Lay young Edward out on table in de parlor. Bells ring and all de people notified what I done an' by 'leven 'clock, 'bout a hundred people crowded 'round Edward, weepin' wid ole Massa an' ole Missus."

I must admit there were tears in the eyes of this old soldier as Andrew finished his tale. More over, it would take a pen more articulate and practiced than mine to record fully the tribute due to this loyal and devoted slave.

Elias and Andrew and all the other faithful body servants! They tend the horses, water and saddle them. Bed them down at night. Bathe the worn places under the saddle blankets. They stay behind the line during battle and cook hot coffee and soup. They minister to the wounded brought back with balls and canister in their bodies. They put up tents, rustle food, shine boots and, at night, when the fighting has ceased and the grey-coated sentries are pacing quietly to and fro, they gather around the campfires and sing to the accompaniment of an old banjo or guitar the haunting strains of the spirituals that are drawn straight from the hearts of a race so close to God.

NOVEMBER 4, 1862—TUESDAY
ON THE TRAIN—NEAR MARION, SOUTH CAROLINA

Here we are on the train at last. This is the first chance I have had at my journal since Elias and I left Pawley's Island last Sunday.

The train north was a luggage train and had two passenger cars attached. I left Elias in one of the boxcars with our luggage and entered one of the crowded cars. By dint of the conductor's earnest packing, the passengers all got in, but it has been anything but a pleasant ride. The car is lower in the roof than usual and the seats are too small and too close together to sleep comfortably. Add to this a wood fire in the stove which fills the air with irritating dryness and the fact that most of the male passengers chew tobacco and enjoy spitting out oceans of the foul juice on every side.

It has been a pleasant day to travel with the sky clear and the sun shining out strongly, so that it was warm and cheering. It took me some time to get used to the rocking motion of the car for the road bed was so uneven that, in places, the car tilted from side to side as if it were going to upset and spill us all out.

Until we reached the great Pee Dee River, there was very little cleared land near the railroad. The bridge over the great Pee Dee is one that has attracted much interest. I knew of its construction and was on the look-out for it. The Pee Dee River is not very broad, but it runs through a swamp and its own bed is sand. The engineers found it impossible to pile it in the ordinary way and were forced to use novel methods. This has been accomplished by sinking great cast-iron cylinders to a depth of eighty feet through the sand and gravel. Once each cylinder had been brought to its place in the bed of the river a receiver was screwed on its top end and the air extracted by an air pump. The consequence of this ingenious method was that the sand and water rose from below and the cylinders sank correspondingly by their own weight as the opposing sand was withdrawn. The engineers then added compartment after compartment to the cylinders. They were sunk until sufficient stability was gained. Two piers were formed in this way in the bed of the Pee Dee supporting the usual form of an unfilled tubular budge of wood. I noticed the bridge vibrate as the train passed slowly over, but the structure appears to be very sufficient. It is a beautiful piece of Southern engineering work, one that any Yankee would surely marvel at.

The inhabitants of the passenger car are a varied lot. Sitting at the front of the car is a handsome middle-aged gentleman in the uniform of a colonel, with a pretty, young girl beside him, who I at once ascertained was his new bride. Although they were surrounded by a number of young officers, she only had eyes for the stalwart cavalier at her side.

Behind me sat two ladies from Charleston. I remember overhearing a conversation between them—one a young wife whose husband was in the army and the other an elderly lady with no husband or son, but with many friends and relatives in marching regiments. The younger lady remarked, "I'm sure I do not hate the Yankees. I earnestly hope their souls may go to heaven, but I would like to blow all their mortal bodies away as fast as they come upon our soil."

"Why, you shock me, my dear," replied the older lady. "I don't see why you want the Yankees to go to heaven. I hope to get there myself someday and I'm sure I shouldn't want to go if I thought I should find any of them there."

The old lady was firmly convinced the South would lose the war and she based this belief on the fact that we had permitted the Yankees to build railroads through the Southern states. "I tell you," she would say, "that's what they built these infernal railroads for. They knew the war was coming and they go ready for it. The railroads will whip us, you may depend on it. What else were they built for? We got on well enough without them and we shouldn't have let the da_ _ Yankees build them."

The most interesting person in the car, however, was a Federal doctor. He had been captured while staying with the wounded of his regiment at Perryville. He had been refused leave to pass through General Bragg's lines and was now on route for Richmond. Both sides, by a very sensible arrangement, have agreed to treat doctors as a non-combatants and not make prisoners of war of them.

The doctor was in full Yankee uniform but was treated with civility by all on the train. I had a long talk with him. He seemed a sensible man and did not attempt to deny the courage and aptitude for war of the Southern people.

Before the war, he was a gentleman of good means in Wisconsin and was accustomed to a life of luxury. He now finds himself in a life he never imagined enjoying the duties of a regimental surgeon with perfect contentment being now totally indifferent to civilization and comfort.

During our time together on the train, the good doctor and I have been making each other's acquaintance by simple good fellowship. For this, after all, is the only true way. If we have agreed on many things, it was soon evident we could find no common ground on the subject of slavery. The doctor was anxious to discuss this with me for he loved much of what he had seen of the South, but not slavery.

The doctor was distressed and indignant over slavery and in his nasal Yankee twang recited the following view of slavery:

> "Put yourself, General Pettigrew, in the slave's place to whatever extent you can. On your slave ship's arrival, say in South Carolina, there was such a stench that it could often be smelled coming from five miles away. Once landed, you were often exposed naked, without distinction as to sexes, to brutal examination by your purchasers. You are driven against your will to work from dusk to dark. Your food and lodging are inadequate. You hear clothes and shoes referred to as Negro cloth or Negro shoes because of their inferior condition. Your stated name is rarely used. You are generally called upon with curse words or by burlesque terms as "Caesar Negro, Angelo Negro or Negro Mary." You watch in despair as your closest friends and relatives are sold without warning. As an added insult, you are often compelled to watch the murderous beating of your fellow slaves, or look on while a kind master forces suicide-minded slaves to eat by breaking their teeth. You watch helplessly when one of your number is whipped because he cried when he witnessed his fellow slave and friend beaten to death.
>
> This is just an introduction, General, but can you not see the evil and hypocrisy of it all? Can not you see that as a slave you could never understand that you had no rights and were not regarded as human, but property?"

I was not unprepared for an answer to this polemic and answered thusly, "Slavery, doctor, is an evil. But under the wise direction of the Almighty, it has become a blessing to the Negroes. Those who enslave them have made them compensation for their sufferings through the gift of Christianity. Yes, doctor, slavery is in the South considered quite a beneficent institution, for it permitted a savage to share the benefits of the white man's civilization. It gives the Negro clothes, houses and food, things more than compensating him in our minds, for the inconvenience of being taken out of previous environments and conditions of life."

The Yankee waited impatiently for me to finish and then twanged the following reply:

"General, as early as 1833, John Rankin wrote that the African was not created for slavery. They are, he testified, rational creatures, human, possessing all the original properties of human nature. I agree with Rankin and furthermore consider the Negro race inferior in mental endowment only to the white race. The Negro is as full of music as a bird is of song and music is allied to poetry and eloquence. No people are closer to God. As a race, they are proverbial for kindness and affection and respect for authority and age. In drollery, they are unequaled and are only slightly inferior to the Irish in wit. If properly taught they would make wonderful orators and musicians. Hence, the Southern aristocrats should emancipate their Negroes and thus retain their affection and their own choice and thus reap all the benefits of slavery without its crime and consequences."

And so the arguments, both pro and con, bounced like the train back and forth. I would like to think I vanquished the Yankee doctor with superior reason and made him see the error of his abolitionist ways, but I think not for he's too obstinate to know the truth when he hears it.

NOVEMBER 6, 1862—THURSDAY
CAMP VANCE—NEAR PETERSBURG, VIRGINIA

The cars were dreadfully crowded all the way to Petersburg and the luxuries of Charleston had spoiled me for train travel as I could not appreciate at their proper value the sparse meals I was able to procure at stops along the way. The Yankee doctor, however, was an agreeable traveling companion and we carried on a pleasant conversation from our position in the tobacco juice.

When we reached the station at Petersburg, I prepared to make my departure, for the doctor was going on to Richmond. His farewell was unexpected. "I will be delighted in the future to meet men from South Carolina, for now I know I shall find in them intelligence and hospitality. God speed, General Pettigrew. I bid you an affectionate goodbye. Perhaps we will meet again for the days ahead should be highly interesting."

Departing from the train, I encountered one of the seemingly ubiquitous provost guards who immediately asked me for my passport.

I have grown increasingly tired of showing my passport at every stop or way station. The provost marshals, guardians of order, travel on trains, loiter around railroad stations, occupy seats on stage lines and take positions anywhere they can intercept travelers to catch spies and traitors. Anyone not able to show a passport is liable to be arrested and held until their identity can be established. It seems that great numbers of able-bodied men who could be serving at the front are employed as provost marshals.

Furthermore, the requirement that all travelers must secure passports has led to great inconvenience for the loyal people of the confederacy, for passport offices are only open at certain hours of the day. Often, soldiers on leave lose days in reaching home because of missing trains while awaiting passports. I become extremely annoyed when I depart from a train and the first words I hear are, "Show your passport." Many of the provost marshals have become little Gods causing great bitterness wherever they operate.

After satisfying the provost marshal, I was not a Yankee spy, Elias and I stood outside the Petersburg station. The lights from the fire of a bevy of pine knots built on the ground outside while illuminating the rough depot and platform left the city beyond in deeper darkness.

Several Negro children, appearing in the darkness like figures carved in ebony, lounged near a large pile of locomotive firewood. A white man smoking a cigar looked out of one of the depot doors and another chewing tobacco leaned against a gatepost in front of the station. I noticed as I neared him that one of his coat sleeves hung empty at his side. He advanced toward me and said, "How d'ye do, General," spitting and slanting with ceremony. "I'm Jim Williams, forage master of the 26th North Carolina and I'm here to take you to Camp Vance. I have an ambulance parked at the front of the depot."

"Very good, Mr. Williams," I replied, "lead the way."

"Thank you, General. Reckon I will. Tom! Tom! Tom! Now, where has that devilish nigger gone again? Tom! Oh To-om! Help the general with his luggage!"

Once in the ambulance, Williams informed us we had quite a piece to go yet. A moment later, Doctor Middleton, surgeon of the 26th North Carolina, rode up on horseback, welcomed me pleasantly, and said he would accompany us to camp. The ride was a dismal one as I was shivering from the cold and yearned sadly for a sight of the pleasant faces and for the sound of the kindly voices to which I had grown accustomed in my old command. At last, a turn in the road brought us in sight of the numberless fires of a large camp. It was a bright scene though, in my opinion, far from gay.

We drove into the camp along an avenue bordered on either side by rows of white tents. Finally, the ambulance drew up before my quarters—a cabin built of logs. Through the open door streamed the cheery light of a wood fire upon which pine knots had been freshly thrown.

Entering, I found a bunk at one side made of puncheons and filled with pine straw. Over which comforters and army blankets had been thrown, hard pillows stuffed with straw, having coarse unbleached cases, a roughly made table before the fire, a lot of boxes marked "Q.M." to serve as seats, and you have my new quarters in its entirety.

Drawing my box up close to the fire, I sat down. Elias in the mean-while stirred the coals and arranged the burning ends of the pines in true country style.

Presently, my supper was brought in, cornbread, cornmeal, coffee, a piece of musty fired salt meat, heavy brown sugar and milk. I was, how-ever, hungry and ate this simple fare with a relish. Elias went off to some region unknown for his super, returning a short while later unsatisfied and highly disgusted with the "hog-whittles" which had been offered to him. Soon, Dr. Middleton called, bringing with him, Captain Louis Young, my old and dear friend from Charleston.

I had not seen the captain since I was wounded at Seven Pines. It was a joyful reunion, especially when I learned that he was to serve as my Aide-de-Camp. It is a strange and indefinable feeling that one has when after a long absence, he once again grasps the hand of an old comrade in arms. It is a mixture of hope and regret, sadness and gladness. Seeing the kind face of Young reminded me how much I miss some faces which used to be familiar. Most are now in other commands, but some have received their final discharge and now sleep where the roar of battle can never disturb their slumbers.

As Young and Dr. Middleton entered, I lit a candle, stuck it into the neck of a whiskey bottle, and placed it on a box. Then we all found seats and cigars to light. Dr. Middleton took a long puff and bade me formal welcome to Camp Vance. He said he was sorry he couldn't stay long, but that in his recent service to the Confederacy, he had acquired a bad case of body lice and they were presently making him quite uncomfortable. He claimed they were so thick that he was afraid to go to sleep for fear that in a weak moment he might snore and the vermin would think it was the dinner gong and eat him up.

He then told the story of a soldier of the 26th who, some time ago, had gone home on furlough. Once on the train, the soldier was seized by a bad case of the scratches. A citizen sitting near him noticed this queer behavior and said quite concernedly, "What is the matter? Have you fleas on you?"

"Fleas?" Said the itching soldier, "Do you think I'm a damn dog? Perhaps I should bark and itch at the same time? I'm no dog, sir, I'm human. They are lice, sir, and hungry ones at that!"

Laughing at the doctor's story, I replied that I feel very clean and comfortable now, but after a few days in camp, I would undoubtedly be scratching away and looking as seedy as any of the boys.

Later, sitting by the flickering candle, I tried to read, but found it hard to concentrate. Soldier life has once again commenced and I find myself in command of a new brigade consisting of the Eleventh North Carolina, Colonel Collett Leventhorpe; the Twenty-Sixth North Carolina, Colonel H. K. Burgwyn; The Forty-Fourth North Carolina, Colonel Thos. C. Singletary; the Forty-Seventh North Carolina, Colonel G. H. Fairbault; and the Fifty-Second North Carolina, Colonel J. K. Marshal.

My brigade comprises men of good stock—farmers, manufacturers, mechanics of almost every trade and men of almost every calling—bookkeepers, clerks, tradesmen—the substantial, intelligent, energetic doers of the South's work. "They will endure no domineering," claimed Captain Young. "Nor will they suffer driving, but officers who set an example of courage they will follow willingly."

The tattoo has sounded and it's time for bed. As I am about to snuff out the candle, I reflect how swiftly life has been passing. One year ago tonight, I commanded the 22nd North Carolina along the banks of the Potomac. Now I command five regiments. Then as now I was writing in my journal, recording the scenes of my everyday life. Hopefully, I will still be doing the same a year hence.

NOVEMBER 17, 1862—MONDAY
CAMP VANCE—NEAR PETERSBURG, VIRGINIA

The members of my staff participated in the brigade shooting practice today. As they were returning to camp, Lieutenant Robertson, my Ordinance Officer, was boasting of his skillful marksmanship. The Lieutenant had placed all of his shots near the center of the target easily outshooting the rest of the staff.

As they walked along listening to Robertson blow his own trumpet, they passed a small field and noticed a large black hog which had been running at large. Believing that fresh meat would be more palatable than the food regularly issued by the quartermaster, they decided to shoot the hog and enjoy a hearty evening meal.

As Lieutenant Robertson had been flaunting his ability as a marksman, he was selected to kill the animal. Carefully loading his rifle, Robertson went in search of the porker, leaving his weapon resting against a fence while he drove the hog to a nearby pen where it was proposed to have it die. During his brief absence, Louis Young withdrew the bullet from Robertson's rifle. When Robertson had driven the hog into the pen, he picked up his rifle and, taking deliberate aim at the unsuspecting swine, not more than ten yards away, blazed away. The loud noise of the shot merely startled the hog, which looked up and grunted. Robertson, amazed to see his victim still standing, looked at the hog, than toward the men who were unable to restrain themselves from laughter. Robertson then reloaded and ended the days of the black hog. The rest of the way to camp, the embarrassed lieutenant had to endure the good natured ribbing of his fellow staff members who now call him "crack-shot" Robertson.

Last week, I issued orders for Captain Jones to take command of the axe-corps—twenty-five men from each regiment in the brigade, each man provided with a sharp new axe. The axe-corps goes out to work every morning at five o'clock—125 men, 10 non-commissioned officers, two lieutenants and Captain Jones. They usually return to the camp at 11:00 in the morning and have the rest of the day to themselves. Jones can somehow accomplish more effective work with a gang of choppers than any other officer in the brigade. He is continually going from squad to squad and personally plans the felling of nine-tenths of the trees.

Yesterday, Captain Jones received orders to proceed in the direction of Waverly to procure wood. The battalion of axe-men, with a large number of teams, marched beyond the Blackwater River to chop trees. By the end of the morning, they had accumulated a large woodpile and began to load all the wagons. When this was accomplished, the teams were headed toward camp accompanied by a strong guard, the balance of Captain Jones' command following slowly in the rear.

As the train proceeded toward camp, the advance guard reported that the enemy were visible in the woods in front, apparently in large numbers. The teams were at once stopped and a scout reported back with the information that the report was correct and that a body of Yankee cavalry were evidently moving into position for the purpose of ambushing our train.

The situation of Jones' command was rather serious in nature. It was readily seen by the officers that it would be nearly impossible to force a passage with a long line of cumbersome wagons loaded with wood. Jones decided that to save the train, prompt action was required. A nearby forest road was fortunately discovered that led away from the Yankee cavalry and to the Blackwater. From the other side of the stream, the road continued toward camp, but this stream, which was usually fordable at certain seasons of the year, was at this time impassable for teams. Our skirmishers were directed to occupy the attention of the Yankees if necessary, while the head of the train was turned into the forest road and a strong detail of men, under Lieutenant Park, worked to throw a bridge across the Blackwater. With great celerity, trees were filled, rails and logs gathered and a rude bridge constructed over which our wagons all managed to cross with safety and were no sooner on the other side then they struck open land and moved rapidly toward camp.

The Yankees, who were some distance away and behind a dense woods, were wholly ignorant of these movements, evidently supposing that the wagons could move to camp only on the main road which they were guarding. They had not even deemed it necessary to attack our skirmishers until they saw our wagons a long distance away, moving across the open country. They then for the first time realized that they had been outwitted and immediately moved forward, deploying to charge. Seeing this, the skirmishers fell back and the command formed in line of battle.

The situation had now changed. The wagons were safe and on their way toward camp. This having been accomplished, the men were unhampered and in condition to give the enemy a warm reception. Inspired by their commander, the Yankees, with wild shouts, made a dash upon our position. Captain Jones, standing in the rear of his line, forbade the men to fire until the enemy was only fifty yards away. Then, at his command, a deadly volley lashed out. The Yankee commander, while waving his sword and shouting to his men to come on, was shot dead. Four others of his brave command suffered the same fate and the survivors fell back to the safety of a small woods. Then, after exchanging a few shots, Jones withdrew his command leisurely back to camp. The Yankees, stung by our volley, declined to follow.

I met Jones and his battalion near an old brick house as I had been informed of the affair by the officer in immediate charge of the train. When I learned from Captain Jones how the movement had been conducted, I was greatly pleased and bestowed warm commendations upon the officers and men of the battalion.

NOVEMBER 24, 1862—MONDAY
CAMP VANCE—NEAR PETERSBURG, VIRGINIA

Very cold today. Water freezes solid in many of the men's canteens as they carry them at their side while on picket.

Cooking utensils are inspected and every man is provided with a new tin plate, tin cup, knife, fork and spoon; and every regiment with its full number of kettles and cooking utensils.

Virginia weather and mud is responsible for nine-tenths of the profanity in the brigade. One of my staff officers has suddenly given up the use of profane language, declaring that "no hard words can possibly do the weather and mud here any degree of justice" and he is tired of trying.

Sisyphus, the mythical king of ancient Corinth, was condemned throughout eternity to roll a heavy boulder up a hill in Hades only to have it roll down again as it neared the top. Also condemned to severest labor were Adjutant Hughes and I as we struggled this morning to complete the daily reports. These descend to the most minute details. The number of men in camp. The number of sick. The number of sick in quarters. The sick in the hospitals. The number in the company present for duty. The number detailed for special service. And who are those absent from camp, whether on passes or furlough. The rations drawn. And they go on. These reports must in all things conform to strict military rule. There must be no mistakes, nothing to be corrected, or left to be understood.

Late in the afternoon, I tired of signing my name and walked about the camp. During this time, I chanced to meet a faithful darky cook. I was astonished to learn he was a slave of George Washington's. Old Amos is a Negro of character and bears a greater dignity being a former member of the most illustrious family. Old Amos told me he was three months old when General Washington died and that the general shortly before his death emancipated all his slaves—three hundred and sixty in number. Despite being free, almost all of them remained with the general, for he was always good to his Negroes and would not permit them to be beaten or sold away from their families.

Before I left to talk to his master, a captain, I asked, "What are you doing, Amos, for another life? Are you a Christian?

"Oh, yes, Gen'rel. Dis nigger b'lieve in de Lord Jesus. Religion de mostest beautiful ting in dis world. Old Amos, he do drink, cuss and swear awful. De Lord, he makes Amos a temperance man and bless my massa who now radder die dan cus. Yes, Gen'rel, religion is de great hope to dis ole nigger."

The captain was a young man about twenty-five years old with black hair and a round face. Curious about old Amos, I sought the captain's opinion.

"He bears a high reputation as a man of truth and piety, is industrious and serves me well. I have found there is more ability and intelligence in these ape-ish-looking Negroes than is commonly supposed" and proceeded to relate the following story.

"I first saw old Amos at a hotel in Petersburg," the captain continued. "He took a-liking to me from some cause and, in order to be near me, engaged in the service of a Lieutenant Glenn. At length, I had the misfortune to lose a very valuable servant and did not know how I should replace him. Servants were plenty enough, but I wanted one who could understand what I wished to have done without being told. Who would have it done almost before I was aware of the necessity. I chanced to wish for a servant in the presence of Lieutenant Glenn who said to me, 'I have just the man you want and though I wouldn't part with him for any other cause, you shall have him.' I accepted his offer and what was my surprise when he introduced me to old Amos."

His eyes twinkled as he continued to speak. "At first I thought it a jest, but soon learned that he had conferred up me a great prize. I have never had such a servant. In a week's time, he understood perfectly all my needs and it is very rare I ever give him a verbal order. I have, like all soldiers, difficulty in getting my washing and ironing properly done, but one day, I noticed my linen looking better than usual. Old Amos had anticipated my want in that respect and learned to wash and iron expressly to please me. He is one of the best washers and ironers I know. I don't think a woman in the Confederacy can beat him. As soon as this art became known, it was in demand and he asked my permission to do the linen of some of my fellow officers, which I granted. He is hard working and provident. And during the year we have been together, he has laid up eight hundred dollars!"

"Thank you, Captain," I replied as I returned his farewell salute. "There are many slaves like old Amos who amaze me. I am always studying these creatures. They are to me inscrutable in their way and past finding out."

NOVEMBER 26, 1862—WEDNESDAY
CAMP VANCE—NEAR PETERSBURG, VIRGINIA

Dined tonight with Major Hawkins and Lt. Col. Lane of the 26th North Carolina. Dinner was splendid. Corn, cabbage, beans, peaches, apple and blackberry pie with buttermilk and sweet milk.

During our repast, Lane reflected upon Burgwyn's ascendancy to the command. "Almost immediately a good many judged that the regiment made an appalling mistake. The colonel was all intensity. The regiment was literally snatched out of bed and shaken to attention."

"At first sight," added Hawkins, "I both admired and feared him."

"It seems as if Providence has almost guided Colonel Burgwyn to his present command," mused the lieutenant colonel. He then relayed to me that Burgwyn had been educated by tutors and hoped to attend West Point, but had decided to attend the University of North Carolina. He graduated at eighteen, the head of his class, and continued his studies at

Virginia Military Institute. One of his teachers there was a professor who has won some current renown, Stonewall Jackson.

When he assumed the position of lieutenant colonel of the 26th, he was a hard and exacting drill master. Many of the men grumbled and swore he would get the proper kind of attention when they fought their first battle.

The morning before the battle of New Bern, Yankee gunboats were coming up the river, shelling the banks. Colonel Vance was placed in command of the right of the line, leaving Lt. Col. Burgwyn in command of the 26th. He suspected the hard feelings the men towards him. He formed the regiment at the point where the breastworks crossed the railroad and addressed them in substance as follows:

> "Soldiers! The enemy are before you and you will soon be in combat. You have the reputation of being one of the best-drilled regiments in the service. Now I wish you to prove yourselves one of the best fighting. Men, stand by me and I will by you."

The response was a heartening "We will!" from the men. The next day, the battle was fought.

At one point, two companies found the Yankees on their flank and getting in their rear. They had to retreat, but found the bridge across the Trent on fire and the only way to escape was to cross Bryce's Creek.

When they got there, only a small boat that would carry four men at a time could be found. Colonel Vance rode his horse in the creek, which refused to swim, and the colonel was nearly drowned trying to swim to shore. When the boat was readied, an officer called to Burgwyn to get in first. He was met with the reply, "I will never cross until the last man of my regiment is over." Nor did he until the last man was over.

"From this point on," concluded Lt. Colonel Lane, "he had the entire confidence of his men and was their pride and love. For the regiment then knew what he would do for the soldiers."

Lt. Colonel Lane and Major Hawkins have left my quarters and, as I write these words, my thoughts are interrupted by the braying of an army mule and the strains of a far-off violin. It is a strange chorus and produces little melody.

As I reflect up the dinner conversation, I find it remarkable how often first impressions can be wrong. I must admit, I greatly underestimated young Burgwyn upon our first meeting. I give my due to the colonel to say that, while he is always active, no effort fatigues him, nor length of march wearies him. He is patient with the men and never permits anyone to be wronged if he knows of it. He is restless, impulsive and fiery in temper and can, at times, be a martinet. But underneath all, there is a warm and generous nature. He has the singular power of infusing his own spirit into the men of his regiment, making the weakest strong and controlling the most turbulent by a glance of his eye, or a wave of his hand. A man whom nature most assuredly designed for the command he occupies. Though only twenty-one, it is obvious that the field is his home, the tent, his house, and war, his business.

The last mail brought news of McClellan's having been relieved of his command and Burnside being assigned to his duty, an unexpected and astonishing step.

It is speculated that McClellan may make his next appearance at the head of a column advancing upon Richmond by the way of Suflock.

General Burnside is the valiant gentleman who came to North Carolina to die or conquer last winter. He issued a proclamation to assure the people of the state he was a "Christian," but his after acts, like many of those who make the like profession, showed that he was either a hypocrite or backslider. Witness the ravages and pillage of his command throughout the eastern part of North Carolina. I hope

General Lee will give this most unworthy Christian a lesson in humility. Lee's position keeps us uneasy, but such confidence is felt in his generalship that we all believe he will inflict a severe blow upon Burnside when they meet.

The South Carolina reserves have been ordered to Charleston and ordered to report to Beauregard who expects an attack soon. If this is true, how I wish I could be transferred south with my magnificent brigade to assist in the defense of the Holy City.

The next entry is a difficult one to write and my hand begins to tremble as I do so. It is a tale, however, that must be told, for it illustrates the nature of the times and the grief and suffering that comes to many in this hard struggle for independence.

Captain Stoodley recently was taken down with jaundice, aggravated by the extreme fatigue and exposure of three days on picket. This was soon complicated by a case of pneumonia and a few days ago, he was evidently near his end.

Dr. Middleton watched over the captain and was glad to find he was not unprepared to die. Stoodley had been a professor of religion for some years and told the doctor he was suffering too much to think on that or any other subject, but he constantly tried to look to God for mercy.

The captain was a gallant and brave officer, yet so kind and gentle to those under his command that his men were deeply attached to him. Many showed their love by coming to the hospital to visit and nurse him.

One night, Dr. Middleton heard coming up from the captain's room a voice pouring forth in the richest and tenderest tones, the words of hope and peace. The doctor was anxious to see who at the midnight hour was filling the air with this hymn of praise.

As he approached the bed, Stoodley ceased singing and opened his eyes to say, "Why, doctor, thank you for coming to see me. I am still here, but I think fast approaching the holy angels and the gates of Heaven. I find that after my first sleep, I am restless and miserable for a time and nothing quiets me like one of the hymns I sing in my church at home. The singing makes me feel better and lifts me closer to the bosom of my Lord."

Dr. Middleton then said a few words about Christ and his free salvation, offering up a fervent prayer in which Stoodley seemed to join. After watching the sad scene for a short time, Dr. Middleton left for the night, apprehending that Stoodley would die before morning, and so it turned out. For at the chaplain's early call, there was nothing in the room but the chilling sight of the empty hospital bed.

The captain was buried that day, in a lonely grave near the edge of camp. This, it was thought, would be the last of this brave and good soldier. But in the dead of night, came hurriedly a single carriage to the front of the hospital. A lone woman, tall, straight and dressed in deep mourning clothes, got quickly out and moved rapidly up the steps into the hospital where, meeting the guard, she asked anxiously, "Where's Captain Stoodley?" Taken by surprise, the guard stammered hesitantly, "Captain Stoodley is dead, madam, and was buried today." This terrible announcement came as a shock to the poor lady and she fainted, falling to the floor as one dead. Awakened by the guard and Dr. Middleton, she began crying at the top of her voice for her husband. Worn down by apprehension and weary from traveling the many miles from western North Carolina by day and night, all the while overcome with grief, she continued to scream and sob, despite the efforts of Dr. Middleton to comfort her.

Weeping and lamenting the loss of her loved one, she told the story of her married life. How her husband was the best man who ever lived. How everyone loved him. How kind he was to all. How devoted to her. How he loved his children. How, from her earliest years almost, she had loved him as no other. When the telegraph brought the dreaded news that he was dangerously ill, she never waited an instant or stopped a moment by the way, day nor night and "Drove as fast as the horses could come from the train depot to this place and now he is dead and buried! I shall never see his face again! What shall I do? But where is he buried?"

Dr. Middleton then told her where.

A look of resolution came over her face, and she announced "I must go there. He must be taken up. I must see him!"

"But, Madam," replied Dr. Middleton, "you can't see him. Don't you understand he has been buried some hours."

"But I must see my husband!" she cried. "I can't live without seeing his face one more time. Please, doctor, help me. I beseech you!"

The doctor finally gave in to her heartfelt pleas and said, "Very well. I don't like it, but I will have your husband brought forth."

The next day, the body was taken up and brought to a room in the hospital to be embalmed. Doctor Middleton entered the building with the wife and was directed by the guard to the northeast room. Once within, the doctor uncovered in the presence of the dead. With the body was a surgeon and a hospital aide. Lying peacefully on a table was the noble Captain Stoodley, who clothed in a handsome uniform with gauntlet hand over breast, emblematic of rest, and sword at side, presented a picture, even in death, of the ideal warrior.

The sorrowing wife walked slowly to the table and looked long at her beloved, then bent down and gently kissed his forehead. She then said, "I must take him home. He must go home with me. The last thing I said to his children was that they must be good children and I would bring their father home. They are waiting for him now."

Dr. Middleton tried to convince her to leave the room, but she watched by her husband until his body was embalmed and everything was ready. She then carried him back to his own house and his children, to seek a grave close by those he loved, among the kindred and friends in the brave old North State he died to defend.

DECEMBER 5, 1862—FRIDAY
CAMP VANCE—NEAR PETERSBURG, VIRGINIA

Orders were received yesterday to be ready to march at any time. We are to join Lee's army at Fredericksburg! All has been bustle and hurry. There are tents after tents as far as the eye can see in any direction. The whole camp of thousands of men has been preparing to move. Many of the men of the brigade are still very sick; they will remain behind with the 52nd North Carolina in camp.

The men have been expecting to remain here during the winter and have taken much pains to fit up their quarters at no little expense, yet the chance to join Lee has all excited. With the 52nd staying to guard the camp, the men are assured that their quarters will be here undisturbed when, and if, they return.

At about nine o'clock this morning, the brigade was ordered to have three days' rations in haversacks and to take 80 rounds of ammunition. We are at last soldiers in full feathers and trappings; ten pounds of gun, eighty rounds per man of ball cartridge, one pound of powder, five pounds of lead, heavy equipment, knapsack, haversack, three-pint canteen—full, three days' rations, rubber blanket, woolen blanket, shelter tent, full winter clothing, tin cup, knife, fork, spoon, et cetera. Too numerous to mention and to carry. But let us make effort to mention the pound of Virginia mud in each shoe. My brigade is now a baggage train, freight train, ammunition train, commissary train, and gravel train, all in one. Thus equipped and armed, we go forth to soon try conclusions with General Burnside somewhere near the besieged city of Fredericksburg.

The day has been spent in preparation. Orders are received to be ready to move early tomorrow morning. Wrapped in my overcoat, I laid down at about ten o'clock to sleep, but a terrible toothache took hold of me and I was compelled to find such relief as I could in walking up and down the road. The moon shone brightly and many campfires glimmered on the nearby hills. Off in the distance, a band was playing "Dixie" and the boys broke into an occasional cheer by way of endorsement.

Standing alone in the dark, I was suddenly overwhelmed by the weight of the responsibility I bore. I could only hope I was prepared with courage and fortitude to lead this magnificent group of men into battle. I walked slowly back toward my quarters hoping to find there a gentle sleep that would make me oblivious to the aching teeth and head, and all other aches and worries that had possession of me.

When almost there, I was reminded of a British author who wrote a novel called *Fortitude*, which I had the pleasure to read while recovering in Charleston. It is the story of a man called Peter whose creed was, "It isn't life that matters, but the courage you bring to it." In Peter's life there were many sorrows, but at the end, on his own mountaintop, he heard a voice, "Blessed be pain and torment and every torture of the body. Blessed be all loss and failure of friends and the sacrifice of love. Blessed be all failure and the ruin of every earthly hope. Blessed be all sorrow and torment, hardships and endurance that demand courage. Blessed be these things—for of these things come the making of a man." After he heard this heavenly voice, Peter knelt in prayer. "Make of me a man…to be afraid of nothing, to be ready for everything. Love, friendship, success…to take it if it comes, to care nothing if these things are not for me. Make me brave. Make me brave."

It is now two o'clock in the morning and I am once again ready for sleep, but still repeating those courageous words, "Make me brave. Make me brave."

DECEMBER 10, 1862—WEDNESDAY
FREDERICKSBURG, VIRGINIA

Burnside and his army can now see the bristling bayonets of the Army of Northern Virginia, over 78,000 strong, surrounding the range of hills that overlook the plain and city of Fredericksburg.

The Federals have a large force on Stafford Heights across the Rappahannock, supported it is rumored by over 300 pieces of artillery. High above the Federal position float two balloons, immense, black and sinister looking, subjecting our position to their disconcerting gaze.

Early this morning, Colonel Burgwyn and I rode to Mayre's Hill where we encountered Colonel Porter Alexander of General Longstreet's staff. Alexander was helping the engineers lay out works for three batteries of the Washington Artillery. The guns were being placed, enbarbette—that is, with the entrenchments only as high as a man's breast or the muzzle of the cannon—but, the gun crews were busy improving upon the work by raising the earth higher and arranging embrasures to fire through.

Alexander was in high spirits and confident that Lee had selected a position of great defensive strength. With his scraggly beard and spreading baldness, he looked a decade older than his twenty-six years. Walking among the guns, he reeked of sweat, leather, tobacco and sour coffee. He paused from time to time to study the Federal positions on Stafford Heights, opposite, using a telescope he carried in a special holder in his saddle.

Down below the heights on the plain south of Fredericksburg, several engineers were busy staking off distances to be marked on the gun-carriages to cut shell-fuse by. "General," Alexander said to me, "we cover that ground now so well that we will sweep it as a fine-tooth comb. A chicken could not live on that field when we open fire on it."

A short time later, as we were standing by the guns, General Longstreet came riding up. Dismounting, he looked over the guns and listened to the complaints of several of the engineers who protested to him that the gun crews were ruining the emplacements by digging them too deep. Longstreet would not agree to order them to stop. "If we only save the finger of a man, that's good enough," he told the engineers, while the cannoneers kept digging.

Longstreet, the commander of the First Corps, presents a most striking figure, being about forty years of age, a soldier every inch and very handsome, tall and well proportioned. His eyes were glint steel blue, deep and piercing. He wore a full, brown beard. I am told he is regarded by his soldiers as the best fighter in the whole army.

Longstreet found religion in the early days of the war, after the death in a single week of his children from Scarlet Fever. Before this tragedy, he had been one of a gay coterie of officers who drank and stayed up most of the night playing poker. After the funeral, he quit his cards, drank so sparingly as to be almost abstentious and became a devout church member. I could only think how indomitable in spirit must be the man who could overcome this tragedy and go on with his life.

Often phlegmatic, the general this morning was in an expansive mood, saying that General Lee preferred the Federals to attack Longstreet's position. Though Lee expected the crossing of the Yankee army to be attempted at some point down river, in which case he intended to challenge it at the water's edge. It was his fervent hope that Burnside would cross at Fredericksburg. In that case, Lee does not intend to contest the crossing itself with any considerable force. The serious challenge will come later, it the Yankees come at him across the open, gently undulating plain, between the town and Mayre's Heights.

Lee has confidence that Longstreet, securely entrenched along the ridge, can repulse the enemy attack. At the present time, the Confederate infantry has the unaccustomed numerical wealth of six men to every yard of the seven-mile line. This, General Lee believes, is enough to not only repulse the Federals, but to enable our troops to launch a counter stroke in the style of Second Manassas. That would drive the bluecoats in a panicky mass and pen them for slaughter against the unfordable river, too thickly clustered for escape across their pontoon bridges and too closely intermingled with our own charging troops for the Union artillery to attempt a bombardment from the opposite heights.

"Gentlemen," concluded Longstreet, "it is unlikely that Burnside will expose his army to the dangers of an attack here. In fact, it is almost too much to hope for. No general could fail to see the danger. But General Lee does hope for it. He hopes for it intensely."

Later, Burgwyn and I shared a meal with Alexander. While eating, he reminisced with us of his days before the war in Georgia. Here he had a French Cook, brought in at great expense from Paris. His dinners, we were told, were a culinary delight. As we bivouacked in the open air and partook of our slice of bacon and dipped our crackers into the grease, Alexander gave a sigh of satisfaction and said, "Ah…General Pettigrew, Isn't this just as delightful as the French cooking. Now we are greased up for another day."

DECEMBER 17, 1862—WEDNESDAY
BATTLE OF FREDERICKSBURG

On the morning of the 11th, at three o'clock when the night was still and all fast asleep, we were rudely awakened by the deep boom of a cannon. Scarcely had the sound of the first gun died away than another report thundered out of the stillness, its echo reverberating from hill to hill and down along the riverside. Having laid down with my sword and pistol buckled around me, I had but to raise up and shake myself and my toilet was made. "Fall in" was the word given and repeated from hill to hill and camp to camp. Drums beat the long roll at every camp while the blast of the bugle called the troopers to "boots and saddles."

Couriers dashed about in the darkness from one general's headquarters to another's. Adjutants and colonel's orderlies were rushing from tent to tent arousing the officers and men to arms, and giving instructions for the great army of General Lee to move.

As I stepped from my tent, I caught sight of Adjutant Hughes coming down the line of the officers' tents, his sharp, distinct voice calling out to each as he came opposite, "Colonel _____, get your regiment ready to move at once."

The brigade was soon in line. I then ordered the 47th and 48th North Carolina to remain in camp in reserve, but ready to move at a moment's notice if needed, and marched with the 11th and 26th North Carolina in the direction of the breastworks at the top of Mayre's heights. We soon reached the top of the hill and the men filed into the waiting works to lend support to the guns of the Washington Artillery. Below our position, I could see the public highway leading to the city of Fredericksburg, curving in a semi-circle around the base of Mayre's Heights. This is called the telegraph road and is here sunken three of four feet below the ground and riveted with stone forming a natural trench. It is just breast high and also at just the height convenient for infantry defense and fire. Here Longstreet had placed Brigadier General Cobb's Georgia brigade. The Georgians were positioned behind the stonewall in two ranks; one rank to fire, then step to the rear to reload while the other would fire.

Once we were in position, daylight was yet some hours off. I tried to see toward the river with my glass, but it was very dark and such a dense fog hung over the river and valley that earth and sky were alike invisible. I could clearly hear the rattle of the rifles of Barksdale's Mississippians, whose turn it was to be on picket in the city, attempting to drive off the enemy's pontoon corps and bridge builders.

Fredericksburg was almost deserted, as General Lee had advised the citizens to leave their homes for safety. Still a few, loathing to leave their worldly possessions to the Yankees, decided to remain and trust in fate. But soon after the firing along the river began, I began to see groups of women and children in the twilight of the morning rushing along the roads out of the city toward the safety of our lines.

One old lady walking by one of the cannon of the Washington Artillery said, "Give it to them damned rascals, boys, when you open fire." The cannoneers promised they would try. At another point, I saw a shadowy apparition through the mists, which materialized into a young mother with a babe in her arms. Colonel Alexander directed the two refugees to a house behind the hill for shelter. Colonel Burgwyn, standing next to me, watched this sad affair and said resolutely, "General, a fire is burning in my heart and pray God I could hasten the sun-rising that I may defend innocent women and children!"

The bridges had reached more than halfway across the four-hundred-foot-wide river before breaks in the fog revealed the Yankee bridge builders to Barksdale's marksmen, concealed in buildings along the waterfront. Now able to see their foe, they sent the pontoniers racing for cover. The sun climbed higher and slowly melted away the morning mist. At midmorning, I looked with my glass at a spectacular view of Burnside's army. There, across the river stood over 100,000 Federal infantry standing in great solid squares upon the hilltops. The whole scene seemed very theatrical concealing the awful grimness of war. It was a view I shall long remember.

At midday, over 200 guns opened on Barksdale's sharpshooters to root them out of Fredericksburg. Battery after battery joined in the dreaded chorus until the very hills shook. I could hear buildings crash under the awful storm of the iron and lead, while the crack of numberless shells marked the sky with hundreds of angry flashes and little ball-like clouds of smoke. Many of the enemy's shells came over far enough to burst near our infantry lines. For several hours, the noise was deafening, the city being battered by the whole fire of the national cannon;

the shots frequently counting as high as one hundred per minute and numbering several thousands in all. Over and over again, we tried to count the cannon shots, but always failing as they mingled in a roar.

We watched in awe as house after house was set on fire; the red flames leapt from roof to roof and the black smoke swirled upwards in dense volumes for two hundred feet, perhaps, before it began to spread horizontally and form a great black canopy.

At dark, the Mississippians were withdrawn from the town and the enemy left in possession of it. I thought it strange that our batteries did not open on the Yankees once they crossed the river, but Alexander told me General Lee was calmly waiting and our batteries would have ample targets soon enough. "We only have to hold our ground," said Alexander, "and one of the greatest victories of the war would be ours."

That night, we slept by our guns and kept a close watch for any sign of a Yankee attack. Now that the enemy was across the river, Longstreet felt sure that they would pass through the town and attempt a surprise attack on our positions. He sent a note to Colonel Alexander instructing that the batteries should open at once on anything that looked like an advance. "Be especially vigilant," wrote Longstreet, "between moon rise and dawn when an attack may be made." Despite the alarm, the night was peaceful.

The next morning, the 12th, as the fog lifted, Stafford Heights and the inclines above the river were one field of blue. Great lines of Burnside's infantry, with waving banners—their bright guns and bayonets glittering in the sunlight—were all slowly marching down the inclines and over the bridges, then down the riverside at a double quick to join their comrades of the night before. Behind the infantry, light batteries of artillery came dashing at break-neck speed down the hillsides, their horses rearing and plunging as if wishing to take the river at a leap. Alexander and I counted at least eight four-gun batteries crossing the river before noon.

Bands of music enlivened the scene by their inspiring strains and when some national air or especially martial piece would be played, shouts and yells would rend the air for miles to be answered by counter yells from thousands of our troops. The Confederate bands were not idle, for as soon as a Federal band would cease playing, some of the Southern bands would join in playing "Dixie." As the music of this great song would be borne over water and hills, the Federals would shout, sing and dance—hats and caps thrown in the air, flags waved in the breeze—because of their especial delight at the sight and sound of "Dixie." The entire spectacle seemed more of a celebration or holiday than the prelude to what I thought would be one of the bloodiest battles of the war.

The night following was cold and a biting wind was blowing while our lines were enshrouded in a thick atmosphere of smoke, proceeding partly from the earlier cannonading and, in part, from the campfires of the armies. As I looked around, I could observe the campfires gleaming on every hill and hillside and along the horizon. Our men joked and laughed around the campfires as they prepared rations for the next day. Everyone expected that the great battle would take place within the next twenty-four hours.

When the night grew late and the two armies finally laid down to sleep, it was with the consciousness that many of the men who were now congregated around the fires of the bivouac would never meet together again, and many a brave soldier, as he gazed upon the stars that were twinkling above him so peacefully, wondered whether or not on the next night they might not gleam upon his lifeless body. The night passed by quietly and except the occasional click of the pick and spade of the engineers who were finishing the field works for the protection of the cannon, or the sighing of the night wind through the branches of the pine trees, nothing was heard to break the stillness that reigned supreme.

The low rumble of artillery passing over frozen ground sounded through the darkness as the eastern sky began to lighten toward six o'clock on Saturday, the 13th. Alexander, with his trained artillery man's ear, had heard Burnside's assault columns forming behind the grey mist of the early morning fog and awoke me from a deep sleep. I eagerly accepted his invitation to accompany him to Lee's field headquarters on Telegraph Hill where we could better view the panorama of the developing battle.

When we arrived, dense fog and smoke covered the plateau before us and the enemy. Nothing could be seen or heard except an indescribable buzz, like the distant sound of swarming bees that so plainly tells the trained soldier that an army is going into battle.

On Telegraph Hill were General Lee and staff, Longstreet and staff, and about one hundred others, largely officers and couriers. I can't recall ever seeing so many worthies and shoulder straps in one place. General Jackson rode up to have a word with Lee. As he dismounted several of the staff officers broke into astonished smiles. He was in a spick-and-span new overcoat, new uniform with rank marks, fine black felt hat and a handsome sword. Alexander remarked he had never seen "Old Stonewall" like this before and gave the general his congratulations on his fine appearance. Jackson said he "believed it was some of his friend Stuart's doings." After saying a few words to General Lee, he went off and leaned against a tree. General Stuart, who had been making a reconnaissance into the fog, trotted up the hill whistling. He was soon joined by generals Wilcox and McLaws. Lee looked at his watch several times and tried to peer through the fog with his glass. General Kershaw, whose South Carolina brigade was in reserve between Telegraph and Mayre's Hill, came up and talked with Longstreet and the hours wore on. It was near ten o'clock when suddenly, "Bang!" went a cannon on our right and then, "Bang! Boom! Bang!"

"There she goes, boys!" said Stuart and, leaping on his horse, he cantered off to the right. The other brigadiers and major generals followed suit to their respective commands. Just as Jackson was ready to mount, Longstreet called out, "Jackson, what are you going to do if the Yankees attack?"

"Sir," said Stonewall, with great fire and spirit, "we will give them the bayonet."

In less than ten minutes, the fog began to whirl upward and in less time than it takes to tell, the whole cloud curtain rolled away, revealing the grandest panorama I have ever seen—an army of nearly one hundred thousand men in battle array. It was a majestic sight and I was reluctant to return to Mayre's Hill with Alexander.

The advance on our right by Franklin's corps soon began while the enemy opened a heavy cannonading along our whole line. The fact of my having ridden to the left and too far distant from the scene of action of the right to make a personal observation will prevent me from giving any detailed account of the gallantry with which A. P. Hill's division repelled every attack by the enemy at that point and finally drove him in disorder from the field.

Returning to Mayre's Heights, we witnessed a Confederate courier riding out of Fredericksburg. As he started along the telegraph road, the enemy's guns opened, forcing the rider to give his horse whip and spur. Two white bags hung across his saddle and they flapped up and down at a great rate. On he came, the shells of the enemy licking at his heels, following him up the road.

"He'll never make it," said Alexander.

The whole command was watching this ride for life. By dint of great exertion, he reached the sunken road and finally safety on the hill to the delight and cheers of the troops stationed there. Here he made his report that he had been visiting a friend in the city when a cannon ball intruded on the conversation and knocked the dining room to "damnation smash." Realizing it was time to leave, his friend provided him with two pillows filled with biscuits for the brave Confederate troops on the hill and two bottles of Barton's Old Maderia. The cannoneers enjoyed the biscuits and drank to Mr. Barton's health, standing by their guns.

At noon, while sitting in the garden of Mayre's house, we were in momentary anticipation of an attack upon our position as the enemy could now be seen in immense force in the town. A note arrived from General Longstreet for General Cobb, but for our perusal. It read:

"If Anderson, on your left, is badly pressed, he will fall back to the second line of heights. Conform to his movements."

Longstreet obviously feared the overwhelming numbers of the Yankees could drive us from our position. Worried, Alexander and I went down the terraced hill and into the sunken road. We found General Cobb near a small house and delivered the order. Cobb read the message carefully and then said, "If they wait for me to fall back, they will wait a long time. A million Yankees couldn't drive me from this position!"

Then, to our amazement, Federal troops began to spread across the open ground below Mayre's Heights. Looking over the stone wall, in the direction of the town, we saw our skirmishers falling back and the enemy's skirmishers advancing. Presently, with loud cries of "Hi! Hi!" columns of the enemy came running through the streets of the city with their muskets at a right shoulder and their colors aslant the shoulders of the color bearers. The Yankees then began to rapidly deploy behind a ridge that partially hid them from our view. It was obvious the ball was about to begin.

We left General Cobb, climbed the hill and mounted our horses. Alexander directed Lieutenant Galbraith, who, with one three-inch rife-gun was close to plank road, to open fire as soon as the enemy came within good range. This order given, we rode to the center of the batteries and joined Captain Squires in his redoubt. Our horses were left with a bugler behind the brick wall of Mayre's graveyard upon the hill, just behind our position.

Finally, the Federals formed their line and began their advance. What a magnificent sight it was! We had never witnessed such a battle-array before; long lines following one another, of brigade front. As they advanced, their musket barrels gleamed brightly in the sunlight, the red, white and blue national flags fluttered in the breeze. The lines advanced at a double-quick and the alignments were beautifully kept. Alexander watched in silent admiration, his jaw firmly set. He then put down his glass, turned to me and said, "They are coming on beautifully. It's a pity I will soon have to blow them to smithereens."

The lines of blue continued to advance. Then the loud full voice of Colonel Alexander rang out, "'tention! Commence firing!" and instantly, the edge of Mayre's Hill was fringed with flame. The cannoneers soon warmed up to their work and aimed and fired coolly and deliberately. It was an awful sight as the shells struck the Federals and burst. The air, for a minute, would be just full of legs and arms and pieces of trunks.

Despite the heavy fire, the Federals continued to advance. Soon they were within canister range and the cannon poured forth of the deadly missiles. They continued to advance and neared the infantry posted in the sunken road. The Georgians and North Carolinians were unseen by the enemy for smoke had covered the battlefield. All at once the infantry below us stood; one moment to aim along the trusty rifle-barrels, then a bright burst of flame lit up the stone wall from end to end and a blast of musketry scorched the Federal line. The infantry fire was devastating and even the boldest and stoutest of hearts could not withstand long this withering blast of bullets and shells. The Yankees fell to the ground and opened upon us a terrific fire, both from the columns in front and the sharp shooters on the housetops in the city. After giving us battle as long as human endurance could bear the ordeal, they at last retreated in confusion. As they fled, I could hear the Confederate infantry below yell derisively, "Set 'em up again!"

The assault had been met and repulsed and the field before us was dotted with patches of blue—the dead and wounded of the Federal infantry. It was a gallant assault, but what imbecile, I wondered, ordered an attack against such a well-fortified position?

After a brief lull, Hancock's division poured onto the field only to meet the same bloody repulse. Then Howard's division came up and again assailed the hill. The enemy moved to the charge heroically, and, once again, the withering fire of the artillery and infantry blew great holes in their ranks.

On they came to within less than one hundred and fifty paces of our line, but nothing could live before the storm of lead that assailed their ranks. They wavered, broke and then retreated from the field. A few, however, more resolute than the rest, lingered under cover of some houses and fences and annoyed us with a scattering, but well-directed, fire.

During this attack, the gallant General Cobb was mortally wounded. General Kershaw, at the head of one of his South Carolina regiments, then dashed into the fight at Mayre's Hill where he assumed command of the troops in the road.

After the third charge, it was clear to us that the Federals had undertaken an impossible task. To charge across 400 yards of open ground broken only by a few houses and garden fences under the direct fire of our artillery and a sizeable body of infantry seemed sheer folly. So confident was Alexander of the strength of our position that, before one assault, he allowed himself to be distracted by a covey of partridges that had been stunned by the noise and were flying about aimlessly. Amidst the shelling, he drew his pistol and shot down a few choice birds for his mess.

The Yankees had made three unsuccessful charges upon our position, leaving their wounded and dead lying in heaps and winding rows from the old railroad cut to the outskirts of town. Our infantry in the road and behind the wall, Cobbs' and part of Kershaw's, were nearly out of ammunition and, during the last charge, had been using that of their dead and wounded. Calls were made on all sides for more ammunition both from the artillery and infantry. Orders and details were soon sent to the ordinance trains to bring supplies to the front. With enough ammunition, we knew we could kill all the Yankees in the Army of the Potomac and end the war right here.

The enemy's batteries were firing at us from positions they had taken on the plain and their sharpshooters sent their lethal balls overhead and around us. A cannoneer, with his sleeves rolled up, had been ramming his gun when, suddenly, he threw up his hands and fell backwards with a ball in his spine. A comrade seized the sponge-staff as it fell and took position. The sharp ring of a bullet, striking the face of the cannon was heard and severely wounded the replacement in the arm.

A cannon shot then came crashing through one of the works and struck the edge of the wall, knocking dirt and brick right and left. A thirty-two-pound shot struck a tree and passed through the center of it taking a private's head entirely off.

Captain John Fuller, crouched down on his knees, was leaning forward looking through his glass. Seeing a large shell descending toward him, I called to him to look out! When he raised his head, the shell was within five feet of him and grazed his back before entering the ground close behind him. He was severely shocked and unfit for duty the rest of the day. Still photographed in my memory is the appearance of the body of one of the Washington Artillery being hauled away on a rear caisson, his head was shot off and over the headless trunk was fastened a bloody white handkerchief.

Shortly, a new Yankee attack formed. In this column of assault was the famous Meager's Irish Brigade of New York—all Irishmen, but undoubtedly the finest body of troops in the Federal Army. When the signal for advance was given, they sprang up and came forward, compact rows of glittering bayonets, in long battle lines.

With a firm and elastic step, this magnificent body of Irishmen moved to the assault determined to break our lines or die trying. Not a shot was fired from this advancing column while the shells from our batteries cut swatch after swatch through their ranks. Where ever did our cannon worked with truer aim or more rapidly? The men stood to their work with powder-grimed faces and hands while sweat steamed from their brows. Clouds of smoke rolled from the mouths of our guns and the roar of the cannon was incessant.

Colonel Alexander watched with pride remarking occasionally, "Handsomely done. Very handsomely done, men."

Then two men were horribly wounded while loading a piece by its premature discharge, each losing both arms and one having also his face and body fearfully mangled.

On the Yankees came, colors fell but rose and floated again, men forward and eagerly grasping the fallen staff, seemingly indifferent to the fate that awaited them. Officers were in front with drawn swords flashing in the gleam of the fading sunlight. It began to look as if they would overrun us, but they could not advance closer than one hundred paces from the wall. The terrible fire from the infantry and our cannon was too much. They too finally yielded to the inevitable and left the field in great disorder.

The last charge against Mayre's Hill was made at dark by determined Yankee regulars of Sykes' division. These troops, out of sheer desperation, charged with the bayonet, but the deadly fire of artillery and musketry broke it after an advance of only fifty yards. Save an occasional cannon shot, or the crack of a sharpshooter's rifle, the battle in front of Mayre's Hill was over.

A flask of spirits in my saddle pocket, behind the graveyard wall was considered the correct thing to have just then and I made a hasty run for it, returned and passed it around. It seemed to do a power of good to all hands.

As it became dark, a heavy, chilling fog settled down upon the plain and we found comfort sitting by a warm fire behind one of the revetments. It had been a fateful day and Alexander remarked that he could not remember what or even whether he had eaten during the battle because the business at hand had consumed him.

Alexander was fortunate, he had over fourteen cannon under his command and enough work to keep ten men busy. My role as observer left me more than ample time to reflect on the dangers of our position. I found the fire of the sharpshooters bothered me not at all, but the shelling, I must admit, was, at times, unnerving. First you hear the sound of a gun instantly followed by a noise between a whiz and a yell. Then, perhaps 20 rods in front and 100 feet in the air, there is the prettiest ball of dense, white smoke the size of a small haycock, eddying and unfolding in all directions.

This is all you usually see, but you know that from 10 to 100 musket balls and ragged pieces of iron will strike within the next two seconds on the acre of ground on which you stand. You hear the explosion, then come the fragments, each one according to its own shape singing a different note, varying from a sharp swiz to a low heavy hiss. There is no use of dodging or moving about. You wonder where will they strike? Will one angry piece of jagged metal tear off the head to which I have grown attached? Will that triangular chap which screams so loud tear out my bowels with one of its sharp points? Will that large piece which makes a heavy, low, rushing sound be satisfied with an arm or leg? Will they all skip you and take someone else? Perhaps they will go too high or to the left. No. Too low. Then it is decided, fate plays its hand. Thump, rattle, boom, smash, dirt and splinters fly on every side. The air clears. I am safe, but looking around, I see from one to a dozen poor fellows rolling headless, or writhing in bloody agony on the ground.

My brigade lost two killed and ten wounded from the shelling of the Federal batteries while we lay in reserve. About midnight, I moved the brigade to the stone wall on the telegraph road, replacing Cobb's Georgians. Orders were sent out to prepare with plenty of ammunition, water and rations under the conviction that the battle of the next day, if made as ordered, would be the last of the Army of the Potomac. It was expected that Burnside would renew the attack and once repulsed, we could go over to the attack and destroy the Yankees who would be trapped and helpless with the river at their back.

The night was cold and quiet. I paced back and forth along the telegraph road. Early in the morning, while still dark, a sentinel on one of the picket posts halted a stump and demanded the countersign. No response being made, he fired. The entire 26th North Carolina sprang to arms. The cannoneers on Mayre's Hill gathered about their guns and thousand of eyes peered into the darkness to get a glimpse of the approaching enemy. But the stump, evidently intimidated by the first shot, did not advance. Soon the men returned to their rest to dream doubtless of the subject of a song very common now in camp, to wit:

"Old General Burnside

"seems not so wise.

"As he looks across the Rappahannock

"With his goggle eyes."

The next day, as if by mutual agreement, was a day of rest. The wounded were gathered in as far as we were able to reach them. The Federal wounded lay within one hundred yards of the stone wall and their piteous calls for help and water were heart rending. Whenever one of my brigade attempted to relieve the Yankees lying close under our portion of the wall, he would be fired on by the pickets and sharp-shooters on the housetops.

On the night of the 15th, the Federal army stole silently across the river. A hard rain fell during the night, lashed by a stiff south wind that carried the sounds of retreat away from us. We heard nothing. Suspected nothing. Dawn revealed an abandoned battlefield.

Late in the morning, I accompanied a party of skirmishers of the 26th North Carolina into Fredericksburg. On the outskirts of town, a white woman appeared in the streets with two small children and all three of them frightened more than half to death. They must have remained in hiding during the bombardment of December 11th and the Federal occupation of the city. They were immediately cared for and sent, at once, to a place of safety.

As we advanced down Caroline Street, one could see that the city was terribly smashed and shattered. Many buildings have been burned. Houses in which shells have burst are a mere heap of rubbish. The Baptist church had more than thirty holes through it. Many of the streets were impassable because of the piles of brick, timber, and rub-bish. There had been some vandalism, but less than one would expect.

Here and there, in the yards about the houses, men were lying. In many places, half a dozen or more together with their coat capes thrown up over their faces—dead. I was shown a cellar where a num-ber of women and children had gone for protection. A shell had burst in their midst—Union or Confederate, no one could tell—but upon the occupation of the city by our troops, it was said that the bodies of ten women and one child were found there, dead. All killed by pieces of shell.

The Yankees have left many of their dead and a few of their wounded in the city. A Confederate soldier looking for wood in a back yard stum-bled over three dead bodies. Not caring to repeat such an experience, he secured the wood elsewhere.

I returned to my command by the road that ran between Mayre's Heights and the stone wall. Just at that fatal point, I halted to look up on the right at Mayre. There was hardly a twig as big as my little finger that had not been scratched by a bullet or shell. In one thin telegraph pole, I counted thirteen minie balls. And then I looked to the left over the wall. The Federal dead lay there, untouched as they had fallen. I stood before the stone wall and looked out over the ghastly scene, literally amazed at the extent of the slaughter. The line of dead began about fifty yards from the wall, piled upon each other and thence extended back for acres. The mutilation of the bodies was of the most terrible description, showing the havoc of grape and canister.

I was repelled by the scene but some morbid curiosity made me venture out onto the field where corpses formed a level carpet over the sodden, open ground. There were only a few surviving wounded. I stooped for a closer look at one miserable Yankee shot in the head, a wound that should have been fatal, as it was directly through the brain. When I spoke to the poor fellow, he replied hoarsely, "Captain. Captain."

Nearby, another wounded Federal was calling out "Water! Water!" He had been shot through the forehead and some of his brains were spilling out. I bent down and asked him where he came from. His eyes were glazed over and he began to shout "New York! New York!" just as he had been crying for water. He kept calling out his home state as long as I could hear.

I approached a party of our men who were gathering the dead. They had dug a long trench six feet wide and three feet deep. Into this trench they were throwing the petrifying bodies of the dead Yankees head first, pell-mell. One confederate would get between the legs of the dead enemy, take a foot in either hand, then two others would each grasp an arm and drag at a run the remains of the dead Federal to the pit, heaving it in. One fellow who seemed to enjoy this ghoulish work sang to himself as he threw body after body into the trench, the verse of which I will forever remember.

> "I asked her if she could and would;
> "I thought she'd say she couldn't;
> "Instead of that she said she could;
> "But rather thought she wouldn't."

In this way, these pits—or ditches—were filled almost to a level of the surface and a little dirt was thrown over them. I watched as one of the trenches was filled with dirt and heard a woman who lived in one of the houses near the stone wall say, "nearly all the Yankee dead have been entirely stripped naked by our troops who are short of clothes. The morning after the battle, the field was blue. But the morning after the Federals withdrew, the field was white."

Returning to the stone wall, I chanced upon a corporal whose regiment was posted behind the wall during the battle. He told me that it was the easiest battle he was ever in. "Why," said he, "we had our ammunition all laid out, handy for use, and all we had to do was load and fire. Load and fire. We stood in no danger from anything but bursting shell. All the Yankee fire went over our head. There was absolutely no chance for the Federals to reach us. They came pretty nigh it once and one brave fellow fell just a few yards from the wall. He was the nearest one I saw."

The night of the 16th, a group of us sat around the fire, cultivating our palates with some cheap whiskey Captain Handfield had commandeered in Fredericksburg. The whiskey was fiery and rough, quite nasty to take, but warming and appreciated on a cold night. The captain had taken the ragged edge off this useful beverage by putting it over the fire and letting it simmer. What disappeared in the smoke was, we supposed, the worst part.

After a few cups of this fusel oil had been passed around the campfire and quaffed in gulps from our tin cups, conversation turned to why General Lee did not attack the Yankees while they were in the exposed position of crossing the river during their retreat. It was generally agreed that it would have been fatal to the Federals. Someone claimed that Jackson proposed a night attack, but many of us doubted this rumor. We realized the enemy's powerful artillery on Stafford heights would have been an efficient aid in resisting an attack on the Federals before and while crossing the river. But they were badly demoralized and probably would not have stood long with the threatening river in their rear and our triumphant forces in the front.

Colonel Burgwyn suggested that perhaps we were deficient in ammunition and that was the logical explanation for our failure to attack.

Colonel Alexander replied, "We had no want of it. We have missed a great opportunity to destroy the Yankee army." And General Lee, in his opinion, failed to read the truest lesson in the Yankee pattern of failure. However badly beaten, the Yankee never relaxes and always comes back again.

DECEMBER 21, 1862—SUNDAY
ROCKY MOUNT, NORTH CAROLINA

The brigade of James Johnson Pettigrew has again taken to the cars and, like firemen to the rescue, is rushing at railroad speed toward Goldsboro. It seems that a large force of Yankees under General Foster have left their base at New Bern and are headed up country toward Kinston and Goldsboro and toward the Wilmington and Weldon Railroad, the great north-south trunk line that is the main artery supply for Lee's army. With the Yankee threat to Richmond ended because of Burnside's defeat at Fredericksburg, large quantities of ammunition and reinforcements are being rushed to North Carolina.

As we made ready to board the cars near Fredericksburg, a number of our sick were led to some open platform cars. The ride to North Carolina on open cars would have been almost a sure death to several of these men and brigade surgeon Amos Sullivan—in whose care they were—protested against such treatment. Protests being of no avail, the good surgeon put his foot down and refused with all the force he could to have them put on the open cars at all. A war of words ensued and a considerable delay was caused, but the affair was finally settled. Several boxcars with a good supply of hay were found and attached to the train, the sick men put in, and we moved finally on toward North Carolina, with most of the men on open platform cars. It took several trains to move the entire brigade and I managed to secure a place in a car near the locomotive of the lead train. Rank has its advantages, but not on a train and I have been doomed to be smoked and sooted and choked as we travel south. Nevertheless, I find car traveling quite tame now and rather enjoy being boxed up on a long passenger car or riding near the engine, watching the flame in the furnace or the black smoke wreathing out of the chimney and talking with the engineer of the wonderful machine they control with such facility.

Army life is often rendered tolerable and even agreeable by the occurrence of incidents that have the flavor of humor and even comicality to make them memorable. Such an incident occurred during one of our frequent stops for water and coal after leaving Virginia. While stopped at a way station, Lieutenant Blount, one of my volunteer aides, wandered from the train and succeeded in buying a turkey at a nearby farmhouse. Blount wrung the neck of the bird and hired a colored mammy to cook the turkey, she agreeing to have it cooked and ready for him as soon as possible so he could eat it on the train. The generous-hearted lieutenant agreed to pay the cook a quarter for her service.

While Lieutenant Blount was making his bargain with the colored cook, he was not aware of the fact that another party was an attentive listener to it. This was Sergeant Fellows, who was concealed in the bushes nearby. The crafty sergeant, taking advantage of the knowledge thus gained, presented himself about fifteen minutes before the train was scheduled to depart and asked. "Is the turkey cooked?" The mammy replied, "Yes, Massa, all ready, Massa." Fellows then said, "Well, here's your quarter and give me the turkey." And she gave the bird to him.

A few minutes after Fellows departed with the bird, Lieutenant Blount appeared and asked for his turkey, but to his surprise and indignation, he learned that someone had got ahead of him and secured the bird. Blount asked the mammy who the thief was, but all the information he could get from her was, "de genman had come paid de quarta and took dat turkey away wif 'im." Blount then asked her to describe the man and what he said when he called for the turkey. To all his inquiries, she replied, "All I know dat he was a sojer and I done thought he wus de same genman dat had gave me de turkey to cook."

Naturally, Lieutenant Blount was extremely upset over the loss of his turkey, which he had paid a dollar and a half for, plus a quarter to the cook. Hunger and anger drove him to complain to Captain Louis Young. Young, ever a diplomat, pacified Blount and told him that if he would keep quiet about the matter, they could perhaps find out who the thief was. Blount agreed to keep silent about it and had not to wait many hours before the culprit was fully known, much to his satisfaction. The crime was solved in the following manner.

At roll call that evening, during another long stop, all the men were ordered from the train and paraded. After the orderly sergeants had called the roll, Young was informed that the name of Sergeant James Fellows had not been called. Young asked why the name of Fellows had not been called? The orderly replied that Fellows was a very sick man. "Trot him out," said Young. And, sure enough, when Fellows was brought from his boxcar, he presented a most pallid appearance. It was obvious that the sergeant was a very sick man.

Captain Young looked at the indisposed soldier before him and asked, "What is the matter with you, Fellows?"

"I don't know," he replied, "but I feel a bit flush."

Young approached Fellows and, with a show of knowing something of medical practice, felt his pulse, looked at his tongue, raised the lid of one eye and looked in. Then, speaking so loud that all who had gathered around could here, he said, "James Fellows, pilfered turkey does not agree with you, does it?"

Fellows looked guilty and hung his head, but made no answer. Then, Captain Young said, "Fellows, you stole Lieutenant Blount's turkey and I'll give you until twelve o'clock tomorrow to pay him one dollar and fifty cents. If you don't pay him, I'll have you court-martialed. Will you do it?"

"I will, sir," was Fellows' answer.

It appears that when he obtained possession of Blount's turkey, Fellows went to the woods and devoured everything of it but the bones. The ravenous Fellows must have eaten three pounds of turkey meat. His illness was no wonder.

The men of Fellows' company, learning of the affair, promptly nicknamed him "Turkey Fellows" and began calling him by that name. Then, when the boys began to joke Lieutenant Blount about his sergeant, James Fellows, and the great turkey heist, the lieutenant replied, "No, no, boys, you are mistaken. That man can't belong to my company. Can't you tell by his appearance, his name and his accent, where he hails from?" To this, Blount added that he knows by all peculiarities referred to, as well as his weakness for poultry, that Turkey Fellows must have been born in the vicinity of Constantinople and that he has the name, the accent, the appearance and some of the habits of the people of that region.

DECEMBER 22, 1862—MONDAY
GOLDSBORO, NORTH CAROLINA

We arrived in Goldsboro early this morning and the snail-like pace with which the crowded trains were compelled to creep along, have extended an ordinary journey of two days into one of nearly a week.

One of the conductors told us that because the rails were worn out, effort was being made to preserve them by running trains at slower speeds. The conductor then facetiously informed us that the speed of the train was so slow and stops so frequent, that the train had been repeatedly passed by an old Negro laden with farm implements. To each and every invitation from the conductor to get on the train as it overtook him, the Negro politely replied, "Much obliged, boss, but I'se in a hurry."

As we left the cars, we rejoiced to hear of the repulse of the enemy in front of Goldsboro, yet they destroyed a portion of the railroad between Goldsboro and Wilmington. We also learned the Federals are retreating on New Bern. It is reported that our loss is small and the enemy's large. Our 3,000 men fought successfully against overwhelming numbers.

Fears for the safety of Goldsboro are now totally dissipated. With the exception of an occasional raid against the railroad here and there—which one hundred thousand men could not prevent—there is nothing to apprehend. Prisoners state that Foster, the Yankee general, brought with him eighteen thousand men, two thousand cavalry and forty pieces of artillery, the object of the expedition being the capture of Goldsboro and the establishment of a base of operations from which he could have moved on Raleigh, Weldon and Wilmington. It was not, as we were originally informed, a mere reconnaissance en force, but a determined effort to secure a strong-hold with the fall of which the whole of North Carolina would, in all probability, have become a prey to the enemy.

A remarkable feature of this brief campaign is the promptness with which we gathered and concentrated troops. I have been told that there have recently arrived in Goldsboro alone nine regiments and several batteries of artillery, while several other brigades are also on their way hither. If one recalls the peculiar nature of all or our campaigns and remembers how much has been done by forces greatly inferior to those of the enemy, the conclusion is at once evident that, except the French, there are no troops in the world more capable of mobility and endurance than those of the South. The campaign of Stonewall Jackson in the Valley, that of General Lee around Richmond, and from Manassas to Maryland, and then to Fredericksburg, and finally the present one in North Carolina, is each a running commentary on the fact.

After leaving the train, we marched a short distance and halted at a rich plantation for the purpose of resting and securing fresh water. I informed the regimental commanders the rest would last for half an hour.

The sudden appearance of almost four thousand Confederate soldiers was a surprise and a source of instant attraction to the hundred or more slaves of the place who poured out to look at us. The darkies, in order to obtain a good view of the brigade, clambered to the roofs of the sheds, the shacks and some of them even up into the trees, perched on the branches like so many crows. One young girl took to the upper rail of a rail fence and was joined by several little niggers who were jaybird naked. The young ones came to the fence very shyly and by degrees; first peeping round the corners and from behind trees as they approached with great hesitation.

A girl appeared who was about seventeen years old, well developed, bright looking, with bright, snappy eyes and a mouthful of handsome teeth as white as ivory. She wanted information and seemed determined on getting it. Seeing Captain Young, she moved toward him, conforming to the zigzag shape of the fence. Finally reaching him, she exclaimed, "Massa! Massa! Has all you uns got naims?"

"Yes, we do," answered Young. "How about you, daughter, what's your name?"

"January," she answered.

"Why January?" asked Young.

"Wa-al, my mammy has a passel of chillun. She name de fo' gals January, May, June an' Augusta, like de months. De boys she name fo' de days of de week. That's my brotha, Monday, o'er thare. Mammy, not happy wit dat name though. She say he oughter been name' Sunday, de day o' rest. He been sittin' down all his life!"

DECEMBER 25, 1862—THURSDAY, CHRISTMAS
NEAR POLLOCKSVILLE, NORTH CAROLINA

The brigade has spent the last several days following the Yankees as they withdrew to their base in New Bern. Of course this did not involve hard fighting and a hundred or so will cover all the dead and wounded.

We had orders to begin the reconnaissance in force and cross the Neuse River early on the morning of the 23rd. I awoke at 4:30. It was raining like mad, dark as a box with thunder and lightning. Not a delightful beginning to the day. I dressed in my India-rubber coat and much-insulated large boots, which kept me relatively dry. By the time we were saddled, it stopped raining and away I went, quite thankful, with a trail of six orderlies and Captain Young. The ground, of course, was very wet and we went slipping and sliding in the red mud for most of the early morning.

We rode to the extreme picket line and took a view. There, sure enough, was Mr. Yank with his picket line about one-third of a mile off. Through the glass I could see clearly a chain of mounted videttes and, behind these, on a little knoll, a picket reserve with their horses tied to trees. We waited some time to give a chance to Colonel Burgwyn on the right and Colonel Leventhorpe to get their troops into the proper positions. Then I ordered an advance. In a few moments, quite as if by magic, the open country was alive with our infantry who deployed and went forward, making a connected line as far as the eye could reach, right and left.

Then followed the supports, in close order, and with and behind them the field batteries, all trooping along at a lively pace. It was now between eight and nine and the sun was bright, so that the whole spectacle was one of the most picturesque possible. Not the least remarkable feature was the coolness of the Yankees under these trying circumstances. Their videttes stared a few moments, apparently without much curiosity, then turned tail and moved off at a slow pace, disappearing over a ridge before us. We rode on about a mile, keeping a little behind the skirmishers. Colonel Burgwyn and his staff were slightly ahead and to the right. To the left we could hear the sound of musketry and cannon, Colonel Leventhorpe having got into a skirmish there.

Then I saw a puff of smoke on a ridge in front of us and then, "hm-m-whz-z-z-z bang!" went a shell, right by Colonel Burgwyn's staff, taking the leg off a young orderly. Pleased with their good shot, the Yankees then proceeded to give my staff a taste and missiles of various kinds began to skip and buzz round us. It was, to me, extraordinary to see the precision with which they fired. All the shot flew near us and several burst close around, pelting us with soft dirt as they struck the ground. Captain Young came riding up and called to me, "General, I don't think the Yankees enjoy our company."

We kept going forward and entered a wooded tract, interspersed with mud holes and springy ground. It was here that the enemy made quite a hard stand, for the town of Kinston lay a couple of miles beyond and they wished to gain time to get off their supplies and wounded by the railroad. Our infantry were coming out of the woods on all sides, moving on the town in the form of a semi-circle. Suddenly, we were aware of a railroad train slowly leaving the depot. Immediately, several cannon were turned on it, but it raced off despite the shells that burst over it.

The Yankees were now retreating in all haste and we rode in at once. We found a good many supplies at the depot with a number of rifles and saddles. As our advance continued, we drove the enemy five miles beyond Kinston, making fifteen miles in all. It was there that I ordered a halt and had pickets thrown out. I made my headquarters at the house of a Mr. Bright. The old gentleman has a fancy for naming his children with the same names of the Southern states. His eldest, a girl, Louisiana, is about twenty years old. The youngest, a mere babe. But his family has well nigh confiscated the entire Confederacy! His house has no glass windows. Square holes are cut and cotton cloth stretched across to admit the light. All can be closed with heavy board shutters. "To keep the wild cats from stealing the children," as he says.

During our supper, a large pig came in and nosed around familiarly among the children, dogs and chickens on the floor. Soon, piggy smelled a large hoe-cake all baking hot in the ashes of the fireplace. Before he could be stopped, his hoof had raked the cake out and, plunging his snout deep into the scalding hot mass, he gave one hoggish bite, one queer shake of his head, one shower of dough, one loud squeal, one tremendous leap for the door—the gay curl of his tail sticking out straight as a candle—and we never saw him more. The family was sorry to lose the hoe-cake, but seemed to regard the affair as nothing particularly unusual in their dining room.

By this time, it was dark and raining guns. Captain Young had a stomachache. Despite Squire Brights' hospitality, we had little in the way of creature comforts but sabers and revolvers. I took from my saddle bag a candle and lighting the same prepared tea from my canteen and produced a loaf of bread and a bologna sausage to the astonishment of the staff who inquired if I had a pontoon bridge with me. Then I rolled myself in my coat and took sleep on the floor.

That night, an ingenious lieutenant of Colonel Leventhorpe's staff thought he emptied a long artillery shell of its powder and then used the shell for an andiron in the fireplace of the log cabin he was utilizing for the night.

About ten o'clock, the shell exploded, demolishing the cabin, lifting the roof, knocking the chimney and fireplace all into pieces, stunning the lieutenant badly and leaving him sprawling on the middle of the cabin floor all out of doors in a driving rain and scared out of his wits. The explosion was taken to be a signal gun announcing an attack by the enemy. It roused much of the brigade which sprang to arms—all this in the dead of night. Guns were manned in short order, regiments ready to fall into line while loud bugle blasts startled cavalry and field artillery to boots and saddles. But orderlies soon began to fly about and explain the cause of the disturbance. Quiet was quickly restored and the men turned in again. There is a moral, of course, don't mix loaded shells and fire if you wish to sleep soundly.

The next morning as I was saddling my horse, stretcher bearers came by carrying a Yankee who had been fatally wounded in our advance. They set down their stretcher near a small group of mounds and began to dig his grave. From their actions, I perceived the man was not yet dead and went to watch them. After digging a hole about two feet deep, they lit their pipes and sat down to smoke and talk over matters and wait for the poor fellow to die.

It saddened me to notice that they betrayed not the least sense of emotion or feeling for the wounded soldier who lay there before them, gasping in the agonies of death, and when he had breathed his last, they roughly tipped him over into the hole and covered him with a few shovels' full of earth. They then picked up their stretcher and went back into the field.

Such scenes are common in war and I have seen many killed who get little more than a blanket for a coffin or as much as a hasty prayer over their burial. And yet all this lack of feeling and sympathy was without malice. No. It was but a result of living night and day within the "valley of the shadow of death."

Our advance this day followed the Trent River and the enemy was some distance ahead of us and only opposed us with a few skirmishers. Near Tranton, our advance was interrupted by a shell which exploded about 100 yards ahead. Then another flew right among my horse's legs without touching me. I rode ahead to reconnoiter the Yankee position, but they have a sharp eye for gold cords round hats and, in a minute, wh-n-n-ng flup! Wh-z-z-z-z! A solid shot struck just in front of us and bounced over our heads. I ordered the staff to disperse about the field so as not to make such a tempting target, but as Captain Young rode off, they sent a shell so near him that one of the orderlies called out, "I guess they think you're somebody pretty distinguished, Captain."

As terrible as the shells sound, there may be a good deal of cannon shooting without many hits. In proof of which I will say that we had a brisk fire of artillery from 10:30 to 2:30, together with a sharp spattering of rifle fire, and yet we only lost a few killed and wounded.

Shortly before dark, we halted and made camp for the night. On the right, Colonel Burgwyn had driven the enemy to within five miles of New Bern. We have taken on our reconnaissance in force about 150 prisoners, three guns and five caissons.

Near one of the captured cannon was a Yankee who had obviously tried to desert. He must have been caught in the act and tied hand and foot. When the Federals saw that they must abandon their cannon, they blew the fellow's brains out. And so our men found him today, nearly headless, still tied and stretched out on the ground near the captured cannon.

DECEMBER 30, 1862—TUESDAY
KINSTON, NORTH CAROLINA

Kinston has a population of two or three thousand inhabitants. It also contains several fine churches and a number of public buildings that show traces of considerable architectural beauty. The streets are wide and well paved and bordered by neatly-laid brick sidewalks. Many beautiful lawns extend from the fronts of dwellings of the street, neatly enclosed by iron palisades and abutting on well-kept garden. Several houses were surrounded with tastefully arranged flowerbeds. Here and there, nice, comfortable-looking arbors and roomy porticos are seen. Just the place an old soldier could comfortably enjoy one's self of a summer evening with a friend, book, cigar or glass of Madeira.

I found the largest hotel in Kinston and entered the barroom. As I was about to sit down, I encountered the seemingly ubiquitous Flex G. de Fontaine, correspondent of the *Charleston Courier*. At first I hardly recognized de Fontaine. He looked so whole and hearty. He was, however, his familiar, smiling, convivial self, although considerably bronzed by exposure.

I learned during our conversation that he had hurriedly left Charleston to cover the battle of Goldsboro for the *Courier*. I asked him the difference between luxuriating among the lovely ladies and other titillations of Charleston and campaigning in the mud and swamps of eastern North Carolina with bullets occasionally flying over head. He thought a moment and then replied thoughtfully:

"General, it is the difference between new corn whiskey and champagne. This thing of going where glory waits you is not what it is cracked up to be by poets who have never smelt powder and pretty women who can very well afford to hurry their heroes off to the wars while they loll on sofas and flirt. Glory forsooth! You know full well, General, there is little glory in war. The fleas give you greeting, the sand ticks and camp itch almost drive you mad, then, maybe, an ugly bullet flies nearby with its cursed song that doesn't make any music at all! To lie in the trenches, mud up to the eyes; to sleep in a ditch of bilge water, with a rock or log for a pillow and snake for a bed fellow; to cook your own rations and sit down to a bit of bacon and hard tack and consider coffee of the blackest description, sans sugar, a luxury for a king; to be shot at by every Yankee that blunders upon a sight of you and be kept from morning 'til night dodging the visits of shells as one dodges a dun around a corner. Now that's one picture.

"But to leave Charleston, ah, that was hard! The night before I left, I was invited out to dine where there were a brace of beauties full of music, love and sympathy. I dined in a saloon with a carpet that melted beneath my tread. There was rosewood furniture and marble slabs and full-length mirrors which reflected satisfaction from every wall. I sat at a table covered with roasts and fricassees and wines and sweet meats, a napkin in my lap and the gentle embraces of an easy chair pressing against me. I drank cafe au lait out of china cups and listened to delicious music. It was heaven and, my God, just thinking of it makes my thirsty."

When we asked for wine, the eyes of the Negro waiter nearly started from their sockets. As in a flurried manner, he assured us that such an article he had not seen for over six months. "Nor whiskey?" we inquired.

"Nor whiskey, sah," he answered. So, at our suggestion, he showed us into a private room. Here I produced my private flask and offered it to de Fontaine. He took the flask, drank and wiped his mouth with the back of his hand, smiled and said, "Brandy?'

"Aye," said I.

After watching this, the darky left the room and de Fontaine and I sat at a small table talking and sharing pulls from the flask. After a short period of time, the darky re-entered the room and seated himself at the table. De Fontaine, astonished at this unceremonious intrusion, exclaimed, "What you doing here, boy!"

"'thought I'd like to try drink ob that dar brandy."

"Hell!" shouted de Fontaine. "Do you suppose I'm going to drink with a damn common nigger? Leave boy, til we're through. We'll save a pull for you."

After our brief sojourn at the hotel, de Fontaine decided to accompany me to the salt warehouse located near the railroad depot. As de Fontaine was temporarily without a horse, we rode in an army wagon drawn by six mules and loaded with molasses, hard tack, salt pork and coffee. A very black Negro drove the team who rejoiced in the name of Socrates. The black philosopher pronounced his name as if it were Succotash.

When we climbed onto the back of the wagon, he dropped a pair of boots from which he was scraping deposits of Kinston mud and gave us a glad welcome.

"I g-g-got plenty of room in de b-b-b-back," he said. He was an inveterate stammerer.

In this lumbering ark, we took passage over a very muddy road. We had gone but a little way when we stuck fast in the mud. Thereupon black Socrates fell into a rage and whipped the mules unmercifully. They kicked and pulled and floundered until, at last, extricating themselves. We started again. We rode but only a short way when, again, we were stuck in the mud. Socrates repeated his previous gestures of whipping and swearing in a most unphilosophic way until I could endure it no longer.

"What are you beating the mules for?" I remonstrated. "Don't you see they are doin" the best they can?"

"L-l-l-lors, Gen'rel, dey onter be l-l-licked. M-m-m-mules is dat mean dey allers won't

p-p-p-pull a bit when dey knows yer g-g-g-oin' somewhar in a hurry."

But I have digressed and must now return to the scene. We were once again on the road and had been making good time when we, unfortunately, once again, got stuck in a deep mud hole. After several attempts to urge the mules forward with his whip, Socrates jumped to the ground and suggested we do the same to lighten the load.

Socrates tried talking to the mules and, at one point, threw back his head, showed all his gleaming teeth, and yelled, "Git goin' t-t-thar m-m-mules! G-g-git goin' or I gonna lick y-y-you!"

With this he drew the whip back over his head, but it slipped out of his hand and fell to the ground behind him. He turned to pick it up, bending over and, unfortunately offering a splendid view of his down-sitter to the lead mule. The mule, as I have stated, no dumb beast, saw his chance and gave a kick, striking the vulnerable darky square in the hind end and sending him head first into a large mud puddle.

Socrates came up spitting mud. He looked at the mules in astonishment and the, while wiping the mud from his face, exclaimed, "L-l-lawdy. I-th-th-th-think dat mule do th-th-that on purpose!"

The rest of the trip was uneventful and we were dropped off at the salt warehouse. We last saw Socrates still ploughing through the mud, but evidently reconciled to his mules as he was sitting aloft on the driver's seat, shouting in a singing recitative:

> "A-a-an' I hope to g-g-gain d-d-de promise lan', g-g-g-lory hall-e-e-lujah!
> "Lod', I-I-I-hope to gain de promise lan', d-d-dat I d-d-d-do!
> "Glory, glory, how I l-l-lub my Savior, d-d-d-dat I do!"

DECEMBER 31, 1862—WEDNESDAY
CAMP—NEAR NEW BERN, NORTH CAROLINA

I managed yesterday to secure two hundred bushels of salt and various other supplies for the brigade. The shortage of salt has been a severe one and, without it, the meat we are able to obtain spoils in a short time. A large supply of salt, over 2,000 bushels had recently arrived from the

Wilmington Saltworks and I was, after much bargaining, fortunately able to induce the quartermaster to send some salt immediately by train.

The trip back to camp in the cars was an interesting one. After securing a place for de Fontaine's and my horse in one of the freight cars, we walked to the train depot and waited for the conductor to assign us to a car. I was much interested in a gang of about one hundred young men, slaves, who were being loaded into the Negro cars. They were, I was informed, being taken to dig entrenchments for Colonel S. D. Pool's battalion of heavy artillery, which is placed at the obstruction in the Neuse River below Kinston.

Most of the slaves were young men between eighteen and twenty-five. They were all comfortably clad in that coarse, but warm and serviceable cloth, called "Negro cloth." Some of the young men seemed reckless and a little merry, but I saw no indications of anything like joy. The general aspect of the group was that of silence, patience and weariness.

There were several overseers in charge of the party, with the head overseer riding at the head of the gang of slaves on a dirty white horse. His assistant, also on horseback, brought up the rear, riding with whip in hand and rifle cocked lest one of the blacks attempt to escape. A tall, well-built Negro led the slaves, each of whom had an iron collar about his neck. A chain of iron a hundred feet in length passed through the hasp of each padlock which held the collar securely. For added security, the slaves were also handcuffed by twos.

As the slaves were being lead into the cars, de Fontaine, ever on the outlook for a story, approached the assistant overseer and engaged him in conversation. He learned that he had been for eight years a driver on a Louisiana plantation where he learned to handle the whip with marvelous dexterity and precision. The overseer said that any slave who did not do his task or failed to be properly submissive was flogged.

He then dismounted and showed his lash to de Fontaine and I, explaining, with some pride, the method he used in selecting the "bull whip."

"I like to find a stock of convenient length, the butt end of which I load with lead to give the whip force. I split the stock to within a foot or so of the butt into twelve strips and take a piece of tanned leather, divided into eight strips, and draw it on to the stock so that the split ends can be plaited together. This is done until the leather tapers down to quite a fine point, the whip being altogether about six feet long and as limber and lithesome as a snake. The thong does not bruise but cuts and I have become quite expert in the use of it. Would you believe I can swing the whip so as to only raise the skin and draw blood or, if provoked, lash through a quarter inch board with one good blow. The whip can also be employed to calm down savage bulls or unruly cattle. I have seen many a horse cut with it right through the hollow of the flank and the animal brought quivering to the ground. Now you see the way to use it is to whirl it around until the thong acquires a certain forward power and then to let the end of the thong fall across the back or legs of the slave. I seldom have to use the whip, but if I am forced to, I will, for I don't mind whipping a nigger more than I would a dog."

We boarded one of the passenger cars of the long train of twenty-six cars, as it stood waiting at the depot. There were two powerful engines attached, which panted and puffed and shrieked as if eager to be off.

The car was filled with officers, many covered and spattered with the red mud which marks everything and everybody. Some were smoking pell-mell and passing around an occasional bottle of vile spirits. Others, wrapped in their blankets, were hoping to enjoy some needed sleep.

A few miles out of Kinston, a couple of officers near us, got into a violent wrangle regarding rumors of incompetency, cowardice and intoxication exhibited by General Evans during the battle of Kinston. As I listened to this argument, which gradually attracted everybody's attention, I noticed that de Fontaine was listening eagerly to the dispute. He kept edging forward a seat at a time, as he had opportunity and was soon sitting near the noisy belligerents.

The officer critical of General Evans repeated all the stereotyped accusations against Evans that are currently in vogue, and asserted that many of the officers in General Evan's command were critical of his actions at Kinston and wanted him to be removed from command. "Any private in the ranks could have carried out things better than General Evans. It was disgraceful the way he acted and sacrificed his men," loudly proclaimed Evan's critic. "He was drunk as usual and it seems he did not know what he was about. He was not too drunk, however, to keep in a safe place and did not show himself once on the battlefield."

At this juncture, de Fontaine arose, stepped in front of the man who professed to have such damaging knowledge of General Evans, and quietly asked the gentleman his name. The latter replied pompously that he was Captain Powers of a South Carolina regiment, giving its number.

"You seem to know all about the battle of Kinston," continued de Fontaine.

"I have a right to know," replied the captain, bracing up, "I went through it from beginning to end."

Two men stood confronting each other in silence, the captain considerably netted by the manner of the questioner, de Fontaine, grim in expression and emitting a torrent of scorn, wrath and hate from his glittering eyes. The correspondent commenced deliberately again, "I am always willing to overlook and forgive misstatements about men and events…"

"But I am not mistaken about what happened and what came under my own observation," hotly interrupted the captain.

"But," replied de Fontaine, "when a man pretending to be a gentleman and an officer makes slanderous charges against a friend of mine, claims to have witnessed what I know never occurred and to have heard orders which I know were never given, I intend to confront his lies on the spot. You are a liar, I know. You are a coward, I believe. I'll be ten to one you were not in the battle of Kinston."

The captain, stung by de Fontaine's accusations, began to bluster and threaten to fight. Some of his comrades urged him to defend his honor by throwing his assailant head foremost through the car window. Every one in the car crowded forward. Until then but two men had avowed their support for General Evans. But the audacity of de Fontaine and his determined defense of Evans against all odds struck a responsive chord in most of those present. A general roar of shouts, yells and guffaws in support of de Fontaine burst from all.

The captain saw the odds against him and wisely adopted the role of discretion at fearful expense to his reputation and valor. He demanded de Fontaine's name, blustered and swore fearfully, but committed no breach of the peace.

"My name is of no consequence," the correspondent replied to all questioners. "If I must get into a public row, I prefer to do so unknown."

Later de Fontaine said to me, "I am aware that I acted strongly in confronting the captain, but not more so than circumstances demanded. And not more so than shall always be the case when I can speak the truth to right a wrong."

JANUARY 1, 1863—WEDNESDAY
CAMP—NEAR NEW BERN, NORTH CAROLINA

The year 1862 has passed away and a new one is upon us. How great the contrast in the condition of our young Republic do I see when compared to what it was twelve months ago. Then, the fall of Fort Donelson, Roanoke and New Bern and the continued success of our foes had cast gloom over the whole Confederacy. These reverses, though, called forth more energy and we have the happy result in the present, bright state of our affairs. The victory at Fredericksburg has sent the Federals reeling back from their third attempt on Richmond. Our capital is still safe. The Yankees endeavoring to cut our line of communication at Goldsboro did little or no material damage and fled hastily back to their fortifications at New Bern. In summation, I must say that the sky is brighter today than it has been since the inception of the revolution.

Late last night, one of the company cooks in Colonel Burgwyn's regiment was severely scalded while cooking rations for the company to use while on picket the next day, by upsetting a kettle of boiling water over his legs. He was carried to his tent and someone ran to the doctor's quarters and asked assistant surgeon Hunter to come and dress the man's injuries. It was a cold disagreeable night and the doctor was comfortable in bed. He refused to get up and gave this heartless answer, "He won't die before the morning and I'm not going to get out in the cold night for any damned soldier in the army."

But there was a surprise in store for Doctor Hunter. Colonel Burgwyn was told of the matter and, in a few minutes, a file of men marched the doctor at bayonet point to where the injured man was. After the poor soldier's hurts were dressed, Doctor Hunter was then escorted to Colonel Burgwyn's tent and told in no uncertain terms that the next time he refused to treat a man, the colonel would have him placed in irons and confined to the guardhouse.

Colonel Burgwyn, though one of the strictest disciplinarians in the army, has a heart as tender as a woman's and will not permit any wrong or injury to be perpetrated on any soldier in the regiment. This is one reason he has the devotion and loyalty of his men.

Our picket lines extend some fifteen miles from camp and about twelve from New Bern. Our pickets and those of the enemy are about five miles apart. We captured more Yankee deserters yesterday. When being asked their reasons for deserting, they generally reply, "Our government has broken faith with us. We enlisted to fight for the union, not to liberate the God damn niggers!"

This entry begins the fourth volume of my journal. I might have easily found events enough to double it, but many incidents occurred when I had little time to take notes. I think I have accomplished my object in this journal—to fix the experiences of my soldiering in time and place that I may easily recall them in years to come, should my life be spared.

JANUARY 3, 1863—SATURDAY
CAMP—NEAR NEW BERN, NORTH CAROLINA

This morning, shortly after breakfast, an orderly brought to my tent a budget of letters, the morning's mail. One announces the shipment of a wagonload of hospital stores that will arrive today. Another scolds roundly because an important letter sent a week ago has not been answered, while a copy of the answer in the copying-book is indisputable proof that it was received attention, but has in some way miscarried. A third is the agonizing letter of a mother and widow, blistered with tears, begging piteously that I will search out and send to her tidings of her only son, who she has not heard from since the battle of Fredericksburg. A fourth is a letter from two nine-year-old girls from Raleigh, who have, between them, earned five dollars and wish to spend it for the "brave soldiers." God bless these two children. A fifth is from the wife of a soldier of the brigade, begging permission to visit her husband. And so on through a package of twenty, thirty, forty, sometimes fifty letters. And this is but the first mail of the day—usually the heaviest however.

Then begins the task of replying to these multitudinous epistles—a work that this morning was interrupted by Captain Young bearing a new letter. The captain informed me it was from General Pender at Fredericksburg and thought it important enough to bring it to me personally.

I thanked the captain, carefully opened the letter and begin reading. It is the worst possible news and my hands trembled as I realized the message it contained.

"Camp Fredericksburg, Virginia

"December 22, 1862

"Dear General Pettigrew,

"I take pen in hand to inform you of the recent death of Chaplain Alfred Keys. I know the high regard you held for the chaplain and the strong bonds of friendship formed between you while he served under your command as Chaplain of the 22nd North Carolina.

'In early December, Chaplain Keys was disappointed in not being able to share the hardships of the campaign with the brigade. The rigors of army life had incapacitated him for duty and sent him to the hospital. There he was reluctantly brought to the conclusion that he must conform to the army surgeon's advice and relinquish his position.

"His taking leave was a melancholy affair. On Sunday, December 7, his regiment was drawn up in a hollow square, at the close of dress parade, for the purpose of holding religious services and hearing the farewell address of Chaplain Keys. The services were deeply moving. Rev. Keys expressed his great regret in parting with the regiment whose officers and soldiers he regarded after so many hardships and perils shared together, as his brothers. Nothing but the state of his health, which had suffered greatly from exposure in the field, induced him to leave them.

"On the 11th day of December 1862, the enemy began to attempt passage of the Rappahannock at Fredericksburg. Chaplain Keys watched the laying of the Yankee pontoon bridges with concern. He had indeed been discharged from all official obligations to the army and was scheduled to leave for Richmond the morning of the 12th.

"It was at this point that he volunteered to join General Barksdale's brigade of Mississippians who were guarding the riverfront and disputing the enemy crossing. The decision to suddenly volunteer was totally unexpected. He was arrayed in the uniform of a staff officer, which made him a special mark for the sharpshooters. I had cautioned him early in the day against exposing himself and reminded him that, as he had his discharge on his person, he would not be exchanged if taken prisoner. Unfortunately, there was no time or place to change his uniform. The last I saw of him was on the outskirts of Fredericksburg, musket in hand, heading for the riverfront.

"I later talked with Captain Dunn of Barksdale's staff and he gave me the following account of Keys' movements.

"'I first saw Chaplain Keys in the streets of Fredericksburg on the 11th December ultimo, at about half-past three, where I was in command of 25 men deployed as sharpshooters. We were near Caroline Street, I think. At this time, Chaplain Keys accosted me with the usual military salute. He had a musket in his hand and said, 'Captain, I must do something for my country. What shall I do?' I replied that there never was a better time than the present and he could take a place on my left. I thought he would give a good account of himself for he was calm and collected. In fact, I have seldom seen a person on the field so calm and mild in his demeanor. I suspected he was a veteran of many battles.

"'His position was directly in front of a grocery store. He fell five minutes after he took it, having fired once or twice. I think he fell from the ball that entered his hip. He was also shot in the arm, but may not have been aware of this wound, as sometimes soldiers are not conscious of wounds in battle.

"'Once the chaplain fell, I detailed a group of men to move him and another wounded man to the rear. I last saw the chaplain being carried toward the rear. He was a brave man and fell with his face to the foe.

"The chaplain was taken to a field hospital in the rear and kindly cared for. After the battle, I was able to visit Rev. Keys on December 16 and felt he was doing well. On my next visit on December 20th, it was obvious the grand-looking man was dying.

"'Can I do anything for you, Chaplain?' I inquired, after the surgeon had examined him for the last time.

"'Too late. Too late, General!' was his only reply, slightly shaking his head.

"'Have you friends to whom you wish me to write?'

"He drew from an inside vest pocket—for his clothing was not removed—a letter enclosing a photograph of a most lovely woman. 'You wish me to write to the person who has sent you this letter?'

"He nodded slightly and feebly whispered, 'My wife.'

"How strange, I thought, for as long as I had known Rev. Keys, I had never heard him mention his wife or even speak that often of his home. How little we sometimes really know about those we work or serve with.

"As I left to talk to the surgeon, I watched him lift the photograph and gaze at it earnestly for a few seconds, press it to his lips and then clasp it in both hands. When I returned to his bed, some ten minutes later, he was still looking upward, his hands still clasping the photograph and his face was irradiated with the most heavenly smile I have ever seen on any face. I spoke to him, but he seemed to hear not and there was a far-away look in the gaze, as though his vision reached beyond my little world. I stood still, awestruck. The ward master approached and laid his finger on the wrist. 'He has rendered his soul to God,' he whispered.

"So ended the life of a noble man of God. He died doing his duty and I for one shall miss him greatly.

"Most truly yours,

"Dorsey Pender, General"

I am indebted to General Pender for his account of the last days of Chaplain Keys. Although I never saw Keys after the battle of Seven Pines, I am proud to say we were friends. I did all I could to show him my appreciation of our friendship as well as to keep our days together with the 22nd in his memory. We wrote to each other often. The drum which we obey said "Roll call" and I left him. This is what makes the life of soldier so hard. You form acquaintances and they become dear friends. The order says, "March" and you know you may never see them again. And now I am haunted by his memory and the knowledge he is gone forever.

JANUARY 5, 1863—MONDAY
CAMP—NEAR NEW BERN, NORTH CAROLINA

Late yesterday afternoon, the staff and I had just finished an inspection of the brigade general hospital and were standing near headquarters assisting ourselves to coffee, bread and cold ham. The day was cold and it was a sight to behold—the officers in big coats and bigger sabres standing talking and laughing with the bright light of the campfire on their faces.

Our feast was interrupted by the arrival of an orderly with a message informing me of a railroad accident that had just been reported about three miles from camp. I quickly issued orders to the brigade surgeons and quartermaster department to assist the survivors. My horse was still saddled, so I gulped down the coffee, clasped the remains of the bread and ham in my saddlebag and in two minutes was off—two orderlies, Captain Young and I winding our way toward the scene of the accident.

When we arrived, we learned from a dazed survivor that the train of ten or twelve cars was passing over a bridge that spanned a small, deep river, when the bridge gave way. The train was midway at the bridge when the first car left the iron and the cars in the rear followed, cutting the ties and bridge timbers nearly off. This precipitated the engine, tender and four cars into the water. The engineer and fireman were killed.

Captain Walsh of the Eighth North Carolina, who was in one of the cars that went into the water, but escaped, had taken charge of affairs around the wreck. When we arrived, he was busily engaged in taking out the dead and burying them.

Those on board the ill-fated train were mostly soldiers on their way to various regiments in Eastern North Carolina. One of the civilians killed was W. P. Grayson, formerly cashier of the Bank of Raleigh. This gentleman had been for some time engaged as an agent for the government buying cotton. When the accident occurred, he had in his possession $40,000 in currency, which was recovered.

The body of Mr. Becham, the engineer, was also recovered and his remains were taken to his residence at Goldsboro. The remains of Mr. Grayson and the 18 soldiers who died were buried near the place where the disaster occurred. Their graves were marked so that they could be identified by friends. Coffins were prepared and the interments conducted with as much respect as possible under the circumstances. The

454   The Long Lost Journal of Confederate General James Johnson Pettigrew

papers and valuables of the deceased were placed in charge of Dr. Middleton, regimental surgeon of the 26th North Carolina. He will endeavor to return the valuables to the appropriate parties.

One of the dead was a young slave named Ed, property of Mr. Grayson. I looked upon Ed's body as it lay by the track. His body was unmarked as he had drowned. He had lost his shirt and I was struck by the fact that, for some reason, his pants were considerably shorter than his shoes. His lifeless eyes were open as well as his mouth, revealing a full set of white teeth. His body was turned over to a party of Negroes and he was buried in a separate place not far from the bridge. As dirt was being shoveled upon the body of poor Ed, the slaves began singing a Negro melody.

> "Ed the slave was of African birth,
> "He was bought for a bagful of gold;
> "He was counted as part of the salt of the earth,
> "But he died today, very young.
> "Twas his last request, so we laid him away,
> "In a grave by the rails.
> "Wake me up was his charge at the first break of day,
> "Wake me up for the great Jubilee.
> "There's a good time comin', it's almost here,
> "Twas long, long, on the way.
> "Now run tell Elijah to hurry up Pomp,
> "To meet us at the gum-tree down by the swamp,
> "To wake Ed today."

If Ed would not wake under the fervency which moved the burial party, melody and volume will do little to accomplish it. I marveled at the power of body and mind that was thrown into this melody which expressed their strong faith in God's ultimate deliverance from the troubles of this world.

One of the survivors was a young soldier who fell off a flat car and had both legs cut off—the left foot above the ankle, the right above the knee. The poor fellow was lying by the tracks when the surgeons arrived to help. It was a most fearful maiming. The lad spoke of his mother as deprived of her only son. "Oh! My mother," he sobbed. "Four children and only one boy and here I am cut down. How I wanted to be a soldier." The he groaned with agony and said, "Oh, how I suffer."

The doctors tried to comfort him. "Possibly you may recover."

He was in great pain and answered, "Oh no. I'll never live to see tomorrow!"

The surgeons gave him whiskey and prepared for the unavoidable operation. The leg bones were ground to pieces like a fingernail for size and there was no hope for either leg. He was then chloroformed and, thankfully, unconscious of his agony. It was no use, the injuries were too severe and he died that night.

The Richmond newspapers received today contain a dispatch from General Bragg which brings all in the camp great joy and causes even enemies to pause and shake hands in the street. Bragg attacked Rosecran's army near Murfreesboro and gained a great victory. He says he drove the Federals from all their positions except in the extreme left. After ten hours of fighting, he occupied the whole of the field except the enemy stronghold on the left. We have captured thirty-one guns, two generals, 4,000 prisoners and 200 wagons. This is a Western dispatch, it is true, but it has Bragg's name to it and he does not willingly exaggerate.

JANUARY 6, 1863—TUESDAY
CAMP—NEAR NEW BERN, NORTH CAROLINA

A short time ago, Captain Gilman was assigned to the command of the axe-corps. Although one of the most corpulent officers of the brigade, he is a fine soldier-like man of about thirty-five with broad shoulders, a florid complexion, and bright eyes. He wears his whiskers and mustaches in the English fashion and is extremely affable. Before I assigned him to the command, I had a short visit with him and was rather surprised when his massive frame proved too much for a feeble camp stool, which caused his sudden disappearance accompanied by a loud crash in the midst of a discussion. Despite his bulk, he has undoubtedly acquired the entire confidence of all the officers and soldiers under him.

This morning a man named Gibbs, who is brave and, when sober, a good soldier but a devil incarnate when drunk, was brought to the guard tent in a state of howling intoxication. He had been imbibing heavily all night and early this morning. As he invariably attacked everyone who came near him when in that condition, he was bound hand and foot and even then it was dangerous to approach him.

Shortly after the arrest and incarceration of Gibbs, Captain Gilman reported to me with a member of his axe company who balked at duty and refused to help in felling trees. The man was reported to be extremely lazy and a coward as well. Gilman suspected that his refusal to work was due to the fact that his company had been fired on the night before.

I had the reluctant soldier brought to me and he made the same positive declination to work which had been previously made to Captain Gilman. He was a stout, heavy fellow of ponderous proportions. As he stood before me, the perspiration ran in rivulets down the creases of his fat physiognomy. He was obviously extremely nervous and a rather comical-looking fellow.

I asked him once more if he still refused to do his duty as a soldier. He then made to me the same positive declination to go on duty, which had previously been made to the captain.

"Very well then," I said. "You will go to the guard tent."

The fat one signified a decided preference for that assignment than to work with Gilman's axe company and walked off with a very satisfied air. I could only smile and think that if my large friend knew who was to be his companion in confinement, he would have not so cheerfully accepted his punishment. The guard tent was a large commodious "Sibley" and the slacker was introduced into it without ceremony. The opening was tightly strapped behind. Captain Gilman and a good many of his men gathered about the tent, for all felt sure that Gibbs would instantly attack anyone who entered it and, even bound as he was, would be formidable. They were not disappointed. In a few seconds, the sound of struggling could be heard within the tent and the sides of it bulged as if someone was being thrown about. Soon after, agonizing cries for help were heard. I was inclined, at first, to give no heed to the pleas for help, but they soon became so vociferous being accompanied by assertions that Gibbs was devouring him, or more accurately, "biting my leg off," that I thought it best to investigate.

When Gilman and I entered, we found the stout one prostrate and Gibbs fastened upon him like a bulldog with his teeth firmly gripping the fleshy part of his plump thigh. Gibbs was a large man of impressive strength and he had seized his unfortunate tent companion and pushed him about until he lost his footing and then immediately nipped him.

It was with some difficulty that we pulled Gibbs off and released his thoroughly frightened victim. After a brief interval, I asked if he was now ready to do duty with Gilman's axe company. He answered firmly that he was still of the same mind and wouldn't do duty.

"Very well, then," I said. "You must go back to the guard tent."

"My God, General!" He howled, perfectly aghast. "You are not going to put me in that tent again with that madman! That cannibal!"

I assured him that I would certainly do so unless he performed his fair share of duty. He pondered the matter for a short time, no doubt wondering if he could survive another go around with the carnivorous Gibbs. He then ruefully consented to go with the axe company. A few minutes afterward, I saw him march away with the others, shouldering an axe and limping slightly. He had a large wet rag bound around his leg.

This afternoon the weather was uncommonly warm and the officers of the various regiments tested the speed of their favorite steeds upon a makeshift racetrack near the camp. Lt. Colonel Lane of the 26th raced a magnificent horse, a light chestnut sorrel with blaze face and "white stockings," named "White Eye." Before the war, he had belonged to different horsey gentlemen in the city of Charlotte. At one time, he was being ridden toward Center Street. The street was blocked by heavy teams, but White Eye would stop for nothing. He jumped, rider and all, over a loaded coal cart to the other side of the street and continued on his way. The lieutenant colonel, needless to say, won most of the races although he was given a good run by Adjutant Hughes on a black horse named "Clodhopper."

The quintessence of the sport was obtained during the last race of the day. This matched four darkies each representing a regiment of the brigade. They were mounted on mules. One of the riders looked familiar. When I heard him reply to a question that his mule's name was "L-L-L-Lightning," I knew it was my old acquaintance, Socrates.

Many bets were of course placed on the outcome of the race and the four mules entered: Flash, Beauregard, Jeff Davis and Lightning. Colonel Burgwyn, foolishly I thought, placed a wager on Lightning. I bet on an athletic-looking darky riding Jeff Davis.

The four mules and their riders were lined up at the starting line and the large throng hushed awaiting the starting signal. The flag was dropped and the mules dashed from the starting line with a roar from the assemblage. All dashed away. That is, except Lightning. He wouldn't budge. With one buck he sent the saddle and Socrates half-way down his neck. After dismounting and coaxing and walking around him to induce as much docility as possible, Socrates again mounted.

With a smile on his face and an attitude of certainty in Lightning's will to show his potential, Socrates yelled, "G-G-Get mule!" and slapped his steed on the rear. The second buck was worse than the first. This time, Lightning bucked the saddle well-nigh to his ears and propelled Socrates on an aerial flight some distance down the track.

Me thinks this marks the end of the legendary racing career of L-L-L-Lightning and his flying black jockey. The mule is reputed to be extremely fast, but seems a little slow off the starting line.

JANUARY 12, 1863—MONDAY
CAMP—NEAR NEW BERN, NORTH CAROLINA

Some time ago, there came into the area a Negro who pretended to be very religious. For a time he visited the various farms and plantations in the area singing and talking to the darkies about the joys of God. His manner was to get upon a stump and sing religious songs, many of his own compositions. He had a good voice, an intelligent manner of speaking and the slaves enjoyed his visits. They would gather around him in large numbers, hear his songs and exhortations, receive his notions, and then he would go to the next plantation and repeat; and so he spent his time.

Major Negley, a cavalry officer, became suspicious when a Negro came to him to report that the stranger was trying to induce the slaves to run away and go to New Bern and enlist in one of the forming Negro regiments. The Negro was such an ignorant fellow that Major Negley could hardly believe his report. He then sent him back telling him to bring us more definite information. He was a field hand, barefooted and very black, but loyal to our cause. "If de stranger, a Yankee spy, I will come back an' tell yer all." With these words, this poor proprietor of a dilapidated pair of pants and shirt started off.

A day or two later, the Negro returned to Major Negley bringing word of a song of the stranger was teaching to the slaves. The words of the song that delighted the darkies were as follows:

"Say, darkies, hab you seen de massa
"Wid de mufftache on him face
"Go down de road somtime dis mornin',
"Like he's goin' to leab de place?
"He seen a smoke way up de ribber,
"Whar de linkun gunboats lay.
"He took his hat an' left berry sudden,
"An' I spec he's rund away!
"De massa run? Ha! Ha!
"De darky stay? Ho! Ho!
"It mus' be now de king-um am a comin', an' de yar ob jubilee!"

The Negro informer reported to the major that the slaves at once caught the melody and spirit of the song and would often sing it as many as a dozen times until the tune and the words stayed with them.

This was enough for Major Negley and he at once had the Negro stranger arrested on suspicion of being a spy. He was put in the provost guardhouse in Kinston, which was a long storeroom. One dark, rainy night, the guard fell asleep and the fellow slipped by him. A citizen, who was walking by, gave the alarm and told the guard to go after the fellow and bring him back. The guard was afraid to leave his post and the rascal would have escaped had not the citizen seized a gun and ran after the Negro and brought him to a halt. After his recapture, he was thoroughly examined and a map of our troop positions and U. S. Army enlistment papers were found on him.

The Negro was a Yankee spy and was soon tried by a military court and sentenced to a spy's fate.

Yesterday morning, the reveille awoke the camps at the first trace of dawn. A "special order" required every enlisted man in the Kinston garrison, not on duty or excused by the surgeon to be present, and hence the entire garrison was formed on three sides of a hollow square on a wide plain outside the town. At six o'clock the funeral cortege moved from the town headed by the provost marshal and a band with a sepulchral dirge. The condemned Negro was preceded by a squad of cavalry, a platoon of infantry, followed by a hollow square of soldiers with reversed arms in which an ambulance moved, containing the manacled victim sitting upon the end of a plain pine box—his coffin.

When the cortege arrived at the gallows, the condemned Negro was marched up the steps to the gallows, while four soldiers bearing his coffin placed it at the rear of the elevated platform.

A large congregation of slaves had been gathered to witness the fate of one who was disloyal to the South. The dirge, the roll of muffled drums, the weeping, haggard darky women and children made it an aggravating scene for weak nerves.

Just before the hood was to be placed over his head, the condemned was asked if he had any last words. Speaking loudly in a brave voice, the spy uttered his final wordy statement. "I entered this world a slave in the midst of a country where most honored writings declare that all men have a right to liberty. I had imprinted upon my body no mark which could be made to signify that my destiny was to be that of a bondsman. Neither was there any angel stood by, at the hour of my birth, to hand my body over, by the authority of heaven, to be the property of a fellow man. No, but I was a slave because my countrymen had made it lawful in utter contempt of the declared will of heaven for the strong to lay hold of the weak and to buy and sell them as marketable goods."

He continued, "Now, you may hang me, but you cannot hang the cause I die for nor can you hang every slave who yearns for freedom, for to do so, you would have hanging lifeless from the gallows all your bondsmen—for all men, if they say or not, yearn to be free. When I consented to assume the dangerous task which I undertook, I knew well its penalty in the advent of capture. I do not deny the charge of being a spy and I am proud of the service I have rendered my race and country. I expect nothing from your hands but death and I meet that fate with the consciousness of having faithfully performed my duty to the best of my ability. While I thank God that I have been successful in doing harm to the Confederacy, I am satisfied with my lot. Though I walk through the valley of the shadow of death, I fear no evil. For his rod and staff comfort me. Go ahead with your hanging."

This speech had a marked effect upon the many slaves gathered to watch the hanging and I'm sure that every Negro's heart throbbed in sympathy with the brave man whose life the cruel mandate of war decreed should be forfeited.

Then, as the rays of the sun broke through a cloud, the fatal word was given. The trap strung and the spy was dangling between earth and eternity. I watched astonished as a change came over one of the old Negro aunties at the scene. Turning about and facing the provost marshal with her large, lustrous eyes blazing with excitement, she spoke in a tone and manner that would have befitted a seer uttering a prophecy.

"Oh Lord! Oh Lord! Tars a day a-comin'! Tars a day a-comin'!" She said with right hand uplifted. "I hear de rumblin' ob de chariots! I see de flashing ob de guns! White folks' blood is a-runnin' on de ground like a ribber an' de dead's heaped up dat high!" She measured up to the level of her shoulder as she continued. "Oh Lord! Aris', in your anger rise up again the rage of my enemies. Awake oh Lord! An' decree justice. Oh Lord! Gib me de pleasure ob livin' til de day when I shall see these such sobers shot down like de wolves when dey come hungry out o' de woods!"

The auntie left the scene followed by a large group of women and children singing a hymn. They sang it with the strong barbaric accent of the native African and, with those indescribable upward turns and those deep gutturals that give such a wild, peculiar power to Negro singing. The auntie, with a powerful voice of great harmony, walked in the center of the crowd and sang alone the first two lines.

"I see de angels beck'nin'. I hear dem call me 'way.

"I see de golden city an' de eberlastin' day!"

Then, the whole group, with a mighty rush of melody and astonishing enthusiasm, joined in the chorus:

"Oh, I'm goin' home to glory—won't yer go along wid me

"Whar de blessed angels beckon an' de Lord my savior be?"

How strange, I thought, they have just stood by helplessly while one of their own has just been hung and not one of them probably has a dollar in their pocket, yet they leave singing joyous songs of praise to God. I may not understand such faith, but I surely admire it.

JANUARY 17, 1863—SATURDAY
GOLDSBORO, NORTH CAROLINA

I took the cars to Goldsboro on military business yesterday morning. Once seated, my attention was drawn to an attentive mother endeavoring to put a hooped skirt under the dress of a young girl without exhibiting to a curious public the small girl's legs, which attempt on her part was a lamentable failure.

During a stop at one of the obscure places on the way, a planter came on board, apparently from a plantation not far from the rails. He sat at the front of the car and soon made several boon companions. They proceeded to do their best to empty a large jug of whiskey. As the drinking progressed, the planter made himself revoltingly conspicuous by his loud, boisterous talk and rowdyism. I left the intoxicated trio when the train arrived at Goldsboro glad to get out of the eminently close locomotive dormitory.

Late in the afternoon, my business completed, I directed my steps to the Webster Hotel on Walnut Street. My favorite staying place in

Goldsboro, the Webster is a massive three-story brick structure, ornamented by two balconies, each with seven wooden pillar supports. Seven massive pillars of brick, plaster coated, resting on the masonry neath the walk, sustain their weight.

Entering the hotel, I passed through the lobby into the bar. This area is composed of two rooms, thrown into one with a massive oak beam across the ceiling. The saloon was a commodious abode with ample light from three large windows and always struck me as a cheerful place for the locals to sit arduously in for serious drinking.

I noticed, much to my surprise, the obnoxious planter still in the flush of his debauch, holding forth at the bar. In loud tones and with a swaggering air, he proclaimed, "When I am dry, I drink whiskey. When I am hungry, I drink whiskey. When I am hot, I drink whiskey. When I am cold, I drink whiskey. I just keep pouring it down all the while. I had rather drink whiskey than eat or sleep! I came to Goldsboro for a bust. I never expect to get nearer to heaven than when I drink whiskey in Goldsboro. If I don't bust it this afternoon, I'll surely do it tonight!"

This was followed by a discourse on his slaves. "The damned niggers! If they don't work well while I am gone, they'll get it. I tell you what I do when I've been gone on a spree. When I go home, if I find the damned niggers have not done good work, I just take 'em and lick 'em like hell! Yes, I lick 'em like hell! God Almighty never yet made a nigger that can get the best of me!"

I could see through a blue haze of cigar smoke to the far corner of the bar and there sat three young men, handsomely dressed, smoking and chatting pleasantly and leisurely. While thus engaged in whiling away the time, the planter steered a course toward them and took a seat at their table. Then, displaying his insolent manners, he managed to intrude into their conversation, turning its course, meanwhile, to the army.

Raising his voice, he began his harangue by demanding, "How is it, gentlemen, that you in the full tide of health with apparently plenty of time and money, well brought up, and all that...how is it that you sit here idly and see others serving in the cause of the Confederacy, fighting...and being wounded and sickened to death for your sake?"

The young men tried to ignore him, but soon realized that it was near impossible to ignore one so deep in his cups. Pounding his hand on the table, he declared, "Well don't just sit there, I demand a response!"

"Sir," responded one, "the army would suit me well enough but for one thing, if you will pull off that neatly fitting shoe and roll up my drawers, you will find a leg made of leather straps and iron ribs. The original, I left at Sharpsburg where I served with A. P. Hill."

"As for me," remarked the second, "if you will take the trouble to feel this left arm, you will discover that it is stiff and almost lifeless. When I stand upon my right foot, also, I am balancing on my toes. The heel is gone. These wounds were the result of Yankee balls at the second battle of Manassas."

The third youth scarcely knew what to say, but looked daggers at the lubricated planter and finally broke out, "I was only sixteen when I joined and on the march to Sharpsburg broke down, got put in one of the meanest hospitals in the South and came out paralyzed on one side." He also held up a shriveled and lifeless arm.

"And may I ask, sir," he added scornfully, "what keeps you out of the service? You seem to be in excellent vigor!"

"Me? I..." The planter paused and then answered, "Why...ahem...I'm not in because of the Overseer Exemption. Now, I gave serious thought at taking a crack at those cowardly Yankees, but I have over 100 Negroes under my care. You see, gentlemen, I manage these slaves well and keep them in proper subjection, but if I am taken away, they would be at large on the community and entirely demoralize the corn crop. Some shallow-minded persons believe that any man can run a plantation and manage the harvesting and a gang of Negroes, but there are few who have the ability to do this. And in my opinion, it requires more sense and talents to direct a large farm and a number of Negroes than it does to be just another faceless number, serving in the ranks. You see, gentlemen, the loss of my crop of corn and wheat would be a serious one to the quartermaster when he wanted supplies in the present scarcity."

He continued, "The present year I sold the Confederate quartermasters 4,000 bushels of corn. The feeding of an army in my opinion is of as much importance as equipping it with arms, for no man can fight without food no matter how well armed."

His haughty speech over, the planter arose, turned on his heel and walked away, appearing eminently satisfied with himself, to join his drinking companions at the bar. One of the young lads gazed at him as he departed and in an angry tone of voice remarked, "It seems this is a rich man's war and a poor man's fight!"

Later, reflecting in the quiet of my hotel room, I realized all too well it is indeed not difficult to get material for a grumble if one will but look about in this world. Such is the case of the exemption for the drunken planter. I know many planters who have left their plantations for the army, but I am also aware that the Exemption Act of 1862 exempted one white male, either owner or overseer, on every plantation with twenty slaves or more. Like most North Carolinians, I abhor this "20 Nigger" law as gross class legislation and discrimination, but the Confederate congress and President Davis seem little inclined to change or modify it.

JANUARY 19, 1863—MONDAY
OLD NORTH STAR HOTEL—WILMINGTON, NORTH CAROLINA

I left Goldsboro under orders this morning to meet with General Whiting who commands at Wilmington and General Beauregard who commands at Charleston. In the advent of a Yankee attack, my brigade may be needed to move by rail rapidly to either place.

I got onto the railway cars at 9:30 a.m. after a lengthy wait in line. A sentry stands at the door of each railway car and examines the papers of every passenger with great strictness. Even after that inspection, the same ceremony is performed by an officer of the provost marshal's department, who accompanies every train.

I found the train crowded with a lot of prosperous and ponderous old gentlemen who were members of the home guard, returning to their homes after being called to duty during the enemy advance on Goldsboro. They wore their uniforms uneasily as a farmer's boy wears his Sunday suit. Most were hampered by muskets which they did not know how to handle. Those who carried sabres experienced much inconvenience when walking on account of the propensity of these weapons to get between their legs. They were all swearing by a multitudinous variety of strange gods that death was preferable to existence under the detested Yankee's rule.

In citizen clothes at my side, sat a wounded cavalry lieutenant from Bragg's army who was returning to his home in Wilmington to recuperate. The wound in his neck gave him great pain and he looked upon the home guard warriors with much contempt. After an outburst of mild invective, he gave this opinion of their value to the cause:

> "You know, General," said he, "there are over 2,000 volunteers in Wilmington regularly drilled and prepared to resist raids. These men are exempted from the conscription, either on account of their age, nationality or other cause, or have purchased substitutes. I have always thought the Northern blood is cold; the Southern is full of life and passion, but the blood of these antiquated fellows runs old. God help us if we have to rely on men such as these."

It was not long before I noticed a farmer sitting not far away who had obviously taken a great fancy to me. He kept staring and pointing toward me while talking to his wife. Finally, he left his seat and approached saying, "I recognized you from your likeness in the papers, General Beauregard, and I've always wanted to shake hands with you. Look Ma, I'm shaking hands with General Beauregard!"

"I'm not General Beauregard," I protested.

"Not Beauregard," he harrumphed, "What general are you then?"

"General Pettigrew."

"But I never heard of General Pettigrew."

"I'm sorry to disappoint you, but I have always rather enjoyed being General Pettigrew."

Obviously disappointed he had shaken hands with a Pettigrew and not a Beauregard, but anxious to learn something of the military situation, he asked how the Confederate cause was progressing.

"Very well," I answered. "We have whipped the Yankees at Fredericksburg and they have retreated from Goldsboro back to New Bern. If our victories continue, our independence will soon be recognized.

The train arrived in Wilmington at nine o'clock in the evening. I stepped onto the platform and boldly asked for a cab. My modest request was greeted with laughter by the few loafers who were there assembled. If the Negro cabmen had not gone to the front, their horses had. Knowing my way, however, I undertook a forced march to the City Hotel only a short distance away.

After registering, I was put into a room in an obscure corner of the top story, accessible only by an enterprising and difficult escalade. It had the advantage of being traversed by certain steam pipes, connected with a large iron tank in the garret. They leaked and gave me the benefit of an atmosphere warmed by escaping steam and flavored with oleaginous vapors. Also of a persistent noise, sounding somewhat like frying sausages.

After depositing my luggage, I went downstairs to get a bite to eat. While I was away, the hotel's functionaries took the liberty of putting a suspicious-looking stranger in my room. There I found him ensconced in a cot and breathing stertorously when I went upstairs for the night.

As they would do nothing about it, I packed my luggage and ventured forth into the night. I had made up my mind. I must either sleep on the wharves of the river, desert to Charleston, commit a breach of peace and get lodging in the watch house, or return by train to Goldsboro. After a short search, I found a quiet little hotel on the corner of Market and Fourth streets.

JANUARY 20, 1863—TUESDAY
OLD NORTH STAR HOTEL—WILMINGTON, NORTH CAROLINA

I arose early and took my breakfast in the hotel dining room. While at my table and musing over a cup of hot coffee, I was joined unbidden by a local undertaker who was in the hotel to measure a coffin for a guest who had died during the night. This visit did little to leave me in a cheerful state of mind, although he was in fine spirits in the anticipation of the demand for his stock in trade.

Presenting me with his card, he politely expressed the hope I would give him my business, if I needed anything in his line. Just before leaving my table, he took a glass of brandy and water. Holding the glass in his hand, which was yet stained with coffin paint, he drank a toast to my health. I viewed this toast with some skepticism, knowing full well that his interests lie in the opposite direction. After he said his farewell and was walking away, I thought to myself, *You won't bury me, you damned rascal, if I do die.*

Also eating breakfast was a "character" I had been introduced to on the train named Captain Wegner. He was in Wilmington to outfit a ship for running the blockade. Cotton purchased at five cents a pound could be shipped from here to England where it sold for fifty-five cents a pound. Wegner claimed to have already made over one hundred thousand dollars in gold running cotton through the blockade.

As he was only sitting a few tables from me and was engaged in conversation with two other speculators, I couldn't help but overhear most of the conversation. Although, perhaps conversation is the wrong word. It was more of a soliloquy by Wegner expressing great satisfaction with his current situation.

"These are hard times," claimed Wegner, "but here I am a rich prosperous man with nothing to do but enjoy myself. Egad, what a blessing this war is to me. Worth over one hundred thousand dollars, I am."
He continued with an absurd, sanctimonious tone:

"Now, one hundred thousand dollars is nothing, yet it is quite a little plum. When the war began, I wasn't worth a cent, unless it was in debts. Now I am well off. I must say I'm no fool. It was a stroke of genius to enlist those darkies in Boston and sell them in Galveston. It made me thirty thousand dollars, it did.

"You know, the Yankees wanted to hang me for selling those darkies. Can you believe that? Hang a white man for selling a bunch of apes from Africa? What was I supposed to do, teach them to read and write, make doctors and lawyers out of 'em? Ha! That's a good one. A darky doctor.

"I'm a business man, I am. Let the poor people enlist and fight for the Confederacy. It takes a smart man to keep out of the war, himself, and entice others to go. Poor fools! They actually want to fight for their country!

"Yes, I have now one hundred thousand dollars in gold in an English bank. This gold averages me eight per cent interest. Eight per cent on one hundred thousand dollars is eight thousand and I get it in gold.

"And the beauty—Oh!—it is. I don't have one cent of taxes to pay. Isn't it nice? I hope the Confederacy and this war go on for a long time. Yes, sir! Rich man hold gold, poor man fight, die and pay taxes. Yes, sir! Isn't it nice!"

I left the dining room in disgust. Wegner gloats over one hundred thousand dollars in blood money while Chaplain Keys and thousands of soldier patriots lie moldering in their graves. Good God! What a world! It's at times like these when the world makes little or no sense that I must tell myself that God has so arranged things so that evil eventually brings judgement on itself. If I did not believe this, I think I would go stark raving mad!

I walked back to the hotel along Water Street that parallels the Cape Fear River. The steamer Sumter was lying at one of the docks. They were taking off her decks in order to get out two enormous English guns, brought from England. These guns were six hundred and forty pounders. One of them, I was told by a dock worker, was to be sent to Charleston. The other was to go to Fort Fisher.

I continued along until I came upon a large gang of Negro stevedores loading cotton onto a blockade runner. As they worked, they sang one of their peculiar songs. I stopped to listen to the rhythmical melody. The blacks were led in their song by a jet-black, or rather I should say, wine-black leader. His complexion was of a sort of rich, clear depth without a trace of spottiness. To my eye, he was very handsome. He was over six feet high, perfectly proportioned and of apparently inexhaustible strength and activity. He strode about the bales like a panther. I never saw such a tread.

The big black would sing the first line of the song solo, follow with the response line, then sang the second solo line. After which the rest of the workers would sing a response. Each line of the solo part, with the exception of an occasional repetition, was different.

So intrigued was I by this singing that I took pencil and pen to record the words.

> *Oh how I hate to load de cotton*
> *Bales so big, this work's done rotten*
> *Big boy, can't you load 'em?*

Big boy, can't you load 'em?
Big boy, can't you load 'em?
Big boy, can't you load 'em?
Here we is to load de cotton

Moses stood on that Sinai Mount,
Praisin' the Lord too many times to count.
Big boy, can't you load 'em?
Big boy, can't you load 'em?
Big boy, can't you load 'em?
Here we is to load de cotton.

Even while loading the large bales, the stevedores were tapping their feet and clapping their hands, for the Negro sings not only with his voice, but his body as well. I listened to the singing for some time and, as I left, I thought that wherever else the Almighty has given to his other children, He has given to the African a capacity for song as responsive to the forces of life as the cock-crow of the rooster is to the newborn dawn.

JANUARY 21, 1863—WEDNESDAY
OLD NORTH STATE HOTEL—WILMINGTON, NORTH CAROLINA

I walked through a chilling rain this morning to General Whiting's headquarters on the northwest corner of Market and Third streets. Entering the plain, wooden two-story dwelling, I found General Whiting with Colonel Duncan, his aide de camp, in the front room on the left side of the hall. In an armchair facing the fireplace was seated a general officer, stout in figure and of medium stature. As I paused to take off my coat, he turned toward the door and, as he did so, I recognized him to be General Beauregard. His face born an expression of weariness, while his clothes were wet and his trousers and top-boots spattered with mud.

Called "Old Bory" by his men, though he is not yet forty-five, the hero of Sumter has twice been relived of important command. First in the east, where he had routed McDowell's invasion attempt at Manassas. Then in the west, where he had saved his badly outnumbered army by giving the federal general Halleck the slip and Corinth. Now he was back on the scene of his first glory as the commander of the forces around Charleston and Savannah.

With General Beauregard were his son, Rene, who served on his staff, and Major A. R. Chisolm, who has served with the general since the bombardment of Fort Sumter.

After greetings and introductions, we all moved to the center of the room where a large map was spread over two tables pulled together.

At General Whiting's request, Colonel Duncan pointed out various positions on the map and described the general military situation. He began by surmising that the Yankees would soon be making one of the most important moves on the chess board of this war, a move on which much is staked, for a success to their arms will prolong the contest, while a signal defeat may do much in bringing it to a speedy close. Shifting the scene of their operations from Virginia to North Carolina, the principal aim of the Federals may now be to obtain possession of our interior lines of communication. As in the western county, they have fruitlessly sought to divide the Confederacy by holding the Mississippi river, so here they could make the same attempt by severing the Weldon and Wilmington Railroad and taking possession of as much of the state as they can hold.

Asking us to glance at the map, Duncan pointed out how the capture of Weldon alone would tend to effect this object. If the Yankees held Weldon, we could in that event go neither to Raleigh and thence south by way of Charlotte and Columbia, or to Wilmington. Our railways would all be rendered useless. Duncan emphasized that the possession of Weldon would give the Yankees a new base of operations against

Petersburg and Richmond from the south and against Raleigh, Warrenton, Hillsboro and other places in North Carolina.

He suggested that Wilmington is also a prize coveted by the Yankees. Capture of this port would close off one of the major arteries to Europe and free additional Yankee ships for the blockade of Charleston.

Because of their base at New Bern, the enemy can strike at any of four important points: Weldon, Goldsboro, Wilmington, and Charleston. To this end, they have a well-organized force that Duncan estimated at sixty thousand men.

"You can see," concluded Duncan, "the effort we will have to make to check this tremendous movement."

During this discussion, General Beauregard sat for some time immovable as a rock and as silent as the sphinx, but listened intently to all that was said. After Duncan finished, he straightened himself up in his chair and his features assumed an air of animation, and, in a tone of voice which manifested deep interest in the discussion, he began to fire whole volleys of questions at the officers present. So intelligent were his inquiries that he made a deep impression on everyone by the quickness of his perception and his knowledge of the situation.

After discussing the possibility of defending Weldon, Beauregard turned to me and asked, "How long will it take to bring your brigade and that of Evans to Wilmington and Charleston?"

I replied, "Three to four days to Wilmington and four to five to Charleston."

He then asked, "Can General Evans be relied on. He is reputed to have been drunk at Kinston?'

"A court martial has exonerated him," I replied. "I feel he will do his duty and do it well."

General Beauregard then had his son place a new map on the table that displayed in some detail the defenses of Charleston. He then began to discuss his plans for the defense of the city. He explained that defying Union sea power, Mobile on the gulf, and Wilmington, Savannah and Charleston on the Atlantic remained in Confederate hands. Of these four, it was clear at least to Beauregard that the one the Federals coveted most was the last, variously referred to in their newspapers and the "cradle of secession."

"If I had been aboard a vessel on the Charleston bar, just outside the harbor in 1861," explained Beauregard, "I would have said that no vessel ever constructed could run the gauntlet to that city. The harbor was impregnable because Fort Sumter was built to knock wooden ships to pieces. Now the Yankees have built iron ships to knock Fort Sumter to pieces.

"On my return to Charleston in September of 1862, to assume command," he continued, "I found the defenses of the city in bad and incomplete condition. A recommendation had even been made by my immediate predecessor that the outer defenses of Charleston Harbor should be given up as untenable against the ironclads and monitors then known to be under construction at the North and that the water line of the city of Charleston should be made the sole line of defense."

The general then told us that the Northern press was so sure that their forces could capture Charleston that they boasted about it in their papers. He had his son read to us a copy of the *New York Tribune* for January 5, 1863, which said:

Doom hangs over wicked Charleston. That viper's nest and breeding place of rebellion will soon be infested with Union arms. If there is any city deserving of holocaustic infamy, it is Charleston. Should its inhabitants choose to make its site a desert, blasted by fire, we do not think many tears would be shed. Travelers of today are quite undecided as to the location of ancient Carthage. Travelers of 2862 may be in the same doubt about Charleston."

Beauregard informed us that he was determined that Charleston should not suffer the fate of New Orleans no matter what force the Yankees brought against it.

To this end, he had been working to make the city as nearly impregnable as military science and Confederate resources would allow. Forts Sumter and Moultrie have been repaired and strengthened. Eight other forts mounting a total of seventy-five guns of various calibers have been erected between the city and the bar. Every buoy has been removed in the channels and the channels obstructed. Across the right hand channel is a cable supported by casks, and to the cable have been hung ropes, nets, torpedoes, and whatever else can be thought of. The left hand channel is filled with piles driving into the bottom and projecting six or eight feet out of the water. In the center is a passage forty feet wide, defended by torpedoes containing twelve hundred pounds of powder. Seven or eight heavy guns can easily be trained on this one spot. Half a mile above the first row was a second and above that, a third. The ship which might safely pass all would be under the fire of the Confederate ironclads, Palmetto State and Chicora, which are stationed near the Charleston docks. "No craft ever built and no commander ever born, not even a vile Yankee, would dare such a passage," claimed Beauregard.

General Whiting then asked if the torpedoes were powerful enough to sink a Yankee ironclad.

"Our first torpedoes were crude affairs," explained Beauregard. "The torpedo itself was a demijohn or a keg and the design was to fire it by percussion. Not one out of eight was of any value. The powder would get damp, or the torpedo would be carried away, or something would occur to render it useless." He then told the story of a Confederate engineer who helped to plant torpedoes in the James River. The engineer witnessed one explode after a steamer had passed over it and was a hundred feet beyond. The explosion threw a column of water fifty feet high and ran a wave over two feet high along the shores for a mile. Had the explosion occurred under the steamer, she would have been lifted high in the air and destroyed.

Beauregard then commented in a most enthusiastic manner on a new device now being used by the Confederacy, the electric torpedo. "In December, 1862, as the Yankee gun boat Cario was steaming up the Yazoo River, she ran a foul of an electric torpedo and was sent to the bottom in six minutes. That river for a space of a dozen miles was defended by these monsters. The torpedo itself was nothing more than a demijohn full of powder, anchored three feet below the surface. The float was a log and this was anchored or held in place by a rope running to the bank of either shore. By pulling, or slackening, these lines, the torpedo could be held at any desired distance from the surface. Anything striking the line on either side sent the galvanic spark straight to the powder.

"Think of the damage this torpedo caused, gentlemen," he continued, "had a battery of six guns been discharged at the Cario and all the missiles struck in one spot. That damage could hardly have been greater. A hole large enough to back a buggy into was torn open in her bows, all her heavy guns upset on their backs, the boilers lifted off their beds, nearly every man knocked down, and several severely injured. There was not time to save a thing before she went down in twenty-five feet of water. Thus in six minutes, at less than fifty dollars expense, the Confederates destroyed over three hundred thousand dollars worth of federal property and cleared the river of a much-dreaded gun boat. I would remind you that there are dozens of these electric torpedoes below the waters of Charleston Harbor."

Not content with this, General Beauregard had set marker buoys at known ranges in the harbor with the corresponding elevations chalked on the breeches of the cannon. He also informed us that Major Chisolm has developed what is called a torpedo ram. This, explained the general, is a small, swift boat with a pole projecting from its brow under water. At the end of the pole is a torpedo. The idea is for the ram to sneak up on a Yankee ironclad, presumably at night, and strike the pole into the most vulnerable part of the ship below the water line. The general believes that these boats will revolutionize naval warfare. With six of these, he feels he can hold Charleston against any naval force the Federals can mount.

As a last ditch measure of defense to be employed if all else fails, the general said he has encouraged the organization of a unit known as the Tigers made up of volunteers whose assignment is to hurl explosives down the smokestacks of such enemy ships that manage to enter the harbor and approach the city docks. "The Yankee ironclads might indeed be invincible," mused Beauregard. "Some say so. Some say not. But one thing is fairly certain, the argument will be likely settled on the day the enemy tries to bring them into Charleston Harbor."

He then pounded his fist on the table and emphasized that Charleston will not be surrendered. "The city will be defended to the least extremity. It will be defended street by street and, if necessary, burned to the ground!"

At ten o'clock, we finished our discussion and General Beauregard arose to leave the table, telling us that as he had arrived from Charleston late last night, he needed to retire to a bed upstairs to get some much-needed rest. As he walked across the floor, his fatigue was very perceptible, but, before he departed, he made an appointment with General Whiting and I to accompany him tomorrow to make a personal inspection of Fort Fisher.

I dined tonight with Colonel Duncan and Major Chisolm. Good company but an unpalatable meal. Shoe leather called beefsteak, bread made of sour milk and poor flour, turkeys born before the flood and companions of Noah. The only redeeming feature of the culinary disaster was the excellent wine. After dinner, we adjourned to another room for cigars, to spend time in pleasant conversation. Both Duncan and Chisolm were wounded at First Manassas and discoursed on their adventures there.

Chisolm says Beauregard is a great man and never was his star higher than after First Manassas. Fantastic stories of his exploits were spread over the press. One Northern journal carried a story that during the battle, he had ridden a headless horse. People wrote to tell him he was the great captain of the Confederacy and the best hope for its independence. Musical composers rushed to the market songs and marches which bore such titles as "The Beauregard Manassas Quick-Step" and "General Beauregard's Grand Polka Militaire."

Chisolm gave us a most interesting account of his service with Beauregard, some of which he has detailed in a journal he kept titled "Journal of Events Before and during the Battle of First Manassas—July, 1861." I was spellbound by many of the things he told us, which enabled me to better understand the events that led to our victory.

JANUARY 22, 1863—THURSDAY
FORT FISHER—NORTH CAROLINA

When I arrived at Wharf Number 10 on Water Street this morning, I found two old ferry boats waiting to receive passengers. One of the ferries was being loaded with a large number of slaves who were going to be transported to work on the fortifications of Fort Fisher. First came, led by a driver carrying a whip, about sixty of the largest and strongest men I have ever seen together. They carried themselves loftily, each having a shovel or pick over the shoulder and walking with a free, powerful swing, like chasseurs on the march. Behind them came about thirty women. They were all in a simple uniform dress of a bluish color. Their skirts reached little below the knee. Their legs and feet were bare. On their heads they wore handkerchiefs, turban fashion. A lean and vigilant white overseer, on a brisk pony brought up the rear. The Negroes were in a jubilant spirit and sang and halloed as they marched down Water Street and onto the ferry.

General Whiting, who was standing near me, watched with interest as the slaves were loaded onto the ferry. "They are a fine-looking lot," he remarked, "and we need more of them. For every Sambo with a shovel frees up a Johnny to carry a gun."

"You're quite right, General," replied Beauregard. "I have had many captured Union soldiers tell me they are tired of attacking Rebel breast-works that are often impregnable. They complain quite loudly about this, finding the Negro with his pick and spade a greater hindrance to their progress than Confederate cannon balls."

Both ferries were soon under way, chugging along reassuringly at seven miles an hour. The staff officers aboard lolled comfortably on bales of hay, smoking cigars and sampling Colonel Duncan's Catawba. Beauregard, Whiting and I chatted pleasantly while enjoying the beauty of river travel.

Going down, we met three steamers coming up the river, having successfully run the blockade, the Lady Davis, the Advance, and the Owl. We exchanged cheers as they passed us, but the great sight is when they come up to the wharves in Wilmington. They all dress up with flags as if for a victory and as the ships which belong to the same company do the same, the spectacle is very gay. The cheering too is vociferous and many a champagne cork is popped in celebration of the enormous profit that a successful trip brings. The moon is the blockade runner's greatest enemy, but these three vessels today had come in, notwith-standing the moon, which did not set til three o'clock in the morning.

As we approached the mouth of the Cape Fear River, a rocket shot up from the shore, signaling our approach to the gun crews at Fort Fisher. Approaching the dock, General Whiting mentioned to General Beauregard that the hardest shore line to blockade was that of the Cape Fear River sector, for the river has two navigable outlets, forty miles apart, both guarded by forts and coastal batteries. Because of this, the Federals have to keep on duty two flotillas requiring almost twice as many ships as the twenty needed to close off Charleston. Even with all these ships, the blockade was ineffective, for in the first two weeks of January alone, blockade runners docked in Wilmington with over 20,000 rifles, 1,000,000 ball cartridges, 2,000,000 percussion caps, 43 cannon, and 400 barrels of cannon powder.

The commander of Fort Fisher is 27-year-old Colonel Lamb. A handsome man of great tact and charm, he told us that he first assumed the command of the fort in July of 1862 and determined at once to build a fort that could withstand the heaviest fire of any guns in the American navy. "I had seen the effect of 11-inch shell," said Lamb, "and read about the force of the 15-inch shell. I believed that their penetrating power was well ascertained and could be provided against."

'Lamb himself sketched out the fort's basic design with help from General Whiting. The colonel employed as many as 1,000 men per day, including every slave he could get, usually working them seven days a week. It was hard work involving long circular lines of wheelbarrows pushed and pulled on wooden scaffolding. "It was very interesting," remarked Lamb, "to see two or three hundred wheelbarrows rolling in unison from the points of loading to those of dumping, returning in a circle and passing the loaders who shovel in hand threw sand in the barrows as they passed by without stopping."

Built in the shape of an up-side-down L, the fort stretches almost a half-mile across Confederate Point, from the river to the ocean, then snakes more than a mile down the beach, heavily armed with artillery all the way. This massive fortress is able to protect blockade runners coming in and out of New Inlet and strong enough to deter any attempt to close the river and formidable enough to resist Yankee land or sea assault.

Lamb was eager to have our party tour and inspect Fort Fisher and led us to Battery Buchan, a massive two-story earthwork, whose four heavy artillery pieces anchor the fort's southern flank. Two large eleven-inch Brooke cannon have been mounted in the battery to compliment its existing ten-inch Columbiads and, today, the guns were being test fired. The Brooke is a cast-iron smooth bore that weighs 25,500 pounds and can fire a 181-pound shot to 5,800 yards. Several months ago, another Brooke was being test fired when it exploded, spraying the gun crew with cast-iron fragments. When the smoke cleared, one artillery man lay headless near the wrecked cannon. Another was lying mangled n the sand with a huge piece of iron embedded in his stomach and sprawled nearby were half-dozen other wounded. Although prone to explode, Lamb has been eager to add the powerful Brookes to the fort's armament in an attempt to strengthen the already powerful fortification. Lamb told us he believed Fort Fisher could not be too strong, for it was vital to the defense of Wilmington and Wilmington was vital to the defense of the Confederacy.

From our starting point at Battery Buchan, it took our party over three hours to inspect the fort. As we stopped at various points, Lamb patiently answered questions from generals Beauregard, Whiting and myself.

While we were inspecting the Armstrong Battery a brief thunderstorm passed over and for awhile the volleys of thunder were resounding. It was at this time that we noticed something that was decidedly curious and which showed the instinct of dumb animals and how they remember their training. The peals of thunder emanating from the darkened sky were short and sharp, like the firing of heavy cannon.

Near the Armstrong Battery were several pieces of field artillery that could be used in case of attack to rush from place to place as an artillery reserve. The horses had been taken some distance from the guns and turned into a small green plot to eat grass. All at once, the heavy crashes of thunder broke over us and, at the first boom, the horses raised their heads, rushed to the guns, where they arranged themselves in their usual positions in the rear of them, evidently taking the peals of thunder for artillery firing.

A telegraph station had been erected at the lower end of the sea face and line had been strung on poles all the way to district headquarters in Wilmington. At the southern end of the sea face, a full mile from the Northeast Bastion, towers a mountainous sixty-foot-high artillery placement known as the Mound Battery.

Lamb informed us that it took three months to construct the Mound Battery. An old lighthouse had been dismantled to provide lumber for the scaffolding and a wall of underbrush had been planted at the Mound's base to retard erosion. To hasten completion, the ingenious Lamb built a small inclined railroad on which a steam-powered mining cart rolled back and forth from dawn to dusk carrying tons of sand to the top. Once the base was complete, Lamb designed a gun pit for the top, mounting a 10-inch Columbiad and a rifled 32-pounder. Both weapons are on moveable carriages and are capable of sustained plunging fire onto the decks of any Yankee ship foolish enough to come within range. Finally, Lamb has hollowed out the base of the Mound Battery to provide a bomb-proof shelter for its crews and also added a signal light on to serve as a marker for the blockade runners.

After we finished out tour, I had the opportunity to talk to many of the soldiers garrisoning the fort, something I always try to do whenever I visit a command. Rations, they said, were often inadequate, drinking water blackish and the "fever" a serious threat in warm weather.

"I am afraid this place is going to be very unhealthy this summer," one soldier told me.

Another said, "The rats get into the cistern in such quantities that the water tastes and smells very strong of the little devils which every body knows is far from being pleasant."

Indeed, the soldiers of the Northeast Bastion were at one time so plagued by rats, they undoubtedly would have welcomed the services of the Pied Piper of Hamlin. The Bastion and the tents in the vicinity of it were overrun with rats. But in this case, the soldiers' ingenuity equaled the magic of the piper's pipes. The scheme for the extermination of the rats originated with a sergeant of one of the gun crews. The homes of the rats were first to be flooded and then, as they sought safety in flight, they were to be clubbed to death. Under the supervision of the sergeant, some twenty men volunteered to carry water in kettles from the ocean to the rat holes. It was a weary job; the ocean was some fifty yards distant and gallon after gallon was emptied into the holes and all to no purpose.

Finally, as the water bearers were losing heart and roughly berating the sergeant for conceiving such a ludicrous plan, a single rat presented himself and quickly fell before the unerring club of the man who stood nearest. The spirits of the exterminators revived.

"More water! More water!" was the cry. More rats, more rats was the response. They came thick and fast, literally hordes of rats were abandoning their holes. Reinforcements were called for and, before the fray was over, one hundred men were engaged in battle.

As the rats continued to dart from their holes, the blows were laid on hard and the battlefield was soon strewn with hundreds of the foul pests. The affair was completely successful. The enemy routed and wholly exterminated, never to reappear. Those of little faith who had mocked the originator of the plan now accorded him his just deserts and were eternally grateful.

This evening between eight and nine, the band of the 36th North Carolina came over and serenaded General Beauregard. Its excellent music soon attracted a crowd of officers who formed a semi-circle around a huge bonfire in front of headquarters, sitting on the ground, standing or reclining as fancy prompted. Outside and a few paces retired was a large throng of the soldiery. Sitting by the fire on camp stools sat Colonel Lamb and his staff, and General Beauregard, Whiting and I. The weird light from the fire cast such a strange unearthly glare over the entire scene as indelibly to stamp it on the memory of all present. Speeches were called for from Beauregard and Whiting and they responded in words no less happy than the occasion demanded. After more music by the band, the speakers, the band and North Carolina were loudly cheered. The gathering then separated, realizing more than ever that they were a single brotherhood engaged in a glorious and just cause.

JANUARY 23, 1863—FRIDAY
OLD NORTH STATE HOTEL—WILMINGTON, NORTH CAROLINA

After the campfire serenade broke up last night, I went to my assigned quarters confident the rhythmic pounding of the waves upon the shore and the brisk ocean air would assure me a pleasant night's sleep, but my well-laid plans were waylaid. During the night, we were favored with quite a disturbance. The officer of the guard, who had pretensions of impressing General Beauregard, suddenly conceived an idea that it was proper for the sentries to call the hours. So we were awakened from our sweet slumber by loud nasal and otherwise discordant cries of, "Post number eight! Half-past twelve! All's well!" at every hour precisely. The sentries evidently considered it a good joke and, as they had to keep awake, determined no one else should sleep. So roared often and loud the sentries. Some of the officers, hastily roused, fancied the camp was on fire. Others conceived the sentinels were inebriated, others that the Yankees were in the camp, and others, again, like myself, didn't think anything about it, but growled and tried to drop off again to sleep.

"What was that howling?" asked General Whiting at breakfast.

"Yes, what did the confounded fools mean?" I interjected.

But the most indignant personage was Beauregard. "Jesus, Joseph and Mary!" he exclaimed. "The whole night I couldn't sleep. Are these guards at Fort Fisher all fools?"

The captain who served as the officer of the guard is now a much wiser lieutenant and Colonel Lamb assured us that will be the last of the singing sentinels.

The morning was further enlivened when two of the darky laborers found what they call "one er dese ere mortisses," by which they would say mortar shell. Their conjecture over this strange object went as follows:

> "Hullo, dars er mortiss. S'pose dat ar'll 'splode. 'splode! 'course it'll 'splode! No it won't. How's goin' to 'splode after it's been shot out er cannon? Bet yer one dollars it'll 'splode. Bet yere it wunt."

Then there was a tremendous report that shredded and blew down a captain's tent. As the smoke cleared, the captain could be seen struggling to free himself from the tent covering him. Miraculously, he had been left uninjured by the blast. At last he escaped and clad only in his drawers, rushed forth and collared a handful of the darks and demanded immediate explanation. Whereunto one replied, with the utmost simplicity, "Didn't mean nuffin', Cap'in. All de fault er dat stupid nigger. Said er mortiss wouldn't 'splode." Because of my great regard for decency, I cannot record here the captain's reply to that explanation.

This evening found me, once again, back in Wilmington and I had the pleasure of dining with one of the more noteworthy blockade runners, Augustus Charles Hobart-Hampden. The captain is a son of the sixth Early of Buckinghamshire and a Victoria Cross recipient (from heroic action in the Crimean War). He was also once the captain of Queen Victoria's yacht. He is an elegant, tall, bearded sea dog who delights in confounding the Yankees by adopting almost as many aliases as he has made voyaged through the blockade. On various occasions, he has called himself Roberts, Gullick, Hewett and Ridge.

We ended our conversation in the early evening, for I had much to do before I departed on tomorrow's early train to return to my brigade. As we parted, he looked at me with his dark eyes dancing and with outstretched hand said confidently, "God speed, General. I hope we meet again." He is a character with a dash and swagger I have seen in few men and I thought to myself that it is no ordinary man who captains a blockade runner. He who makes a success of it must have the cunning of a fox, the patience of Job, and the courage of a Spartan warrior.

JANUARY 24, 1863—SATURDAY
NEAR ROSE HILL, NORTH CAROLINA

When I arrived at the railroad depot early this morning, I was surprised to see a large crowd gathered around one of the passenger cars of the down train from Weldon. Approaching the train, I observed the undertaker's wagon drawn up and several men removing the body of a darky dressed in a Confederate uniform from one of the cars.

Curious as to what was transpiring, I stopped one of the departing passengers and learned firsthand of the tragic event which had occurred on the train last evening.

It seems that at about seven p.m. yesterday at the Everettsville depot, a large number of soldiers who were going home to Wilmington on leave got on board. As no arrangements had been made for their transportation, there was not a sufficiency of cars to accommodate them all with seats. Most of the soldiers had imbibed freely of liquor and were ripe for any rumpus. On passing through the cars in search of seats, some of them came across a Negro who occupied a seat in one corner of the car. This proved too much for them and they ordered him to get up and let white folks sit down. To this the Negro refused, telling them he was a free Negro and a soldier in the 16th Virginia Infantry and, as such, entitled to his seat. Angered by what they felt was nigger insolence, several of the soldiers seized the Negro by his clothes and made an effort to jerk him out of his seat.

The Negro resisted the drunken intruders and tried to push them away. Then, one of the soldiers struck the Negro a violent blow in the face whereupon the darky rose to his feet, pulled out pistol and, before it could be wrestled from his hand, discharged it at his antagonist who escaped injury, but the ball struck and passed through the left shoulder of another soldier who had taken no part in the affair. Immediately the Negro was set upon by half a dozen soldiers who wrestled him out to the car's platform and endeavored to thrust him down between the cars while the train was at full speed. Had they succeeded in their purpose, the Negro would have been literally cut or torn to pieces. However, the Negro was a large fellow of very powerful frame and held for dear life onto the iron railing until the train was stopped when he slipped off and tried to make his escape. The soldiers and a number of passengers started in pursuit and, as the Negro had been pretty well bruised in the scuffle, he was soon overtaken. As he turned to confront his pursuers, he picked up a large stick lying close by and began to swing it violently at those nearest him. It was at this point that one of the soldiers drew his revolver and fired. The ball struck the Negro in the forehead killing him instantly.

The name of the dead Negro was Pompay Tucker, who it was learned had gone to war as a body servant. During the Seven Days campaign, his master confessed his fright to his superior officer and Pompay received permission to take the coward's rifle and place. Pompay gave a good account of himself during the battle by killing several Union soldiers with his accurate marksmanship. In the winter of 1862, officers of the 16th Virginia Infantry had posted Pompay to guard the regiment's rations. While on duty, he mortally wounded a white private who tried to steal the supplies and only the intervention of General William Mahone prevented Pompay from being lynched.

One of the soldiers who was engaged in the affray with the Negro asserted that the black had no business on board the train and that no Negro should be allowed to sit down in any car where he was as long as a white man had to stand. Another reasoned that it was too bad the Negro was killed as he was a valuable one and might have sold for $1,500.

I later heard a small group of bystanders contending for the rights of the Negro, saying he had not fired until struck violently in the face. While others said they did not see anyone strike the Negro.

They were still arguing the matter as the undertaker's wagon with poor Pompay lying dead in back, drove away from the station. Whatever the cause of the argument, it was very clear who had lost it.

I left Wilmington at one p.m. The train was typical of those you see in the Confederacy these days. The engine was, for lack of a better word, a curiosity. The conductor called it a hunchback. It was an old worn-out machine loaded with clanking parallel rods, levers and valve gears very short and heavy, and flashing headlights as they dashed past vividly suggested pandemonium. Needless to say, it was impossible to sleep for any length of time under these conditions.

Seeking relief from boredom, I found two editions of the *Richmond Whig*. They abound in stories of the war. One account recounted a Yankee correspondent's talk with a lady from South Carolina about the policy of forming nigger regiments. I have copied from the article, which caused me no little amusement, below.

The lady was obviously furious." Just think how infamous it is that our gentlemen would have to go out and fight niggers and that every nigger they shoot is a thousand dollars out of their own pockets! Was there ever anything so outrageous?"

JANUARY 30, 1863—FRIDAY
CAMP NEAR NEW BERN, NORTH CAROLINA

Returned safely to camp yesterday. Found headquarters still in the same old place. I was also rather delighted to receive the warmest kind of welcome from my staff. I was in capital spirits until Captain Young entered my tent with a smug smile on his face and carrying a pile of papers. "New and unfinished business," he said and I soon found myself sitting at my desk laboring away at a mountain of paper.

I preserve here for prosperity some of the affairs I as an underpaid and overworked brigade commander must attend to.

The replacements who arrived during the night on January 14th have by and large fit in well with the brigade. They are fast on their way to becoming soldiers; however, one of the replacements, I understand, is a very curious specimen. He wears long hair and believes in universal peace and abhors blood shedding. It seems he wishes to tender his resignation and addressed me a note, of which the following is a copy.

"General,

"I want to report to you that I do lay down my arms, feeling myself entirely unfit for duty on account of my health and, also, conscientiously pledged to my church not to take up arms to kill. Also, I am no soldier. When I first heard the command "Order arms!" I dropped my musket and, taking out my notebook, began drawing an order on the government for what arms I needed. The sergeant didn't understand my confusion and ordered me to the guardhouse where I have spent much of the time since joining the brigade.

"I hope you will consider favorably my request.

"Yours truly."

I denied this request. We need all the soldiers we can get, even those who order arms from the Confederacy.

Another order of business concerned the copy of an application for a furlough from a private sent directly to me.

"January 27, 1863

"Camp Near New Bern, N.C.

"11th Reg. N.C. Vol.

"General Sir. I request a furlow 20 days to visit my home in Charlotte to arrange some unsettled business, also to make some important famley arrangements of grate impotance to myself and famley.

"Respectfully yours."

I learned from Colonel Leventhorpe the private had six children, the youngest a year old, and "General Sir" granted him a "furlow" immediately.

The next missive concerned the following complaint:

"General Pettigrew,

"Among the many evils prevalent in our brigade, there are two or three which I desire to call to the attention of the commanding general in order that they may be speedily remedied. The first of which I would speak is the great number of men employed on "extra duty" as wagoners, blacksmiths, butchers, artisans and hostlers, whose services are needed in the ranks, while the duties they are now performing might be easily supplied by Negroes hired for that purpose. Most of the men referred to are able-bodied, athletic soldiers, and would do excellent service with guns in their hands. There are a large number of Negro men in the South whose masters would be glad to hire them in the brigade for a very small recompense. They are equal if not superior to white men in manual labor. The general has only to issue an order directing the regimental quartermasters to hire Negro drivers, blacksmiths, et cetera, and order the men now doing those duties to report to their companies. You will see the brigade increased by over three hundred men capable of bearing arms and killing Yankees.

"The second subject that demands your attention is the manner in which post surgeons at camps of instruction receive substitutes who are physically incapacitated to perform military duty in the place of conscripts, who are feasting at home while their comrades are barring their breasts to the storm of battle. A letter from the general to the Secretary of War or President Davis might help end this evil practice.

"It is useless for me to say more concerning these evils—their pernicious and injurious effects are self-evident, and ought to be immediately corrected. A word to the wise is sufficient.

"Concerned"

I would have appreciated the letter from "Concerned" more if he would have had the courage of his convictions and signed his name. I do not acknowledge unsigned letters.

Lastly, I received this interesting letter from an officer of the 44th North Carolina.

"General Pettigrew,

"I am a bob-tailed second lieutenant paid eighty dollars per month. I was disabled by a wound received at Fredericksburg and sent to the rear. No government hospital being then open to me because I was an officer. Not being able to pay hotel or public house charges for board, necessity, as well as to see the dear ones at home, drove me to the far South to spend the period of my disability. My railroad fee to Mobile amounted to $65.25. The balance of a month's pay was left me to pay for my meals on the route at prices ranging from $1.50 to $2.00—as well as to splurge on when I got home. The same experience attended my return trip, thirty days afterwards. As I then compared my situation with that of a wounded friend who accompanied me—an "enlisted man"—whose traveling expenses were borne by the government, my reflections led me to depreciate the advantages of rank. Late experience since my return confirms the correctness of my incipient reflections. The greatest of the privileges enjoyed by officers at government prices from the commissary is a limited amount of government provender, provided there remains a surplus after issuing the regular rations to enlisted men and that this is a privilege you will appreciate for as you know our only other sources of supplies are the Kinston or Goldsboro markets. Supplied by the commissary, my mess bill for the next month including cook's wages and an occasional bunch of greens and a little vinegar to keep off scurvy, will amount to $79. The commissary informs me prices will go up soon. Now to come to the thrilling part of my appeal, where am I to get my next set of clothes (gold lace, according to the regulations included), my shoes, my hat—not to mention the luxuries of tobacco, of buying a daily paper, of responding to the next contribution for the suffering of ____, or orphans of ____, or having my clothes washed and the means of sustaining the dignity and responsibilities of my position. Alas! To all those a long farewell.

"I know nothing else to propose than that we all, from general down to bob-tails like myself, descend from the dignity of our high rank and, surrendering alike its responsibilities, its privileges and its honors, share and share alike with the private—food, clothing and eleven dollars a month furnished by the government.

"Faithfully yours,

Lieutenant Rob Mitchell."

This officer has a point of legitimate concern! The Confederate paper currency has suffered from depreciation. As a result, the pay of the officers is in reality a pittance and those without other resources are often in straits. Many boxes and hampers, however, come to the camp from home and are of some help to all.

I know that while I was in Wilmington, both General Whiting and General Beauregard told me they had sent petitions to the war department asking that rations might be issued to the officers the same as they are to the private soldiers. General Beauregard in his petition said that at existing prices, the pay of company officers was worth less than that of a private soldier, a point well verified by Lieutenant Mitchell.

It is now late and Friday has almost slipped away. The wind is high and my small stove smokes prodigiously. I am not sure if my eyes are blurry from the smoke or the multitude of paperwork I have waded through. Nevertheless, it is probably better to freeze to death than to be smoked to death, so I shall extinguish the fire and freeze.

FEBRUARY 1, 1863—SUNDAY
NEW CAMP—NORTH CAROLINA

Yesterday, we moved our headquarters camp to this place. It is located on the left of the road about three miles from our old camp. The twenty-sixth North Carolina lies quite near us. The 11th and 44th are still from two to three miles off, but very much closer than our old camp. Major Collins, the Quartermaster, picked this spot for our camp and has made a good selection. It is far enough off the road not to be disturbed by persons passing by and the tents are pitched under the brow of a small hill which, being crowned with small pines, shuts off all the cold north wind.

A recent editorial in the *New York Herald* says that the true Yankee policy should be to occupy every Southern port, open the Mississippi River and keep a couple of armies in strong, comfortable and healthy positions on the frontier of the South. Once their armies are in position, the Yankees will say to President Davis, "We are not going to advance into your jungle over your muddy roads. If you want a fight, you must come to us. If you don't want it, stay where you are and let us see which party will first be starved and wearied into submission."

Now, on to news of a lighter nature. In yesterday's *Richmond Whig*, I read with interest the following item:

"Matrimonial…comely young lady, of good education and high standing, desires to form the acquaintance of some young gentleman, that hath the love of women in his soul, in pursuance of matrimony.

Anyone desirous of forming an alliance through this novel medium will please address: Miss Evline Maxim, 59 James River Avenue, Richmond, Virginia."

Me thinks I felt my heart beat a bit faster as I read the missive of the fair Evline. Could such a flower of the South care for a hitherto hopeless bachelor with the frosts of many winters tingeing his patriarchal beard? If so, he could behold the glimmering prospect of change in his lonely manner of life loom up before him.

Here is a young lady of good education and of high standing who desires to marry somebody. I have just apprehended something, I'm somebody! She could marry me! I always did have an excessive weakness for high standing females and even some who had no standing.

Evline wants a young man with the love of women in his soul! I'm your man fair Evy—dear, gallant James Johnson Pettigrew—soul chuck full of love and overflowing—ready to be married and be converted into a quiet, respectable husband within 24 hours time. Summon my staff! Love has blinded me and I'm ready to resign my command and ride my charger to Richmond to claim my beloved.

Just thinking about it makes my hands tremble and my breath come in short gasps. How can I be expected to send a telegraph to Evline with my accustomed composure after the perusal of her card. I'm in an ecstasy of matrimonial excitement, nothing matters anymore except the beautiful Evline.

If this journal entry rambles and is an incoherent jumble of words, I must attribute it to the shattered condition of my nerves at the present writing. The matrimonial of Evline awakens emotions in my breast that were believed by my most distant elderly female relatives to have been smothered, years ago. The days of my early bachelorhood loom up grandly in my memory. And I take from my trunk my small mirror to see if any traces are left of my former beauty, but alas and alack, I recognize nary a trace.

Oh! Evy—Evy. Forget my looks and write to this old cuss won't you? Don't put your matrimonial in the papers anymore. Those abominable dashing young officers will be running all over Richmond after you. Beware of them, innocent, pure Evline. Beware of them. They're all married. They'll tell you they ain't, but don't believe them. If they annoy you, telegraph me. I shall fly to your side and be your champion. Till then, stay pure my love.

Stage lights dim. Brigadier General Pettigrew sits at his desk and stares longingly toward Richmond. He sighs, reads Evline's matrimonial once again and tucks it into a pocket near his heart. Scene closes. Stage lights go out. Curtain falls.

FEBRUARY 4, 1863—WEDNESDAY
NEW CAMP—NORTH CAROLINA

Colonel Burgwyn took supper with me tonight. It was a pleasant repast marred only by an altercation in the culinary department. Elias had secured a nigger boy, new to the camp to wait on our table. He was an extraordinary youth of muscular proportions, but unlike most darkies very solemn. It would, however, appear that beneath this serious and very black exterior worked a turbulent soul. The diminutive Elias, our chef, had informed me that the waiter was extremely indolent and had a marked antipathy to washing out dishes after the meal. This observation interested me as it is my observation that the washing of dishes by the camp darkies often tended rather to dirty than to cleanse the platter. When Elias reproved the lad for not washing the crockery, he replied with rude words. On being reproved again, he proposed to smite Elias, remarking that he would have no trouble knocking down a crippled nigger. This was too much and I had the sergeant of the guard remove him to the guardhouse where he could cool his passions for the night.

The colonel and I are quite fond of sitting awhile and talking after meals. Tonight was no exception and we had barely finished lighting our cigars when he told me the tale of three privates of his regiment who were arrested yesterday.

It seems the three, becoming bored with the routine of camp life, had rigged themselves out in outlandish outfits and went over to another regiment. As they approached the sentinel, he halted them and demanded, "who goes there?"

The leader replied in a theatrical voice, "The devil with the countersign."

The sentinel was a bit confused, but regained his composure enough to reply, "Advance one devil and give the countersign."

The leader advanced, gave the correct countersign and the guard said, "Pass devils."

Merrily they went to the next sentinel who demanded, "Who goes there?"

To this challenge, the leader replied, "A flock of sheep."

The guard, a veteran of many campaigns, immediately replied, "Advance, old buck and give the countersign."

The leader advanced and said, "Baa." Then the old veteran replied, "Advance sheep who have lost your way."

Thinking this great fun, the three were on their way to the next guard station when they were nabbed by Captain Porter, who had been alerted to the pranksters. The three devilish sheep are now mending their ways in the guardhouse…Baa…Baa…Baa.

FEBRUARY 6, 1863—FRIDAY
NEW CAMP—NORTH CAROLINA

I read with interest today an item in the *Charleston Mercury* on Captain Hazzard, whose exploits on St. Simons and other sea islands I have recorded previously in this journal. The captain is on a lecture tour to raise money to build another iron-clad for the Confederate Navy. It seems the captain has become quite zealous in his appearances, but to quote from the *Mercury*:

"The public is becoming a good deal disgusted with the recent behavior of the intrepid Captain Hazzard. The Richmond Examiner voices a growing sentiment when it says that 'Hazzard should be called in.' It adds: 'Captain Hazzard is zigzagging all over the South performing many one-night shows, delivering lectures on his sea island exploits and winding up the performance by kissing a lot of silly and maudlin young women who had better have stayed at home and behaved themselves.'

"Nor, it appears, does Captain Hazzard confine his labors to kissing women in the lecture hall. His appetite has apparently grown with what it feeds on and he now makes a practice of stopping at every railroad station, getting out on the platform and kissing all the girls within his reach. He does not, according to accounts, simply stand still and receive the salutes of the emotional females, but grabs them around the waist, throws their heads back on his shoulder and delivers the kisses in a manner which much practice has made highly effective. He exhibited a new technique recently in Savannah when several hours after an early afternoon lecture he rode his horse through the bar room of the Sumter Hotel scattering patrons left and right. Many were incensed at his conduct and all the more so when he bowed gently from his horse to kiss several comely bar-maids. 'He was intoxicated of course,' said one of the maids, 'but isn't he a marvelous smoocher and splendid rider.' However, at a stop in

Georgetown, it is said that several young women who were assaulted by Hazzard in a kissing frenzy were highly indignant and actually shed tears over the indignity.

"It was all well enough when the first enthusiastic hero-worshiping female imprinted a tender kiss upon Hazzard's handsome countenance. He was taken by surprise and blushed accordingly. But that innocent kiss created a phenomenon who now seems intent on kissing all the females south of the Mason-Dixon line.

"It is this newspaper's opinion that Hazzard is making an ass of himself and the Mercury's advice to the War Department and General Beauregard who commands this region is to call a halt to Hazzard's antics. It is stating the case rather mildly to say that Hazzard is rapidly alienating the respect of the Southern people and diminishing his heroic proportions by his barnstorming tour and, worst of all, by his nauseous osculation of the semi-hysterical women who throng to see or hear him. He is making himself both cheap and tiresome. He is diluting the worth of military achievement and clothing renown in the cheap habiliments of theatrical display. The country is sick of the whole tawdry, melodramatic performance and sensible and thoughtful men are wondering why his military superiors permit such melancholy nonsense."

The sentiments of the editors of the *Mercury* and *Examiner* aside, it appears that Captain Hazzard met his match several days ago in Charleston after a lecture at the Charleston Hotel. According to the newspapers, Hazzard was up to his usual antics of smooching all the females in sight. He had just planted a kiss on the full, ruby-red lips of a young belle when a shout was heard across the room. The kissing subsided at once and every eye in the hall was fixed upon a tall, almost Amazon, female who stood over six feet high, head erect with eyes fixed on Hazzard. She spoke in deep tones, which though not loud reached every ear in the hall and away through the throng at the doors and windows.

Hazzard looked at her aghast as she walked toward him saying, "Well, Captain, at last I have found you."

"Do I know you?" asked the captain, surprised at the sudden appearance of this spitfire.

Ignoring his question, she addressed Hazzard in the following manner, "There are those who say that a woman needs to be helped into carriages and lifted out of ditches and to have the best place everywhere. But no man ever helps me into carriages or out of mud puddles, or gives me the best place!" And then, standing next to Hazzard, she rose to her full height and, her voice to a pitch like rolling thunder, asked, "Ain't I a woman, Captain? Ain't I more woman than these frail creatures you have been spooning? Look at me! Look at my arm! (She then bared her right arm to the shoulder exposing her tremendous muscular power). "I have plowed and planted and gathered into barns and no man could head me! But I hear tell, Captain, that you are a man among men. Well, hearing this, I decided to come and get me one of those kisses you are throwing around. Now ain't I a woman? So kiss me!" Than, amid rows of applause, she puckered her lips and leaned toward a flabbergasted Captain Hazzard. It seems the great kisser then decided he had done enough work for one day, for he turned and darted toward the rear door, leaving the hall as the crowd laughed and jeered.

FEBRUARY 7, 1863—SATURDAY
NEW CAMP—NORTH CAROLINA

I slightly burned one of my feet yesterday. I was sitting by the fire with Captain Young making morning coffee. We each have a small tin kettle holding three pints or so, fitted with a tight cover. We call them muckets for want of a better name. By the way I believe I would throw away my field glasses before I would my mucket, it is so indispensable.

The cover of one was crowded down so tight there was no room for the steam to escape. It swallowed the indignity with commendable patience for a time, but finally lost all self-control and exploded, throwing hot coffee in all directions, but particularly in the direction of my left foot. It was not very badly scalded and I hope will be as good as new in a few days.

During our discussion Wednesday, Colonel Burgwyn and I decided to send a detail of soldiers to break up a Negro cabin located not far from his regiment. This place has been much frequented by soldiers of the lower type and is the source of much drunkenness, sickness and general mischief. In charge of the detail sent to arrest the parties was the brave and handsome Adjutant Hughes.

After reaching the cabin, it looked strangely deserted and Hughes decided to enter alone to scout out the situation. He had no sooner entered the cabin when he was seized from behind by a strong and quite good-looking young Negro wrench, spry and lithe as a cat. She threw both of her arms around him, under his own arms and gave him a hug like a bear, exclaiming, "Oh my handsome soldier! You are so young and handsome!" And much more of the same appreciative sort. Then, all pandemonium broke loose as Adjutant Hughes struggled to free himself from his new-found admirer. Trying to break loose, Hughes lost his balance and they both fell to the floor where there ensued an exhibition of Anglo-African wrestling and struggling altogether past description. The darky would give no quarter and held on to Hughes with a grip of steel. The wrestlers rolled and lunged all over the room, kicking over the chairs and tables, breaking dishes, covering the floor with food, butter, slops and water, rolling into the fireplace, scattering the ashes and becoming both of them thoroughly bedaubed with the dirt upon the floor. It was a battle, but finally, Hughes managed to gain the upper hand over the amorous darky. The contest over, the cabin, its contents and its crew went speedily beyond further opportunities for mischief in our vicinity. On the return to camp, the adjutant reported the mission's success to Colonel Burgwyn, but requested that some other more-deserving officer might be sent to "mop up the next old Negro cabin that must be cleaned out."

Anarchy reigns in parts of Eastern North Carolina. The cause of this unrest is companies of North Carolina Unionists armed and supplied by the Yankees., There are also partisan bands of those opposed to conscription and deserters from both armies—sometimes joined together—who operate under little or no higher authority and whose sole aim is survival.

Some of these outlaws perform conventional military service for the Federals. The Yankee General Foster arms them and outfits them with uniforms. These Unionists provide him with information and form a loosely knit network of outposts inside the area around Plymouth and Washington.

Whether they are Union regulars, deserters or common bandits, these men have become known to the fearful and unprotected civilians as "Buffaloes." The origin of this term can, I believe, be traced to the description of one of the native Unionist companies who are dressed in sky-blue pants and dark blue coats. The uniforms made them appear so large that the people began calling them "buffaloes."

Most of the Buffalo camps are located deep in the swamps where Confederate forces scarcely dare to venture. Once located there, they subsist mostly by stealing. At first, the desperados stole mostly food and a few horses, but as the war continues, they have begun to steal anything and everything that isn't protected by well-armed men. If anyone betrays them or tries to fight them off, they return some dark night and administer their own form of rough and ready vengeance.

FEBRUARY 19, 1863–THURSDAY
NEW CAMP–NORTH CAROLINA

Brigade Surgeon Sullivan and Doctor Charles Macgill spent an hour with me this morning discoursing about matters and things in general. The doctors both attended the Medical University in Baltimore and have been life-long friends. Surgeon Macgill, a large, portly fellow who speaks with a lisp, serves with Archer's Brigade in the Army of Northern Virginia. His regimental commander is Birkett Fry, an excellent soldier who has already been wounded three times.

Macgill entertained us with several stories of life in Lee's army, but the one I found most enjoyable concerned Colonel Fry and one of his pre-war adventures.

In the late 1850's, Fry, urged by the love of adventure, which was so strong in his nature, accompanied William Walkers filibustering expedition which invaded Nicaragua. He remained there some months and, when he returned, brought back with him a considerable stock of experience and a large and very intelligent monkey. This animal was much attached to Fry and used to follow him like a dog. Birkett reciprocated the ape's affection and was very fond of making him display the tricks he had learned. Unfortunately, the monkey finally met with an untimely end, due to having unduly gratified the inquisitive curiosity which characterizes these most human-like of creatures.

Birkett was living with his father at the old Fry homestead, one of the handsomest places about Charlottesville. His mother, a kind lady, was also a notable housewife and manager, and took special pride in her poultry. She raised every spring a large multitude of chickens, and would never suffer them to be molested. Fry used to complain that the chickens were allowed more privileges than members of the family. They not only strolled and scratched everywhere on the premises as pleased them, but had the audacity to enter the house, the doors of which were always open in warm weather. No one was allowed to drive them out but the old lady herself and this was always done in a very strange manner. She always kept a fire burning, at all seasons, in the dining room. Over the mantel in this room hung a powder horn full of powder, a reminiscence of the pioneer period, not at all uncommon at that time in Virginia.

Not wishing to violently alarm her prize chickens, but only give them a gentle hint to leave, she would when they gathered too thickly in the room, pour a touch of powder into the palm of her hand and throw it on the fire. The consequent flash and sputter would effectually disperse the chickens. Fry's pet monkey was often an interested spectator of this unusual proceeding and, one day, when the chickens had invaded the room in unusual numbers and no one was present to prevent him, the monkey determined to drive the chickens from the room himself. A monkey has, of course, little sense of proportion. Instead of throwing a small amount of powder upon the fire, he hurled the entire contents of the horn into it. A tremendous explosion ensued. The room was wrecked, the air was filled with feathers and the monkey completely disappeared.

Fry mourned the loss of his pet monkey and spoke of the catastrophe with great emotion. "I made a diligent search for his remains," he said, "to give him a decent Christian burial in the family graveyard. All I could find, and that under a pile of singed feathers, was one of his front teeth."

FEBRUARY 25, 1863—WEDNESDAY
NEW CAMP, NORTH CAROLINA

It has rained and snowed here, with the exception of a few days, for the last two weeks. The mud, at the present, is more than a foot deep on all the roads, offering a serious impediment to locomotion.

Quite an interesting incident happened to Adjutant Hughes a few days ago. The said adjutant is a very handsome and gallant fellow who is always extremely polite to the ladies and, in his present isolated situation not having many opportunities to pay his respects to the fair sex is, of course, all the more attentive when such opportunity does occur.

This much, by way of preface; now to the story.

An officer of the 26th Regiment stopped at a house where Adjutant Hughes had taken dinner the day before. The lady and her daughter had moved into the house sometime ago having been forced to flee their home during the battle of Fredericksburg.

As the officer was about to take his leave, the lady asked him if he knew the adjutant.

"Yes, madam. Why do you ask?"

"What kind of man is he?" asked the woman.

"One of the politest men in the army, madam. A perfect gentleman."

"Well, I think he puts on a heap of style."

"Madam, I am surprised to hear you don't like Adjutant Hughes. He is very popular with the ladies. A general favorite in fact."

"I didn't know he was a general!"

"No, madam, he's a general *favorite*."

"Well, general or not, I don't like the way he talked to me."

"There must be a mistake somewhere, madam. What did he say?"

"I don't know where he stays."

"No, madam, what did he SAY," replied the officer rather loudly, suddenly becoming aware that the lady was a bit hard of hearing.

"Why, he used insulting language toward me."

"Impossible, madam. I can't believe for a moment that the adjutant would do anything of that kind. He is the pink of politeness."

"Ha! He thinks of politeness then tries to blackguard me."

"What did the adjutant say?"

"Well, if I must tell, I will. I thought he was a gentleman for he often used mighty big words, but he asked me what the state of my virginity was and if that ain't insulting language, I don't know it when I hear it."

Here, the daughter, a pert miss of sixteen, mostly feet and ankles, put in. "Mother, I was there. He asked you what made you leave the state of Virginny."

"See! Even my daughter heard it."

It would seem to be a case of miscommunication between the soft spoken adjutant and the rather deaf lady of the house. However, I think it will be sometime before my staff lets Adjutant Hughes forget the State of "Virginity."

I must end this entry on a melancholy note. Old Maurice, the remarkable mule of the 26th North Carolina, has taken sick. The mule, who is called "Mo" for short, is remarkable for his great coolness under fire. He seems to care no more for the whistling of cannon balls and shells than if they are so many blue-bellied flies. "Mo" has been wounded four times. He has a bullet hole through each ear and a minie rifle ball shaved off his tail close to his body. At the battle of New Bern, a ball entered his hip and came out in the middle of his back, but, notwithstanding all this, he soon recovered again and was ready for duty. About three days ago, "Mo," having been transferred from the "Jackass Battery" to a baggage wagon, found some wild cucumber on the road, which had been thrown from a bottle of bitters. After partaking freely of the vegetable, he became so intoxicated that the driver had to discharge him from duty. It is hoped that "Mo" will soon recover from his intoxication and re-enlist for the remainder of war.

FEBRUARY 28, 1863—SATURDAY
NEW CAMP, NORTH CAROLINA

I received by telegraph today news that on February 25th, General Lee appointed General Longstreet commander of the Department of Virginia and North Carolina. This move, I believe will herald a more aggressive posture for our forces in eastern North Carolina. Both Lee and Longstreet are very aware of how vital the agricultural products of the region are to the Army of Northern Virginia and of how vulnerable the supply lines are because of their proximity to the Union garrisons on the coast.

To command in North Carolina, Longstreet has selected General D. H. Hill. The new commander is a native North Carolinian and a proven commander. I hope this appointment signals that, at long last, a serious campaign will be mounted to recapture the coastal cities of New Bern and Washington.

A short time after learning of Hill's appointment, I received via the telegraph an address to his new command. I have ordered the address read by all company commanders to their men. A short time after General Hills' address was read to the various regiments of the brigade Colonel Burgwyn came riding up to my headquarters on his black charger. "General!" he shouted, "The men greeted the address with the greatest enthusiasm. They cheered and yelled and shouted 'Hurrah for old Daniel H.!' It looks as though we got ourselves a fighting general. I just hope his bite is as good as his bark."

"He has a high and well-deserved reputation as a fighter," I answered.

"This is a great day for us, General," enthused Burgwyn. "We have had vastly too much strategy, too much science, and too much digging in North Carolina. Had we less of these and more fighting, the Yankees might not be holding garrisons at New Bern and Washington."

I took an affectionate farewell of young Burgwyn and walked back to my tent musing on what this change of command would mean. I had been told that General Hill is an extraordinary man, gifted with courage and determination and a perfect faith in Providence that he is destined to destroy the enemy.

I could only hope this will turn out to be true. Our cause has suffered only anguish and anxiety in North Carolina and the heart of the people seems heavy with despair. But if General Hill is the leader he appears to be, we will confront the Yankees with a burning desire to avenge our previous defeats and drive them forever from our soil. Though it should cost another thirty years of war and a generation of lives, the red work we have begun must be completed. Ultimate failure is impossible; ultimate triumph is certain.

MARCH 5, 1863—THURSDAY
NEW CAMP, NORTH CAROLINA

A sunny but very cold day. General inspection is at 9 a.m., company drill, forenoon, regimental drill in the afternoon.

The burden of the winter camp affects some of the men more than others. There is one of them in the 26th, a man who has become depressed while burying several of his comrades who have died of disease. Something must be done with this man to break the spell. Kindness, scolding or extra duty have had no effect. So, on this exceedingly sharp, frosty morning at roll call about daylight, the poor fellow is ordered to step three paces to the front and then turn about and face his company in line.

A lieutenant and two privates fall in beside the man. Colonel Burgwyn then directs them to procure soap and to take the man at once to a nearby stream to strip him and scrub him from head to foot with the soap and water as they would scrub a dirty floor. The brook is frozen over and the water is icy cold.

They started for their work but about half-way to the stream, the man offered to keep himself "satisfactorily clean" if he can be spared the punishment. The colonel relents and the man is allowed to try for himself and directed to report within two hours.

The time expired and there, in front of Colonel Burgwyn, stood the dearest dandy in the regiment.

With General Hill now in command, rumor fills the camp. The men will be glad to escape this boring camp life and enter upon an active campaign, to strike into the business for which they enlisted, to do their part to close this war and return to the callings of civilian life, in a Southern Confederacy.

A mule has just broken the stillness of the night by a most discordant bray and I am reminded that all horses are to be turned over to the cavalry and mules used in the teams instead. Mules are far better for the wagons than horses. They require less food, are hardier, and stand up better under rough work and irregular feeding.

Speaking of mules, one of the chaplains has been preaching the Gospel among all who will listen. One of his converts, rejoicing in the conviction that he had at last found the truth, went down to the river in company with many others and received baptism by immersion. Now this convert was none other than the darky mule driver Socrates. After the immersion, everything went well as long as the mules did well and Socrates seemed in the enjoyment of unalloyed happiness. But the Lord warned that in this world, we would have tribulation. Sure enough, the day came in an unguarded moment, when the mules became obstreperous, Socrates lost control of his temper and his old habit of profanity got the upper hand.

"D-D-Damn to h-h-hell dem m-m-mules!" the inveterate stammerer was heard to exclaim, all pretense of piety gone. After this slip, knowing that he had publicly disgraced his profession, he was heard to say, "A m-m-man can't be a C-C-Christian and drive m-m-mules too." Then, as if all of the pent-up oaths of the past few weeks were clamoring for an opportunity to give emphasis to the sentiment, he broke forth into such unrestrained profanity as is seldom heard in this sinful world. The tirade over, he seemed to feel better and was heard to say, "De s-s-spirit is willing, but de f-f-flesh is so weak."

MARCH 10, 1863—TUESDAY
KINSTON, NORTH CAROLINA

Yesterday morning, I received the following order by telegraph from General Hill:

"Goldsboro, North Carolina, March 9, 1863

"Brig. Gen. J. J. Pettigrew:

"I wish you to take all the rifled guns in your own brigade. Daniel's and the reserve artillery and the Whitworth gun from Wilmington (if arrived) and move your brigade to the north side of the Neuse River in readiness to attack Fort Johnson. Get all of your guns in position, if possible, without observation and open a concentrated fire upon the enemy's fort. It is thought that the fort can be reduced; if so, push up your guns to it after its fall and open upon the Yankee shipping and barracks in New Bern. It is important that the bombardment shall begin on Saturday and your brigade must move part of the way tomorrow. I will take General Daniel's brigade and attack on the south, or city, side of the river. General Robertson's cavalry brigade will attack by a third route. It is proper for you to know that there is to be a combined movement from the James River to the Cape Fear and you are to begin it. Upon your success depends very much the success of the scheme. I most earnestly hope there will be no obstacle in your way. I have written to General Garnett at Greenville that you will begin your attack on Thursday. Everything is entrusted to your skill, prudence and good management.

"With great respect,

"D. H. Hill

"Major General"

The receipt of the telegram found us all in motion. Our time of inactivity was over. In less than an hour, the brigade was marching away from new Camp. Behind us the remnants of once what was our home. Empty quarters of officers and men and rude chimneys standing out like ghosts. Not even a dog or camp left behind, only silence. We let camp early in the morning and marched until noon when we reached our present temporary camp on the outskirts of Kinston.

With the entire brigade under marching orders, for daylight tomorrow, the men are in high spirits. As to the officers, you would suppose they were all going on a merry making, to hear them when the order was issued. Our object is to fight the enemy, which I pray we may do, and with success.

The task will not be an easy one, however, as the distance is about fifty-seven miles through densely wooded and marshy country, with numerous lakes and bodies of stagnant waters. Wherever the land emerges from the swamp, the soil at once assumes a light sandy character, with forests of pine, oak, black walnut and ash.

The marshes are bottomless swales, where vegetable mold has accumulated for ages, until sufficient consistency has formed to push the bilious waters into meandering streams and pools of stagnant water. Into these slimy depths, huge cone-shaped roots from the cypress plunge for sustenance and support, while monster trees rise with distended, paunch-like trunks, towering high above as if attempting to escape from their foil surroundings. High vines hang from the trunks like serpents, crossing from tree to tree and mingling in myriad snarls, while the thick undergrowth forbids admission to, or exit from, these confines. The river banks are low, disappearing almost imperceptibly at the water line. Near the rivers and creeks are a scattering of fishermen's homes, the scant clearing around them showing they calculate little on the soil for substance.

Major John Cheves Haskell, who is to command the artillery battalion, called this evening and remained for an hour. We had a very agreeable time. The young major is a native of South Carolina and a veteran of some of the hardest campaigns of the Army of Northern Virginia, having lost an arm at Gaines Mill.

My admiration for Major Haskell is boundless. I believe if I had been wounded as badly as him, I would think I had done my duty and would have never returned. His terrible wound entitled him to a pension and gratitude from the country for the balance of his life. Such is his high degree of patriotism that he has returned. This can only aid our cause and set a high example of courage and dedication for the men.

MARCH 20, 1863—FRIDAY
HOOKERTON, NORTH CAROLINA

The attempt to capture New Bern has ended in failure and we have returned safely to this place. We have had a very trying time through anxious and laborious days and sleepless nights, such as I fancy would make old age come prematurely. For ten days I have not been able to change clothes and only now and then to washing my face, sleeping under trees or on unsheltered earth, and generally vagabonding up and down the Neuse River.

On the morning of the 11th, camp was broken at six a.m. by a bugle signal from brigade headquarters. As the men were preparing to march, a desperate situation occurred at the camp of the 26th. One of the soldiers was quite drunk and refused to heed the call to assembly. Major Harkins tried in vain to restore the soldier to the ranks and was facing a one-man mutiny. The major could do nothing with him and the scene was growing more and more exciting as the mutiny gained strength from his companions. How it would terminate was hard to foresee and the authority of a superior officer was in very serious jeopardy. As the excitement grew, the circle grew also and it was difficult for the other officers to reach the major or the soldier in mutiny. Finally, news of the affair reached Colonel Burgwyn. He mounted his horse, put spurs to him and rushed through and over the crowd with a drawn sabre in his hand. When he reached the soldier, he ran him through. In an instant the soldier lay bleeding and dying on the ground. A shudder passed through his companions who immediately left to join their ranks. Colonel Burgwyn rode off satisfied he had put a stop to disobedience. This action is hard to contemplate and many would cry out it was inhuman. The colonel, however, had strong reasons for such a severe measure, especially when the brigade was beginning an active campaign against our hated enemy.

The morning was damp and as we crossed the bridge over the muddy Neuse, I looked back at Kinston enveloped in a misty canopy of fog and wondered if I should ever see it again. But we were on the march at last. On perhaps to capture New Bern. At least on. And every step brought us nearer.

We passed through Airy Grove at noon and halted for a short rest and dinner just beyond. The men were standing the march very well although many found they had overestimated their pack-horse ability and a few overloaded knapsacks disgorged a portion of their contents.

Early in the afternoon, thick black clouds began to gather and soon they obstructed the sun. Heaven's artillery then opened fire and the continuous peal made the solid earth tremble. It soon grew dark, the lightning dazzled and flashed and the succeeding darkness was all the blacker. A vivid flash, a deafening crash and a few big drops like the "advance guard" of an army warned us of the torrents they preceded. We had four miles yet to march before we were to halt. I looked up at the ominous sky and thought, "Be merciful oh ye black clouds! Keep the wash tub right side up with care until we reach our bivouac, build our fires and crawl under shelter." The rain ignored my plea however, and we marched through a thunderstorm of an hour's duration. Every soldier knows what such a storm brings and how wet a man may get that is exposed to it.

We reached the spot designated for a bivouac and halted for the night, making ourselves as comfortable as our wet clothing and wet beds would permit. We took the rails from the fences and made our fires, laid rails alongside of them, ourselves upon the rails, and attempted to sleep. Soon all was still. When the lightning glared for a moment, I could see groups of sleeping men in the attitudes in which they fell with their loosened burdens oblivious of all, unmindful of the distant thunder and lightning, now receding to the east, slumbering as only tired soldiers can slumber.

For me it was too cold to sleep. As fast as I would fall into a doze, the chill of the atmosphere would steal through my blanket and remind me of my location. Half-sleeping and half-waking, I dreamed of many places and things. I had visions of Charleston, standing on the battery watching the shells explode over Fort Sumter, of my bloody experience at Seven Pines, of burning dwellings at Fredericksburg and many other scenes of this war. These dreams followed each other with a rapidity that far outstripped the workings of the electric telegraph.

Just before dawn, Captain Young warned me it was time to rise. To make my toilet, I pulled the sticks and wet leaves from my hair and beard and brushed my overcoat with a handful of moss. I breakfasted on hardtack and a spoonful of whiskey. I gave my horse "Tarheel" a handful of corn and some oats. The men began to stir just as I had done so. The brigade would soon begin to move and I was ready to attend upon its fortunes.

We resumed our march at 6:30 a.m. The road was very muddy. We worked all day to get twelve miles, such floundering in bottomless holes, such whipping, hallowing and swearing. It was enough to make a lady blush. The twenty-pound Parrots weigh almost two thousand pounds and many times they stuck fast inextricably and could only be pulled free with the aid of heavy ropes and many mules. We watched one driver who was driving six mules with a single line while whipping and cursing away "like sixty," as the saying goes, when Major Haskell, a religious man feeling it his duty called out, "Young man, do you know you are a son of God?"

"What?" said the driver, stopping a minute from his whipping and cursing.

"Do you know you are a son of God?" repeated the major, this time in a very loud voice.

"That well may be," said the driver, "but this lead mule is a son of a b_ _ _ _!"

Lifting his great army whip, he struck the leading mule on the ear with a snap that sent blood flying. "Get on there!" he cried, "Before I whip your damned hide again!"

"I think," said the major, "mule drivers are beyond redemption."

"That may be," I countered, "but if he can get those mules to pull that cannon loose, I'll pray doubly hard for his salvation."

The road on both sides was for the most part hemmed in by dense and impassable pine thickets. Through this, man and beast were obliged to flounder along the best way possible. If the deep mud was remarkable, so were the immense flocks of crows that for several mornings darkened the sky in the flight to their feeding grounds and again at night as they returned to their roosts in the abundant forest. Near Brownville, we found the pike literally black with them, save one lone sentinel who perched aloft on a large tree-top keenly watched our approach until at his shrill signal the large gathering rose in a single cloud and flew away.

Johnson's Mill, where we camped at night, is like many small hamlets in this region of North Carolina, a place of four old homes, a small dilapidated courthouse, and a jail about eight feet square. It is surrounded by interminable stunted pine and evergreen thickets.

516   The Long Lost Journal of Confederate General James Johnson Pettigrew

During the night, the wind subsided somewhat, but with the approach of morning it rose again so that when the camp began to stir itself, the weather was very severe. Careless soldiers who had forgotten to empty the water from their canteens found them split in twain. Our shoes which had received a liberal coating of soft mud inside as well as out were, of course, frozen stiff and hard. Some of the staff were already awake and made a fence rail fire as large as a small cottage and apparently hot enough to keep a naked man warm at the North Pole. It felt agreeable to stand by the blaze while drinking my morning coffee, turning first one side and then the other to the fire to keep warm.

An unfortunate incident occurred at this time when one of the Negro cooks tripped while carrying a boiling hot kettle of water. Most of the water fell upon the foot of assistant quartermaster Cornelius Tolles, badly scalding his foot. The incident reminded my of my unfortunate scalding a short time ago, but the injury to Tolles was much worse. When the sock was removed by one of the surgeons, much of the skin came off with it. Tolles was in great pain and we sent him and a lieutenant suffering from a malignant form of typhoid fever back to Kinston in a small ambulance with a darky driver.

When the teams stopped that night, they sank axle deep in the soft mud and thus were frozen solid in the morning. Captain Gilman and men of his ax squad were detailed to chop them out and clear fallen trees from portions of the road ahead.

It was now the morning of the 13th and if we were to keep to General Hill's schedule and begin the attack on time, we would have to make haste and do some hard marching.

Despite the cold weather and the roughness of the road, the brigade moved forward. An occasional log cabin was the only indication that the country was inhabited. By early afternoon, we had made 14 miles.

Gilman's pioneers had cleared an old road over Sudley Hill for the artillery, but the mud was something appalling. The wagons were moved over this portion with the greatest difficulty. The light artillery managed to pull through this new mud road, but when the heavy Parrott guns tried the road, the movement stopped. The first gun was very stuck in the mud. Teams from the other guns were brought forward until twenty-four horses were hooked to the one gun, but they could not, or would not, pull it out. I then halted the nearest column of infantry and men of the 52nd regiment were ordered over to help them out. The regiment stacked arms and unslung knapsacks. The horses were all taken away and a heavy rope one hundred and fifty feet long was fastened to the gun. The regiment lined up in the road which was a stream of mud for which, however, they cared not, as no more mud could hang to their shoes or pant legs. With some grumbling, the men took hold of the rope from both sides all ready.

"Go!" came the command. The rope grew taunt and the cannon moved, raising high on root or rock, this side or that, or both, to plunge down again axle deep in mud, the axles loudly pounding in the boxes. With much straining and pulling there was no halt made until the top of the hill was reached. In this way, the four Parrott guns were drawn up by the men until the entire battery stood on top of the hill. The horses, six to a gun, were again hooked on, the 52nd returned to its place in the column and the brigade was once more on the move.

At four, I halted the brigade for ten minutes. The men rested against the fences eating some of their rations. Many did feast on the army hard bread made of flour, salt and water, though a trifle harder, it probably more nearly resembles the sunburnt bricks of ancient Babylon than any other modern sustenance. The men break off small, irregular, jagged pieces of this bread, put them into their mouths and chew the unyielding mass, looking for all the world like cattle eating corn on the cob. This is what is meant by "gnawing hardtack." Once in a while, a good fat maggot appears in a hardtack and then the lucky owner must encourage his appetite despite the queasy feeling in his stomach. Colonel Burgwyn claims that maggots in army bread prove it is a good article.

At six o'clock, we reached a swollen stream which crossed the road diagonally in a torrent, covering the track for at least twenty rods. The bridge had been swept away and we had to search for a place to affect a crossing. We finally found the shallowest part which was breast deep. Many of the men shouldered their accoutrements and dashed in. While others crossed slowly upon felled trees. It took quite some time, but, at last, all were over and I gave the men a rest and chance to dry off.

It was at this time when a detachment of Major Whitford's scouts came riding up. These men are employed in the hazardous duty of collecting information and engaging in reconnaissance of the enemy's whereabouts. They are a fine-looking lot of men—wild and very picturesque in appearance.

They brought the sad news that a Yankee cavalry detachment had swooped down on the ambulance conveying Assistant Quartermaster Tolles and the sick lieutenant to Kinston. Captain Faulkner, one of the scouts, described the incident.

> "The Yankees must have been dispatched from Washington and, riding behind our advance, struck a prize in the ambulance proceeding south on the pike 2 miles south of Blount's Mill. The Yankee descent on the ambulance was sudden and took the occupants completely by surprise. A sad feature of the affair was the tragic end to the two occupants of the vehicle, Tolles and the lieutenant. The two had only themselves to blame for they lost their heads and sprang from the wagon, attempting to escape instead of remaining quiet. As a result, they were shot down while running."

Following the questioning of the darky driver, the Yankees released him and he was found by Captain Faulkner and his men wandering some distance from the site of the ambush. After burying the two unfortunates, they brought the old Negro to me. I questioned him and learned the following story.

"Well, massa, I will tell you how it was. You see, I was goin' toward Kinston out on that road unbeknownst that the Yankees was there. Well, fo' sure, some of dem Yankees on horseback cried, 'Stop dar!' Then they fired shots in the air. Master Tolles and the lieutenant jump wagon and run. Yankees holler, 'Stop!' and then they shoot. End of dem two fellows. They then asked me where I was goin'. I told how it was and they said, 'Come along, old man' and they took me to the colonel. He was in a house sitting on a sofa and he says to me, 'Are you from Kinston?' I says, 'Yes, master.' And then he says, 'Take a seat here.' So I got down just this way. He was on this side of me and I was, as it might be, on the other side of him. He looked kind to me and says to me, 'You know we are friends of the colored people and so you must tell me the truth.' Then he says, 'Mose—for I had done told him my name—Mose, are there many soldiers in the force advancing on New Bern?' I told him there was more men than I had ever seen in my life. Then he asks me, 'Mose, have they much caba'ry?' 'Caba'ry? What you mean by dat?' I says. 'Have they many men on horses?' he says. And I says, 'Bless your soul, master, I neber have seen as many blackbirds in de cornfields as dey have horses thar. Everywhere yous go you see dem men on horses.' 'Have they many guns?' he says. 'Sure do. Think ebery man hab a gun.' I says. 'You don't understand me, Mose.' he says. 'Have they many cannon on wheels?' Then I ups and tells the Yankee how when dem cannon went out of Kinston I sot on de ground on my knees in a joint of fence in a cornfield on the other side de road and looks through de rails and counts them and dar war for sure just sixty-four of dem. Next he asks me what ginrals were there. I told him I ain't partic'larly 'quainted with dem, but that I heard tell of Ginral Longstreet and Ginral Stonewall or something like dat. Then, after thinking for some time, he called a soldier and told him to take me back to de pike and let me go. Once free, bless the Lord, I come onto Captain Faulkner and am back to where I belong."

Whether the Yankees were influenced by the information they got from old Mose, I know not, but such was the old Negro's story as he relayed it to me.

After this halt, the regiments were again formed and moved onto the road and by seven, we were again under way. The exhaustion of the march none of us will soon forget as fatigue wore proportionately upon us. Tramp. Tramp. Tramp. Eyes seeing nothing and feet moving only by habit while the ear dulls to the clanking of bayonet and canteen until roused by the hoarse "Close up!" or still less agreeably by a smart thud from the musket of some sleepy comrade or stumbling upon the heels of the man ahead.

Some time after ten, we made a halt of a half-hour near James Ferry. Many of the men slept soundly until it was time to fall in again. While others hurriedly boiled their coffee and ate a paltry ration of hardtack before they sought to snatch a little rest.

The infantry reached a point six miles from Fort Johnson at midnight and I intended to begin the last march to the fort at one o'clock, but a swamp some three miles in the rear of the halt changed under the supply and artillery train to quicksand. The men worked vainly all night in the freezing water to repair it. It was, however, necessary to bridge the swamp in a new place which was done under the superintendence of Lieutenant Koerner of the topographical engineers and Captain Gilman and his axe-men. About 3:00 a.m., Saturday, the bridge was finished. The infantry then marched to the fort, arriving early in the morning, but the twenty pounders having mired, the artillery was detained until late in the morning.

At about noon, Major Haskell, Captain Young and I rode out to see the enemy's position and, at 400 yards, we came, for the first time, in view of the fort. What I now saw before me in my field glasses was an earthwork on the bank of the river immediately opposite New Bern. It was flanked by a swamp of 3 or 4 miles on the right and a swampy creek on the left so that it could only be approached in front by a causeway a quarter of a mile long and only wide enough for a small wagon.

Major Haskell estimated the garrison of the fort at 300 men and felt that if we charged they would only be able to fire one volley, costing us 50 or 100 men. I therefore decided to display my force, demoralize the Yankees by a heavy fire and demand a surrender, thus saving my own men and not unnecessarily killing theirs.

Upon my order, the 26th regiment advanced with skirmishers in front driving in the Yankee pickets. I then gave the command to bring the four light batteries up. As the infantry pressed eagerly forward, the cry was passed along from the rear of "Give way, right and left for artillery!" As the infantry fell back on each side of the road, we could see the batteries approaching in the distance. As they drew near,, the leader shouted, "Gallop!" and on they came, the horses on the full run, the guns rattling and jumping, the men clinging to their seats for dear life, to prevent being dismounted by some extra jounce, but smiling as if going to parade. Cheer after cheer greeted each successive gun as it rushed through our ranks on to the front and we all felt sure that, with such support, the fort would soon be ours.

The guns were deployed at 300 yards from the fort and opened upon it a rapid and well-directed fire.

I and my staff watched with interest the progress of the artillery fire. Shouts and cheers would go up whenever a well-aimed shot struck the fort.

"There. Take that will you?"

"A splendid shot! Hit 'em again!"

"Hurrah! We've set one of their houses on fire!"

Such were the remarks freely made as different pleasing incidents occurred. We were particularly delighted upon seeing a party of Yankee officers who had been examining our position from the peak of a small house inside the fort suddenly dislodged by a shell exploding under the roof which sent shingles, rafters and men into the air.

The enemy offered no opposition to our bombardment. After several minutes of this, I ordered a halt to the artillery fire and sent Captain Young forward under a flag of truce to demand a surrender. This was a mistake on my part and I now regret it very much.

Captain Young met with Lieutenant Colonel Hiram Anderson of the 92nd New York. Young then galloped back to our lines wearing a rather troubled air. He handed me the paper with Anderson's request for a cease fire so he could consult General Foster in New Bern.

"It's a trick," said Major Haskell. "They are stalling for time."

Young was even more adamant saying, "We must charge the fort. It will only cost the lives of a few men."

I then looked at him and replied, "Are you, Captain Young, willing to be one of the few?"

I decided to grant Anderson the time he needed and sent back Captain Young to inform him of my decision. However, it soon became apparent that the Yankee colonel was stalling for time and I decided to resume the artillery fire with the light batteries and the twenty pounders.

Major Haskell asked for the honor of firing the first shot with the twenty pounders and I granted his request. The ground beyond the Neuse River toward New Bern is almost dead level. Haskell put just enough powder into the gun to send the round shell fairly across the river. He then cut the fuse, sighted the gun and sent the shell rolling over the smooth ground beyond the river. As I watched through my field glasses, I saw it roll into an old cellar and burst there. A dozen or so Yankees scrambled out and made the best time on record to a near-by brick house. Now for the house. Haskell tried again with a heavier load of powder and sent his shell ricocheting over there where it lodged within the house and burst. Again, another scattering of Yankees. After firing the two shots and, without saying a word, Haskell turned, saluted and marched off with the air of an actor leaving the stage.

But before long, we could see the smoke of the enemy's gunboats coming up the river. One was soon in range and *Bang!* went the deck cannon. Then *Boom! Boom!* From their 100-pounders and then *Bang! Boom! Bang!* pretty generally. The first shell burst high over our heads and every one of us, for a moment expected to catch a piece of one of the little balls as they rattled down among the pine trees. But no one was hit. About one-third of this shell, in one piece, came down and struck the ground with a loud noise, about ten feet to the rear of our colors.

The artillery duel that ensued was entirely one-sided as the performance of the twenty pounders was execrable. Half the shells burst just outside the guns or turned over the air and were perfectly harmless to the enemy. At length the axle of one of these guns broke and it became unserviceable. Then another burst wounded three men, one of them mortally. It was soon evident that the twenty pounders were worse than useless. The light guns would have been effective against the gunboats in an ordinary-sized river, but the Neuse at New Bern is so wide as enable them to fire upon us from distances of a mile or two.

The men of the 26th Regiment were placed some sixty feet behind the guns and the shells from the enemy's guns could be seen for a half a mile or more before reaching us, coming generally end over end. Many of them passed entirely beyond us and stirred up the musicians, cooks and all who made it a business to stay in the rear during a fight.

Many of the shells fell, however, among the battery men or horses, or passing them, dropped among the infantry. Occasionally, a shell plowed under some of our boys who were lying down, threw them into the air and emerged from the earth to burst in the rear. Things became very exciting, for the enemy had the range of our position and was cutting his fuses so accurately that nearly every shell burst in our midst. Finally a shell penetrated a caisson that was full of ammunition and caused it to explode in a deafening roar, sending its contents in every direction, killing a horse and wounding two men. I was deeply affected as the boys carried Private Newton, one of the wounded on a stretcher to the rear to die, by his calling out, "Good-bye, General!" One feels so helpless in the presence of death.

It was a powerless feeling to endure the shelling for of all the devils in war, the scream of a shell is the wickedest. A bombshell flies with a long *W-o-o-o-o-sh!* Something like the rush of a big skyrocket and there are shells used by the light artillery which fly with a loud rush of air, not too terrifying. But the man who hears the scream of a 100-pound shell from a gunboat will never forget the sound to the day of his death. It begins afar off like the sound of a coming freight train. It comes nearer and fills the air with an ear-piercing, reverberating roar and then explodes with a jarring crash.

Several of our men were killed by these shells and I firmly believe that all of them were so terrified by the sounds that they suffered nothing in the moment of death. One could tell after a short time, whether the shell was in the direct line or to the right or left, but the coming brought a feeling of utter helplessness—a sort of dumb terror which held the limbs captive. One could not have run away if he had so desired, but where could one run to anyway? Who could say where these death-dealing devils would fall after their flight or the instant they were to explode and send their fragments hither and thither to search out and claim their prey.

At one time during the shelling, I watched a new Yankee ship steam into the fray and a puff of smoke rise from the deck. It was apparent this was a mortar-boat and had opened fire. Of this I was soon convinced on casting my eyes aloft. Never shall I forget the sight that met my astonished vision. Shooting upward at an angle of forty-five degrees, with the rapidity of lightning, small globes of scarlet flame could be seen sailing through the azure sky, not a steady, unfading flame, but coruscating like the nighttime gleam of a firefly—now visible and soon invisible. Soon the terrible missile—a thirteen-inch shell—neared its zenith up and still up, higher and higher. Its flight then became much slower until reaching its utmost altitude when it suddenly fell earthward. Down, down it came until it exploded in the midst of one of the twenty pounders, killing one man and wounding three others.

The mortar shell in falling straight down had entered the top of the unfortunate soldier's head passed through his body and exploded, literally tearing him to pieces.

The explosion left a good-sized hole and there was blood on the grass, bits of burned clothing a short distance away and a lock of hair here and there with a bit of scalp attached. Those were the only relics left of what had once been a human being.

To be killed by a shell in this way means more than death. It means such complete annihilation as can be effected in no other manner on earth except by the explosion of gun powder or nitroglycerine. The victim may see a flash, hear a roar, but it happens in the fiftieth part of a second. Those to the right and left see a flash of flame and hear an explosion and the *Whing!* of shell fragments, but the victim has been blotted off the face of the earth as if he never existed.

The horror of the mortar shells was too much for one of the men of the battery and he ran from the shelling in a terribly frightened condition. Colonel Burgwyn ran to stop him demanding in an official tone, "Where are you going, sir?"

"B-a-a-back!"

"Are you wounded?'

"N-n-n-no!"

"Then return to your battery!"

"Oh," said he, "do not send me back! I am not wounded, but I am fearfully demoralized!"

`And indeed his appearance showed that. As he broke free from Burgwyn and passed rapidly toward the woods, he was losing not only his courage, but also everything most useful to him—even his hat. It was useless to send him back. We had no time to waste. As he ran, he kept looking back with nervous twitches and continued to the rear quite as badly demoralized as a half-drowned hen.

`It was obvious the principal object of the expedition was doomed to failure. With the Yankees alerted and more of their gunboats with heavy guns coming around from the Trent River, we could no longer hope to capture New Bern. The only question was whether I should carry Fort Anderson before withdrawing. The 26th was at hand and would have done it in five minutes. The advantage of doing so would have been the capture of 300 Yankees with their arms. The disadvantage was the probable loss of a certain number of men 60 miles from our hospitals. I decided against it. It cost me a struggle after so much labor and endurance to give up the campaign, but I felt that my duty to the country required me to save my men for some operation in which sacrifices would be followed by consequences, not in capturing a few Yankees and holding temporary possession of the fort, however brilliant the operation may be. I, therefore, decided to withdraw my command.

The 26th retired some distance to the rear and bivouacked that night in deep woods. A large detail was sent on picket and the balance of the regiment settled down to rest in pitchy darkness. The excitement, hard work and danger of the day had left many of the men in a state of exhaustion and the rest was most welcome.

Probably the 26th had never seen during all of its previous service a more unsatisfactory day than this one. There was apparently no head, tail or order to the work—a nebulous fight. They had to fight without winning and advance without going ahead. I cannot too highly express my admiration of the manner in which they stood the furious shelling of the enemy without flinching.

It was interesting to observe the different spirit in which the men met the discomforts of that night in the woods. I found my way among several small groups of men sitting by their fires and one of the privates addressed me saying, "Now, General, is not this as bad as it could be?'

"No," I said, "it is not as bad as it could be."

"Well, how could it be any worse?" growled the soldier.

"If we had made an assault today," I replied, "and been repulsed and had two or three hundred wounded men to bring along back through the swamps to Kinston, that would have been a good deal worse."

The grumbler had nothing more to say.

Late that night, Major Haskell and I spread our two rubber blankets between two pine trees and laid down together. Pulling our woolen blankets over ourselves, we lost no time in seeking sleep. But as I write these reflections, I recall how I had trouble sleeping that night, despite my fatigue. The shadow of the whole wasted campaign came over me and I remember how my spirit reflected the mood of Dante at the beginning of *The Inferno*, which I give you in his own deep echoing words.

> *Midway the path of life,*
> *I found myself in a gloomy wood,*
> *where the right way out was perplexed.*

The next morning, we began our retreat. Back we went over the same road as yesterday. We passed the bridges and saw men with fuel prepared to set them on fire as soon as we passed. There was little laughter or mirthfulness. The knapsacks were heavy and the men were sullen. We halted for a while and everyone was on his back in a moment. But fewer men fell out, for they feared capture by the enemy should Yankee cavalry be following us. In the middle of the afternoon, it began to rain. The road became a deep puddle and the gutters were rivers. The brigade splashed on through the rain, dreary and disheartened. About eight o'clock, we reached a field to camp. Then, through the evening dark as pitch, we went stumbling about to find wood for fuel. There was more rain and, when morning came at last, such a half-drowned, haggard set of men I have never seen. But there was spunk in the old brigade yet and we were soon on the march again.

We went on very well and arrived at Hookerton Tuesday night. We accomplished little in the campaign—sent a few souls to heaven, exceedingly rejoiced, it may be, to be out of this wicked world and my only consolation was that as far as human weakness goes, all tried to do their duty to their fellow man in their time of need, either of soul or body. Now the brigade is in camp and, as the full realization of our failure sets in, most are very blue.

MARCH 22, 1863—SUNDAY
HOOKERTON, NORTH CAROLINA

We have rather shabby accommodations here in Hookerton and I long for the comforts of New Camp. I think yesterday was as glum a day as I have had in camp. The failure of the move on New Bern still hangs heavy in my thoughts and the terrific showers of lightning, thunder, wind and rain did little to lift my spirits. It was as muddy and nasty and sticky about the camp, in general, and headquarters, in particular, as it could be.

The two funerals of Alfred Clapp and Major Turner also did little to promote cheerfulness. The sudden and accidental death of the major was particularly tragic. His horse had come up lame and, therefore, Captain Thomas generously lent him his. The horse's mouth was tender from a change of bit that had been made a day or two before and the major had hardly pulled the reins before the animal reared. Major

Turner fell off backwards, striking his head on a large rock. The horse also fell over backwards and the pommel of the saddle came down on the major's left leg with the entire weight of the animal. This ruptured the main artery. Either of these blows would have proved fatal yet between them both, the good major lingered in great agony until after 4:00 p.m. Those of us who stood near him during his last hours will not soon forget his thanks to us for our attention, nor his appeals to remember the men of his regiment.

Although he suffered great pain to the end, his noble Christian nature forbade him to complain. He put his arms around us one after another with great affection, inquired our names (the blow on the head had blinded him) and said as his last words, "Tell all the soldiers to be Christians. They then can die in peace."

The body was embalmed by Dr. Sullivan and this morning was sent south in charge of Captain Blake, a friend of the major and his family. The officers and men of his regiment subscribed $420 to pay the expenses of transportation and to present the remainder to the widow.

As we watched the coffin loaded into the wagon to be taken to the train depot, I asked Chaplain Pender of the 52nd how he bore up under the duty of so much death and sadness.

"I bear up very well for it is important to me, General," he answered. "To minister to the bodies and souls of men who live with constant hardship and who frequently face the prospect of their own death with an immediacy seldom experienced by those in civilian life."

He continued, "I think the world would be a very much poorer place, if there were not those who cared intensely about the sorrows and sufferings of others. In my case, this concern began very simply. When I was a boy in Raleigh, I was going along the street one day and I came upon a pauper's funeral. The coffin was a shoddy, ill-made box. It was on a hand-barrow. The barrow was being pushed by a quartet of men who were drunk, and as they pushed the barrow along, they were singing ribald songs and joking and jesting among themselves. As they pushed the barrow up the hill, the box, which was the coffin, fell off the barrow and burst open. I saw this horrid affair and said to myself, 'When I grow up, I'm going to give my life to see that things like that don't happen.' Since that time, I have dedicated my life to caring for others."

The mail service here is abominable. Three days ought to bring mail from Charleston or Raleigh, but letters come along anywhere from four to twelve days late, any time that best suits the careless, lazy mail carrier or the ever-watchful mail censor.

Nothing can exceed or describe the often pathetic scenes connected with the soldier's mail. A letter is opened by a man and gives the news of his child's, wife's or near relative's death, sudden and unexpected. He instantly seems dazed and goes to his tent in silent, hopeless sorrow as a man in chains and mourns for many days. He is not soon, if ever again, the man he was. Another suddenly learns that his wife has been unfaithful to him. He tears the letter to shreds and almost seems to sink into the ground. In a few days, he has turned into a dullard or drunken brute and is never again the man he was.

Out of three Richmond papers I receive by mail, only one came today. There were no full particulars yet of the late attacks and repulses of the Yankees at Port Hudson and Fort Pemberton. The Yankee gunboats made two attempts at Fort Pemberton and were repulsed effectively in each. With this repulse, it appears another of Grant's efforts against Vicksburg has come to an end.

Another item of interest concerned the opinions of the Yankees in New Bern about the condition of the Negroes in the South. Most of these men were New Englanders and were, therefore, on their arrival in New Bern, curious to see the Negroes on their native heath. They were surprised, it seems, to find them so well-dressed and to note that their manners were good and their intelligence far above the conventional

Northern description. An officer of the 24th Massachusetts was quoted as saying, "The darkies are, of course, of all shades of color. Mental development is as a rule in direct ratio to the proportion of white blood. I fancy the brutishness of the black fieldhand of the Gulf States is rare in our part of North Carolina. On the other hand, some house-bred yellow girls have manners and more particularly language which for correctness and even elegance would do credit to any education."

The Yankees are also reported to find the Negroes a source of endless amusement. They keep the swarming idlers dancing, singing and telling the quaint stories so common to their race.

In such a manner do the Yankees in New Bern spend their time. If the battery of Whitworth guns sent from Wilmington had reached me on time I could have used them, instead of the defective twenty pounders during the attack on New Bern. Under the fire of these cannon, I could have sunk their gunboats, captured Fort Anderson, and afforded them far more amusement than their captive darkies.

MARCH 26, 1863—THURSDAY
HOOKERTON, NORTH CAROLINA

I have tried several times today to write in this journal, but have not been well. A dull headache and kind of slow fever in the bones have kept me feeling a kind of discomfort and unrest, which I am quite unable to shake off. To add to my discomfort, last night, I was awakened in the small hours by a most frightful diarrhea, which has also troubled my day. I presume it is the result of a sudden change of water and diet. I have one thing in my favor and that is a very slim appetite. I shall try fasting, or at least abstemiousness for a time and hope soon to be all right again.

Last night, after one of my many visits to the sinks, I lay in bed wide awake and became for some reason which I was quite unable to control, very worried by personal matters. In consequence of the war, I have become quite concerned about property and pecuniary matters. Most of my estate, valued at $63,000 has been put into bonds of several railroads, the city of Charleston and my house on Tradd Street. With the Yankees about to mount a major attack on Charleston, my mind has been full of suspense and anxiety for I could lose all in the advent that Charleston falls or is reduced to rubble. These are hard times, but I must strive for cheerful contentment with my lot, be it what it may and put a firm reliance upon God who will give us all things needed for us. I must keep courage. All will be right! Courage, and keep a cheerful heart.

In the late morning, I bestirred myself enough to make a visit to Colonel Burgwyn, who, as the day was rather mild, was lying in his tent neatly attired in his shirt and drawers. With a quaint hospitality, he besought me to take off my coat and make myself at home, which I did avail of no further than to sit down. He said his men were rested and he was ready for another campaign.

I told him he might not have long to wait as General Hill had telegraphed that I should ready my command for a start and send all superfluous baggage to the rear. We were to cook five day's rations and supply each man with forty rounds of ammunition.

"Rumor has it we are going to join Lee at Fredericksburg," said the colonel.

"Rumor also has it we are going to Charleston to join Beauregard," I countered. "All we can do is prepare and wait."

After leaving the colonel, I sent off a scouting detail to reconnoiter the roads leading from Hookerton in all directions. I wanted to be ready regardless of where we were ordered. As I watched the scouts ride off, it occurred to me that we live very much after the way of the Arabs, when you think of it, nomadic, staying sometimes a day, sometimes a month in a place and then leaving it with all the bowers and wells that cost so much pains.

I read in the recent Richmond papers that a most fiendish Federal expedition left Port Royal a short time since, destination unknown, supposed Florida, with the open and avowed object of inciting the Negroes to revolt. The Northern papers actually glory in it and gloat over the adversity and misfortune that is to come upon the people of Florida. God avert their infamous acts. The Yankees declare that they are in correspondence with the slaves throughout a large and populous portion of the Confederacy, who only await their arrival to rise against their masters and strike a blow for the Union and freedom.

Some think this is balderdash, that Sambo knows nothing of freedom and cares little for it. Nor do they believe the Negroes will rise at the bidding of the Yankees. They take for granted the loyalty of the slaves.

But the slaves are also men and, like all men, carry within their hearts the idea that they were born to be free. This idea is allied to their hope of immortality. It is the eternal part of their nature which oppression cannot reach. It is the torch lit up in their soul by the hand of the Deity and never meant to be extinguished by the hand of man.

I have spent much time around the slaves and have overheard them praying morning and night for deliverance. Some of them would stand up in the fields or bend over the cotton and rice and pray out loud for God to help them. Down in South Carolina, near Charleston it is said among the darkies that there was a praying ground where the grass never had a chance to grow for the troubled knees that kept it crushed down.

This is a desperate time and I fear many of the slaves feel they owe no allegiance to a country which grinds them under its iron heel and treats them like dogs. So they wait, I fear, with the unnerving patience so peculiar to the race for a deliverer to come, singing their portentous song:

> "Gwine to write to Massa Jesus,
> "To send som valiant soldier,
> "To turn back Pharaoh's army. Hallelu!"

And although the mass insurrection that many have expected has not yet taken place, there have been limited risings in many parts of the South and hundreds of acts of individual resistance. Near Columbia, South Carolina, last month, whites became suspicious of an increasing number of black funerals and followed a group of mourners to a cemetery where it was discovered that the coffin contained arms which were being removed and hidden in a vault. Here in nearby Goldsboro, a young black woman tried to blow up her master's house by dropping a live coal into a cask of gun powder. She succeeded and I can only conclude that she had counted it as worthwhile, the cost of the serious injury she sustained.

APRIL 19, 1863—SUNDAY
GREENVILLE, NORTH CAROLINA

We have set up camp about a mile south of the Tar River. The brigade is camped in line on a big hill and headquarters is located in a large orchard overlooking the line. It is a splendid place and the day has been sunny and warm. I have pitched the headquarters tent under a large pine that offers shelter from the sun. A mocking bird offered a sweet serenade most of the afternoon, much to my pleasure.

The men look clean and well cared for. Everything has been restored to the order of a well-regulated camp. Parades and company drill, regimental and battalion are again the order of the day. We may remain here a month yet or we may not stay 24 hours. I see no present indication of a move, unless General Hill would once again attempt to capture New Bern.

I received two letters today to break the boredom of camp life. The first was from Judge Petigru.

"Charleston, April 10, 1863

"Dear Johnson,

"You see in spite of Yankee Monitors and Yankee shells, I am still in Charleston. The Yankees made their attack on Fort Sumter on

April 7th. I watched it all from the cupola of the Exchange and, with my glass, saw almost every shot. We did not know at the time how much their iron-clads were damaged, but the next day, one of them, the Keokuk, sank about 500 yards from Morris Island and we learn from reliable information that all the others were more or less damaged.

"The attacking force consisted of the iron-clad ocean steamer frigate New Ironsides and 8 or 9 iron-clad Monitors. The Monitors are almost invulnerable to balls or shells from the heaviest artillery. They lie so flat and low on the water that very little of the vessel is exposed to be struck except the turret, and that and every other part are so covered with iron plates as to be impenetrable to any missiles. The firing from the Yankee ships was rapid and was replied to by our batteries on Morris and Sullivan Islands, and by forts Moultrie and Sumter. The Ironsides, at 4:30 p.m., withdrew from the action, apparently badly injured, and retreated out of range of our guns. At 5:00 p.m., the fire from the monitors slackened and soon after they retreated out of range. The early renewal of the attack was confidently expected, but never materialized. There was intense excitement in Charleston among the crowd on the promenade battery viewing the fight. It reminded me of the glorious days of '61 when Sumter was shelled by our batteries.

"During the combat, I had only one fear that the enemy's iron-clads, relying on their impenetrability, would pass as rapidly as they could steam by the fortifications and under our heaviest fire to go to, or above, the city and destroy it and defeat our weaker, rear defenses by bombardment. But, thank God, this mode of attack was not attempted. It was a most signal defeat for the Yankees, as evidenced by the fact that their fleet has retired to Port Royal and their army, which had landed on Coe's

Island and Folly Island, has evacuated these points and has suspended the attack for the present, probably for 3 or 4 months, perhaps forever.

"We now feel that Charleston has been proved impregnable from the water and the fights at Secessionville and Pocataligo were such complete victories over greatly superior forces in point of numbers that we are now perfectly confident of our ability to hold the city against any forces they can bring against it.

"I sleep now at home, which I have all to myself. I also breakfast and dine ($2.50 each) at the Charleston Hotel. After breakfast, I walk to Tradd Street and spend some time at your house where Ruth makes me a cup of tea with some crackers. I get along very well with this routine. The afternoon I spend tucked away codifying the civil statutes of South Carolina.

"I am obliged to confess to having been quite unwell recently. I have had a bothersome cough and have had to give up my daily walks along Meeting and Broad streets as I tire easily and become quite short of breath. Today I am most happy to say I feel quite well again. It must be the advances of old age that tires me so. Nevertheless, I am determined to keep active when health permits.

"Write, Johnson, and stay safe,

Louis Petigru"

APRIL 26, 1863—SUNDAY
GREENVILLE, NORTH CAROLINA

The newspapers report bad news from Vicksburg. Five of the enemy's gunboats have succeeded in running past our batteries. Eight made the attempt but three were sunk by our guns. An attack upon

Vicksburg seems eminent. A new Yankee battery mounting Parrot guns has opened on the fortifications. So General Grant's late abandonment of the canal and the post opposite Vicksburg was only a ruse, in hope of catching the defenders off their guard.

There is also a report that the Yankees now pretend that their late advance on Charleston was a "reconnaissance in force" to get the range of our guns. If so, why then were so many transports needed and so many troops landed on Cole's and Folly Island? Why too were bets so freely offered and refused by army officers in Washington as to their success?

Doctor Sullivan, Major Haskell and I had a discussion tonight on the question whether the Negro has any love of liberty, whether he desires freedom or merely imagines more personal comfort in being free. We submitted the following test question to William, to Jeff, to James, to Moses, to Tom and to Ceceil, all the darkies accessible: "Which would you prefer, to be a slave with a good master, not much work to do, plenty of hog and hominy, and a coon dog, or be a free man, live in Yankeedom and have to scratch for a living?" William said it would be nice to be free, but Moses, who has much influence among our camp servants, followed the coon dog and the rest of them followed Moses.

Moses argues that if he could pick his master, he had better be a slave than President Davis. These was no better position. It involved "no 'sponsibility." If the master was a "heavy coon dog" it was all the better.

"What do you mean by a 'heavy coon dog'?"

"Why, ye see," said Moses, "when a man owns a big plantation and a heap o' darkies, and carries a heavy pocket, den we call him a heavy coon dog."

"And," said I, "you like life on the heavy coon dog's plantation?"

"De slaves on our plantation," said James, "liked workin' for old master. He didn't want no more freedom than us was gittin' on our plantation already. Us knowed too well dat us was well taken care of, wid plenty of vittles to eat and tight log and board houses to live in. De slaves where I lived didn't want no freedom 'cause they could not eat, wear, or sleep it. Yes sir, they thought dat freedom ain't nothing less you is got somethin' to live on and a place to call home. Dis livin' is freedom is lak young folks livin' on love after they gits married. It just don't work."

"But," said I, "what chance do you have to amount to something in this world if you are a slave?"

"Gen'rel," said Tom. "I is kinda glad I is a black man 'cause you knows dere ain't much expected of them no how and dat, by itself, take a big and heavy burden off der shoulders."

"So you are happy and contented on the plantation," said Haskell. "But what if your master died?"

"That might be bad," said Moses, "because with massa we had something, an' dat security. Yassuh. With massa, we had somebody to go to when we was in trouble. We had a massa dat would fight fo' us an' help us an' laugh wid us an' cry wid us. We had a missus dat would nuss us when we was sick, an' comfort us when we hadda be punished."

"Besides," added Cecil, "a free nigger was d'spized everywhere he had ever been."

"Dat your opinion," replied William. "Every time I think of slavery and if it done the nigger any good, I think of the story of the coon and the dog who chanced to meet. The coon said to de dog. 'Why is it you're so fat and I be so poor and we is both animals?' The dog replied, 'I lays around massa's house and let him kick me and he gives me a piece of bread right on.' Said the coon to de dog, 'Better than that, I stay poor.' Dats my feeling. I'm lak dat coon. I don't believe in abuse."

Later in the day, Captain Young and I rode to a neglected graveyard on the outskirts of Greenville.

"This is where Quartermaster Tolles, the poor fellow, is buried— right here, General."

I thanked the caretaker and looked round upon the graves. I thought of Tolles who had by chance burned his foot and then lost his life when shot in a Yankee raid upon the wagon carrying him to the hospital in Kinston. I thought of this good and kind man and of the household benefit of his presence.

"You see them green spots over you covered with weeds? Them are the graves of Yankees killed in the battle of Goldsboro."

"Do you know who they were?" I asked.

"Might of, but the last time I was here, there was a nigger plowing and every time he came to a grave, he would just reach over his plough, jerk up the lead board, and throw it behind him as he ploughed along. All the time he never stopped whistling his tune."

After the caretaker left Captain Young and I, I placed a small vase of flowers on Tolles' grave. As we left, I thought if these graves could speak what a history they could disclose. But the small mounds of earth are rigid and still. Even the winds seem to hush their whispers about this place of death. All is silence and the heart of the visitor is constrained to silence also.

MAY 2, 1863-SATURDAY
GREENVILLE, NORTH CAROLINA

Early yesterday morning, a buoyant Major Haskell came to my tent with the news that he was being transferred to Longstreet's Corps. Army of North Virginia. "At last," said the delighted one, "away from the back-water of North Carolina to a fighting general and a fighting army!"

Later, while the major was in his tent at breakfast, the first sergeants of the 26th quietly called out the regiment. The men surround the tent where Haskell was and surprised him with three cheers and then three times three. He came out and tried to make a speech but broke down in tears. The men gave him three times three more cheers.

In the afternoon when the major left to join his new command, the men of the 26th formed a line to properly honor him as he left camp. I was standing at the end of the line and, as the major rode up, he smiled and waved his sword towards me as he passed by. I called out to him wishing him good luck and so he went on, and when we shall meet again, only God knows.

At about ten o'clock tonight, one of our pickets was suddenly startled by a loud cry for help from the darkness near his post. Rushing to the spot he discovered a Yankee deserter, stuck fast in a swampy place. Reading out his musket he managed to pull the Yankee out of the mud hole and brought him to headquarters. He was a man about fifty years old and until conscripted into the Yankee army had been a physician practicing his profession somewhere in Connecticut. He was enormously fat, wore a wig and spectacles and false teeth, all of which he had lost in the mud hole. Covered with mud and dirt, he presented a ludicrous and pitiable spectacle. After he had wiped the mud from his face and eyes and blown it from his mouth, he drank a cup of coffee and proceeded in a most deliberate and solemn manner to deliver his opinion of Yankeedom.

As he began his conversation, he must have been extremely nervous for great beads of sweat fell from his forehead and he took out his handkerchief frequently to wipe his brow. The energy which this Connecticut doctor anathematized his Northern government was astonishing. He cursed it individually from Abe Lincoln and his cabinet down through its congress and public men to the lowest pothouse politician who advocated its cause; he cursed its army from generals Hooker and Foster down to the army mule; he cursed that army in its occupation of Washington and New Bern and said it had no business being in North Carolina or Virginia; he cursed its artillery and its muskets, its banner, bugles and drums; he cursed the Abolitionists, who had brought about the war and he invoked the direct calamity woe and disaster upon the Black Republicans and Lincoln and all they represented; while the earnestness, force and sincerity with which it was delivered made it one of the most effective speeches I ever heard and this together with his comical appearance and the circumstances of his capture afforded Captain Young and I ample opportunity for laughter.

Just as the corpulent Yankee was finishing his outburst, Major Whitford of the partisan battalion rode up to my tent for a pow-wow. He is an excellent cavalry officer, having served with Ben McCullock's Texas Rangers in the Mexican War. A more reckless, devil-may-care looking soldier it would be impossible to find this side of the infernal regions. Imagine if you will a compactly-built man of middle height with tawny moustache and fierce, wild eyes, whose expression is determined, if not sinister. His ancient corduroys are tucked into a pair of muddy cowhide boots, with a huge revolver thrust into one, a Bowie knife into the other. Strapped over his shoulder he carries a sawed-off double-barreled shotgun.

Captain Martin of General Hill's staff knew Whitford when both served in the Texas Rangers during the 1840s. He often tells a tale concerning Whitford and those desperate almost lawless days.

Martin recalled how one evening he sauntered into the Old Exchange Hotel, a noted drinking and gambling saloon in San Antonio, Texas. The barroom was crowed with rangers, Mexicans, townsfolk, some ladies of the night, and a few Indians. Tables and benches were arranged about the room and these were well patronized by the motley crowd of desperate characters who filled the saloon.

Martin sauntered from table to table, watching with interest the wild characters who were engrossed in gambling. Oaths and cigar smoke filled the air, and now and then a dispute led to knives being drawn, but no blood was spilt as friends would interfere before the disputants resorted to cold steel.

At a small table sat two men playing euchre for the drinks. Martin quickly identified one of the men as Whitford, who was quietly playing his hand in a mild way, utterly at variance with the hardened, rugged appearance he presented. His opponent in the game was a noted desperado short in height, thick in body, face bronzed by exposure to the hue of a Indian, with eyes deeply sunken and bloodshot, coarse black hair hanging in snakelocks down his back. His costume was that of a Mexican herdsman, made of leather with a Mexican blanket thrown over his shoulder. A dispute soon attracted the attention of all in the room to the table, when the desperado threw a glass of liquor in Whitford's face and sprang to his feet, drew his revolver and placed it against the breast of Whitford, and swore with fearful oaths that if he did not apologize he would "blow a hole through him a rabbit would jump through!" Whitford did not move from his seat, but replied, "Shoot and be damned, but if you miss I won't miss you."

Martin expected the desperado to back out, for he usually stood up only to those he knew he could intimidate, but with a quivering lip he pulled the trigger, but only the cap exploded! The desperado looked at his revolver, which had misfired, a look of terror on his face as Whitford sprang up, his huge Bowie knife flashing in the candlelight, and the desperado fell with a sickening thud to the floor a corpse! His neck was cut half through. Whitford, with eyes glaring like a wildcat, threw over the table and placing one foot on the fallen desperado said, "Strangers! Does anyone wish to take up this man's fight? If so, step out, if not we'll drink."

As no one seemed disposed to accept Whitford's challenge, all hands went with him to the bar, his hands smearing his glass with the blood of the desperado, whose yet warm body was dragged out. Sawdust was sprinkled over the blood-stained floor, Whitford carefully wiped his knife on the leather sleeve of his jacket, and matters in the Old Exchange Hotel resumed their usual course.

"Who is that?" asks the fat Yankee, looking almost in awe as Whitford dismounts.

"Major Whitford, of the partisan battalion," answers Captain Young. "He caught a notorious spy last winter and hung him to a tall tree with the inscription 'this man to hang three days: he who cuts him down shall hang the remaining time.'"

"You know," said Young, "there have been many cases of Yankees pretending to desert and hating their cause only to spy on their captors. You're not a spy, are you?"

At this suggestion, the Yankee looked as if he had an attack of apoplexy. He turned suddenly pale and I swear his knees buckled a bit, while he sweated all the more profusely.

"He'd be a tough one to hang," said Whitford. "We'd need a large tree and a thick rope."

This was too much for the captive and he fell to his knees almost in a swoon. Captain Young, feeling the jest had gone far enough, called the guards to take the Yankee away and I doubt if ever there was a prisoner happier to be taken to the guardhouse.

I have in the past written in this journal of a soldier named Gibbs of my brigade who, when sober is a good soldier, but who loves his toddy. Gibbs has of late been following the straight and narrow path of good behavior, but a recent incident illustrated that Gibbs is never far from temptation.

Several days ago, a teamster new to our camp brought in a load of supplies in a large army wagon pulled by six large, shaggy mules. The teamster named John was the owner of two bottles of old bourbon, forbidden in camp, which Gibbs fortuitously discovered and resolved to possess. Being aware that the teamster's presence was an impediment to his ownership of the bourbon, he hit upon a plan to get rid of him.

Approaching John, who was busy currying his mules, he accosted him with, "I say, old fellow, what are you doing there?"

"Can't you see?" replied John gruffly.

"Certainly," responded Gibbs, "but that is not your business. It is after tattoo and my regiment, the 26th, has a fellow hired by Colonel Burgwyn, who curries all the mules and horses brought in after tattoo."

The teamster bit at once and asked Gibbs where this hairdresser kept himself. Gibbs then directed John to Colonel Burgwyn's tent with the assurance that there was where the fellow "hung out."

"You can't mistake the man," said Gibbs. "He looks very young, but despite his youth he is very experienced at combing down mules. Unfortunately he is also lazy for a man in his business. Once comfortable in his tent, it is hard to move him. He will probably refuse to do it and tell you to go to the devil, but don't mind that. He has been drinking today. Make him come out for it is his duty."

"Does he drink excessively for one so young?" asked the teamster.

"Yes," replied Gibbs. "It is very sad for he once was a promising youth, but now when in his cups acts as though he is one in authority."

John posted off and entered the tent where Colonel Burgwyn sat with his back to the entrance reading a recent issue of the *Charleston Mercury*. Approaching the unsuspecting colonel, John slapped him on the back with a good degree of force. Surprised, the colonel sprang to his feet and accosted his uninvited guest with "Well sir, who in the world are you and what the devil do you want?"

"Young man, I've got a job for you now. Six mules to be combed down and right off, too," said the captain of the mules, undaunted at the flashing eye of young Colonel Burgwyn.

"Do you have any idea of whom you are addressing, sir?" asked the exasperated commander.

"Yes," said the teamster, elevating his voice to a pitch which rendered the words audible to a distant quarter. "You are the fellow hired by Colonel Burgwyn to clean mules and I won't have any foolishness from one so young. Clean them mules and I'll give you a drink of Old Hennessy."

"You idiot!" yelled Burgwyn, now perfectly furious. "I am Colonel Burgwyn, Commander of the 26th Regiment!"

"Of course you are," replied the teamster, "and I'm Jeff Davis, President of the Confederacy. Now go clean those mules!"

This was too much for Colonel Burgwyn and he pulled his sword from its nearby scabbard as a thoroughly terrified John darted from the tent just in time to save his head.

As John dashed away, Gibbs, watching from a discreet distance, drank to the mule driver's health from his newly acquired bourbon.

Later that night, a thoroughly inebriated Gibbs was once again thrown into the guardhouse. The story of his masterful deceit soon got out and has become the popular joke of the season. None, I might add, enjoying it more that Colonel Burgwyn when he learned the full depth of Gibbs' duplicity.

I received a report from Colonel Burgwyn this morning that the health of his regiment is remarkably good. "On yesterday," he wrote, "I had 1,020 men present, more I suppose than any regiment in the Confederate service."

MAY 3, 1863—SUNDAY
HALIFAX, NORTH CAROLINA

My brigade was ordered north for Richmond late last night. It is not certain but I suspect that we may go right on to Fredericksburg to join Lee's army. There are reports that the Yankee army under Hooker has crossed the Rappahannock about fifteen miles above Fredericksburg. It is thought he hopes to outflank us and cut off our communications with Richmond. I can only hope we can join Lee's army before the great battle begins. I want something more than the minor skirmishes that took place in North Carolina. Colonel Burgwyn and I expect a big fight on the left flank of our Fredericksburg position and hope to be in at the death.

We have had an enforced layover at Halifax while repairs are being made on the train. Colonel Burgwyn, Dr. Sullivan, Louis Young and I shared a noon meal together at the Willie Jones House, the finest and only establishment for dining in Halifax.

It is now early evening and the train rumbles northward. I have tried to get comfortable on my seat and undertake to sleep, but I have already slept too much. I light up my cigar and try to read over yesterday's newspaper, yawn and throw it down and conclude things are confoundedly dull. Captain Young is sleeping in the seat in front of me and I hear a slight snort or two. Then, several minutes later, the captain is snoring diligently away. And such deep, unearthly snores they are! The loud noise comes up from his lungs and rushes like a hurricane through his wide open mouth in tones as unmusical as the rasping of a saw. Who can sleep amidst such thunder. "Breathe through your nostrils, Captain Young," I advise quietly over the seat. I am answered with a loud snort worse than the thunderous report of a 15-inch Rodman Smoothbore. "Confound him," I mutter, resigned to my fate.

Yes it is dull and loud, but great armies are on the move and we are rushing toward the scene of the action. I can only pray we will arrive in time to be of some service to our great cause.

MAY 5, 1863—TUESDAY
NEAR ASHLAND, VIRGINIA

As we passed through Richmond on the cars we learned that the Yankee cavalry under General Stoneman has made a dash into our lines and avoiding Stuart have penetrated into the heart of Virginia, cutting up telegraph wires and tearing up railroad tracks. To prevent further destruction we have been rushed to Hanover Junction, the vital rail center north of Richmond. I have been placed in command of all the troops in the immediate area in anticipation of a Yankee raid on the railroad bridges over the North and South Anna rivers. I have presently dispersed my command in company sized formations over a wide area to better guard the lengthy railroad line and the bridges.

In the afternoon I rode out to the picket line near the Jericho Bridge. Dismounting I approached a soldier of the picket line and brusquely and sharply demanded his gun and extended my hand to receive it. The picket instantly dropped his gun to a 'charge bayonet' position and positively refused to part with it. I left him and tried another man a little farther down the line. This soldier's gun came down to a 'charge bayonet' position with a quick determined snap and I had once again received another refusal, even more emphatic than the previous one. The men of the picket line this afternoon, are not generous with their guns, but I am nevertheless very pleased. Any sentinel while on duty in presence of the enemy will risk less by refusing to part with his musket, no matter who demands it, than by giving it up to anyone.

I moved on again and while resting at a crossroads a detachment of Stuart's cavalry come by. A rougher, more torn and battered collection of men, horses and equipment I have never seen, but the men are jovial, joking and merry and appear to be thoroughly enjoying the staring by our pickets as they pass. Rough riders they seem to be much more warlike than General Robertson's cavalry I served with in North Carolina.

I learned from one of Stuart's officers that the Yankee cavalry under General Stoneman have been reported only a few miles from Richmond and the excitement in the city is rumored to be terrible. Alarm bells have been rung, the citizens armed and sent out to man the batteries; extemporaneous cavalry companies have been sent out and women are reported to be crying and wringing their hands on the streets. This is the most daring raid the Yankees have yet attempted and should put us on our guard against despising our enemy.

As I rode back toward headquarters, I studied carefully the lay of the land and reflected on what I would do if my brigade should be needed against the Yankee cavalry. I thought through all the contingencies of the situation. Proper orders for the surgeon and quartermaster would have to be quickly decided upon, provision made for the sick in camp, transportation, rations and ammunition would all require attention. Then as we marched to the enemy, I would have to ask myself, "What would you do if the enemy should attack from that ridge? What commands would I give? Where would I place the battery and what would I do with the supply train?" Once thought through I then proceeded to criticize my arrangements trying to determine the best course of action to take. Thus did I pass the time until I rode into camp, my brain racked from thinking about these perplexing subjects.

Shortly after reaching camp, we were agreeably surprised by the return of Adjutant Matt Hare. He was wounded at New Bern in March. While in the hospital he had cut out of his shoulder a piece of shell over two inches long, three fourths of an inch wide and half an inch thick, weighing between three and four ounces. The surgeons at first refused to cut the jagged piece of iron out. Finally after carrying in there in a festering wound deep near his shoulder blade for over six weeks the surgeons finally operated and cut it out. He declares that: "It would have killed me long ago if I hadn't been so d _ _ _ awful mad all the time."

MAY 8, 1863—FRIDAY
NEAR ASHLAND, VIRGINIA

News of a glorious victory from the Rappahannock! Hooker crossed the river with 159,000 men about 15 miles above Fredericksburg. He strongly entrenched that wing of his army which rested upon the river, but Stonewall Jackson, making a rapid march, got into Hooker's rear beyond Chancellorsville whilst Lee made an attack upon his other wing. Thus pressed, his left flank was doubled up upon his right, the slaughter being terrific. General Lee in his official report speaks of it as a "signal victory." Our army was smaller than usual as Longstreet was still in Suffolk with two divisions and could not get up in time. It is pretty certain that Hooker—fighting Joe!—had two men to Lee's one and was defeated. The victory is tempered, however, as General Jackson was wounded severely. The great Stonewall has been lost to us for a time; his left arm has been amputated and there is a severe wound in his right hand. The best surgical skill of the army, the sympathy and anxiety of the whole South, and the prayers of the country are his.

When the headquarters staff filed around with their tin plates and cups this morning for their breakfast, there was much grumbling over the brigade once again missing the chance to partake in a great battle. "We have, however," said Captain Young, with a touch of sarcasm in his voice, "managed to guard the railroad in grand style."

I recently had over two dollars worth of stamps and many envelopes ruined in a sudden rain storm. Feeling the need to replenish my supply, I rode the short distance to Ashland to buy the needed articles.

Ashland is a sprawling little town with its Central Street cluttered by the tracks of the Richmond, Fredericksburg and Potomac railroad. As I rode down the main street, it was enveloped in clouds of dust from the passing freight wagons. There was also a crowd of pedestrians passing to and fro. Among these I noticed a number of Negroes with little bundles on their backs. One of them, a very old man, was sitting by the railroad track taking a rest.

"Well, Uncle, how are you getting along?"

"Tolerable, Massa. Only tolerable." And he lifted his tattered cap from his white head with a grace of politeness any gentleman might have envied.

"Where are you going?"

"I's gwine to Richmond, Massa."

"That's some distance from here."

"I's hears tell."

"What do you expect to do there, uncle?"

"I don't know right well. I thought I couldn't be no wus off than whar I was; and I hadn't no place to go."

"How so, uncle?"

"Yo see, a de Yankees burn my massa's house down and de barn also. Now I gots to find a new home."

"Where did you come from?"

"Dinwiddie County."

"You have walked all the way from Dinwiddie County?"

"Yes, Massa. I's walked over fo'ty mile. But I don't mind that."

"You're very old, uncle."

"Yes. I've a right good age, Massa. It's hard to a man o' my years to be burned out of his home. I don't know what I shall do, but I reckon the Lord will take keer of me."

The tone of patience and cheerfulness in which he spoke was very touching. I stayed near him and drew from him by degrees his story. The Yankees, part of the cavalry of General Stoneman, rode up bravely to the house, where they knew they would find only women and children. They ransacked the house, fed their horses at the barns, and took the horses from the stables, shot the pigs, sheep and other stock, and left them dead in the field. Then, after stealing the silver spoons and forks and whatever valuables they could find, they set fire to the barns and rode brazenly on their way. With no means of support, the Negroes were forced to leave, this old man among them.

"There was," he said, "no use for old wore-out niggers. I served my massa and his father befo' nigh on to sixty year; and he never give me a dollar. Now I'm old and wore-out and forced to leave. It's right hard, massa!"

"What will you do, uncle?"

"I heard I can gets wok in Richmond. Dem that pays, offers wages a man can live by."

"It does seem you will be better off in Richmond," I suggested.

"I don't know, Massa. I'd sooner be back on de farm, but de Yankees take care ob dat."

I came back past the tracks on my way back to camp some time later. The old Negro was gone and I surmised he had headed toward Richmond walking south along the railroad track, his bundle on one arm and his faith in God on the other. I could only hope all would go well for him.

MAY 11 1863—MONDAY
NEAR ASHLAND, VIRGINIA

Late last evening, we received by telegram the following message sent by General Lee to all commands:

> With deep grief, the commanding general announced the death of Lieutenant General Jackson, who expired on the 9th at 3:15 p.m. The daring, skill and energy of this great and good soldier by a decree of an all-wise providence are now lost to us. But while we mourn his death, we feel that his spirit lives and will inspire the whole army with his indomitable courage and unshaken confidence in God as our hope and strength.

> Let his name be a watchword for his corps., who have followed him to victory on so many fields. Let officers and soldiers imitate his invincible determination to do everything in the defense of our beloved country.

A chill went through my heart as I read the telegram. He died of pneumonia, eight days after the amputation of his arm, died in the fullness of his reputation, the brightness of his glory.

The men are stunned and each person seems to feel as if he had lost a relative. I feel more disheartened about the war than I have ever felt before. I think the death of Jackson has affected us all and I can't help thinking it will put new life into the enemy and give him courage to make another attempt to capture Richmond.

This evening as I sat by the campfire, the sweet fragrance of Magnolia drifted through the trees. Then, off in the distance, the brigade bugler sounded sharp notes which reverberated through the soft and balmy spring air and as his melody faded into the night, I thought seldom has nature seemed so beautiful and serene.

I stirred the fire and the sparks whirled upward drifting away into the darkness. Off in the distance, I could see other campfires where the bright red flames flickered shadows on the pensive faces of the men. Not far away, a little group of soldiers are sitting around a campfire entertaining each other with stories and otherwise. Just now, one of them lifts up his voice in a melancholy refrain and remembers the fallen Jackson and other myriad killed and wounded friends as he sings:

"Soon with angels I'll be marching
With bright laurels on my brow.
"I have for my country fallen
Who will care for mother now?"

While I write he strikes into another air and these are the words as I hear them:

"I'm gui-en home. I'm gui-en home, to d-I-e no mo.'"

Strangely in the midst of all this tranquility, a poignant feeling crept over me. I lighted a new cigar and as the white smoke drifted about my head and vanished upward, the bugle sounded again and I found myself wandering back year by year into my past. It was a profound experience and I was once again in Charleston, then in my student days at the University of North Carolina. I cannot find the words to adequately describe the moment, but it seemed that all the vicissitudes of life passed in review before my mind. Then the bugle sounded again and, as the tones died softly away in the distant hollows of the surrounding hills, I dwelt on the unknown but wondrous scenes of the future. I realized this war has been the despair and ruination of many a man, but I resolved then and there to meet it head on come what may.

I sat lost in my reverie late into the night, finally retiring to bed with a heart full of emotion and a mind somewhat exhausted from too much thinking, hopefully to dream of home and friends far away.

MAY 17, 1863—SUNDAY
NEAR ASHLAND, VIRGINIA

This evening, I was agreeably surprised by a call from Captain Frank Bennett of the 23rd North Carolina, who has just recovered from his dreadful wound received at Sharpsburg. The captain is returning for duty with his regiment, encamped near Fredericksburg.

I had known Frank Bennett before the war at the University of North Carolina. He has light, sandy hair, florid complexion, steel blue eyes, sharp features and chin and is spare built and wiry. He was a comical character. According to his own story, he had one day received orders with his command to repair a broken bridge over the Chickahominy River during the Peninsula Campaign. Once of General D. H. Hills aides rode up, full of anxiety and demanded, "Who commands here?"

Captain Bennett, who stutters considerably at times, especially when nervous, replied, "I-I-I do."

"I want to know, sir, can artillery pass over?"

"Ye-yes, s-s-sir, if they are f-f-flying artil-l-lery!" Casting a glance over the broken bridge as he made the answer.

Bennett was the life of his company and kept many a depressed spirit in good humor. It was astonishing that he could remain so light-hearted under the grave and trying circumstance of Gaines Mill, Malvern Hill and the other bloody battles of the Seven Days Campaign.

I soon saw during our conversation that Captain Bennett's spirits had undergone a change and for once he was like many others—quiet, depressed, nervous, anxious and apprehensive. A strange gloom had come over quaint Frank Bennett's soul and his small steel blue eyes no longer twinkled nor did he seem inclined to joke.

I told the captain I didn't mean to pry but that there had been a sudden and complete change in his manner.

"Yes," he replied, "this war has changed me—it has changed us all. I think it began after I was wounded at Sharpsburg—yes, terrible Sharpsburg. That was, I think, the birth of my fear."

"It is hard to bear in mind what occurred after I was wounded, but suffice it to say I was eventually taken to a house on Clay Street in Richmond as all the hospitals were filled. I had been shot in the shoulder and my femur fractured by a Minie ball. It was at the house on Clay Street my leg was amputated. I was nursed by a young widow named Hennrietta Aiken and she was an angel on earth. I will never forget her large and lustrous black eyes. It was hard for any man to resist their influence."

"Several days after I lost my leg, Major George Robb was brought to the house on Clay Street. He had been shot near the Dunker Church leading his men. The surgeons did not think him mortally wounded. He asked me to write a letter to his mother. Afterward he said he had another letter to write but that he wished to sleep first—he felt so exhausted. At his request, Hennrietta then turned his face from the light and left him. Some time later, when she came again to look after him, she found him dead. He had been dead a long time. He was a true specimen of our old regime—gallant, gay, unfortunate. These are sad and unfortunate memories and I have tried to run away from them. But as my recovery went on fear was no longer an occasional visitor but a permanent settler in my midst.

"So you see through God's blessing, I am yet alive and able to return to duty. But when alone at night, I feel strange things stirring in the darkness. Strange feelings and I listen anxiously hardly able to sleep. I now believe I cannot hope to pass safely through another campaign. I will do my duty, but I am weary of this war.

"On my way here, I passed some hunters 'on a stand' for deer. What a thrill of old associations the sight of those hunters awakened

Remembrances of dreamy October days, of woods flush of gorgeous coloring, of repose deep, untroubled and serene, of quiet broken only by the hoot of an owl, the singing of a bird, or the sigh of the wind through the trees, of plenty and prosperity, cornfields with bended heads awaiting the gatherer's hand, or, to sum it all in one word, peace. And now, I look within my own mind torn by anxiety with wearying care for the future, distressed for my wounded and dying countrymen, sympathizing with the anguish of lonely and broken hearts, with the cares of mothers for food for their children, with the sorrow which oppresses the manly bosoms of our soldiers separated from their loved ones and forced to live in peril and my own heart is heavy within me and I can only pray for the blessed tidings of peace."

MAY 30, 1863—SATURDAY
NEAR ASHLAND, VIRGINIA

This guarding of the railroad is doleful. My command is so scattered I have only several companies at headquarters. I miss the parades, drills, music and company of a concentrated brigade and I am anxious to get the regiments together again.

The great topic of interest from the newspapers I receive in camp concerns Grant's victories in Mississippi. From the time he ran the blockade at Vicksburg with his vessels and landed down the Mississippi River at Port Gibson, he seems to have marched from one victory to another. The newspapers mention five distinct battles in seventeen days.

Many here fear the worst for Vicksburg and we cannot understand what important use there can be in our continuing to hold and defend the city. The safety of the position and of the large garrison are now greatly endangered by the Yankees in their rear, with all supplies and communication likely to be cut off.

The close approach of the sickly season—doubly to be dreaded by the Yankees because of their having laid all the low country under water that will soon be stagnant—will hurry Grant's operations. What ever can be done by him must be done in a few weeks, or disease will probably so weaken his army to frustrate his plans and render all the gigantic preparations useless. The same danger threatens the Yankee army of Seabrook and Folly islands in South Carolina. Except immediately on the seashore, this region is dangerously unhealthy before June. Yet, as Dr. Middleton pointed out to me, it is true and strange that the Yankee forces were able to remain on the South Carolina seacoast and also in New Orleans through the last summer without suffering greatly by disease.

Yesterday morning a small freight train stopped near here. As I approached, I noticed an unusually animated and cheerful group of soldiers. They were gazing at something hidden from my view with great interest. Near the train I looked and, behold! Several of the freight cars were laden with stained coffins. They were obviously going to be used for those killed at Chancellorsville. I was rather amazed and bewildered at the feelings manifested by such a sight. Before turning to leave, I caught the following language from the soldiers, standing near the train. "I'm glad my time didn't come until the coffins got here. I tell you tis dreadful hard to think of being carried on a board and buried in a duty blanket."

"That's so," said another. "'taint human to be buried like a dog as some of them fellers was at Chancellorsville. Death doesn't seem half so bad since I've seen these coffins."

Troops continue to pass along the railroad from North Carolina and Suffolk, Virginia (Longstreet's men). They are going north to reinforce Lee. Stuart is also gathering a large body of cavalry. From what I have observed, it appears General Lee is upon the point of advancing to attack Hooker. That he will once again whip Hooker I have no doubt in the world. When the achievements of the Army of Northern Virginia are written by an impartial historian, I believe they will compare favorably with those of the Romans or to Napoleon's Imperial Guard.

Lee is now stronger than at Chancellorsville. It is said that General Lee will have from 33,000 to 37, 000 reinforcements. Thus his force will soon number almost 80,000 men. These are effective men, all present for duty. Hooker's army will not be in as good a condition as it was before the battle for six months or more. With all this taken into consideration, my opinion is that six weeks will find General Lee's army once again in Maryland, embarked upon another invasion of Yankee soil.

A box of cigars sent to me by Judge Petigru still holds out. Whenever I am in great straits for a smoke, I try one, but I have not yet succeeded in finding a good one. I affect to be very generous when entertaining and pass the box around freely, but all who have tried the cigars once insist that they do not smoke. They will probably last to the end of the war, even if that proves to be a hundred years from now.

There is at this moment a lively discussion in progress between two African gentlemen in regard to religious matters. It is mainly devoted to the case of one of their number who had died two nights before and who was regarded around the camp as a notorious thief and who Israel Lewis unhesitatingly declared, "was in hell." Old Hanson replies, "Oh hush. Yer don't know what you're talking about, nigger."

"I's don't," replies Israel. "Whar you 'spect Uncle Jim done gone? Thursday night at half-past ten o'clock…" (the hour at which the man died) "…Uncle Jim done gone to hell. Now he roll about on de red— not sheet—iron floor thar an' he climb up de red-hot walls an' fall back agin—no escaping from hell."

It was a most vivid picture Israel had painted of hell. I must confess that after I heard the punishment given to Uncle Jim and his unpleasant predicament, I didn't hesitate to say a short prayer in consideration that God would pardon the damned and release him from perdition.

JUNE 2, 1863—TUESDAY
HANOVER JUNCTION, VIRGINIA

At long last my brigade has been transferred to the Army of Northern Virginia. We received the news by telegraph yesterday and it set off a wave of rejoicing among the staff and men.

My brigade has been assigned to A. P. Hill's corps and General Henry Heth's division. The other brigades in our division are Archers, Brockenbrough and Davis. The other divisions of our corps are commanded by General R. H. Anderson and my old friend Major General Dorsey Pender.

Our camp here at Hanover Junction is probably a very temporary one. The village itself extends half a mile along the railroad track, the dwellings occupying principally the sides of the street, amply shaded by trees lining the curbs. The houses are squat two-story affairs built principally of stone and coated with rough cast. Every second building seems to have been at one time a public house. One of the locals informed us that Hanover was one of the relays going toward Maryland and the national Road, in ye good old days when teaming was in vogue before the steam horse supplanted that industry.

From my headquarters most of the staff stroll over to a tavern directly after breakfast and remain much of the day. The building is fronted by a beautiful lawn sloping to the west, shaded by the aspen, the fir, the linden, the spruce pine and the magnolia; whilst the spring roses just blossoming into fragrance and the climbing vines of the sweet-scented honeysuckle all combine to make this a charming spot.

Late this afternoon, the division of General Pickett came within sight of Hanover—the troops swinging along the road, marching at ease and all the bands of the regiments playing "The Bonnie Blue Flag."

The column moved through the town, every man in his place, stepping jauntily as on parade with arms at "right shoulder shift," with the rays of the afternoon sun flaming on polished bayonets. The division moved down the broad main thoroughfare and wheeled on to its camping ground. The men of my brigade by the thousands had gathered on either side to see these storied veterans of the Army of Northern Virginia pass.

It was about an hour later when I observed a group of mounted officers ride up the road and stop at the pathway leading to the Hanover Tavern. One of the sentinels pointed his arm towards the veranda where I and several of my staff were enjoying the cooling late afternoon breezes.

One of the officers who walked up the path was a stalwart man who strode along with the nonchalant air of one who had wooed Dame Fortune too long to be cast down by her frowns. Suddenly, Captain Young, sitting by me, sprang from his chair with a cry of "General Pickett!"

"Why Louis!" was echoed back and a warm embrace was exchanged. Captain Young had last parted from Pickett in the Pacific Northwest or some other place where the pleasant pre-war business of killing Indians was going on and now fraternized with his old friend of long ago.

Before me stood one of the most singular figures in the Army of Northern Virginia. He was ordinary enough in size, well-built in the full vigor of mature manhood, erect, alert, quick, the beau ideal of a soldier.

But the head, the hair, was extraordinary! I had never seen anything quite like it on an officer of the Confederate Army. Long ringlets flowed loosely over his shoulders, trimmed and highly perfumed; his beard was likewise curling and perfumed to give out the scents of Avaby.

After their greeting, Captain Young brought the general to me and said, "General Pettigrew, General Pickett."

The general took me by the hand and said, "General, your reputation has preceded you. I have heard of your gallantry at Seven Pines."

"Thank you, General Pickett," I replied. "Your men march magnificently."

"I am a fortunate man, General Pettigrew, for never was there such a division as the one I command, such an uncomplaining, plucky body of men…never. Many of them are without shoes or blankets or overcoats and they have not uttered one word of complaint, nor one murmuring tone; but cheerily singing or telling stories, they have tramped, tramped, tramped. To crown it all, you should have seen our march through Richmond several days ago. We marched through the city, the home of many of my men, without a halt, with not a straggler, greeted and cheered by sweethearts, wives, mothers and friends. 'God bless you, my darling.' 'God bless you, my son.' 'Hello, old man.' 'Howdy, Charley.' rang all along the line. Lunches, loaves of bread, bottles of milk or hot coffee were thrust into grateful hands by the dear people of Richmond as the men hurriedly returned the greetings and marched on. You would hardly recognize these ragged, barefoot soldiers as the trim, tidy boys who went to war two years ago in their handsome gray uniforms, with shining equipment and full haversacks and knapsacks."

Then, after a bow, General Pickett excused himself, saying it was time to look after the men of his division.

As he walked away, one of my staff said to no one in particular, "He seems quite the aromatic dandy."

"He may seem that way," blistered Captain Young in reply, "for looks are deceiving but he always has been the soul of gallantry. If George Pickett is given the order, he will storm the gates of hell."

"Or hold those gates if necessary," I added.

"There have been many strange twists of fate in this civil war," remarked Captain Young, "but General Pickett is a partner to perhaps one of the strangest worries of all. It would probably astound all of you to know the man most responsible for getting him to West Point was none other than Abraham Lincoln, the present president of the United States. Although a native of Virginia, Pickett was living in Illinois in 1842 with his uncle and Lincoln's friend and fellow lawyer, Andrew

Johnson. It was at this point that Lincoln urged Congressman John Stuart to appoint Pickett to the academy. It seems Lincoln and Pickett took a liking to each other and for all I know may still be friends."

JUNE 9, 1863—TUESDAY
FREDERICKSBURG, VIRGINIA

We arrived at Fredericksburg yesterday on the cars and were shortly placed in the trenches overlooking the Rappahannock River. We are on the far right of the Army of Northern Virginia and should Lee move north toward the Shenandoah Valley, we would be among the last to leave the trenches and join the march. One of my great concerns is that General Lee will leave us here to guard Fredericksburg and divert the Yankees while the army moves north and thus miss the campaign.

My worrying aside, everything is perfectly quiet here at present. Today is a perfectly lovely day. The sun shines calmly and warmly and all the realm of nature seems fairly teeming with life. The trees have put forth their luxurious foliage and the little birds are twittering happily through the branches. How such a day reminds me of many I have spent in old Charleston. And to think, the pleasures and joys occasioned by such scenes could be quickly destroyed by the din of battle and the agonizing cries of the wounded and dying. War in many ways is such a paradoxical joke.

Some of our campsites are visited everyday by an aged, jovial darky. He comes dressed in a stovepipe hat, walking with a cane. With him he brings a large basket of pies and cakes. As he approaches our tents, he calls our, "Here's your pies and cakes and apples. Pay me today and I'll trust you tomorrow!" He usually quickly sells his wares and leaves vowing to return the next day.

This strange aberration is reportedly a free Negro and told Dr. Sullivan this morning that to enjoy freedom, a poor man had to work for himself: "It is sho' worth somethin' to be boss," is his philosophy.

Always interested in the workings of the African mind, Dr. Sullivan asked the peddler if being free wasn't a rather hard life and would it not be better to live under the protection and care of the white man.

To this the darky thought a bit and then replied: "No sir. I tink it betta to be free. For I tink dose dat are slaves are treated in de south much worse dan de children of Jacob by de Egyptians. Does not de white man hold de darky slave to be descended originally from de tribes of Monkeys or Orang-Outangs and treat dem so."

Late this afternoon, I mounted my horse and rode towards Fredericksburg. On the brow of a hill overlooking the town is the Marye Estate, one of the finest about Fredericksburg before the blast of battle struck it. As I stood near the house my mind drifted back across time to the halcyon days of December, 1862. I remember that the house was large and elegant then, occupying a beautiful site surrounded by terraces. That was before the mounds of freshly turned earth appeared affording protection for Colonel Alexander's Washington Artillery. Our two or three tiers of shallow trenches then seem modest now by present standards, but between the infantry in the sunken road and the artillery on these heights, the Yankees were mowed down in swaths!

Now, as I look around the house and witness the results of artillery and infantry firing, I observe the great damage that has been done. The pillars of the porch, built of brick and covered with a cement of lime and white sand, are speckled with the marks of bullets. Shells and solid shot have made havoc with the walls and woodwork inside. The windows are shivered, the partitions torn to pieces and the doors perforated.

I walked down the hill to the stone wall and looked out onto the plain below. A captain standing nearby invited me to go out onto the field and see where the dead were buried. Near the middle of the field a strip some fifteen yards long and four wide was devoid of grass or growth of any kind. "There's a thousand Yankees buried in his hole," said the captain. Some distance below this he showed me the cellar of an ice-house in which five hundred Federals were buried. And yet these were but a portion of the slain, all the surrounding fields were scarred with graves.

I left the captain and walked back up the heights to the Mayre House. From there I turned and commanded a view of Fredericksburg and the battlefield. And as I stood there, I once again saw in my imagination the battle reenacted: the Yankee pontoniers at their work in the misty morning; the sharpshooters in the rifle-pits and horses driving the Yankees from the pontoon bridge with their murderous fire; the shelling of the town; the troops crossing; the terrible roaring battle; the spouting flames; the smoke; the charging Federals and the horrible slaughter. I saw and heard it all again and felt like a pallbearer at a ghastly funeral. Verily war is cruel and none more terribly so than this which was forced upon us. God forgive those Yankees who started it. They knew not what they did.

JUNE 13, 1863—SATURDAY
FREDERICKSBURG, VIRGINIA

The Army of Northern Virginia is moving! Ewell's corps is in the lead and the immediate objective is believed to be Winchester. The corps of General Longstreet is following Ewell and only A. P. Hill and the Third Corps is left at Fredericksburg to confront the Yankees.

Our men are confident of success and there is not an officer or soldier in the army who does not believe we are able to drive the Yankee army into the Atlantic Ocean. The *Richmond Whig* editorialized today "that an artificial leg ordered some months ago awaits General Ewell's arrival in the city of Philadelphia."

My brigade and the rest of A. P. Hill's corps is still guarding Mayre's Heights and the other hills above Fredericksburg in the event the Federals should attempt to advance upon Richmond as General Lee moves northward.

General Heth claims we will follow Longstreet and the rest of the army as soon as General Hooker withdraws the Yankee army northward to protect Baltimore and Washington City. I certainly hope so for in my own case, I can sensibly feel the inspiration of going forward! I am in good spirits and haven't growled a single time today. Indeed, with the prospect of taking the war to the North, all the chronic grumblers have shut their mouths and every eye beams with cheerful anticipation.

Yesterday afternoon, Captain Young, Adjutant Hughes and I rode over to the camp of Colonel Leventhorpe. His regiment is away from the rest of the brigade and is strung out along the railroad guard it from any possible Yankee cavalry raid.

As we rode toward the camp, we came to an old log house where as usual at this time, the only occupants were women and children. The family consisted of the middle-aged mother, a tall, slab-sided, long-legged girl seemingly eighteen or nineteen years old, and two little children. The mother said they had lived there fifteen years and found it very comfortable. Before her husband left to join the army, he tilled a small farm and ha earned sufficient money to purchase three slaves. As the armies passed back and forth over the area, the slaves had run off and the ladies were left to their own efforts.

The house was small but comfortable and the mother invited us in while we watered our horses. The young girl was bare-footed and wearing a dirty white sort of cotton gown that looked a good deal like a big gunny sack. From what came under my observation later, I think I can safely say it was the only garment she had on. The young lass was quite attractive even though a bit dirty. We asked for some butter and inquired if they had any they could sell us. The mother replied that they were just going to churn and if we would be so kind to wait until that was done she could furnish us a bit. We waited and when the job was finished Adjutant Hughes handed the young girl a pint tin cup from his saddlebag which she proceeded to fill with butter. As she walked towards the adjutant to hand over the cup of butter, her bare feet slipped on a grease spot on the floor and down she went on her back with her gown distinctly elevated showing a prodigal display of limbs. At the same time, the cup fell from her hand and the contents rolled out onto the floor, like melted lard. The girl arose to a sitting posture, surveyed the wreck, and to our astonishment, laid down on one side and exploded with laughter, while kicking. He mother, shocked by the girl's behavior, exclaimed, "Why, Sallie, you dirty slut! Get a spoon and scrape that butter right up!"

Sallie rose slowly to her feet, still giggling over the mishap and the butter was duly "scraped up," restored to the cup, and this time safely delivered.

After we paid for the butter, the mother asked if we wished some snuff before we departed as her and Sallie were about to enjoy some. As we watched, they engaged in a practice known as "dipping," which is disgusting in the extreme. Sallie took a stick the size of a common pencil and chewed at one end until the fibers were separated. In this condition, it formed a brush. They then moistened the brush with saliva and plunged it into the snuff. The fine powder which adhered was then rubbed on the gums and the teeth. A species of partial intoxication for both Sallie and mother will be the result.

Once on our mounts and leaving mother and Sallie far behind, Adjutant Hughes tried to put the past events into perspective by saying, "One good thing the war has brought among many evils is that it has brought us into contact with many people we should never have known otherwise."

"Yes, Sallie was certainly charming," laughed Captain Young, "but I must say I have little admiration for her toilet."

JUNE 15, 1863—MONDAY
NEAR CHANCELLORSVILLE, VIRGINIA

Shortly after noon today we received orders to pack up and move and soon all was hurley burley. We were ordered to have three day's cooked rations in haversacks and three day's more in the wagons. The division wagon train would carry one or two day's more.

What a fine appearance the brigade made as it marched out from its bivouac above Fredericksburg. We took the plank-road to Chancellorsville and as far as the eye could reach, both in front and rear, the road was crowded with men. A score of bands filled the air with martial strains, while the afternoon sun brightened the muskets and made the flags look more cheerful and brilliant. The day was warm and pleasant and with the men beaming in their splendid uniforms, everything seemed propitious of success.

Three miles out of Fredericksburg, a young and very pretty girl stood in the doorway of a handsome farmhouse and waved the flag of the Confederacy. Cheer after cheer rose along the line. Officers saluted. Soldiers waved their hats and the band of the 26th struck up "Dixie." That loyal girl captured several thousand hearts and I trust that some day, a young gallant, the flower of Southern manhood, will return to the young damsel's abode and claim her as his own.

The march was hard on us for we had just begun to get fat and lazy in camp again. As we approached the Chancellorsville farm, the road runs through a large open field bounded by woods. The marks of hard fighting from the battle in May were visible from far off. The ground everywhere, in the field and in the woods, was strewn with mementos of the battle—rotting knapsacks and haversacks, battered canteens and tin cups and fragments of clothing. On each side of the road were breastworks and rifle-pits extending into the woods. Of the Chancellorsville House, formerly a large brick tavern only the half-fallen walls and chimneystacks remained. Here the Yankee General Hooker had his headquarters until the wave of battle on Sunday morning rolled so hot and near that he was compelled to withdraw. The house was soon after fired by one of our shells and burned.

After inspecting the ruins of the Chancellorsville House I mounted my horse and rode a short distance to the turnpike to watch the slow columns of moving infantry. These are the veterans of New Bern and Washington. Veteran soldiers of the march. They all carry a well-stuffed knapsack, surmounted by a rolled gray blanket, the worse for wear. From their belt is slung a big cartridge box with forty rounds and at their side hangs a haversack quite bursting with three day's rations. Hello! What has that lanky fellow dangling at the end of his musket? A coffee pot! An immense tin coffee pot! And there is another, a short fellow, with a small frying pan more precious to them than gold. And there goes a squad of cavalry, the riders almost obscured by the bags of oats and the blankets and coats piled on pommel and crupper. Their carbine hangs on one side and their sabre clatters from the other.

Several inhabitants of the area who lived near the Van Wert House watched the men march past with delight but seemed to be surprised by our numbers. One old gentleman who from an upper window of his house was busily engaged in waving a Confederate flag as he gazed down the long turnpike and saw the grey-clad column come marching steadily on, kept shouting as if in wonder, "Still they come! Still they come!"

The march was hard on the men and dust covered their clothing. It is interesting to observe, however, that however dirty or slovenly the men may be, their muskets always shine like silver. They know it is the most important item they carry.

As we neared the end of our march about half a mile from the Wilderness Tavern, the men began to straggle. Tired and overburdened with the temperature above ninety degrees, weary man after weary man yielded to the inevitable and dropped by the wayside. The brigade had, it seemed, an endless stream of stragglers. The sergeant of the color guard of the 26th Regiment fell in complete exhaustion and Colonel Burgwyn himself bore the standard to the bivouac.

One weary, dusty private, trudging solemnly and slowly along the turnpike near sunset struggling against the heat and his demoralized condition, came to me and with a salute said, "General Pettigrew, can you tell me where the 26th North Carolina is?"

"Certainly, my man," I replied, "everywhere between here and Fredericksburg."

It was almost dark when the brigade went into bivouac about three miles west of the Chancellorsville House after marching about 12 miles. Our camp is in a place called the Wilderness. It is a wild and weird region. All around us is dense and trackless forest. As we make our campfires, the piercing cry of the whip-poor-will rings through the somber pines and the screech of the owl echoes from the treetops.

Most of the brigade is camped in a large meadow behind the Wilderness Tavern. It is in this meadow that we had a field hospital during the battle of Chancellorsville and in that field the doctors amputated the arm of Stonewall Jackson.

That the scattered commands and straggling soldiers might be directed to their proper bivouacs I have ordered the regimental headquarters at intervals throughout the night to sound their respective bugle calls. A tedious search by each straggling soldier for his command will thus be avoided and the sleeping soldier saved the use of profane replies in response to inquiries from his roving companions and the latter will not be missed by the sulphurous directions usually given them under such circumstances.

Early this evening, a courier brought cheerful intelligence from corps headquarters. General Ewell with the first corps, has been marching rapidly the past week, entering the Shenandoah Valley via Front Royal Gap where his leading division commanded by General Rhodes drove in the Yankee pickets and carried them so fast that a brigade in camp near Berryville didn't get warning until Rhode's men were upon them with the bayonet. Of course the Yankees scattered like sheep, leaving their camps, baggage, etc. at our disposal. These were part of the Federal General Milroy's command. He who enjoys the unenviable pre-eminence of being only second to Bully Pope in brutal vandalism to non-combatants and women.

The remainder of Milroy's army occupied Winchester and were also surprised. Ewell threw forward Early's division to storm the town where upon the cowardly Milroy fled, leaving 3,500 prisoners and 40 pieces of artillery in our hands, besides large amounts of stores, wagons, camp equipage, etc. Milroy with a small body of cavalry effected his escape through the fields and spurring frantically fled to Harpers Ferry.

Standing by the campfire after the evening meal, I was drawn to the sight of a pile of whitening bones in the distance.

"What are those?" I asked.

"This here was a grave," answered Elias. "I looked at it some time ago. The hogs must have rooted it up."

I picked up a skull lying loose on the ground. It appeared to be that of a young man. The teeth were all splendid and sound. The eye-sockets were filled with dirt and there was another large hole above the right eye where a bullet had probably entered.

"Maybe it was one of Stonewall's men," said Elias. "He could have died at the field hospital and been buried here."

I turned the skull in my hand wondering who had been its unfortunate owner. Then moved by a gloomy impulse I thought to myself, "Let him who has never thought seriously of human life look at it through the vacant eye-sockets of a human skull. This whitened bone that I hold in my hand could be what I am coming to before this campaign is over." I placed the skull back on the ground and walked toward my tent. Off in the woods the whip-poor-wills continued their remote mournful whistling. It was late and I needed sleep for tomorrow would bring much to do.

JUNE 18, 1863—MONDAY
NEAR THORTON'S GAP—BLUE RIDGE MOUNTAINS

We did not receive orders until late last night to resume our march. Accordingly reveille was beaten so early this morning that when I popped my sleepy head out of the tent there were the stars, most magnificent, especially Venus who sat above the moon and looked like a fireball.

Elias had breakfast ready by the time it was light and after eating, I hurriedly completed my toilet and flattered myself that my appearance was considerably peacock.

Then this morning, "Forward march!" The brigade streamed toward Yankeedom—weather fine and everyone hearty. After we crossed the Rapidan River at Germanna Ford, the sun began to rise higher in the horizon and I could tell that today's heat would be excessive.

The first several hours of the march were quite orderly, the men preserving their places in the ranks and marching in solid column, but soon some lively fellow began to whistle an air and someone else started a song. Then the whole column broke out with roars of laughter. Route step took the place of orderly march and the jolly singing, laughing, talking and joking that took place were more than my feeble pen can describe.

We halted for an hour at noon near Stevensburg to give the men a rest and a chance to cool off and get the sand and gravel out of their shoes. This time was spent by the wise in absolute repose, but some were too lively and laughed and joked the time away. There was a small stream nearby and many took this opportunity to bathe their feet and face.

We resumed our march early in the afternoon and although we only had about ten more miles to march I knew it would be a difficult one because the day was hot and sultry. We were marching through Culpeper County, a beautiful area of hills and dales, and pure running brooks, fine farmhouses and barns, rich lands with a promising crop of wheat and clover. Off in the distance we had glimpses of the Blue Ridge Mountains which looked more like a bank of dark clouds or smoke low down on the horizon than a range of mountains, but intensely blue.

Despite the beauty around us and the panoramic view ahead, the men soon became oblivious to all but the heat and dust. As we marched, a choking cloud of dust arose and settled in volume on every perspiring face and hand. It penetrated everywhere—eyes, ears, nostrils, hair and skin—until its power of annoyance was almost unbearable!

The men's clothing was soon utterly saturated with perspiration mixing with the dust into a grimy paste. This annoyance combined with the weight of the heavy musket, cartridge and cap boxes and the chaffing canteen straps forced men to drop out by the scores.

It is strange but true that men laden and hot as they were could actually outlast a horse. Colonel Burgwyn's "noble steed" broke down on the march while the men of his regiment trudged on amid the dust and heat.

We reached Sperryville at about six o'clock where we were to camp for the night. Here at last was the opportunity for the men to bathe their blistered feet in the clear waters of a creek, for cooling their throbbing temples and drinking refreshing draughts, even though most were well nigh dead with heat and exhaustion.

It pained me that I had to march the men so hard today in the oppressive heat, but my orders were to camp in the vicinity of Sperryville, the gateway to Thorton's Gap. I felt it would have been far better to cover the distance in a more gradual and leisurely manner, starting early and giving frequent rests and always halting a few minutes when passing near a stream or convenient spring. Yet there was not time for such thoughtful consideration today. "Why couldn't we have spent some of the day in rest?" I heard one poor fellow ask another.

"You don't suppose old Pettigrew cares whether his men live or die," was the reply. Such are the burdens of command and I could not deviate from my orders, for we are in the midst of a campaign where the life of the nation is at stake.

JUNE 20, 1863—SATURDAY
BERRYVILLE, VIRGINIA

When I last made an entry in this journal we had made camp for the night near Thorton's Gap, one of the gateways to the Shenandoah Valley.

That night we camped in a large meadow covered with a dense growth of red clover which made a splendid bed for the tired and dusty men. A short distance to the west were the mountains which seemed to us in the gathering darkness of a cloudy evening to reach the heavens.

Here we watched with awe a grand scene. A storm had been gathering for some time. The sky had become dark and ominous and we prepared as best we could to take a summer drenching, but fortunately for us, very little rain fell, but we were spectators to a grand electrical display. The peals of thunder were rapid and terrible and so powerful that they seemed to shake the mountains to their center. Amid the echoing booms of thunder, vivid flashes of lightning played up and down the mountainside, blinding to the eye and beautiful and grand beyond description. We watched the warring elements until the storm passed over us moving slowly to the east while the rumbling thunder in the distance lulled the tired soldiers to sleep.

The morning of the 19th broke sharp, clear and cloudless. The men turned out at six to the sharp, clear sound of the brigade bugle call, hastily followed by the reveille and "general." Soon after this we were struggling up the slopes of Thorton's Gap in the Blue Ridge.

As we neared the summit, a courier informed us that Stuart has been skirmishing with Yankee cavalry under General Buford—the latter having been sent by Hooker to seize the Blue Ridge passes and prevent us from joining General Ewell in the Shenandoah Valley.

As we marched along the base of the ridge, the sound of cannonading a few miles to the north put every man on the alert for news which soon arrived to the effect that Stuart was holding the Yankees in check with a small brigade, but could soon be overpowered and need assistance.

I halted the brigade for a rest and dismounted for a conversation with Lt. Koerner of the topographical engineers. As we talked we were interrupted by the approach of two men in Yankee uniforms bearing a white flag. They rode up to us and removed their hats, the older one of the two saying, "General Stuart sends his compliments, sir. He has driven the Yankees off and the pass is clear."

I then learned that I was talking with two of General Stuart's scouts. These were the men upon whom General Stuart relied to be kept informed as to the enemy's plans and movements that they were rugged characters I had no doubt and were equipped for the warpath as revealed by the pistol butts peering from their holsters convenient for instant use.

Stuart's scouts are under the command of Major Henry Young. They are forty-five in number and are often clothed in blue uniforms which they obtained from captured Yankees. They mingled with the prisoners, thus obtaining knowledge of their regiments, brigades, divisions and corps.

They often while clad in Yankee blue led the advance of Stuart's cavalry and continued into the enemy's lines with their prepared false reports, etc. The scouts are all known to each other by nicknames such as "Barefoot," "Jim Crow," "Big Foot," etc.

I learned that I was talking to two of the more famous scouts, corporals Jim Campbell and Harry Rowlands. These two daring men had been instrumental in the capture of the famous Yankee raider Captain George Stump who had organized the 18th West Virginia cavalry. The Yankee Captain was nicknamed "Stump's Battery" because he always carried several revolvers and a carbine. When they captured the infamous Yankee, their orders were not to bring him in alive if captured. Stump was given a choice of ten feet and his mount and a chance to break for liberty. He had not gone twenty feet before he was riddled.

Such was the nature of the men who stood before me. They informed me that Stuart with three brigades has been fighting the whole Federal cavalry for several days and was rather pressed this afternoon by mounted infantry and artillery. Stuart took 400 prisoners and several colors, but lost 500 men in killed, wounded, and captured. The Yankees, they said, had now retreated in the direction of Middleburg.

By noon, with Stuart's two scouts guiding us, we rested upon the summit of the mountains and feasted our eyes upon the magnificent valley of the Shenandoah. Bounded by the Blue Ridge on the east and the Alleghenies on the west, we beheld an amphitheater that stretched for 120 miles from Staunton in the south to the Potomac River in the north. Down the center of the valley rose Massanutton Mountain.

This was the scene of Stonewall Jackson's valley campaign of 1862, where he played a deadly game of hide and seek with various Yankee armies. "Old Stonewall knew this valley," Corporal Campbell said as I looked out over the beautiful valley with my field glasses. "Its geography and the distance between the towns were burned into his brain. He seemed to know every hole and corner of it.

"I think," continued Campbell, "he knew every cow path and goat track as if he had made it or at least as if it had been designed for his own use."

Looking to the north, I could easily make out Winchester, a quaint old town of some five thousand inhabitants, which is the business and agricultural center of the lower valley. Other villages and hamlets

dotted the beautiful landscape while here and there stood monu-
ments to the destruction of war—lone chimneys, where once stood
handsome farmhouses sheltering happy families.

Our descent down the mountains was much easier and quicker than
our ascent. As we left the mountains the great valley of Virginia was
before us in all its beauty. There were fields of wheat spread far and
wide, interspersed with woodlands, bright in their robes of green.

As late afternoon became to come on, the men began to wonder
when we were going to camp and I would hear, "General, when are
we going to stop for the night?" "How long do you think we'll camp
for?" Sometimes these questions were in jest but generally they
betrayed anxiety of some sort and a close observer could easily detect
the mood of the men by the nature of their questions.

As we neared Berryville, we had to cross a wide stream at least 30 feet
broad and fully four feet deep. The storm of yesterday chilled the water
to winter temperature and the passage was like wading through the
same amount of ice water. So we were half-frozen and dripping with
water when we presented ourselves to the fair maidens of Berryville
who, notwithstanding the daily tramp of soldiers through their village,
turned out to greet us with bouquets and refreshments.

Once through the village, we camped for the night on both sides of
the pike. After the bivouac was made, the still-lingering daylight kept
animate objects moving about the wooded hillside beyond the camp
well in view. Their location for the night definitely fixed, a number of
men of a regiment that shall go unnamed, prompted by a desire for
investigation, or with a view to better their diet, went with rifle in hand
strolling about the near vicinity. Some hogs had broken their cover and
were straggling through the woods seeking food. It required but a slight
effort of imagination, even in this well populated, well-tilled country, to
consider such strolling beasts as wild. To the men, the idea of fresh pork
after a long march was mouth watering. Shots rang out sharply in the

evening air and two well-rounded porkers fell victims to unerring aim. Soon the smell of pork, fried and toasted, filled the air and many a soldier gorged themselves to restfulness with fresh pig before the evening shadows faded into the depths of night.

It is late and the termination of a long day's march has greatly exhausted us all, though I shall not complain even to myself since I presume it was entirely necessary. And I have always said that I shall bear any necessary hardship or privation without a murmur. But Oh! I dread tomorrow's march and its effect on my tired men.

JUNE 25, 1863—THURSDAY
NEAR WILLIAMSPORT, MARYLAND

On the morning of the 23rd, reveille sounded at daybreak and the morning meal was soon disposed of. Then, "Attention! Fall in men! Forward! March!"

The column moved at seven o'clock, my brigade leading the division. There was no improvement in temperature. The sun beat down relentlessly and the dust rose in the same thickening, suffocating masses. The men marched stiff and sleepy, carrying their muskets, knapsacks, blankets, bayonets, cartridges and cap boxes, canteens, tin cups, frying pans, etc., which weighted them down and chaffed their perspiring skin.

By early afternoon, the column had trudged along to that degree of weariness when a painful stillness follows real fatigue. Sergeant Peter Bayard, a strong, well-proportioned man yet in his twenties was aware of the haggard condition of the men. He has a rich melodious voice—clear, round and ringing. Suddenly, his ringing voice rolled out amidst the quietude in notes full, free and true, in the melodious strains of the entrancing song, "I came from the Old North State." Each verse concluded with a chorus and ended in "boom, boom, boom!"

The effect was instantaneous and the inspiration catching. Gradually Bayard's regiment caught the strain, fatigue was forgotten and the summer air was sonorous with melody. It spread beyond the regiment through the whole column of the brigade. I sat sideways, woman fashion, on my horse watching the long lines of singing men. I marveled at the influence one man could have for as the "boom, boom boom!" died away in my brigade, another took it up and it spread through the whole division until, at last, it subsided in the distance. The effect manifested by enlivened spirits and quickened step was wonderful. It continued through the remainder of our march and brought the command to their destination a better, happier set of men.

We camped that night near Charlestown. As we were making camp a Mr. Blackford appeared and invited me to his house in the neighborhood. A devoted supporter of our cause, he asked me to honor him by having supper at Dewberry, his residence.

The house was a little distance from our camp and I asked Adjutant Hughes, Dr. Middleton and Captain Young to accompany me. The ride there was delightful as we passed through a region that had not yet been touched by war. Flowering plants and rose trees in full bloom attested the glorious wealth of June.

On the broad portico, to welcome us stood the host with his charming wife and a grey-haired darky butler. The house was full of company, principally of young ladies, only one of whom I now remember: Miss Lucy Nelson.

Greetings over with, another darky butler appeared on the portico and, with his smiling face beaming with hospitality, advanced holding a large tray on which rested four huge silver goblets filled with Virginia's nectar—mint julep. Quantities of cracked ice rattled refreshingly in the goblets. Sprigs of fragrant mint peered above the broad rims. A mass of white sugar, too sweetly indolent to melt, rested on the mint and luscious strawberries crowned the sugar. Ah! That julep after the scant fare of camp and march along with the cordial hospitality made it seem a drink from heaven.

Dinner was announced and what a dinner! A long table, snowy white table cloth, damask napkins and, above all, the lovely and gracious manner of the ladies and our host, Mr. Blackford, and how they made us feel the sincerity of their welcome. 'Twas an idyll in the midst of stern realities of war! The table was covered with a variety of food. The main course was an elegant quarter of mutton dressed with drawn butter, eggs and green pickle. One of the young ladies, a lovely woman in crisp gown with more and handsomer roses on her cheek than her garment, proposed a toast to General Lee, in which all gratefully joined.

Then sable servitors brought in more food and drinks and dinner was served. I ate rather moderately but the performance of Adjutant Hughes and Captain Young was gargantuan.

After the meal, the parlor was thrown open and we observed in the corner of the room an elegant piano open with numerous sheets of music upon it. Dr. Middleton had no sooner seen the piano than he approached Miss Lucy and begged her to sing a patriotic air "that he might hear a woman's voice again."

Miss Lucy then sang the grand song "My Maryland." Other songs followed to the delight of us all.

Duty all too soon dragged us from this Eden and we were escorted by our host and Miss Lucy to the portico. Before we could say our adieus, Miss Lucy said, "Gentlemen, we invite you to come again. It is seldom we have such gallant company."

She then gave us a graceful bow and I could only think to myself *look well at her for you have never seen and will probably never see again so beautiful a woman.*

She was of magnificent form. Her neck and shoulders perfect as if from the sculptor's chisel. She wore a pink rose in her alluring auburn hair. I have seldom seen such color on a woman's cheek. Dressed in her lovely dress of pure white she is truly an angel of the South.

Just before mounting, Mr. Blackford approached and said to me, "I pray we win this war, General. To lose it would mean the abolition of slavery and a poverty that would render our way of life here almost impossible. To lose our slaves would do a cruel wrong to many of the fine ladies you met this evening. They know nothing of working with their hands and consider such knowledge disgraceful. Can you imagine Miss Lucy sweating in the kitchen? If our slaves are taken from us, our ladies will be helpless and all will be gone. The luxurious living and the genial hospitality."

"I can only pray, sir," I replied, "that you will have faith in God and General Lee. Our cause is just and if success crowns our efforts here and at Vicksburg, it may mean the end of the war."

Then, thanking him for his generous hospitality, we mounted our horses and rode cheerfully back to camp, talking with great gusto along the way bout the delights of the evening and the charm of our hosts.

We turned out at six o'clock on the morning of the 24th, got breakfast and were ready to march at seven, but the brigade, now being ordered to take the rear, stood waiting over two hours for the division and transportation to pass.

Soon after getting underway, the sun popped out from behind a cloud. The band struck up and we were "en route" for Maryland. Late in the morning, we marched through the streets of Shepherdstown, whose fair daughters cheered us with gladsome smiles, waving their handkerchiefs and little Confederate flags.

We crossed the Potomac at the ford about two miles below the village. The passage of the broad river was a novel spectacle and occasioned a good deal of enthusiasm among the men and offices.

The river was rather high and very muddy but all made the crossing safely. While wading across, the men by the thousands sang, "The Bonnie Blue Flag" and "Maryland, My Maryland." The regimental bands played their liveliest airs. The musicians dressed in their best birthday suits, each with a bundle of clothes on top of his head to keep them dry tooting with louldly at their brass horns. What a sight to behold! Several regiments crossed together with colonels on horseback, flags fluttering and the forest of bright muskets glistening in the afternoon sun. This added a holiday fare to the scene. Many citizens, including women and Negroes of all ages, occupied the high ground near the river and watching us come over.

As I sat on my horse watching the command cross into Maryland, I returned the salute of my men, many of them beardless boys. I could hardly help noticing that I have never seen the brigade in such fine condition. The feeling then came over me that I would rather command this brigade than the division, even the corps. They are a magnificent body of men. God help any Yankees that should get in our way.

Continuing our march, we soon passed through Sharpsburg and moved on the main pike toward Hagerstown. I found Sharpsburg to be a dirty dilapidated old village that still shows many marks of the great battle fought near it last September.

We reached our campground near Williamsport late in the afternoon. I was glad to learn that we had marched from Berryville to here with scarcely a straggler and the report from every division is the same.

It is the opinion of many that our destination is Harrisburg, Pennsylvania, but of course none can tell where coming events will land us. How I wish I had the power to draw aside the dark curtain of the future and read the pages of history that will be written within the next few weeks!

Tonight my bedroom will be as grand as that ever occupied by a prince. The ground is carpeted with soft, green, velvety grass. For walls, I have the surrounding pine trees with their drapery of luxuriant foliage. The ceiling, reaching to the vault of heaven, is studded with stars innumerable. With such lavish accommodations, who could not easily sleep the night away?

JUNE 28, 1863—SUNDAY
NEAR FAYETTEVILLE, PENNSYLVANIA

We moved here early this morning. Our camp is now located about six miles east of Chambersburg and on the west side of South Mountain. Just as we were going into camp an accident occurred and it is to be wondered that several of our men were not killed. Near the camp of the 47th Regiment, a percussion shell in the limber chest of one of the artillery batteries exploded and that spreading to the other shells (fifty in number, one pond each) made a pretty big blow. The explosion caused a great deal of excitement and scarred the Hades out of the men, but when the smoke cleared, it was found no one was seriously hurt.

Upon our march here, we met about 125 Federal soldiers. They were captured east of here a few days before and are now on their way home. Noticing that nearly all of them were without shoes, I naturally inquired of them why it was.

"We were captured by a Rebel named Johnson and I reckon he wanted our shoes for his men. He might have took our shirts, too, but he didn't."

This evening I had a surprise visitor to my headquarters in the person of John Cheves Haskell. I had not seen the major since the days of our forlorn campaign in North Carolina. I hold the major in great affection and was delighted to see him. This appearance put me in mind of a story I had recently heard about Haskell, who has so distinguished himself in many battles and suffered the loss of his right arm. He was in Richmond last February when Hood's troops were passing through and was standing on a porch with some ladies on Franklin Street, very handsomely dressed and with a short military cloak covering his shoulders. As Hood's veterans passed by, they laughed and shouted amongst themselves and guyed the people on each side with rough jokes. As they passed the porch they began making jokes about Haskell's fine dress.

One of the soldiers shouted, "Ho don't come down in the mud, Major, you'll soil your fine clothes." This was followed by a derisive laugh by his comrades.

Suddenly Haskell stepped off the porch into the sidewalk and, facing them, threw back his cloak showing his empty sleeve. The effect was electric. The men took off their hats and one continuous cheer greeted him as the division passed each regiment catching the inspiration from the one ahead of it. I wish I had seen it but I did not. Fortunately it was told to me by one who did.

As we talked it was obvious Haskell was tired but he dismissed the fatigue. The flickering candlelight illuminated his delicate features and I thought how hard it must be to bear the labors of a hard campaign with only one arm.

I learned from our conversation that General Lee was in distress over his missing cavalry. General Stuart had not been heard from for many days. Haskell claimed that General Lee was prone to discuss the absence of Stuart with every officer who visited him. "Can you tell me where General Stuart is?" He will say, or, "Where on earth is my cavalry?" or "have you any news of the enemy's movements? What is the enemy going to do?" Lee repeatedly observed, remarked Haskell, that the Yankee army must still be in Virginia as he had heard nothing from Stuart.

These statements about the cavalry were misleading, I reminded Haskell, for they implied that no troopers were available to keep close watch on the enemy, where as in fact two brigades were at hand. Unfortunately, they were commanded by General Robertson, who had performed so poorly in North Carolina. It seems that Stuart and his three brigades have ridden off somewhere out of the main theatre of operations. Hearing this, I could only recall the warning Peter Alexander of the Savannah Republican had given a week earlier concerning Stuart's unfitness to command so large a cavalry force.

JUNE 29, 1863—MONDAY
CASHTOWN, PENNSYLVANIA

The report of a spy has altered our invasion of the North. General Heth gave me the particulars early this morning. It seems that late last night, Lt. Colonel Moxley Sorrel was roused by a detail of the provost guard bringing in a suspicious prisoner, a weary, bedraggled civilian who seemed to have no business near the outpost line. Sorrel recognized the man instantly. It was Harrison, General Longstreet's favorite scout whom the general had set out to spy on the Yankees before the army left Culpeper.

To Longstreet, Harrison gave a complete account of the enemy's movements. Longstreet was surprised to learn that the Federals were moving north, that they had crossed the Potomac and that the head of the enemy column was at Frederick City on our right. Harrison also informed Longstreet of the removal of General Hooker and the appointment of George Meade to command the Army of the Potomac.

Longstreet, alarmed by the news, immediately forwarded Harrison to General Lee whose headquarters were close by. The general listened to Harrison and then took great pains to satisfy himself of the honesty and soundness of the stranger. He was pleased with the man's candid manner and his story bore an air of consistency and truth.

It was on the report of this single scout that Lee has decided that he is now presented with an entirely new tactical situation. Lee immediately sent orders to bring General Ewell's corps back from Harrisburg to Cashtown. Longstreet's corps will not march north as planned but follow General Hill's corps, which will move east of South Mountain toward Cashtown. Thus the army will concentrate east of the mountains to threaten Baltimore and Washington City and force the Federals to protect those cities. Cashtown offers the perfect point at which to gather our forces and await the Federals next move. From there, General

Lee can maneuver to the east or take the tactical defensive in the mountain gap if the enemy comes up and chooses to attack.

During the morning as we were marching toward Cashtown, a mounted man clad in grey uniform rode up to General Heth, commanding the division, and told him that General Longstreet had sent him to say he was to halt his column where it was and not to proceed to Cashtown. As Heth was under the orders of A. P. Hill, he couldn't understand why Longstreet should send him orders of any kind, especially as it was known Lee had issued the orders to march, not Longstreet.

Suspicion was aroused and the man was ordered at gunpoint to dismount, his person examined, and a memorandum book found containing an account of all of our movements since we had entered Pennsylvania. A cipher alphabet was also found. One barrel of his pistol was empty. Last night, one of General Hill's couriers was joined on the road by a man whose description corresponded with this man. After riding a short distance with Hill's courier, the stranger dropped a little to the rear and shot the courier through the back. He fell from his horse, apparently dead, and was robbed of his dispatches. He was discovered in the morning still alive and told his story.

Further examination of the man's clothing showed the uniform not to be of the Confederate regulation. The cuffs and collar of his jacket were black instead of yellow. His under-clothing, boots, and spurs were unmistakably those furnished the enlisted men of the United States Army. A drumhead, court martial was convened and he was tried and confessed. He was then sentenced to be hung as a spy. He took his sentence quite calmly and gave his name as Thomas Leopold of Philadelphia, Pennsylvania. The spy was a brave man. He was most sensible of the perils of his service. To pass between hostile lines in lone hours of the night, to be halted by cavalry and pickets with guns aimed at him and finally to meet and satisfy the anxious, keen-eyed, heart-searching inquiries of the officers of our army was a mental and physical demand that could not long be sustained.

General Hill's couriers requested permission to carry out the sentence of the court and to avenge their fallen comrade, shot in cold blood by Leopold. He was marched to the woods, placed on a mule, had a rope looped around his neck and its end thrown over the limb of a tree. Then, after a brief prayer by one of the chaplains, a stalwart courier with a heavy stick struck the rump of the mule, causing him to surge ahead. Thomas Leopold, spy and cold-blooded assasin,was left swinging. This affair of but little moment in the history of our army detained the division nearly two hours.

Despite the delay, the division reached Cashtown early this afternoon. The divisions of Pender and Anderson will follow and join us tomorrow. We are now camped on the eastern side of Cashtown Gap, some eight miles west of a small college town named Gettysburg.

JUNE 30, 1863—TUESDAY
BETWEEN CASHTOWN AND GETTYSBURG, PENNSYLVANIA

Late last evening, I beheld couriers going to and fro from General Heth's headquarters and I thought, well we shall be marching somewhere tomorrow. Just before I went to bed, a courier brought me the anticipated order from General Heth placing the entire brigade under marching orders. My orders were to take the brigade to Gettysburg, search the town for army supplies (shoes especially) and return the same day." It was told to me by Heth's aide that I might find the town in possession of a home guard, which we would have no difficulty driving away, but if, contrary to expectations, I should find any portion of the Army of the Potomac, we should not attack it. My orders were peremptory, not to precipitate a fight.

At five o'clock A.M., I was awakened in my tent by Adjutant Hughes shaking me vigorously and saying, "Wake up! Wake up, General!

Reveille will be blown soon." Fancy the comforts of such a life as this! Roused rudely at dawn and be forced to take my bath in a sawn-off barrel while drawing my wardrobe from a single trunk, which contains underclothes, a spare uniform and a spare pair of boots.

Bugler Bill blew reveille at 5:30 o'clock and staff officers were soon dashing about while the men ate a hurried breakfast, and then dried off their gear which was wet from the rain that fell last night.

How we have reduced our equipment during this campaign! Knapsacks have been voted a bore and have been thrown aside. A blanket snugly rolled inside of a rubber cloth, the ends tied together and thrown over one shoulder, now hold the necessary clothing: the haversack carries the crackers and bacon, the comb, the soap, and the towel and the toothbrush decorates the bottom-whole of the jacket, together with the tobacco bag.

The brigade was then mustered for pay and the regiments ordered to leave behind their blanket-rolls and any men not able to make a force march. We were traveling light and expected to return to our camp sometime later today.

I expected that once in Gettysburg we might find large quantities of supplies so I had directed 27 wagons to accompany the brigade. In addition, I considered in prudence to take along three cannon of the Donaldsonville Artillery of Louisiana.

Once troops, wagons and guns were assembled, the column stretched for a mile and a half on the Chambersburg Pike. At 6:30 o'clock, I gave the order and we began our march, the 11th North Carolina in front proceeded by skirmishers.

To make sure all was going smoothly, I rode toward the rear of the column. While doing so, I came across one of the artillery pieces stuck fast against a fallen tree just off the road. How it became stuck was a mystery to me, but nevertheless there it was. Despite some pushing and shoving there was a delay in moving it on. While I watched from a distance the effort to move the cannon, an irate staff officer rode up and began finding fault with the men attempting to move the piece. This annoyed the sergeant and he called out, "Who are you anyhow?" to which the officer replied, "I am Captain A. Coward of General Heth's staff. Who are you?"

"I am Sergeant A. Hero of the Donaldsonville Artillery."

This interesting meeting and exchange of names soon spread along the column and put all hands in a good humor.

To be successful in battle, a general has to be as knowledgeable as possible of the terrain, roads, streams, bridges, possible defensive positions and other minutiae necessary to rapidly maneuver over a strange terrain. During our march, Captain Young and I paid particular attention to these items and transferred our observations onto a notebook the captain carried. Once we returned to camp, we would give the information to Lieutenant Koerner who could then transfer the information into an accurate two-dimensional map.

About two miles west of Gettysburg, our advance party arrested a well-mounted civilian and asked about Federal troops in the vicinity. The man, a physician, was questioned closely by Colonel Leventhorpe. To his surprise, the doctor claimed there were between four and five thousand Federal troops in the area and a much larger Federal force a few miles distant.

This statement alarmed Leventhorpe. He halted the column until he could consult with me. As we discussed this unexpected information, we could only wonder if he was merely repeating a false rumor, or was he exaggerating purposely to deceive us. We decided to proceed, but cautiously in case of a possible ambush.

Some distance closer to Gettysburg, we came across Harrison, Longstreet's spy, riding toward us. He had obviously been on another of his mysterious prowlings and what new information he had gathered, we could only guess. As he rode up to us shouting his greeting, we beheld a tall, slender, black-eyed, impressive-looking man with a commanding presence and a tremendous brass voice. He was nonchalantly munching corn-cake and dressed like a Dutch farmer of Adams County. I knew, of course, that change of costume is an old device among spies and he looked very rural in his current disguise.

"Gentlemen," he boomed, "I have had a perfectly magnificent time today strolling about Gettysburg. It was exciting in the extreme."

"What have you learned?" I asked.

"I'm mighty tired, gentlemen," said Harrison, ignoring my question, "but I had a first-rate time of it. I fooled the Feds, as usual, and had a jolly spree in Gettysburg; talked to the ladies...had lots of tip-top whiskey and cigars...went wherever I darned pleased."

What's the news, Harrison?" demanded Leventhorpe.

"Yes," I chimed in. "What information have you brought us?"

"Well, boys," said Harrison, now filling his pipe. "You had better be careful for there are a bunch of blue-bellies in Gettysburg."

"Militia," countered Leventhorpe. "They'll run at the first hint of trouble."

"Would you call over 3,000 Federal cavalry, led by General John Buford, militia, Colonel?"

"Are you sure?" asked Leventhorpe, shocked by Harrison's information.

"Colonel, being sure is my business and I assure you that there are blue-bellies thick as flies around cow-dung up ahead and if Old John Buford is in Gettysburg, it is likely the Army of the Potomac is not far behind."

After pondering this perplexing information, I determined to send a dispatch back to General Heth informing him of the information we had learned from Harrison and requesting further instructions. After about an hour's wait, I received a message in reply which was simply a repetition of my previous orders coupled with an expression of disbelief that any portion of the Army of the Potomac was in Pennsylvania.

Being reassured, we continued on until I halted the brigade near Willoughby Run at about ten o'clock. I then rode forward with an advance party to a rise of ground called Seminary Ridge where we could obtain a good view of the surrounding country. From the ridge, we peered through our field glasses for any sight of the enemy. Gettysburg lay drowsing in a peaceful valley with golden fields of wheat stretching north and south. Beyond the town, broken wooded hills were capped by a jutting round promontory at the southern end. Through my glass, I gazed intently at the village and I could see clearly numerous civilians gathering at the public square. They looked almost near enough to speak to.

Observing that the city was unoccupied by Federals, I was preparing to move the brigade forward when Colonel Leventhorpe lowered his glass and said calmly, "Look to the south, General, at the road leading into town."

I turned my glass in the direction as suggested and there on the road from Emmitsburg was a long dark column. Through my glass I was able to identify it as Federal cavalry. Captain Young felt they were infantry supported by cavalry, but at such a great distance we couldn't be sure.

"What do you think, General?" inquired Leventhorpe, still gazing through his glass toward the south of town.

"I am more than willing to fight Yankee cavalry, even if supported by local militia, Colonel, but my orders forbid fighting any organized force. Discretion would appear to be the better part of valor at this moment."

I could see the disheartened look on Leventhorpe's face and those of the surrounding staff, but I was determined not to bring on a general engagement. Colonel Leventhorpe reluctantly concurred that it was foolhardy to continue our advance given our orders and our uncertainty of the enemy we faced. The only thing that remained was: "The King of France with forty thousand men marched up a hill and then marched down again."

As we reluctantly countermarched back toward Cashtown, I found we were being followed at a distance by enemy cavalry and I detained Captain Young and Lieutenant Robertson to remain in the rear of the column and observe carefully the movements of the enemy.

Our retreat, if it be called that, was an orderly one. After we had countermarched about four miles, I posted a strong line of pickets under Colonel Burgwyn on the west side of Marsh Creek to resist any belated pursuit by the enemy. The rest of the command I moved near McKnightstown where we camped in ready supporting distance of the 26th.

Late in the afternoon, I rode toward General Heth's headquarters feeling about as blue as indigo. Riding up to the general's headquarters, I met Captain Young who had proceeded me. Sensing my mood, he inquired, "What's the matter, general? Not satisfied with the day's results?"

"What results?" I answered. "About all I accomplished was to wear out the shoe leather of 2,800 of my infantrymen on a futile foraging expedition which involved a round trip march of 16 miles or more in hot, sultry weather. It was not one of the war's great marches, Captain."

"No, but perhaps it was one of the wisest. You obeyed your orders not to bring on a fight, which I feel was important because without a cavalry escort, there would have been the added risk of falling into a trap. Lastly and most importantly, you have obtained useful information about the presence of the Yankee army."

General Heth listened attentively to my report remarking only that he doubted the Federals I observed in Gettysburg were units of the Army of the Potomac. We were still conversing when General A. P. Hill rode up from his headquarters at Fayetteville.

General Heth directed me to repeat my report to the corps commander. I did so once again relating my observations in great detail. General Hill listened tight lipped, eyes to the floor, shaking his head slowly now and then at one of my statements.

When I finished, he replied, "The only Yankee force at Gettysburg is cavalry, probably a detachment of observation. I have just come from talking to General Lee and the information he has from his scouts corroborates what I have received from mine—that the enemy are still at Frederick City, Maryland, and have not yet struck their tents."

In the discussion that followed, both Hill and Heth continued to doubt my insistence that there were Federal infantry in Gettysburg. I felt that I had as much chance of being believed as did Jesus before the Jerusalem Sanhedrin. I expected them at any moment to rent their uniforms and cry "blasphemy!"

Finally in exasperation, I called in Captain Young for support. I thought that the captain's observations might carry some weight with General Hill as he had served in Hill's division as a staff officer to Major General Dorsey Pender during most of 1862. General Hill asked Young the character of the troops he observed at Gettysburg and Young replied that their movements were undoubtedly those of well-trained troops, not a home guard.

Despite Young's assertion, it was obvious, General Hill was unwilling to believe our report. He had deliberately shut his mind to a truth that he did not wish to accept. Then, after pondering our words for a short while, General Hill asserted with more candor than knowledge, "I cannot believe any portion of the Army of the Potomac is in our front, but I indeed hope it is, as that is exactly the place where I want the Yankees to be."

Just as Captain Young and I prepared to leave, General Heth held up the June 29th issue of the *Gettysburg Compiler*, which carried the advertisement of a huge sale at McIlhany's Shoe Factory featuring men's fine calf boots, Galmorals, Wellingtons, and Brogans. "There are shoes in Gettysburg, gentlemen," said Heth, pointing to the newspaper. "General Hill, if there is no objection, I will take my division tomorrow, go to Gettysburg, and get those shoes."

General Hill asked for the newspaper and examined the article closely. Then, he responded, "I have no objection, General, none in the world."

JULY 1, 1863—WEDNESDAY
SEMINARY RIDGE—GETTYSBURG, PENNSYLVANIA

After a long, rough day, one of unspeakable triumphs and calamities, I have very little energy for note taking and tonight I confess to being as nearly worn out as a man can be without actually breaking down. The fighting has now been over for at least five hours, yet so accustomed had I become since this morning to the rattle of musketry that there is a constant "*Crack! Crack! Crack!*" ringing through my ears as I sit down to write. Yet I must find the strength to record in my limited way the momentous events of today's battle.

Late last evening, I received the order to have the men cook one day's rations, have it in haversacks and be ready to march at 5:30 o'clock the next morning. I then sought out General Archer, whose brigade by the normal process of rotation would lead the march towards Gettysburg. I had brought along the notebook which Captain Young and I filled full of information; using this as a reference, I described to General Archer minutely the topography of the country about Gettysburg.

I explained that the first ridge west of Gettysburg was wooded Seminary Ridge, running north and south, about three-quarters of a mile from town. It was named for the Lutheran Theological Seminary located there between Chambersburg Pike and Hagerstown Road. North of the railroad grading this ridge is called Oak Ridge, because it is largely covered with a grove of Oak trees. Oak Ridge terminates in a prominent knob known as Oak Hill, which is approximately one-and-one-quarter miles northwest of the town.

About 500 yards west of Seminary Ridge by my calculations is McPherson's Ridge, named for the McPherson farm buildings located on the ridge south of the pike. McPherson Ridge is open except for a small orchard near the barn and a much larger triangular-shaped grove of trees south of the farm buildings known as McPherson Grove, or woods.

Approximately 900 yards west of McPherson Ridge is Herr Ridge, named for Herr's Tavern, which is situated on the south side of Chambersburg Pike. A narrow crossroad runs along Herr Ridge perpendicular to the pike and crosses it at the tavern.

Between McPherson and Herr ridges, running north and south, is Willoughby Run, a small stream which I pointed out as fordable at almost any point except for a few scattered woods and copses. The country, unlike Virginia, is largely open, being chiefly meadows and cultivated fields.

I then told General Archer that with the use of my field glasses I could make out several important heights south of the town. A villager told us one of the heights was named Cemetery Hill and the others about two miles away were called Little Round Top and Big Round Top. I could add little information about these heights because I did not have the advantage of personal observation as I did the area west of town.

Archer sat at his desk looking up occasionally while I talked, but mostly concentrated on going through a great pile of papers one a minute, signing some, others ruthlessly thrown in the waste basket. When I had finished, he looked up and said, "You say the Yankee army is at Gettysburg, yet General Lee and General Hill tell me the Yankees are at Frederick City. Who am I to believe, the commanders of a dozen glorious battles with this army or an inexperienced brigadier general, fresh from the back water of North Carolina?"

"You are to believe the truth, sir."

"General Lee and General Hill do not know the truth?"

"I think they are misinformed, or perhaps not informed as Stuart hasn't been heard from in some time.

"Was General Lee misinformed at Fredericksburg? Chancellorsville? Why should he be misinformed now?"

"General Archer, my only motive is to alert you to any possible danger and to inform you of the truth."

"General, I mean no offense to you, but here is the truth or what I strongly suspect the truth to be. I think General Hill and General Heth have planned this foray into Gettysburg to bag a few thousand Yankee militia, return to Cashtown and present them to General Lee. They are new to corps and division command and this will affirm their new rank and advance their careers. They may say they're after shoes, but I think they are after glory."

"Shoes or glory. I know not or care not. Perhaps there may be a little of both. But I warn you once again, be prepared. The Army of the Potomac may be up!"

It is sad to say Archer listened but believed not and marched toward Gettysburg unprepared.

By 5:00 a.m., we were on the march toward Gettysburg. In our column, General Archer's brigade was in the lead. He was followed by General Davis' brigade and then by my brigade. Bringing up the rear of the march was Colonel Brockenbrough's brigade. Also in the line of march were the reserve artillery battalions of Major W. J. Pegram and Major D. G. McIntosh. Prudently, General Hill directed General Pender's division to follow within supporting distance.

I sat on my horse by the roadside as the long column advanced down the pike, observing that the men looked like scarecrows in their calico shirts, patched brown trousers and worn leather belts. Many marched with bare feet. Their uncut hair stuck out in shocks through holes in their misshapen slouched hats. Despite their appearance, their esprit de corps was high and they marched with a spring in their step. Many were laughing and joking. As one group of lean, tanned men passed, one of their numbers held up a copy of the *Charleston Courier* of a late date and shouted of an advertisement carried on the front page. It read, "Good news to soldiers! Airtight coffins! Good news to soldiers!"

Soon Archer was about a mile in front and in the usual pattern, he sent out skirmishers on each side of the road in advance. The men, their rifles at the ready, hopped over fences, darted through underbrush, and often disappeared momentarily in the woods as they led the division eastward.

It was a lovely morning. A soft breeze rippled over the ripe wheat fields stretching on either side of us. The column moved forward leisurely and Captain Young and I enjoyed smoking and chatting as we rode along.

Then, at about 7:30 o'clock, the column ground to a halt and we heard a faint *"Crack!"* Then *"Pop! Pop! Pop!"* far in the distance. We all wondered what this meant when a courier came riding by and shouted that Archer's skirmisher's had encountered dismounted cavalry and had to drive them off before we could resume our advance.

By my watch it then took us almost two hours to negotiate the distance from Marsh Creek to Herr Ridge. The Federal cavalry kept up an incessant fire with their breech-loading carbines—a fire that was answered by our skirmishers. The sound of the musketry reverberated back toward us. It was hard to know what was happening up ahead, but obvious we were proceeding slowly in case of an ambush.

At nine o'clock, we began to hear the loud, regular boom of artillery with the occasional crackling noise of a rifle volley. Overhead in the distance, we could see the smoke of battle curl away in small, snow-white clouds. Word soon came back that Federal cannon had begun to shell our men and in response General Heth had ordered Major Pegram to unlimber his twenty-gun battalion and return the fire.

Looking up the pike, I observed a courier galloping forward, a cloud of dust trailing in his wake. He rode up to me, pulled hard rein, saluted and said, "General Heth sends his compliments sir. He desires you and the other brigade commanders to join him on Herr Ridge. He requests you immediately deploy your brigade in reserve here, south of the pike."

I turned toward Colonel Burgwyn who was at the head of the 26th Regiment, which was leading the brigade, and gave the command, "Echelon by battalion, the 26th Regiment by the right flank!"

Colonel Burgwyn gave his regiment the command, "March!" As the 26th followed by the other regiments marched off the pike the Federals were sweeping the road with their artillery and there was a sudden panic among some of the men as several round shot came bounding over, but it soon disappeared as Colonel Burgwyn riding along the line in his grandest style, commanded in his clear firm voice, "Steady boys, steady."

Once the brigade was positioned in the woods to the south of the pike I rode toward Herr Ridge accompanied by Captain Young where I found General Heth with General Archer and General Davis.

From where we were positioned we could see McPherson's Ridge about a half mile distant. General Heth then ordered General Davis to deploy his brigade in line of battle north of the pike and General Archer to do the same south of the pike.

"I am determined to make a forced, reconnaissance to ascertain what force the enemy has on that ridge." said General Heth.

Archer looked intently at the position for a long time with his field glasses and then turned to Heth expressing the opinion, "There are only a thousand men in my brigade and we could easily be overwhelmed so far in advance of any support."

"General Archer, sir," replied the determined Heth, "I do not believe the meek will inherit the earth or in this case, Gettysburg. I saw no evidence of Federal Infantry. It is my opinion that only a thin screen of cavalry stand between us and the town. Deploy your brigade and go forward as ordered!"

General Archer and Davis then rode off to deploy their men. I watched intently as Archer formed his men for the attack. At that time, the enemy opened a battery on the ridge with solid shot, several of which came ricocheting around us.

In the confusion caused by the shells, I recollect I turned just then and saw Henry Rison of General Archer's staff sitting on horseback not far off. He waved and smiled at me. Immediately after he rode off to join General Archer further to the south on Herr Ridge. Shortly hereafter a round shot passed through Archer's staff and struck Rison in the side. He fell dead from his horse. He was a fine young man and beloved by all in the division. When I rode that evening to the corps hospital and saw poor Rison lying face up on the ground, it made me think of Chaplain Keys, almost a year ago. This war is not a place for friendships for it is the same thing over and over again. And strange too, this seeing a young friend in full flush of robust health and the next moment nothing that we can make out but the broken body that the soul once put in motion.

Soon the brigades of Archer and Davis were advancing in line of battle over a half mile long. It was really a magnificent sight. The country is almost destitute of forests and was so open that it was easy to see what was transpiring about us.

As my brigade was half a mile in the rear, I rode back to rejoin it thinking that as soon as Archer and Davis swept the ridge clear of cavalry, we would reform on the pike to continue our march into Gettysburg. I had scarcely got back when *br-r-r-r-ang!* Went the musketry in front of Davis and Archer, which for the next half hour was continuous. First several long volleys, then a continuous crackle now swelling and now abating and interspersed with occasional cannon.

Very soon the wounded could be seen heading back from the battle. All had the same question over and over again, "How far to the corps hospital?"

Then I saw coming towards me a mounted officer—his face was covered with blood and he was kept in the saddle only by an officer who rode beside him.

"Hello, General!" he cried in a wild way that showed he was wandering. "Here I am. Hurt a little. Not much. I am going to lie down a few minutes and then I am going back again! We must salvage the day!"

"What does he mean?" I asked his companion, perplexed.

"We have been routed, General."

"Routed? Impossible!"

"No. It's true. It was those damned black-hatted fellows. 'twas no militia up thare. 'twas the Army of the Potomac."

Poor Archer. Not only had he unexpectedly encountered the Army of the Potomac, but had collided head on with the most formidable unit in that army. "Those damned black-hatted fellows" were the Crack Iron Brigade—made up of men from Wisconsin, Michigan and Indiana. They had battled through the bloody cornfield at Antietam and fought Stonewall Jackson's troops at Groveton for over two hours at a maximum distance of 75 yards until their dead lay on the ground as on dress parade. Their bodies on the ground, their spirits in the care of the great God who was the source of their courage. These seasoned veterans were mindful of their past glories and their reputation for valor. They had routed poor, unprepared Archer in less than thirty minutes.

Seeking to learn greater detail, I hailed another wounded soldier passing to the rear, Private Moon of the 13th Alabama.

"Brigades been cut to pieces," he offered. "General Archer was captured along with many others. Can't quite say what happened, but it seemed to me that out of nowhere came 20,000 Yanks hallowing surrender."

Gradually, the musketry died away; and, shortly after one o'clock, General Heth rode up—his face was stern and flushed, as well it might be considering that our foray to Gettysburg had ended with two of his brigades in shambles and one of his brigadiers captured.

He has several very sensible officers on his staff and several very fool-ish ones who have talked and laughed flippantly about our presumed holiday march to Gettysburg. But they had now changed their note and I heard no more of their facetiousness. The more experienced officers were sober, like men who knew that hard work was ahead.

General Heth told me he had conferred with General Hill, some-thing I felt he should have done in the beginning once we encoun-tered the Yankee cavalry, and that Hill had ordered General Pender to form his brigades behind Heth's to prepare for an assault. And so we were getting into it! And everybody has been ordered up, including Anderson's division.

I was directed to mass my brigade to the right of Brockenbrough's in the shade of the woods that cover the east slope of Herr ridge. The batteries of Pegram and McIntosh were then brought into action and began to shell the Yankees with their 53 cannon.

As the shells began to drop into the Yankee positions, both sides began to send out skirmishers and sharpshooters. We began to hear the sharp staccato cracks of the musketry. Captain Young, standing beside me, found the danger strangely exhilarating and shouted, "Come, boys, choose your partners! The ball is about to open! Don't you hear the music!"

Suddenly, there was a loud yell to our front and one of the skirmish-ers literally flew into the air. A Yankee Minie ball had struck his car-tridge box, tearing it apart and igniting his cartridges. As he was carried to the rear, we could see he was rendered unconscious, his hands and face burned black, his eyelashes and eyebrows singed off.

As our skirmishers engaged the enemy, General Hill was bringing up his corps and placing it in position. Colonel Burgwyn, sitting by a pine tree, grew tired of the delay and became quite impatient to engage the enemy, saying we were losing precious time. Another officer, stoically smoking his briarwood pipe, said, "Maybe the delay will offer the Yankees a chance to retire south of the town."

To this Colonel Burgwyn replied, "Ah! You are wrong, sir. That is the Iron Brigade on that ridge and they will not leave unless driven from it."

Here it is proper to say something of the situation that confronted us. In front of us was a wheat field about a fourth of a mile wide. Beyond this was Willoughby Run with thick underbrush and briars skirting the banks. Beyond this was McPherson's Ridge. The ridge to the front of us was defended by three Federal brigades: Stone's Pennsylvania brigade was posted south of the pike to the woods, the Iron Brigade was posted in McPherson's Woods, and with my field glasses I could easily distinguish individual Yankee soldiers. They wore tall, bell-crowned black hats, which made them conspicuous in the Federal line. To our right of the woods was posted Briddle's Pennsylvania brigade. There were also two Yankee batteries on the ridge in a position to sweep any portion of the field.

The sun was long past the meridian when General Ewell's corps came up on our left and the sound of guns on Oak Ridge announce the arrival of his first column, Rode's Division, by the Middletown road. They soon formed on the left at nearly right angles to our line and began to engage the enemy. Never was a grander sight beheld. The lines extended more that a mile, all distinctly visible from our position on Herr Ridge. The roar of the artillery, the crack of musketry and the shouts of the combatants added grandeur to the scene.

Suddenly, up rode a staff officer of General Heth's. "Who commands this brigade?"

"I do," I replied, springing up from the ground where I had been sitting.

"Well," remarked the officer, "are you ready to move in?"

Startled by his question, I paused a bit and then asked, "Will you give me the order to go in now?"

"Yes! General Heth desires you to move forward and drive the Yankees from yonder ridge."

He made a salute and I returned it by lifting my hat then announced somewhat melodramatically, "Tell General Heth that if my brigade cannot drive the enemy from that ridge, where will he find one that can!"

The order was soon relayed to the various regiments and I then gave the long-waited command to go forward. Now the orders rang out, "Attention! Load at will. Load!" Harsh. Stern. Determined. In quick succession and obeyed with alacrity. I watched with admiration as the gallant officers of the 26th went to their stations—Colonel Burgwyn in the center, Lieutenant Colonel Lane on the right, Major Jones on the left. The gallant standard bearer went to his post with the color guard four paces to the front, the blood red battle flag of the Confederacy swinging loosely in the strong July sun.

Accordingly, the word rang out from one end of the brigade to the other, "Forward march!" and, giving the familiar piercing rebel yell—incapable of description, conceivable only by those who know it—the advance began.

I watched with admiration as for a mile up and down the open field in front the splendid lines of my veterans swept toward the enemy. Their bearing was magnificent. They maintained their alignments with great precision. In many cases the colors of the regiments were advanced several paces in front of the line.

The attack was met by a furious storm of shells and canister. One shell struck in the midst of the 47th, killing three men and wounding five more. Another shell soon followed and exploded under one of the file closers and literally cut him in two leaving his heels in contact with his head.

The 26th kept good order until they reached Willoughby Run. Here the briars, reeds, and underbrush made it difficult to pass and there was some crowding in the center. A Yankee battery opened an enfilade fire and the loss was frightful but the men crossed in good order and immediately were in proper alignment again. Up the hill they went, firing accurately and with good execution.

The engagement in front of McPherson's Woods soon became desperate. The bullets were flying thick as hail stones. To add to the confusion, the men had difficulty maintaining their ranks in the ghastly confusion and killing gunfire on that field of blood. The air was soon completely filled with smoke, so much so that the position of the enemy could only be seen by the sudden flashes of light across our front as volley after volley filled the air in an almost continuous roar. Standing erect, the men would reply with a deliberate volley, rush forward, crouch, and load while the return volley swept over them. The 26th fought like savage, wild animals and yet, despite their bravery, many were slaughtered, shot down in droves.

Still, our line advanced, delivering its steady fire amid the rebel yells, and closed with the first line of the enemy. Here we had to stride over the bodies of the Yankees, who lay just as they fell, in regular line. At his post on the right of the regiment and ignorant as to what was taking place and the left, Lt. Colonel Lane hurried to the center. He was met by Colonel Burgwyn who informed him, "it is all right in the center and on the left. We have broken the first line of the enemy!"

The reply was given, "We are in line on the right, Colonel!"

To the right, the 11th North Carolina was able to flank the left of the 19th Indiana and force it back. This then uncovered the left of the 24th Michigan and forced it to withdraw under a murderous fire.

The men were engaged in a frantic struggle to shoot fast. Everybody tears cartridges, loads, passes guns or shoots. The line pushes forward and there is a rattling fusillade and loud cheers. "Advance" is the word. The men are loading and firing with demonical fury as they push ahead.

As the 26th entered McPherson's Woods, the men fought from tree to tree, often standing erect, taking deliberate aim and firing, instantly bending low or crawling several feet or yards to the next tree, rapidly loading, waiting for return fire, and judging the distance by the line of legs visible under the dense battle smoke, which did not fall within two feet of the ground.

The day was a hot one and as the men advanced slowly through the woods, they had difficulty in ramming down their cartridges so slick was the iron ram-rod in hands thoroughly soaked with perspiration. All expedients were resorted to, but mainly jabbing the ram-rods against a tree or rock.

On they advanced, yelling and pressing forward. Their mouths and faces were blackened with powder from furiously tearing open the paper cartridges with their teeth. Many were splattered with blood, brains and pieces of flesh or bone from comrades who had been shot beside them. The atmosphere was suffocating with the heat of the intense sun and the men were soaked in sweat, but they fought on, intent on victory.

As I watched the fierce struggle from my place in the rear of the lines, I was in a very belligerent state of mind, and much excited. I was recalled to my senses by an orderly who was following me, calling out: "No use going any closer, General." We had approached the front too closely, and the minies were flying about our ears; evidently the sharp-shooters were taking notice of us.

One of our batteries was firing from a small knoll to the rear. I gave my horse the spur and rode back toward them, pulling up near the first cannon where I once again took out my field glasses to observe the advance. "The men are fighting with great courage, general," said Lt. Raymond, one of my orderlies.

Soon up rode Lt. Owens, sent by Colonel Burgwyn. "Sir!" The 26th is hard pressed and low on ammunition!" "Tell the Colonel to keep advancing." I shouted over the din, "I will order up more ammunition."

"The fight in the woods is terrific," said Owens. "It is like no fight I ever heard of. But damn 'em! We'll beat 'em yet, God damn 'em! Before the day is out!"

Then with a salute Owens rode rapidly away as the sounds of the musketry in the woods seemed to awaken with double violence.

I turned to Sergeant Smalley and shouted, "Go, and tell Captain Wagner to bring ammunition forward at once."

Then a whistling ball seemed to pass just under my ear, and before I commenced to congratulate myself upon the escape, a shell with a revolving fuse came toward us and burst a short distance in front. Soon a few other shells dropped here and there as the battery was drawing fire. A caisson suddenly blew up, tearing the horses to pieces. Close by an ammunition wagon exploded and the air seemed to be filled with fragments of wood, iron and flesh. An officer stood by the side of the battery, helping with the shells; suddenly a shell, which we could not see, exploded in a piece of woods, mutilating the trees.

Lt. Raymond sat astride his horse with folded arms so near I could have reached to touch him; a loud zinng! Followed by a muffled Thud! And he fell beneath my horse's head. Another orderly rushed to Raymonds' side and bathed his bow with cool water, but I saw that the bullet had taken effect. His hands were stretched stiffly by his side, his feet were rigidly extended and death was hardening into his bleached face. The white eyeballs glared sightlessly upward: he was looking into the other world. I wonder as I calmly recall these episodes now, how lucky I was to escape the death that played about me.

The fighting in the woods continued in intensity. By the time the 26th struck the second line of the enemy, the colors had been cut down ten times, the color guard all killed and wounded. The fighting at this point was fierce. The killing proceeded in deadly earnest. Adjutant Hughes of my staff rushed forward, carrying a message. He spoke to Colonel Burgwyn with anxiety in his voice, "Colonel! General Pettigrew wishes to tell you your regiment has covered itself with glory today!"

Delivering these encouraging words, Adjutant Hughes then seized the fallen flag and, waving it aloft, advanced to the front and yelled, "Come on boys! Come on boys! Quick is the word! Here they are before us. You cannot miss them!"

For his bravery the adjutant was shot through the heart and fell, bathing the sacred banner in his life's blood.

Lieutenant Wilcox then rushed forward and, pulling the flag from under the body of Adjutant Hughes, he mounted a stump and waved the banner, hollering above the rattle of musketry, "For God's sake, boys, rally around the colors!"

In a few seconds, he also fell with two wounds in his body.

The men hesitated. The crisis is reached. Who will lead the colors forward? It is the peerless Colonel Burgwyn who seizes the banner from the lifeless hands of the gallant Wilcox and advances, shouting the order, "Dress on the colors!"

It is just like Burgwyn, ever in front regardless of danger. Following his example, the men moved forward, the minie balls whizzing thick around them. Private Honeycut rushed forward from the ranks and asked the honor to advance the flag. Turning to hand the colors to the gallant private, there was a *Zip! Purrrrr!* and a ball slammed into the colonel on the left side, which, tearing through both lungs, the force of it spun him around. He was caught in the folds of the flag as he fell and carried it with him to the ground. Private Honeycut survived only a minute more. A ball struck him in the forehead, knocking him backward, dead to the ground.

Lieutenant Colonel Lane rushed to the side of the fallen colonel and, taking his hand, asked, "My dear Colonel, are you severely hurt?"

As a trickle of blood ran from the corner of his mouth, Burgwyn, in great pain, could only nod towards his left side and squeeze Lane's hand to indicate that he was hurt badly.

Lieutenant Colonel Lane now boldly took charge of the regiment and rushed to the right through the battle smoke. He met Captain McLaughlin and gave the order, "Close your men quickly to the left. We will give the damn Yankees the bayonet!"

He then hurried to the left giving a similar order and returned to the center to find the colors still lying on the ground, Colonel Burgwyn and Private Honeycut lying nearby. As he looked down at his comrades with both anguish and anger, Colonel Lane bravely raised the colors.

Lieutenant Blair, seeing the act of bravery, rushed out saying, "Colonel, no man can take those colors and live."

Lange replied, "It is my time to take them now!" and advanced, waving the banner and shouting at the top of his voice, "Twenty-Sixth! Follow me!"

Inspired by the act of courage, the men answered with a yell and pressed forward.

The men of the 26th aided on the right by the 11th soon pushed their redoubtable black-hatted foe back to yet a third line on the other side of a slight ravine. No sooner was the line formed than Nat Chandler, a young drummer boy and quartermaster's clerk was shot down. Despite Colonel Burgwyn's firm order to remain in the rear, he had grabbed a musket and a pocket full of ammunition and had joined the attack where he was eventually mortally wounded in the right hip.

Determined to overcome this latest line of enemy resistance, Lane once again urged the men forward, shouting, "Move forward! Sustain an unbroken line! Fire low!"

With a loud cheer, the men obeyed the command to advance and rushed on to drive the enemy from the woods. The Yankee withdrawal was no panic, however, this was the Iron Brigade and as they fell back toward Seminary Ridge, they stopped every five steps to turn and fire another volley. Lt. Colonel Lane was still in the lead carrying the regimental color and, as he turned to see if his regiment is following him, a ball struck him in the back of the neck just below the brain and ripped through his jaw and mouth. For the 14th and last time, the colors were down.

On the right, the 47th and 52nd North Carolina had, after bitter fighting, driven Briddle's Pennsylvania Brigade from the ridge and at last McPherson's Ridge is ours, but at a cost that has literally torn the brigade to shreds.

General Hill, closely watching the action, now sent Pender's division forward. They made a well-ordered advanced through our exhausted ranks. The Federal line assaulted from the north and west soon broke. The Federal soldiers fled through Gettysburg to the rear.

During the Yankee retreat, we began to meet Yankee prisoners coming to our lines in considerable numbers. Many of them were wounded. Among them was a Pennsylvania colonel suffering from a wound in his face. In answer to my question he remarked, "We've pretty nigh whipped already, by Lord. I wish those stay-home gentlemen in the North, who cannot understand why we can't overwhelm you with numbers, could only see...only see...a Rebel brigade in all their rags and squalor. If they had eyes, they would know your men are like wolfhounds and not to be beaten by turnspits and foreign mercenaries."

JULY 2, 1863—THURSDAY
SEMINARY RIDGE—GETTYSBURG, PENNSYLVANIA

I once again take up my pen to continue my account of yesterday's battle. I wanted to finish last night but made the mistake of closing my eyes to rest a bit and went fast asleep and never woke till it was too late for more writing! The fact is that is had been a day of extraordinary events and I had been up at half-past two that morning. I felt a great deal done-in by the day's work.

While Pender's division drove the Yankees through the town, I ordered the brigade to stack arms at the Lutheran Theological Seminary. It was here that I learned I now commanded the division as General Heth had been wounded in the attack on McPherson's ridge. It appears that the new hat he captured at Cashtown saved his life. The general was struck by a minie ball on the head which passed through his hat but was slowed by the paper which had been placed in the hat to make it fit. Even so, the ball broke the outer coating of his skull and knocked him senseless.

Shortly after four o'clock, we noticed a party of officers riding up the pike from Cashtown. The horsemen drew up on Seminary Ridge where the pike reaches the summit and their leader took out his field glasses and looked down on the town of Gettysburg, then across at the range of hills south of town where he could see the enemy retreating pursued by our men with loud yells.

Many of my men pulled themselves to their feet and took off their hats. There was no cheering. My men were too exhausted to manage anything but a silent salute. But the word soon spread all along the line that our gallant and beloved commander General Lee had reached the field.

A number of general officers and staff officers were assembled about General Lee. The occasional crack of a rifle, the boom of a cannon, the groans of wounded men being carried by on stretchers, made it a scene not soon to be forgotten.

General Lee was talking to General Hill when I approached. I heard Lee ask in his quiet way, "Well, General, what do you make of the situation?"

Hill gave his impression that the Yankees were "entirely routed."

"I'm not so sure," replied Lee. "The Federal position, from what I can see of it, looks formidable, especially if it is assaulted from the town."

An aide then arrived on lathered horse bringing a message from General Ewell, requesting Hill to press the enemy in front, while he performed the same operation on his front.

Enough daylight remained for one more attack that might completely rout the Yankee army. Lee turned to Hill and asked if his men could advance from their present position across the town valley and seize the opposite hills.

"Nature has it limits," replied Hill, "and we have reached ours with fearful sacrifice."

He then explained that the divisions of Heth and Pender had taken frightful losses. The men still in line had been marching and fighting since five in the morning. In addition, they were almost out of ammunition and no replenishment was in sight. Anderson's division was still three or more miles from Gettysburg and would not be up before dark. "No, General," concluded Hill, "my men have had all they can take for one day."

General Hill's reply seemed out of character. Although new to the corps command, he had won a reputation in the Army of Northern Virginia as a fearless and able fighter without peer as a division commander and with an unquenchable thirst for battle. Perhaps his aggressive nature was tempered by the fact that he had been unwell all day. I thought he looked rather pale, in fact, almost as white as a ghost.

I must record that General Hill unfortunately suffers from frequent attacks of illness and often feels poorly, especially in the aftermath of strenuous forced marches or a hard battle. Camp rumor has it that he suffers from biliousness aggravated by Yellow Fever contracted during his service in the Everglades of Florida in the early 1850's. Dr. Middleton, however, told me it is common knowledge among the corps surgeons that General Hill suffers from the lingering complications of gonorrhea, which he contracted on furlough while a cadet at West Point. This has led to frequent pelvic pain, fever and difficulty in urinating. It seems the General's brief night of passion has had an unfortunate effect on his health even to this day. The effects of his chronic poor health are most evident upon his features. His cheeks are pronouncedly sunken and a weary gaze often covers his once-flashing hazel eyes.

Just then, General Longstreet rode up, smoking the cigar, which he usually held all day, unlighted between his clenched teeth, as was his custom when business was pressing and urgent. General Lee now dismounted and stepped forward as Longstreet dismounted and, grasping him by the hand, said, "Ha! Here is Longstreet. Here's my old war horse!"

Lee and Longstreet then made a careful scrutiny of the Federal position, especially south of the cemetery. Lee asked Longstreet about the locations of the First Corps divisions and was informed that the leading division McLaws was still six miles from the field.

Since General Hill had told Lee that his corps could not continue the battle and Longstreet's corps was not yet up, Lee decided Ewell's would have to make the attack. He then sent Colonel Taylor of his staff to suggest to Ewell that he push the enemy and seize Cemetery Hill.

Longstreet continued to study the ground with his field glasses. He seemed surprised to learn that Lee wanted to continue fighting an offensive battle. To Longstreet, the opportunity seemed perfect to throw the army around to the Federal left and interpose between the Federals and Washington.

"Finding our objective is Washington, the Yankees will be sure to attack us. When they attack, we shall beat them!" said Longstreet, pounding a clenched fist into his open palm for added emphasis.

Lee replied, "If the enemy is there tomorrow, we must attack him. Attack and we shall beat them!"

To which Longstreet retorted, "If he is there, it will be because he is anxious that we should attack him, a good reason in my judgement for not doing so."

Later, Captain Young and I felt compelled to return to the battlefield on McPherson's Ridge. As we rode up the pike, we met a constant stream of troops marching towards the battlefield and had great difficulty in passing through. When Captain Young's horse ran against some infantrymen, he was saluted by curses loud and strong and it was supposed that he was a "cavalryman leaving the battlefield and going after buttermilk."

At length, we reached the summit and steered for the wooded grove. As we neared the spot, we paused to contemplate, a young Confederate fully accoutered who lay stretched on his back behind an isolated hickory with arms extended and a bullet through the center of his forehead. He had evidently met his fate as a sharpshooter.

Upon entering the woods, we found it a veritable slaughter pen. The timber was literally crowded with dead and wounded. We had to guide our horses carefully to avoid trampling upon the poor fellows strewn in all directions. We soon came upon a Yankee sitting against a stump. From the insignia on his distinctive high-topped black felt hat with the left side brim turned up, we could see he was a member of the 24th Michigan. His eyes were open and he had a strange smirk upon his face. I asked Captain Young to dismount and find out what that fellow means by grinning that way.

"If he answers decently, help him," I added.

"Why, he's dead, General."

"That can't be," I replied. "See where he's hit."

Young then investigated more closely. The black hat, when taken off, brought away with it a mass that sickened us. A small bullet—from a revolver, probably—had gone through the inner corner of his eye leaving no visible wound, but the whole back of his head was blown off and the skull entirely emptied.

Leaving the pathetic scene, we turned and soon gained the south margin of the woods where we halted our horses, attracted by the unusual number of Confederate and Union dead at the spot, evidence of the vicious close-quarter fighting which occurred here. It was strange to note the position of the dead. As they lay strewn about the area, nine out of ten were on their backs with arms outstretched and feet pointing all round. Men shot in the head strike this attitude invariably. Men shot below the neck usually have one leg drawn up and their fingers clenched.

Some yards south of the woods lay a stiff stark naked Union soldier, his clothing having been appropriated by a Confederate to replace his ragged garments. This was the only body I was stripped on this part of the field and here was war indeed in all its naked horror.

We were trying to find the spot where Adjutant Hughes fell when we stopped to look at a dead infantry officer. Captain Young at once recognized the man as Captain William McCreery of the 26th, a brave and gallant officer. He lay on his back with his right hand grasping his head where the ball had entered that led to his demise. The agonizing look that distorted his features and the wild-eyed haunting glassy stare made it a most unpleasant sight. Even through accustomed as we were to such horror, we turned from the gory spectacle.

Fifty or so paces away from Captain McCreery we finally found the body of Adjutant Hughes. He lay face up on the ground, the grass around him red with his blood. His eyes were fixed and the ashen color of death was on his face. It was a disheartening sight, but a common one on that day.

As we rode slowly through the woods, the groans of the wounded were heart rendering, and the hospital-corps liter bearers and others were everywhere, busy, while now and then a sufferer would pass in a blood-stained blanket, being carried to the corps hospital by four companions. Near the pike spades were being handed out for interning the dead and men of the pioneer corps, pipe or cigar in mouth, consigned many to a humble grave without tears or words.

Among the many who perished on this occasion, none was more regretted than Colonel Burgwyn, who had gloriously fallen at the head of his regiment. All regretted the death of this valiant soldier and many a stout heart was wrung with anguish when it was whispered, "Poor Burgwyn is gone!" When dying, he had just one request, "Bury me on the battlefield, boys! Bury me on the battlefield!"

His last words were, "The Lord's will be done." Thus he died, very quietly and resignedly. He was interned beneath a lonely, wide-spreading walnut tree not far from where he had fallen. A crude headboard was placed at the site of the grave on which his men carved the following:

Henry King Burgwyn
COL 26th Reg. N.C.
Aged 22 years
Fell at Gettysburg, July 1, 1863
The Lord Gave
And
the Lord Hath Taken Away

There are no words I can use to express how deeply I feel his passing. I earnestly desired and tried to be with him after he fell but I could not leave my post which was with the brigade. I feel as though I have lost a brother, but it is for his family that I feel most deeply.

As we were leaving the woods, a member of the pioneer corps informed us that several Federal officers had been captured near the northwestern border of the woods. Curious, we rode in that direction and soon saw that the captives were medical personnel who had elected to stay behind and treat the wounded. We dismounted and approached one of the doctors who was about to probe for a bullet. He noticed our approach and extended his hand saying, "Why hello,

General Pettigrew. Dr. Ayres 7th Wisconsin Volunteers. We meet again! Have you found the day to be highly interesting?"

Astonished at his greeting, I could only stammer, "D-Do I know you, sir?"

"Why, General, don't you recall? We spent some time together last November on a train going to Richmond."

"Last November, hmmm?"

"Yes, General, I had been captured at Perryville and was being exchanged through Richmond."

The word Perryville jogged my memory and I smiled and extended my hand. "Yes, Doctor, now it comes to me. I remember you with affection." Then glancing around at the numerous wounded lying about and seeing the doctor was deprived of medical supplies, I asked if he could use some whiskey for his patients.

Ayres responded, "Does a duck like to swim?"

"I will have two pails full of whiskey sent immediately, Doctor."

"My patients will be most appreciative," Ayres replied.

"I regret you have been captured once again, Doctor, But your captivity may not last long as the day is ours and your forces routed. This war may soon be over."

"That depends on your willingness to surrender, General. We Yankees have set about this work very slowly. Fighting was not our choice, only our necessity, but we won't stop until we finish. I have a young son. I am going to stick to this war as long as I live and teach my boy to take my place when I'm gone and tell him to teach his children to do the same if it be necessary to put down this rebellion. That is the time we mean to stop and not before."

"I have no children, Doctor, and can only speak for myself but I will tell you if I had a thousand lives, I would rather lose them all than for the cause of the South to be lost."

"As usual, General, we disagree."

"As usual."

After I mounted, the doctor shook my hand and said, "God bless you, General. You won't forget the whiskey, will you?"

"You will have your whiskey, Doctor, count on it."

Lt. Colonel Lane who had been grievously wounded, had been taken to the corps hospital, a large stone house located near Herr Tavern. We found the house occupied by some thirty wounded soldiers. They lay in their blankets on the floors—pale, hollow-eyed—making low moans at every breath. Two or three were feverishly sleeping and as the flies reveled upon their open wounds, they stirred uneasily and moved their hands to and fro. A few attendants were brushing off the insects with rolled up paper, laving the sores or administering cooling draughts.

We found Lane in a corner near the rear door. He was lying on his back and I knelt by him, taking his hand. Twitches of keen pain shot across his face now and then, but he received me with a simple courtesy that made his suffering thrice heroic. I said to him that one of the surgeons had informed me his wound would have been fatal had the bullet passed a quarter-inch further to the left.

"Ah, General," he whispered, "the quarter-inches are in the hands of God."

Before we left, his thoughts turned to his fallen colonel and he eulogized Burgwyn saying in his halting, labored voice, "No braver man fell today on McPherson's Ridge. Neither the regiment nor the brigade, nor the division can furnish a man to fill his place with equal valor. If it was young Harry's fate to die in battle, no grander field, no greater battle, nor more decisive victory could his blood have brought." Tears slowly filled his eyes and he seemed to wander a bit, but soon regained his composure and, grasping my hand once again, he whispered, "Through

God's blessing I am still alive, but, Oh General, I pray God that I may never witness such another slaughter as took place today."

Outside the house, upon a pile of lumber and some heaps of fence rails close by, sat some dozens of wounded men, mainly Federals with bandaged arms and faces and torn clothing. There was one shot in the foot, who howled at every effort to remove his boot. The blood leaked from a tear in the side and at last the leather was cut, piecemeal from the flesh. A table for amputations was set up in the open air and I could see several products of that ghastly place sitting by a tree, bloody bandages covering their stumps. On the pike, the ambulances came and went, while in anticipation of further carnage, the white-covered ammunition wagons creaked eastward.

Several of the ambulance wagons were drawn up off the roadside near where we had tied our horses and, in passing, one whose driver was attempting to fix a broken wheel, I noticed a soldier wearing a sergeant's chevrons seated on the front seat of the vehicle whittling slowly at a stick. It did not occur to me that the sergeant was wounded until I glanced up and observed that the poor fellow's whole lower jaw had been evidently blown off, carrying tongue and teeth with it, leaving the moustache, clotted with blood, arching over a raw, tangled mass of muscles and arteries. The drippings from the horrid wound ran down over his chest in a sheet of bloody, clotted gore, saturating waistcoat, shirt and pantaloons! Yet the sergeant sat upright and whittled as calmly as if unhurt. I thought the wound worse than the grievous one sustained by Lt. Col. Bull at Seven Pines. Like Bull, he would have to fight for his life as there was no way by which food could be conveyed down his throat. How he could sit on that wagon seat and whittle with half his face shot away was something I marveled at, for I know that Lt. Colonel Bull's wound completely prostrated him and the exceedingly severe pain almost drove him mad.

I placed my bedroll last night near a tree by the theological seminary. A scant supply of rations had reached us and we found an abundance of hardtack of the Yankee army. This, though as hard as flint, when soaked in coffee is exceedingly nutritious. There were dead Yankees everywhere. I judged that they had recently been paid for on most of them were found sums of money. Before I went to sleep I walked around the seminary, noticing groups of savage looking soldiers gathered around the fires relating tales of the horrors of the day's battle, while others were engaged in gambling with the spoils obtained from the dead. Others were watching by the side of some wounded comrade, the fires throwing their shadows in gigantic proportions on the high walls. Tired and sleepy, I laid down near a dead Yankee and soon utterly exhausted fell asleep. All night in my dreams I fought the battles of the day before, over again. Sometimes I was engaged in a desperate struggle for life with a Yankee, who would suddenly change into some former acquaintance. My slumbers did not refresh me, sleeping among the dead was only too suggestive of the shortness of life and the nothingness of fame, and I awoke towards morning cold and quite worn out. It was yet dark, the fires had dwindled down to a few dying embers, men alive and dead lay stretched out on the hillside, the loud snores of some only distinguishing them from those who slept their final sleep.

I breakfasted a little before daylight. Elias had captured some Yankee coffee and General Pender joined me by the fire for an early morning cup. Pender said he had been unable to sleep being troubled by our failure to seize the high ground south of town. He commented that through the night, he had heard the ominous sound of Yankee soldiers with picks and shovels digging trenches on the hills and the rumbling of cannon being put into position. He forecasted that the dawn would witness ranks of Federals behind heavy works supported by cannon frowning down upon us, and that it might now cost us 10,000 men to drive them from their new positions.

At six a.m. I was standing by the north side of the Theological Seminary when a strange figure approached. He looked like a highly independent mounted newsboy. He was attired in a flannel-checked shirt, a threadbare pair of trousers, and an old grey kepi, with a field glass belt about his body. His features wore a familiar warm smile. It was nonetheless than my old friend, Lt. Colonel Arthur James Lyon Fremantle.

"Hello, General Pettigrew. I've just arrived from Chambersburg," he shouted in his particularly British manner.

"Hello, old friend," I answered, right royally delighted to see him, for I was always glad when Fremantle was about.

"I have heard your brigade covered itself with glory yesterday."

"Yes, my brigade was in it good, but it was glory purchased at too dear a price. One more such battle and I shall have few, if any, men to command."

Fremantle and I decided to ride to the south of town where it was said we could get a good view of the Yankee positions. Upon our arrival, we could see the enemy occupied a series of high ridges. Their right, which was east of the cemetery, rested on a steep, rocky hill, the top of which was covered with trees. From the cemetery, their line curved southward and their left appeared to rest upon a high rocky hill called Round Top.

After surveying the position for some time, Fremantle said, "The Yankee general has chosen his position well."

"Too well," I replied, surveying the Yankee position carefully. I didn't like the looks of it one bit. The Yankees held the high ground and interior lines. They could shift their forces from one point to another with ease while we enclosed them in a sort of semi-circle, covering five or six miles at least. I felt General Lee would not attack a more numerous enemy force holding higher ground. He must see the enemy position cannot possibly be carried by an attack in front, and would depend upon Longstreet and Ewell to outflank them.

It would help if Stuart and the cavalry were here. All wonder where that vain, glorious fool is.

We were unexpectedly joined by three vulgar and very able-bodied newspaper correspondents who I suppose had joined the army to experience our triumphant march in Cashtown and, hearing little musketry, they concluded it would be quite safe to go further to the front. "There," said one in a flippant way, "there are the Yankee positions". Riding a short distance ahead of us they dismounted for a better look. All was quiet, but these braves had hardly begun their look-see when a Yankee gun opened and a shell came with fearful precision over their heads. One correspondent, a fat man, rushed wildly to his horse, convulsively clutched the mane and tumbled on the saddle, galloping hotly off; but, it so happened that two more well-aimed shells, passing with their hideous screams, burst just behind his horse, giving him the wings of panic! The other correspondents, quite paralyzed, ran wildly to a nearby rock and flung themselves down flat behind it; after a few minutes of quiet, one of them looked up at us and, with a cold sweat rolling off him, exclaimed, "Oh! I wish they would stop! Don't you think, General, they will stop pretty soon?" He finished just short of an approaching shell. "Time to get!" I shouted to Fremantle and as we turned to ride off, the shell exploded with an ear-splitting thunderclap about twenty yards away. Fremantle and I were unscathed but my horse received a sharp piece of metal through the nose and, as we galloped away, he kept up a constant snorting and blowing of blood on Fremantle and myself. Once we reached Seminary Ridge, I was able to stop and upon examination, found that the wound fortunately was not serious. After some minor repairs, he would be available for further service.

I spent the remainder of the morning tending to various military duties attempting to restore the brigade to a semblance of military efficiency. Reports have been written, rolls called and the dead buried. I have gone around to the hospitals and rousted our all the men who could walk and returned them to duty. I then armed the cooks and other non-combatants and put them in the ranks. To further restore the spirit of the men, I have ordered the band of the 26th, one of the best in the army, to play. The trumpets, drums and trombones sounded all morning and by early afternoon, the survivors of my brigade inspired by the stirring music and return of the lightly wounded, raised a cheer.

Shortly before one o'clock, an aide from General Hill rode up and handed me an order directing me to march the division a mile to the south toward the army's right and move into position on Seminary Ridge, adjoining the left of Longstreet's First Corps and behind our massed artillery batteries. Just as the aide was about to depart, he handed me two letters. Now to receive two letters in the army at any time was quite an event, but here? Away in the enemy's country? In the face of their frowning guns? This was quite something. One of the letters I recognized as being from Judge Petigru. The other aroused my curiosity. The envelope was written in a feminine hand and was very neat, but the end had been burned off and the contents were held in place by a narrow red ribbon daintily tied.

Who, I wondered, could have sent me such an unusual letter? Could it be some fair maiden, a secret admirer perhaps? Even though I was in a conspicuous place, surrounded by staff officers, curiosity got the best of me and I carefully opened the precious missive and read the following.

"Your are cordially invited to be present at the commencement exercises of the Charleston Female Seminary on the evening of July 3, 1863 at eight o'clock p.m. Compliments of the President."

My feelings were inexpressible. How I longed to be there! Unfortunately the ceremony would have to proceed without me. I have been temporarily detained by events in Pennsylvania, but I am sure the young ladies will understand and forgive my absence.

By two o'clock, the division was in position and we made our camp near Spangler's Woods, well back of Seminary Ridge. Shortly after our arrival, I had a brief conversation with General Longstreet, who after a long consultation with General Lee, was riding down with his staff towards the front.

Longstreet and I sat on our horses in the shade and conversed about the Yankee position on Cemetery Ridge. Although I had only been with the army a short while, I had grown quite fond of the general. He reminds me in some ways of Judge Petigru, forthright and honest, a man of honor. He is a handsome man, about forty years of age, a soldier every inch, tall and well proportioned. He wears a full brown beard, which helps, give prominence to his glint steel-blue eyes. Like all of us at this stage of the campaign, his uniform looks the worse for wear, even the three stars upon the throat being dingy and ragged, while his common brown felt hat would not bring half a dollar at any place in times of peace.

Longstreet is a thorough soldier and in battle some say that he is slow to start. But once engaged, all agree, that he is a magnificent fighter, handling his men well, getting from them everything they have. His troops have a confidence in their commander unsurpassed in the army and no battle is ever considered decisive until Longstreet and his troops, who acknowledge no superior in endurance and courage, have measured strength with the enemy.

As we talked, the general appeared weary and I reasoned he could have not had much rest for he said he was up at 3:30 a.m., had his breakfast and reached Seminary Ridge by 5:00 a.m. He mentioned that he was most unhappy over the prospects of an offensive against the Yankees in their positions along Cemetery Ridge and he had more the look of gloom than I ever noticed before. He then leaned forward in his saddle and explained that General Lee seemed a little nervous today.

"He wishes me to attack. I do not wish to do so without Pickett's division. I never like to go into battle with one boot off."

With a salute, he rode off to converse with General Kershaw, whose men were marching along nearby. I could only think that Longstreet was highly disturbed about the whole proposition. Probably because the frontal attack he opposed was becoming more and more inevitable.

Hour after hour rolled on until we began to think that Longstreet had deferred the attack until tomorrow. In front of us our skirmishers and those of the enemy kept a continual popping and first one side is driven back, then the other. I procured a good position on the branch of a tree and with my field glasses watched the movements of both armies with no little interest.

All was relatively quiet until about 4:15 in the afternoon. Then, far away on the right, the boom of a heavy gun betokened the commencement of Longstreet's attack. One by one the artillery on his left joins in with a hearty will and our line becomes a living sheet of flame. A puff of white smoke is seen on the enemy's line—another and another and the deadly cannon balls come hurling and screaming through the air, busy on their mission of death.

As I watch intently from my precarious perch, Fremantle comes riding by and asks me to join him on the right to get a good view of the battle. The suggestion strikes my fancy and I descend and am soon mounted and we are on our way, continually aware of the hellish scream of the shells as they pass over us or explode high in the air in a puff of white smoke.

To reach the position of our artillery, we will have to pass some distance under this heavy shelling. As we halted to ascertain the most direct route, I was suddenly aware of my legs trembling and, looking at them rather contemptuously, I muttered, "legs if you could see the danger into which I am going to take you, you would tremble more." We continued to ride and whether from fatigue, loss of sleep, or what, I was nervous as a lady. When we reached the artillery position, I told Fremantle I was no more good than a frightened deer. He laughed and replied, "Nonsense! 'Tis Elias' strong coffee. Better give it up."

We soon located Colonel Alexander commanding Longstreet's artillery. He had pushed his guns up close to a Yankee position in a peach orchard by the Emmitsburg Road, figuring his unreliable ammunition will work better at shorter ranges.

Alexander was near one of his batteries where the fire was hottest, with the reins on his horse's neck seemingly in prayer, but only, I think, trying to calculate the exact range. Attracted by my approach, he said in a loud voice, better to be heard above the din, "Delightful excitement!" I replied that it was pleasant to learn he was enjoying himself, but thought he might have indigestion of such fun if his guns did not soon silence the Yankee batteries.

The guns boomed and the shells burst in and around the Yankee positions. The shellfire soon became too hot for the Federals and they soon abandoned the area. As the cannoneers cheered and the enemy retreated, a fuse ignited accidentally at an ammunition limber. To prevent an explosion near the limbers, Corporal Willard carried the shell away and pulled the burning fuse from it with his bare hands. I felt this courageous act saved many lives.

A short time later, I watched intently as one four-gun battery of Frank Huger's dueled with the Yankee guns in the orchard. Each man in the battery worked as if success depended on is individual efforts, while Huger and Lieutenant Vincent galloped back and forth among the guns, urging the men to their best efforts. The Yankees responded with a weight and accuracy that surprised us. One shell I noticed particularly as it burst in a tremendous crack of flame and smoke. One of its fragments struck Lt. Vincent's horse near the middle of the hip, tearing an ugly hole from which there spurted a stream of blood the size of a man's wrist. To dismount, before his horse fell, required quick work, but he lieutenant was equal to the occasion.

Behind us, Barksdale's Mississippi brigade was getting ready to go in. His troops formed for the attack. The general, his long white hair flowing in the wind, rode up to Alexander and said, "As soon as Longstreet lets me go in I will take that battery in five minutes."

"Wait a little," replied Alexander, "you will be ordered in shortly."

Barksdale's men were as eager as their leader and those in the front line began to pull down the fence behind which they were positioned.

"Don't do that or you will draw the enemy's fire!" shouted Barksdale. Soon afterwards, Barksdale received the order to attack and called for his horse, mounted, rode to the front of his men, gave the word, waving his hat and led the line forward himself.

It was a glorious sight. The men who had been lying down sprang to their feet and went in with a will. Forward swept Barksdale's brigade, breaking out with a yell as they came face to face with the foe. True to Barksdale's word, the guns in the peach orchard were pounced upon and half of them taken. The rest limbered up and made a hasty retreat.

Quite suddenly, the Yankee line began to give away in the peach orchard and along the western edge of the wheat field. Alexander dismounted and, in his shirt sleeves, had taken his stand a few paces to the left of the guns and with his field glasses, was intently observing the progress of the battle. Seeing the Yankee's waver, Alexander shouted for the dead and wounded animals to be cut away from the teams, freeing the batteries to accompany the infantry. As the Yankees began to retreat, the battle looked to be in its final phase. Alexander mounted his horse and rode along the guns, urging the men to limber to the front as rapidly as possible, telling them we would "finish the whole war this afternoon!"

The guns started forward and the dust and smoke were fearful. The boys were covered with it as we trot toward the peach orchard; there is no drawing of rein while straining our eyes in the direction of the battle smoke, as our ears take in the sound of the musketry. As we neared the Emmitsburg Road, the bugler sounded the "Gallop." We rattled past some wounded soldiers and were cheered. It made my heart leap to hear them. We crossed the road into the peach orchard, the drivers whipping the gaunt, undernourished artillery horses into a lather. The exhilaration of the charge is heart-pounding. Guns bouncing, sparks flying, we gained the eastern edge of the orchard, pulled up, loaded the guns, and began losing shotgun blasts of canister into the Yankees.

Alexander has dismounted and I ride over to where he is standing. He has trained his field glasses on the Yankee position. Suddenly he lowers his glasses and says to me in a disappointed tone, "General, it is not the enemy's main line we have broken, but only the position of the Yankee Third Corps. I can see beyond a ridge giving good cover and on it enemy batteries in abundance, and troops marching up to it as reinforcements."

Our attack stalls, Hood has been wounded and General Barksdale killed and at the very moment of apparent victory, we hesitate and then fall back. It has been a frightful battle but we have gained decided advantages, taking many prisoners and getting possession of the ground up to the foot of Little Round Top.

Night came on. The crash of musketry and the roar of cannon finally ceased. At about ten o'clock, Fremantle and I rode back to my headquarters where we fed our horses a late supper.

After taking care of the horses, we sat around the campfire and tried to put the day's events in perspective. We well knew the work is still unfinished and today's fight has accomplished little towards the grand result. We know that to gain a great victory we must not only drive the Yankees from their position, but must destroy Meade's powerful army—or the war will likely be protracted many years.

Later we were joined by Captain Ross, the Englishman serving in the Austrian Army who has joined our army as an observer. He had spent most of the day observing the battle with General Lee. He noted that as soon as the firing began, Lee joined Hill and Heth near the seminary and stayed there nearly all the time during the battle. He had just returned from General Lee's headquarters and was full of news and camp gossip. Lee's headquarters' cottage was, he reported, crowded with officers some seeking orders, some greeting friends from other commands, some seeking gossip. Adjutants coming and going. Altogether a bit of a madhouse that made passage to and from the little house difficult. Outside the yard, crowds of soldiers hovered in the area, eager to learn what the army's next move might be.

At ten o'clock, a stir of excitement passed over the crowd as two muddy, fatigued generals, and their staffs, dismounted on the Cashtown Pike and walked through the yard and into the headquarters building.

Most present immediately recognized General Stuart. He wore no insignia of command, a common black felt hat turned down in front and up behind, a much splattered overcoat tightly buttoned, elegant riding boots covering the thigh, a handsome sabre carelessly slung by his side and a heavy pair of Mexican spurs that jingled and rattled as he walked were all that Ross could see of this dashing leader. The cavalry chieftain was followed by Fitzhugh Lee and Major Henry McClellan. They had arrived to report to the commanding general.

One of the adjutants inside the building told Ross that when Stuart approached Lee, the commanding general raised his arm in a gesture of frustration and said, "General Stuart, where have you been? Not one word from your command has been received by me! Where have you been?"

Fremantle who was listening intently then interrupted, "Me thinks I feel sorry for General Lee. He did not choose this battleground with the Federals yonder holding a string of high places. Add to this Stuart off glory seeking with the cavalry that should have informed Lee of the enemy's whereabouts."

"What you say may well be true," replied Ross, "but it has been my observation that General Lee has not been himself here at Gettysburg. The Confederates have shown great courage and assaulted with great elan, but Lee seems to have abandoned the great turning movements that have brought him victory after victory. Here he has fought as he has never fought, a relentless hammering of a numerically superior enemy. Such a strategy can only lead to disaster for the South."

It is late and I am struggling to finish this entry. I should try to sleep, but who can sleep upon a battlefield? One may sleep when almost prostrated by fatigue, but it is not the gentle sleep that brings rest to the weary body. Off in the distance the sentinels occasionally exchange shots. I can see the flash of the guns and hear the whistle of an occasional bullet above my head. The two armies are too near to sleep comfortably, or even safely, so the boys cling to their muskets and keep ready for action. It will be a long night, but by God's good grace, it will thankfully come to an end.

JULY 5, 1863—SUNDAY
NEAR CASHTOWN PASS—PENNSYLVANIA

Well, it is all over now. The battle of Gettysburg is lost! I have come safely through the terrible engagement on the fatal Third of July, but my splendid brigade is almost destroyed.

I have been more or less under fire for three straight days, and it has not been very pleasant or good for the nerves. But now that there is a quiet day, I thought I would make an attempt to describe the sad bloody work of the third day's battle that has been so fatal to our cause.

The morning of Friday, July the Third (or rather the night—for we were up by starlight) was mild, forecasting a warm day to come. As I awoke, I clearly heard the courthouse clock in Gettysburg strike four. By daylight we had had our breakfast and were ready to see what the day would bring.

At about seven o'clock I rode over to General Hill's headquarters. When I arrived, the general was sitting close to a campfire. I was seriously alarmed at the expression of his face as he waved hello. After saluting, I said, "What is the matter?"

He seemed entirely unnerved as he replied, "They hit General Pender yesterday and, my God, I'm afraid he is seriously wounded."

I soon learned the details. General Pender with a carelessness of consequences for which he was well known, had gone forward yesterday to get a clear view of the land over which his division would charge. He had just raised his field glasses to his eyes when a shell exploded nearby and sent a large fragment of metal into his thigh. He tried to get back on his horse but found the feat impossible and thus for the first time ever, he was forced to leave the battlefield. It is not known when he will be able to return.

After he had informed me of Pender's wound, the general's spirits slowly returned. His health had improved and the smell of battle always exhilarates him. He said to me, "We have just had our coffee and you will find some left for you." Then, taking a critical look at my bespattered and worn clothes he added, "You look weary, General Pettigrew. I wish you could rest and refresh yourself, but General Heth is still not able to resume command and I am afraid you will have to command the division until further notice."

No one could conjecture what the next move would be, but both General Hill and I felt a certainty that Lee would not yield to a drawn battle without at least another attempt to breach the Yankee lines. After the battle of yesterday, and the heavy casualties, the men were still eager to fight. There was no despondency. Each and every soldier felt—while he had done his best the day before—still he was equal to that before him today.

Later, I learned that Lee intended to renew the battle using Pickett's fresh division as a spearhead. There were no details, but my impression was that the assault would take up just north of the peach orchard. I was delighted we were going to renew the attack, for I believed it would succeed because General Lee had planned it and the spirit that pervaded our troops was invincible.

At about nine o'clock on this beautiful midsummer morning, I was ordered to the crest of Seminary Ridge. Standing out in an open field in range of Federal cannon, I found General Lee, A. P. Hill, Longstreet and members of Lee's staff. Lee pointed to a clump of trees near the center of the Union line and explained his plan of attack. The gathering soon became a conference in which the mode of attack and the troops to make it were thoroughly debated.

Lee's attack plan was simple—to use Pickett's fresh division, reinforced by mine, to breach the Federal center. "Generals Pickett and Pettigrew will advance on the same line," said the noble Lee. "Two brigades will be added from Pender and two from Anderson, Stuart and the cavalry will be sent to the Yankee rear to aggravate and pursue the Federals should Pickett and Pettigrew achieve a break-through."

"How many men," asked Longstreet, "did the general expect to have in the attacking force?"

When Lee gave a figure of 15,000, Longstreet made a sweeping gesture with his arm toward the ridge and the ground leading to it. He then exclaimed vehemently, "I have been a soldier, I may say, from the ranks up to the position I now hold. I have been in pretty much all kinds of skirmishes from those of two or three soldiers up to those of an army corps and I think I can safely say there never was a body of 15,000 men who could make that attack successfully."

I thought Longstreet's reply close to insubordination, but Lee, my beau ideal of a soldier, chose not to regard it so. He answered in his firm, quiet, determined voice, "The enemy is there, General Longstreet, and I am going to strike him."

Later, after the meeting, Pickett, Longstreet, and I stared across at the Union line on Cemetery Hill. Attacking it would not be easy. The Yankees were massed there, across that empty valley, at the clump of trees, where the focus of our attack must be made. A skirmish line nearly as heavy as a single line of battle was thrown out all across the Federal front. On the ascending slope behind, two tiers of artillery frowned and two lines of infantry waited. Beyond, on the crest of the ridge, heavy reserves of infantry were massed in double column.

A low stone wall fronted sections of the ridge, behind which the Union infantry crouched. One hundred yards from the stone wall was the Emmitsburg Road leading out of Gettysburg. Along either side of the road were post and rail fences, which would have to be scaled on the way to the stone wall. From Seminary Ridge where Pickett's and my division would emerge from the cover of the woods to the Union position, the infantry would have to cross fourteen hundred yards of pasture and grain lands. Over this empty, treeless space, our men would be exposed to cannon fire from the full two-mile length of Cemetery Ridge.

"Gentlemen," said Longstreet," I don't wish to make this attack, but I have been ordered to do so. It looks to me like a truly forlorn hope on an extensive scale."

Pickett didn't agree with Longstreet's assessment. As he studied the terrain closely, he agreed the attack would cost lives. He saw the undeniable strength of the Federal position, but nevertheless was full of hope and confident of victory. He argued that his division had seen little action at Fredericksburg and had not been at Chancellorsville. Although missing two brigades, the men were ready and were supported by the entire power of the invincible Southern Army led by Robert E. Lee. "I am confident this attack will succeed," said the undaunted Pickett, "and I feel lucky to have the chance to breach the Yankee line."

By eleven o'clock, our men were in position to make the assault. Pickett drew up his division in the hollow behind the line of batteries, which now crowned Seminary Ridge. Pickett's column of assault consisted of Garnett's brigade on the right, Kemper's on the left and Armistead supporting both. Wilcox's brigade of Anderson's division, which was to accompany the assaulting column as a cover to Pickett's flanks, was already in contact with the Federal skirmishers, having been sent forward early in the morning to protect the batteries on the ridge. It lay almost in front of Pickett's right brigade, ready to rise and go forward when Pickett's men passed on their way to charge the Yankee positions.

My division was formed from north to south: Brockenbrough, Davis, Marshall (commanding my old brigade), Archer. The division was also drawn up in a line of regiments, with each regiment having half its companies in the first line and half in the second. The second line was posted a hundred yards or more behind the first. Behind my division, the two brigades of Pender's (Scales and Lanes) formed a single line, the intent being that they should reinforce the right or left wing of the assaulting column as occasion might require.

After the division was formed, I paid a visit to Colonel Birkett Davenport Fry who was in temporary command of General Archer's brigade.

I told Colonel Fry of Lee's plans. After a heavy cannonade, we would assault the Union line. The Yankees, of course, would return the fire with all the guns they had. "We must shelter the men as best we can at this time," I told Fry. "They will be less exposed to the Federal fire if they lie down." I then ordered Colonel Fry to go at once to Pickett and work out an understanding about dressing the lines in the coming assault since his brigade backed on Pickett's division.

Soon after Fry rode off, I walked to a secluded spot at the crest of Seminary Ridge and there deliberately surveyed the field from Round

Top on my right to the spires of Gettysburg on my left. I then took another long look at the point on Cemetery Ridge where my division would strike the enemy provided our advance be made in a straight line. I had only commanded the division two days and I hoped I was equal to the task ahead. Realizing full well what was before me and the brave men under my command (and at one of the most serious moments in my life) I asked aloud the question, "James Johnson Pettigrew, your soul may this day be required of you. Are you ready to make that sacrifice if your duty requires it?" The audible answer was "No matter how desperate the situation, I shall do my duty, for I have sworn a solemn oath to God and my country and, should I perish in this undertaking, I will fear no evil, for God has limited the wickedness of man for he cannot kill the soul." After I responded to my own question as to doing my duty, a change of feeling immediately took possession of me. All dread even passed away and from that moment to the close of that disastrous struggle, I was free of fear and my actions were as calm and deliberate as if upon dress parade.

Captain Young and I ate a Spartan lunch and, after lighted cigars and under the flickering shade of a very small tree, discoursed of the incidents of yesterday's battle and of the probabilities of the day. Our horses were hitched to some nearby trees munching some oats. A great lull rested upon the field, broken only by the occasional arrival of an officer or orderly carrying a message. I yawned and looked at my watch. It was five minutes before one o'clock. I returned my watch to its pocket and thought the midday bell would just be ringing from St. Michael's steeple in far away Charleston and kind-hearted Judge Petigru would just be coming up Meeting Street, finishing his after-lunch constitutional.

What sound was that? I was wrenched from my reverie. The thunder of two signal shots echoed across the valley and I observed directly above the crest of Cemetery Ridge in the distance the smoke of a bursting shell.

There soon followed the loud booming report of gun after gun in rapid succession as our artillery opened fire upon the enemy positions.

The guns leaped and bucked with each discharge and soon the Yankee batteries responded, tentatively at first, then with increasing weight. The air was soon filled with screeching projectiles. Every now and then, a solid shot from the Yankee cannon would crash through the neighboring trees, or go hoppity-hop along the open field. I could watch them skip as they whizzed along. It would be odd if they were not so dangerous for if used against a mass of men these cast iron balls can be horribly effective. I recall reading that at the battle of Zorndorf in 1758, one of them had caused forty-eight casualties. After they have gone some distance and lost their velocity, I could see them plainly, provided I was in front of, or behind, them. They dash with a great whish, hit the ground, make a great hop, and go *skip skip skip* till they lose their energy and then tumble down raising a small cloud of earth. The long rifled shells careen in with more of a rush and scream. If I looked intently I could see them, high in the air above, upsetting and tumbling end over end.

I went to my horse, which was still tied to a tree, still eating oats with an air of the greatest composure. Anxious alone for his oats, while I put on the bridle and adjusted the halter, he delayed me by keeping his head down. The shells still made music around me as I buckled up my saddle and put my foot upon the stirrup. Suddenly two shells exploded together, just short of us and a little high. The whirling and whizzing of fragments filled the air and they tore up the ground around. One shard ripped a button off my coat and another tore away half of Captain Young's sleeve. Young and I were unharmed, but a two-inch square piece struck my horse, Tar Heel, with a loud spat. I had been told somewhere that a once-wounded horse hit again will always squeal in a certain characteristic pitch. Tar Heel now let out a shriek unlike anything human or animal I had ever heard. Blood spurted from her neck and she reared high in the air. Luckily, I was able to throw myself clear. She landed heavily on all fours, shocked and disoriented and began to race around wildly.

Seeing the commotion, the ubiquitous Fremantle galloped up to volunteer his services. "General, she's mortally wounded," Fremantle called out. "Shall I put her out of her misery?"

Reluctantly, I gave the OK.

The Englishman drew his revolver and took aim.

"Hold on!" I yelled at the last second. "I guess she'll live to carry her own saddle to the rear and avoid our carrying it."

It was a lucky guess, for upon examination, Tar Heel turned out to have a flesh wound, ugly but treatable. She was soon led to the rear and I transferred my accoutrements to my other horse, Dixie.

After mounting, I rode among my men ordering them to lie down. This was the command everywhere on Seminary ridge. The men didn't need to be told that and it hardly mattered. There was no place to hide. A shell crashed through the trees raining branches down upon us and directly two men bolted and sought to get shelter in an excavation nearby where some dead horses killed in the prior day's battle had been thrown. Seeing this and hoping to avoid any further panic, I yelled, "My men, do not leave your ranks to get shelter here. All these matters are in the hand of God and nothing that you can do will make you safer in one place than another."

The men gave a hearty cheer and I knew all would be right.

Riding back toward the crest, I said to Fremantle, "I am a somewhat lucky person you know, and I have always had a strong religious feeling. I always believe that I am in the hands of God and that I should be unharmed or not according to his will. For this reason, I am always ready to go into the thick of it, no matter how great the danger."

By two o'clock, a hundred and twenty five of our guns were concentrating their fire on the position of the enemy Second Corps. The

Yankees replied with over a hundred guns and soon both ridges were covered with smoke which drifted out into the valley between. The sun which had been so brilliant at midday was now eclipsed and out of the cloud came the screaming shot and shell and the air was thick with murderous iron. From my position at the edge of the woods, I could see only the dense black smoke and flashes of orange flame, while the ground trembled and shook beneath me. It seemed to me that men could not live under that artillery fire and perhaps the Yankee line would be completely smashed.

There was little to do except listen and wait. I tried to count the exploding shells but lost count after 500. All things must end. At about three o'clock the last shot hummed and bounded to earth and the great cannonade was over.

Soon the clouds of black powder began to drift away and it was to be the infantry's turn. I watched intently as General Longstreet rode slowly across the field from right to left directly in front of the prone infantry. Only Colonel Moxley Sorrel, the general's adjutant, was with him. Longstreet was in full view of all as he inspected the line. It was a brave act for rifle balls from Yankee skirmishers whistled past him. The men called out to him, "Go to the rear…we'll fight without you leading us!" Longstreet said nothing. He rode leisurely and calmly into the woods and disappeared.

Colonel Marshall and Colonel Fry rode up and reported little loss in their regiments from the artillery. Colonel Fry, however, had been hit for the fourth time in the war, by a shell fragment in his shoulder. The wound was painful but not serious and he stated resolutely he would retain his command.

"General," Fry asked, "tell me what you think of this attack."

"Well, Colonel Fry," I said, "it is mostly a question of support. I think we'll be able to get there. The real difficulty will be in staying there after we arrive, for we will be most unwelcome guests and the whole infernal Yankee army is up there in a bunch."

At last the order came to prepare for the attack and my voice was subdued as I said to Marshall and Fry and the assembled staff, "Make your peace with God and mount, Gentlemen. General Lee has a hot place picked out for us today."

I then called the division to attention in my loudest voice and the order was passed to pile knapsacks, blankets—anything that would encumber the march—into company heaps. Then began the task of aligning the brigades and divisions. This was not easy as one does not launch nine brigades by saying, "Follow me, men!"

Pickett's division was on the right, Kemper in front, Garnett to his left, and Armistead immediately behind in support—three brigades, 4,500 men. To General Garnett's left, the gallant Brickett Fry's brigade, on which all would dress, stepped into lines and to his left the rest of my division—four brigades in all, 5,000 men. In support of my division were two brigades of Pender's division, temporarily under the command of General Trimble, with 2,500 men. On Pickett's extreme right, to cover his flank if needed was Wilcox with 1,200 men.

With the exception of Colonel Fry and myself, almost all of the officers were on foot as General Lee had ordered them to dismount so as to not draw enemy fire.

At almost regular intervals, about a hundred yards apart, the single flag of each regiment stood above the line and the men waited impatiently for the order to advance, as almost anything would have been a relief from the strain upon them. Many knelt in prayer for there were many God-fearing men in the regiments and they wished to go into the battle at peace with their Maker.

I noticed the flaming red battle flag of the 26th North Carolina with the blue Saint Andrews cross bearing thirteen white stars and the words "26th N.C. Inf'y" in white painted letters. The flag was the very soul of the regiment and I reflected on how the lamented Colonel Burgwyn had fell while holding it. How he would have wished to have been here today, leading his men in this great assault. I rode to Colonel Marshall who now commanded the regiment and he asked if there were any last minute instructions as I rode up.

"No, James, I believe not, unless it be to advise you to make good time crossing the valley. It is a devilish ugly place over yonder and we can't afford to be too long in getting there."

Then the command to advance came from the colonels, "Fix bayonets! Attention! Dress in line men! Steady in the center! Guide upon your right men! Forward! March!" There was soon the murmur and jingle of thousands of men beginning to move forward. The cannoneers sat astride their smoking guns to make room for the infantry who must pass between them.

Soon I could see the whole line a moving wall of steel at intervals the red battle flags floating high above the bayonet points. Here and there an officer motioning with his sword to perfect the alignment which in general looked as ordered as a holiday parade. The two divisions marched forward in a uniform steady step, stirring the dry stubble into a cloud of dust.

I rode up close behind the last line of the division. This was the first time I had ridden Dixie into battle and she was nervous. I kept tight rein and hoped she wouldn't bolt when the Yankees greeted our advance with their artillery. I looked along the line watching the flags flutter and snap, the glaring sunlight gleaming upon the thousands of burnished bayonets. Who could see this grand array marching resolutely forward without feeling pride in it.

The batteries in front were quiet yet, but we still had a long way to go. My division would have to advance several hundred yards further than Pickett's, for the stone wall angled away on our part of the front. I looked to the right and observed that Colonel Fry knew his business for he was making sure Pickett's left brigade dressed on his line, which would be the center of the attack.

As I rode forward, I took out my field glass and looked at the Yankee positions in the distance. It was an imposing and frightening sight for behind the low stone wall was an array of bristling Union muskets and cannon. I reasoned the artillery fire wouldn't be too bad until we were within 300 yards of the enemy's line. That is when they would begin to open on us with canister. This type of ammunition consists of a big tin can billed with cast-iron balls about an inch in diameter. On firing, the can disintegrates and the discharge thus becomes that of a large shotgun. At about 250 yards the canister begins to be really lethal and at 150 years, the gunners switch to double canister, or two cans fired at one shot. This horrific blast can literally disintegrate a line of infantry. No wonder the soldiers call it "canned hell-fire."

Suddenly, there was a loud report in the distance and a ponderous shell screamed across the valley, striking the ground in front of our advancing line, showering the men with dirt. Two men limped away to the rear.

"Close up men!" shouted the captain and immediately the gap is closed. The Federal artillery, which had stood quietly by as we began our advance, now began to open upon us with a savage fury. Shot, shell, shrapnel, spherical case—every missile conceived of by man—came shrieking and hurtling through the air in horrible density.

Dixie was proving difficult. Her ears were erect, eyeballs distended and her nostrils were tremulous with fright. A shell, so perfectly in range that I held my breath and felt my heart grow cold, came toward and passed me. It exploded some distance behind.

Bang! Whiz! Came one, two, three shells.

"My God!" said Young. "They have opened upon us with batteries from Round Top!"

As the shells exploded around us, there came the sensation of a tremendous blow and I sank forward on my horse who ceased prancing when my hold was loosened on the bridle reins. I looked at my left hand and saw a severe and ragged wound. A piece of shell had gouged a path along the back of the hand and the index and middle finger. Captain Young stopped to express regret for my wound and helped me to dress it with a piece of cloth from my saddlebag.

The wound was painful but it was my duty to go on and so I put spurs to Dixie and rejoined the advance. Unexpectedly, once she felt the spurs, Dixie reared and plunged. It did not occur to me she had been hit. I drew tighter rein and once again gave her the spur. To my surprise, she fell heavily on her haunches. I scrambled form the ground where I had been thrown sprawling. The gallant mare also struggled to her feet and hobbled toward the rear. She had been struck in the breast by a shell fragment which penetrated seven inches. For the rest of the battle, I was on foot.

Even as the shot and shell fell upon us, the men moved steadily on without a waver or break. We soon reached a fence and this was quickly toppled over by hand and upon the points of bayonets. A short distance ahead we came upon a second fence and, as I approached, the men were trying to topple it to the ground. Then to my horror a man's head bounced towards me like a football, sprinkling blood in all directions. A solid shot had struck a portion of the top rail of the fence driving it with terrible force across the neck of the man behind, cutting off his head as if severed by an axe and pitching the gory mass some distance to the rear.

We marched on soon reaching the fences that bordered the Emmitsburg Road. As the men scaled them, they reformed and began advancing again. Now the moment of truth had come! From my position west of the road, I looked up the slope at the stone wall fronting the Federal position and watched as a dense blue line rose from behind the wall where they had laid in comparative safety. For an instant the sheen of the bright musket barrels caught my eye, then the Federal line erupted in a withering, blinding sheet of fire that rained destruction upon the advancing troops. The slaughter that took place was almost inconceivable. The hiss of bullets was incessant and men fell at every step. The ground in front of me was covered with scores of dead and dying. Then came a fearful blast of canister further shattering and mutilating as fine a body of Southern soldiers that ever trod a battlefield. Still the men went forward and I could hear Colonel Marshall's booming voice roaring above the tumult, "Forward, men! Forward! For God's sake forward!"

As Colonel Marshall led the advance toward the stone wall, Captain Brewer, always a dashing leader, fell dead when struck in the chest by canister. Colonel Marshall continued on but when his regiment, the 26th reached to within about forty yards of the enemy's works, it had been reduced to a skirmish line.

Seeing the men approach near the enemy line, I climbed over the fence along the road and, waving my sword, I gave the command, "Align on colors! Close upon the colors! Close up on the colors!"

I was now close enough to see the stone wall clearly. I looked to the right through the drifting battle smoke and could see that some of Pickett's men had passed over the angle and were inside. If supports would now come up, the day could yet be ours.

A Yankee color was waving defiantly behind the stone wall in our front and a heroic ambition to capture it took possession of several of the men. Corporal Smith sprang forward to seize it and was shot and mortally wounded. Private Cozart then swung his musket at the Yankee who had shot Smith but missed with a wild swing and was shot down at the base of the wall. Sergeant Brooks and Private Thomas, the latter carrying the flag, reached the enemy's works, but were soon confronted by a dozen Federals who called out to them, "Come over on this side of the Lord," and took them prisoner rather than needlessly shooting them down. Colonel Marshall was not so fortunate. This gallant soldier was shot down just as he reached the wall.

For five, perhaps ten minutes, we held our ground and looked back and prayed for support. Unfortunately, there was no help coming over the storm-raked field we had just crossed—no support at all from the rest of the Army of Northern Virginia.

All was lost and the Yankees threw out a brigade to sweep along our flank and gobble up the feeble remnants of the division. Many of the brave men chose to surrender rather than run the gauntlet of the enemy's fire, but I refused to once again become a Yankee prisoner and started for the rear, one of the last I believe to leave.

As I retreated back toward the Emmitsburg Road, Captain Cureton of the 26th approached and asked, "General, the men are falling back, shall I rally them?"

"No, Captain," I replied. "Most of the field and staff officers in the division have been killed or wounded. The best thing we can do is get our brave men out of this."

On reaching the sunken bed of the Emmitsburg Road, for some strange reason I stopped to count the dead lying up the slope. Truly in the midst of life we are in death! I thought, after I stopped counting at 75.

The captain and I, with bullets whistling about our heads, set a speed record retiring up the same long, gentle slope down which we had advanced so confidently only half an hour before. At last we reached the safety of our lines and it seemed as if I must fall through sheer exhaustion and frayed nerves. My hand throbbed with pain and the division was shattered. I thought I had never known a more disagreeable situation. As I sat down to rest upon a pile of fence rails, General Lee rode up and asked, "Are you wounded?"

"Yes, General, but it is a minor wound compared to many suffered today."

There was the saddest imaginable expression on his face as he leaned from the saddle and grasped my good hand. "We did all that mortal men could do, General," I said.

"Ah, yes. It was too much for us," he replied. "We were not strong enough. It was all my fault and I am very sorry, but we will try to repair it."

By dusk, we had a substantial skirmish line established in case of an enemy counterattack. But it seems the Federals had won enough glory for one day and they made no attempt to follow up our repulse and the battle of Gettysburg was over.

There was little sleep for any of us that night as time passed wearily by. Campfires burned brightly, but quietness reigned throughout the lines undisturbed by and demonstration by the enemy. Friends met friends around the fires and spoke of dangers past. This officer was reported dead and that one wounded. One had lost his leg. Another his arm. It was hard to walk twenty paces without seeing many with heads or arms bandaged. In one place, a youth was lying near a campfire dying, the embers lighting up his pale features as his comrades watched over him. To the rear, all the horrible sights of a battlefield were frequent and heart-rendering, while groans reached the ear from every barn and every house.

I met a dazed General Pickett at one campfire. We shook hands. "I thought you were dead," I said.

"I almost wish I was," he replied. "I am ruined. My division is gone. It is destroyed. Armistead and Garnett are dead and Kemper is mortally wounded."

"But your division covered itself with glory today," I responded. But for Pickett, it was empty consolation. His magnificent division had been hopelessly shattered and his hopes with it.

I returned to my camp to seek some much-needed sleep, but I couldn't remove the vision of the disconsolate Pickett from my mind. The glories of war seemed almost ludicrous now. The gay parade, with battle flags gracefully floating in the evening breeze, the nodding plumes, gaudy uniforms with brightly polished buttons, which were the admiration of the fair sex, the inspiring notes of the military band and all the pomp and glamour of the days of our innocence that shone so beautifully as we left our beloved Southland seemingly ages ago had lost their charm. The reality of this cruel war was the shattered and torn bodies which now littered the field between Seminary and Cemetery ridges. From the distance, I could hear the pathetic notes of "the girl I left behind me." Its haunting melody perfectly fitted my mood and I tried in vain to understand for some time, before I drifted off to sleep. Why all this misery and human suffering?

This morning refreshed by sleep a mood of determination and defiance slowly returned as I positioned the men to stand watch behind Colonel Alexander's grim guns. About noon, I heard the news of the surrender of Vicksburg but still believe we are far from whipped. In fact, if yesterday's assault had succeeded, the Yankees would now be suing for peace. For some reason, I cannot explain why General Lee did not throw the full power of the Army of Northern Virginia at the enemy line on Cemetery Ridge. Only eleven infantry brigades made the attack. Another 27 were not used. Many merely watched. For all that bravery, sacrifice and blood, it was nothing but a forlorn hope.

Yesterday, I had the pleasure or pain of announcing that I turned 35 years of age. For obvious reasons, it was a sad birthday. The soul-arousing question occurs, where will I be on July 4th of 1864?

I most sincerely pray that the answer may be, once again, enjoying the delights of home and Charleston. But alas, the uncertain tomorrow! My bones may be bleaching on the battlefield or have found a soldier's grave 'neath the soil of Virginia. Nevertheless, I have no concern for the morrow, whatever the case may be, for the Lord's will, not mine, be done.

JULY 9, 1863—THURSDAY
NEAR HAGERSTOWN, MARYLAND

Although I am sure there were many reasons for us to retreat from Gettysburg the order to do so still came as a shock and a surprise. If General Lee had so ordered, I would have willingly once more marched across that valley of death and essayed to break the Federal lines on Cemetery Ridge.

At two o'clock on the morning of the 5th, we commenced our backward movement towards old Virginia. It was a murky, disagreeable morning and we marched through a chilly, drenching rain on the Fairfield Road in the direction of Hagerstown. The scene of the first day's battle was still a scene of horror, as many of the Yankee First Corps men were yet unburied and dead men with blackened faces were thickly strewn over the field.

This retreat had been a hard one and the men have even a more dirty appearance than usual. As for myself, I have never been so dirty before in all my life. For what reason I do not know, our corps headquarters wagons have not been seen since the first day's fight. Eight days without a change of drawers or even a clean pocket handkerchief is awful. I had to stop by a brook yesterday and wash mine, hanging it over my head as we rode along. I also forgot my dignity as a general for once and washed my feet by the roadside like a private. But in spite of my best endeavors, I felt horribly nasty.

It would be impossible to describe the horrors and hardships of these last days, from the first night's long march to the present hour. The long wagon trains, the artillery, the assortment of vehicles of all kinds, impressed from the farmers and loaded to their utmost capacity with our wounded men have added to the discomforts of our march.

The other day, I rode to the front of a long wagon train and in all that time, I was never out of hearing of the groans and cries of the wounded and dying. Scarcely one in a hundred had received adequate medical aid, and many had been without food for thirty-six hours. Very few of the wagons had even a layer of straw in them and all were without springs. The road was rough and rocky and from nearly every wagon came the heart-wrenching cry of the wounded.

"Oh, God! Why can't I die?"

"My God, will no one have mercy and kill me?"

No heed could be given to any of these appeals. To stop would have meant capture by the Yankee cavalry.

We are now camped near Hagerstown and nothing of importance has occurred since the 7th, save an occasional picket fight and the loss of a few forage wagons. The Yankee cavalry has worried us a little and our pontoon bridge at Falling Waters has been destroyed, whether by a rise in the Potomac River or the enemy, I know not. Thus far, General Lee has evinced no haste in crossing the river and the hostile armies are cautiously watching the movements of each other.

This afternoon, I rode over to visit Lt. Colonel Lane who is resting at one of the temporary hospitals which have been put in place until we cross the river. As we retreated from Gettysburg, the wagon train in which he was carried was ambushed by Yankee cavalry. He at once got out of the wagon, mounted his horse and made his escape, though at the time he was unable to speak or receive any nourishment in the natural way. He is still very weak from the swollen and inflamed condition of his throat and mouth. I wonder if it will ever be possible for him to recover.

Speaking in a hoarse whisper, he told me of a strange incident, which occurred, after he was wounded on July 1st. He was carried from the field and taken to a brick house being used as a field hospital. A wounded officer of a Georgia regiment was lying near him and had been delirious all afternoon.

The Georgian finally fell quiet at about 3:00 p.m., and, after a silence of some minutes, Lane heard him say in a perfectly rational tone of voice, "There now. There now. Vicksburg has fallen. General Lee is retreating and the South is whipped. The South is whipped." He ceased speaking and died a short time later. At the time, Lane thought nothing of it, but in the light of subsequent events, he finds the prediction most startling.

Tonight after supper, I took up my pen and wrote the following letter to Governor Vance:

"Knowing that you would be anxious to hear any news of your regiment, the 26th, I embrace an opportunity to write you a hasty note. You should be so proud of this gallant regiment. At Gettysburg it covered itself with glory. It fell to the lot of the 26th to charge one of the strongest positions possible. They drove three regiments out of the woods with a gallantry unsurpassed. It must be remembered that these were not Yankee regiments of Dutchmen or foreign mercenaries, but regiments of the renowned Iron Brigade, the crack unit of the Federal army.

"Both on the first and third days of the battle, your old command did honor to your association with them and to the state they represent. Their loss has been heavy, very heavy as you can see from the following examples.

"Company A went into action with 92 men and lost 11 killed and 66 wounded on the first day; and on the third day, 1 killed and 10 wounded and missing for a total of 88.

"Company E took into battle on the first day 82 men. Of these, 18 were killed and 52 wounded. Of the 12 men who made the assault on the third day, only two escaped injury or capture.

"Company F went into battle with 3 officers and 88 men. Sad to say every man was killed or wounded, with 31 dead and 60 wounded. There were three sets of twins in this company. At the end of the battle, 5 of the 6 lay dead on the field.

"Company G marched down the Cashtown Pike with 91 men. At the end of the third day, 12 were dead and 58 reported wounded or missing.

"Company H had 78 men present for duty and suffered losses of 17 killed and 55 wounded.

"Company K entered Pennsylvania with 103 men. There are now present for duty 16 rank and file.

"If our figures are correct, Captain Young and I put the loss of this regiment at Gettysburg at 88 percent.

"As I pondered these staggering casualties, I wondered why this gallant regiment behaved so nobly on the field of battle? The answer I believe is devotion. Devotion to their righteous cause and to each other.

"In closing I must not forget to mention the gallant colonel of the 26th. How can I ever forget Harry Burgwyn who died on a blood-stained Pennsylvania ridge? At darkest night on the second day of the battle. A group of us led by several Negro cooks and body servants went to the burial place of young Harry. Here, with the darkness illuminated by pinewood torches, held by the slaves, we knelt for a brief service. As we were preparing to leave this hallowed spot, Elias raised the melody that all the slaves knew:

"Goodbye forever, I hope the Lord will bless you,

"Till we meet again

"I know I will never see you here any more,

"but I pray we meet you again

"On Canaan's happy shore."

"The soldiers who had gathered, wept. And so I weep. For Colonel Burgwyn and all the lost brave lads of the 26th. I weep and hope I meet them again someday on Canaan's happy shore."

Your obedient servant,

James Johnson Pettigrew

JULY 12, 1863—SUNDAY
NEAR WILLIAMSPORT, MARYLAND

This morning, we moved to within three miles of Williamsport. Our troops are now in line of battle awaiting the advance of the enemy. The most serious difficulty under which we labor is the scarcity of ammunition, especially for rifled artillery. The Potomac River is not yet fordable, though falling, and a pontoon bridge the engineers are building is not yet finished. If, by some chance, the Yankees attack and break our line, our situation will be critical indeed—with a swollen river in our rear and a superior enemy in front of us and our artillery ammunition nearly exhausted.

I have in hand the *Richmond Enquirer* of July 7, 1863. On the front page in bold print is news of a message from the superintendent of the telegraph office in Martinsburg. Major J. T. Caldwell, who reports that General Meade is retreating toward Baltimore, pursued by Lee and that in a continuation of the battle on Sunday, July 5, Ewell and Longstreet have captured 40,000 prisoners. The *Enquirer* goes on to report that the population of Richmond is considerably excited by these messages and that Confederate flags are being hung from every window in celebration of our victory.

This news is followed by an editorial of the *Enquirer* which reads in part:

"General Lee's magnificent victory at Gettysburg has, doubtless cost us very dear, as many will come to know when the sad details come in. At present we have only the great and glorious result—the greatest army of the Yankee nation swept away, trampled under foot and all but annihilated upon its own soil—the best part of Pennsylvania laid under contribution to support our army. Philadelphia open to our armies and already reckoning up the number of millions it must pay to ransom it from pillage and conflagration; our own city of Baltimore waiting for its deliverance and Washington, that foul den of thieves, expecting the righteous vengeance of heaven for the hideous crimes done within its walls. How the whole brood of Lincoln and his rascal ministers must turn pale—how their knees smite together as they hear from afar off the roar of their grand Army of the Potomac rolled back in bloody rout and dismay, and see flashing through their guilty dreams the avenging bayonets of those they dared call "rebels!" Ha! Does their monstrous crime weigh heavy on their souls today? Yes. For sure they begin to feel they were in the wrong. That there was a mistake somewhere. And, for the first time, they pray for peace.

"But this is only their first lesson. It is probable that our peace commissioners will have several other such to administer before the Yankees shall be perfectly satisfied that there is no possible peace for them until they withdraw every soldier from the soil of every state, including Missouri, Kentucky, Maryland and Delaware and yield up to their lawful owners every town and fort they hold all around our borders. Cincinnati for example would, we are assured, burn well!!

"After peace is made, the following epitaph from the grave-stone of an infant should be placed upon the monument of the Yankee General Meade:

"If so soon I'm done for,

Wonder what I was begun for."

Me thinks bewilderment will give way to disillusionment when the good citizens of Richmond learn that Lee is back in Hagerstown instead of on the road to Baltimore and that the number of prisoners as reported from Martinsburg has shrunk from 40,000 to 4,000.

I still cannot get over the feeling that the invasion of the enemy's territory however tempting was the wrong policy for us, but at the same time, I believed General Lee must know better than I. The wisdom of our invasion will be long debated and will be the cause of much disagreement. The fact is, however, that we have brought nothing from Pennsylvania which can be considered even partial compensation for what we left at Gettysburg.

JULY 13, 1863—MONDAY
FALLING WATERS, MARYLAND

General Heth once again commands the division and I have rescinded command of my old brigade. We arrived here last evening. The night was dark. Roads were ankle deep in mud and rain. We have halted on a hill overlooking the Potomac where troops that proceeded us have thrown up entrenchments. About one mile away, at Falling Waters, our wagons and artillery are crossing on the pontoon bridge into Virginia.

The division is in line of battle on either side of the road and Pender's division is in our rear in column of brigades. We are the rear guard of the army. The men have stacked arms, some sit in the trenches while others have found more comfortable spots and are attempting to catch up on their sleep. There is little else to do except wait patiently for our turn to cross the river.

Once again, as has happened with some of the earlier battles of the war, disparaging statements about the performance of North Carolina regiments by Virginia newspapers has aroused the lire of many of the men of Heth's division. The men, in particular, object to biased account in the July 11, 1863 issue of the *Richmond Enquirer* by a correspondent only identified by the initial A regarding what is being called "Pickett's Charge." I have the paper before me and record below what correspondent A. claims he saw:

"Now Pettigrew's command emerge from the woods upon Pickett's left and sweep down the slope of the hill to the valley beneath and some two or three hundred yards in rear of Pickett. I saw by the wavering of this line as they entered the conflict that they wanted the firmness of nerve and steadiness of thread which characterized Pickett's gallant men. Pettigrew's command were mostly raw troops which had been recently brought from the South and who had perhaps never been brought under fire—who certainly had never been in any severe fight and I trembled for their conduct.

"But on press, Pickett's brave Virginians and now the enemy open upon them, from more than fifty guns, a terrible fire of grape, shell and canister. On they move in unbroken line, delivering a deadly fire as they advance. Now they have reached the Emmitsburg Road and here they meet a severe fire from the heavy masses of the Yankee infantry posted behind the stone wall. Now again they advance. They storm the stone wall. The Yankees fly. The enemy's batteries are one by one silenced in quick succession as Pickett's men deliver their fire at the gunners and drive them from their guns. I see Kemper and Armistead plant their banners in the enemy's works. I hear their glad shout of victory.

"Let us look after Pettigrew's division. Where are they now? I turn my eyes to the left and there, all over the plain, in utmost confusion is scattered this strong division. Their line is broken. They are flying, apparently panic stricken to the rear. The gallant Pettigrew is wounded but still retains command and is vainly striving to rally his men. Still the moving mass flee pell-mell to the rear and Pickett is left along to contend with the hordes of the enemy now pouring in upon him from every side. Garnett falls, killed by a Minie ball and Kemper, the chivalrous, reels under a mortal wound and is taken to the rear. Pickett gives the order to fall back and his men reluctantly obey doggedly contesting every inch of ground. The enemy follow closely our retreating line. Armistead is shot down and left in the enemy's hands.

"So ended the attempt by Pickett and his brave Virginians to storm the enemy line. It was doomed to failure once Pettigrew's division failed to support it. In fact, this correspondent has learned that had the cowardly North Carolinians not been told they faced only Pennsylvania militia, they would not have charged at all."

The supposed eyewitness account of Correspondent A. (Does the A. stand for Ass?) confirms my opinion that many of the newspaper accounts of this war are hackneyed, hastily conceived and deficient in clarity and perception.

The North Carolinians in my command feel the name Pickett's charge given by the Richmond press is a misnomer. Pickett's division made up less than half of the 3rd day's attack force. Only 15 of the 42 regiments that made the assault.

It was said in the *Enquirer* that my division did not advance as expected and that it was because they were not of the same fine quality as those of Pickett…that they were raw and undisciplined. Yet two days before these raw, undisciplined troops had fought around McPherson's Grove for hours in a struggle with the crack Yankee first corps that is unsurpassed for bravery and endurance.

In the final reckoning, the casualties tell the story. My brigade lost over 1,100 killed or wounded in the Gettysburg campaign. This was 208 more casualties than the next highest brigade in the army and nearly twice as many as the heaviest hit brigade in Pickett's division. The casualties in Heth's division were over 2,300. Those in Pickett's division, which was smaller as two of its brigades remained in Virginia, were over 1,300.

Simply put, no General every commanded a more magnificent body of men than I had the honor to command at Gettysburg. There were in fact no better troops in the Confederacy. Their accomplishments during that bloody three-day battle are eloquent testimony to that fact.

JULY 15, 1863
FALLING WATERS, MARYLAND

Several nights ago, Captain Young came to my tent for a short visit. It was a black moonless night and, after we lit our cigars on a tallow candle, we walked outside and drew up our chairs around a campfire. General Heth joined us and soon Captain Harrison strolled over from his nearby bivouac and sat next to Heth.

As we talked, General Heth caught sight of a pale face which was unusually gloomy. It proved to be General Pickett and my eyes were drawn to the earnest, mournfully solemn lines of his face. Since the last day at Gettysburg, the general has been most disconsolate and seems no longer the gay Virginia cavalier. He walked by our little gathering, head down, looking as if the weight of the world was on his shoulders.

Later in the evening, I sat alone by a small table writing by candle-light when there was a light knock on my door.

"Enter," I said. Much to my surprise, my nocturnal visitor was General Pickett. Motioning him in, I cleared a space for him by my table.

"Lee said I should write a report of the whole campaign," said Pickett in the discontented voice of a schoolboy who has been set a long exercise. "I don't want to write a report of the whole campaign. My division wasn't in action until that last fatal day at Gettysburg. What I have written is the account of the third day. Could you listen while I read it and give me your opinion?"

I then moved to the edge of my cot and sat in shirt and drawers and listened to his report. He read slowly, pausing for effect now and then, always with a sort of sad squint upon his face. When he finished, he smiled like one who had done a good thing and said, "I swear on my honor as a gentleman and officer in the Army of Northern Virginia,

General, that my report is the truth as I saw it. There will be those who will undoubtedly attempt to suppress or deny it, or become angry because I told unpleasant truths about them and abuse me for it, but nevertheless, it is the truth!"

He then gave me a copy saying, as he rose to leave, that he wanted me to read it over once again and make any needed suggestions before he gave it to General Lee.

Immediately after General Pickett left, I sat down and read his report, the most controversial portion I have copied below.

"..... a note was handed to me from Colonel Alexander. After reading it, I handed it to General Longstreet, asking if I should obey and go forward. He looked at me for a moment then held out his hand. Presently, clasping his other hand over mine without speaking, he bowed his head upon his breast. I shall never forget the look in his eyes, nor the clasp of his hand when I said, 'Then, General, I shall lead my division on.'

"My brave men were full of hope and confident of victory as I led them forth, forming them in column of attack, and though officers and men knew the odds against them, they advanced resolutely at route step—110 to a minute—accompanied by four of my aides. I rode about 20 yards to the rear of the assault force, a good position from which to keep an eye on things and issue orders.

"The advance was magnificent. My brave Virginians charged across a space nearly a mile in length, moving with the steadiness of a dress parade. Each commander was in front of his command leading and cheering on his men.

"As we neared the Emmitsburg Road, we came under canister fire—no long range pummeling, but murderous shotgun blasts. It was obvious the time was past for a parade ground march with dressed lines. Many of the mounted officers were down and the flags were dropping and coming up again. The lines were ragged, but still my brave Virginians came on! Now many of the soldiers marched in a half stoop, with their heads bowed, as if walking into storm.

"As my division marched on toward enemy lines, I rode to the right of the column to take a position that commanded a full view of the field. I came to the Codori house and there I halted. It was the job of the brigadiers and colonels to lead the charge. It was my job to stay alive and direct it.

"Two lines of the enemy's infantry were driven back, guns taken, a narrow wedge driven into the Federal line at the clump of trees. I watched as my Virginians seemed on the verge of victory; but suddenly there was only defeat. Where was the rest of the army? Where was our promised support?

"At the muster of my division the next morning, not a thousand survivors answered the call. Four of every five of my men had been either killed, wounded or captured. General Garnett rode his horse into battle, declining to dismount and was killed, instantly falling from his horse. General Kemper was desperately wounded. Dear old Lewis Armistead, God bless him, was mortally wounded at the head of his command after planting the flag of Virginia within the Federal lines. Seven of my colonels were killed and one was mortally wounded. Nine of my lieutenant colonels were wounded and three lieutenant colonels were killed. Only one field officer of my whole command, Colonel Cabell, was unhurt and the loss of my company officers was in proportion.

"In retrospect, the task the commander of the army assigned to my division was too great. As a result of the attack, my division was practically destroyed. We squandered a great opportunity, for if the charge made by my gallant Virginians on the third of July had been supported, or even if my two other brigades had been with me, we would now be in Washington City and the war ended. But it was not to be, the Almighty has willed otherwise and I wish that we had never crossed the Potomac and entered into Pennsylvania."

General Pickett returned this evening to see me. His despondency had given way to anger as he said to me, "General Lee has decided to suppress my report of Gettysburg." He then once again affirmed that he had written his report with the purest of motives and handed me a letter he had just received from General Lee. I took the letter, unfolded it carefully and seated myself while I read:

"General George E. Pickett, Commanding,

You and your men have crowned themselves with glory; but we have the enemy to fight and must carefully at this critical moment guard against dissensions which the reflections in your report would create. I will, therefore, suggest that you destroy both copy and original, substituting one confined to casualties merely. I hope all will yet be well.

I am, with respect, your obedient servant,

R. E. Lee, General"

Pickett then said to me, "In accordance with Lee's wish, I will destroy my report, but I do so with reluctance. Lately I can't think of anything but the desolate homes in Virginia and the unknown dead in Pennsylvania."

I listened respectfully to him and then said, "General, you and your gallant troops did all that mortal men could do."

His face then flushed and, seeming to become a bit unnerved, he answered, "At the beginning of the fight, I was so sanguine, so sure of success. Early in the morning I was assured by Colonel Alexander that General Lee had ordered every brigade in his command to charge Cemetery Hill, so I had no fear of not being supported. Alexander also assured me of the support of his artillery which would move ahead of my division in the advance, but, alas, the attack took place under conditions that left no chance of success."

"Did you protest to General Lee your concerns about your report?" I asked.

"Yes. I went to his tent with Captain Arnold of my staff. The conversation was cold and formal, rather embarrassing to both of us. I took Lee's manner as a rebuff and left his tent. As we came to our horses, I complained to Arnold about General Lee's uncompromising attitude and that he had my division massacred at Gettysburg. I was not mollified by Captain Arnold's rejoinder, 'the assault has made your name immortal.'"

Later, after General Pickett left, I sat alone in my tent and wondered what future generations would say of Gettysburg. Any historian who reads over the various reports of the battle and accepts them as reliable and permits himself to be guided by them through all the windings of the three-day battle, with the expectation of finally allotting to over forty brigades or ten divisions, their rightful credit, will probably not be successful. But by then, perhaps the contentions and disagreements of this world, like its glories, will have passed away.

JULY 18, 1863
BUNKER HILL, VIRGINIA

Brigadier General James Johnson Pettigrew is dead! I was at his bedside yesterday in the home of the Henry Boyd family in Bunker Hill when he passed away from a wound he received during a skirmish with Yankee cavalry at Falling Waters, Maryland on July 14th.

Begun as a "private record" for friends and kindred, the keeping of this journal was important to General Pettigrew and he put as much time and effort into it as his duties would allow. A highly intelligent man with a keen sense of history, the General was a perceptive observer of the momentous events of the day. I often watched him write at odd moments or late at night, working with a kind of frantic desperation to set down all he had observed and felt. Whether his writing was good, bad, or indifferent, he did, I think, not care. He wrote for his own purpose without prospect of ultimate publication or reward.

Before time dims of my memory, I wish to intrude upon the General's journal and record the sad events of the last days of his life. He would, I believe, not object for he once told me that "anything once begun, should not be left undone."

On July 14th, Pender's division received orders to cross the Potomac. General Pettigrew was placed in charge of the rear guard and told by General Heth that a body of Confederate cavalry was soon to be approaching Falling Waters. Unknown to General Heth, the cavalry had encountered two Federal cavalry brigades that had gone upstream to cross at Williamsport.

I soon observed a body of cavalry a considerable distance away, rapidly deploying. This seemed a strange maneuver and I called this to the attention of generals Heth and Pettigrew. They asked me if they were our cavalry or that of the enemy. General Heth made the opinion they were ours, but should they prove to be Yankees, we could easily drive them off. General Pettigrew then ordered me to get his command under arms and to draw in the pickets on our left.

Suddenly a troop of forty or fifty cavalry made their appearance in our front and rode straight at a gallop toward General Pettigrew and the small group of officers with him. Someone gave the order to fire, but General Heth quickly countermanded the order. He believed the cavalry were Confederates. As they came forward, I looked at them carefully with my glasses and discovered they were Federal cavalry. I then gave the command to fire. At almost the same time, the Federals opened fire. General Pettigrew rushed to his horse and attempted to mount with his one good hand. His horse reared and he fell.

There then ensued a hand-to-hand fight and General Pettigrew watched in dismay as a Yankee trooper shot several of our men with his revolver. The general called to the men near him to shoot the Yankee, but they were busy with the enemy in their midst so the general drew a small pistol from his coat pocket and advanced on foot toward the man. At about eight feet, he stopped, aimed and pulled the trigger. A misfire!

The Yankee fired his Colt and the general fell wounded in the stomach. Someone shot the Federal's horse and he jumped free and ran, firing as he went. Shots were fired after him, but he was finally brought down by a clubbed musket to the head. In a few moments, the fight was over and all of the Federal cavalry were dead or captured.

Our loss in number was very small, but the loss of General Pettigrew to the army was irreparable. General Heth came to me that night and said he had lost nearly his entire division, but the loss of Pettigrew was greater than all else.

General Pettigrew was examined by Dr. Sullivan and carried across the river to a nearby house. It was found that the pistol ball had entered his abdomen on the left side, just above the hip, and, passing downward, came out behind. The wound was a large one and he had lost a great deal of blood.

Dr. Sullivan thought almost immediately that the wound would prove fatal as few recovered from a stomach wound. Mortification was bound to set in and the end would not be then far away. We suggested to General Pettigrew that he stay at the house and that Federal surgeons would soon find him there. But the general let us know in no uncertain terms he would rather die than be captured again.

On the night of July 16th, the general was placed in the Boyd home at Bunker Hill. The next day he was much weaker, but bore his pain calmly. He was not afraid to die for he took the changes and chances of this mortal life like the gallant soldier he was.

By late afternoon of the 17th, he had grown quite weak and, as the afternoon faded into dusk, mortification began to set in. He was given morphine by Dr. Sullivan to ease the pain. For quite some time, he hardly moved. At 8:00 p.m., he stirred, "It's time to be going," he said faintly to me and ceased to breathe.

Sometime later, as Elias and I prepared his body to be placed in a coffin, I took from his breast pocket a blood-stained sheet of paper containing a poem. I knew it to be his favorite by Prentice. I opened the paper and read aloud the following lines over the mortal remains of one whose shameless spirit I knew stood before the throne of God:

A NAME IN THE SAND
"Alone I walked the ocean strand,
A pearly shell was in my hand;
I stopped and wrote upon the sand,
My name, the year, the day;
As onward from the spot I passed,
One lingering look behind I cast,
A wave came rolling high and fast,
And washed my lines away.
And so, me thought, 'twill quickly be,
With every mark on earth from me
A wave of dark oblivion's sea
Will sweep across the place
Where I have trod the sandy shore
Or time, and been, to be no more of me,
Of my day, the name I bore,

To leave no track as trace.
And yet with him who counts the sands,
And holds the waters in his hands,
I know a lasting record stands,

Inscribed against my name.
Of all this mortal part has wrought,
Of all this thinking soul has thought,
And from these fleeting moments caught,
For glory or for shame."

> Captain Lewis Young
> Aide de Camp
> Pettigrew's Brigade
> Army of Northern Virginia

About the Author

Dan Bauer is the author of *Great American Fighter Aces* and over 25 articles on military history.These Articles have been published in such magazines as: Military History,Civil War Times llustrated,World War II, Civil War Magazine and Air Classics Magazine.

Dan received his undergraduate degree from the University of Wisconsin-Whitewater,and his MA From the University of Denver, Denver, Colorado. He also has an M. A. in School Administration From California State University at San Bernardino, San Bernardino, California. He currently Serves the Monroe, Wisconsin Public Schools as the Director of Special Education/Principal Monroe Alternative Charter School.

He may be reached by email at dbauer@tds.net

Printed in the United States
29041LVS00006BA/74